Lecture Notes in Computer Science 11844

More information about this series at http://www.springer.com/series/7412

George Bebis · Richard Boyle ·
Bahram Parvin · Darko Koracin ·
Daniela Ushizima · Sek Chai ·
Shinjiro Sueda · Xin Lin ·
Aidong Lu · Daniel Thalmann ·
Chaoli Wang · Panpan Xu (Eds.)

Advances in Visual Computing

14th International Symposium on Visual Computing, ISVC 2019
Lake Tahoe, NV, USA, October 7–9, 2019
Proceedings, Part I

 Springer

Editors
George Bebis
University of Nevada
Reno, NV, USA

Bahram Parvin
University of Nevada
Reno, NV, USA

Daniela Ushizima
Lawrence Berkeley
National Laboratory
Berkeley, CA, USA

Shinjiro Sueda
Texas A&M University
College Station, TX, USA

Aidong Lu
University of North Carolina
at Charlotte
Charlotte, NC, USA

Chaoli Wang
Notre Dame University
Notre Dame, IN, USA

Richard Boyle
NASA Ames Research Center
Moffett Field, CA, USA

Darko Koracin
Desert Research Institute
Reno, NV, USA

Sek Chai
Latent AI
Palo Alto, CA, USA

Xin Lin
Louisiana State University
Baton Rouge, LA, USA

Daniel Thalmann
École Polytechnique Fédérale
de Lausanne
Lausanne, Switzerland

Panpan Xu
Bosch Research North America
Palo Alto, CA, USA

ISSN 0302-9743   ISSN 1611-3349   (electronic)
Lecture Notes in Computer Science
ISBN 978-3-030-33719-3   ISBN 978-3-030-33720-9   (eBook)
https://doi.org/10.1007/978-3-030-33720-9

LNCS Sublibrary: SL6 – Image Processing, Computer Vision, Pattern Recognition, and Graphics

This Springer imprint is published by the registered company Springer Nature Switzerland AG
The registered company address is: Gewerbestrasse 11, 6330 Cham, Switzerland

Preface

It is with great pleasure that we welcome you to the proceedings of the 14th International Symposium on Visual Computing (ISVC 2019), which was held in Lake Tahoe, Nevada, USA, during October 7–9, 2019. ISVC provides a common umbrella for the four main areas of visual computing including vision, graphics, visualization, and virtual reality. The goal is to provide a forum for researchers, scientists, engineers, and practitioners throughout the world to present their latest research findings, ideas, developments, and applications in the broader area of visual computing.

This year, the program consisted of 13 oral sessions, 2 special tracks, 3 tutorials, and 6 keynote presentations. We received 163 submissions from which we accepted 62 papers for oral presentation and 29 papers for poster presentation. Special track papers were solicited separately through the Organizing and Program Committees of each track. A total of 9 papers were accepted for oral presentation in the special tracks.

All papers were reviewed with an emphasis on the potential to contribute to the state of the art in the field. Selection criteria included accuracy and originality of ideas, clarity and significance of results, and presentation quality. The review process was quite rigorous, involving three independent blind reviews followed by several days of discussion. During the discussion period we tried to correct anomalies and errors that might have existed in the initial reviews. Despite our efforts, we recognize that some papers worthy of inclusion may have not been included in the program. We offer our sincere apologies to authors whose contributions might have been overlooked.

We wish to thank everybody who submitted their work to ISVC 2019 for review. It was because of their contributions that we succeeded in having a technical program of high scientific quality. In particular, we would like to thank the ISVC 2019 area chairs, the organizing institutions, the industrial sponsors, the international Program Committee, the special track organizers and their Program Committees, the keynote speakers, the reviewers, and especially the authors who contributed their work to the symposium. In particular, we would like to express our appreciation to Springer for sponsoring the Best Paper Award this year.

We sincerely hope that ISVC 2019 offered participants opportunities for professional growth.

September 2019

George Bebis\
Richard Boyle\
Darko Koracin\
Bahram Parvin\
Daniela Ushizima\
Sek Chai\
Shinjiro Sueda\
Xin Li\
Aidong Lu\
Daniel Thalmann\
Chaoli Wang\
Panpan Xu

Organization

Steering Committee

George Bebis   University of Nevada, Reno, USA
Richard Boyle   NASA Ames Research Center, USA
Bahram Parvin   University of Nevada, Reno, USA
Darko Koracin   Desert Research Institute, USA,
         and University of Zagreb, Croatia

Area Chairs

Computer Vision

Daniela Ushizima   Lawrence Berkeley National Lab, USA
Sek Chai   Latent AI, USA

Computer Graphics

Shinjiro Sueda   Texas A&M University, USA
Xin Li   Louisiana State University, USA

Virtual Reality

Aidong Lu   UNC Charlotte, USA
Daniel Thalmann   École Polytechnique Fédérale de Lausanne,
         Switzerland

Visualization

Chaoli Wang   Notre Dame University, USA
Panpan Xu   Bosch Research North America, USA

Publicity Chair

Ali Erol   Eksperta Software, Turkey

Local Arrangements Chair

Alireza Tavakkoli   University of Nevada, Reno, USA

Special Tracks Chairs

Gholamreza Amayeh   Arraiy, USA
Zehang Sun   Apple, USA

Tutorials Chairs

Fabien Scalzo   UCLA, USA
Emily Hand   University of Nevada, Reno, USA

Awards Chairs

Amol Ambardekar   Microsoft, USA
Leandro Loss   Quantaverse, USA

Web Master

Isayas Berhe Adhanom   University of Nevada, Reno, USA

Program Committee

Emmanuel Agu   Worcester Polytechnic Institute, USA
Touqeer Ahmad   LUMS, Pakistan
Kostas Alexis   University of Nevada, Reno, USA
Amol Ambardekar   Microsoft, USA
Mehdi Ammi   University of Paris 8, France
Mark Apperley   University of Waikato, New Zealand
Antonis Argyros   Foundation for Research and Technology – Hellas,
                         Greece
Vijayan K. Asari   University of Dayton, USA
Vassilis Athitsos   University of Texas at Arlington, USA
Melinos Averkiou   University of Cyprus, Cyprus
George Baciu   The Hong Kong Polytechnic University, Hong Kong,
                         China
Selim Balcisoy   Sabanci University, Turkey
Reneta Barneva   SUNY Fredonia, USA
Ronen Barzel   Independent, UK
George Bebis   University of Nevada, Reno, USA
Michael Behrisch   Tufts University, USA
Alexander Belyaev   Heriot-Watt University, UK
Jan Bender   RWTH Aachen University, Germany
Bedrich Benes   Purdue University, USA
Ayush Bhargava   Clemson University, USA
Harsh Bhatia   Lawrence Livermore National Laboratory, USA
Sanjiv Bhatia   University of Missouri–St. Louis, USA
Ankur Bist   Govind Ballabh Pant University of Agriculture
                         and Technology, India
Ayan Biswas   Los Alamos National Laboratory, USA
Dibio Borges   Universidade de Brasília, Brazil
Alexandra Branzan Albu University of Victoria, Canada
Jose Braz Pereira   EST Setúbal/IPS, Portugal

Min H. Kim	Korea Advanced Institute of Science and Technology, South Korea
Benjamin Kimia	Brown University, USA
James Klosowski	AT&T Labs Research, USA
Steffen Koch	University of Stuttgart, Germany
Elena Kokkinara	Inflight VR, Spain
Stefanos Kollias	National Technical University of Athens, Greece
Dimitris Kosmopoulos	University of Patras, Greece
Igor Kozintsev	Facebook, USA
Jens Krueger	SCI Institute, USA
Arjan Kuijper	TU Darmstadt, Germany
Yoshinori Kuno	Saitama University, Japan
Tsz Ho Kwok	Concordia University, Canada
Hung La	University of Nevada, Reno, USA
Yu-Kun Lai	Cardiff University, UK
Robert S. Laramee	Swansea University, UK
D. J. Lee	Brigham Young University, UK
Robert R. Lewis	Washington State University, USA
Frederick Li	University of Durham, UK
Xin Li	Louisiana State University, USA
Jie Liang	Sydney University of Technology, Australia
Kuo-Chin Lien	XMotors.ai, USA
Chun-Cheng Lin	National Chiao Tung University, Taiwan
Stephen Lin	Microsoft
Peter Lindstrom	LLNL, USA
Lars Linsen	Westfälische Wilhelms-Universität Münster, Germany
Zhanping Liu	Old Dominion University, USA
Manuel Loaiza	Universidad Católica San Pablo, Peru
Benjamin Lok	University of Florida, USA
Leandro Loss	QuantaVerse, ITU, ESSCA
Joern Loviscach	University of Applied Sciences, Germany
Aidong Lu	UNC Charlotte, USA
Xun Luo	Tianjin University of Technology, China
Brendan Macdonald	NIOSH, USA
Anthony Maeder	Flinders University, Australia
Sokratis Makrogiannis	Delaware State University, USA
Luigi Malomo	ISTI – CNR, Italy
Rafael M. Martins	Linnaeus University, Sweden
Yoshitaka Masutani	Hiroshima City University, Japan
Kresimir Matkovic	VRVis Research Center, Austria
Stephen Maybank	Birkbeck, UK
Tim Mcgraw	Purdue University, USA
Qurban Memon	UAE University, UAE
Daniel Mestre	Aix-Marseille University, France
Xikui Miao	Brigham Young University, UK
Gabriel Mistelbauer	Otto-von-Guericke University, Germany

Filip Sadlo	Heidelberg University, Germany
Punam Saha	University of Iowa, USA
Naohisa Sakamoto	Kobe University, Japan
Kristian Sandberg	Computational Solutions, Inc., USA
Allen Sanderson	SCI Institute, USA
Alberto Santamaría-Pang	General Electric Research, USA
Nickolas S. Sapidis	University of Western Macedonia, Greece
Muhammad Sarfraz	Kuwait University, Kuwait
Andreas Savakis	Rochester Institute of Technology, USA
Jacob Scharcanski	UFRGS, Brazil
Thomas Schultz	University of Bonn, Germany
Mohamed Shehata	Memorial University, USA
Yun Sheng	East China Normal University, China
Gurjot Singh	Fairleigh Dickinson University, USA
Sandra Skaff	NVIDIA, USA
Alexei Skurikhin	Los Alamos National Laboratory, USA
Pavel Slavik	Czech Technical University in Prague, Czech Republic
Dmitry Sokolov	Université de Lorraine, France
Fabio Solari	University of Genoa – DIBRIS, Italy
Paolo Spagnolo	National Research Council, Italy
Jaya Sreevalsan-Nair	IIIT Bangalore, India
Diane Staheli	Massachusetts Institute of Technology, USA
Chung-Yen Su	National Taiwan Normal University, Taiwan
Shinjiro Sueda	Texas A&M University, USA
Changming Sun	CSIRO, Australia
Guodao Sun	Zhejiang University of Technology, China
Zehang Sun	Apple inc., USA
Tanveer Syeda-Mahmood	IBM, USA
Carlo H. Séquin	University of California, Berkeley, USA
Ahmad Tafti	Mayo Clinic, USA
Alireza Tavakkoli	University of Nevada, Reno, USA
João Manuel R. S. Tavares	INEGI, University of Porto, Portugal
Daniel Thalmann	École Polytechnique Fédérale de Lausanne, Switzerland
Holger Theisel	Otto-von-Guericke University, Germany
Yan Tong	University of South Carolina, USA
Thomas Torsney-Weir	Swansea University, UK
Stefano Tubaro	Politecnico di Milano, Italy
Georg Umlauf	HTWG Konstanz, Germany
Daniela Ushizima	Lawrence Berkeley National Laboratory, USA
Dimitar Valkov	University of Muenster, Germany
Jonathan Ventura	California Polytechnic State University San Luis Obispo, USA
Athanasios Voulodimos	National Technical University of Athens, Greece
Chaoli Wang	University of Notre Dame, USA
Michel Westenberg	Eindhoven University of Technology, The Netherlands

Benjamin Weyers	Trier University, Germany
Alexander Wiebel	Worms University of Applied Sciences, Germany
Thomas Wischgoll	Wright State University, USA
Kin Hong Wong	The Chinese University of Hong Kong, Hong Kong, China
Panpan Xu	Bosch Research North America, USA
Wei Xu	Brookhaven National Lab, USA
Goshiro Yamamoto	Kyoto University, Japan
Xiaosong Yang	Bournemouth University, UK
Yueming Yang	Baldwin Wallace University, USA
Hsu-Chun Yen	National Taiwan University, Taiwan
Lijun Yin	State University of New York at Binghamton, USA
Zeyun Yu	University of Wisconsin-Milwaukee, USA
Chunrong Yuan	Technische Hochschule Köln, Germany
Xiaoru Yuan	Peking University, China
Xenophon Zabulis	FORTH-ICS, Greece
Jiri Zara	Czech Technical University in Prague, Czech Republic
Wei Zeng	Florida International University, USA
Dong Zhang	NVIDIA, USA
Zhao Zhang	Hefei University of Technology, China
Ye Zhao	Kent State University, USA
Yuanjie Zheng	Shandong Normal University, China
Changqing Zou	University of Maryland, USA

Special Tracks

ST1: Vision for Remote Sensing and Infrastructure Inspection

Hung M. La	University of Nevada, Reno, USA
Alireza Tavakkoli	University of Nevada, Reno, USA
Trung-Dung Ngo	University of Prince Edward Island, Canada
Trung H. Duong	Colorado State University-Pueblo, USA

ST2: Computational Vision, AI and Mathematical Methods for Biomedical and Biological Image Analysis

Sokratis Makrogiannis	Delaware State University, USA
Alberto Santamaria-Pang	General Electric Global Research, USA

Tutorials

T1: Analysis and Visualization of 3D Data in Python

Daniela Ushizima	Berkeley Institute for Data Science, UC Berkeley, USA
Alexandre de Siqueira	Berkeley Institute for Data Science, UC Berkeley, USA
Stéfan van der Walt	Berkeley Institute for Data Science, UC Berkeley, USA

T2: Computer Vision for Underwater Environmental Monitoring

Alexandra Branzan Albu   Electrical and Computer Engineering,
University of Victoria, Canada
Maia Hoeberechts   Ocean Networks Canada, Canada

T3: Visual Object Tracking Using Deep Learning

Mohamed H. Abdelpakey   Memorial University of Newfoundland,
St. John's, Canada
Mohamed S. Shehata   Memorial University of Newfoundland,
St. John's, Canada

Additional Reviewers

Ahmed, Habib
Alderighi, Thomas
Grieβer, Dennis
Han, Jun
Hazarika, Subhashis
Heinemann, Moritz
Helm, Daniel
Hermann, Matthias
Hong, Seokpyo
Huang, Jida
Li, Yan Ran
Loizou, Marios
Mera Trujillo, Marcela

Muralidharan, Lakshmi Priya
Nayeem, Raihan
Nefian, Ara
Oagaz, Hawkar
Parakkat, Amal Dev
Penk, Dominik
Pulido, Jesus
Sabri, Sinan
Schoun, Breawn
Shead, Timothy
Vrigkas, Michalis
Wang, Li

Sponsors

Keynote Talks

Dense 3D Face Correspondence for Deep 3D Face Recognition and Medical Applications

Ajmal Mian

University of Western Australia, Australia

Abstract. In this talk, I will present our research on dense 3D face correspondence which is a core problem in facial analysis for many applications such as biometric identification, symptomatology for the diagnosis of Autism and Obstructive Sleep Apnoea and planning for facial reconstructive surgery. From a morphometric point of view, we are interested in performing dense correspondence based purely on shape without using texture. This makes the problem challenging but the correspondences and subsequent analyses more precise. The idea is to start from a sparse set of automatically detected corresponding landmarks and propagate along the geodesics connecting nearby points. By anchoring on the most reliable correspondences for propagation, accurate dense correspondences are iteratively established between hundreds of faces without using a prior model. Thus, we are able to construct population specific deformable face models for symptomatology and patient specific morphs to facial norms for reconstructive surgery. Moreover, by establishing dense correspondences between different facial identities and expressions, we synthesize millions of 3D faces with varying identities, expressions and poses to learn a deep Convolutional Neural Network (FR3DNet) for large scale 3D face recognition. FR3DNet achieves state-of-the-art results, outperforming existing methods in open-world and close-world face recognition, on a dataset four times the largest dataset reported in the existing literature.

Approaches to Massive Scientific Data Visualization and Analysis

James Ahrens

Los Alamos National Laboratory, USA

Abstract. Science is advancing via the development of highly-precise scientific simulations that are run on the world's largest and fastest supercomputers. The goal of these simulations is to better understand complex physical processes at all scales from the quantum level to the workings of our universe. In this talk, I will describe a set of approaches to analyzing the massive scientific data generated by these simulations, by transforming it into visual knowledge to support scientific understanding. By looking at the massive data visualization and analysis problem abstractly and asking questions about (1) What computing and human resources are available, (2) What are the strengths and limitations of these resources, different solutions emerge. These approaches include data parallelism, data streaming, data reduction operators and reduced size data representations, and in-situ analysis. I will summarize these approaches and discuss how emerging trends, such as, machine learning, data science and hardware accelerated ray-tracing, will a play an important role in future work.

Fast, Accurate and Stable Simulations for Interactive VR Training

Sheldon Andrews

École de Technologie Supérieure, Université du Quebec, Canada

Abstract. Physical simulations are an ubiquitous component in modern computer graphics applications, and over the past several decades a plenitude of specialized algorithms have been developed for solving the linear systems that govern their dynamical behavior. Methods in the field have trended toward iterative techniques that are well-suited to GPU parallelization, yet some applications require alternative approaches. In this talk, I will present our recent results for improving the tractability of stiff and highly coupled multibody simulations that are CPU bound. Our work focuses not only on techniques to improve the computational performance, but also preserving physical and numerical traits. I will motivate the work with some challenging examples and postulate about open problems that lie ahead for the community.

The State of Modern Computer Vision
(Banquet Keynote Talk)

David Forsyth

University of Illinois at Urbana-Champaign, USA

Abstract. Computer vision has gone through major changes over the last seven years. The vision community can solve classification and regression problems with astonishing accuracy and relative ease, as long as enough data is available. Many very important practical problems, like object detection, can be wrangled into either a Classification or a regression problem. Furthermore, we have a spectacular grasp of the relations between 3D worlds and 2D images. I will review the main problems we can currently solve, describe very roughly how we solve them, and sketch out the domain of important unsolved problems.

Bone Microstructural Imaging in Osteoporosis – Recent Developments and Translational Studies

Punam Saha

University of Iowa, USA

Abstract. Osteoporosis is a common age-related disease characterized by reduced bone density and increased fracture-risk. Nearly 40 percent of women and 13 percent of men suffer one or more fragility fractures in their lifetime, and the fracture prevalence will further rise with continued increase in life-expectancy. Osteoporotic hip fractures reduce life expectancy by 20 percent and add an annual healthcare cost of nearly 19 billion dollars in the United States only. Early and accurate diagnosis of osteoporosis and assessment of fracture-risk is fundamental to handle the disease, and bone imaging plays an important role to accomplish this goal. Dual-energy X-ray absorptiometry (DXA) measured bone mineral density (BMD) is clinically used to characterize osteoporosis. It is known that BMD explains 60–70% of the variability in bone strength and fracture-risk, and the remaining variability comes from collective effects of other factors such as cortical and trabecular bone distribution, and their micro-structural basis. Accurate and robust measurement of effective cortical and trabecular bone microstructural features, associated with bone strength and fracture-risk, is of paramount clinical significance. State-of-the-art imaging modalities for bone microstructural assessment include magnetic resonance imaging (MRI), high-resolution peripheral quantitative computed tomography (HR-pQCT), flat-panel cone beam CT (CBCT), and whole-body multi-row detector CT (MDCT). Different research groups have applied various methods for characterization of bone microstructure related to cortical porosity and thickness, trabecular volume, network area, spacing, number, star volume measure, structure model index, connectivity number etc. Our research group has developed unique methods for *in vivo* clinical CT-based assessment of cortical porosity and trabecular plate-rod and longitudinal-transverse micro-architecture. This talk presents the principles and basis of these methods, experimental results evaluating their fidelity, generalizability, and impact on translational and clinical research studies.

Perception and Affordance Research Inspired Design of Virtual Self-Representation in Near-Field Virtual Reality Interactions

Sabarish Babu

Clemson University, USA

Abstract. In this keynote, I will be highlighting a body of work that was conducted over a decade in the investigation of spatial perception and fine motor actions in near field or personal space virtual reality simulations, and its implications to the design of interaction metaphors and self-avatars. In our initial research, we studied near field distance estimation in real and virtual environments via visually guided reaching and speech based responses. We found that distances are systematically misperceived in immersive virtual environments and the real world in the near field. We then investigated how visuo-motor recalibration or adaptation can overcome depth misperceptions in near field virtual reality, via calibration to congruent and divergent visual and haptic feedback. In multiple experiments, we found evidence that congruent and divergent visuo-haptic feedback not only differentially affected distance estimation, but also affected the properties of fine motor actions such as velocity, accuracy and path length of the end effector's movements in open and closed loop experiences in VR. Building upon these findings, we investigated the effect of anthropomorphic and anthropometric fidelity of self-avatars, which are self-representations of the user in VR, on spatial perception and affordances in near field interactions. In this recent thrust, we found evidence of the presence of a malleable embodied body schema that is adaptable based on alterations to the self-avatar, and subsequently scaling our perceptions of distance and the participants' reach envelope in VR interactions. More recently, we have been investigating the effects of the presence or absence of self-avatars in contemporary VR experiences on the affordance of passability, and comparing the results to that of real world viewing situations. Our initial results seem to suggest that the difference in viewing has a larger impact on perceived affordances in the medium field, than the presence or absence of body scaled virtual embodiment. Finally, I will end my talk by highlighting our ongoing research on the effects of congruent and divergent visuo-haptic feedback on size perception and near field affordances in VR. The results of our work have profound implications to the design of VR interactions in fine motor training such as surgical simulation, mechanical skills trainers, as well as tangible devices and interaction metaphors.

Contents – Part I

Segmentation/Recognition

Video Analysis and Event Recognition

Visualization

ST: Computational Vision, AI and Mathematical Methods for Biomedical and Biological Image Analysis

Biometrics

Virtual Reality I

Applications I

ST: Vision for Remote Sensing and Infrastructure Inspection

Computer Graphics II

Contents – Part II

Virtual Reality II

Object Recognition/Detection/Categorization

Posters

Deep Learning I

Application of Image Classification for Fine-Grained Nudity Detection

Cristian Ion[(✉)] ⓘ and Cristian Minea ⓘ

Bitdefender, Bucharest, Romania
{cion,cminea}@bitdefender.com
https://www.bitdefender.com/

Abstract. Many online social platforms need to use an image content filtering solution to detect nudity automatically. Existing solutions only focus on binary classification models to detect explicit nudity or pornography, which is not enough to distinguish between a great number of various racy outfits that people wear (swimsuit, summer outfit, etc.) that might be considered inappropriate according to user's own preferences. This paper addresses the problem by proposing a robust technology which detects fine-grained human body parts (chest, back, abdomen, etc.) and assigns a level of nudity for each part using a multi-label image classification model.

Since existing datasets were not sufficient for the given problem, we created a new dataset with a total of 37.872 images and 4.879.517 annotated labels that describe human body parts and nudity level (6 labels for each body part).

We fine-tuned multiple state-of-the-art convolutional neural network models (VGG, ResNet, MobileNet) on our dataset for multi-label image classification. Our solution has a total accuracy of 98.1% on the test dataset and a low false positive rate of 0.8%.

Keywords: Dataset · Deep learning · Image classification · Nudity · Pornography

1 Introduction

The fast growth of digital media has exposed us to enormous quantities of non-textual data like images, audio, and video. This data must be analyzed to decrease exposure to unwanted content and there is a definite need for personalized selection of information.

A particular case of unwanted content is images with pornography or nudity. Technologies that address this problem are not created adequately to suit the variety of use-case scenarios. For example, in a scenario swimwear nudity is restricted but in another scenario topless photos are accepted.

This paper describes an algorithm for detecting many types of nudity in images. We went through multiple stages to develop our application, the most

Supported by organization Bitdefender.

G. Bebis et al. (Eds.): ISVC 2019, LNCS 11844, pp. 3–15, 2019.
https://doi.org/10.1007/978-3-030-33720-9_1

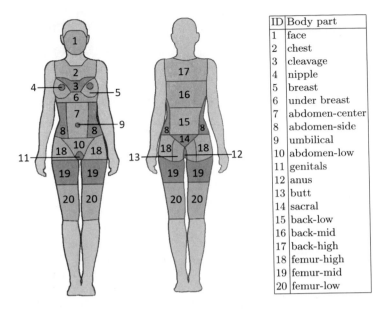

ID	Body part
1	face
2	chest
3	cleavage
4	nipple
5	breast
6	under breast
7	abdomen-center
8	abdomen-side
9	umbilical
10	abdomen-low
11	genitals
12	anus
13	butt
14	sacral
15	back-low
16	back-mid
17	back-high
18	femur-high
19	femur-mid
20	femur-low

Fig. 1. The parts of the human body used to detect nudity

significant being: label selection, dataset image selection, image annotation techniques, classifier type selection, and fine-tuning of classifier architectures.

At each stage, we improved the known techniques in order to achieve better results for this particular problem of nudity detection. We have created a new task-specific dataset and many of the methods described in the paper are relevant and applicable to the creation process of other datasets.

We chose a convolutional neural network (CNN [9]) architecture for the classifier because it is state-of-the-art in image classification (ImageNet), it is efficient in using memory and CPU, it is easy to incorporate in software products (mobile, PC application, cloud based service), and it is a general method to create robust models for many computer vision applications.

2   Related Work

This paper is related to image classification and nudity detection. Based on our findings, no current solution detects components of the human body as fine-grained as our technology. This enables our technology to cover more use-case scenarios than current alternatives.

Image segmentation is an image processing technique that groups pixels with regard to certain distinctive or computed properties, such as color, intensity or texture. This method was implemented for nudity detection by Belém, Karavarsamis et al. [1,7]. To discover skin regions in the picture, a skin color distribution model based on the RGB and HSV color spaces is used. The proposed

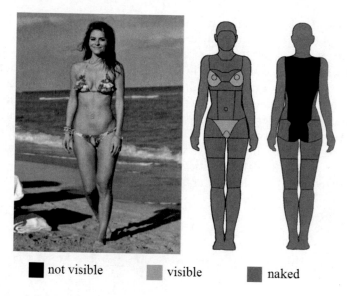

not visible   visible   naked

Fig. 2. Image (left) and nudity detection results (right) for the body parts (Fig. 1). Green is used for visible parts which are not naked, red is used for naked body parts and black is used for components which are not visible. (Color figure online)

skins regions are analyzed for clues that indicate nudity or non-nudity, such as the sizes and relative distances between them. An image is classified nude or non-nude on the basis of these clues and the percentage of skin in the image.

The most commonly used dataset related to the detection of fine-grained human body parts is the PASCAL-part dataset [3], which is used for human body parsing [4]. This dataset can not be used as benchmark though, because nudity labels are lacking.

CNN architectures are the state-of-the-art for image classification [5,8,11] and can be used to classify images directly as nude or non-nude. This method shows superior results compared to the previous approach, and it closely resembles our solution, which also uses a CNN.

Our solution improves on the previous works by enhancing the amount of nudity refinement through the detection of fine-grained labels that are not accessible in any current dataset or technology (Fig. 2). We also adjusted state-of-the-art CNN architectures, leading to improved accuracy and low false-positive error rates compared to methods that do not use deep learning.

3 Dataset

The dataset is a significant element of our solution, and as there is no current dataset accessible for the classification of multiple body parts nudity, this was our primary concern in the application advancement.

The labels defined in our dataset represent, given an input image, the expected output for the algorithm for fine-grained nudity detection. To specify our labels, we selected 20 parts of the human body presented in Fig. 1. The body parts which are not numbered in Fig. 1 are not considered in our dataset.

Each human body part is labeled with 6 expected probabilities: the body part is visible, it is a female body part, it is a male body part, it is a naked body part, it is a naked female body part, and it is a naked male body part.

Our dataset currently consists of 37.872 images and 4.879.517 annotated labels. We created plots that indicate the number of images for all human body parts similarly to Fig. 3. This statistic was used to find patterns of human body parts that were not present in the dataset, which helped extend the dataset with new images.

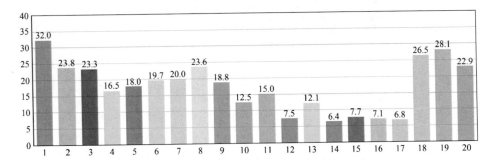

Fig. 3. The percentage of naked body parts in the dataset are shown on the vertical-axis. Numbers from the horizontal-axis represent the 20 human body part IDs from Fig. 1.

3.1   Labels

In other datasets and implementations for image classification, labels are either 0 or 1. As the experiments suggest, we improved the annotation of more difficult images (Fig. 4) by using a less restrictive method to assign expected probabilities. This improved annotation technique is also a great improvement for the training of the model, which achieves a lower error rate.

For a label, the expected value is a range of accepted probabilities that we defined as the target interval. The target interval t consists of a lower (t_a) and upper (t_b) boundary. Any value inside the interval is considered acceptable.

$$t = [t_a, t_b], \text{ where } t_a, t_b \in [0, 1] \text{ and } t_a \leq t_b \tag{1}$$

We have integrated Eq. 1 in the training loss function in a way that the neural network will be corrected if there are any predictions outside the interval.

In the annotation system, labels defined as $[0, \epsilon]$ are considered negative and the ones defined as $[1 - \epsilon, 1]$ are considered positive, where $\epsilon = 0.1$. This separation eases the process for extending the dataset because we focus on adding examples which are false negatives (FN) or false positives (FP).

Fig. 4. Example where the lower body parts (10, 11, 18, 19, 20 from Fig. 1) are difficult to label

3.2 Dataset Annotation

The dataset was developed by creating an initial collection of images with nudity and non-nudity. The dataset continued to grow in a continuous process which consisted of adding new images targeted at correcting and balancing the dataset for each part of the human body. The dataset was annotated by eighteen human annotators.

The dataset was built using annotation tools that helped us identify the problems more easily. Therefore we created some scenarios when an image may be marked for revision:

- An image is annotated differently by multiple annotators.
- An image annotation differs substantially from the prediction of a previously trained model.
- An image is classified differently by at least two previously trained models.

A more advanced method that we applied for corrections was to cluster the dataset using k-means clustering [6] on human annotations, so all images in a cluster are expected to have a similar pattern of visible body parts. We manually analyzed clusters and marked for revision images that did not match the other images in the cluster (e.g. In Fig. 5 the face was mislabeled and therefore went in a wrong cluster of negative examples for all human body parts).

We used the trained models from Table 2 to help us identify and correct problems in the train dataset. Using the data from Table 1 we analyzed the positive and negative errors and identified the body parts that have a lower amount of positive examples (e.g. back-high) leading to higher positive error. The problem was corrected by adding more images which contain particular body parts.

Fig. 5. The image containing a face was placed in a cluster of images without any visible human body parts, indicating a false-positive (FP).

In order to minimize the training time we limited the expansion of the dataset by only adding images which are misclassified by our models. The basic approach is to gather multiple new images, then simply add the misclassified ones to the dataset.

The FP rate of the proposed models was reduced by regularly evaluating a large collection of negative examples and appending the misclassified images to the training dataset. This was our main focus because the FP rate was critical for the application.

An optimization to adding more misclassified images to our dataset was to cluster unlabeled images using model predictions (k-means clustering [6]). We looked into clusters for images that were wrongly placed (Fig. 5) and uploaded them in the annotation system.

4   Nudity Detection Algorithm

In order to predict labels defined in our dataset, we trained a CNN model. The proposed architecture was inspired by state-of-the-art results for image classification [5,8,11] and we refined the existing methods to improve our results on the fine-grained nudity detection dataset. The dataset annotation and model training were conducted simultaneously, so the model immediately benefited from changes to the dataset and vice versa.

Table 1. The training dataset errors for some body parts according to a classifier. The errors are obtained by using Eq. 8. The highest errors are underlined and the lowest errors are bold.

Body part	Positive count	Negative count	Positive error	Negative error
Face	9883	21387	**1.1%**	0.3%
Abdomen-center	9229	22815	1.9%	0.5%
Back-mid	2840	30340	4.8%	**0.2%**
Chest	9631	22291	1.6%	0.4%
Cleavage	10469	22805	1.6%	0.4%
Breast	11055	21648	1.8%	0.5%
Back-high	2515	30490	<u>5.3%</u>	**0.2%**
Genitals	9824	20793	1.8%	<u>1.0%</u>

4.1   Input Image Preprocessing

CNN architectures have the best results for image classification when trained on RGB (Red, Green, Blue) images as observed in the ImageNet challenge [5,8,11]. We applied mean normalization for the image, as done previously by VGG [11], and also resized the input image according to different strategies in order to find the best approach that ensures the model's efficiency (RAM and CPU), the best accuracy, and constant run time.

In our initial implementation, the image was resized along its largest dimension (width or height) in order to fit a fixed-size square, as required by the CNN architecture. For example, an image of 1024 × 256 (256 Kilopixels) was resized to 256 × 64 (16 Kilopixels, 16 times less data than the original image) to fit in a 256 × 256 square image (64 Kilopixels).

In the improved version we resize images with bilinear interpolation so the total area of the image is less or equal to 64 Kilopixels. This leads to a minimal loss of information when resizing images which are not square shaped and helps to maintain a constant run time. For example, an image of 1024 × 256 (256 Kilopixels) will be resized to 512 × 128 (64 Kilopixels, 4 times less data than the original image), meaning 4 times more pixels than in the initial approach.

In some use-cases, special techniques are used to encode images (mostly GIF and PNG formats) to bypass the detection system. For example in Fig. 6 image content was hidden through a special use of the alpha channel. The left part of the image can be seen on black background and the right part of the image can only be seen on white background. We solved this problem by adding the alpha channel (A) to the input of our CNN architecture, obtaining RGBA.

We previously innovated other technologies (e.g. face detection) by using the ideas presented in the work of Canny Edge Detection [2]. The addition of the gradient magnitude channel (Edge) to the input image led to improved results and this inspired us to implement it in the CNN architecture.

Fig. 6. Systems which ignore the alpha channel, using only RGB (left), will wrongly miss the image, while ours (center) will detect it using the alpha channel. Systems which render the image using alpha over black background (right) can only analyze half the image correctly.

We used the gradient magnitude channel to reduce the loss of information about edges, which is the downside of decreasing the image resolution at the resize step in preprocessing. First we obtain the gradients along the x-axis (G_x) and the y-axis (G_y) for the red, green, blue and alpha channels for the initial image I, before resize.

$$G_x^{red}(x, y) = -\frac{1}{2} \cdot I^{red}(x - 1, y) + \frac{1}{2} \cdot I^{red}(x + 1, y) \tag{2}$$

$$G_y^{red}(x, y) = -\frac{1}{2} \cdot I^{red}(x, y - 1) + \frac{1}{2} \cdot I^{red}(x, y + 1) \tag{3}$$

The G_x and G_y are obtained by the weighted sum of the gradient channels.

$$G_x = 0.317 \cdot G_x^{red} + 0.416 \cdot G_x^{green} + 0.267 \cdot G_x^{blue} + 0.333 \cdot G_x^{alpha} \tag{4}$$

$$G_y = 0.317 \cdot G_y^{red} + 0.416 \cdot G_y^{green} + 0.267 \cdot G_y^{blue} + 0.333 \cdot G_y^{alpha} \tag{5}$$

To obtain the gradient magnitude channel E (Edge), the resize ratio factor is multiplied by the distance between G_x and G_y orientation components. The target resolution for the resized image is marked by R. The E channel is resized to match the resized image, and it is used as input to the CNN architecture along the RGBA channels.

$$E = r \cdot \sqrt{G_x^2 + G_y^2}, \text{ where } r = \frac{I_{width} \cdot I_{height}}{R_{width} \cdot R_{height}} \tag{6}$$

4.2 The CNN Architecture

The proposed architecture is inspired by the ResNet [5] and MobileNetV2 [10] architectures. The input of our CNN architecture is an image with RGBAE (Red, Green, Blue, Alpha, Edge) channels. The ResNet architecture is reducing the feature maps resolution by using a 7×7 convolution with a stride of 2, followed by a max pooling operation with a stride of 2, leading to 16 times less spatial information than the input image. By using the first five stacked convolutional layers in Fig. 7, we add more non-linearity in the beginning which is important for analyzing more details of the input image.

For the same reason, we use a 2×2 max pooling (MP) with a stride of 2 in Bottleneck1 (Fig. 7), rather than downsampling by a 1×1 convolution with a stride of 2, as done previously by the ResNet architecture. We apply the Bottleneck2 block as it was previously implemented by the ResNet architecture. Batch normalization and ReLU are placed after each convolution [5]. The average pooling layer reduces w and h to 1×1, regardless of the output dimensions of the previous layer. The network ends with a fully connected layer with 120 outputs, which is the number of trained classes. In the final version we used the depthwise separable convolutions from the MobileNetV2 architecture to lower the computational cost of the standard 3×3 convolutions.

4.3 Training Algorithm

We train the entire network inspired by practices [5,8,11] previously implemented for ImageNet. In our training algorithm, we have experimented with two versions to preprocess the images. The first technique is to resize images with a fixed resolution of 256×256. We improve on this method by using scale augmentation. At each training iteration we randomly select a resolution from the Gaussian distribution with a mean of 256 and a scale of 32, which is clipped to the $[192, 320]$ interval. The images are resized with the largest side to the selected resolution and are padded in order to be placed in a minibatch. This makes the model more robust to resizing and contributes to lowering the negative error rate, as observed in the last row of Table 2. For the images in a minibatch, we randomly select an image augmentation technique (rotation, flip, saturation and brightness adjustments) to use in the next iteration. The network is trained by SGD with momentum having an initial learning rate of 10^{-2}, which is reduced by half when the network cost does not improve for 40 consecutive training epochs.

We use the function L to compute the neural network cost for the predicted values y, given the network parameters θ. $[t_a, t_b]$ is the target interval (Eq. 1) and m is the length of a batch. For predicted values outside the target interval, the expected value is set to t_a or t_b. The predicted values which lie inside the interval do not contribute to the total error.

$$L(\theta) = \frac{1}{2m} \sum_{i=1}^{m} (max(t_a^{(i)}, min(t_b^{(i)}, y^{(i)})) - y^{(i)})^2 \qquad (7)$$

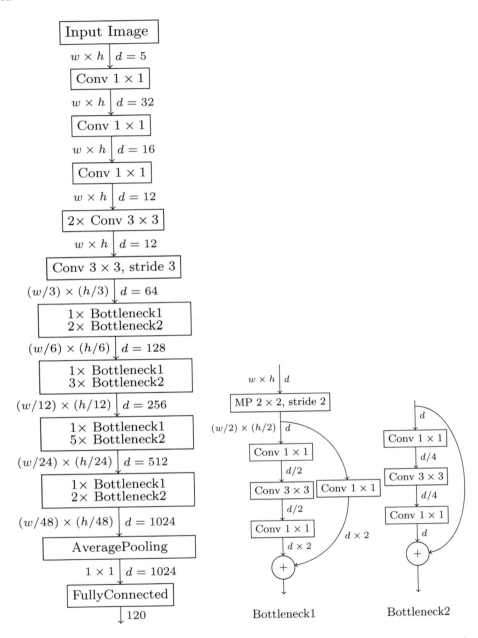

Fig. 7. The CNN architecture. w (width), h (height), and d (depth) represent the output dimensions.

To select the best model and identify high bias and high variance problems of the learning algorithm we evaluate the error at the end of each epoch on the validation dataset, which consists of 5% samples from our initial training dataset. Using the validation error (Fig. 8) we selected the best model based on the lowest over-fitting epoch.

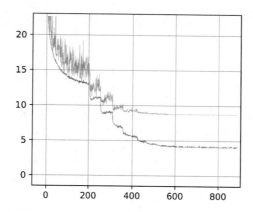

Fig. 8. The train (bottom line) and validation (bottom line) errors by epoch. The horizontal-axis indicates the epoch. The vertical-axis shows the corresponding error percentage.

Table 2. Results on the test dataset. $Error_{positive}$ is similar to the FN rate and $Error_{negative}$ is similar to the FP rate.

Model version	Model date	$Error_{total}$	$Error_{positive}$	$Error_{negative}$
V1	2017-05-05	23.0%	36.41%	16.07%
V2	2017-11-28	13.64%	20.99%	9.98%
V3	2018-06-14	8.19%	16.96%	4.36%
V4	2019-01-09	5.95%	7.23%	5.63%
V5	2019-03-04	5.07%	6.78%	3.91%
Paper	2019-05-13	1.89%	4.72%	0.81%

5   Testing and Results

The comparative testing process uses a test dataset of 3000 images, which were annotated using the same system as for the train dataset.

The results from Table 2 and Fig. 9 are gathered from the first test dataset, in order to have comparable models over time. At each date, the best model was picked based on a frozen training dataset. At different dates we used improved

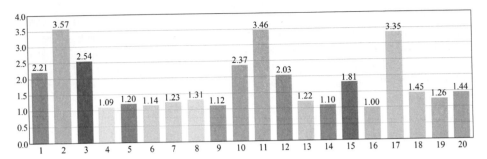

Fig. 9. The test error for each part of the human body using the Paper model version

datasets, which contain annotation corrections and new samples, hence the big improvement from the oldest model compared to the most recent one.

The final results from Table 2 were computed using Eq. 8 to obtain $Error_{total}$, $Error_{positive}$, and $Error_{negative}$. $Error_{positive}$ is the computed error for the subset of labels which satisfy the condition of $t_a + t_b \geq 1$, meaning that the arithmetic mean of the lower and upper bound of annotated interval t is ≥ 0.5. $Error_{negative}$ is the computed error for the subset of labels which satisfy the condition of $t_a + t_b < 1$.

$$Error = \sqrt{\frac{\sum\sum(max(t_a, min(t_b, y)) - y)^2}{\#dataset\_labels}} \qquad (8)$$

The results from Table 2 reflect the performance of the models achieved during technology development.

In model version V1 we fine-tuned the VGG-16 architecture by training only the fully-connected layers. The model was trained on a small dataset and only 40 body parts were used as labels. The model version V2 was trained using the same architecture as V1. It was trained on a larger dataset which consisted of 12500 samples, and only 40 body parts were used as labels.

The dataset has been increased from version V3 until the paper version and the strategies for image augmentation in the training algorithm have been enhanced.

In model version V3 we introduced the architecture proposed in Fig. 7. It was trained using 23000 samples, with 90 augmentations applied to each image. In model version V4 the train dataset contained 35630 images and we replaced the standard 3×3 convolutions form Bottleneck1 and Bottleneck2 blocks with the depthwise separable convolutions from the MobileNetV2 architecture. In model version V5 we improved the results by increasing the depth (d) of the convolutional layers by $1.2 \times d$ and the model was trained with a dataset of 37239 samples.

For the Paper model version in Table 2, we introduced the advanced image preprocessing strategies in the training algorithm, and observed an improvement to the negative error rate.

6   Conclusion and Future Work

Even though our modifications to the architecture improved the results on our test dataset, we can not state that the modifications will apply equally successfully to other datasets or problems. In future works, we look to further replicate our experiments on other available datasets and similar problems to better support our results.

References

1. Belém, R.J.S., Cavalcanti, J.M.B., de Moura, E.S., Nascimento, M.A.: Snif: a simple nude image finder. In: LA-WEB, pp. 252–258. IEEE Computer Society (2005). http://dblp.uni-trier.de/db/conf/la-web/la-web2005.html#BelemCMN05
2. Canny, J.F.: A computational approach to edge detection PAMI-8. IEEE Trans. Pattern Anal. Mach. Intell. **6**, 679–698 (1986)
3. Chen, X., Mottaghi, R., Liu, X., Fidler, S., Urtasun, R., Yuille, A.: Detect what you can: detecting and representing objects using holistic models and body parts. In: IEEE Conference on Computer Vision and Pattern Recognition (CVPR) (2014)
4. Fang, H., Lu, G., Fang, X., Xie, J., Tai, Y., Lu, C.: Weakly and semi supervised human body part parsing via pose-guided knowledge transfer. CoRR abs/1805.04310 (2018), http://arxiv.org/abs/1805.04310
5. He, K., Zhang, X., Ren, S., Sun, J.: Deep residual learning for image recognition. In: 2016 IEEE Conference on Computer Vision and Pattern Recognition (CVPR), pp. 770–778, June 2016. https://doi.org/10.1109/CVPR.2016.90
6. Kanungo, T., Mount, D.M., Netanyahu, N.S., Piatko, C., Silverman, R., Wu, A.Y.: An efficient k-means clustering algorithm: analysis and implementation (2000). IEEE Trans. Pattern Anal. Mach. Intell. **24**, 881–892 (2002)
7. Karavarsamis, S., Pitas, I., Ntarmos, N.: Recognizing pornographic images. In: Li, C., Dittmann, J., Katzenbeisser, S., Craver, S. (eds.) Multimedia and Security Workshop, MM&Sec 2012, Coventry, UK, 6–7 September 2012, pp. 105–108. ACM (2012). https://doi.org/10.1145/2361407.2361425
8. Krizhevsky, A., Sutskever, I., Hinton, G.E.: Imagenet classification with deep convolutional neural networks. Commun. ACM **60**(6), 84–90 (2017). https://doi.org/10.1145/3065386
9. LeCun, Y., et al.: Backpropagation applied to handwritten zip code recognition. Neural Comput. **1**(4), 541–551 (1989). https://doi.org/10.1162/neco.1989.1.4.541
10. Sandler, M., Howard, A.G., Zhu, M., Zhmoginov, A., Chen, L.: Inverted residuals and linear bottlenecks: Mobile networks for classification, detection and segmentation. CoRR abs/1801.04381 (2018), http://arxiv.org/abs/1801.04381
11. Simonyan, K., Zisserman, A.: Very deep convolutional networks for large-scale image recognition. CoRR abs/1409.1556 (2014)

DeepGRU: Deep Gesture Recognition Utility

Mehran Maghoumi[1,2]([⊠]) and Joseph J. LaViola Jr.[2]

[1] NVIDIA, Santa Clara, CA 95051, USA
[2] University of Central Florida, Orlando, FL 32816, USA
{mehran,jjl}@cs.ucf.edu

Abstract. We propose DeepGRU, a novel end-to-end deep network model informed by recent developments in deep learning for gesture and action recognition, that is streamlined and device-agnostic. DeepGRU, which uses only raw skeleton, pose or vector data is quickly understood, implemented, and trained, and yet achieves state-of-the-art results on challenging datasets. At the heart of our method lies a set of stacked gated recurrent units (GRU), two fully-connected layers and a novel global attention model. We evaluate our method on seven publicly available datasets, containing various number of samples and spanning over a broad range of interactions (full-body, multi-actor, hand gestures, *etc.*). In all but one case we outperform the state-of-the-art pose-based methods. For instance, we achieve a recognition accuracy of 84.9% and 92.3% on cross-subject and cross-view tests of the NTU RGB+D dataset respectively, and also 100% recognition accuracy on the UT-Kinect dataset. We show that even in the absence of powerful hardware, or a large amount of training data, and with as little as four samples per class, DeepGRU can be trained in under 10 min while beating traditional methods specifically designed for small training sets, making it an enticing choice for rapid application prototyping and development.

Keywords: Deep learning · Gesture recognition · Action recognition

1 Introduction

With the advent of various input devices, gesture recognition has become increasingly relevant in human-computer interaction. As these input devices get more capable and precise, the complexity of the interactions that they can capture also increases which, in turn, ignites the need for recognition methods that can leverage these capabilities. From a practitioner's point of view, a gesture recognizer would need to possess a set of traits in order to gain adoption: it should capture the fine differences among gestures and distinguish one gesture from another with a high degree of confidence, while being able to work with a vast number of input devices and gesture modalities. Concurrently, a recognition method should enable system designers to integrate the method into their workflow with the least amount of effort. These goals are often at odds: the recognition power of a recognizer usually comes at the cost of increased complexity and decreased flexibility of working across different input devices and modalities.

The original version of this chapter was revised: the name of an author was tagged incorrectly. The correction to this chapter is available at https://doi.org/10.1007/978-3-030-33720-9_54

© Springer Nature Switzerland AG 2019, corrected publication 2020
G. Bebis et al. (Eds.): ISVC 2019, LNCS 11844, pp. 16–31, 2019.
https://doi.org/10.1007/978-3-030-33720-9_2

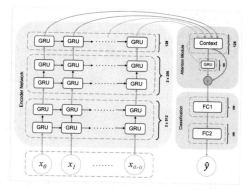

Fig. 1. Our proposed model for gesture recognition which consists of an *encoder network* of stacked gated recurrent units (GRU), the *attention module* and the *classification* layers. The input $\mathbf{x} = (x_0, x_1, ..., x_{(L-1)})$ is a sequence of vector data of arbitrary length and the output is the predicted class label $\hat{y}$. See Sect. 3 for a thorough description.

With these contradicting goals in mind, we introduce *DeepGRU*: an end-to-end deep network-based gesture recognition utility[1] (see Fig. 1). DeepGRU works directly with raw 3D skeleton, pose or other vector features (*e.g.* acceleration, angular velocity, *etc.*) produced by noisy commodity hardware, thus requiring minimal domain-specific knowledge to use. With roughly 4 million trainable parameters, DeepGRU is a rather small network by modern standards and is budget-aware when computational power is constrained. Yet, we achieve state-of-the-art results on various datasets.

Contributions. Our main contributions are devising a novel network model that works with raw vector data and is: (**1**) intuitive to understand and easy to implement, (**2**) easy to use, works out-of-the-box on noisy data, and is easy to train, without requiring powerful hardware (**3**) achieves state-of-the-art results in various use-cases, even with limited amount of training data. We believe (**1**) and (**2**) make DeepGRU enticing for application developers while (**3**) appeals to seasoned practitioners. To our knowledge, no prior work specifically focuses on model simplicity, accessibility for the masses, small training sets or CPU-only training which we think makes DeepGRU unique among its peers.

2   Related Work

Recognition with Hand-Crafted Features. Despite the success of end-to-end methods, classical methods that use hand-crafted features to perform recognition have been used with great success [18,21,49–51]. As Cheema *et al.* [9] showed, these methods can achieve excellent recognition results. They compared the performance of five algorithms (AdaBoost, SVM, decision trees *etc.*) on Wii controller gestures and concluded that, in some cases, the seemingly simple linear classifier can recognize a set of 25

---

[1] Reference implementation is available at: https://github.com/Maghoumi/DeepGRU.

gestures with 99% accuracy. Weng *et al.* [51] leveraged the spatio-temporal relations in action sequences with naïve-Bayes nearest-neighbor classifiers [6] to recognize actions. Xia *et al.* [53] used hidden Markov models (HMM) and the histogram of 3D joint locations to recognize gestures. Vemulapalli *et al.* [49] represented skeletal gestures as curves in a Lie group and used a combination of classifiers to recognize the gestures. Our approach differs from all of these methods in that we use the raw data of noisy input devices and do not hand-craft any features. Rather, our encoder network (Sect. 3.2) learns suitable feature representations during end-to-end training.

Recurrent Architectures. The literature contains a large body of work that use recurrent neural networks (RNN) for action and gesture recognition [10, 14, 16, 23, 24, 29, 33, 43, 48, 52]. Shahroudy *et al.* [38] showed the power of recurrent architectures and long-short term memory (LSTM) units [20] for large-scale gesture recognition. Zhang *et al.* [55] proposed a view-adaptive scheme to achieve view-invariant action recognition. Their model consisted of LSTM units that would learn the most suitable transformation of samples to achieve consistent viewpoints. Avola *et al.* [2] used a LSTM architecture in conjunction with hand-crafted angular features of hand joints to recognize hand gestures. Contrary to these methods, we only use gated recurrent units (GRU) [12] as the building block of our model. We show that GRUs are faster to train and produce better results. Also, our method is designed to be general and not specific to a particular device, gesture modality or feature representation. Lastly, we leverage the attention mechanism to capture the most important parts of each input sequence.

Attention Mechanism. When using recurrent architectures, the sub-parts of a temporal sequence may not all be equally important: some subsequences may be more pertinent to the task at hand than others. Thus, it is beneficial to learn a representation that can identify these important sub-parts to aid recognition, which is the key intuition behind the attention model [3, 31]. Even though the attention model was originally proposed for sequence to sequence models and neural machine translation, it has been adapted to the task of gesture and action recognition [5, 28, 41]. Liu *et al.* [28] proposed a global context-aware attention LSTM network for 3D action recognition. Using a global context, their method selectively focuses on the most informative joints when performing recognition. Song *et al.* [41] used the attention mechanism with LSTM units to selectively focus on discriminative skeleton joints at each gesture frame. Baradel *et al.* [5] leveraged the visual attention model to recognize human activities purely using image data. They used GRUs as the building block of their recurrent architecture.

Contrary to some of this work, DeepGRU only requires pose and vector-based data. Our novel attention model differs from prior work in how the context vector is computed and consumed. GCA-LSTM [28] has a multi-pass attention subnetwork which requires multiple initialize/refine iterations to compute attention vectors. Ours is single-pass and not iterative. Our attention model also differs from STA-LSTM [41] which has two separate temporal and spatial components, whereas ours has only one component for both domains. VA-LSTM [55] has a view-adaptation subnetwork that learns transformations to consistent view-points. This imposes the assumption that input data are spatial or view-point dependent, which may prohibit applications on non-spatial data (*e.g.* acoustic gestures [36]). Our model does not make any such assumptions. As we show later, our single-pass, non-iterative, spatio-temporal combined attention, and device-agnostic architecture result in less complexity, fewer parameters, and shorter training time, while achieving state-of-the-art results, which we believe sets us apart from prior work.

3 DeepGRU

In this section we provide an in-depth discussion of DeepGRU's architecture. In our architecture, we take inspiration from VGG-16 [39], and the attention [3,31] and sequence to sequence models [42]. Our model, depicted in Fig. 1, is comprised of three main components: an encoder network, the attention module, and two fully-connected (FC) layers fed to softmax producing the probability distribution of the class labels. We provide an ablation study to give insight into our design choices in Sect. 5.

3.1 Input Data

The input to DeepGRU is raw input device samples represented as a temporal sequence of the underlying gesture data (*e.g.* 3D joint positions, accelerometer or velocity measurements, 2D Cartesian coordinates of pen/touch interactions, *etc.*). At time step t, the input data is the column vector $x_t \in \mathbb{R}^N$, where N is the dimensionality of the feature vector. Thus, the input data of the entire temporal sequence of a single gesture sample is the matrix $\mathbf{x} \in \mathbb{R}^{N \times L}$, where L is the length of the sequence in time steps. Each input example sequences could have different number of time steps. We use the entire temporal sequence as-is without subsampling or clipping. When training on mini-batches, we represent the ith mini-batch as the tensor $\mathbf{X}_i \in \mathbb{R}^{B \times N \times \widetilde{L}}$, where B is the mini-batch size and $\widetilde{L}$ is the length of the longest sequence in the ith mini-batch. Sequences that are shorter than $\widetilde{L}$ are zero-padded.

3.2 Encoder Network

The encoder network in DeepGRU is fed with data from training samples and serves as the feature extractor. Our encoder network consists of a total of five stacked unidirectional GRUs. We prefer GRU units over LSTM units [20] as they have a smaller number of parameters and thus are faster to train and less prone to overfitting. At time step t, given an input vector x_t and the hidden state vector of the previous time step $h_{(t-1)}$, a GRU computes h_t, the hidden output at time step t, as $h_t = \Gamma\big(x_t, h_{(t-1)}\big)$ using the following transition equations:

$$
\begin{aligned}
r_t &= \sigma\left(\left(W_x^r\, x_t + b_x^r\right) \;+\; \left(W_h^r\, h_{(t-1)} + b_h^r\right)\right) \\
u_t &= \sigma\left(\left(W_x^u\, x_t + b_x^u\right) \;+\; \left(W_h^u\, h_{(t-1)} + b_h^u\right)\right) \\
c_t &= \tanh\left(\left(W_x^c\, x_t + b_x^c\right) \;+\; r_t\left(W_h^c\, h_{(t-1)} + b_h^c\right)\right) \\
h_t &= u_t \circ h_{(t-1)} \;+\; \left(1 - u_t\right) \circ c_t
\end{aligned}
\tag{1}
$$

where σ is the sigmoid function, $\circ$ denotes the Hadamard product, r_t, u_t and c_t are reset, update and candidate gates respectively and W_p^q and b_p^q are the trainable weights and biases. In our encoder network, h_0 of all the GRUs are initialized to zero.

Given a gesture example $\mathbf{x} \in \mathbb{R}^{N \times L}$, the encoder network uses Eq. 1 to output $\bar{h} \in \mathbb{R}^{128 \times L}$, where $\bar{h}$ is the result of the concatenation $\bar{h} = \begin{bmatrix} h_0; & h_1; & \dots; & h_{(L-1)} \end{bmatrix}$. This compact encoding of the input matrix $\mathbf{x}$, is then fed to the attention module.

3.3 Attention Module

The output of the encoder network, can provide a reasonable set of features for performing classification. We further refine this set of features by extracting the most informative parts of the sequence using the attention model. We propose a novel adaptation of the global attention model [31] which is suitable for our recognition task.

Given all the hidden states $\bar{h}$ of the encoder network, our attention module computes the attentional context vector $c \in \mathbb{R}^{128}$ using the trainable parameters W_c as:

$$c = \left(\frac{\exp\left(h_{(L-1)}^{\mathsf{T}} W_c \bar{h} \right)}{\sum_{t=0}^{L-1} \exp\left(h_{(L-1)}^{\mathsf{T}} W_c h_t \right)} \right) \bar{h} \tag{2}$$

As evident in Eq. 2, we solely use the hidden states of the encoder network to compute the attentional context vector. The hidden state of the last time step $h_{(L-1)}$ of the encoder network (the yellow arrow in Fig. 1) is the main component of our context computation and attentional output. This is because $h_{(L-1)}$ can potentially capture a lot of information from the entire gesture sample sequence. However, since the inputs to DeepGRU can be of arbitrary lengths, the amount of information that is captured by $h_{(L-1)}$ could differ among short sequences and long sequences. This could make the model susceptible to variations in sequence lengths. To mitigate this, we jointly learn a set of parameters that given the context and the hidden state of the encoder network would decide whether to use the hidden state directly, or have it undergo further transformation while accounting for the context. This decision logic can be mapped to the transition equations of a GRU (see Eq. 1). Thus, after computing the context c, we additionally compute the auxiliary context c' and produce the attention module's output o_{attn} as follows, where Γ_{attn} is the attentional GRU of the our model:

$$c' = \Gamma_{\text{attn}}\big(c, h_{(L-1)}\big) \qquad o_{\text{attn}} = \begin{bmatrix} c; & c' \end{bmatrix} \tag{3}$$

We believe that the novelty of our attention model is threefold. First, it only relies on the hidden state of the last time step $h_{(L-1)}$, which reduces complexity. Second, we compute the auxiliary context vector to mitigate the effects of sequence length variations. Lastly, our attention module is invariant to zero-padded sequences and thus can be trivially vectorized for training on mini-batches of sequences with different lengths. As we show in Sect. 5, our attention model works very well in practice.

3.4   Classification

The final layers of our model are comprised of two FC layers (F_1 and F_2) with ReLU activations that take the attention module's output and produce the probability distribution of the class labels using a softmax classifier:

$$\hat{y} = \text{softmax}\left(F_2\left(\text{ReLU}\left(F_1(o_{\text{attn}}) \right) \right) \right) \tag{4}$$

We use batch normalization [22] followed by dropout [19] on the input of both F_1 and F_2 in Eq. 4. During training, we minimize the cross-entropy loss to reduce the difference between predicted class labels $\hat{y}$ and the ground truth labels y.

4   Evaluation

We evaluate our proposed method on five datasets: UT-Kinect [53], NTU RGB+D [38], SYSU-3D [21], DHG 14/28 [13,15] and SBU Kinect Interactions [54]. We believe these datasets cover a wide range of gesture interactions, number of actors, view-point variations and input devices. We additionally performed experiments on two small-scale datasets (Wii Remote [9] and Acoustic [36]) in order to demonstrate the suitability of DeepGRU for scenarios where only a very limited amount of training data is available. We compute the recognition accuracies on each dataset and report them as a percentage.

Implementation Details.   We implemented DeepGRU using the PyTorch [35] framework. The input data to the network are z-score normalized using the training set. We use the Adam solver [25] ($\beta_1 = 0.9, \beta_2 = 0.999$) and the initial learning rate of 10^{-3} to train our model. The mini-batch size for all experiments is 128, except for those on NTU RGB+D, for which the size is 256. Training is done on a machine equipped with two NVIDIA GeForce GTX 1080 GPUs, Intel Core-i7 6850 K processor and 32 GB RAM. Unless stated otherwise, both GPUs were used for training.

Regularization.   We use dropout (0.5) and data augmentation to avoid overfitting. All regularization parameters were determined via cross-validation on a subset of the training data. Across all experiments we use three types of data augmentation: (**1**) random scaling with a factor[2] of ± 0.3, (**2**) random translation with a factor of ± 1, (**3**) synthetic sequence generation with gesture path stochastic resampling (GPSR) [45]. For GPSR we randomly select the resample count n and remove count r. We use n with a factor of ($\pm 0.1 \times \tilde{L}$) and r with a factor of ($\pm 0.05 \times \tilde{L}$). We additionally use a weight decay value of 10^{-4}, as well as random rotation with a factor of $\pm \frac{\pi}{4}$ on NTU RGB+D dataset. This was necessary due to the multiview nature of the dataset.

---

[2] A factor of ± 0.3 indicates that samples are randomly and non-uniformly (*e.g.*) scaled along all axes to [0.7, 1.3] of their original size.

4.1   UT-Kinect

This dataset [53] is comprised of ten gestures performed by ten participants two times (200 sequences in total). The data of each participant is recorded and labeled in one continuous session. What makes this dataset challenging is that the participants move around the scene and perform the gestures consecutively. Thus, samples have different starting position and/or orientations. We use the leave-one-out-sequence cross validation protocol of [53]. Our approach achieves state-of-the-art results with the perfect classification accuracy of 100% as shown in Table 1.

4.2   NTU RGB+D

To our knowledge, this is the largest dataset of actions collected from Kinect (v2) [38]. It comprises about 56,000 samples of 60 action classes performed by 40 subjects. Each subject's skeleton has 25 joints. The challenging aspect of this dataset stems from the availability of various viewpoints for each action, as well as the multi-person nature of some action classes. We follow the cross-subject (CS) and cross-view (CV) evaluation protocols of [38]. In the CS protocol, 20 subjects are used for training and the remaining 20 subjects are used for testing. In the CV protocol, two viewpoints are used for training and the remaining one viewpoint is used for testing. We create our feature vectors similar to [38]. Also, note that according to the dataset authors, 302 samples in this dataset are corrupted which were omitted in our tests.

Our results are presented in Table 2. Although DeepGRU only uses the raw skeleton positions of the samples, we present the results of other recognition methods that use other types of gesture data. To the best of our knowledge, DeepGRU achieves state-of-the-art performance among all methods that only use raw skeleton pose data.

Table 1. Results on UT-Kinect [53] dataset.

Method	Accuracy	Method	Accuracy
Histogram of 3D joints [53]	90.9	GCA-LSTM *(direct)* [28]	98.5
LARP + mfPCA [1]	94.8	CNN + Feature maps [47]	98.9
ST LSTM + Trust gates [29]	97.0	GCA-LSTM *(stepwise)* [28]	99.0
Lie group [49]	97.1	CNN + LSTM [33]	99.0
ST-NBNN [51]	98.0	KRP FS [11]	99.0
DPRL + GCNN [43]	98.5	**DeepGRU**	**100.0**

Table 2. Results on NTU RGB+D [38] dataset.

Modality	Method	Accuracy		Modality	Method	Accuracy	
		CS	CV			CS	CV
Image	Multitask DL [32]	84.6	–	Pose	STA model [41]	73.2	81.2
	Glimpse clouds [5]	**86.6**	**93.2**		CNN + Kernel feature maps [47]	75.3	–
Pose + Image	DSSCA - SSLM [37]	74.9	–		SkeletonNet [23]	75.9	81.2
	STA model (Hands) [4]	82.5	88.6		GCA-LSTM *(direct)* [28]	74.3	82.8
	Multitask DL [32]	**85.5**	–		GCA-LSTM *(stepwise)* [28]	76.1	84.0
Pose	Lie group [49]	50.1	52.8		DPTC [52]	76.8	84.9
	HBRNN [17]	59.1	64.0		VA-LSTM [55]	79.4	87.6
	Dynamic Skeletons [21]	60.2	65.2		Clips + CNN + MTLN [24]	79.6	84.8
	Deep LSTM [38]	60.7	67.3		View-invariant [30]	80.0	87.2
	Part-aware LSTM [38]	62.9	70.3		DPRL + GCNN [43]	83.5	89.8
	ST LSTM + Trust Gates [29]	69.2	77.7		**DeepGRU**	**84.9**	**92.3**

4.3 SYSU-3D

This Kienct-based dataset [21] contains 12 gestures performed by 40 participants totaling 480 samples. The widely-adopted evaluation protocol [21] of this dataset is to randomly select 20 subjects for training and the use remaining 20 subjects for testing. This process is repeated 30 times and the results are averaged and presented in Table 3.

4.4 DHG 14/28

This dataset [13] contains 14 hand gestures of 28 participants collected by a near-view Intel RealSense depth camera. Each gesture is performed in two different ways: using the whole hand, or just one finger. Also, each example gesture is repeated between one

Table 3. Results on SYSU-3D [21].

Method	Accuracy	Method	Accuracy
Dynamic skeletons [21]	75.5	VA-LSTM [55]	77.5
ST LSTM + Trust gates [29]	76.5	GCA-LSTM *(stepwise)* [28]	78.6
DPRL + GCNN [43]	76.9	**DeepGRU**	**80.3**

Table 4. Results on DHG 14/28 [13] with two evaluation protocols.

Protocol	Method	Accuracy		Protocol	Method	Accuracy	
		C = 14	C = 28			C = 14	C = 28
Leave–one–out	Chen *et al.* [10]	84.6	80.3	SHREC'17 [15]	HOG^2 [15,34]	78.5	74.0
	De Smedt *et al.* [14]	82.5	68.1		HIF3D [7]	90.4	80.4
	CNN+LSTM [33]	85.6	81.1		De Smedt *et al.* [15,40]	88.2	81.9
	DPTC [52]	85.8	80.2		DLSTM [2]	**97.6**	**91.4**
	DeepGRU	**92.0**	**87.8**		**DeepGRU**	94.5	**91.4**

to ten times yielding 2800 sequences. The training and testing data on this dataset are predefined and evaluation can be performed in two ways: classify 14 gestures or classify 28 gestures. The former is insensitive to how an action is performed, while the latter discriminates the examples performed with one finger from the ones performed with the whole hand. The standard evaluation protocol of this dataset is a leave-one-out cross-validation protocol. However, SHREC 2017 [15] challenge introduces a secondary protocol in which training and testing sets are pre-split. Table 4 depicts our results using both protocols and both number of gesture classes.

4.5   SBU Kinect Interactions

This dataset [54] contains 8 two-person interactions of seven participants. We utilize the 5-fold cross-validation protocol of [54] in our experiments. Contrary to other datasets, which express joint coordinates in the world coordinate system, this dataset has opted to normalize the joint values instead. Despite using a Kinect (v1) sensor, the participants in the dataset have only 15 joints.

We treat action frames that contain multiple skeletons similarly to what we described above for the NTU RGB+D dataset, with the exception of transforming the joint coordinates. Also, using the equations provided in the datasets, we covert the joint values them to metric coordinates in the depth camera coordinate frame. This is necessary to make the representation consistent with other datasets that we experiment on. Table 5 summarizes our results.

4.6   Small Training Set Evaluation

The amount of training data for some gesture-based applications may be limited. This is especially the case during application prototyping stages, where developers tend to rapidly iterate through design and evaluation cycles. Throughout the years, various methods have been proposed in the literature aiming to specifically address the need for recognizers that are easy to implement, fast to train and work well with small training sets [26,27,44,46]. Here, we show that our model performs well with small training sets and can be trained only on the CPU. We pit DeepGRU against Protractor3D [27], $3 [26] and Jackknife [46] which to our knowledge produce high recognition accuracies with a small number of training examples [46].

Table 5. Results on SBU Kinect Interactions [54].

Method	Accuracy	Method	Accuracy
HBRNN [17]	80.4	Clips + CNN + MTLN [24]	93.5
Deep LSTM [38]	86.0	GCA-LSTM *(direct)* [28]	94.1
Co-occurance deep LSTM [56]	90.4	CNN + Kernel Feature Maps [47]	94.3
STA Model [41]	91.5	GCA-LSTM *(stepwise)* [28]	94.9
ST LSTM + Trust gates [29]	93.3	**VA-LSTM** [55]	**97.2**
SkeletonNet [23]	93.5	DeepGRU	95.7

Table 6. Rapid prototyping evaluation results with T training samples per gesture class.

Dataset	Method	Accuracy		Dataset	Method	Accuracy	
		$T = 2$	$T = 4$			$T = 2$	$T = 4$
Acoustic [36]	**Jackknife** [46]	**91.0**	94.0	Wii Remote [9]	Protractor3D [27]	73.0	79.6
	DeepGRU	89.0	**97.4**		$3 [26]	79.0	86.1
					Jackknife [46]	**96.0**	98.0
					DeepGRU	92.4	**98.3**

We examine two datasets. The first dataset contains acoustic over-the-air hand gestures via Doppler shifted soundwaves [36]. This dataset contains 18 hand gestures collected from 22 participants via five speakers and one microphone. The soundwave-based interaction modality is prone to high amounts of noise. The second dataset contains gestures performed via a Wii Remote controller [9] and contains 15625 gestures of 25 gesture classes collected from 25 participants. These datasets are vastly different from other datasets examined thus far in that samples of [36] are frequency binned spectrograms (165D) while samples of [9] are linear acceleration data and angular velocity readings (6D), neither of which resemble typical skeletal nor positional features.

For each experiment we use the user-dependent protocol of [9,46]. Given a particular participant, T random samples from that participant are selected for training and the remaining samples are selected for testing. This procedure is repeated per participant and the results are averaged across all of them. We evaluate the performance of all the recognizers using $T = 2$ and $T = 4$ training samples per gesture class to examine a setup with limited training data. Even though deep networks are not commonly used with very small training sets, DeepGRU demonstrates very competitive accuracy in these tests (Table 6). We see that with $T = 4$ training samples per gesture class, DeepGRU outperforms other recognizers on both datasets.

5 Discussion

Comparison with the State-of-the-Art.[3] Experiment results show that DeepGRU generally tends to outperform the state-of-the-art results, sometimes with a large

---

[3] Refer to our supplementary material for more details: https://arxiv.org/abs/1810.12514.

Table 7. Ablation study on DHG 14/28 dataset (14 class, SHREC'17 protocol). We examine (respectively) the effects of the usage of the attention model, the recurrent layer choice (LSTM vs. GRU), the number of stacked recurrent layers (3 vs. 5) and the number of FC layers (1 vs. 2). Training times (seconds) are reported for every model. Experiments use the same random seed. DeepGRU's model is boldfaced.

Attn.	Rec. Unit	# Stacked	# FC	Time (sec)	Accuracy	Attn.	Rec. Unit	# Stacked	# FC	Time (sec)	Accuracy
-	LSTM	3	1	162.21	91.78	✓	LSTM	3	1	188.29	92.74
-	LSTM	3	2	164.07	91.07	✓	LSTM	3	2	192.12	92.02
-	LSTM	5	1	246.47	91.90	✓	LSTM	5	1	277.32	92.38
-	LSTM	5	2	251.67	89.52	✓	LSTM	5	2	283.35	92.26
-	GRU	3	1	143.87	93.45	✓	GRU	3	1	170.48	94.12
-	GRU	3	2	148.08	93.33	✓	GRU	3	2	174.00	93.81
-	GRU	5	1	210.83	93.69	✓	GRU	5	1	243.10	93.93
-	GRU	5	2	212.99	93.81	✓	**GRU**	**5**	**2**	**248.66**	**94.52**

Table 8. DeepGRU training times (in minutes) on various datasets. DeepGRU training times (in minutes) on various datasets.

Device	Configuration	Dataset	Time	Device	Configuration	Dataset	Time
CPU	12 threads	Acoustic [36] ($\mathcal{T} = 4$)	1.7	GPU	2 × GTX 1080	SHREC 2017 [15]	5.5
		Wii Remote [9] ($\mathcal{T} = 4$)	6.9			NTU RGB+D [38]	129.6
					1 × GTX 1080	SHREC 2017 [15]	6.2
						SYSU-3D [21]	9.0
						NTU RGB+D [38]	198.5

margin. On the NTU-RGB+D [38], we observe that in some cases DeepGRU outperforms image-based or hybrid methods. Although the same superiority is observed on the SBU dataset [54], our method achieves slightly lower accuracy compared to VA-LSTM [55]. One possible intuition for this observation could be that the SBU dataset [54] provides only a subset of skeleton joints that a Kinect (v1) device can produce (15 compared to the full set of 20 joints). Further, note that VA-LSTM's view-adaptation subnetwork assumes that the gesture data are 3D positions and viewpoint-dependent. In contrast, DeepGRU does not make any such assumptions.

As shown in Table 4, classifying 14 gestures of the DHG 14/28 dataset [13] with DLSTM [2] yields higher recognition accuracy compared to DeepGRU. As previously mentioned, DLSTM [2] uses hand-crafted angular features extracted from hand joints and these features are used as the input to the recurrent network while DeepGRU uses raw input, which relieves the user of the burden of computing domain-specific features. Classifying 28 classes, however, yields similar results with either of the recognizers.

Generality. Our experiments demonstrate the versatility of DeepGRU for various gesture or action modalities and input data: from full-body multi-actor actions to hand gestures, collected from various commodity hardware such as depth sensors or game controllers with various data representations (*e.g.* pose, acceleration and velocity or frequency spectrograms) as well as other differences such as the number of actors, gesture lengths, number of samples and number of viewpoints. Regardless of these differences, DeepGRU can still produce high accuracy results.

Ease of Use. Our method uses raw device data, thus requiring fairly little domain knowledge. Our model is straightforward to implement and as we discuss shortly, training is fast. We believe these traits make DeepGRU an enticing option for practitioners.

Ablation Study. To provide insight into our network design, we present an ablation study in Table 7. We note depth alone is not sufficient to achieve state-of-the-art results. Further, accuracy increases in all cases when we use GRUs instead of LSTMs. GRUs were on average 12% faster to train and the worst GRU variant achieved higher accuracy than the best LSTM one. In our early experiments we noted LSTM networks overfitted frequently which necessitated a lot more parameter tuning, motivating our preference for GRUs. However, we later observed underfitting when training GRU variants on larger datasets, arising the need to reduce regularization and tune parameters again. To alleviate this, we added the second FC layer which later showed to improve results across all datasets while still faster than LSTMs to train. We observe increased accuracy in all experiments with attention, which suggests the attention model is necessary. Lastly, in our experiments we observed an improvement of roughly 0.5%–1% when the auxiliary context vector is used (Sect. 3.3). In short, we see improved results with the attention model on GRU variants with five stacked layers and two FC layers.

Timings. We measured the amount of time it takes to train DeepGRU to convergence with different configurations in Table 8. The reported times include dataset loading, preprocessing and data augmentation time. Training our model to convergence tends to be fast: GPU training of medium-sized datasets or CPU-only training of small datasets can be done in under 10 min. We also measured DeepGRU's average inference time per sample both on GPU and on CPU in *micro*seconds. On a single GPU, our methods takes 349.1 µs to classify one gesture example while it takes 3136.3 µs on the CPU.

Limitations. Our method has some limitations which we plan to address in the future. The input needs to be segmented, nonetheless adding support for unsegmented data is straightforward and requires some changes in the training protocol as demonstrated in [8]. In our experiments we observed that DeepGRU performs better with high-dimensional data, thus application on low-dimensional data may require further effort from developers. Although we used a similar set of hyperparameters for all experiments, other datasets may require some tuning.

6   Conclusion

We discussed DeepGRU, a deep network-based gesture and action recognizer which directly works with raw pose and vector data. We demonstrated that our architecture, which uses stacked GRU units and a global attention mechanism along with two fully-connected layers, was able to achieve state-of-the-art recognition results on various datasets, regardless of the dataset size and interaction modality. We further examined our approach for application in scenarios where training data is limited and computational power is constrained. Our results indicate that with as little as four training samples per gesture class, DeepGRU can still achieve competitive accuracy. We also showed that training times are short and CPU-only training is possible.

References

1. Anirudh, R., Turaga, P., Su, J., Srivastava, A.: Elastic functional coding of human actions: from vector-fields to latent variables. In: 2015 IEEE Conference on Computer Vision and Pattern Recognition, pp. 3147–3155 (2015)
2. Avola, D., Bernardi, M., Cinque, L., Foresti, G.L., Massaroni, C.: Exploiting recurrent neural networks and leap motion controller for the recognition of sign language and semaphoric hand gestures. IEEE Trans. Multimed. 21, 234–245 (2018)
3. Bahdanau, D., Cho, K., Bengio, Y.: Neural machine translation by jointly learning to align and translate. In: Proceedings of ICLR (2015)
4. Baradel, F., Wolf, C., Mille, J.: Human action recognition: pose-based attention draws focus to hands. In: 2017 IEEE International Conference on Computer Vision Workshops (ICCVW), pp. 604–613 (2017)
5. Baradel, F., Wolf, C., Mille, J., Taylor, G.W.: Glimpse clouds: human activity recognition from unstructured feature points. In: The IEEE Conference on Computer Vision and Pattern Recognition (2018)
6. Boiman, O., Shechtman, E., Irani, M.: In defense of nearest-neighbor based image classification. In: 2008 IEEE Conference on Computer Vision and Pattern Recognition, pp. 1–8 (2008)
7. Boulahia, S.Y., Anquetil, E., Multon, F., Kulpa, R.: Dynamic hand gesture recognition based on 3D pattern assembled trajectories. In: 2017 Seventh International Conference on Image Processing Theory, Tools and Applications (IPTA), pp. 1–6 (2017)
8. Caputo, F.M., et al.: Online gesture recognition. In: Eurographics Workshop on 3D Object Retrieval (2019)
9. Cheema, S., Hoffman, M., LaViola, J.J.: 3D gesture classification with linear acceleration and angular velocity sensing devices for video games. Entertain. Comput. 4(1), 11–24 (2013)
10. Chen, X., Guo, H., Wang, G., Zhang, L.: Motion feature augmented recurrent neural network for skeleton-based dynamic hand gesture recognition. In: 2017 IEEE International Conference on Image Processing (ICIP), pp. 2881–2885 (2017)
11. Cherian, A., Sra, S., Gould, S., Hartley, R.: Non-linear temporal subspace representations for activity recognition. In: Proceedings of the IEEE Conference on Computer Vision and Pattern Recognition, pp. 2197–2206 (2018)
12. Cho, K., et al.: Learning phrase representations using rnn encoder-decoder for statistical machine translation. In: Proceedings of the 2014 Conference on Empirical Methods in Natural Language Processing (EMNLP), pp. 1724–1734 (2014)
13. De Smedt, Q., Wannous, H., Vandeborre, J.P.: Skeleton-based dynamic hand gesture recognition. In: Proceedings of the IEEE Conference on Computer Vision and Pattern Recognition Workshops, pp. 1–9 (2016)
14. De Smedt, Q., Wannous, H., Vandeborre, J.-P.: 3D hand gesture recognition by analysing set-of-joints trajectories. In: Wannous, H., Pala, P., Daoudi, M., Flórez-Revuelta, F. (eds.) UHA3DS 2016. LNCS, vol. 10188, pp. 86–97. Springer, Cham (2018). https://doi.org/10.1007/978-3-319-91863-1_7

15. De Smedt, Q., Wannous, H., Vandeborre, J.P., Guerry, J., Le Saux, B., Filliat, D.: Shrec'17 track: 3D hand gesture recognition using a depth and skeletal dataset. In: 10th Eurographics Workshop on 3D Object Retrieval (2017)
16. Devineau, G., Moutarde, F., Xi, W., Yang, J.: Deep learning for hand gesture recognition on skeletal data. In: 2018 13th IEEE International Conference on Automatic Face Gesture Recognition (FG 2018), pp. 106–113 (2018)
17. Du, Y., Wang, W., Wang, L.: Hierarchical recurrent neural network for skeleton based action recognition. In: 2015 IEEE Conference on Computer Vision and Pattern Recognition, pp. 1110–1118 (2015)
18. Fernández-Ramírez, J., Álvarez-Meza, A., Orozco-Gutiérrez, Á.: Video-based human action recognition using kernel relevance analysis. In: Bebis, G., et al. (eds.) ISVC 2018. LNCS, vol. 11241, pp. 116–125. Springer, Cham (2018). https://doi.org/10.1007/978-3-030-03801-4_11
19. Hinton, G.E., Srivastava, N., Krizhevsky, A., Sutskever, I., Salakhutdinov, R.R.: Improving neural networks by preventing co-adaptation of feature detectors. arXiv preprint arXiv:1207.0580 (2012)
20. Hochreiter, S., Schmidhuber, J.: Long short-term memory. Neural Comput. 9(8), 1735–1780 (1997)
21. Hu, J., Zheng, W., Lai, J., Zhang, J.: Jointly learning heterogeneous features for rgb-d activity recognition. IEEE Trans. Pattern Anal. Mach. Intell. 39(11), 2186–2200 (2017)
22. Ioffe, S., Szegedy, C.: Batch normalization: Accelerating deep network training by reducing internal covariate shift, pp. 448–456 (2015)
23. Ke, Q., An, S., Bennamoun, M., Sohel, F., Boussaid, F.: Skeletonnet: mining deep part features for 3-D action recognition. IEEE Signal Process. Lett. 24(6), 731–735 (2017)
24. Ke, Q., Bennamoun, M., An, S., Sohel, F., Boussaid, F.: A new representation of skeleton sequences for 3D action recognition. In: 2017 IEEE Conference on Computer Vision and Pattern Recognition, pp. 4570–4579. IEEE (2017)
25. Kingma, D.P., Ba, J.: Adam: A method for stochastic optimization. arXiv preprint arXiv:1412.6980 (2014)
26. Kratz, S., Rohs, M.: The $3 recognizer: Simple 3D gesture recognition on mobile devices. In: Proceedings of the 15th International Conference on Intelligent User Interfaces (2010)
27. Kratz, S., Rohs, M.: Protractor3D: a closed-form solution to rotation-invariant 3D gestures. In: Proceedings of the 16th International Conference on Intelligent User Interfaces (2011)
28. Liu, J., Wang, G., Duan, L., Abdiyeva, K., Kot, A.C.: Skeleton-based human action recognition with global context-aware attention lstm networks. IEEE Trans. Image Process. 27(4), 1586–1599 (2018)
29. Liu, J., Shahroudy, A., Xu, D., Wang, G.: Spatio-temporal LSTM with trust gates for 3D human action recognition. In: Leibe, B., Matas, J., Sebe, N., Welling, M. (eds.) ECCV 2016. LNCS, vol. 9907, pp. 816–833. Springer, Cham (2016). https://doi.org/10.1007/978-3-319-46487-9_50
30. Liu, M., Liu, H., Chen, C.: Enhanced skeleton visualization for view invariant human action recognition. Pattern Recogn. 68(C), 346–362 (2017)
31. Luong, M.T., Pham, H., Manning, C.D.: Effective approaches to attention-based neural machine translation. In: Proceedings of the 2015 Conference on Empirical Methods in Natural Language Processing (2015)
32. Luvizon, D.C., Picard, D., Tabia, H.: 2D/3D pose estimation and action recognition using multitask deep learning. In: The IEEE Conference on Computer Vision and Pattern Recognition, vol. 2 (2018)
33. Núñez, J.C., Cabido, R., Pantrigo, J.J., Montemayor, A.S., Vélez, J.F.: Convolutional neural networks and long short-term memory for skeleton-based human activity and hand gesture recognition. Pattern Recogn. 76(C), 80–94 (2018)

34. Ohn-Bar, E., Trivedi, M.M.: Joint angles similarities and HOG2 for action recognition. In: 2013 IEEE Conference on Computer Vision and Pattern Recognition Workshops (2013)
35. Paszke, A., et al.: Automatic differentiation in pytorch. In: NIPS-W (2017)
36. Pittman, C.R., LaViola Jr., J.J.: Multiwave: complex hand gesture recognition using the doppler effect. In: Proceedings of the 43rd Graphics Interface Conference. pp. 97–106 (2017)
37. Shahroudy, A., Ng, T., Gong, Y., Wang, G.: Deep multimodal feature analysis for action recognition in RGB+D videos. IEEE Trans. Pattern Anal. Mach. Intell. **40**(5), 1045–1058 (2018)
38. Shahroudy, A., Liu, J., Ng, T.T., Wang, G.: NTURGB+D: a large scale dataset for 3D human activity analysis. In: IEEE Conference on Computer Vision and Pattern Recognition (2016)
39. Simonyan, K., Zisserman, A.: Very deep convolutional networks for large-scale image recognition. CoRR abs/1409.1556 (2014)
40. Smedt, Q.D., Wannous, H., Vandeborre, J.: Skeleton-based dynamic hand gesture recognition. In: 2016 IEEE Conference on Computer Vision and Pattern Recognition Workshops, pp. 1206–1214 (2016)
41. Song, S., Lan, C., Xing, J., Zeng, W., Liu, J.: An end-to-end spatio-temporal attention model for human action recognition from skeleton data. AAAI. **1**, 4263–4270 (2017)
42. Sutskever, I., Vinyals, O., Le, Q.V.: Sequence to sequence learning with neural networks. In: Advances in Neural Information Processing Systems, pp. 3104–3112 (2014)
43. Tang, Y., Tian, Y., Lu, J., Li, P., Zhou, J.: Deep progressive reinforcement learning for skeleton-based action recognition. In: The IEEE Conference on Computer Vision and Pattern Recognition (2018)
44. Taranta, II, E.M., LaViola Jr., J.J.: Penny pincher: a blazing fast, highly accurate $-family recognizer. In: Proceedings of the 41st Graphics Interface Conference, pp. 195–202 (2015)
45. Taranta II, E.M., Maghoumi, M., Pittman, C.R., LaViola Jr., J.J.: A rapid prototyping approach to synthetic data generation for improved 2D gesture recognition. In: Proceedings of the 29th Symposium on User Interface Software and Technology, pp. 873–885. ACM (2016)
46. Taranta II, E.M., Samiei, A., Maghoumi, M., Khaloo, P., Pittman, C.R., LaViola Jr., J.J.: Jackknife: a reliable recognizer with few samples and many modalities. In: Proceedings of the 2017 Conference on Human Factors in Computing Systems, pp. 5850–5861 (2017)
47. Tas, Y., Koniusz, P.: CNN-based action recognition and supervised domain adaptation on 3D body skeletons via kernel feature maps. In: BMVC (2018)
48. Tewari, A., Taetz, B., Grandidier, F., Stricker, D.: Two phase classification for early hand gesture recognition in 3D top view data. In: Bebis, G., et al. (eds.) ISVC 2016. LNCS, vol. 10072, pp. 353–363. Springer, Cham (2016). https://doi.org/10.1007/978-3-319-50835-1_33
49. Vemulapalli, R., Arrate, F., Chellappa, R.: Human action recognition by representing 3D skeletons as points in a lie group. In: 2014 IEEE Conference on Computer Vision and Pattern Recognition, pp. 588–595 (2014)
50. Vrigkas, M., Mastora, E., Nikou, C., Kakadiaris, I.A.: Robust incremental hidden conditional random fields for human action recognition. In: Bebis, G., et al. (eds.) ISVC 2018. LNCS, vol. 11241, pp. 126–136. Springer, Cham (2018). https://doi.org/10.1007/978-3-030-03801-4_12
51. Weng, J., Weng, C., Yuan, J.: Spatio-temporal naive-bayes nearest-neighbor (ST-NBNN) for skeleton-based action recognition. In: 2017 IEEE Conference on Computer Vision and Pattern Recognition, pp. 445–454 (2017)
52. Weng, J., Liu, M., Jiang, X., Yuan, J.: Deformable pose traversal convolution for 3D action and gesture recognition. In: Ferrari, V., Hebert, M., Sminchisescu, C., Weiss, Y. (eds.) ECCV 2018. LNCS, vol. 11211, pp. 142–157. Springer, Cham (2018). https://doi.org/10.1007/978-3-030-01234-2_9

53. Xia, L., Chen, C., Aggarwal, J.: View invariant human action recognition using histograms of 3D joints. In: 2012 IEEE Computer Society Conference on Computer Vision and Pattern Recognition Workshops, pp. 20–27. IEEE (2012)
54. Yun, K., Honorio, J., Chattopadhyay, D., Berg, T.L., Samaras, D.: Two-person interaction detection using body-pose features and multiple instance learning. In: 2012 IEEE Computer Society Conference on Computer Vision and Pattern Recognition Workshops. IEEE (2012)
55. Zhang, P., Lan, C., Xing, J., Zeng, W., Xue, J., Zheng, N.: View adaptive recurrent neural networks for high performance human action recognition from skeleton data. In: 2017 IEEE International Conference on Computer Vision (ICCV), pp. 2136–2145 (2017)
56. Zhu, W., Lan, C., Xing, J., Zeng, W., Li, Y., Shen, L., Xie, X.: Co-occurrence feature learning for skeleton based action recognition using regularized deep LSTM networks. In: Proceedings of the Thirtieth AAAI Conference on Artificial Intelligence, pp. 3697–3703 (2016)

Delineation of Road Networks Using Deep Residual Neural Networks and Iterative Hough Transform

Pinjing Xu[ID] and Charalambos Poullis[(⊠)][ID]

Immersive and Creative Technologies Lab, Department of Computer Science and
Software Engineering, Gina Cody School of Engineering and Computer Science,
Concordia University, Montreal, QC, Canada
charalambos@poullis.org
http://www.theICTlab.org

Abstract. In this paper we present a complete pipeline for extracting
road network vector data from satellite RGB orthophotos of urban areas.
Firstly, a network based on the SegNeXt architecture with a novel loss
function is employed for the semantic segmentation of the roads. Results
show that the proposed network produces on average better results than
other state-of-the-art semantic segmentation techniques. Secondly, we
propose a fast post-processing technique for vectorizing the rasterized
segmentation result, removing erroneous lines, and refining the road network. The result is a set of vectors representing the road network. We
have extensively tested the proposed pipeline and provide quantitative
and qualitative comparisons with other state-of-the-art based on a number of known metrics.

Keywords: Road network extraction · Residual neural networks ·
Semantic segmentation

1 Introduction

The automatic extraction of road networks from remote sensor imagery has long
been a challenge not just to the GIS but also the computer vision communities.
The vast variations in the road functions [e.g. rural, urban, highways, etc.], colors
[e.g. dirt road, asphalt], shapes [e.g. winding mountain roads, straight highways],
and sizes, make it an extremely challenging task. Recent attempts using deep
learning techniques have shown promising results [12,14], the majority of which
reformulate the problem as a pixel classification problem and employ semantic
segmentation techniques. Although this is useful in some cases, the majority of
the applications employing road network data, e.g. autonomous driving, GIS,
etc., require that the network is in vector form; and in fact, it is this vectoriza-
tion or linearization of the road network pixels that is perhaps one of the most
challenging tasks.

© Crown 2019
G. Bebis et al. (Eds.): ISVC 2019, LNCS 11844, pp. 32–44, 2019.
https://doi.org/10.1007/978-3-030-33720-9_3

In this paper we present a novel approach for extracting road networks in vector form. A deep convolutional neural network based on the SegNeXt architecture is trained to classify road pixels in satellite images of urban areas. This architecture offers a reduced number of parameters and high localization accuracy therefore eliminating the need for the typical refinement of the segmentation results using MRF-based techniques. Furthermore, a novel loss function is proposed which provides better results than the typical loss functions used. The segmentation result is then vectorized and refined using a fast post-processing technique. During the post-processing, linear road segments are extracted using an iterative patch-based Hough transform technique which tracks the segments from one patch to the other. Next, a refinement process ensures that the nearby linear road segments are connected together to form a larger road network, and conflicting/overlapping parallel segments and other small segments are removed. The final result of the proposed technique is a road network in vector form which can be readily used in any GIS-based application.

Paper Organization. The paper is organized as follows: Sect. 2 provides a brief overview of the state-of-the-art in the area. In Sect. 3 we present an overview of the system. The network architecture is presented in detail in Sect. 4 including the training and validation tests. Section 4.4 explains the post-processing refinement process which converts the classified road pixels into the final road network vectors. Finally, Sect. 5 shows the comparisons of the proposed pipeline and the current state-of-the-art, and Sect. 6 presents the conclusion and future work.

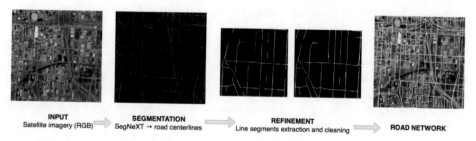

INPUT   SEGMENTATION   REFINEMENT
Satellite imagery (RGB)   SegNeXt → road centerlines   Line segments extraction and cleaning   ROAD NETWORK

Fig. 1. System overview. The input RGB image is processed using SegNeXt and results in a grayscale classification image of road and non-road pixels. The classification image is then divided into patches which are further processed. The refinement process involves an iterative application of patch-based Hough transforms which results in a set of extracted lines. Erroneously extracted lines resulting from misclassification are removed, and nearby lines are either connected (if not parallel) or suppressed (if parallel). The result is a set of vectors representing the road network in the input image shown in yellow overlaid on the input image. (Color figure online)

2   Related Work

Below we provide a brief overview of the state-of-the-art in the area.

For many years the majority of the road extraction techniques relied solely on procedural approaches [1,6,7]. Of the most recent, is the work in [8] where the authors propose a technique for extracting the urban roads from satellite images by using orientation histograms and morphological profile features to guide a binary partition tree, thus achieving a higher accuracy.

Perhaps one of the first works on training deep neural networks for extracting large-scale road networks from satellite images is the work presented in [11]. The authors present a network trained on a challenging dataset with large context (i.e. larger sized patches containing a large number of urban features) in order to better differentiate between what is a road vs a non-road pixel.

Recently, more studies are following the semantic segmentation approach [4,9,15,18]. The authors in [3] propose a fully convolutional network based on the U-Net family architecture with pre-trained ResNet-34 as the encoder. They optimize a loss function which combines the binary cross entropy and the intersection over union. During the test phase they report that data augmentation helps improve the prediction results even further.

In [17] the authors present a network which combines the ResNet and U-Net architectures to address the road network extraction. Their network employs skip connections within the residual units and between the encoding and decoding paths of the network to facilitate propagation of information, and also reduce the number of the generic U-Net's parameters by 75%.

The authors in [10] propose a semantic segmentation technique based on the ResNet architecture consisting of an encoder that compresses the image into a small feature map, and a fully convolutional decoder for generating the segmentation output. They also propose a post-processing technique for refining the segmentation result. Their approach relies on heuristics to connect and refine the roads (i.e. gap distances, accumulated error resulting from the first network's classification) which in some cases makes it hard to get complete and well optimized road networks.

At the time of writing this manuscript the best performing road network extraction technique is RoadTracer presented in [2]. The authors follow a new paradigm in which a CNN is used as a decision tool for tracing the road network in the image instead of using the neural network for semantic segmentation. Their approach has the pre-condition that the starting point lies on a road otherwise the tracing fails. Problems also arise in cases where tracing the road network runs out of points to process e.g. happens often when a bridge is reached. In this case, the result will be partial and disjoint from the entire road network and hard to recover the missing parts.

3   System Overview

The input to our system is an RGB image which is fed forward into a deep autoencoder network (SegNeXt) with aggregated residual transformations.

The network outputs a semantic segmentation of the image in the form of a grayscale image in which each pixel is classified into a *road* or *non-road* classes. The classification image is then divided into patches which are further processed. During the refinement process, an iterative patch-based Hough transform is applied. Extracted lines are tracked from one patch to the other. Erroneously extracted lines resulting from misclassification are removed, and nearby lines are either connected (if not parallel) or suppressed (if parallel). The result is a set of vectors representing the road network in the input image. Figure 1 summarizes the system overview.

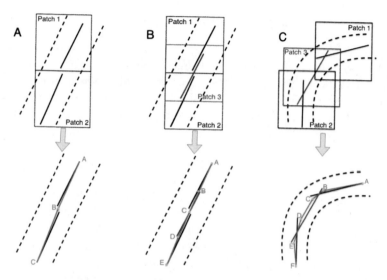

Fig. 2. Refinement process. Three cases are considered. A: no overlap between two windows, move the two nearby end points to the average location to connect these two line segments; B: 50% overlapping between windows, in addition to merging nearby end points of line segments, the merging of nearby points-to-lines is also needed; C: extract a curve by merging nearby lines. Smaller windows size and larger overlapping area will yield smoother result.

4   Network Architecture

The network architecture resembles that of a SegNeXt network [5] but with grayscale output and is shown in Fig. 3. The network consists of three deep convolutional encoders and corresponding number of decoders with feed-forward links and cardinality-enabled residual-based building blocks. In each residual block the input data is split into multiple groups onto which different kernels are applied. A dilation of 2 is applied during convolution to introduce more spatial context. The feed-forward links from the encoders to the decoders help to retain high frequency information and improve the boundary delineation resulting in a smoother segmentation result therefore eliminating the need for any

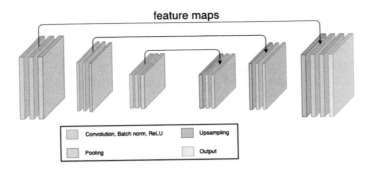

Fig. 3. SegNeXt-variant architecture

subsequent post-processing with conditional random fields (CRF), etc. In [16] these cardinality-enabled residual-based blocks used in shallow networks were shown to surpass in terms of performance other deeper CNNs. Thus, using these blocks the network can be shallower resulting in a smaller number of trainable network parameters therefore making the training process more effective.

4.1 Dataset

For the training, validation and testing of the network we follow a similar approach as in [10]. A large number of satellite images acquired from Google Maps with resolution of 4096×4096 and ground sampling density of $60 \frac{cm}{pixel}$ are used. These images are randomly selected in the $24\,km^2$ surrounding area of the GPS locations of 40 major cities. Training and validation is performed using images of 25 of these cities, and testing is performed on the images of the remaining 15 cities. Thus, there are no images of the same city between the training and testing datasets. The ground truth data is road center line extracted from the OpenStreetMap [13], width of road lines in ground truth images is 10 pixels.

4.2 Training

The network was trained on the images of the 25 cities. In order to maximize the training dataset we decided not to use a validation set during training but rather calculate the loss based after each epoch on three randomly selected patches from the training set. The training took 48 h on a single NVIDIA GTX 1080Ti with an adaptive learning rate. We have used Keras API (with Tensorflow as backend engine) for the development of the network and the code will be made available as open source.

Input. The input to the network is a batch of 32 patches of size 200×200. Patches are selected using random sampling in order to ensure appropriate coverage.

Data Augmentation. We apply a series of different data augmentation operations on the input patches. A histogram equalization is first applied to all patches in order to reduce possible high contrast resulting from the sun which appears as deep black shadows. Next, a number of transformations is performed consisting of random rotations in the range of $[0, \frac{\pi}{2}]$ degrees, scaling up/down by up to 70%, and random flipping on the vertical/horizontal axis.

Loss Function. Perhaps the most widely used loss functions when dealing with a classification problem are the (a) Mean square error (MSE), and (b) Intersection over Union (IoU). However, due to the characteristics of MSE (takes the sum of a patch but ignores the positional relationships), it tends to result in a lot of noise in the segmentation output, and often yields bad performance. On the other hand, the use of an IoU loss function results in many gaps in the results as it was also recently reported in [2]. To address the aforementioned limitations, we propose a new loss function which comprises of both MSE and the inverse of IoU, and combines them as follows,

$$L = MSE \times \frac{union}{intersection} \tag{1}$$

Intuitively, the MSE is good at indicating whether a pixel is road or non-road, and the inverse of the IoU helps to reduce the noise.

4.3 Testing

During testing, we run the network on the image with a sliding window, with a window size of 200×200 and a step size of 100. Instead of thresholding the semantic segmentation result similar to many other semantic segmentation techniques, we remove the noise and extract roads by applying Hough transform to extract line segments in each window based on the network predictions. Since we have overlaps between the sliding windows, extracted line segments may not agree in different windows. Thus, a few more steps are needed to refine the result and get a clean road network.

4.4 Post-processing Refinement

Figure 2 shows all possible cases handled by our refinement process and what the resulting line segments will be. For a simple case, if there's no overlap between two windows (patches), extracted Hough lines will be like case A with no crossing over or overlap on one another. In this case, we merge all nearby line end points by moving them to their average location. Next, we consider the case of overlapping patches similar to case B in the Fig. 2. If the extracted Hough lines on two patches do not "agree" with each other, intersection or misalignment will occur. To address the misalignment issue, we perform the following steps:

1. Merge all nearby line end points similar to case A;
2. For each line end point, search around itself for nearby lines, if there is a line **ab** passing by this end point, merge this end point into the line in the following steps:

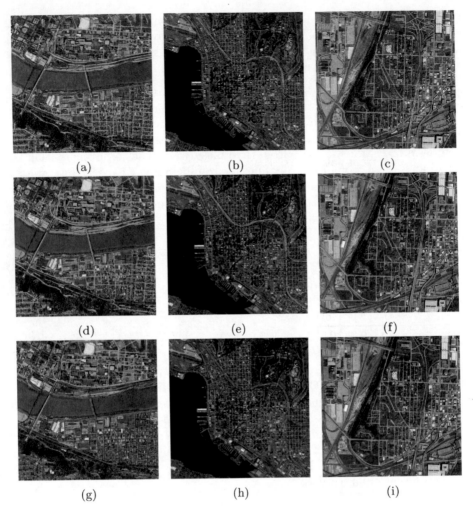

Fig. 4. Comparison between the proposed technique (a, b, c), DeepRoadMapper [10] (d, e, f), and RoadTracer [2] (g, h, i) for the cities of Pittsburgh (left column), San Diego (middle column), and Kansas City (right column). Green: true positives. Red: false positives. Blue: false negatives. Ground truth: OpenStreetMap [13]. The full resolution comparison results for all 15 cities and the source code can be downloaded from http://theictlab.org/lp/2019Re_X/ (Color figure online)

- break the line **ab**;
- find the middle point **p** between the end point and the line;
- move the end point to **p**;
- connect the two end points **a** and **b** with point **p**, forming two new lines **ap** and **pb**

This procedure is repeated on all line end points in the image which results in all misaligned lines being removed. An advantage of this procedure is that Hough transform cannot extract curved roads from the network prediction but by extracting short line segments on each patch a curved road can be approximated as a set of piece-wise linear segments connected to each other. By merging nearby points-to-points (e.g. case A) and points-to-lines (e.g. case B), we can reconstruct a curved road or a circle with Hough lines (e.g. case C).

Iteratively looking through the entire image space could be a time consuming process, but since we are using sliding window technique during testing, only neighbours of current patch are in the searching range to merge nearby points and connect line segments. Meanwhile, in most cases, only one or two line segments will be found on road patches. Thus, this searching and merging progress is actually very fast.

Table 1. F1 Score, IoU and Junction metrics on 15 test cities. [2] RT: RoadTracer, [10] DRM: DeepRoadMapper (implementation provided in [2])

City	Ours			[2] RT			[10] DRM		
	F1	IoU	Junction	F1	IoU	Junction	F1	IoU	Junction
Amsterdam	0.28	0.16	0.16	0.01	0.01	0.01	0.22	0.13	0.04
Boston	0.71	0.55	0.58	0.67	0.51	0.74	0.77	0.62	0.66
Chicago	0.58	0.41	0.41	0.69	0.52	0.77	0.68	0.51	0.51
Denver	0.71	0.56	0.57	0.69	0.53	0.73	0.46	0.30	0.35
Kansas City	0.82	0.69	0.70	0.76	0.61	0.82	0.85	0.74	0.76
Los Angeles	0.68	0.51	0.51	0.73	0.57	0.79	0.73	0.58	0.61
Montreal	0.73	0.57	0.55	0.78	0.63	0.80	0.69	0.53	0.56
New York	0.51	0.34	0.35	0.73	0.57	0.84	0.42	0.26	0.29
Paris	0.59	0.42	0.26	0.67	0.51	0.71	0.41	0.26	0.31
Pittsburgh	0.71	0.55	0.57	0.41	0.26	0.48	0.69	0.58	0.57
Salt Lake City	0.75	0.60	0.65	0.73	0.58	0.79	0.58	0.41	0.47
San Diego	0.72	0.56	0.62	0.66	0.49	0.77	0.79	0.65	0.72
Tokyo	0.38	0.24	0.11	0.56	0.39	0.60	0.42	0.27	0.34
Toronto	0.69	0.53	0.48	0.76	0.61	0.74	0.79	0.65	0.69
Vancouver	0.41	0.26	0.25	0.65	0.49	0.70	0.45	0.29	0.29
Average	0.63	0.47	0.45	0.63	0.49	0.69	0.60	0.45	0.48

5 Evaluation

As of writing this manuscript the state-of-the-art in the area is considered to be the work presented in [2]. The authors have shown that they outperform all previously top performers in road extraction. Hence, we use the custom *junction metric* proposed by them in [2] and the well-known Intersection over Union (IoU) metric to evaluate our work and compare our results. The junction metric involves measuring the precision and recall based on the detected junctions in the inferred map. Furthermore, we report on additional metrics typically used in road extraction such as completeness, correctness, precision, recall, and F1 score.

Table 1 shows the comparison between the proposed approach and the two state-of-the-art RoadTracer [2] and DeepRoadMapper [10]. The F1 Score and IoU metrics shown are for the 15 test cities. As it can be seen, our method outperforms the DeepRoadMapper on the overall test set in both F1 score and IoU metrics. Our technique also surpasses the RoadTracer in accuracy on at least half of the cities. We attribute this to the fact that our approach initially results in a very high number of classified roads which the refinement process then prunes down leading to a lower error rate than the other techniques.

In terms of the junction metric, the results show that both semantic segmentation methods (ours and DeepRoadMapper) have the same level of performance in detecting the junctions, whereas the RoadTracer performs better because it seldom misclassifies road pixels around junctions.

As shown in the results shown in Fig. 4, the road network resulting from our proposed method has relatively high completeness factor, and higher continuity than the results of DeepRoadMapper for the same areas. The images of some of the cities in the test dataset such as Tokyo and Amsterdam exhibit considerably different characteristics when compared to the images of other cities in the training set. As shown in Fig. 5, the building density in Tokyo is much higher than other cities and the roads are narrower, therefore tall buildings produce shadows which occlude large parts of the roads. Amsterdam on the other hand has a different color temperature (tone). Both of these examples are seldom seen in the dataset during the training process, hence their presence in the testing dataset results in a higher misclassification rate. This is also evident from the reported metrics shown in Table 1.

Table 2 shows the effect on the performance of the proposed post-processing method. A set of experiments were conducted to determine how the iterative Hough transform post-processing affects the accuracy and completeness of the extracted road network. First, we applied our pipeline on the aforementioned 15 cities with- and without- the proposed post-processing. Furthermore, we applied our post-processing method on the results of DeepRoadMapper by replacing its own post-processing steps. As it can be seen from the reported metrics the proposed post-processing method has a significant and positive effect on the evaluation results. Specifically using our network, in Tokyo where the network performs the worst the F1 score increased by 30% and IoU increased by 19% when using our post-processing method, while the overall F1 score increased

Table 2. F1 score, IoU on 15 test cities with and without post-processing. [10] DRM: DeepRoadMapper (implementation provided in [2]). DRM (w/PP): DeepRoadMapper, but replace its own post-processing with our post-processing. w/PP: with our post-processing. w/o PP: without our post-processing

City	Ours (w/PP)		Ours (w/o PP)		DRM [10]		DRM (w/PP)	
	F1	IoU	F1	IoU	F1	IoU	F1	IoU
Amsterdam	0.28	0.16	0.26	0.15	0.22	0.13	0.21	0.12
Boston	0.71	0.55	0.62	0.45	0.77	0.62	0.80	0.67
Chicago	0.58	0.41	0.44	0.29	0.68	0.51	0.74	0.58
Denver	0.71	0.56	0.64	0.47	0.46	0.30	0.55	0.38
Kansas City	0.82	0.69	0.78	0.64	0.85	0.74	0.88	0.79
Los Angeles	0.68	0.51	0.57	0.39	0.73	0.58	0.77	0.63
Montreal	0.73	0.57	0.69	0.52	0.69	0.53	0.74	0.59
New York	0.51	0.34	0.41	0.26	0.42	0.26	0.42	0.27
Paris	0.59	0.42	0.30	0.18	0.41	0.26	0.42	0.27
Pittsburgh	0.71	0.55	0.59	0.42	0.69	0.58	0.75	0.60
Salt Lake City	0.75	0.60	0.72	0.56	0.58	0.41	0.64	0.47
San Diego	0.72	0.56	0.64	0.47	0.79	0.65	0.83	0.71
Tokyo	0.38	0.24	0.08	0.04	0.42	0.27	0.42	0.26
Toronto	0.69	0.53	0.67	0.51	0.78	0.65	0.83	0.71
Vancouver	0.41	0.26	0.35	0.21	0.45	0.29	0.47	0.31
Average	0.63	0.47	0.52	0.37	0.60	0.45	0.63	0.49

by 10%, and IoU increased by 9%. For DeepRoadMapper, the average performance improved by 4% on both F1 score and IoU after substituting their post-processing method with ours. It should be noted that DeepRoadMapper uses a post-processing method which relies on training yet another deep neural network to recover the missing segments and connect the gaps in the raw segmentation result. The authors indicate that the training of this second network takes at least a day to reach a good performance score. Thus, our iterative Hough transform method is not only improving the overall performance, but also takes less time to perform the task. All measurements shown in Table 2 are based on the F1 score and IoU metrics.

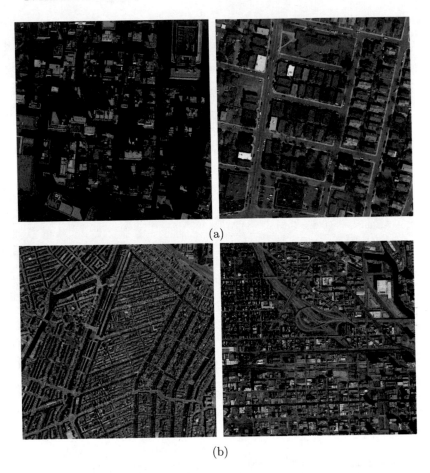

(a)

(b)

Fig. 5. Cities exhibiting different characteristics i.e. patterns, building densities, building heights, etc. The most commonly occurring city pattern/density in the training dataset looks like Boston (a)-right and Chicago (b)-right. Unique cases appearing in the test dataset none similar to which were seen by our network during training such as Tokyo (a)-left and Amsterdam (b)-left. Tokyo (a)-left is shown at the same zoom-level as Boston (a)-right; has much higher road and building density, roads are narrower, tall buildings produce shadows which occlude large parts of the roads. Amsterdam (b)-left is shown at the same zoom-level as Chicago (b)-right. The majority of the images used in training have similar color temperature (tone) as Boston and Chicago; in contrast Amsterdam has more green and gray areas. (Color figure online)

6   Conclusion

We presented a novel approach for road extraction. Uniquely, the proposed approach leverages cardinality-enabled neural networks with feed forward links in order to achieve high accuracy in the semantic segmentation. The classification result is then further processed using a novel post-processing refinement process which iteratively applies a Hough-transform on a per-patch basis which results in a set of linear segments. The segmented are further refined by connecting nearby segments together and removing erroneous segments resulting from mis-classification. We compared our approach with state-of-the-art techniques and we have shown that it can produce on average comparable results and in some cases better. We also compared the post-processing techniques and showed our proposed iterative Hough-transform post-processing method brings significant improvements for semantic segmentation results.

Acknowledgement. This research is based upon work supported by the Natural Sciences and Engineering Research Council of Canada Grants DG-N01670 (Discovery Grant) and DND-N01885 (Collaborative Research and Development with the Department of National Defence Grant).

References

1. Barzohar, M., Cooper, D.B.: Automatic finding of main roads in aerial images by using geometric-stochastic models and estimation. In: 1993 Proceedings IEEE Computer Society Conference on Computer Vision and Pattern Recognition, CVPR 1993, pp. 459–464. IEEE (1993)
2. Bastani, F., et al.: Roadtracer: automatic extraction of road networks from aerial images. In: Computer Vision and Pattern Recognition (CVPR) (2018)
3. Buslaev, A., Seferbekov, S., Iglovikov, V., Shvets, A.: Fully convolutional network for automatic road extraction from satellite imagery. In: The IEEE Conference on Computer Vision and Pattern Recognition (CVPR) Workshops (2018)
4. Cheng, G., Wang, Y., Xu, S., Wang, H., Xiang, S., Pan, C.: Automatic road detection and centerline extraction via cascaded end-to-end convolutional neural network. IEEE Trans. Geosci. Remote Sens. **55**(6), 3322–3337 (2017)
5. Forbes, T., Poullis, C.: Deep autoencoders with aggregated residual transformations for urban reconstruction from remote sensing data. In: 2018 15th Conference on Computer and Robot Vision (CRV), pp. 23–30. IEEE (2018)
6. Hinz, S., Baumgartner, A.: Automatic extraction of urban road networks from multi-view aerial imagery. ISPRS J. Photogramm. Remote Sens. **58**(1–2), 83–98 (2003)
7. Hu, J., Razdan, A., Femiani, J.C., Cui, M., Wonka, P.: Road network extraction and intersection detection from aerial images by tracking road footprints. IEEE Trans. Geosci. Remote Sens. **45**(12), 4144–4157 (2007)
8. Li, M., Stein, A., Bijker, W., Zhan, Q.: Region-based urban road extraction from vhr satellite images using binary partition tree. Int. J. Appl. Earth Obs. Geoinf. **44**, 217–225 (2016)
9. Long, J., Shelhamer, E., Darrell, T.: Fully convolutional networks for semantic segmentation. In: Proceedings of the IEEE conference on computer vision and pattern recognition, pp. 3431–3440 (2015)
10. Máttyus, G., Luo, W., Urtasun, R.: DeepRoadMapper: extracting road topology from aerial images. In: The IEEE International Conference on Computer Vision (ICCV) (2017)
11. Mnih, V., Hinton, G.E.: Learning to detect roads in high-resolution aerial images. In: Daniilidis, K., Maragos, P., Paragios, N. (eds.) ECCV 2010. LNCS, pp. 210–223. Springer, Heidelberg (2010). https://doi.org/10.1007/978-3-642-15567-3_16

12. Noh, H., Hong, S., Han, B.: Learning deconvolution network for semantic segmentation. In: Proceedings of the IEEE International Conference on Computer Vision, pp. 1520–1528 (2015)
13. OpenStreetMap contributors: Planet dump retrieved from https://planet.osm.org. https://www.openstreetmap.org (2017)
14. Sherrah, J.: Fully convolutional networks for dense semantic labelling of high-resolution aerial imagery. arXiv preprint arXiv:1606.02585 (2016)
15. Singh, S., et al.: Self-supervised feature learning for semantic segmentation of overhead imagery. In: BMVC (2018)
16. Xie, S., Girshick, R., Dollár, P., Tu, Z., He, K.: Aggregated residual transformations for deep neural networks. In: Proceedings of the IEEE Conference on Computer Vision and Pattern Recognition, pp. 1492–1500 (2017)
17. Zhang, Z., Liu, Q., Wang, Y.: Road extraction by deep residual U-Net. IEEE Geosci. Remote Sens. Lett. **15**, 749–753 (2018)
18. Zhou, L., Zhang, C., Wu, M.: D-LinkNet: LinkNet with pretrained encoder and dilated convolution for high resolution satellite imagery road extraction. In: Proceedings of the IEEE Conference on Computer Vision and Pattern Recognition Workshops, pp. 182–186 (2018)

DomainSiam: Domain-Aware Siamese Network for Visual Object Tracking

Mohamed H. Abdelpakey[1](✉) and Mohamed S. Shehata[1,2]

[1] Computer Engineering and Applied Science, Memorial University of Newfoundland,
St. John's, NL, Canada
mha241@mun.ca
[2] Department of Computer Science, Math, Physics, and Statistics,
University of British Columbia, Kelowna, BC, Canada
m.shehata@ubc.ca

Abstract. Visual object tracking is a fundamental task in the field of computer vision. Recently, Siamese trackers have achieved *state-of-the-art* performance on recent benchmarks. However, Siamese trackers do not fully utilize semantic and objectness information from pre-trained networks that have been trained on image classification task. Furthermore, the pre-trained Siamese architecture is sparsely activated by the category label, which leads to unnecessary calculations and overfitting. In this paper, we propose to learn a Domain-Aware that fully utilizes semantic and objectness information while producing a class-agnostic using a ridge regression network. Moreover, to reduce the sparsity problem, we solve the ridge regression problem with a differentiable weighted-dynamic loss function. Our tracker, dubbed *DomainSiam*, improves the feature learning in the training phase and generalization capability to other domains. Extensive experiments are performed on five tracking benchmarks, including OTB2013 and OTB2015, for a validation set as well as VOT2017, VOT2018, LaSOT, TrackingNet, and GOT10k for a testing set. *DomainSiam* achieves a *state-of-the-art* performance on these benchmarks while running at 53 FPS.

Keywords: Object tracking · Siamese network · Ridge regression network · Dynamic loss

1 Introduction

Tracking is a fundamental task in many computer vision tasks such as surveillance [18], computer interactions [30] and image understanding [22]. The objective of tracking is to find the trajectory of the object of interest over time. This is a challenge since the object of interest undergoes appearance changes such as occlusions, motion blur, and background cluttering [1,43]. Recent deep trackers such as CFNet [39] and DeepSRDCF [10] use pre-trained networks that have been trained on image classification or object recognition.

© Springer Nature Switzerland AG 2019
G. Bebis et al. (Eds.): ISVC 2019, LNCS 11844, pp. 45–58, 2019.
https://doi.org/10.1007/978-3-030-33720-9_4

In recent years, convolutional neural networks (CNNs) have achieved superior performance against hand-crafted trackers (e.g., CACF [31], SRDCF [11], KCF [16] and SAMF [26]). Siamese trackers such as SiamFC [4], CFNet [39], SiamRPN [23], and DensSiam [29] learn a similarity function to separate the foreground from its background. However, Siamese trackers do not fully utilize semantic and objectness information from pre-trained networks that have been trained on image classification. In image classification, the class categories of the objects are pre-defined, while in object tracking tasks, the tracker needs to be class-agnostic while benefiting from semantic and objectness information. Moreover, the image classification increases the inter-class differences while forcing the features to be insensitive to intra-class changes [25].

In this paper, we propose DomainSiam to learn Domain-Aware, which fully utilizes semantic and objectness information from a pre-trained network. DomainSiam consists of DensSiam with a self-attention module [29] as a backbone network and a regression network to select the most discriminative convolutional filters to leverage the semantic and objectness information. Moreover, we develop a differentiable weighted-dynamic domain loss function to train the regression network. The developed loss function is monotonic, dynamic, and smooth with respect to its hyper-parameters, which can be reduced to l_1 or l_2 during the training phase. On the other hand, the shrinkage loss function [27] is static, and it can not be adapted during the training phase. Most regression networks solve the regression problem with static loss such as the closed-form solution if the input to the network is not high-dimensional or minimizing l_2. The results will be made available[1].

To summarize, the main contributions of this paper are three-fold.

- A novel architecture is proposed for object tracking to capture the Domain-Aware features with semantic and objectness information. The proposed architecture enables the features to be robust to appearance changes. Moreover, it decreases the sparsity problem, as it produces the most important feature space. Consequently, it decreases the overhead calculations.
- A differentiable weighted-dynamic domain loss function is developed specifically for visual object tracking to train the regression network to extract the domain channels that are activated by target category. The developed loss is monotonic with respect to its hyper-parameters, and this will be useful in case of high-dimensional data and non-convexity. Consequently, this will increase the performance of the tracker.
- The proposed architecture tackles the generalization capability from one domain to another domain (e.g., from ImageNet to VOT datasets).

The rest of the paper is organized as follows. Related work is presented in Sect. 2. Section 3 details the proposed approach. We present the experimental results in Sect. 4. Finally, Sect. 5 concludes the paper.

---

[1] https://vip-mun.github.io/DomainSiam.

2   Related Work

In this section, we firstly introduce the *state-of-the-art* Siamese-based trackers. Then, we briefly introduce the gradient-based localization guidance.

Siamese-Based Trackers

Recently, Siamese-based trackers have received significant attention, especially in realtime tracking due to its balanced accuracy and speed. However, Siamese-based trackers drift to the background due to lack of semantic and objectness information about the positive samples. Siamese-based trackers always provide a heat map which encodes the most important channels for the object category as well as the sparse channels. Consequently, the heat map is sparsely activated by the category label. In general, a Siamese network consists of two branches: the target branch and the search branch, and both branches share the same parameters. The score map, which indicates the position of the object of interest, is generated by the last cross-correlation layer.

The first Siamese network was first proposed in [6] for signature verification. The pioneering work that uses Siamese in object tracking is SiamFC [4]. SiamFC searches the target image in the search image. Siamese Instance Search [38] proposed SINT, which has a query branch and a search branch, and the backbone of this architecture is inherited from AlexNet [21]. CFNet [39] enabled SiamFC to be re-trained once per frame instead of using an offline pre-trained network. CFNet integrated a correlation layer to back-propagate gradients through an online learning. improved SiamFC by adding a correlation layer to the target branch. SA-Siam [15] proposed two Siamese networks: the first network encodes the semantic information, and the second network encodes the appearance model. This is different from our architecture, which has only one Siamese network. SiamRPN [23] formulated the tracking problem as a local one-shot detection. SiamRPN consists of a Siamese network as a feature extractor and a region proposal network that includes the classification branch and regression branch. DensSiam [29] used the Densely-Siamese architecture to make the Siamese network deeper while maintaining the performance of the network. DensSiam allows the low-level and high-level features to flow within layers without vanishing gradients problems. Moreover, a self-attention mechanism was integrated to force the network to capture the non-local features. SiamMask [41] improved the offline training of Siamese networks by using augmentation loss to produce a binary segmentation mask. In addition, the binary segmentation mask locates the object of interest accurately. ATOM [8] formulated the tracking as a target estimation problem. ATOM proposed a Siamese network with explicit components for target estimation and classification. The components are trained offline to maximize the overlapping between the estimated bounding box and the target. Siamese-based trackers provide a heat map which is sparsely activated by the category label due to lack of the semantic and objectness information.

Gradient-Based Localization Guidance

It turns out that the gradient can be used to determine the importance of each channel in the heat map in Siamese networks. Moreover, the global average pooling of the gradients acts as Attention to locate the target from the heat map. In this category of learning, the objective is to determine the most important channel of the network with respect to the object category. In an object classification task, each category activates a set of certain channels. Grad-CAM [36] used a gradient of any target logit (e.g., "cat") and, using this gradient, determined the active category channel for this logit. The work in [45] demonstrated that the global average pooling of the gradients is implicitly acting as Attention for the network; consequently, it can locate the object of interest accurately.

3 Proposed Approach

We propose DomainSiam for visual object tracking. The complete pipeline is shown in Fig. 1. The DensSiam with the Self-Attention network is used as a feature extractor; however, in any Siamese network, these features do not fully utilize the semantic and objectness information. Furthermore, the channels in Siamese networks are sparsely activated. We use the ridge regression network with a differentiable weighted-dynamic loss function to overcome the previous problems.

3.1 Ridge Regression Network with Domain-Aware Features

In Fig. 1, the pipeline is divided into three blocks: the input block to the target branch and the search branch; the DensSiam block, which has the same architecture in [29]; and the ridge regression network. The DensSiam network produces two feature maps for target and search images, respectively. Imbalanced distribution of the training data makes the feature maps produced by Siamese networks less discriminative, as there is a high number of easy samples compared to the hard samples. Siamese networks use pre-trained networks that have been trained on other tasks (e.g., classification and recognition). These networks increase inter-class differences and are also insensitive to intra-class variations. Consequently, this property decreases the performance of Siamese networks, as the tracker needs to be more discriminative to the same object category. Moreover, the pre-trained network is sparsely activated by the object category. In other words, in the feature channels/maps there are only a few active channels that correspond to the object category. The regression network in Fig. 1 highlights the importance of each channel in the feature map to the object of interest and discards the others.

In Fig. 1, the ridge regression network regresses all samples in the input image patch to their soft labels by optimizing the following objective function.

$$\arg \min_{w} \|W * X_{i,j} - Y(i,j)\|^2 + \lambda \|W\|^2 \qquad (1)$$

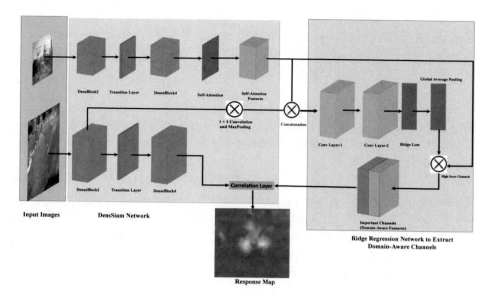

Fig. 1. The architecture of DomainSiam tracker. It consists of three blocks: the input images block, which includes the target image and search image; the DensSiam network with a Self-Attention module at the end of the target branch; and the Ridge Regression Network, which highlights the important channels and produces the Domain-Aware features. The response map is produced by the correlation layer, which is the final layer. The correlation layer calculates the correlation between the Domain-Aware channels and search branch features and is represented by DenseBlock4.

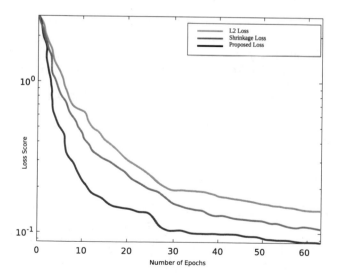

Fig. 2. A comparison of convergence speed on L_2 loss, Shrinkage loss [27], and our proposed loss function. The average loss is calculated on a batch of eight samples on VOT2018 [19] dataset.

Where $\| * \|$ denotes the convolution operation, W is the weight of the regression network, $\mathbf{X} \in \mathbb{R}^{N \times D}$ is the input features and $\mathbf{Y} \in \mathbb{R}^{N \times D}$ is the soft label. Gaussian distribution is used as a soft label map, and its centre is aligned to the target center and $\lambda > 0$ is the regularization parameter.

$$Y(i,j) = e^{-\frac{i^2+j^2}{2\sigma^2}} \tag{2}$$

Where (i,j) is the location corresponding to the target location and σ is the Gaussian kernel width. The closed-form analytic solution for Eq. 1 is defined as

$$W = \left(X^\top X + \lambda I\right)^{-1} X^\top Y \tag{3}$$

The optimal solution of W can be achieved by Eq. 3; however, solving this equation is computationally expensive as $X^\top X \in \mathbb{R}^{D \times D}$. Instead, we use the ridge regression network with the proposed loss function to solve Eq. 1.

3.2 Ridge Regression Optimization

In Fig. 1, the ridge regression network consists of two convolutional layers, ridge loss and the global average pooling. The global average pooling encourages the proposed loss function to localize the object of interest accurately compared to the global max pooling. It is worth mentioning that both global average pooling and global max pooling have similar performances on object classification tasks. As shown in Fig. 1, in the last block, the Domain-Aware feature space is calculated by

$$\delta_i = GAP(\partial L/\partial F_i) \tag{4}$$

Where δ is the Domain-Aware non-sparse features; GAP is the global average pooling; L is the domain-dynamic loss function, which will be discussed later; and F is the input feature channel of the ith channel to the ridge regression network. Let the objective function of the ridge regression network be x

$$x = \|W * X_{i,j} - Y(i,j)\|^2 + \lambda\|W\|^2 \tag{5}$$

We propose a differentiable weighted-dynamic loss function for visual object tracking to solve Eq. 5. This is inspired by [2], who uses a general loss function for the variational autoencoder, monocular depth estimation, and global registration, as follows.

$$L(x,\alpha) = \frac{|\alpha - 2|}{\alpha} e^{ay} \left(\left(\frac{x^2}{|\alpha - 2|} + 1 \right)^{\alpha/2} - 1 \right) \tag{6}$$

where $a \in [0,1]$ is a hyper-parameter, y is the regression target of a sample, and $\alpha \in \mathbb{R}$ is the parameter that controls the robustness of the loss. The exponent term in this loss function tackles the imbalanced distribution of the training set by assigning a higher weight to hard samples. The imbalanced data occurs when the number of easy samples (background) is extremely higher than the hard samples (foreground).

The advantage of this loss function over Eqs. 1 and 3 is that it can automatically adjust the robustness during the training phase. This advantage comes from the α parameter. For example, at $\alpha = 2$ the Eq. 6 becomes L_2

$$\lim_{\alpha \to 2} L(x, \alpha) = \frac{e^{ay}}{2} x^2 \tag{7}$$

Similarly, when $\alpha = 1$, the Eq. 6 becomes L_1

$$L(x, \alpha) = (\sqrt{x^2 + 1})e^{ay} - 1 \tag{8}$$

Another advantage of Eq. 6 is becoming Lorentzia loss function [5] by allowing $\alpha = 0$ as follows

$$\lim_{x \to 0} L(x, \alpha) = \log \left(\frac{1}{2} x^2 + 1 \right) e^{ay} \tag{9}$$

As noted before, the proposed loss function is dynamic, which allows the network to also learn a robust representation. The gradient of the Eq. 6 with respect to α is always positive. Consequently, this property makes the loss monotonic with respect to α and useful for non-convex optimization.

$$\frac{\partial L}{\partial \alpha}(x, \alpha) \geq 0 \tag{10}$$

The final proposed loss function is given by

$$L(x, \alpha) = \begin{cases} \frac{e^{ay}}{2} x^2 & \text{if } \alpha = 2 \\ \log \left(\frac{1}{2}(x)^2 + 1 \right) e^{ay} & \text{if } \alpha = 0 \\ (1 - \exp \left(-\frac{1}{2}(x)^2 \right)) e^{ay} & \text{if } \alpha = -\infty \\ \frac{|\alpha - 2|}{\alpha} e^{ay} \left(\left(\frac{(x)^2}{|\alpha - 2|} + 1 \right)^{\alpha/2} - 1 \right) & \text{otherwise} \end{cases} \tag{11}$$

Figure 2 shows that the optimization over the proposed loss function achieves faster convergence speed, while in the Shrinkage loss function proposed in [27] and the original ridge regression loss function 1 (l_2), the convergence speed is slower. The importance of each channel in the feature map is calculated by plugging Eq. 11 into Eq. 4. It is worth noting that the output feature map of the ridge regression network contains only the activated channels that have the most semantic and objectness information corresponding to the object category. The Domain-Aware features and the feature channels from denseBlock4 are fed into the correlation layer to calculate the similarity and produce the response map.

4   Experimental Results

The benchmarks are divided into two categories: the validation set including OTB2013 [42] and OTB2015 [43] and the testing set including VOT2017 [20], VOT2018 [19], and GOT10k [17]. We introduce the implementation details in the next sub-section and then we compare the proposed tracker to the *state-of-the-art* trackers.

Table 1. Comparison with the state-of-the-art trackers on VOT2017 in terms of Accuracy (A), expected Average Overlap (EAO), and Robustness (R).

Tracker	A↑	EAO↑	R ↓	FPS
CSRDCF++	0.453	0.229	0.370	>25
SAPKLTF	0.482	0.184	0.581	>25
Staple	0.530	0.169	0.688	>80
ASMS	0.494	0.169	0.623	>25
SiamFC	0.502	0.188	0.585	86
SiamDCF	0.500	0.473	0.249	60
ECOhc	0.494	0.435	0.238	60
DensSiam	0.540	0.350	0.250	60
DomainSiam (proposed)	**0.562**	**0.374**	**0.201**	53

4.1 Implementation Details

We used the pre-trained DensSiam network (DenseBlock2 and DenseBlock4) that has been trained on Large Scale Visual Recognition Challenge (ILSVRC15) [35]. ILSVRC15 has over 4000 sequences with approximately 1.3 million frames and their labels. DomainSiam, which has been trained on 1000 classes, can benefit from this class diversity. We implemented DomainSiam in Python using a PyTorch framework [34]. Experiments are performed on Linux with a Xeon E5 @2.20 GHz CPU and a Titan XP GPU. The testing speed of DomainSiam is 53 FPS, which is beyond realtime speed.

Training. The ridge regression network is trained with its proposed loss function separately from the Siamese network with 70 epochs. The highest scores associated with 100 channels are selected as the Domain-Aware features. The training is applied with a momentum of 0.9, a batch size of 8 images, and the learning rate is annealed geometrically at each epoch from 10^{-3} to 10^{-8}.

Tracking Settings. The initial scale variation is O^s where $O = 1.0375$ and $s = \{-2, 0, 2\}$. We adopt the target image size of 127×127 and the search image size of 255×255 with a linear interpolation to update the scale with a factor of 0.435.

4.2 Comparison with State-of-the-Art Trackers

In this section, we use five benchmarks to evaluate DomainSiam against *state-of-the-art* trackers. We use VOT2017 [20], VOT2018 [19], LaSOT [12], TrackingNet [32], and GOT10k [17].

Table 2. Comparison with *state-of-the-art* trackers on VOT2018 in terms of Accuracy (A), expected Average Overlap (EAO), and Robustness (R).

Tracker	A↑	EAO↑	R↓	FPS
ASMS [40]	0.494	0.169	0.623	25
SiamRPN [23]	0.586	0.383	0.276	160
SA_Siam_R [15]	0.566	0.337	0.258	50
FSAN [19]	0.554	0.256	0.356	30
CSRDCF [28]	0.491	0.256	0.356	13
SiamFC [4]	0.503	0.188	0.585	86
SAPKLTF [19]	0.488	0.171	0.613	25
DSiam [14]	0.215	0.196	0.646	25
ECO [7]	0.484	0.280	0.276	60
DomainSiam (proposed)	**0.593**	**0.396**	**0.221**	53

Table 3. Comparisons with *state-of-the-art* trackers on TrackingNet dataset in terms of the Precision (PRE), Normalized Precision (NPRE), and Success.

Tracker	PRE ↑	NPRE ↑	SUC.↑
Staple_CA [31]	0.468	0.605	0.529
BACF [13]	0.461	0.580	0.523
MDNet [33]	0.565	0.705	0.606
CFNet [39]	0.533	0.654	0.578
SiamFC [4]	0.533	0.663	0.571
SAMF [26]	0.477	0.598	0.504
ECO-HC [7]	0.476	0.608	0.541
Staple [3]	0.470	0.603	0.528
ECO [7]	0.492	0.618	0.554
CSRDCF [28]	0.480	0.622	0.534
DomainSiam (proposed)	**0.585**	**0.712**	**0.635**

Results on VOT2017 and VOT2018

We used the standard metrics on short-term challenge on the VOT dataset. The results on the VOT dataset shown in Tables 1 and 2 are given by the VOT-Toolkit. DomainSiam outperforms the *state-of-the-art* trackers listed in both tables. It is worth mentioning that DomainSiam is about 2% higher than the DensSiam tracker in terms of Accuracy (A) and Expected Average Overlap (EAO) in Table 1 while running at 53 frames per second. Table 2 shows that DomainSiam is ranked as the best tracker in terms of accuracy with 0.593 and gain of 0.7% compared to the second-best tracker, which is SiamRPN. In terms of expected average overlap, DomainSiam is ranked as the best tracker with score

Table 4. Comparison with *state-of-the-art* trackers on LaSOt dataset in terms of the Normalized Precision and Success.

Tracker	Norm. Prec. (%)↑	Success (%)↑
MDNet [33]	46.0	39.7
DaSiam [46]	49.6	41.5
STRCF [24]	34.0	30.8
SINT [38]	35.4	31.4
StrucSiam [44]	41.8	33.5
SiamFC [4]	42.0	33.6
VITAL [37]	45.3	39.0
ECO [9]	33.8	32.4
DSiam [14]	40.5	33.3
DomainSiam (proposed)	53.7	43.6

Table 5. Comparison *state-of-the-art* trackers on GOT10k dataset in terms of Average Overlap (AO), and Success Rates (SR) at overlap thresholds of 0.50 and 0.75.

TRACKER	DomainSiam (proposed)	CFNet	SiamFC	GOTURN	CCOT	ECO	HCF	MDNet
AO	**0.414**	0.374	0.348	0.347	0.325	0.316	0.315	0.299
SR (0.50)	**0.451**	0.404	0.353	0.375	0.328	0.309	0.297	0.303
SR (0.75)	**0.214**	0.144	0.098	0.124	0.107	0.111	0.088	0.099

of 0.396 while the score of the second-best tracker is 0.383 with gain of 1.3%. In terms of robustness, the number of failures per sequence, DomainSiam achieves the best score of 0.221, which is about 5% higher than the second-best tracker (SiamRPN) while working in realtime speed.

Results on TrackingNet Dataset

This is a large-scale dataset that was collected from YouTube videos. Table 3 shows that DomainSiam outperforms MDNet, which is the second-best tracker on the TrackingNet dataset with 2% in terms of precision and about 3% in terms of success. DomainSiam outperforms all other trackers on the TrackingNet dataset.

Results on the LaSOT Dataset

The average sequence length in this dataset is about 2500 frames. Table 4 shows that DomainSiam achieves the best success score with over 2% from the second-best tracker (DaSiam). Our tracker significantly outperforms DaSiam with 4% in terms of normalized precision.

Results on GOT10k Dataset

This dataset has 180 test sequences. We tested the proposed tracker against seven trackers as shown in Table 5. DomainSiam outperforms CFNet, which is the best tracker in terms of Average Overlap (AO) with 4%. It is worth noting that DomainSiam achieves the best performance among all trackers in terms of Success Rate (SR) at thresholds of 0.50 and 0.75.

5   Conclusions and Future Work

In this paper, we introduced DomainSiam tracker, a Siamese with a ridge regression network that fully utilizes semantic and objectness information for visual object tracking while also producing a class-agnostic. We developed a differentiable weighted-dynamic loss function to solve the ridge regression problem. The developed loss function improves the feature learning, as it automatically adjusts the robustness during the training phase. Furthermore, it utilizes the activated channels that correspond to the object category label. The proposed architecture decreases the sparsity problem in Siamese networks and provides an efficient Domain-Aware feature space that is robust to appearance changes. DomainSiam does not need to be re-trained from scratch, as the ridge regression network with the proposed loss function is trained separately from the Siamese network. DomainSiam with the proposed loss function exhibits a superior convergence speed compared to other loss functions. The ridge regression network with the proposed loss function can be extended to other tasks such as object detection and semantic segmentation.

References

1. Alahari, K., et al.: The thermal infrared visual object tracking VOT-TIR2015 challenge results. In: 2015 IEEE International Conference on Computer Vision Workshop (ICCVW), pp. 639–651. IEEE (2015)
2. Barron, J.T.: A general and adaptive robust loss function. In: Proceedings of the IEEE Conference on Computer Vision and Pattern Recognition, pp. 4331–4339 (2019)
3. Bertinetto, L., Valmadre, J., Golodetz, S., Miksik, O., Torr, P.H.: Staple: complementary learners for real-time tracking. In: Proceedings of the IEEE Conference on Computer Vision and Pattern Recognition, pp. 1401–1409 (2016)
4. Bertinetto, L., Valmadre, J., Henriques, J.F., Vedaldi, A., Torr, P.H.S.: Fully-convolutional siamese networks for object tracking. In: Hua, G., Jégou, H. (eds.) ECCV 2016. LNCS, vol. 9914, pp. 850–865. Springer, Cham (2016). https://doi.org/10.1007/978-3-319-48881-3_56
5. Black, M.J., Anandan, P.: The robust estimation of multiple motions: parametric and piecewise-smooth flow fields. Comput. Vis. Image Underst. **63**(1), 75–104 (1996)
6. Bromley, J., Guyon, I., LeCun, Y., Säckinger, E., Shah, R.: Signature verification using a "siamese" time delay neural network. In: Advances in Neural Information Processing Systems, pp. 737–744 (1994)
7. Danelljan, M., Bhat, G., Khan, F.S., Felsberg, M.: Eco: efficient convolution operators for tracking. In: Proceedings of the 2017 IEEE Conference on Computer Vision and Pattern Recognition (CVPR), Honolulu, HI, USA, pp. 21–26 (2017)

8. Danelljan, M., Bhat, G., Khan, F.S., Felsberg, M.: Atom: accurate tracking by overlap maximization. In: Proceedings of the IEEE Conference on Computer Vision and Pattern Recognition, pp. 4660–4669 (2019)

9. Danelljan, M., Bhat, G., Shahbaz Khan, F., Felsberg, M.: Eco: efficient convolution operators for tracking. In: CVPR (2017)

10. Danelljan, M., Hager, G., Shahbaz Khan, F., Felsberg, M.: Convolutional features for correlation filter based visual tracking. In: Proceedings of the IEEE International Conference on Computer Vision Workshops, pp. 58–66 (2015)

11. Danelljan, M., Hager, G., Shahbaz Khan, F., Felsberg, M.: Learning spatially regularized correlation filters for visual tracking. In: Proceedings of the IEEE International Conference on Computer Vision, pp. 4310–4318 (2015)

12. Fan, H., et al.: LaSOT: a high-quality benchmark for large-scale single object tracking. In: Proceedings of the IEEE Conference on Computer Vision and Pattern Recognition, pp. 5374–5383 (2019)

13. Galoogahi, H.K., Fagg, A., Lucey, S.: Learning background-aware correlation filters for visual tracking. In: Proceedings of the 2017 IEEE Conference on Computer Vision and Pattern Recognition (CVPR), Honolulu, HI, USA, pp. 21–26 (2017)

14. Guo, Q., Feng, W., Zhou, C., Huang, R., Wan, L., Wang, S.: Learning dynamic siamese network for visual object tracking. In: Proceedings of IEEE International Conference on Computer Vision, pp. 1–9 (2017)

15. He, A., Luo, C., Tian, X., Zeng, W.: A twofold siamese network for real-time object tracking. In: Proceedings of the IEEE Conference on Computer Vision and Pattern Recognition, pp. 4834–4843 (2018)

16. Henriques, J.F., Caseiro, R., Martins, P., Batista, J.: High-speed tracking with kernelized correlation filters. IEEE Trans. Pattern Anal. Mach. Intell. **37**(3), 583–596 (2015)

17. Huang, L., Zhao, X., Huang, K.: Got-10k: a large high-diversity benchmark for generic object tracking in the wild. arXiv preprint arXiv:1810.11981 (2018)

18. Kendall, A., Grimes, M., Cipolla, R.: PoseNet: a convolutional network for real-time 6-DOF camera relocalization. In: 2015 IEEE International Conference on Computer Vision (ICCV), pp. 2938–2946. IEEE (2015)

19. Kristan, M., et al.: The sixth visual object tracking VOT2018 challenge results. In: Leal-Taixé, L., Roth, S. (eds.) ECCV 2018. LNCS, vol. 11129, pp. 3–53. Springer, Cham (2019). https://doi.org/10.1007/978-3-030-11009-3_1

20. Kristan, M., et al.: The visual object tracking VOT2017 challenge results. In: Proceedings of the IEEE International Conference on Computer Vision, pp. 1949–1972 (2017)

21. Krizhevsky, A., Sutskever, I., Hinton, G.E.: ImageNet classification with deep convolutional neural networks. In: Advances in Neural Information Processing Systems, pp. 1097–1105 (2012)

22. Lenc, K., Vedaldi, A.: Understanding image representations by measuring their equivariance and equivalence. In: Proceedings of the IEEE Conference on Computer Vision and Pattern Recognition (CVPR) (2015)

23. Li, B., Yan, J., Wu, W., Zhu, Z., Hu, X.: High performance visual tracking with siamese region proposal network. In: Proceedings of the IEEE Conference on Computer Vision and Pattern Recognition, pp. 8971–8980 (2018)

24. Li, F., Tian, C., Zuo, W., Zhang, L., Yang, M.H.: Learning spatial-temporal regularized correlation filters for visual tracking. In: Proceedings of the IEEE Conference on Computer Vision and Pattern Recognition, pp. 4904–4913 (2018)

25. Li, X., Ma, C., Wu, B., He, Z., Yang, M.H.: Target-aware deep tracking. In: Proceedings of the IEEE Conference on Computer Vision and Pattern Recognition, pp. 1369–1378 (2019)
26. Li, Y., Zhu, J.: A scale adaptive kernel correlation filter tracker with feature integration. In: Agapito, L., Bronstein, M.M., Rother, C. (eds.) ECCV 2014. LNCS, vol. 8926, pp. 254–265. Springer, Cham (2015). https://doi.org/10.1007/978-3-319-16181-5_18
27. Lu, X., Ma, C., Ni, B., Yang, X., Reid, I., Yang, M.-H.: Deep regression tracking with shrinkage loss. In: Ferrari, V., Hebert, M., Sminchisescu, C., Weiss, Y. (eds.) Computer Vision – ECCV 2018. LNCS, vol. 11218, pp. 369–386. Springer, Cham (2018). https://doi.org/10.1007/978-3-030-01264-9_22
28. Lukezic, A., Vojir, T., Zajc, L.C., Matas, J., Kristan, M.: Discriminative correlation filter with channel and spatial reliability. In: Proceedings of the IEEE Conference on Computer Vision and Pattern Recognition, vol. 2 (2017)
29. Abdelpakey, M.H., Shehata, M.S., Mohamed, M.M.: DensSiam: end-to-end densely-siamese network with self-attention model for object tracking. In: Bebis, G., et al. (eds.) ISVC 2018. LNCS, vol. 11241, pp. 463–473. Springer, Cham (2018). https://doi.org/10.1007/978-3-030-03801-4_41
30. Molchanov, P., Yang, X., Gupta, S., Kim, K., Tyree, S., Kautz, J.: Online detection and classification of dynamic hand gestures with recurrent 3D convolutional neural network. In: Proceedings of the IEEE Conference on Computer Vision and Pattern Recognition, pp. 4207–4215 (2016)
31. Mueller, M., Smith, N., Ghanem, B.: Context-aware correlation filter tracking. In: Proceedings of IEEE Conference on Computer Vision on Pattern Recognition (CVPR), pp. 1396–1404 (2017)
32. Müller, M., Bibi, A., Giancola, S., Alsubaihi, S., Ghanem, B.: TrackingNet: a large-scale dataset and benchmark for object tracking in the wild. In: Ferrari, V., Hebert, M., Sminchisescu, C., Weiss, Y. (eds.) ECCV 2018. LNCS, vol. 11205, pp. 310–327. Springer, Cham (2018). https://doi.org/10.1007/978-3-030-01246-5_19
33. Nam, H., Han, B.: Learning multi-domain convolutional neural networks for visual tracking. In: Proceedings of the IEEE Conference on Computer Vision and Pattern Recognition, pp. 4293–4302 (2016)
34. Paszke, A., Gross, S., Chintala, S., Chanan, G.: Pytorch: tensors and dynamic neural networks in python with strong GPU acceleration. PyTorch: Tensors and dynamic neural networks in Python with strong GPU acceleration 6 (2017)
35. Russakovsky, O., et al.: Imagenet large scale visual recognition challenge. Int. J. Comput. Vis. **115**(3), 211–252 (2015)
36. Selvaraju, R.R., Cogswell, M., Das, A., Vedantam, R., Parikh, D., Batra, D.: Grad-CAM: visual explanations from deep networks via gradient-based localization. In: Proceedings of the IEEE International Conference on Computer Vision, pp. 618–626 (2017)
37. Song, Y., et al.: Vital: visual tracking via adversarial learning. In: Proceedings of the IEEE Conference on Computer Vision and Pattern Recognition, pp. 8990–8999 (2018)
38. Tao, R., Gavves, E., Smeulders, A.W.: Siamese instance search for tracking. In: 2016 IEEE Conference on Computer Vision and Pattern Recognition (CVPR), pp. 1420–1429. IEEE (2016)
39. Valmadre, J., Bertinetto, L., Henriques, J., Vedaldi, A., Torr, P.H.: End-to-end representation learning for correlation filter based tracking. In: 2017 IEEE Conference on Computer Vision and Pattern Recognition (CVPR), pp. 5000–5008. IEEE (2017)

40. Vojir, T., Noskova, J., Matas, J.: Robust scale-adaptive mean-shift for tracking. Pattern Recogn. Lett. **49**, 250–258 (2014)
41. Wang, Q., Zhang, L., Bertinetto, L., Hu, W., Torr, P.H.: Fast online object tracking and segmentation: a unifying approach. In: Proceedings of the IEEE Conference on Computer Vision and Pattern Recognition, pp. 1328–1338 (2019)
42. Wu, Y., Lim, J., Yang, M.H.: Online object tracking: a benchmark. In: Proceedings of the IEEE Conference on Computer Vision and Pattern Recognition, pp. 2411–2418 (2013)
43. Wu, Y., Lim, J., Yang, M.H.: Object tracking benchmark. IEEE Trans. Pattern Anal. Mach. Intell. **37**(9), 1834–1848 (2015)
44. Zhang, Y., Wang, L., Qi, J., Wang, D., Feng, M., Lu, H.: Structured siamese network for real-time visual tracking. In: Ferrari, V., Hebert, M., Sminchisescu, C., Weiss, Y. (eds.) ECCV 2018. LNCS, vol. 11213, pp. 355–370. Springer, Cham (2018). https://doi.org/10.1007/978-3-030-01240-3_22
45. Zhou, B., Khosla, A., Lapedriza, A., Oliva, A., Torralba, A.: Learning deep features for discriminative localization. In: The IEEE Conference on Computer Vision and Pattern Recognition (CVPR), June 2016
46. Zhu, Z., Wang, Q., Li, B., Wu, W., Yan, J., Hu, W.: Distractor-aware siamese networks for visual object tracking. In: Ferrari, V., Hebert, M., Sminchisescu, C., Weiss, Y. (eds.) ECCV 2018. LNCS, vol. 11213, pp. 103–119. Springer, Cham (2018). https://doi.org/10.1007/978-3-030-01240-3_7

Reconstruction Error Aware Pruning for Accelerating Neural Networks

Koji Kamma[✉] and Toshikazu Wada

Wakayama University, 930 Sakaedani, Wakayama-shi, Wakayama 640-8510, Japan
kanma@vrl.sys.wakayama-u.ac.jp
http://vrl.sys.wakayama-u.ac.jp/

Abstract. This paper presents a pruning method, Reconstruction Error Aware Pruning (REAP), to reduce the redundancy of convolutional neural network models for accelerating the inference. REAP is an extension of one of the state-of-the-art channel pruning methods. Our method takes 3 steps, (1) evaluating the importance of each channel based on the reconstruction error of the outputs in each convolutional layer, (2) pruning less important channels, (3) updating the remaining weights by the least squares method so as to reconstruct the outputs. By pruning with REAP, one can produce a fast and accurate model out of a large pretrained model. Besides, REAP saves us lots of time and efforts required for retraining the pruned model. As our method requires a large computational cost, we have developed an algorithm based on biorthogonal system to conduct the computation efficiently. In the experiments, we show that REAP can conduct pruning with smaller sacrifice of the model performances than several existing state-of-the-art methods such as CP [9], ThiNet [17], DCP [25], and so on.

Keywords: Neural network · Pruning · Biorthogonal system

1 Introduction

In various areas of Computer Vision, Convolutional Neural Network (CNN) has become a key technology. For example, some recent CNN models (e.g. M2Det [27]) conduct object detection with high accuracy, and are expected to be used in assorted applications. However, can we use those models as they are in the embedded systems, such as an object detection and classification system for in-vehicle camera? At this point, we need strong computational resources such as GPUs to use the large CNN models. For the future applications, it is important to produce fast CNN models without degrading their performances.

A major approach for producing a fast CNN model is to conduct pruning on a pretrained large model. Some early works aim for holistic network optimization based on the unified criteria across the layers, e.g. magnitude based criteria [8], loss function based one [14], and so on. However, most of these methods use the heuristic criteria, which does not guarantee the optimality of the results.

© Springer Nature Switzerland AG 2019
G. Bebis et al. (Eds.): ISVC 2019, LNCS 11844, pp. 59–72, 2019.
https://doi.org/10.1007/978-3-030-33720-9_5

On the other hand, some recent works propose the pruning methods that focus on layer-wise optimization based on theoretically sound criteria [9,17,25]. The weakness of the layer-wise methods is that the pruning ratio for each layer has to be determined manually. Although, in [10], reinforcement learning is employed to determine the pruning ratio for each layer, which enables us to achieve holistic network optimization using the layer-wise methods. Therefore, the layer-wise methods have been more successful recently.

Among the family of the pruning methods, "CP" [9] is a strong one. CP prunes channels based on the error of the outputs in each convolutional layer, and tunes the remaining weights so as to reconstruct the outputs by the least squares method, as shown in Fig. 1. This is why CP can prune the models without spoiling their performances. However, the problem is that the channels are selected based on the error *before* reconstruction, which does not guarantee the minimal error *after* reconstruction.

The solution of this problem is obvious. We need to select the channels so as to minimize the reconstruction error. However, this approach requires a tremendous computational cost. We need to solve the least squares problem to compute the reconstruction error repeatedly. Therefore, we also propose an algorithm to compute the reconstruction errors efficiently.

We conduct the experiments with several CNN models and datasets. The results show that our method can conduct pruning with smaller sacrifice of the model performances than the other methods do.

2   Related Works

The existing approaches on CNN acceleration can be categorized into 5 groups: (1) Factorization, (2) Sparsification, (3) Quantization, (4) Weight pruning and (5) Channel pruning.

Factorization. The most fundamental method in the factorization group is presented in [21]. They apply SVD to large weight matrix, and approximate it by the product of small matrices by discarding the components with small singular values. This results in reducing the parameters with small sacrifice of accuracy. For example, assume that a $m \times n$ matrix is approximated by the product of a $m \times o$ matrix and a $o \times n$ matrix. If $o \ll m, n$, the number of the parameters reduces from mn to $(m + n)o$. Some other methods [22,23] also belong here.

Sparsification. Sparsification methods make the weight tensors sparse by training the models with L1 regularization [1,15,20]. The theoretical weak point of sparsification is that L1 regularization shifts the global minimum of the cost function and sacrifices the model performances. Besides, in order to take the advantage of the sparsified models, the special hardwares and libraries are required for executing the computations on only non-zero weights.

Quantization. The methods in this group reduce the redundancy of each bitwise operation [3,6,24], e.g. changing the floating point precision from 32-bit to 8-bit. The quantized models require the special hardwares and libraries to be deployed.

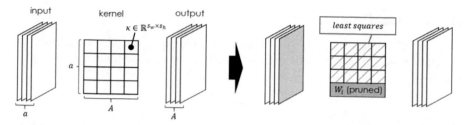

Fig. 1. The idea behind CP (and REAP). When we prune a channel, the whole weights which connect to the pruned channel are also pruned. The remaining weights are updated by the least squares method so as to reconstruct the outputs.

Weight Pruning. The idea of weight pruning is to remove the weights based on their saliencies [1,5,6,14]. Similarly with sparsification methods, these methods aim to reduce the number of non-zero weights and do not aim to reduce the sizes of the weight tensors, therefore, the special hardwares and libraries are required when the pruned models are deployed.

Channel Pruning. The methods in this group prune the whole weights that belong to the same channels of the convolutional layers [9,16,17,19,25]. Therefore, the sizes of the weight tensors get smaller, which results in saving the computational cost for inference without any special hardwares and libraries. In this group, CP [9], which our work stands on, is one of the strongest methods. CP can produce a fast and accurate model out of the pretrained large model, because CP prunes the channels while it conducts reconstruction to compensate the impact of pruning. Therefore, CP can achieve good model performances after pruning as well as save the computational cost for retraining the pruned models. Recently, some methods [19,25] marginally outperform CP. However, as they use heuristic pruning criteria without theoretical guarantees, it is reasonable to say that their performances rely on retraining rather than pruning itself. Thus, to our best knowledge, CP is still theoretically the strongest method.

As our method is an extension of CP, it belongs to the channel pruning group. However, it is possible to combine our method and the ones from other groups (e.g. quantization, factorization) to achieve further acceleration.

3   From CP to REAP

We explain CP [9], and show how this strong method gets even stronger by our strategy. We also show the algorithm to accelerate the computation of REAP.

Both CP and REAP aim for channel pruning in the convolutional layers. Although, in principle, they can be applied to fully connected layers as well. We first explain the basics of these methods on the fully connected layers, and then, we explain how our method can be applied to the convolutional layers, since we think it is easier to understand.

3.1   Channel Pruning (CP)

Let c and C denote the numbers of neurons in a layer and the next layer, and N denote the number of the input images. The forward propagation formula is given by

$$Y = \sum_{i \in Z} \boldsymbol{x}_i \boldsymbol{w}_i^\top, \tag{1}$$

where $\boldsymbol{x}_i \in \mathbb{R}^N$ denotes the outputs of the ith neuron corresponding to N input images, $\boldsymbol{w}_i \in \mathbb{R}^C$ denotes the weights going from the ith neuron to the ones in the next layer, $Y \in \mathbb{R}^{N \times C}$ denotes the inner activation levels in the next layer, and $Z = \{1, \cdots, c\}$ is the set of the neuron indices. The goal is to reduce the number of neurons to the desired number while keeping Y as unchanged as possible.

In CP, the neuron selection and the reconstruction are conducted in two separated steps. Let $\boldsymbol{\beta} = (\beta_1, \cdots, \beta_c)^\top$ denote the coefficient vector used for neuron selection, and $c'(0 < c' < c)$ denote the desired number of the neurons. The neurons are selected by Lasso Regression while the weights ($\boldsymbol{w}s$) are fixed:

$$\boldsymbol{\beta}^* = \underset{\boldsymbol{\beta}}{\operatorname{argmin}} \left\| Y - \sum_{i \in Z} \beta_i \boldsymbol{x}_i \boldsymbol{w}_i^\top \right\|_F^2 + \lambda \|\boldsymbol{\beta}\|_1 \quad \text{subject to } \|\boldsymbol{\beta}\|_0 \leq c'. \tag{2}$$

The hyper-parameter λ has to be controlled to satisfy $\|\boldsymbol{\beta}\|_0 \leq c'$. If $\beta_i^* = 0$, the ith neuron is pruned. Then, $\boldsymbol{\beta}$ is fixed to $\boldsymbol{\beta}^*$, and $\boldsymbol{w}s$ are tuned so as to reconstruct the outputs:

$$\{\boldsymbol{w}_i^* | i \in Z'\} = \underset{\boldsymbol{w}_i}{\operatorname{argmin}} \left\| Y - \sum_{i \in Z'} \beta_i^* \boldsymbol{x}_i \boldsymbol{w}_i^\top \right\|_F^2, \tag{3}$$

where $Z' \subset Z$ denotes the set of the selected neurons' indices. This is a classic least squares problem. The final solution is obtained as $\{\beta_i^* \boldsymbol{w}_i^* | i \in Z'\}$.

CP is powerful because of its reconstruction strategy based on the least squares method. However, its neuron selection criteria could be improved. The neurons are selected based on the error *before* reconstruction, which does not guarantee the minimal error *after* reconstruction. Besides, a minor problem is that CP controls the number of the selected neurons via the hyper-parameter λ in Eq. (2), which often requires cumbersome manual parameter tuning.

3.2   Reconstruction Error Aware Pruning (REAP)

In REAP, we use the consistent strategies for neuron selection and reconstruction. We select the neurons to be pruned based on the reconstruction error:

$$Z^* = \underset{Z'}{\operatorname{argmin}} \, \underset{\boldsymbol{w}_i}{\min} \left\| Y - \sum_{i \in Z'} \boldsymbol{x}_i \boldsymbol{w}_i^\top \right\|_F^2 \quad \text{subject to } |Z'| \leq c'. \tag{4}$$

In Eq. (4), the weights ($\boldsymbol{w}$s) are optimized before we fix Z' to Z^*. Therefore, its solution provides the neuron set that minimizes the reconstruction error of the outputs. This is the essential difference from CP.

We solve this problem in a greedy fashion. We define the cost function P such that $Z^* = \mathrm{argmin}_{Z'} P(Z')$:

$$P(Z') = \min_{\boldsymbol{w}_i} \left\| Y - \sum_{i \in Z'} \boldsymbol{x}_i \boldsymbol{w}_i^{\top} \right\|_F^2 . \tag{5}$$

We prune the neurons one by one so that $P(Z')$ stays as small as possible. This greedy solution makes it easy to control the number of the selected neurons, while one needs to do the manual efforts on parameter tuning in CP.

3.3   Efficient Computation for REAP

For the greedy solution of REAP, we need to compute the reconstruction error of Y by solving the least squares problem defined by Eq. (5) repeatedly. In order to be efficient, we use the biorthogonal system to compute the reconstruction error caused by pruning each neuron. Once we have the reconstruction error of each neuron, we can easily compute the reconstruction error that is caused by pruning two or more neurons by using some linear algebra tricks.

Computing Reconstruction Error Caused by Pruning Each Neuron
For computing the reconstruction error caused by pruning each neuron, we need to compute the following for all $j \in Z$.

$$P(Z\backslash\{j\}) = \min_{\boldsymbol{w}_i} \left\| Y - \sum_{i \in Z\backslash\{j\}} \boldsymbol{x}_i \boldsymbol{w}_i^{\top} \right\|_F^2 . \tag{6}$$

When there are a lot of neurons, this would be computationally expensive. In order to solve this problem, we introduce its subproblem.

Subproblem of Eq. (6). As Eq. (6) shows, $P(Z\backslash\{j\})$ is the reconstruction error of Y after pruning the jth neuron. This can be easily computed after we solve the subproblem of reconstructing $\boldsymbol{x}_j$ from $\{\boldsymbol{x}_i | i \in Z \setminus \{j\}\}$:

$$\{v_{ji}^* | i \in Z\backslash\{j\}\} = \mathrm{argmin}_{v_{ji}} \left\| \boldsymbol{x}_j - \sum_{i \in Z\backslash\{j\}} v_{ji} \boldsymbol{x}_i \right\|^2 , \tag{7}$$

where v_{ji} denotes the coefficient for reconstructing $\boldsymbol{x}_j$ from $\boldsymbol{x}_i$.

By using the solution of Eq. (7), Eq. (6) can be easily solved. Let $\boldsymbol{r}_j$ denote the residual of $\boldsymbol{x}_j$:

$$\boldsymbol{r}_j = \boldsymbol{x}_j - \sum_{i \in Z\backslash\{j\}} v_{ji}^* \boldsymbol{x}_i. \tag{8}$$

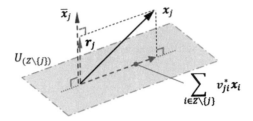

Fig. 2. Illustration of the projection of x_j onto a subspace $U_{(Z\setminus\{j\})}$ spanned by $\{x_i | i \in Z\setminus\{j\}\}$. Computing the orthogonal projection of x_j onto $U_{(Z\setminus\{j\})}$ is equivalent to solving the problem of reconstructing x_j from $\{x_i | i \in Z\setminus\{j\}\}$ by the least squares method. The residual r_j is linearly dependent on $\bar{x}_j$, the dual basis for x_j.

By using Eqs. (1) and (8), the solution of Eq. (6) is given by

$$P(Z\setminus\{j\}) = \left\| r_j w_j^\top \right\|_F^2 . \tag{9}$$

Therefore, $P(Z\setminus\{j\})$ can be easily computed after solving Eq. (7).

Solution of Eq. (7). Equation (7) is the problem of minimizing the error of x_j reconstructed from $\{x_i | i \in Z\setminus\{j\}\}$, which is equivalent to computing the orthogonal projection of x_j onto the subspace $U_{(Z\setminus\{j\})}$ spanned by $\{x_i | i \in Z\setminus\{j\}\}$, as shown in Fig. 2. Therefore, r_j is equivalent to the projection residual of x_j.

We obtain r_j by using biorthogonal system. Let $\{\bar{x}_i | i \in Z\}$ denote the set of the dual bases for $\{x_i | i \in Z\}$. The biorthogonal system is defined by

$$\langle x_j, \bar{x}_i \rangle = \begin{cases} 1 & (i = j) \\ 0 & (otherwise) \end{cases} \tag{10}$$

where $\langle \cdot, \cdot \rangle$ denotes inner product. The biorthogonal expansion for r_j is given by

$$r_j = \sum_{i \in Z} \langle r_j, x_i \rangle \bar{x}_i. \tag{11}$$

Obviously, $\langle r_j, x_i \rangle = 0$ holds for all $i \in Z\setminus\{j\}$, because r_j is orthogonal to $U_{(Z\setminus\{j\})}$ spanned by $\{x_i | i \in Z\setminus\{j\}\}$. Thus, Eq. (11) can be rewritten as

$$r_j = \langle r_j, x_j \rangle \bar{x}_j + \sum_{i \in Z\setminus\{j\}} \langle r_j, x_i \rangle \bar{x}_i = \langle r_j, x_j \rangle \bar{x}_j. \tag{12}$$

Equation (12) means that r_j is linearly dependent on $\bar{x}_j$. Therefore, we can obtain r_j by computing the orthogonal projection of x_j onto $\bar{x}_j$, as shown in Fig. 2.

On implementation, we compute r_j for all $j \in Z$ at once. Let $X = [x_1 \cdots x_c]$ and $\bar{X} = [\bar{x}_1 \cdots \bar{x}_c]$. By definition of dual bases, $\bar{X}$ is given by

$$\bar{X} = (X^g)^\top , \tag{13}$$

where X^g denotes the generalized inverse of X. Since r_j is the orthogonal projection of x_j onto $\bar{x}_j$, we have $r_j = (\langle x_j, \bar{x}_j \rangle / \|\bar{x}_j\|^2) \bar{x}_j = \bar{x}_j / \|\bar{x}_j\|^2$. Let D denote a diagonal matrix whose (i, i) entry is given by $1/\|\bar{x}_i\|^2$, and $R = [r_1 \cdots r_c]$. Then, we have

$$R = \bar{X}D. \tag{14}$$

Let V^* denote a matrix, and its (j, i) entry is v_{ji}^* $(i \neq j)$, which would be obtained by solving Eq. (7), and $v_{ii}^* = 0$. At this point, we have not actually solved Eq. (7), however, the following equation must hold because of Eq. (8):

$$X = R + XV^{*\top}. \tag{15}$$

Thus, we get $V^{*\top} = I - X^g R$, where I is an identity matrix.

As above, instead of solving Eq. (7) for every possible j, we only need a few matrix operations to obtain the equivalent solutions.

Computing Reconstruction Error When We Prune Another Neuron

Assume that we have pruned the jth neuron. As we want to solve Eq. (4) in a greedy fashion, the next step is to compute $P(Z \backslash \{j, k\})$ for all $k \in Z \backslash \{j\}$ so that we can select the neuron to be pruned next. The naive approach might be solving the least squares problem defined by Eq. (5) for the case of $Z' = Z \backslash \{j, k\}$ for every possible k, which is costly. We try to obtain $P(Z \backslash \{j, k\})$ more efficiently.

Let r_j' and r_k' denote the residual of x_j and x_k reconstructed from $\{x_i | i \in Z \backslash \{j, k\}\}$. Fortunately, the solution of Eq. (5) for the case of $Z' = Z \backslash \{j, k\}$ is given by

$$P(Z \backslash \{j, k\}) = \|r_j' w_j^\top + r_k' w_k^\top\|_F^2. \tag{16}$$

Therefore, if we have r_j' and r_k', we can easily compute $P(Z \backslash \{j, k\})$.

We obtain r_j' and r_k' with some linear algebra tricks. Here in below, we only show how to compute r_k', since r_j' can be computed in the same manner. We already have

$$x_j = r_j + v_{jk}^* x_k + \sum_{i \in Z \backslash \{j, k\}} v_{ji}^* x_i. \tag{17}$$

$$x_k = r_k + v_{kj}^* x_j + \sum_{i \in Z \backslash \{j, k\}} v_{ki}^* x_i, \tag{18}$$

After pruning both the jth and the kth neurons, we cannot use x_j for reconstructing x_k. Thus, we substitute Eqs. (17) to (18) and get

$$x_k = \frac{r_k + v_{kj}^* r_j}{1 - v_{jk}^* v_{kj}^*} + \sum_{i \in Z \backslash \{j, k\}} \frac{v_{ki}^* + v_{kj}^* v_{ji}^*}{1 - v_{jk}^* v_{kj}^*} x_i. \tag{19}$$

Obviously, we have $\langle x_i, r_j \rangle = 0$ and $\langle x_i, r_k \rangle = 0$ for all $i \in Z \backslash \{j, k\}$. Therefore, $\langle x_i, (r_k + v_{kj}^* r_j)/(1 - v_{jk}^* v_{kj}^*) \rangle = 0$ holds for all $i \in Z \backslash \{j, k\}$, which means the first term of the RHS of Eq. (19) denotes the residual of $\boldsymbol{x}_k$ reconstructed from $\{\boldsymbol{x}_i | i \in Z \backslash \{j, k\}\}$. Thus, we have

$$r'_k = \frac{r_k + v^*_{kj} r_j}{1 - v^*_{jk} v^*_{kj}}, \tag{20}$$

We compute $\boldsymbol{r}'_j$ as well as $\boldsymbol{r}'_k$, substitute them to Eq. (16), and obtain $P(Z \backslash \{j, k\})$, which denotes the error of Y reconstructed from $\{\boldsymbol{x}_i | i \in Z \backslash \{j, k\}\}$.

At the same time, we update the coefficients for reconstruction. Let $\{v'_{ki} | i \in Z \backslash \{j, k\}\}$ denote the coefficient for reconstructing $\boldsymbol{x}_k$ from $\{\boldsymbol{x}_i | i \in Z \backslash \{j, k\}\}$. Then, we have

$$v'_{ki} = \frac{v^*_{ki} + v^*_{kj} v^*_{ji}}{1 - v^*_{jk} v^*_{kj}}. \tag{21}$$

As above, we can compute $P(Z \backslash \{j, k\})$ without directly solving the least squares problem defined by Eq. (5). We find k that minimizes $P(Z \backslash \{j, k\})$ and prune the kth neuron. If we have to prune yet another neuron, we just repeat the same procedures above.

Greedy Algorithm

To sum up, our algorithm can be described as below.

1. Initialize $Z' \leftarrow Z$ and $v^*_{ii} \leftarrow 0$ for all $i \in Z$. Compute r_i, v^*_{ji} for all $i, j (i \neq j)$.
2. Compute $P(Z' \backslash \{j\})$, $\boldsymbol{r}'_k$ and v'_{ki} for all $j \in Z'$, $i \in Z' \backslash \{j\}$ and $k \in Z \backslash \{j\}$ as
   $\boldsymbol{r}'_k = (\boldsymbol{r}_k + v^*_{kj} \boldsymbol{r}_j) / (1 - v^*_{jk} v^*_{kj})$,
   $v'_{ki} = (v^*_{ki} + v^*_{kj} v^*_{ji}) / (1 - v^*_{jk} v^*_{kj})$,
   $P(Z' \backslash \{j\}) = \| \sum_{m \in Z \backslash (Z' \backslash \{j\})} \boldsymbol{r}'_m \boldsymbol{w}^\top_m \|^2_F$.
3. Find j that minimizes $P(Z' \backslash \{j\})$, and update such that
   $\boldsymbol{r}_k \leftarrow \boldsymbol{r}'_k$ for all $k \in Z \backslash \{j\}$,
   $v^*_{ki} \leftarrow v'_{ki}$ for all $i \in Z' \backslash \{j\}$ and $k \in Z \backslash \{j\}$,
   $Z' \leftarrow Z' \backslash \{j\}$.
4. If $|Z'| > c'$ (c' is the desired number of the neurons), do step 2 and 3 again.

3.4   Applying REAP to Convolutional Layers

Same with "im2col" method implemented in cuDNN [26], we can describe the sliding window operations in the convolutional layers by the sum of the matrix multiplications. Let a and A denote the numbers of the input channels and the output channels, t_w and t_h denote the width and the height of the feature maps, s_w and s_h denote the width and the height of the weight tensor. The sliding window operation with a $N \times a \times t_w \times t_h$ tensor, which denotes the feature maps corresponding to the N input images, and a $A \times a \times s_w \times s_h$ tensor, which denotes the weights, can be alternatively written as

$$Y = \sum_{i \in B} \Phi_i \Psi^\top_i = \sum_{i \in B} \sum_{m \in T} \phi_{i(m)} \psi^\top_{i(m)}, \tag{22}$$

where $B = \{1, \cdots, a\}$ denotes the set of the indices of the input channels, the matrix $\Phi_i \in \mathbb{R}^{Nt_w t_h \times s_w s_h}$ denotes the ith channel of the reshaped input feature maps, where each row of Φ_i denotes the sub-tensor of the original feature maps, the matrix $\Psi_i \in \mathbb{R}^{A \times s_w s_h}$ denotes the reshaped weight tensor, $T = \{1, \cdots, s_w s_h\}$ denotes the set of the column indices of Φs and Ψs, $\phi_{i(m)}$ and $\psi_{i(m)}$ denote the mth columns of Φ_i and Ψ_i.

For convolutional layers, we conduct channel-level pruning, in other words, we remove $\phi_{i(m)}$ and $\psi_{i(m)}$ for all $m \in T$ at the same time for pruning the ith channel. The rest of the procedures are the same with the ones on the fully connected layers.

Generally, Φs are very large vertical matrices and are highly redundant. Thus, we sample some rows from each Φ and the corresponding rows from Y so that we can conduct channel selection efficiently.

4   Experiments

We first conduct the preliminary experiments to compare REAP and its baseline method CP. Then, we compare REAP with some state-of-the-art methods including CP on the experiments with the well known CNN models and datasets.

4.1   Preliminanary Experiments for Comparing REAP and CP

The major concern about REAP might be that it selects the channels to be pruned in a greedy fashion, which probably raises the following questions:

1. Do the channels selected in REAP cause actually smaller reconstruction error than the channels selected by Lasso Regression in CP?
2. Although REAP takes an efficient algorithm for channel selection, does the computation finishes within reasonable time?

In order to answer these questions, we conduct the experiments with VGG16 [18]. For pruning, we use 5000 images randomly selected from ImageNet training dataset, and take 10 rows per image from the feature maps (Φs). The images are resized so that the shorter side becomes 256, then 224×224 center crop is applied. We prune *conv1-1, conv2-1, conv3-1, conv4-1* with several pruning ratios, and observe the layer-wise reconstruction errors ($P(Z')$ in Eq. (5)) and measure the computational time spent on channel selection. For determining the hyper-parameter in CP, we use binary search algorithm as we found out it was the fastest. All the methods are implemented with python3.6 and tested on Intel(R) Core(TM) i7-2600K CPU @ 3.40 GHz.

As shown in Fig. 3, REAP suffers consistently smaller error than CP. Besides, the trend is that the higher the pruning ratios are, the larger the error gaps between REAP and CP are. Because REAP selects channels based on the reconstruction error, we suffer consistently smaller reconstruction error than CP, despite we use greedy algorithm for channel selection.

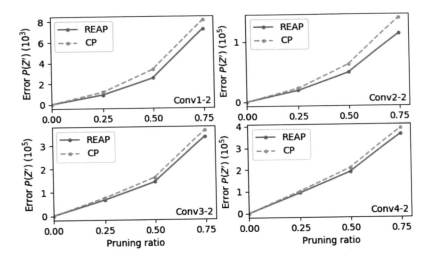

Fig. 3. Layer-wise analysis for VGG16 on ImageNet. The channels selected by REAP cause consistently smaller reconstruction error than the channels selected by CP.

Table 1 shows the results of computational time measurements. In *conv4-1* that has 512 channels, REAP consumes more computational time than CP. However, REAP requires 1872 s at the pruning ratio of 0.75, which we think is acceptable enough. When the number of channels is not greater than 256 (in *conv1-1*, *conv2-1*, and *conv3-1*), REAP is fast enough.

Table 1. Time (sec.) spent for channel selection in *Conv1-1*, *Conv2-1*, *Conv3-1* and *Conv4-1* (channels# in the parentheses), at the pruning ratios of 0.25, 0.5, 0.75.

Method	*Conv1-1* (64)			*Conv2-1* (128)			*Conv3-1* (256)			*Conv4-1* (512)		
	0.25	0.50	0.75	0.25	0.50	0.75	0.25	0.50	0.75	0.25	0.50	0.75
REAP	21	22	24	35	44	53	116	168	229	777	1307	1872
CP	90	84	83	117	130	120	209	226	220	385	434	418

4.2   Experiments with Classification Models

We conduct experiments with several CNN models and datasets (VGG16 [18] on ImageNet [4], ResNet-56 [7] on cifar-10 [13]), and DenseNet-121 [11] on Stanford Dogs [12] to compare REAP with several state-of-the-art methods.

As already mentioned, one of the advantages of REAP is that it can preserve the performances of the pruned models, which saves the efforts on retraining the models after pruning. In order to verify this advantage, we evaluate the model performances before retraining as well as the performances after retraining.

Table 2. VGG16 on ImageNet. The changes of top-5 accuracy from the baseline (89.5%) are reported (The greater, the better.). In this table, "rt" stands for "retraining".

Speed-up ratio	Method	Acc. before rt	Acc. after rt	Retrain epoch#
×2	REAP	**−2.0%**	**+0.2%**	10
	CP [9]	−2.7%	0.0%	10
	[a]ThiNet [17]	−65.0%	−1.0%	10
	SPP [19]	−	0.0%	−
×5	REAP	**−9.4%**	**−1.3%**	10
	CP [9]	−22.0%	−1.7%	10
	[a]ThiNet [17]	−88.8%	−3.4%	10
	SPP [19]	−	−2.0%	−

[a]Our implementation.

VGG16 on ImageNet. We conduct experiments with VGG16 on ImageNet. We prune the convolutional layers until the theoretical speed-up ratio (the ratio of the floating point multiplications before and after the pruning) becomes ×2 and ×5. The pruned models are fine-tuned for 10 epochs with the learning rate 10^{-5}. The momentum is set to 0.9, the minibatch size is set to 128, and the dropout rate in the fully connected layers is set to 0.5. The rest of the setups, including the pruning ratio for each layer, are aligned with [9].

The results are shown in Table 2. REAP performs consistently better than the existing methods. In the accuracy after retraining, we marginally outperform the other methods at ×2 speed-up. At ×5 speed-up, the existing methods suffer even larger accuracy drop than we do.

An important observation is that we only suffer 9.4% accuracy drop at ×5 speed-up, and we have NOT retrained the model at this point. On the other hand, CP suffers 22.0% drop and ThiNet spoils the model performance. This is because we use consistent strategy for channel selection and reconstruction to preserve the performances of the pruned models. Therefore, we can achieve higher accuracy after the same retraining. To put this observation differently, REAP enable us to achieve a certain accuracy with fewer epochs of retraining, which means that we can save time and efforts for retraining.

It is also worth noting that the model pruned by REAP, at ×2 speed-up, after retraining, is better than original VGG16. This is most likely because we removed the redundant parameters, the remaining parameters had smaller chance of being trapped in the local minima during the retraining.

ResNet-56 on cifar-10. We prune the pretrained model taken from [2]. For pruning, we use 6400 randomly sampled training images. ResNet-56 has 27 residual units that have 2 sequential convolutional layers and a shortcut path. The pruning ratios in the first 9 units, the second 9 ones and the rest are set to approximately 3:2:1. The pruned models are retrained for 100 epochs, beginning with the

Table 3. ResNet-56 on cifar-10. The changes of top-1 accuracy (baseline: 93.4%) are reported (The greater, the better.).

Speed-up ratio	Method	Acc. before rt	Acc. after rt	Retrain epoch#
×2	REAP	**−1.9%**	−0.5%	100
	[a]CP [9]	−3.7% ([b]−2.0%)	−0.9% ([b]−1.0%)	100
	[a]ThiNet [17]	−56.9%	−1.9%	100
	DCP [25]	−	**−0.3%**	400

[a]Our implementation.
[b]Results taken from [9].

Table 4. DenseNet-121 on Stanford Dogs. The changes of top-1 accuracy (baseline: 84.6%) are reported (The greater, the better.).

Speed-up ratio	Method	Acc. before rt	Acc. after rt	Retrain epoch#
×2	REAP	**−3.1%**	**−3.3%**	20
	[a]CP [9]	−4.7%	−3.5%	20
	[a]ThiNet [17]	−63.7%	−4.9%	20

[a]Our implementation.

learning rate 10^{-2} and dividing it by 10 every 25 epochs. The rest of the training setups are aligned with [7]. Since we want to compare REAP with CP in the same conditions, we try to evaluate CP on our own and put the results reported in [9] just for reference (The pretrained model used in [9] is not available, and the experimental setups are not clearly mentioned in [9].).

The results are shown in Table 3. Before retraining, we easily outperform the existing methods. We suffer only 1.9% accuracy drop without retraining, while CP suffers 3.7%. After retraining, we are slightly worse than, although competitive with, DCP [25]. However, while DCP needs 400 epochs of retraining to achieve this result, we only need 100 epochs to achieve the competitive result. In this way, the fact that we can save efforts on retraining is a strength of REAP.

DenseNet-121 on Stanford Dogs. Finally, we conduct experiments on DenseNet-121 fine-tuned with StanfordDogs dataset. For transfer learning, we set the learning rate to 10^{-2} for the first 30 epochs and set it to 10^{-3} for 20 more epochs. For retraining after pruning, we set the learning rate as 10^{-3} and train the models for 10 epochs, then repeat another 10 epochs with learning rate 10^{-4}. We set the pruning ratios in Block1, Block2, Block3 and Block4 to 5:5:4:3. The rest of the setups are aligned with Sect. 4.2.

The results are shown in Table 4. Similarly with other experiments, REAP preserves the model accuracy better than the other methods. It is also remarkable that the model pruned by REAP without retraining is as accurate as the model after retraining. REAP preserves the model performances so well that we sometimes do not even need to retrain the pruned models.

5   Conclusion

We have proposed REAP, a channel pruning method to accelerate the inference of CNNs. REAP is an extension of the currently state-of-the-art pruning method CP. REAP prunes the channels based on the reconstruction error of the outputs, then reconstruct the outputs by the least squares method. Thus, REAP can reduce the computational cost of CNNs while maintaining their performances, which not only makes it possible to produce a compact and accurate models but also saves the time and efforts required for retraining the pruned models. On the experiments, we could confirm these strengths of REAP.

Acknowledgment. This work was supported by JSPS KAKENHI Grant Number 19K12020 and the Environment Research and Technology Development Fund (3-1905) of the Environmental Restoration and Conservation Agency of Japan.

References

1. Aghasi, A., Abdi, A., Nguyen, N., Romberg, J.: Net-Trim: convex pruning of deep neural networks with performance guarantee. In: Advances in Neural Information Processing Systems, vol. 30, pp. 3177–3186. Curran Associates Inc. (2017)
2. akamaster. Proper implementation of resnet-s for cifar10/100 in pytorch that matches description of the original paper (2019)
3. Courbariaux, M., Bengio, Y., David, J.-P.: BinaryConnect: training deep neural networks with binary weights during propagations. In: Advances in Neural Information Processing Systems, vol. 28, pp. 3123–3131. Curran Associates Inc. (2015)
4. Deng, J., Dong, W., Socher, R., Li, J., Li, K., Fei-Fei, L.: ImageNet: a large-scale hierarchical image database. In: CVPR (2009)
5. Dong, X., Chen, S., Pan, S.: Learning to prune deep neural networks via layer-wise optimal brain surgeon. In: Advances in Neural Information Processing Systems, vol. 30, pp. 4857–4867. Curran Associates Inc. (2017)
6. Han, S., Mao, H., Dally, W.J.: Deep compression: compressing deep neural networks with pruning, trained quantization and Huffman coding. In: Proceedings of International Conference on Learning Representations, pp. 1–14 (2016)
7. He, K., Zhang, X., Ren, S., Sun, J.: Deep residual learning for image recognition, pp. 770–778 (2016)
8. He, T., Fan, Y., Qian, Y., Tan, T., Yu, K.: Reshaping deep neural network for fast decoding by node-pruning, pp. 245–249 (2014)
9. He, Y., Zhang, X., Sun, J.: Channel pruning for accelerating very deep neural networks. In: Proceedings of International Conference on Computer Vision (2017)
10. He, Y., Lin, J., Liu, Z., Wang, H., Li, L.-J., Han, S.: AMC: AutoML for model compression and acceleration on mobile devices. In: Ferrari, V., Hebert, M., Sminchisescu, C., Weiss, Y. (eds.) ECCV 2018. LNCS, vol. 11211, pp. 815–832. Springer, Cham (2018). https://doi.org/10.1007/978-3-030-01234-2_48
11. Huang, G., Liu, Z., van der Maaten, L., Weinberger, K.Q.: Densely connected convolutional networks, pp. 2261–2269 (2017)
12. Khosla, A., Jayadevaprakash, N., Yao, B., Fei-Fei, L.: Novel dataset for fine-grained image categorization. In: First Workshop on Fine-Grained Visual Categorization, IEEE Conference on Computer Vision and Pattern Recognition, Colorado Springs, CO, June 2011

13. Krizhevsky, A., Nair, V., Hinton, G.: Cifar-10 (Canadian institute for advanced research)
14. LeCun, Y., Denker, J.S., Solla, S.A.: Optimal brain damage. In: Advances in Neural Information Processing Systems, vol. 2, pp. 598–605. Morgan-Kaufmann (1990)
15. Liu, B., Wang, M., Foroosh, H., Tappen, M.F., Pensky, M.: Sparse convolutional neural networks, pp. 806–814 (2015)
16. Liu, Z., Li, J., Shen, Z., Huang, G., Yan, S., Zhang, C.: Learning efficient convolutional networks through network slimming. In: Proceedings of International Conference on Computer Vision (2017)
17. Luo, J.-H., Wu, J., Lin, W.: ThiNet: a filter level pruning method for deep neural network compression. In: Proceedings of International Conference on Computer Vision (2017)
18. Simonyan, K., Zisserman, A.: Very deep convoolutional networks for large-scale image recognition. In: Proceedings of International Conference on Learning Representations, pp. 1–14 (2015)
19. Wang, H., Zhang, Q., Wang, Y., Hu, H.: Structured probabilistic pruning for convolutional neural network acceleration. In: Proceedings of British Machine Vision Conference (2018)
20. Xie, G., Wang, J., Zhang, T., Lai, J., Hong, R., Qi, G.-J.: Interleaved structured sparse convolutional neural networks. In: Proceedings of Computer Vision and Pattern Recognition (2018)
21. Xue, J., Li, J., Gong, Y.: Restructuring of deep neural network acoustic models with singular value decomposition. In: INTERSPEECH (2013)
22. Ye, J., et al.: Learning compact recurrent neural networks with block-term tensor decomposition. In: Proceedings of Computer Vision and Pattern Recognition (2018)
23. Yu, X., Liu, T., Wang, X., Tao, D.: On compressing deep models by low rank and sparse decomposition. In: The IEEE Conference on Computer Vision and Pattern Recognition (CVPR), July 2017
24. Zhou, A., Yao, A., Wang, K., Chen, Y.: Explicit loss-error-aware quantization for low-bit deep neural networks. In: Proceedings of Computer Vision and Pattern Recognition (2018)
25. Zhuang, Z., et al.: Discrimination-aware channel pruning for deep neural networks. In: Proceedings of Advances in Neural Information Processing Systems (2018)
26. Chetlur, S., Woolley, C., Vandermersch, P., Cohen, J., Tran, J., Catanzaro, B., Shelhamer, E.: cuDNN: efficient Primitives for Deep Learning. Technical report (2011)
27. Zhao, Q., et al.: M2Det: a single-shot object detector based on multi-level feature pyramid network. In: Proceedings of AAAI Conference on Artificial Intelligence (AAAI) (2019)

Computer Graphics I

Bioinspired Simulation of Knotting Hagfish

Yura Hwang[1], Theodore A. Uyeno[2], and Shinjiro Sueda[1(✉)]

[1] Department of Computer Science and Engineering, Texas A&M University,
College Station, TX, USA
{chizuru97,sueda}@tamu.edu
[2] Department of Biology, Valdosta State University, Valdosta, GA, Georgia
tauyeno@valdosta.edu

Abstract. Hagfish are capable of not only forming knots, but also sliding them along the length of their bodies. This remarkable behavior is used by the animal for a wide variety of purposes, such as feeding and manipulation. Clearly of interest to biologists, this knotting behavior is also relevant to other fields, such as bioinspired soft robotics. However, this knot-sliding behavior has been challenging to model and has not been simulated on a computer. In this paper, we present the first physics-based simulation of the knot-sliding behavior of hagfish. We show that a contact-based inverse dynamics approach, motivated by the biological concept called *positive thigmotaxis*, works very well for this challenging control problem.

Keywords: Simulation · Biology · Physics-based · Knots

1 Introduction

Hagfish are incredibly flexible animals. Their flexibility is best demonstrated by their ability to tie their long skinny bodies into knots and effectively manipulate those knots for many purposes: they wipe their bodies clean by passing knots from one end to the other [1]; they can use knots to extricate themselves from burrows and holes [31,40]; and knots are used to generate leverage in order to tear off chunks of food [11]. This last function of knotting is interesting because hagfish evolved prior to the evolution of vertebrate jaws, and yet they are able to remove considerable morsels while scavenging carrion, such as the decaying carcasses of whales. This is achieved by first embedding the teeth of an eversible toothplate into the food item, forming a knot at the tail, and then *sliding this knot* anteriorly until a loop of the knot passes over the hagfish's head. This loop is pressed up against the food item and is used as powerful leverage to tear out the morsel [12,37].

While there are other vertebrates that are capable of knotting, namely sea-snakes (e.g. [27]) and moray eels (e.g. [24]), hagfish seem to be the most ready to employ knotting behaviors and are capable of tying the greatest variety of

© Springer Nature Switzerland AG 2019
G. Bebis et al. (Eds.): ISVC 2019, LNCS 11844, pp. 75–86, 2019.
https://doi.org/10.1007/978-3-030-33720-9_6

knots. This may be because they possess extensive adaptations for creating and manipulating body knots. First, their bodies are flexible and extremely elongate; their lengths are typically over twenty times that of their widths [16]. Second, hagfish have no fins or other projections that extend from their rope-like bodies. Third, their skins lack the outer layer that produce rough scales, resulting in a smooth skin with low friction [3]. Fourth, their skins are extremely baggy and loosely connected to the musculature of the body wall, which precludes the tough skin from binding during knotting maneuvers [10]. Fifth, the body does not have a spinal column, or any bones at all, to stiffen the body; instead a flexible, cartilaginous rod (the notochord) that extends down the length of the inextensible body accounts for most of the body stiffness [22].

The extreme flexibility represents a neural control problem that is poorly understood, because controlling such flexibility may theoretically require an enormous amount of neural input [38]. Such models and organisms are described as "hyper-redundant" [36]. As a result, researchers have not only been unable to characterize how hagfish control their bodies during this *knot formation and manipulation* process, but they also have struggled to develop a computer simulation of knotting that appears realistic or biologically informative.

The key to developing a realistic simulation of a knotting hagfish rests on a behavioral characteristic known as "positive thigmotaxis," which describes an animal's drive to be in direct physical contact with solid objects in its local environment. Our own observations of hagfish in aquaria confirm that they seem to prefer to be pressed up against the edges or touching others, rather than be alone or in the center of the aquarium. This positive thigmotaxis may stem from their real world behaviors of living in shallow burrows or crevices in the dark zones of the ocean or packing tightly into cavities of whale carcasses [23, 40]. In reviewing high speed videos of knotting hagfishes, Haney noticed that the tail exhibits positive thigmotaxis during all stages of knot formation and manipulation [16]. The type of knots that hagfish make depends on the number of crossovers that the tail forms. Interestingly, mathematicians who study knots also categorize them by the number and organization of crossovers [2]. The key feature that we have noticed is that as the hagfish slide a given knot anteriorly or posteriorly along the body, the constituent crossovers do not change in relation to each other. Our contact-based inverse dynamics approach is motivated by this observation.

In this paper, we present a novel graphics testbed for simulating a knotting hagfish. Our main contribution is that our work is the first demonstration of the knot forming *and sliding* behavior. We use reduced coordinate rigid body dynamics to model the hagfish with parameters taken from real-world measurements (Sect. 3.1). We then apply a contact-based inverse dynamics controller based on positive thigmotaxis that produces a realistic and bioinspired knot sliding movement of the hagfish (Sect. 3.2).

2   Related Work

Knotting of Hagfish. The knotting behavior of hagfish was first documented by Adams [1], who observed that *Myxine glutinosa*, or Atlantic hagfish, formed a knot to clean off slime from its body. He also observed that the movement can be reversed—the knot can slide toward the head or the tail. Ever since, most works focused on specific functional uses of knotting behavior, which hagfishes exploit for their survival. These include wriggling out of burrows and leveraging retractile force against the surface to tear out morsels of food [11,12,37,40]. There are also some works that looked into the biomechanisms involved in the knotting process. Haney [16] focused on different kinds of knots that hagfish are capable of formulating, and Evans et al. [14] analytically examined the body flexibility of hagfish based on biometric data [22]. In this paper, we use their observations and measurements to simulate the knot forming and sliding.

Simulation of (Sliding) Rods and Cables. There exist many approaches for the dynamic simulation of rods and cables that could be used for hagfish simulation [6,7,13,25,32]. In our work, we use rigid body dynamics, which has been an active research area for decades [15]. In computer graphics, the classical work by Baraff presented an efficient method for computing contact and friction forces acting on rigid bodies [4]. In the past decade, a number of works have studied how to combine rigid and deformable bodies [17,19,21,29,39]. In our work, we use only the rigid degrees of freedom, and deform the skin mesh using splines, which is used for contact with the environment and itself. Our dynamics simulator uses the REDMAX formulation by Wang et al. [39]. However, our *positive thigmotaxis* approach can be used by any simulator as long as it supports inverse dynamics with contact. Frictional contact [18] is out of scope of our work, since hagfish possess smooth, water-lubricated skin that effectively eliminates friction. Finally, some researchers have specifically studied knot tying [9,26], but their systems cannot be used for knot *sliding*, which is the focus of our work.

Neural Control. The extreme flexibility exhibited by hagfish represents a neural control problem that is poorly understood by biologists, although several studies have begun to investigate several examples. For example, Sumbre et al. presented a motor primitive of an octopus reaching its arm toward a 3D target point [34]. Motivated by biology, roboticists have worked on designing and controlling soft robots [28,30,36]. In biomechanics, the standard approach for computing the control signal of skeletal animals has been to use computed muscle control [35], and in computer graphics, similar methods have been proposed [20,33]. However, these methods do not consider knot forming or sliding, which is the primary focus of our work.

3   Methods

In this section, we first describe our simulation framework (Sect. 3.1), followed by our control strategy for knot forming and sliding (Sect. 3.2).

3.1 Simulator

We use 100 rigid bodies and joints, aligned along the X-axis. Although hagfish
are flexible, using rigid bodies is a reasonable approximation, since their cartilaginous spine is flexible and inextensible. These rigid bodies are connected with
X-revolute joints and YZ-universal joints in an alternating fashion. This allows
us to apply our biometric data on twisting limits on revolute joints and bending
limits on universal joints (Fig. 1), which is difficult to do with spherical joints.
These and other parameters of the simulation are obtained from real-world measurements, and are listed in Sect. 4.

We use forward Euler integration to advance the rigid bodies in time. When
there are no constraints, we solve the following linear system:

$$M\dot{q} = M\dot{q}_0 + hf, \tag{1}$$

where M is the mass matrix, $\dot{q}$ is the new velocity vector we are solving for,
$\dot{q}_0$ is the velocity from the last time step, h is the fixed time step, and f is the
force vector, which includes all internal, external, and Coriolis forces. Once the
velocities are computed, we update the positions as

$$q = q_0 + h\dot{q}. \tag{2}$$

During the course of a simulation, we encounter various types of constraints.
Bilateral constraints are used to fix the head to the wall, to match the video.

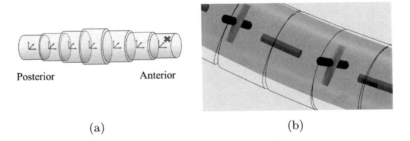

Posterior   Anterior

(a)   (b)

Fig. 1. The simplified representation of our hagfish model (a), and a zoomed view of
hagfish anatomy (b), where it consists of revolute joints and universal joints.

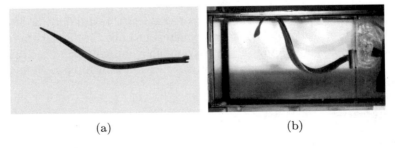

(a)   (b)

Fig. 2. We fixed our hagfish's head to the wall (a), to match the video (b).

(See Fig. 2; the head was gently held by a rubber collar in order to facilitate imaging.) This constraint may be released during the simulation to allow the head to release from the wall. Unilateral constraints are used for joint limits, contact with the wall, and self-contact. If there exists only bilateral constraints, we solve the problem using Karush-Kuhn-Tucker (KKT) system [8]:

$$\begin{pmatrix} M & G^\top \\ G & 0 \end{pmatrix} \begin{pmatrix} \dot{q} \\ \lambda \end{pmatrix} = \begin{pmatrix} M\dot{q}_0 + hf \\ 0 \end{pmatrix}, \tag{3}$$

where G is the Jacobian of the constraints, and λ is the vector of Langrange multipliers. If there exist both bilateral and unilateral constraints, we solve the following quadratic program:

$$\begin{aligned} \underset{\dot{q}}{\text{minimize}} \quad & \frac{1}{2}\dot{q}^\top M\dot{q} - \dot{q}^\top \left(M\dot{q}_0 + hf\right) \\ \text{subject to} \quad & G\dot{q} = 0, \quad C\dot{q} \geq 0, \end{aligned} \tag{4}$$

where G and C are the Jacobians of bilateral and unilateral constraints, respectively. Since the constraints are enforced at the velocity level, the system may drift away from the constraint manifold. To counter this, we stabilize the positions when necessary [5].

Contact Handling. Collision detection and contact handling are important aspects of this work, given that our work is inspired by positive thigmotaxis. Collisions can come from either self collisions during knotting, or from the body hitting the head plate of the tank.

For collision detection, we use a Catmull-Rom spline curve passing through the center of each rigid body, which represents the cartilaginous spine of the hagfish (Fig. 3a). We first find two colliding rigid bodies using bounding spheres around each rigid body. Once colliding spheres are detected, we find the closest points between these two segments of the spline curve using Newton's method, by looking for the zero of the following function:

$$f(t_i, t_j) = \begin{pmatrix} x'(t_i)^\top (x(t_j) - x(t_i)) \\ x'(t_j)^\top (x(t_j) - x(t_i)) \end{pmatrix}, \tag{5}$$

where t_i and t_j are the parameters of the spline curve; $x(t_i)$ and $x(t_j)$ are positions along the curve; and $x'(t_i)$ and $x'(t_j)$ are derivatives, respectively. Once these points are computed, we check if the distance between them are shorter than the sum of the radii at these two points. If so, the contact constraint is added to the unilateral constraint matrix, C, in Eq. 4.

3.2   Controller

The controller consists of two independent steps: forward dynamics and inverse dynamics, for knot forming and knot sliding, respectively.

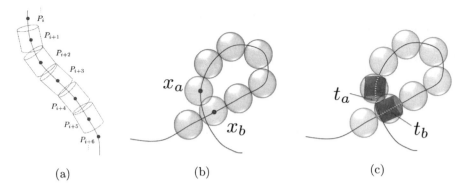

Fig. 3. Illustration of overall collision detection process. (a) We represent our hagfish using spline curve. (b) We find two colliding rigid bodies using bounding spheres. (c) The exact colliding points of collided rigid bodies are computed using Newton's method.

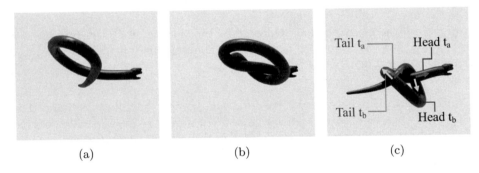

Fig. 4. Simulation of knot formulation. We closely follow each kinematic steps of hagfish behavior: (a) body crossover, (b) tail wrap, and (c) tail insertion. The labeled tangents in (c) are for the thigmotaxic constraints used in knot sliding.

Knot Forming. To form the knot, we use forward dynamics with scripted forces. In order to formulate a knot, we follow the kinematic steps of body crossover, tail wrap, and tail insertion. For each time step, we apply a sequence of scripted forces on the terminal body of the hagfish to manipulate the behavior, as shown in Fig. 5. Although torques can be applied as well, we found that linear forces were enough to produce the initial knot. Forming a knot using a sequence of scripted forces is time consuming, but fairly easy to achieve. On the other hand, the same method cannot easily be used for sliding the knot along the body, which we discuss next.

Knot Sliding. There is no intuitive way to apply forces or torques to make the knot slide. We overcome this difficulty by using a novel *contact-based inverse dynamics* approach based on positive thigmotaxis, which is the main technical contribution of this paper.

Fig. 5. Illustration of knot manipulation. We manipulate the terminal body to form a knot.

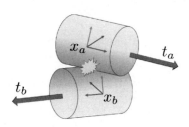

Fig. 6. Illustration of our contact-based inverse dynamics.

Once we detect self collisions due to the tail forming the knot, we switch the controller from forward dynamics to inverse dynamics. In inverse dynamics, we compute the forces and torques given a specified motion. This can be cast as a constraint to be applied to the motion [39]. Specifically, for self-collision points, we require that the projection of the relative velocity between the two contacting points onto the tangent direction be greater than some value. Mathematically, this can be written as:

$$t_a^\top (\dot{x}_a - \dot{x}_b) \geq v_a$$
$$t_b^\top (\dot{x}_b - \dot{x}_a) \geq v_b, \tag{6}$$

where t_a and t_b are the unit tangent vectors of the colliding rigid bodies, $\dot{x}_a$ and $\dot{x}_b$ are the world velocities of the colliding points, and v_a and v_b are scalar parameters to control the sliding motion in tangential directions. Figure 6 illustrates these quantities. All of these quantities can be computed as functions of the current generalized positions and velocities, q and $\dot{q}$ [39]. These constraints are added to the unilateral constraint matrix in Eq. 4.

In general, there are many self-collisions during a knotting process. We do not use all of them, as this could lead to an overly constrained problem. Instead, we sort the collisions by the parametric distance from the head, and apply the thigmotaxic constraint to only the first and last collisions. These two constraints with their respective tangents (t_a and t_b) are shown in Fig. 4c. We can manipulate the knot by changing the v_a and v_b parameters of these two constraints. We use two substeps. First, we tighten the knot by using different values between the two constraints, which shortens the portion of the hagfish tied into the knot. Once the knot is sufficiently tight, we set the parameters to be the same for both constraints, which forces the hagfish to slide the knot along its body toward the head. The parameters used in our simulation are listed in Table 1.

The forces computed by the inverse dynamics solver can be calculated with the Lagrange multipliers of the quadratic program in Eq. 4. Let λ be the vector of Lagrange multipliers corresponding to the inequality constraints. Let us also divide the unilateral constraint Jacobian and the Lagrange multiplier into three parts corresponding to the joint limits, collisions, and thigmotaxis:

$$C = \begin{pmatrix} C_{\text{limits}} \\ C_{\text{collision}} \\ C_{\text{thigmo}} \end{pmatrix}, \qquad \lambda = \begin{pmatrix} \lambda_{\text{limits}} \\ \lambda_{\text{collision}} \\ \lambda_{\text{thigmo}} \end{pmatrix}. \tag{7}$$

Then the inverse dynamics force from positive thigmotaxis can be computed as:

$$f_{\text{thigmo}} = \frac{1}{h} C_{\text{thigmo}}^{\top} \lambda_{\text{thigmo}}. \tag{8}$$

4   Results

We implemented our simulation using C++, and ran our experiments on a consumer desktop with an Intel Core i7-7700 CPU 3.6 GHz and 16 GB of RAM. We used Eigen for linear algebra computations and Mosek for quadratic programs.

Table 1. Biometric data and inverse dynamics parameters. The specimen was measured at 20% increments in length; the four values for circumference and bending limit are for 20%, 40%, 60%, and 80%, respectively, from head to tail. Intermediate values are linearly interpolated. The twisting limit was measured for the whole body, and was divided by the number of rigid bodies.

Data	Values	Units
Length	42.4	cm
Mass	80	g
Circumference	5.6, 5.5, 5.6, 4.3	cm
Bending limit	21, 75, 45, 51	deg
Twisting limit	48	deg
v_a, v_b (tightening, head)	0.0, 0.0	cm/s
v_a, v_b (tightening, tail)	0.5, 2.0	cm/s
v_a, v_b (sliding, head)	2.0, 2.0	cm/s
v_a, v_b (sliding, tail)	2.0, 2.0	cm/s

Table 1 lists the biometric data and parameters for inverse dynamics that were used in our simulation. Figure 7 shows a visual comparison between our simulation and real hagfish restrained in the tank. Our method is able to simulate the sliding movement of the knot realistically. The first three pairs of images show the real and virtual animal form the knot with the tail. During this stage, the

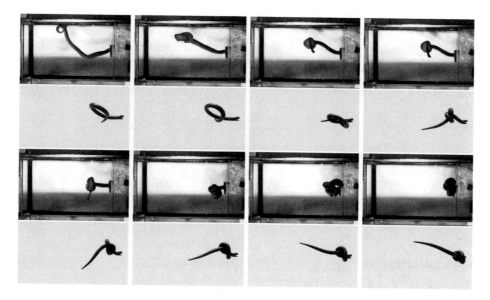

Fig. 7. Our result of knotting hagfish with *positive thigmotaxis*. The above row shows the actual video of hagfish restrained in a tank, and below shows our simulation.

virtual hagfish is driven using a manually scripted forward dynamics controller. The next five pairs of images show the animal sliding the knot toward the head. During this stage, the virtual hagfish is driven using our contact-based inverse dynamics controller.

Figure 8 shows the plot of force with time and joints during the knot sliding phase. The three subfigures are the X, Y, and Z torques, respectively. The vertical axis shows the force computed by the inverse dynamics controller. The two horizontal axes show the time in seconds and the joint number (head = 0, tail = 50).[1] As is typically the case, the forces produced by inverse dynamics is noisy. However, we can see some interesting patterns. First, as the knot moves toward the head over time, the forces acting on joints closer to the tail become zero, as expected. This is because once the knot has passed over a joint, that joint no longer needs to be controlled to move the knot. In the graph, this can be seen as a flat triangular region to the right of each graph. Second, more force is required when the knot approaches the head. This is because the head is attached to the plate, and so manipulating the knot requires moving the whole length of the animal from head to tail. Third, even though the forces rapidly change along the temporal dimension, the force is smooth along the spatial dimension. Therefore, it may be possible to represent the control signal using a reduced set of basis (e.g., the Fourier basis), rather than with a different value for each indi-

---

[1] There are 50 revolute joints (z rotation) and 50 universal joints (x and y rotations) for a total of 100 joints.

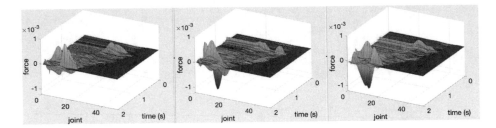

Fig. 8. Sliding force in inverse dynamics in x-axis, y-axis, and z-axis, respectively.

vidual segment. This may be an important clue for how a real hagfish controls its muscles while sliding the knot.

5   Conclusion

We presented a simulation technique for modeling a knotting hagfish. The simulator uses real-world biometric data that were collected from hands-on experiments. Our most significant contribution is our successful implementation of *positive thigmotaxis* using newly devised contact-based inverse dynamics. This allowed our hagfish model to slide the knot along the length of its body, which had not been successfully achieved using existing approaches. We hope that our work will enable researchers to characterize how hagfish control their bodies and to further develop better simulators that are biologically informative. Although the focus of this paper is on biological simulation, the positive thigmotaxic constraint may also be applicable to soft-robotics applications [28, 30, 36].

There are several features we would like to develop as future work. First, our current framework uses torques directly, rather than using muscle fibers. Adding contractile muscle fibers and computing the required activations would be an important next step toward a more biologically accurate simulator. We suspect that these activations can be represented by a reduced basis, as was the case with our torque-based simulation. Also, it would be interesting to model the deformable flesh with continuum mechanics, which would enable us to generate more accurate contact geometry. Next, we have only tried plain overhand knots for simplicity. It would be an interesting challenge to formulate other, more complicated knots that have been observed in nature. Lastly, the initial controller based on forward dynamics is hand crafted by trial and error. If we can obtain biologically correct muscular control signals, we would be able to generate much more realistic motions.

Acknowledgements. We thank Austin Haney for helping to record video of knotting Pacific hagfish, *Eptatretus stoutii* and Washington Department of Fish and Wildlife officer Donna Downs for their procurement. This work was supported in part by the National Science Foundation (IOS-1354788 to T.A.U. and CAREER-1846368 to S.S.).

References

1. Adam, H.: Different types of body movement in the hagfish, myxine glutinosa l. Nature **188**(4750), 595–596 (1960)
2. Alexander, J.W., Briggs, G.B.: On types of knotted curves. Ann. Math. **28**(1/4), 562–586 (1926)
3. Andrew, W., Hickman, C.P.: Histology of the Vertebrates: A Comparative Text. Mosby, Saint Louis (1974)
4. Baraff, D.: Fast contact force computation for nonpenetrating rigid bodies. In: Proceedings of the 21st Annual Conference on Computer Graphics and Interactive Techniques, SIGGRAPH 1994, pp. 23–34. ACM, New York, NY, USA (1994)
5. Baumgarte, J.: Stabilization of constraints and integrals of motion in dynamical systems. Comput. Methods Appl. Mech. Eng. **1**, 1–16 (1972)
6. Bergou, M., Wardetzky, M., Robinson, S., Audoly, B., Grinspun, E.: Discrete elastic rods. ACM Trans. Graph. **27**(3), 63:1–63:12 (2008)
7. Bertails, F., Audoly, B., Cani, M.P., Querleux, B., Leroy, F., Lévêque, J.L.: Super-helices for predicting the dynamics of natural hair. ACM Trans. Graph. **25**(3), 1180–1187 (2006)
8. Boyd, S., Vandenberghe, L.: Convex Optimization. Cambridge University Press, New York (2004)
9. Brown, J., Latombe, J.C., Montgomery, K.: Real-time knot-tying simulation. Vis. Comput. **20**(2), 165–179 (2004)
10. Clark, A.J., Crawford, C.H., King, B.D., Demas, A.M., Uyeno, T.A.: Material properties of hagfish skin, with insights into knotting behaviors. Biol. Bull. **230**(3), 243–256 (2016)
11. Clark, A.J., Summers, A.: Ontogenetic scaling of the morphology and biomechanics of the feeding apparatus in the Pacific hagfish Eptatretus stoutii. J. Fish Biol. **80**, 86–99 (2012)
12. Clubb, B.L., Clark, A.J., Uyeno, T.A.: Powering the hagfish "bite": the functional morphology of the retractor complex of two hagfish feeding apparatuses. J. Morphol. **280**(6), 827–840 (2019)
13. Deul, C., Kugelstadt, T., Weiler, M., Bender, J.: Direct position-based solver for stiff rods. Comput. Graph. Forum **37**(6), 313–324 (2018)
14. Evans, E., Hwang, Y., Sueda, S., Uyeno, T.A.: Estimating whole body flexibility in pacific hagfish. In: The Society for Integrative & Comparative Biology, 3–7 January 2018
15. Featherstone, R.: The calculation of robot dynamics using articulated-body inertias. Int. J. Robot. Res. **2**(1), 13–30 (1983)
16. Haney, W.A.: Characterization of body knotting behavior in hagfish. Master's thesis, Valdosta State University, May 2017
17. Jain, S., Liu, C.K.: Controlling physics-based characters using soft contacts. ACM Trans. Graph. **30**(6), 163:1–163:10 (2011)
18. Kaufman, D.M., Sueda, S., James, D.L., Pai, D.K.: Staggered projections for frictional contact in multibody systems. ACM Trans. Graph. **27**(5), 164:1–164:11 (2008)
19. Kim, J., Pollard, N.S.: Fast simulation of skeleton-driven deformable body characters. ACM Trans. Graph. **30**(5), 1–19 (2011)
20. Lee, Y., Park, M.S., Kwon, T., Lee, J.: Locomotion control for many-muscle humanoids. ACM Trans. Graph. **33**(6), 218:1–218:11 (2014)

21. Liu, L., Yin, K., Wang, B., Guo, B.: Simulation and control of skeleton-driven soft body characters. ACM Trans. Graph. **32**(6), 1–8 (2013)
22. Long, J.H., Koob-Emunds, M., Sinwell, B., Koob, T.J.: The notochord of hagfish myxine glutinosa: visco-elastic properties and mechanical functions during steady swimming. J. Exper. Biol. **205**(24), 3819–3831 (2002)
23. Martini, F.H.: The ecology of hagfishes. In: Jørgensen, J.M., Lomholt, J.P., Weber, R.E., Malte, H. (eds.) The Biology of Hagfishes, pp. 57–77. Springer, Netherlands (1998). https://doi.org/10.1007/978-94-011-5834-3_5
24. Miller, T.J.: Feeding behavior of echidna nebulosa, enchelycore pardalis, and gymnomuraena zebra (teleostei: Muraenidae). Copeia, 662–672 (1989)
25. Pai, D.K.: Strands: interactive simulation of thin solids using cosserat models. Comput. Graph. Forum **21**(3), 347–352 (2002)
26. Phillips, J., Ladd, A., Kavraki, L.E.: Simulated knot tying. In: IEEE International Conference on Robotics and Automation, vol. 1, pp. 841–846. IEEE (2002)
27. Pickwell, G.V.: Knotting and coiling behavior in the pelagic sea snake pelamis platurus (l.). Copeia **1971**(2), 348–350 (1971)
28. Rus, D., Tolley, M.T.: Design, fabrication and control of soft robots. Nature **521**(7553), 467 (2015)
29. Shinar, T., Schroeder, C., Fedkiw, R.: Two-way coupling of rigid and deformable bodies. In: Proceedings of SCA 2008, pp. 95–103 (2008)
30. Simaan, N.: Snake-like units using flexible backbones and actuation redundancy for enhanced miniaturization. Proceedings of ICRA 2005, pp. 3012–3017 (2005)
31. Strahan, R.: The behaviour of myxinoids. Acta Zoologica **44**(1–2), 73–102 (1963)
32. Sueda, S., Jones, G.L., Levin, D.I.W., Pai, D.K.: Large-scale dynamic simulation of highly constrained strands. ACM Trans. Graph. **30**(4), 39:1–39:10 (2011)
33. Sueda, S., Kaufman, A., Pai, D.K.: Musculotendon simulation for hand animation. ACM Trans. Graph. **27**(3), 83:1–83:8 (2008)
34. Sumbre, G., Fiorito, G., Flash, T., Hochner, B.: Octopuses use a human-like strategy to control precise point-to-point arm movements. Current Biol. CB **16**, 767–72 (2006)
35. Thelen, D.G., Anderson, F.C.: Using computed muscle control to generate forward dynamic simulations of human walking from experimental data. J. Biomech. **39**(6), 1107–1115 (2006)
36. Trivedi, D., Rahn, C.D., Kier, W.M., Walker, I.D.: Soft robotics: biological inspiration, state of the art, and future research. Appl. Bionics Biomech. **5**(3), 99–117 (2008)
37. Uyeno, T.A., Clark, A.J.: Muscle articulations: flexible jaw joints made of soft tissues. Integr. Comp. Biol. **55**(2), 193–204 (2015)
38. Vladu, I., Strîmbeanu, D., Ivănescu, M., Bîzdoacă, N., Vladu, C., Florescu, M.: Control system for a hyper-redundant robot. IFAC Proc. Vol. **45**(6), 853–858 (2012)
39. Wang, Y., Weidner, N.J., Baxter, M.A., Hwang, Y., Kaufman, D.M., Sueda, S.: REDMAX: efficient & flexible approach for articulated dynamics. ACM Trans. Graph. **38**(4), 104:1–104:10 (2019)
40. Zintzen, V., Roberts, C.D., Anderson, M.J., Stewart, A.L., Struthers, C.D., Harvey, E.S.: Hagfish predatory behaviour and slime defence mechanism. Sci. Rep. **1**, 131 (2011)

Interactive 3D Visualization for Monitoring and Analysis of Geographical Traffic Data of Various Domains

Daniil Rodin$^{(\boxtimes)}$ (ID), Oded Shmueli (ID), and Gershon Elber

Technion, Haifa, Israel
{daniil.rodin,oshmu,gershon}@cs.technion.ac.il

Abstract. Visual interactive tools are of great importance for monitoring and analysis of geographical data, and, in particular, traffic data. Substantial research effort goes into visualization techniques of various kinds of geography-bound traffic data. Unfortunately, such techniques are very domain-specific and often lack useful features. We propose an interactive visualization system for monitoring and analyzing traffic data on a 3D globe. Our system is general and can be transparently used in different domains, which we examplify by two simulated demonstrations of use cases: Logistic Service and Data Communication. Using these examples, we show that our approach is more general than the current state of the art, and that there are significant similarities between several domains in need of interactive visualization, which are mostly treated as completely separate.

Keywords: Geovisualization · Transport visualization · Network visualization · Visual analysis

1 Introduction

The concept of traffic appears in many areas and performing analysis and monitoring of traffic-related data and processes is often an absolute necessity. Visualization is an invaluable tool for analysis and monitoring tasks with visualization of movement data being a research topic of high interest [3].

There are several domains in need of visualization which deal with traffic data that can be naturally mapped onto the globe. These domains include transportation of goods, vehicles, people, data, money, etc. with each such domain requiring visualization tools. While much research in visualization of such domains is performed, it is mostly very domain specific.

In this work, we present a generic visualization system based on primitives that we believe can be applied to many different domains of traffic visualization. Our system visualizes traffic as an interactive animation on a 3D globe where the user can both navigate the globe, interact with various visualization primitives, and control movement on the time scale as well. More importantly, the user can query the data using the provided API, causing the visual primitives

© Springer Nature Switzerland AG 2019
G. Bebis et al. (Eds.): ISVC 2019, LNCS 11844, pp. 87–98, 2019.
https://doi.org/10.1007/978-3-030-33720-9_7

to be filtered, highlighted, and/or selected, and/or causing the camera to move towards the primitives representing the resulting data. The primitives include sites (static locations), pipes (fixed routes between sites), and packages (dynamic items representing whatever is being transported), all of which are organized into a spatial hierarchy. In this work, we demonstrate that these primitives can describe use cases from various, potentially hierarchical, domains. We thus further demonstrate that our system is well-suited for visualizing use cases from various, potentially hierarchical, domains, as it is based on the aforementioned primitives.

This work is structured as follows. In Sect. 2, we give an overview of related work. In Sect. 3, we describe the system architecture. We present two examples of use cases of the system, in Sect. 4, and then conclude and discuss future work, in Sect. 5.

2   Related Work

The need in geographical traffic visualization is similar to a need that arises in various fields. The research, however, is often focused on a specific domain. In this section, we discuss works that are relevant to our system, separated into two main domains, namely, vehicle traffic and traffic in computer networks.

2.1   Vehicle Traffic Visualization

With geo-positioning data for transport vehicles becoming increasingly available (with the notable example of GTFS[1]), so are visualization, monitoring, and analysis tools for such data. [8] presents a visual interactive tool for analyzing taxi trips using queries optimized for spatio-temporal data. [10] proposes a technique for optimizing visualization by detecting and utilizing spatial patterns when working with origin-destination type data. [13] provides a visual system for analysis of transportation data aimed at helping municipalities and transport companies. A recent survey of such systems and techniques can be found in [2].

However, all of the above approaches work with aggregated data, while our goal is to provide a system capable of real-time monitoring. Various local public transport information systems, such as [7], provide real-time information about current bus locations to the end users. TRAVIC[2], which is an implementation of [4], is a system that allows monitoring public transport around the world (data provided through GTFS) in real time with playback capabilities. These systems are, however, still heavily domain-specific.

2.2   Visualization of Traffic in Computer Networks

Another domain of geographical traffic visualization is visualization of traffic in computer networks. The benefits of geographical visualization of networking

---

[1] https://developers.google.com/transit/gtfs/.
[2] https://tracker.geops.ch/.

data as well as a prototype implementation of a network monitoring system are discussed in [11]. [1] visualizes geo-referenced networks (not necessarily computer networks) on a 3D globe while using surface deformation to reduce data clutter. This approach is expanded by [6], which also adds a method of 'peeling' slices of the Earth surface to show occluded regions. [12] unifies the ideas of [11] and [1] in a single system that provides analytical tool for geo-referenced computer networks. Neither of these systems, however, combines the capabilities of real-time monitoring, 3D visualization, and domain-independence.

3   System Architecture

In this section, we discuss our system from the technical standpoint. First, we give a brief overview of the architecture in Sect. 3.1. Then we describe what kind of input data the visualizer uses in Sects. 3.2 to 3.4. We mention how the visualizer and the data provider communicate in Sect. 3.5. Finally we discuss the capabilities of the visualizer in Sect. 3.6.

3.1   Architecture Overview

In this subsection, we describe the overall architecture of the system, which is shown in Fig. 1. We discuss each subsystem in detail in the next subsection.

The main part of the system is the visualizer, which is a client-side object responsible for taking the data from the data provider (described next) and generating an interactive 3D visual representation of the data inside the browser. The visualizer in our system is implemented using the Cesium library [5], which gives the end user the ability to navigate on the globe, navigate though the timeline (seeking, playback forward or backward at a given speed), explore the data, etc. The visualizer also provides a client-side API to allow integration with higher level management and analytics systems, which in turn allows operations such as filtering and highlighting the data that meets user-specified criteria.

The visualizer gets the data to visualize from the data provider (Fig. 1(b)). From the point of view of the visualizer, the data provider is also a client-side object, but in real world scenarios this object will be a simple proxy to a remote server that sends the data using a network transfer protocol, like HTTP.

The data is largely separated into a static and a dynamic part. The static data is provided directly as is and does not change over time. The dynamic data, on the other hand, can change over time and is thus provided in the form of events. Each event has a timestamp and information about a piece of dynamic data being created, modified, or deleted. This allows the system to be used for both retrospective analysis and real-time monitoring.

3.2   Static Data

We start our in-depth description of the system with the static data. As stated in the overview, the static data does not change over time. While it can be loaded

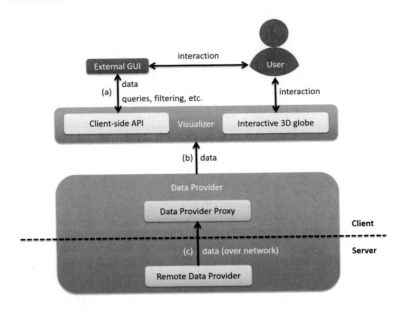

Fig. 1. Architecture overview (Color figure online)

partially on-demand, and its visual representation can change (e.g., collapse or expand, based on the viewing distance), the underlying data is considered unchanged and is provided directly.

Spatial Nodes. All the static data is defined within a hierarchy of what we denote as "spatial nodes", defined as follows.

Definition 1. *A **spatial node** is a named position and orientation in 3D space that represents a certain location or region. Together, spatial nodes form a tree structure denoted as **spatial node tree**. The root spatial node is the Earth itself. Each non-root spatial node can either be defined as an absolute position and orientation (i.e., as latitude, longitude, altitude, heading, pitch, and roll) or using position and orientation relative to its parent spatial node.*

An example of such a hierarchy is Earth, continents, countries, regions, cities, neighborhoods, buildings, floors, and rooms. All the other static data (and most of the dynamic data) is defined over the spatial node hierarchy.

In addition, each spatial node can specify a view distance such that when the camera is further from the node than that distance, the node is considered 'collapsed' and has a different visual representation (we discuss how visual representations are specified in Sect. 3.4). When a spatial node is collapsed, its descendants are not shown at all. This is necessary to reduce visual clutter when looking at complex node trees from afar.

Sites and Pipes. To further help structure the data and thus provide a stream-lined API for placing dynamic data, we introduce two additional static data types, defined below.

Definition 2. *A **site** is a special spatial node that can be used as a storage for dynamic data.*

Examples are airports which can hold airplanes, servers which can hold pieces of data, etc. A site also has a user-visible name and a description in the form of HTML. Each spatial node can either be a site or not.

Definition 3. *A **pipe** is a bi-directional connection between two sites.*

The pipes serve two main purposes. First, a pipe can be used as a relative position for a piece of dynamic data thus removing the burden of always dealing with absolute positions (see Sect. 3.3). Second, the pipe is visible to the user, which helps to understand at a glance the origin and the destination of dynamic data moving along the pipe. Pipes can be specified in three forms: as geodesic lines, geodesic arcs (i.e., with the middle part elevated), and as explicit sequences of points in space, interpolated with a given degree of continuity. Together, sites and pipes effectively form a graph.

3.3 Dynamic Data

Every piece of dynamic data in our system is represented as a 'package', defined as follows:

Definition 4. *A **package** is a piece of data that has a name, description, position and orientation in space, visual representation (discussed in Sect. 3.4), and any kind of custom properties. All of these properties can change over time.*

The most important dynamic property of a package is its position in space. It can be set in several forms:

- Absolute position on the Earth.
- Absolute position relative to a spatial node.
- In a pipe with a given relative position (interpolation amount between the beginning and the end of the pipe).
- On a site.
- Inside another package (obviously, prohibiting circular nesting).

The last option allows us to dynamically nest packages inside each other and thus enable such use cases as people inside airplanes flying between airports (representing both people and planes with packages) and pieces of data inside data transfers between data centers (again, pieces of data and transfers are represented with packages), etc.

Since the properties of packages may change over time, the data about packages is provided to the visualizer in the form of events. Each event has a timestamp, a package ID, and what happened to that package at that timestamp, i.e., being created, deleted, or having some of its properties changed. This also enables real-time visualization by sending events as they happen in real life.

3.4   Visual Elements

Spatial nodes and packages can have visual representations in the form of lists of visual elements.

Definition 5. *A **visual element** is an atomic piece of visual representation of an object (site, package, etc.).*

We heavily base our visualizer on the Cesium library [5], and thus, visual elements are identical to the visual properties of entities in Cesium. The visual element types include:

- Billboard: a screen-space image with a given pixel size and Z offset (for depth ordering).
- Model: a 3D model (in glTF format[3]) with support for dynamic scaling in the form of minimum pixel size and maximum scale.
- Polygon: a flat shape specified by its border points.
- Wall: a wall-like shape specified as vertical extrusion of a given polyline by a given height.
- Box: an embedded cube model.

All the above visual element types can be colored and textured. 3D models can also be animated.

3.5   Data Provider

As the name implies, the role of the data provider is to provide the relevant data (discussed in the previous sections) to the visualizer.

Definition 6. *The **data provider** is the part of the system that provides the data (spatial nodes, sites, packages, etc.) as shown in Fig. 1(b).*

From the point of view of the visualizer, the data provider is simply a client-side object that provides the capabilities described in the rest of this section.

Providing Metadata. To be able to request from the data provider the actual data to visualize (e.g., sites and packages), the visualizer first has to know some global information about the data. We denote this global information as 'metadata'.

Definition 7. *Metadata is the global information, describing the actual data that the data provider provides. The metadata includes the overall timespan of the process being visualized, the ID of the root spatial node, a textual description of the process the data represents, and custom properties to cover the use cases we have not foreseen.*

---

[3] https://www.khronos.org/gltf/.

Providing Static Data. As discussed in Sect. 3.2, all the static data is bound to the spatial node tree, and thus acquiring the static data simply means acquiring the spatial node tree itself. However, there may be cases when the whole tree contains much more information than what the end user actually needs or can interact with in real time. For example, a spatial node tree might contain detailed information about buildings in 100 different cities, but the end user is going to zoom-in on only one or two of those cities. In such cases, it is useful to support on-demand loading of spatial node subtrees.

Acquiring static data is thus implemented as a method that returns a subtree of a spatial node tree starting at a node with a given ID. When returning descendants of this subtree root, the data provider may decide to mark some of them as 'details-on-demand' instead of returning them completely. The visualizer then may request them separately or ignore those that the user never gets too close to.

We have also considered an option of letting the visualizer decide the needed level of detail, but decided to let the data provider decide, since it has much more information about the data. It is theoretically possible to let the visualizer provide an abstract "level of detail" numeric value, which the data provider would consider to decide which nodes to mark as details-on-demand, but we leave it for the future work.

Providing Dynamic Data. As discussed in Sect. 3.3, in our system, dynamic data is represented as packages and is provided in the form of events. To enable provision of events in real-time, the event provision is implemented via subscription. The visualizer subscribes to events by giving the data provider a callback function that is called for every event received.

API. The described capabilities of the data provider are exposed as the following narrow API. This API is used to provide the data to the visualizer, as shown in Fig. 1(b).

- **getMeta**(): returns the metadata (asynchronously).
- **getSpatialSubtree**(*subtreeRootId*): returns (asynchronously) a spatial node subtree starting at the node with ID *subtreeRootId*.
- **subscribe**(*eventCallback*): subscribes to dynamic data events.
- **unsubscribe**(*eventCallback*): unsubscribes from dynamic data events.

As discussed in Sect. 3.1, in real life scenarios, this client-side object is likely to be a simple proxy to a remote server that exposes these same capabilities as a web API.

3.6   The Visualizer

Definition 8. *The **visualizer** is the client-side component responsible for visualizing the data and responding to user input. (Green rectangle in Fig. 1.)*

The visualizer provides two ways of interaction: the 3D globe, with which the user can directly interact, and the client-side API.

Interactive 3D Globe. The main goal of our system is presenting the data to the user in a visual and interactive form, which is one of the responsibilities of the visualizer. We employ the Cesium library to render various data on top of the 3D globe, in a browser. The visualizer is thus responsible for converting the data it received from the data provider to Cesium entities and Cesium primitives that are actually rendered. This is true for both static and dynamic data.

An important feature of the visualizer that is offered directly to the end user is the ability to smoothly navigate through time in the form of playback controls, whereas the user controls the direction and speed of animation. The visualizer is thus also responsible for correctly placing packages in both space and time, and also correctly handling cases of package nesting.

Client-Side API. The necessary capabilities are, however, not limited to what can be done by directly interacting with the 3D globe. (Note that hereafter, we sometimes refer to spatial nodes, sites, pipes, and packages as 'objects' when discussing capabilities not unique to one type only.) There is an obvious need for capabilities such as filtering, highlighting, and tracking objects that satisfy certain criteria. By 'filtering' and 'highlighting' we mean the following.

Definition 9. *Filtering is hiding and showing objects based on a given criterion (filter), usually supplied as a function that takes an object and returns a boolean value indicating whether that object should be visible or not.*

Definition 10. *Highlighting is temporarily modifying visual properties of some objects to make them visually distinguishable. The exact visual change is defined by custom functions.*

These capabilities are provided through the client-side API of the visualizer, which is shown below. This API is meant to be used by arbitrary external GUI, as shown in Fig. 1(a).

- **spatialNodes**: a filterable collection of spatial nodes.
- **sites**: a filterable collection of sites.
- **pipes**: a filterable collection of pipes.
- **packages**: a filterable collection of packages.
- **defineHighlighting**(*highlight, unhighlight*): sets the functions that would be used to highlight objects.
- **registerCustomVisual**(*name, visual*): registers a visual representation to use for a visual element named *name*, effectively extending the list of visual elements (Sect. 3.4) that can be provided by the data provider.
- **highlight**(*objects*): highlights a given set of objects using the highlighting method defined with **defineHighlighting**.
- **select**(*object*): selects the given object.
- **navigateTo**(*objects*): navigates the camera to show the given set of objects.

Each of the filterable collections of objects serves as a sub-API with the following methods:

- **visibilityFilters**: a modifiable collection of filters that determine visibility of objects within the 3D view. A filter is a function that takes an object and returns a boolean value indicating whether the object should be visible.
- **queryVisible**(*filter*): returns all visible objects that satisfy the given filter.
- **query**(*filter*): returns all objects (including invisible ones) that satisfy the given filter.

The client-side API also allows the system to be used as an embedded visualizer for higher level data analysis systems such as Elastic Search [9].

4   Examples

In this section, we present two example use cases for our system. First is a logistic service that governs delivery of parcels (Sect. 4.1), and the second is communication between data centers (Sect. 4.2). Note that the only difference between the examples is the data returned by the data provider (spatial nodes, sites, pipes, and packages). Everything else stays the same, which makes our system quite universal.

4.1   Logistic Service

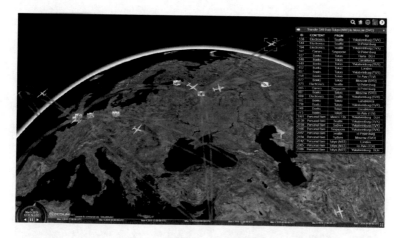

Fig. 2. The Logistic Service use case example. On the top right, you can see the contents of the selected airplane, i.e., the parcel packages bound to that airplane package.

The first example that we present is the Logistic Service (Fig. 2). It demonstrates how our system can be used in monitoring and analyzing parcel delivery around the globe. In this example, the sites are storage and sorting centers (including ones in airports) and there are two types of packages: parcels and transportation means for those parcels (e.g., airplanes).

First, we establish the spatial node tree in the form of countries, cities, and sorting facilities within cities. Then, demand in various places on the globe for various goods and items from other places on the globe is generated. For each instance of such demand, a parcel which is delivered through the various means of transportation (mainly flights) is created. We also added a case of door-to-door delivery, which, in addition to generated transport, also uses explicit coordinates to simulate GPS tracking of a delivery mini-truck (Fig. 3).

Fig. 3. A package that follows the path specified with absolute coordinates, representing a delivery mini-truck with GPS tracking.

Each parcel is a package and each plane or truck that carries it is also a package since both of these data types are dynamic. Our ability to place packages within other packages allows us to directly model the concept of placing parcels inside airplanes and mini-trucks. This, in turn, allows an intuitive way of executing Client API commands such as "highlight all parcels carrying electronics from Taiwan", which will visually highlight all planes, trucks, and sites that contain such parcels, as well as the parcels themselves.

4.2 Data Center Communication

Fig. 4. The Data Center Communication use case example. Different shapes and colors of the items represent different categories of data transfers and network events.

The second example is communication between data centers (Fig. 4). Here, we have a network of data centers which constantly exchange various kinds of data.

In this case, the data centers are sites, direct connections between them are pipes, and the data transfers (possibly consolidated) between them are packages.

Another thing represented as a package in this simulation is the data itself, and an interesting type of such data is cache data for load balancing. Consider a simulated scenario where each data center is supposed to serve data to the closest customers, but the data requested may be stored in another data center. The data centers therefore exchange the data and store it as a cache, thus allowing several instances of the same data to exist.

For monitoring and analyzing the performance of the data centers and of load balancing, we believe it is useful to be able to track data instances and transfers that contain them. Fortunately, it is straightforward to do this within our system. Furthermore, the request to show all the sites and network transfers that contain specific data is conceptually no different from a request to show all the sorting centers and transport vehicles containing

Fig. 5. Zooming in on a building to monitor the communication inside.

parcels with a certain type of product, which was discussed in the previous section.

This example also demonstrates the benefit of 3D and the hierarchical structure by allowing the visualization of some buildings from the inside as 3D primitives and models (Fig. 5). This allows to monitor and investigate what is happening on the building level in the most intuitive way.

5   Conclusions and Future Work

We have presented a generic visualization system that allows monitoring and data analysis for geographical traffic data of various domains on a 3D globe with the ability to navigate in both space and time in a continuous (and thus visually coherent) way. Our infrastructure manages all static and dynamic hierarchical data, and exploits the Cesium library for rendering 3D geometry on a 3D globe, time controls, mouse-based spatial navigation, and basic GUI.

We have presented two simulated examples from two completely different domains (a logistic service and a data center communication) implemented in a very similar way based on the same set of abstractions. We, thus, demonstrate that there are significant similarities between these, and potentially more, domains in need of interactive visualization that are mostly treated as unique.

Needless to say, there is a lot of room for improvement. First and foremost, there is a potential for more use cases for traffic visualization. Examples include visualization of traffic of money, electricity, natural resources (e.g., oil), etc.

We define pipes as static data that connects sites. However, one can easily envision scenarios where allowing pipes to have dynamic properties is desirable, such as showing current availability, throughput, or other properties of a pipe. Having unidirectional pipes is also a possible future extension.

Another aspect that can be improved is additional GUI. We provide the default GUI supported by Cesium for spatio-temporal navigation and viewing properties. We also support a client-side API of the visualizer to attach any additional GUI the specific use case requires. Nevertheless, the burden of creating additional GUI can be lifted if one designs and implements a large enough set of universal GUI widgets that can be used with our system.

References

1. Alper, B., Sümengen, S., Balcisoy, S.: Dynamic visualization of geographic networks using surface deformations with constraints. In: Proceedings of the Computer Graphics International Conference (CGI). Computer Graphics Society, Petrópolis, Brazil (2007)
2. Andrienko, G., Andrienko, N., Chen, W., Maciejewski, R., Zhao, Y.: Visual analytics of mobility and transportation: state of the art and further research directions. IEEE Trans. Intell. Transp. Syst. **18**(8), 2232–2249 (2017)
3. Andrienko, N., Andrienko, G.: Visual analytics of movement: an overview of methods, tools and procedures. Inf. Vis. **12**(1), 3–24 (2013)
4. Bast, H., Brosi, P., Storandt, S.: Real-time movement visualization of public transit data. In: Proceedings of the 22nd ACM SIGSPATIAL International Conference on Advances in Geographic Information Systems, pp. 331–340. ACM (2014)
5. Cozzi, P., Bagnell, D.: A WebGL globe rendering pipeline. GPU Pro 4: Advanced Rendering Techniques, vol. 4, pp. 39–48 (2013)
6. Debiasi, A., Simões, B., De Amicis, R.: GeoPeels: deformation-based technique for exploration of geo-referenced networks (2015)
7. Farkas, K., Nagy, A.Z., Tomás, T., Szabó, R.: Participatory sensing based real-time public transport information service. In: 2014 IEEE International Conference on Pervasive Computing and Communication Workshops (PERCOM WORKSHOPS), pp. 141–144. IEEE (2014)
8. Ferreira, N., Poco, J., Vo, H.T., Freire, J., Silva, C.T.: Visual exploration of big spatio-temporal urban data: a study of new york city taxi trips. IEEE Trans. Vis. Comput. Graph. **19**(12), 2149–2158 (2013)
9. Gormley, C., Tong, Z.: Elasticsearch: The Definitive Guide: A Distributed Real-Time Search and Analytics Engine. O'Reilly Media Inc., Sebastopol (2015)
10. Guo, D., Zhu, X., Jin, H., Gao, P., Andris, C.: Discovering spatial patterns in origin-destination mobility data. Trans. GIS **16**(3), 411–429 (2012)
11. Hofstede, R., Fioreze, T.: SURFmap: a network monitoring tool based on the Google Maps API. In: 2009 IFIP/IEEE International Symposium on Integrated Network Management, pp. 676–690. IEEE (2009)
12. Hu, H., Zhang, H., Li, W.: Visualizing network communication in geographic environment. In: 2013 International Conference on Virtual Reality and Visualization, pp. 206–212. IEEE (2013)
13. Liu, S., Pu, J., Luo, Q., Qu, H., Ni, L.M., Krishnan, R.: VAIT: a visual analytics system for metropolitan transportation. IEEE Trans. Intell. Transp. Syst. **14**(4), 1586–1596 (2013)

Propagate and Pair: A Single-Pass Approach to Critical Point Pairing in Reeb Graphs

Junyi Tu[1] , Mustafa Hajij[2], and Paul Rosen[1]($\boxtimes$)

[1] University of South Florida, Tampa, FL 33620, USA
{junyi,prosen}@mail.usf.edu
[2] The Ohio State University, Columbus 43210, USA

Abstract. With the popularization of Topological Data Analysis, the Reeb graph has found new applications as a summarization technique in the analysis and visualization of large and complex data, whose usefulness extends beyond just the graph itself. Pairing critical points enables forming topological fingerprints, known as persistence diagrams, that provides insights into the structure and noise in data. Although the body of work addressing the efficient calculation of Reeb graphs is large, the literature on pairing is limited. In this paper, we discuss two algorithmic approaches for pairing critical points in Reeb graphs, first a multipass approach, followed by a new single-pass algorithm, called Propagate and Pair.

Keywords: Topological Data Analysis · Reeb graph · Critical point pairing

1 Introduction

The last two decades have witnessed great advances in methods using topology to analyze data, in a process called Topological Data Analysis (TDA). Their popularity is due in large part to their robustness and applicability to a variety of domains [17]. The *Reeb graph* [21], which encodes the evolution of the connectivity of the level sets induced by a scalar function defined on a data domain, was originally proposed as a data structure to encode the geometric skeleton of 3D objects, but recently it has been re-purposed as a tool in TDA. Beside their usefulness in handling large data [12], Reeb graphs and their non-looping relative, contour trees [5], have been successfully used in feature detection [24], data reduction and simplification [7,22], image processing [16], shape understanding [2], visualization of isosurfaces [3] and many other applications.

One challenge with Reeb graphs is that the graph may be too large or complex to directly visualize, therefore requiring further abstraction. Persistent homology [13], parameterizes topological structures by their life-time, providing a topological description called the *persistence diagram*. The notion of persistence can be applied to any act of birth that is paired with an act of death. Since the Reeb graph encodes the birth and the death of the connected components of the level sets of a scalar function, the notion of persistence can be applied to critical points in the Reeb graph [1]. *The advantage of this approach is simplicity and scalability—a large Reeb graph can be reduced to a much easier to interpret scatterplot.* Figure 1 shows an example, where a mesh with a scalar function (Fig. 1(a)) is converted into a Reeb graph (Fig. 1(b)). After that,

© Springer Nature Switzerland AG 2019
G. Bebis et al. (Eds.): ISVC 2019, LNCS 11844, pp. 99–113, 2019.
https://doi.org/10.1007/978-3-030-33720-9_8

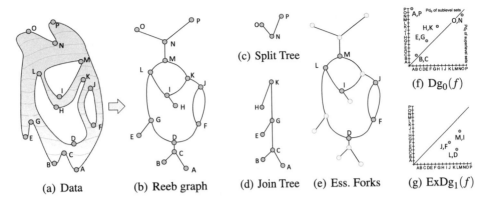

(a) Data   (b) Reeb graph   (d) Join Tree   (e) Ess. Forks   (g) ExDg$_1(f)$

(c) Split Tree

(f) Dg$_0(f)$

Fig. 1. (a) A mesh with a scalar function being processed into (b) a Reeb graph, where critical points are paired. In the multipass approach, (c) a split tree and (d) a join tree are first extracted for non-essential pairing. Next, the (e) essential forks are paired, one at a time. (f) The persistence diagram and (g) extended persistence diagram provide a visualization of the pairings.

the critical points are paired, and the persistence diagram displays the data (Fig. 1(f) and (g)). This final step can be challenging, particularly when considering *essential critical points*—those critical points associated with cycles in the Reeb graph—that each require an expensive search. While many prior works [8–11, 14, 15, 18, 20, 25] have provided efficient algorithms for the calculation of Reeb graph structures, to our knowledge, none have provided a detailed description of an algorithm for pairing critical points.

In this paper, we describe and test 2 algorithms to compute persistence diagrams from Reeb graphs. The first is a multipass approach that pairs non-essential (non-loop) critical points using branch decomposition [19] on join and split trees, then pairing essential critical points also using join trees. This leads to our second approach, an algorithm for pairing both non-essential and essential critical points in a single-pass.

2   Reeb Graphs and Persistence Diagrams

2.1   Reeb Graph

Let X be a triangulable topological space, and let $f : X \to \mathbb{R}$ be a continuous function defined on it. The Reeb graph, R_f, can be thought of as a topological summary of the space X using the information encoded by the scalar function f. More precisely, the Reeb graph encodes the changes that occur to connected components of the level sets of $f^{-1}(r)$ as r goes from negative infinity to positive infinity. Figure 1(a) and (b) show an example of a Reeb graph defined on a surface. For the sake of simplicity we plot the Reeb graph using the height function indicated by the vertical coordinate in the figure.

The function f can be used to classify points on the Reeb graph as follows. Let x be a point in R_f. The *up-degree* of x is the number of branches (1-cells) incident to x that have higher values of f than x. The down-degree of x is defined similarly. A point x on R_f is said to be *regular* if its up-degree and down-degree are equal to one. Otherwise it is a *critical point*. A critical point on the Reeb graph is also a *node* of the Reeb graph.

A critical point is called a minimum if its down-degree is equal to 0. Symmetrically, a critical point is said a maximum if its up-degree is equal to 0. Finally, a critical point is said to be a down-fork/up-fork if its down-degree/up-degree is larger than 1.

2.2 Persistent Homology

The notion of persistent homology was originally introduced by Edelsbrunner et al. [13]. Here we present the theoretical setting for the computation of the persistence diagram associated with a scalar function defined on a triangulated topological space. Consider the p-dimensional homology class H_p of a space, where H_0 are components, H_1 are tunnels/cycles, H_2 are voids, etc. Persistent homology evaluates a sequence of vector spaces: $0 = H_p(X_0) \rightarrow H_p(X_1) \rightarrow \cdots \rightarrow H_p(X_n) = H_p(X)$, where $X_i = X_{\leq f_i}$, recording the birth and death events. In particular, the p-th *ordinary persistence diagram* of f, denoted as $\mathrm{Dg}_p(f)$, is a multiset of pairs (b, d) corresponding to the birth b and death d values of some p-dimensional homology class.

Since the homology $H_p(X)$ may not be trivial in general, any nontrivial homology class of $H_p(X)$, referred to as an *essential homology class*, will never die during the sequence. These events are associated with the cyclic portions of the Reeb graph. We refer to the multiset of points encoding the birth and death time of pth homology classes created in the ordinary part and destroyed in the relative part of the sequence as the *p-th extended persistence diagram* of f, denoted by $\mathrm{ExDg}_p(f)$. In particular, for each point (b, d) in $\mathrm{ExDg}_p(f)$ there is an essential homology class in $H_p(X)$ that is born in $H_p(X_{\leq b})$ and dies at $H_p(X_{\geq d})$. Observe that for the extended persistence diagram the birth time b for an essential homology class in $H_p(X_{\leq b})$ is larger than or equal to death time d for the relative homology class in $H_p(X_{\geq d})$ that kills it.

2.3 Persistence Diagram of Reeb Graph

Of interest to us are the persistence diagram $\mathrm{Dg}_0(f)$ and extended persistence diagram $\mathrm{ExDg}_1(f)$. Pairing critical points can be computed independently of the Reeb graph. However, it is more efficiently computed by considering the Reeb graph R_f. We give an intuitive explanation here and refer the reader to [4] for more details.

First, we distinguish between 2 types of forks in the Reeb graph, namely the ordinary (non-essential) forks and the essential forks. Let R_f be a Reeb graph and let s be a down-fork such that $a = f(s)$. We say that the down-fork s is an *ordinary fork* if the lower branches of s are contained in disjoint connected components C_1 and C_2 of $(R_f)_{<a}$. The down-fork a is said to be *essential* if it is not ordinary. The ordinary and essential up-forks are defined similarly.

Ordinary Down-Forks of a Reeb Graph. We first consider pairing down-forks using sublevel set filtration. We track changes that occur in $H_0((R_f)_{\leq a})$ as a increases. A connected component of $(R_f)_{\leq a}$ is created when a passes through a minimum of R_f. Let C be a connected component of $(R_f)_{\leq a}$. We say that a local minimum a of R_f *creates* C if a is the global minimum of C. Every ordinary down-fork is paired with a local minimum to form one point in the persistence diagram $\mathrm{Dg}_0(f)$ as follows. Let s be an ordinary down-fork with $f(a) = s$ and let C_1 and C_2 be the connected components of $(R_f)_{<a}$. Let x_1 and x_2 be the creators of C_1 and C_2. Without loss of generality we assume that $f(x_1) < f(x_2)$. The homology class $[x_2]$ that is created at $f(x_2)$ and dies at $f(s)$ gives rise to a point (x_2, s) in the ordinary persistence diagram $\mathrm{Dg}_0(f)$. Note, a pair occurs when the minimum is a branch in the Reeb graph, hence we name it a *branching feature*.

Ordinary Up-Forks of a Reeb Graph. Ordinary up-forks are paired similarly using superlevel set filtration, pairing each up-fork with a local maximum to form points in the persistence diagram, $\mathrm{Dg}_0(f)$, with the following variations. For an ordinary up-fork, s, with $f(a) = s$, connected components C_1 and C_2 now come from $(R_f)_{>a}$. Assuming that $f(x_1) < f(x_2)$, the homology class $[x_1]$ that is created at $f(x_1)$ dies at $f(s)$ and gives rise to a point (x_1, s) in $\mathrm{Dg}_0(f)$.

Cycle Features of a Reeb Graph. Let s be an essential down-fork. We call the down-fork s a creator of a 1-cycle in the sublevel set $(R_f)_{\leq a}$. As shown in [1], s will be paired with an essential up-fork s' to form an *essential pair* (s', s), and a point (s', s) in the extended persistence diagram $\mathrm{ExDg}_1(f)$. The essential up-fork s' is determined as follows. Let Γ_s be the set of all cycles born at s, each corresponding to a cycle in R_f. Let γ_s be an element of Γ_s with largest minimum value of f among these cycles born at s. The point s' is the point that the function f achieves this minimum on the cycle γ_s.

3   Conditioning the Graph

Our approach is restricted to Reeb graphs where all point are either a minimum, maximum, up-fork with up-degree 2, or down-fork with down-degree 2. Fortunately, graphs that do not abide by these requirements can be conditioned to fit them. We define the $J : K$ degree of a node as the J up-degree and K down-degree.

There are 4 node conditions to be corrected: **1:1 nodes**—Nodes with both 1 up- and 1 down-degree are regular. Therefore, they only need to be removed from the graph. This is done by removing the regular point and reconnecting the nodes above and below, as seen in Fig. 2(a). **0:2 (and 2:0) nodes**—Nodes with 0 up-degree and 2 down-degree (or vice versa) are degenerate maximum (minimum) nodes, in that they are both down-fork (up-fork) and local maximum (minimum). As shown in Fig. 2(b), this condition is corrected by added a new node for the local maximum ϵ higher value, where ϵ is a small number. This type of degenerate node rarely occurs in Reeb graphs, but it frequently occurs in approximations of a Reeb graph, such as Mapper [23]. **2:2 nodes**—Nodes with both 2 up- and 2 down-degree are degenerate double forks, both down-fork and up-fork. Figure 2(c) shows how double forks can be corrected by splitting into 2 separate forks, one up- and one down-fork, ϵ distance apart. **1:N > 2 (and N > 2:1) nodes**—Nodes with down-degree (or up-degree) 3 or higher, are difficult forks to pair. These forks correspond to complex saddles in f, such as monkey saddles. A single critical point pairing to these forks just reduces the degree of down-fork by 1, requiring complicated tracking of pairs. To simplify this, as seen in Fig. 2(d), these forks can be split into 2 forks ϵ apart. The upper down-fork retains 1 of the original down edges. The new down-fork connects with the old and takes the remaining down-edges. For even higher-order forks, the operation can be repeated on the lower down-fork.

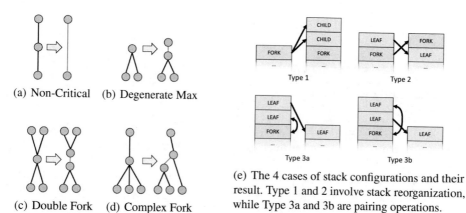

(e) The 4 cases of stack configurations and their result. Type 1 and 2 involve stack reorganization, while Type 3a and 3b are pairing operations.

(a) Non-Critical   (b) Degenerate Max

(c) Double Fork   (d) Complex Fork

Fig. 2. (a–d) Before pairing, the nodes of Reeb graph are conditioned considering 4 node configurations. New nodes and edges are shown in blue. (e) For non-essential fork pairing in the multipass algorithm, the 4 cases for stack processing are illustrated with their resulting configurations. (Color figure online)

Beyond these requirements, the Reeb graph is assumed a single connected component. If not, each connected component can simply be extracted and processed individually. Finally, all nodes on the Reeb graph are assumed to have unique function values. If not, some processing order is arbitrary, and 0-persistence features may result.

4   Multipass Approach

The persistence diagram $Dg_0(f)$ can be obtained by pairing the non-essential fork nodes of the Reeb graph. The extended persistence diagram $ExDg_1(f)$ can be obtained by pairing of essential fork nodes. We demonstrate these 2 steps using Fig. 1 as an example.

4.1   Non-essential Fork Pairing

Identifying the non-essential forks can be reduced to calculating join and split trees on the Reeb graph (see Fig. 1(c) and (d)), in our case, using Carr et al.'s approach [6]. Next, a stack-based algorithm, based upon branch decomposition [19], pairs critical points. The algorithm operates as a depth first search that seeks out simply connected forks (i.e., forks connected to 2 leaves) and recursively pairs and collapses the tree.

The algorithm processes the tree using a stack that is initially seeded with the root of the tree. At each iteration, 1 of 3 operation types occurs, as seen in Fig. 2(e). Operation Type 1 occurs when the top of the stack is a fork. In this case, the children of the fork are pushed onto the stack. Operation Type 2 occurs when the top of the stack is a leaf, but the next node is a fork. In this case, the leaf and fork have their orders swapped. Finally, operation Type 3 has 2 variants that occur when 2 leaf nodes sit atop the stack. In both variants, one leaf is paired with the fork, and the other leaf is pushed back onto the stack. The pairing occurs with the leaf that has a value *closer* to the value of the fork. The stack

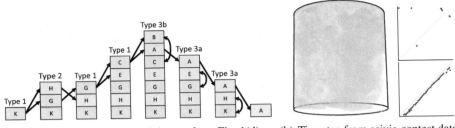

(a) Example processing the join tree from Fig. 1(d).   (b) Timestep from scivis_contest data.

Fig. 3. (a) An example pairing of the join tree from Fig. 1(d) shows the stack at each processing step, from left to right. (b) Timestep (066) from the scivis_contest data is shown with concentration mapped to color (left), along with Dg_0 (top) showing up-forks in blue and down-forks in red; and the $ExDg_1$ (bottom) showing cycles in purple. (Color figure online)

is processed until only a single leaf node remains, the global minimum/maximum of the join/split trees, respectively. The algorithm operates identically on both join and split trees. Finally, the unpaired global minimum and maximum are paired.

Figure 3(a) shows an example for the join tree in Fig. 1(d). Initially the root K is placed on the stack. A Type 1 operation pushes the children, G and H, onto the stack. Next, a Type 2 operation reorders the top of the stack. G, a down-fork, in now atop the stack, pushing its 2 children, E and C, onto the stack. Another Type 1 pushes C's children, A and B onto the stack. In the next 3 steps, a series of Type 3 operations occur. First B and C are paired, followed by E and G, and finally H and K. At the end, A, the global minimum, is the only point remaining on the stack. The assigned pairs, B/C, E/G, and H/K, appear in the $Dg_0(f)$ in Fig. 1(f), along with the split tree pairing, O/N, and the global min/max pairing, A/P.

4.2 Essential Forks Pairing

The remaining unpaired forks are essential forks, as seen in Fig. 1(e). We developed an algorithm from the high-level description of [4] to pair them. The essential fork pairing algorithm can be treated as join tree problem, processing forks one at a time. For a given up-fork, s, the node can be split into two temporary nodes, s_L and s_R. A join tree can be computed by sweeping the superlevel set. At each step of the sweep, the connected components are calculated. The pairing for a selected essential up-fork occurs at the down-fork that merges s_L and s_R into a single connected component.

Figure 4 shows the sweeping process for the up-fork D. Initially (Fig. 4(a)), D is split into D_L and D_R, which are each part of separate connected components, denoted by color (Fig. 4(b)). As the join tree is swept past E (Fig. 4(c)), a new connected component is formed. In Fig. 4(d), F is added to the connected component of D_R. As the join tree is swept past G (Fig. 4(e)), the E and D_L connected components join. The process continues until Fig. 4(h), where 3 connected components exist. The purple and yellow components join at K (Fig. 4(i)). Finally at L (Fig. 4(j)), both D_L and D_R are part of the same connected component. This indicates that D pairs with L.

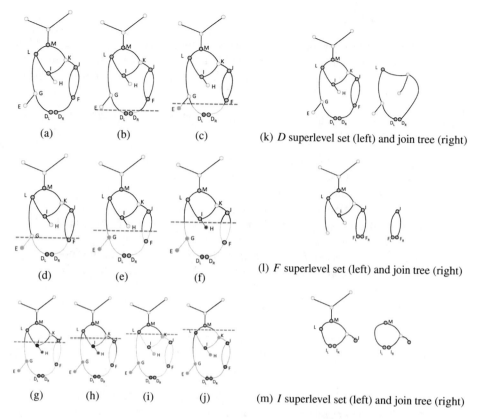

(k) *D* superlevel set (left) and join tree (right)

(l) *F* superlevel set (left) and join tree (right)

(m) *I* superlevel set (left) and join tree (right)

Fig. 4. Essential fork pairing in the multipass algorithm for the example Reeb graph from Fig. 1. (a–j) The join tree-based essential fork pairing for up-fork D. (a) D is initially split into D_L and D_R. (b–i) The colors indicate different connected components as the join tree is swept up the superlevel set. (j) The pairing is found when D_L and D_R are contained in the same connected component. (k–m) Each up-fork (D, F, and I, respectively) is split into 2 pieces and a join tree calculated from the superlevel set to find the partner.

Figure 4(k–m) shows the superlevel sets and associated join trees for the up-forks D, F, and I. The pairing partner L/D, J/F, and M/I can all be seen in the $\mathrm{ExDg}_1(f)$ in Fig. 1(g).

5 Single-Pass Algorithm: Propagate and Pair

In the previous section, we showed that the critical point pairing problem could be broken down into a series of merge tree computations. For non-essential forks this was in the form of join and split trees, which are merge trees of the superlevel sets and sublevel sets, respectively. For essential saddles, it came in the form of a special join tree calculation for each essential up-fork. A natural question is whether these merge tree calculations can be combined into a single-pass operation, which is precisely what follows.

5.1 Basic Propagate and Pair

The Propagate and Pair algorithm operates by sweeping the Reeb graph from lowest to highest value. At each point, a list of unpaired points from the sublevel set is maintained. When a point is processed in the sweep, 2 possible operations occur on these lists: *propagate* and/or *pair*.

Propagate. The job of propagate is to push labels from unpaired nodes further up the unprocessed Reeb graph. 4 cases exist.

- For <u>local minima</u> a label for the current critical point is propagated upward. In the examples of Fig. 5(a) and (b), both A and B are propagated to C.
- For <u>local maxima</u> nothing needs to propagate.
- For <u>down-forks</u> all unpaired labels are propagated upwards. In the example of Fig. 5(c), the critical points B and C are paired, thus only A is propagated to D.
- For <u>up-forks</u> all unpaired labels are propagated upwards. Additional labels for the current up-fork are created and tagged with the specific branch of the fork that created them (in the examples with subscripts L and R). This tag is critical for closing essential cycles. In the example of Fig. 5(d), the labels A and D_L are propagated to G, and labels A and D_R are propagated to F.

Pair. The pairing operation searches the list of labels to determine an appropriate pairing partner from the sublevel set. The pairing operation only occurs for local maxima and down-forks.

- For <u>local maxima</u> the labels list is searched for the unpaired up-fork with the largest value. Those critical points are then paired. In Fig. 5(o), for local maximum O, the list is searched and N_L is determined to be the closest unpaired up-fork.
- For <u>down-forks</u> two possible cases exist, essential or non-essential, which can be differentiated by searching the available labels. First, the list is searched for the largest up-fork with both legs. Both legs indicate that the current down-fork closes a cycle with the associated up-fork. In the example, Fig. 5(m), the list of M is searched and labels I_L and I_R found. If no such up-fork exists, then the down-fork is non-essential. In this case, the highest valued local minimum is selected from the list. In the example of Fig. 5(c), no essential up-forks are found for C, and the largest local minimum, B is selected instead.

5.2 Virtual Edges for Propagate and Pair

The basic propagate and pair will fail in certain cases, such as in Fig. 6(a). The failure arises from the assumption that the superlevel set is the only thing needed to propagate labels. In this case, label information needs to be communicated between E and F, which are connected by the node D in the sublevel set. To resolve this communication issue, virtual edges are used. Virtual edges have 4 associated operations.

Virtual Edge Creation. Virtual edges are created on all up-fork operations. For example in Fig. 6(b), when processing B, the endpoints of the fork, E and F are connected

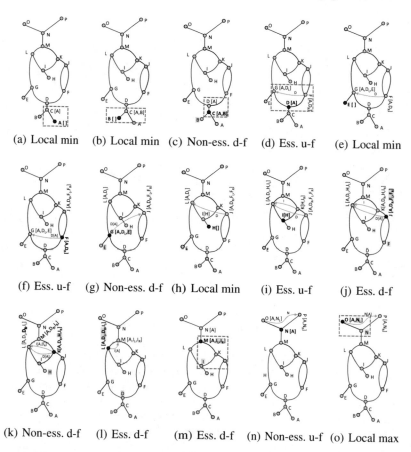

(a) Local min   (b) Local min   (c) Non-ess. d-f   (d) Ess. u-f   (e) Local min

(f) Ess. u-f   (g) Non-ess. d-f   (h) Local min   (i) Ess. u-f   (j) Ess. d-f

(k) Non-ess. d-f   (l) Ess. d-f   (m) Ess. d-f   (n) Non-ess. u-f   (o) Local max

Fig. 5. Propagate and Pair algorithm on the Reeb graph from Fig. 1. At each step, the node being processed is in bold; propagated edges are shown in brackets; pairing is shown in blue; and virtual edges are shown in orange. (ess.: essential; non-ess.: non-essential; d-f: down-fork; u-f: up-fork) (Color figure online)

with virtual edge V_B. Similarly, in Fig. 6(c), when processing up-fork D, another virtual edge V_D is created connecting the endpoint, E and F.

Label Propagation. Propagating labels across virtual edges is similar to standard propagation with one additional condition. A label can only be propagated if its value is less than that of the up-fork that generated the virtual edge. In other words, for a given label X and a virtual edge V_Y, X is only propagated if $f(X) < f(Y)$. Looking at the example in Fig. 6(d), for the virtual edge V_B, only A is propagated because $f(A) < f(B)$. For the virtual edge V_D: A, B_L, and C are all propagated, since they all have values smaller than D.

Virtual Edge Merging. When processing down-forks, all incoming virtual edges need to be pairwise merged. Figure 6(k) shows an example. When processing down-fork N,

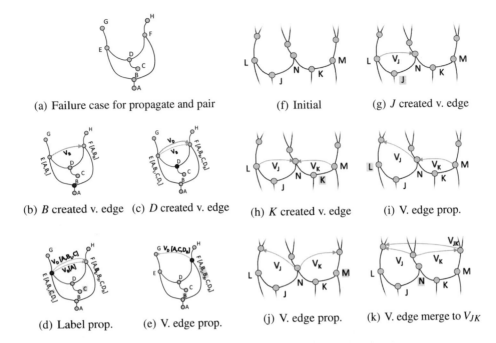

(a) Failure case for propagate and pair   (f) Initial   (g) J created v. edge

(b) B created v. edge   (c) D created v. edge   (h) K created v. edge   (i) V. edge prop.

(d) Label prop.   (e) V. edge prop.   (j) V. edge prop.   (k) V. edge merge to V_{JK}

Fig. 6. Example where the basic propagate and pair algorithm fails. (a–e) In this case, B and F should pair but do not. To overcome this limitation, (b–c) virtual edges are created as up-forks are processed. (d) Labels can then be propagated across virtual edges. (e) The virtual edges themselves are propagated and redundant edges removed. (f–k) An example requiring virtual edge merging. (g–h) Virtual edges are created. (i–j) Virtual edges are propagated. (k) At the down-fork N, virtual edges V_J and V_K are propagated and merged into V_{JK}.

the virtual edges V_J and V_K are merged into a new virtual edge V_{JK}. For the purpose of label propagation, the virtual edge uses its minimum saddle, in this case J.

Virtual Edge Propagation. Finally, virtual edges themselves need to be propagated. For up-forks, all virtual edges are propagated up to both neighboring nodes. In the case of down-forks, all virtual edges are similarly propagated, as we see in Fig. 6(e). During the virtual edge propagation phase, redundant virtual edges can also be culled. For example, the virtual edge V_D is a superset of V_B. Therefore, V_B can be discarded. The necessity of the virtual edge process can also be seen in Fig. 5. In Figs. 5(i)–(l), the pairing of L with D is only possible because of the virtual edge created by I in Fig. 5(i).

6   Evaluation

We have implemented the described algorithms using Java. Performance reported in Table 1 was calculated on a 2017 MacBook Pro, 3.1 GHz i5 CPU, 8 GB RAM.

We investigate the performance of the algorithms using the following:

- Synthetic split trees, join trees, and Reeb graphs generated by a Python script. Given a positive integer n, where $n = \{100, 500, 1000, 3000, 5000\}$, the script creates a fork G_1 consisting of a node with valency 3 and 3 nodes with valency 1 linked to the 3-valence node. At each iteration $i < n$, another fork is generated, and 1 or 2 of its 1 valency nodes are glued to the nodes in G_{i-1} with valency 1. Constraining the gluing to a single node at each iteration results in a split tree.
- Reeb graphs calculated on publicly available meshes in Fig. 8 and meshes provided by AIM@SHAPE Shape Repository. Reeb graphs were extracted using our own Reeb graph implementation in C++.
- Time-series of 120 Mapper graphs taken from the 2016 SciVis Contest[1], a large time-varying multi-run particle simulation, in Fig. 3(b). Our evaluation took one realization, smoothing length 0.44, run 50, and calculated the Mapper graphs for all 120 time-steps using the variable *concentration*. Our video, available at https://youtu.be/AcJX4GdzBZY, shows the entire sequence. The Mapper graphs were generated using a Python script that follows the standard Mapper algorithm [23].

Table 1. Performance for all datasets tested. Bold indicates the faster algorithm.

Data	Figure	Mesh		Reeb graph nodes		Cycles	Multipass time (ms)	Single-pass time (ms)
		Vertices	Faces	Initial	Cond			
random_tree_100				401	204	0	2.45e–02	2.71e–02 (split)
								9.06e−03 (join)
random_tree_500				2001	1004	0	0.13	0.18 (split)
								4.90e−02 (join)
random_tree_1000				4001	2004	0	0.42	0.30 (split)
								0.11 (join)
random_tree_3000				12001	6004	0	1.10	1.98 (split)
								0.39 (join)
random_tree_5000				20001	10004	0	2.11	3.39 (split)
								0.75 (join)
random_graph_100				401	112	46	1.90e–02	**1.76e−02**
random_graph_500				2001	542	231	**0.48**	0.57
random_graph_1000				4001	1010	497	**0.55**	0.59
random_graph_3000				12001	3014	1495	**1.71**	1.91
random_graph_5000				20001	5204	2400	**14.35**	24.45
4_torus	Figure 8(d)	10401	20814	23	10	4	2.06e–03	**1.47e−03**
buddah	Figure 8(c)	10098	20216	33	14	6	1.61e–03	**1.16e−03**
david	Figure 8(e)	26138	52284	8	8	3	7.82e–04	**4.17e−04**
double_torus	Figure 8(a)	3070	6144	13	6	2	5.29e–04	**2.80e−04**
female	Figure 8(b)	8410	16816	15	8	0	7.82e–04	**3.45e−04**
flower	Figure 8(h)	4000	8256	132	132	65	2.80e–02	**2.43e−02**
greek	Figure 8(f)	39994	80000	23	10	4	8.62e–04	**4.81e−04**
topology	Figure 8(g)	6616	13280	28	28	13	4.34e–03	**4.02e−03**
scivis_contest	Figure 3(b)	194k (avg)	–	117 (avg)	178.2 (avg)	81.3 (avg)	**3.82** (total)	4.18 (total)

[1] https://www.uni-kl.de/sciviscontest/.

Overview of Results. The performance for the algorithms can be seen in Table 1. These values were obtained by running the test 1000 times and storing the average compute time. The persistence diagrams of both the single-pass and multipass algorithms were compared in order to verify correctness. For most cases, the single-pass approach outperformed the multipass approach. The exceptions being the random split tree, random graph, and SciVis contest data, each of which we will discuss.

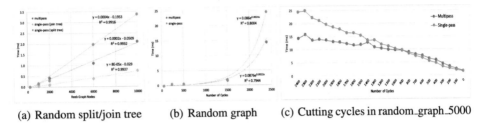

(a) Random split/join tree   (b) Random graph   (c) Cutting cycles in random_graph_5000

Fig. 7. Plots of the compute time for various input sizes to (a) the random split/join tree and (b) the random graph for Table 1. (c) Performance results when cutting cycles in the random_graph_5000. As more cycles that are cut, the single-pass algorithm begins to outperform the multipass variant.

Random Split Tree vs. Join Tree. We compared the exact same tree structures as split trees and join trees by negating the function value of the input tree. The performance observed in Table 1 and Fig. 7(a) shows that the join tree performs significantly better than the split tree. The explanation for this is quite simple. The join tree consists of exclusively down-forks, while the split tree consists of exclusively up-forks. Since only up-forks generate virtual edges, the split tree created and processed many virtual edges, while the join tree has none. In fact, split trees represent one worst case by generating many unneeded virtual edges. From a practical standpoint, the algorithm can avoid situations like this by switching sweep directions (i.e. top-to-bottom), when the number of up-forks is significantly larger than the number of down-forks.

Random Graph. We next investigate the performance of randomly generated Reeb graphs, shown in Table 1 and Fig. 7(b). These Reeb graphs consist predominantly of cycles. This represents another type of worst case, since many up-forks generate virtual edges, which are then merged into even more virtual edges at the down-forks. To verify this, we ran an experiment, as seen in Fig. 7(c), that randomly cuts n cycles in the starting Reeb graph random_graph_5000 containing 2400 cycles. The break even was about 900 cycles (about 25% essential and 75% non-essential forks).

SciVis Contest Data. The SciVis contest data was "cycle heavy" as can be seen in the persistence diagram of Fig. 3(b). Given the random graph analysis, it is unsurprising that the performance of the single-pass approach was lower than the multipass approach.

7   Discussion and Conclusion

Pairing critical points is a key part of the TDA pipeline—the Reeb graphs capture complex structure, but direct representation is impractical. Critical point pairing enables a

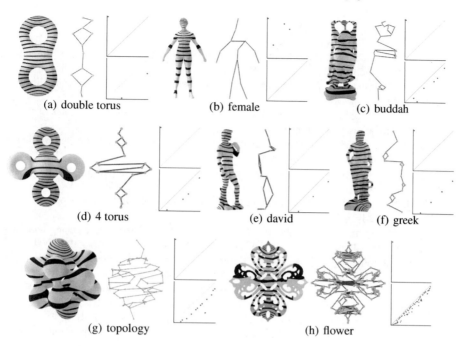

Fig. 8. The meshes colored by the scalar value (left), Reeb graphs (middle), Dg_0 with up-forks in blue and down-forks in red (top), and $ExDg_1$ cycles in purple (bottom) are shown for evaluation. (Color figure online)

compact visual representation in the form of a persistence diagram. The value of representing a dataset with the persistence diagram is the simplicity and efficiency. Persistence diagrams avoid the occlusions problems of normal 3D datasets (e.g., the internal structure of Fig. 3(b)), and they avoid the potential confusion of direct representation of the Reeb graph (e.g., the Reeb graph of Fig. 8(h)). In addition, they provide sharp visual cue for time-varying data (see our video).

Our results showed that although the single-pass algorithm tended to outperform the multipass algorithm, there was no clear winner. We point out some advantages and disadvantages for each. The multipass algorithm has an advantage in simplicity of implementation. Once the merge tree and branch decomposition are implemented, the only necessity is repeated calls to those algorithms. This approach also has a potential advantage for (limited) parallelism. First, processing join and split trees in parallel, then all essential up-forks. The single-pass algorithm showed a slight edge in performance, particularly for data with a balance between essential and non-essential forks. The other significant advantage of the approach is that it is in fact a single-pass approach, only visiting critical points once. This is useful for streaming or time-varying data, where the critical points arrive in order, but analysis cannot wait for the entire data to arrive.

Acknowledgments. This project was supported in part by National Science Foundation (IIS-1513616 and IIS-1845204). Mesh data are provided by AIM@SHAPE Repository.

References

1. Agarwal, P.K., Edelsbrunner, H., Harer, J., Wang, Y.: Extreme elevation on a 2-manifold. Discrete Comput. Geom. **36**(4), 553–572 (2006)
2. Attene, M., Biasotti, S., Spagnuolo, M.: Shape understanding by contour-driven retiling. Vis. Comput. **19**(2), 127–138 (2003)
3. Bajaj, C.L., Pascucci, V., Schikore, D.R.: The contour spectrum. In: Proceedings of the 8th IEEE Visualization, p. 167-ff (1997)
4. Bauer, U., Ge, X., Wang, Y.: Measuring distance between Reeb graphs. In: Symposium on Computational Geometry, p. 464 (2014)
5. Boyell, R.L., Ruston, H.: Hybrid techniques for real-time radar simulation. In: Proceedings of the November 12–14, Fall Joint Computer Conference, pp. 445–458 (1963)
6. Carr, H., Snoeyink, J., Axen, U.: Computing contour trees in all dimensions. Comput. Geom. Theory Appl. **24**(2), 75–94 (2003)
7. Carr, H., Snoeyink, J., van de Panne, M.: Simplifying flexible isosurfaces using local geometric measures. In: Proceedings of the 15th IEEE Visualization, pp. 497–504 (2004)
8. Cole-McLaughlin, K., Edelsbrunner, H., Harer, J., Natarajan, V., Pascucci, V.: Loops in Reeb graphs of 2-manifolds. In: Symposium on Computational Geometry, pp. 344–350 (2003)
9. Doraiswamy, H., Natarajan, V.: Efficient output-sensitive construction of Reeb graphs. In: Hong, S.-H., Nagamochi, H., Fukunaga, T. (eds.) ISAAC 2008. LNCS, vol. 5369, pp. 556–567. Springer, Heidelberg (2008). https://doi.org/10.1007/978-3-540-92182-0_50
10. Doraiswamy, H., Natarajan, V.: Efficient algorithms for computing Reeb graphs. Comput. Geom. **42**(6), 606–616 (2009)
11. Doraiswamy, H., Natarajan, V.: Computing Reeb graphs as a union of contour trees. IEEE Trans. Visual Comput. Graphics **19**(2), 249–262 (2013)
12. Edelsbrunner, H., Harer, J., Mascarenhas, A., Pascucci, V.: Time-varying Reeb graphs for continuous space-time data. In: Symposium on Computational Geometry, pp. 366–372 (2004)
13. Edelsbrunner, H., Letscher, D., Zomorodian, A.: Topological persistence and simplification. In: Symposium on Foundations of Computer Science, pp. 454–463 (2000)
14. Harvey, W., Wang, Y., Wenger, R.: A randomized O (m log m) time algorithm for computing Reeb graphs of arbitrary simplicial complexes. In: Symposium on Computational Geometry, pp. 267–276 (2010)
15. Hilaga, M., Shinagawa, Y.: Topology matching for fully automatic similarity estimation of 3D shapes. In: SIGGRAPH, pp. 203–212 (2001)
16. Kweon, I.S., Kanade, T.: Extracting topographic terrain features from elevation maps. CVGIP Image Underst. **59**(2), 171–182 (1994)
17. Munch, E.: A user's guide to topological data analysis. J. Learn. Analytics **4**(2), 47–61 (2017)
18. Parsa, S.: A deterministic $O(m \log m)$ time algorithm for the Reeb graph. In: ACM Symposium on Computational Geometry (SoCG), pp. 269–276 (2012)
19. Pascucci, V., Cole-McLaughlin, K., Scorzelli, G.: Multi-resolution computation and presentation of contour trees. In: IASTED Conference on Visualization, Imaging, and Image Processing, pp. 452–290 (2004)
20. Pascucci, V., Scorzelli, G., Bremer, P.T., Mascarenhas, A.: Robust on-line computation of Reeb graphs: simplicity and speed. ACM Trans. Graph. **26**(3), 58.1–58.9 (2007)
21. Reeb, G.: Sur les points singuliers dune forme de pfaff completement intgrable ou dune fonction numrique. CR Acad. Sci. Paris **222**, 847–849 (1946)
22. Rosen, P., et al.: Using contour trees in the analysis and visualization of radio astronomy data cubes. In: TopoInVis (2019)

23. Singh, G., Mémoli, F., Carlsson, G.E.: Topological methods for the analysis of high dimensional data sets and 3D object recognition. In: Eurographics SPBG, pp. 91–100 (2007)
24. Takahashi, S., Takeshima, Y., Fujishiro, I.: Topological volume skeletonization and its application to transfer function design. Graph. Models **66**(1), 24–49 (2004)
25. Tierny, J., Vandeborre, J.P., Daoudi, M.: Partial 3D shape retrieval by Reeb pattern unfolding. Comput. Graphics Forum **28**(1), 41–55 (2009)

Real-Time Ray Tracing with Spherically Projected Object Data

Bridget Makena Winn, Reed Garmsen, Irene Humer⬭,
and Christian Eckhardt⁽⬭⁾ ⬭

California Polytechnic State University, San Luis Obispo, CA, USA
ceckhard@calpoly.edu

Abstract. As raytracing becomes feasible in regards to computational costs for real-time applications, new challenges emerge to achieve sufficient quality. To aim for an acceptable framerate, the amount of consecutive rays is strongly reduced to keep the workload on the GPU low, but sophisticated approaches for denoising are required. One of the major bottlenecks is finding the ray intersection with the geometry. In this work, we present a fast alternative by pre-computing a spherical projection of an object and reduce the cost of intersection-testing independent of the vertex count by projecting the object onto a circumscribed sphere. Further on, we test our Spherical Projection Approximation (SPA) by implementing it into a DirectX Raytracing (DXR) framework and comparing framerates and outcome quality for indirect light with DXR's native triangle intersection for various dense objects. We found, that our approach not only hails comparable quality in representing the indirect light, but is also significantly faster and consequently provides a raytracing alternative to achieve real-time capabilities for complex scenes.

Keywords: Real-time raytracing · DiretX Raytracing · Intersection shaders

1 Introduction

In modern real-time Computer Graphics, the trend to enhance render quality, in specific light bleeding and reflections for real time applications is still ongoing. While techniques such as direct lighting, pre-computed light maps and more sophisticated methods like ambient occlusion are still broadly standard, other techniques that support real-time global illumination already exists, accompanied with certain limitations. Common examples are Voxel Cone Global Illumination (VXGI) [1], Light Propagation Volumes (LPV) [2] and Reflective Shadow Mapping (RSM) [3]. However, VXGI and LPV quanitize the involved geometry, making it challenging to find a reasonable balance between quality, memory usage and frame-time and suffer under artifacts due to the voxelization, especially for moving objects. RSM is a post-processing technique and as such difficult

Supported by organization x.

G. Bebis et al. (Eds.): ISVC 2019, LNCS 11844, pp. 114–126, 2019.
https://doi.org/10.1007/978-3-030-33720-9_9

to implement off-screen light-information effectively. Raytracing [4], one of the oldest rendering technique, was hardly considered to be used in real-time applications due to its heavy computational workload. According to the render equation [5], respectively the Bidirectional Reflectance Distribution Function (BRDF) [6], theoretically every primary ray (cast from the camera view) intersecting with geometry casts an infinite number of secondary rays, invoking even more rays on each consecutive hit. Modern render-programs strongly reduces the ray count leading to a noisy outcome, with a need to be post-processed with competent denoising algorithms.

Recently, new graphic card generations (NVidia Titan V, 20XX) are designed to hardware-accelerate real-time ray-tracing. Supporting that, DirectX Raytracing (DXR) [7] is a Microsoft developed API based on DirectX 12. The DXR shader table and state objects allow the GPU to spawn rays and shaders in parallel [11] and its acceleration structure for efficiently finding the correct intersection-triangle per ray even allows multi-object ray intersections [12]. Several games implemented DXR ray-tracing into their render pipeline utilizing a single secondary reflection ray, improving the quality of reflective surfaces. Using more than one secondary ray has still a significant impact on the real-time capabilities. State-of-the-art ongoing research investigates effective GPU denoise algorithms aiming to produce high quality results with just a small set of secondary rays. Further on, studies have been done to accelerate shadow computations in DXR [10]. Noteworthy, there are several other, less efficient methods to approximate object color and position during raytracing, with and without precomputation [13,14].

In this work, we present a different approach to reduce the workload for real-time raytracing with DXR. The DXR programmable interface allows the coding of intersection-shaders, which are called to evaluate if a ray hits an object. Since objects in modern 3D graphics consist of up to several hundreds of thousands of triangles, a highly effective ray-triangle intersection testing as well as a fast hierarchical data structure for finding the right triangle is intrinsic for DXR, but still a bottleneck regarding real-time. Our approach reduces the complexity of any object by projecting it to a circumscribed sphere. Hence, all triangle testing per object is reduced to one ray-sphere intersection. For this publication, we present the implementation as well as the qualitatively and quantitatively results comparing objects of different vertex count.

2 Methodology

2.1 Testing Environment

We utilized DXR to run real-time raytracing on NVidia Titan V graphics card (10XX series) (+ model, CPU, GPU). We used the OpenGL graphics API to generate textures on a MacBook Air 2015. Code was developed on Visual Studio 2019.

2.2 Direct-X 12 Raytracing Overview

To achieve global illumination in real-time, we use DirectX Raytracing (DXR with DirectX 12), an expert-level graphics API that takes advantage of driver and hardware support for raytracing on the GPU.

In the DXR pipeline, we implement an additional *intersection shader* to define behavior between a ray and a sphere geometric primitive. Further on, we also implement a *closest hit shader* to process the hit, after DXR determined the closest object in case a ray intersects multiple objects. When the ray intersects a geometric primitive, DXR chooses the corresponding shader to intersect the geometric type and uses the closest hit shader to accumulate light.

2.3 Spherical Model Projection Overview

The raytracing algorithm sends rays from a camera into the scene and shades pixels based on ray-object intersections and several bounces. It is used recursively to generate global illumination. During global illumination, every primary ray that intersects an object must send secondary rays to collect global light information. Depending on implementation, each secondary ray may invoke tertiary rays and so on. Each ray sent into the scene may intersect objects of different face density. Consequently, the performance depends on the number of rays, as well as the scene objects' vertex count. The algorithm presents challenges when implemented in real-time. In our implementation, we are concerned only with primary and secondary rays, as a minimum requirement to approximate global illumination.

DXR geometry acceleration structure is driver defined and works on an NVidia card with bounding volume hierarchy to increase computational efficiency to find the correct triangle for the ray intersection. However, depending on the complexity of the object, approaching real-time capabilities with reflection rays as well as diffuse light rays is challenging.

In our approach, we contain an object in a bounding sphere and project its complex shape to the sphere's surface. Consequently, we reduce every ray intersection to one test per object, without further searching in a bounding volume hierarchy for the specific triangle. Our implementation aims to achieve a diffuse light quality that is comparable to traditional raytracing.

During raytracing, each primary ray may hit an object containing several triangles. Secondary rays hit bounding spheres instead of hitting the enclosed object. Once a ray intersects a bounding sphere, we sample precomputed spherical textures to approximate the color, position, and normal of the contained object at the hit point. We use the values from the spherical texture to approximate diffuse light contributing to global illumination.

We precompute spherical textures for each object in our real-time scene. To project a 3D object onto the surface of a sphere, we developed a program to scan the object's surface properties and store depth, surface normal, and non-shaded texture color in textures. A camera follows a spherical path around the object and outputs information to each texture. As a result, the output quality of our approach depends on the complexity of the object's shape. The projected depth is the perpendicular distance from the sphere surface to the object, and the depth consistently entails the point closest to the sphere surface. Consequently, surface points behind this will be neglected, see Fig. 1.

In this work, we investigate and show the quality performance under these constraints. The inside of e.g. doughnut-shaped objects will not be visible, although its contribution to secondary rays is less prominent than the outside surface. Thus the spherical intersection algorithm allows developers to further divide an object into separate parts, which are represented by spheres.

Our algorithm aims to work with static as well as with animated objects. Simple static objects may be contained in one sphere. Thus to obtain global illumination with animated objects, each sub-mesh associated with an animation-bone can be contained in its own sphere.

During raytracing, secondary rays intersect bounding spheres to approximate contributing diffuse light. After a ray hits the bounding sphere, we perform a subsequent collision test to determine if the ray intersects the projected object contained in the sphere. For that, we construct a test ray n from the center of the object S_{center}, perpendicular to the incoming ray r, see Fig. 1(a). If the length d_2 of n is less than the distance d_1 from S_{center} to the geometry surface along n, we detect a hit, see Fig. 1(b). d_1 is stored in the pre-computed spherical texture on uv-coordinates derived from n on the sphere's surface.

As can be seen in Fig. 1(b), rays such as r_2 are incorrectly detected as miss if only considering one perpendicular test ray n. Our solution is to increase the number of test rays, see Fig. 1(c): r_1 trajectory through the sphere is smaller than r_2 and its minimum distance to S_{center} is greater, consequently less test rays are necessary to cover the same area or the object. Thus, the amount of test rays is proportional to this minimum distance and yield at a value between 1 and a set maximum of 50 test rays. We use a boot object to test our algorithm with a non-uniform shape, see Fig. 2. We use a texture emphasizing contrasting colors for both side of the boot, in order to evaluate the quality outcome of color bleeding. Due to our model projection, the boot tip takes up a very small portion of the spherical texture, is a known limitation of SPA and the boot is intentionally chosen for comparing our approach to traditional raytracing.

2.4   Spherical Texture Generation

We generate two spherical textures of a resolution of 640×480 with four bytes per pixel. The first texture stores the unshaded texture color in the red, green, and blue channel as well as scaled depth in the alpha channel. The other texture stores the surface normals in the red, green, and blue channel and sets the alpha channel to 1.

For each pixel of the spherical textures, we rotate the camera view around the centered object along a spherical trajectory and render the object into a frame buffer. The view target is set to the center of the object. The middle pixel of each frame buffer is stored into the spherical textures with uv-coordinates depending on the camera position relative to the object. Further on, the distance of the

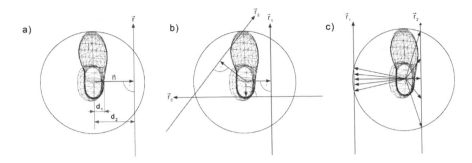

Fig. 1. Spherical Projection Approximation algorithm: (a) Ray r hitting the sphere; a perpendicular test-ray n with the length d_2 is constructed from the minimum distance point on r towards the sphere center S_{center} and is tested against the stored depth information d_1 to determine if a hit occurred. (b) Several cases of hit (r_3) and miss (r_1, r_2). Evidently, r_2 should hit the boot but hails a negative result with one perpendicular test ray. (c) Several test rays are generated between the two enter/exit points of the secant ray towards S_{center}. (Color figure online)

middle pixel is divided by the sphere's radius to normalize its value, suiting to be stored as (color) byte. From the fragment shader, the non-shaded texture color as well as the normalized distance is stored into one of the spherical textures, while the surface normal is stored into the other one. Later on, to retrieve the real distance, the sphere's radius must be known.

Finally, we bind our spherical color/depth and normal textures to DXR to run our SPA approach in real-time.

2.5   SPA Integration in DXR

In DXR, we implement two shaders: The *intersection shader* defines our ray-sphere intersection and overwrites DXR's intrinsic triangle-intersection. The *sphere closest hit shader* calculates diffuse lighting after a ray-sphere intersection.

DXR allows the implementation of *intersection shaders*, so that rays can intersect user-defined geometry [9]. We implement a sphere intersection shader to define ray behavior with our bounding spheres. On a positively detected hit with the bounding sphere, our algorithm further tests if the contained object has been hit, see Fig. 1.

Since the depth values of the spherical texture are normalized, for each test ray, as described in Sect. 2.3, it's length needs to be divided by the sphere's radius in order to compare it's value with the depth value of the spherical texture. To access the spherical textures data, we calculate the uv-coordinates based on the test ray direction as well as through the model-matrix of the object.

If the length of the test ray is less than or equal to the sample depth, we consider this an object hit. Else, if all test rays miss, we consider this an object miss.

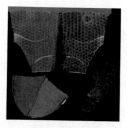

Fig. 2. We are using a simple boot object, as it represents a simple, yet non-spherical object as test-mesh with different vertex count: 326, 1317, 5233, 20865, 83329, 333057, and 1131713. The texture splits the boot into an orange and a blue half. (Color figure online)

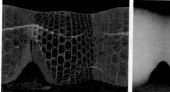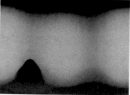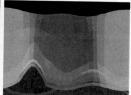

Fig. 3. Spherical texture generation with a resolution of 640 × 480: (left) texture color of the boot object spherically scanned. (Middle) the distance from the boot to the sphere surface is stored as alpha-value by dividing it by the sphere-radius. (Right) Normals are scanned spherically, no tangent space is needed.

After DXR determines which type of object primitive was intersected closest, the corresponding *closest hit shader* is in charge of diffuse shading at the hit point. Here, the non-shaded texture color as well as the surface normal is loaded from the two spherical textures in order to shade the pixel.

3   Results and Discussion

In raytracing, primary rays are reflected by the objects and dependent on the objects' material yield to the reflection and to indirect light. Reflections are usually performed with one secondary ray, while diffuse light requires collecting colors from different directions, which is computationally expensive. To reduce the workload on the GPU, only a small number of secondary rays is sent out and leads to a strong noise in the outcome. To aim for high quality results, a sophisticated denoise step needs to be performed [16]. Nevertheless, to better illustrate the outcome of our approach, we do not perform denoising, but rather keep the result from the ray intersection.

In Fig. 4, we present shadow ray casting using DXR triangle intersection versus SPA to demonstrate the accuracy of our approach. One has to note, we would not recommend using SPA for shadows, since primary rays are used and the difference in computational cost is marginal. To display the shadows, the boot is positioned against a white wall in Fig. 4, with DXR triangle intersection ray-casted shadow (right) compared with the SPA shadow (left). The boot is lit from the front, and global illumination has been disabled to study the shadow only. The SPA algorithm is able to produce shadows that show distinct sections of the boot, including the heel underneath. The SPA shadow is also warped towards the poles of the sphere due to the spherical approximation: The distance projected onto the spheres' surface is measured by a point on the sphere to the spheres' center, which in the case of the cylindrical shape of the upper parts of the boot leads to an increasing steepness towards the pole. Counteraction to this warping is part of a further investigation and entails different shapes, such as cylinders and boxes depending on the base object.

Fig. 4. Shadow mapping by ray intersection to illustrate the effectiveness of the SPA (left) compared to raytracing (left). The detail of the heel is clearly visible.

We created images using test ray counts of 1, 3, 5 and 10. When compared with results yield from raytracing, our images most accurately recreate color bleeding with test ray counts 5 and above. Our algorithm is able to reproduce distinct colors from the boot faces. In Fig. 5 one can see a comparison between raytracing Fig. 5(a) and our spherical projection approximation Fig. 5(b). The boot is placed close to the edge between two adjunct, white walls. We are using 10 test rays with a boot being perpendicular orientated towards the left wall. The boot texture is most prominent on both sides and the tip, where it is most illuminated from the top-positioned light source. Consequently, indirect light will be collected from the frontal area of the boot rather than from the back, as can be seen in both images Fig. 5(a) and (b) by the dark gap between the orange and blue color areas. Notably is the overall less pronounced indirect color bleeding in the SPA. This is due to the color-distribution on the spherical texture, see Fig. 3, were the color-intense parts of the boot-tip are inhabiting less space as a side effect of our approach. However, the color distribution pattern is noticeable comparable. A different angle in the same setting is displayed in Fig. 5(c) and (d) with flipped colors on the boot, where the tip is oriented towards the edge between the walls. Besides having a weaker color bleeding analog to the previous image, the lack of color close to the tip for the SPA image is evident. Here, the SPA sphere already contacts the walls surface, and is the reason for a less intense color concentration at the boots' tip. To further test the light distribution, we rotated the boot in order to increase the direct illuminated surface area of the boot for both methods and compared them in Fig. 5(e) and (f), and Fig. 5(g) and (h). In Fig. 5(e) and (f), both different colored sides of the boot are contributing to the indirect light on the wall.

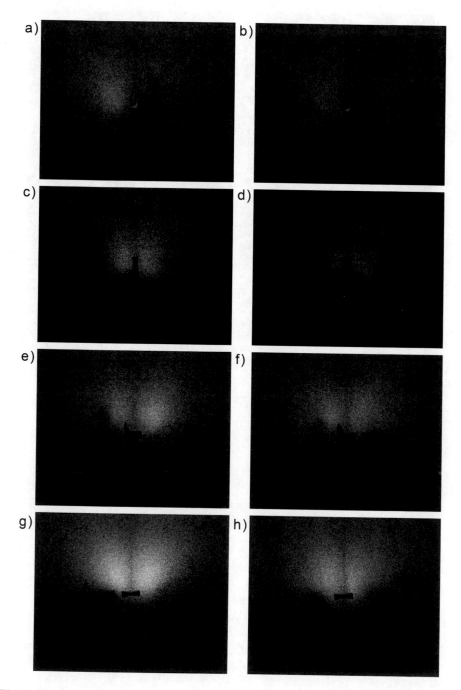

Fig. 5. Color bleeding of the boot under different angles with raytracing (left column) vs SPA (right column) against a corner of a white wall. The light-source is at the top of the boot. (Color figure online)

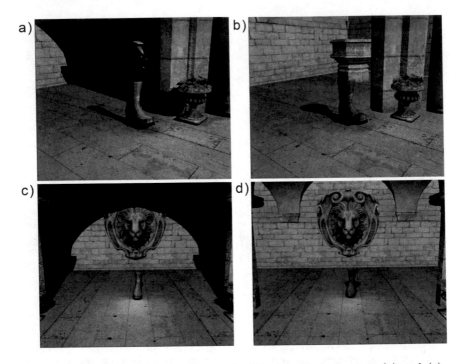

Fig. 6. Comparing color bleeding of the boot in the Sponza scene: (a) and (c) ray-tracing, (b) and (d) SPA. The shadow mapping for the Sponza objects SPA-image is turned off due to using primary and secondary rays with SPA only.

Due to the spherical projection, the boot tip takes up a small portion of the spherical output texture. As a result, our algorithm does not reproduce as much color bleeding from the boot tip. Figure 6 demonstrates the boot object with raytracing (a) and (c) and SPA (b) and (d), lit from above in the Sponza scene, taking a boot texture that yields the boot half blue and half orange. In Fig. 6, the DXR raytracing color bleeding produces blue and orange colors on the ground plane as well as on the surroundings. Compared with SPA Fig. 6(b), both methods achieves the same color bleeding distribution from the boot tip. However, the effect from the spherical texture in SPA, storing less pixels from the boot tip as discussed in Fig. 5 is clearly visible in the difference of color intensity. One will also notice that the scene in Fig. 6(b) lacks shadows from the Sponza objects onto itself; our pipeline uses SPA for both secondary bounces and shadow rays of the boot, while primary rays on the Sponza object are turned off. However the pipeline could be altered to include shadows from triangle intersections. In Fig. 6(c) and (d), we rotated the camera to face the boot tip and rotated the boot down by 20° in order to see the top of the tip from the front view. This angle further demonstrates the color bleeding distribution and amount of color from the boot tip for both methods, DXR triangle intersection and SPA.

We have run the SPA algorithm on identically shaped boots of differing vertex count (326 up to 1131713 vertices), produced by the loop-subdivision surface algorithm. Figure 7 displays the frames per second (FPS) for each boot model. To adequately measure the FPS, we perform SPA with primary and secondary ray intersections, and compare it with DXR ray-triangle primary and secondary intersections.

Figure 7(a) displays the boot vertex count versus FPS for 8 secondary samples per primary ray. For each SPA curve, we use different amounts of test rays, see Fig. 1. The (green), (blue), (orange), and (grey) lines represent our SPA algorithm with test ray density of 1, 3, 5, and 10 respectively. The yellow line represents raytracing using DXR ray-triangle intersection. Test ray counts of 1, 3, 5, and 10 each begin at an FPS of 55.4, 49.7, 45.8, and 42.5 respectively for the boot with 326 vertices, see Tables 1, 2, 3, 4, 5, 6 and 7. Evidently, the maximum gain in FPS for using the SPA yields at boots with approximately 80 K vertices, where we find a FPS rate of 56 compared with DXR triangle intersection of 29 FPS. It is clearly visible, that the DXR triangle intersection is strongly dependent on the vertex count, as it decreases steadily with increasing vertex density. We anticipated this effect due to the ray-triangle intersection pipeline, in which every ray may intersect one of millions of triangles per object. Further increasing the vertices leads to a dependency of the SPA as well, which is due to the vertex processing stage becoming a dominant factor in the shader pipeline. Figure 7(b) displays the vertex count and FPS for 32 recursive samples. Test ray densities of 1, 3, 5, and 10 begin at FPS of 16.8, 14.5, 13.2, and 12.2 respectively for the smallest boot. The highest relative gain in FPS is observed again at objects with 80 K vertices comparing one step SPA with DXR ray-triangle intersection.

Figure 7 involves all boots for Fig. 7(c) 128 and Fig. 7(d) 256 recursive samples respectively. In these figures, there are some fluctuation in FPS due to a steadily decreasing FPS rate, making it difficult to get accurate FPS results, since we need to measure over a longer period of time. In Fig. 7(c) we see the vertex count and FPS for 128 recursive samples. For this many secondary samples, we do not observe a dependency of vertex count for the SPA, since the GPU is mostly occupied with solving ray-intersections compared with vertex processing. All data points can be read from the Table 1 through 7.

Table 1. 326 vertices

		Samples			
		8	32	128	256
	0	128.8	43.6	13.3	6.7
	1	55.4	16.8	4.5	2.3
test rays	3	49.7	14.5	3.8	1.7
	5	45.8	13.2	3.3	1.6
	10	42.5	12.2	2.9	1.4
	ray	42.1	12.3	3.3	1.6

Table 2. 1317 vertices

	Samples		
8	32	128	256
130.5	49.5	12.5	6.1
55.7	16.9	4.4	2.2
47.6	14.6	3.4	1.8
46.8	13	3.2	1.4
41.6	11.8	2.8	1.3
42.3	12.8	3.1	1.5

Table 3. 5233 vertices

	Samples		
8	32	128	256
127	45.3	12.6	5.8
56.2	17.1	4.4	2.3
46.2	13.8	3.7	1.7
43.8	12.7	6.7	1.4
40.7	11.6	3.3	1.4
35.8	10.7	2.4	1.3

Table 4. 20865 vertices

		Samples			
		8	32	128	256
test rays	0	127.2	45.8	12.4	6.2
	1	56.7	17.4	4.2	2.3
	3	47.8	14.2	3.6	1.7
	5	44.3	13.1	3.1	1.6
	10	41.3	11.9	3.2	1.5
	ray	32.9	9.5	2.4	1.1

Table 5. 83329 vertices

Samples			
8	32	128	256
121.1	44.7	13.5	6.6
56.6	18.3	4.8	2.1
48.4	14.6	3.8	1.8
44.6	13.8	3.4	1.6
41.4	12.3	2.9	1.5
28.8	8.5	2.2	0.9

Table 6. 333057 vertices

Samples			
8	32	128	256
98.5	42.6	13.4	6.4
51.2	17.7	4.8	2.2
44.0	14.7	3.6	1.9
38.8	12.9	3.4	1.3
38.1	12.3	2.7	1.3
24.9	7.4	1.9	0.3

Table 7. 1331713 vertices

		Samples			
		8	32	128	256
test rays	0	48.6	31.1	11.7	6.3
	1	38.5	15.9	4.8	2.1
	3	33.6	13.3	3.7	1.8
	5	32.2	12.2	3.4	1.9
	10	30.2	11.3	3.2	1.7
	ray	20.9	6.9	1.6	0.2

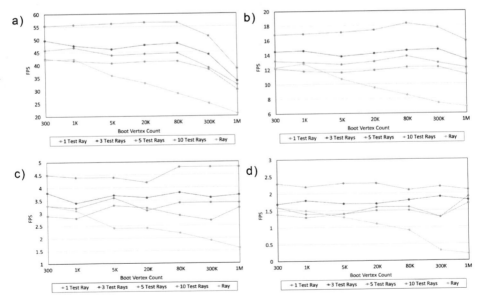

Fig. 7. Boot vertex count versus FPS for (a) 8, (b) 32, (c) 128 and (d) 256 samples samples using different amount of test rays for SPA. (Color figure online)

4   Conclusion and Future Work

In this work, we presented a spherical projection approximation (SPA) algorithm. By spherically scanning complex objects and storing their diffuse color, normals, and depth-to-sphere-surface in textures, and substitute the objects with its bounding sphere for ray-collision detection, we were able to reduce all triangle intersection tests per object to one sphere intersection. Further on, we tested our algorithm compared with DXR triangle intersection raytracing for feasibility regarding computational workload as well as quality outcome and found striking results for both aspects. In a best case scenario for high density objects (80K+ vertices), our algorithm yields up to double the FPS rate compared with DXR. Taking shadow mapping as a test case, SPA holds a sufficient degree of detail, yet due to the spherical approach, objects are warped towards the sphere's poles.

Future work entails different approximation objects such as cylinders and boxes depending on the base objects' shape.

References

1. Crassin, C., Neyret, F., Sainz, M., Green, S., Eisemann, E.: Interactive indirect illumination using voxel cone tracing. In: Computer Graphics Forum (Proceedings of Pacific Graphics 2011), vol. 30, 7 September 2011
2. Kaplanyan, A., Dachsbacher, C.: Cascaded light propagation volumes for real-time indirect illumination. In: Proceedings of the 2010 ACM SIGGRAPH symposium on Interactive 3D Graphics and Games (I3D 2010), pp. 99–107. ACM, New York, NY, USA. https://doi.org/10.1145/1730804.1730821
3. Dachsbacher, C., Stamminger, M.: Reflective shadow maps. In: Proceedings of the 2005 Symposium on Interactive 3D Graphics and Games (I3D 2005), pp. 203–231. ACM, New York, NY, USA. https://doi.org/10.1145/1053427.1053460
4. Appel, A.: Some techniques for shading machine renderings of solids. In: Proceedings of the April 30-May 2, 1968, Spring Joint Computer Conference (AFIPS 1968 (Spring)), pp. 37–45. ACM, New York, NY, USA. https://doi.org/10.1145/1468075.1468082
5. Kajiya, F.T.: The rendering equation. In: Evans, D.C., Athay, R.J. (eds.) Proceedings of the 13th Annual Conference on Computer Graphics and Interactive Techniques (SIGGRAPH 1986), pp. 143–150. ACM, New York, NY, USA. https://doi.org/10.1145/15922.15902
6. Nicodemus, F.E.: Directional reflectance and emissivity of an opaque surface. Appl. Opt. 4, 767–775 (1965)
7. Microsoft DirectX Raytracing. https://blogs.msdn.microsoft.com/directx/2018/03/19/announcing-microsoft-directx-raytracing/. Accessed 15 July 2019
8. SIGGRAPH 2018 NVIDIA talk. http://intro-to-dxr.cwyman.org/presentations/IntroDXR_RaytracingShaders.pdf. Accessed 15 July 2019
9. SIGGRAPH 2018 NVIDIA talk. https://developer.nvidia.com/rtx/raytracing/dxr/DX12-Raytracing-tutorial-Part-2. Accessed 15 July 2019
10. Boksansky, J., Wimmer, M., Bittner, J.: Ray traced shadows: maintaining real-time frame rates. In: Haines, E., Akenine-Möller, T. (eds.) Ray Tracing Gems, pp. 159–182. Apress, Berkeley (2019). https://doi.org/10.1007/978-1-4842-4427-2_13

11. Wyman, C., Marrs, A.: Introduction to DirectX raytracing. In: Haines, E., Akenine-Möller, T. (eds.) Ray Tracing Gems. Apress, Berkeley (2019). https://doi.org/10.1007/978-1-4842-4427-2_3

12. Gribble, C.: Multi-hit ray tracing in DXR. In: Haines, E., Akenine-Möller, T. (eds.) Ray Tracing Gems. Apress, Berkeley, CA (2019). https://doi.org/10.1007/978-1-4842-4427-2_9

13. Akenine-Möller, T., Nilsson, J., Andersson, M., Barré-Brisebois, C., Toth, R., Karras, T.: Texture level of detail strategies for real-time ray tracing. In: Haines, E., Akenine-Möller, T. (eds.) Ray Tracing Gems. Apress, Berkeley, CA (2019). https://doi.org/10.1007/978-1-4842-4427-2_20

14. Szirmay-Kalos, L., Aszódi, B., Lazányi, I., Premecz, M.: Approximate ray-tracing on the GPU with distance impostors. Comput. Graph. Forum **24**, 695–704 (2005). https://doi.org/10.1111/j.1467-8659.2005.0m894.x. https://onlinelibrary.wiley.com/doi/abs/10.1111/j.1467-8659.2005.0m894.x

15. Barré-Brisebois, C., et al.: Hybrid rendering for real-time ray tracing. In: Haines, E., Akenine-Möller, T. (eds.) Ray Tracing Gems. Apress, Berkeley (2019). https://doi.org/10.1007/978-1-4842-4427-2_25

16. Liu, E., Llamas, I., Cañada, J., Kelly, P.: Cinematic rendering in UE4 with real-time ray tracing and denoising. In: Haines, E., Akenine-Möller, T. (eds.) Ray Tracing Gems. Apress, Berkeley (2019). https://doi.org/10.1007/978-1-4842-4427-2_19

Underwater Photogrammetry Reconstruction: GPU Texture Generation from Videos Captured via AUV

Kolton Yager[1]([⊠]), Christopher Clark[2], Timmy Gambin[3], and Zoë J. Wood[1]

[1] Computer Science Department, California Polytechnic State University, San Luis Obispo, CA, USA
{kjyager,zwood}@calpoly.edu
[2] Engineering Department, Harvey Mudd College, Claremont, CA, USA
clark@g.hmc.edu
[3] Department of Classics and Archeology, University of Malta, Msida, Malta
timmy.gambin@um.edu.mt

Abstract. Photogrammetry is a useful tool for creating computer models of archaeological sites for monitoring and for general public outreach. Modeling archaeological sites found in the marine environment is particularly challenging due to danger to divers, the cost of underwater photography equipment and lighting challenges. The automatic acquisition of video footage of underwater marine archaeology sites using an AUV can be an advantageous alternative, yet also incurs its own obstacles. In this paper we present our system and enhancements for applying a standard photogrammetry reconstruction pipeline to underwater sites using video footage captured from an AUV. Our primary contribution is a GPU driven algorithm for texture construction to reduce blur in the final model. We demonstrate the results of our system on a well known wreck site in Malta.

Keywords: Photogrammetry · Texture generation · Autonomous underwater vehicles · Marine archaeology · Color correction

1 Introduction

Marine archaeologists work to discover and map historical archaeological sites in the challenging environments of our oceans and seas. This setting creates unique challenges that technology has greatly aided in recent years. For example, the use of photogrammetry to create 3D reconstructions of underwater sites, has drastically increased the ability of marine archaeologists to map and share data about their discoveries [16,22].

Photogrammetry is a useful tool for creating computer models of archaeological sites of interest from discrete frames showing the target site from various views. There is a wide body of work addressing the use of photogrammetry pipelines for archaeological site mapping [13,16,22]. Our work focuses on the marine setting and specifically the use of an AUV to capture video of archaeological sites of interest such as historical ship or plane wrecks. As diving for a human camera operator can be both dangerous

G. Bebis et al. (Eds.): ISVC 2019, LNCS 11844, pp. 127–138, 2019.
https://doi.org/10.1007/978-3-030-33720-9_10

and expensive, the use of an AUV provides advantages [12,17,21], such as operating in deep waters and deployment from a distance.

The fieldwork for this research was conducted off the coastal waters of Malta, using the OceanServer Iver3 AUV. The AUV was equipped with a GoPro HERO4 camera to capture video of the sites of interest. The work presented here focuses on resolving some of the limitations of camera paths and video quality due to the underwater setting.

Unique Challenges. The underwater setting introduces challenges both to the collection of imagery for photogrammetry, and to the typical photogrammetric pipeline. The need for camera equipment that is both waterproof and compact enough to be mounted onto an AUV limits hardware choices and the maximum acuity of captured imagery. Likewise, continuous capture, the recommended style for photogrametry [26], is made difficult by AUV maneuverability constraints. Instead video capture is limited to predominantly linear paths which cover only portions of the subject. This division of footage into discontinuous segments can lead to significant inconsistencies later in the pipeline when portions are joined into a full reconstruction.

In addition, as light travels through water, certain wavelengths are blocked, reducing colors whilst particulate in the water can reduce visibility. Furthermore the falloff of visibility due to the water volume necessitates shorter distance between camera and the target, and reduces the amount of information collected along most paths about the subject. Overly blue images and blur proves challenging for photogrammetry pipelines that typically rely on pixel correlation primarily using color and in addition can result in textures which are visually unappealing and unduly homogeneous.

To address these challenges we present our pipeline and view dependent texturing algorithm to produce high quality models from applying a photogrammetry pipeline to video data acquired in an underwater setting using an AUV. Specifically, our contributions include a novel GPU based algorithm for improved texture creation in the spirit of view dependent texturing to minimize blur caused by excessive smoothing for the final model's texture and a general system for enhancing photogrammetry reconstruction using data captured using an AUV and GoPro camera.

2   Related Work

There is a rich body of work addressing the field of photogrammetry [13,16,22], and AUV trajectory planning [8,10,15,19,20] and a growing body of work addressing trajectory planning specifically for photogrammetry [23,25,26].

Additionally, there is a wide body of related work on texturing. Debevec's work [11], was foundational for texture mapping through projection in combination with a view-dependent blending function primarily based on view angle. The more recent work of Waechter et al. [24] presents a sophisticated approach with several stages, including, an analysis of the gradient of each photo to disqualify regions with less captured detail. To address issues with inaccurate camera alignment or a moving subject, a mean shift algorithm is used to filter image sources whose colors vary too greatly from the rest of the set. Similarly, Callieri et al. [7] presents a system which uses a variety of metrics to judge the quality of source photos, ultimately creating a single final mask on each photo which determines the photo's weight at the time of final projection.

The problem of color correcting underwater photography has been tackled widely but often with similar core assumptions. Commercially available camera lens filters designed to mitigate discoloration in underwater footage are not appropriate with our set up and site depths. Software solutions generally include an operation which attempts to mitigate discoloration caused by the attenuation of light underwater. The result of this operation typically produces result images which resemble the original, but which have ambient illumination close to the gray scale instead of an original blue or cyan/green tint. The methods of both Bazeille et al. [6] and Iqbal et al. [14] re-balance the images colors towards gray using only the characteristics of the image itself. Conversely, Petit et al. [18] takes a more involved approach which first establishes a Beer-Lambert model of the scenes attenuation with a coefficient set from experimental data.

Related work of particular interest are several papers focused on improving texturing for 3D reconstructions, [4, 5, 9]. In particular, the multi-band approach could provide future directions for image enhancements in our system, however, this work is the first that we know of in which the scale of input images from an underwater setting and the use of the GPU for texture production is explored to this level.

3   Algorithms

We present our algorithm for using the graphics pipeline for creating an improved final texture for models reconstructed using a photogrammetry pipeline in an underwater setting using data captured from an AUV and GoPro camera. To address the unique demands of underwater photogrammetry, over time we have developed a system for managing some of the specific challenges of the marine setting. Figure 1 illustrates the general system used to reconstruct models.

Photogrammetry Reconstruction Pipeline from AUV Video Data: In general using an AUV for video capture requires multiple passes over the site. To minimize geometric distortion in the reconstruction we decompose and group the video data into select regions. Each of the localized regions of the site are individually reconstructed in turn and only later merged together into a final complete model. Figure 2 shows the result of combining several regions of the HMS Maori shipwreck to create a whole model. This historic World War 2 destroyer was bombed in 1942 and broke in half. The entire ship measured 115 m long and this portion is approximately half that length and is located

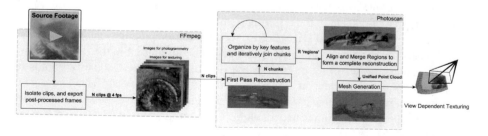

Fig. 1. Overview of our system for improved textured reconstructions from AUV video data

in 16 m deep water near Valletta, Malta. Core tools in the reconstruction pipeline are Agisoft Photoscan [3] for photogrammetry and FFmpeg [1] for image processing. The reconstruction as shown in Fig. 2 captures the shape of the wreck, however, the textures suffer from a fair amount of texture blurring from combining video segments from multiple passes of the AUV. Our primary contribution is our novel GPU based texturing algorithm written in OpenGL and GLSL, which we now present.

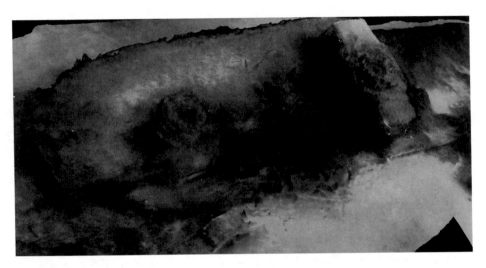

Fig. 2. Example results from our reconstruction pipeline which accurately models the shape of the WW2 wreck, however, the texture is overly smoothed, lacking details found the original images.

3.1   GPU Driven Texture Creation via Parallel View Dependent Selection

Texturing is one of the most critical stages in a reconstruction pipeline with the intent to produce a visually appealing and realistic reconstruction. Texture generation in photogrammetry is almost always done through projection mapping of the scene photos onto the reconstruction. This allows for the original surface and lighting information from the real world scene to be transferred directly onto the reconstruction. Under the assumption that the reconstruction of camera positions is accurate, points on the projected image will line up precisely with their location on the real world subject allowing for a high degree of realism in the resulting texture.

Textures generated using our general reconstruction pipeline using *Photoscan* yielded results missing much of the high frequency detail present in the collected photographs. In general, texturing processes that do not sufficiently disqualify photos or blurred regions of image data are likely to manifest a number of artifacts and potentially loose a significant degree of captured surface detail. The inherent loss of visibility and accurate color information in underwater scenes introduces unique challenges to the typical process due to the shear amount of video data with low image quality. In addition, with AUV video collection the lighting may change significantly between video passes over the site of interest. This variance in the lighting of the video footage in combination with subtle alignment errors leads to blurry textures as shown in Fig. 2.

To create a new less blurred textured, our GPU based algorithm selects pixels from the closest camera (where closest is measured as Euclidean distance). As our input is thousands of frames (and thus camera positions) from the video camera as it moves through the water on the AUV, our system needs to be able to handle large datasets efficiently.

System Overview: Our texturing system starts with the aligned cameras and reconstructed mesh from the photogrammetry pipeline and reconstitutes the scene within our own C++ and OpenGL application. The system generates a new improved texture for the target mesh through a multi-pass pipeline with the goal of forming the clearest texture using the best image information available. Most stages within the pipeline operate on individual texels of image buffers mapped to the mesh.

The challenge in creating an ideal texture for the reconstructed mesh from 2700 input images is identifying the best view of the geometry from the large number of potential input images. To tackle this problem, the mesh and corresponding texture are first partitioned into *cells* which are discrete local regions of the surface which share the same nearest cameras. As such these cells act as a fundamental unit for both resource allocation and computation allowing for some exploitation of locality. This organization is utilized during the final sampling of colors from the source images, when the assets needed by each cell are first loaded into a caching system. Once all assets are loaded, projection from the cell's cameras are used to sample colors from their photographs. These samples are then blended to produce the texturing for all the texels of the cell. The cells partition the entire mesh so processing them all yields a complete texture. A diagram of the system can be seen in Fig. 3. The CPU must handle the allocation and management of resources for this process, but the majority of computation is handled by the GPU. The only task which requires a significant portion of CPU time is the task of sorting unstructured cell neighborhood data.

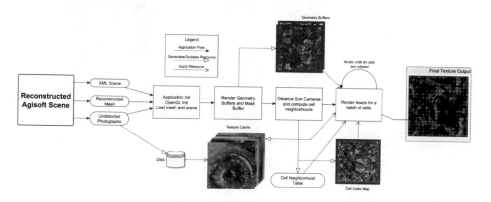

Fig. 3. GPU based view dependent texture generation

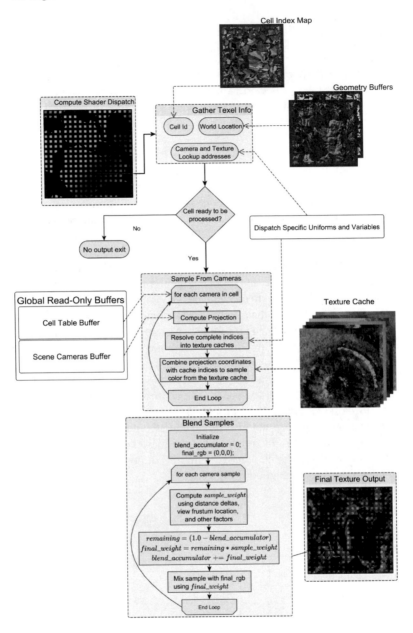

Fig. 4. Process of generating a single texel of texture. Many texels are processed in parallel during the final stage.

Scene Management: The input to our algorithm is the pose and parameters of all the aligned cameras within the scene (which can, for example, be generated with a photogrametry pipeline, in our case from Agisoft Photoscan). Undistorted images are used, thus our system is able to treat each camera as if it were an ideal pinhole camera. Holding all of the potential views (input images) in memory simultaneously is typically not feasible due to the quantity of images (≈ 2700). To work around memory limitations as well as the texture limits of OpenGL, we consume whatever memory is available using large OpenGL *texture arrays*. Our algorithm fills and continuously updates array entries with the images needed for a particular stage or iteration. These arrays are managed automatically by a caching system we developed which uses *least recently used* replacement. This caching is critical as the time cost of loading images from disk greatly overshadows computations in our system. Furthermore this cache structure allows the system to easily adjust to the quantity of memory available.

The reconstruction is loaded as a triangle mesh and oriented within the same coordinate space as the cameras. The mesh must have a parameterization provided as this mapping is critical to our systems design. Meshes with parameterizations mapping to multiple images will be automatically split and processed as several individual meshes. Resources which are cached during the generation of each texture persist in the cache during run-time, so the performance gained during the generation of one mesh's texture can carry over to the next.

Geometry and UV Mask Buffers: Before any coloring or analysis of the mesh is done, our system computes and stores some basic information about the layout of the texture being generated. This stage, like almost all that follow it, operates on intermediate image buffers which match the dimensions of the texture being generated, but which hold non-color information. The parameterization of the mesh being textured provides a mapping between the image and the mesh's surface such that computations can be run in 2D image space which correspond to the 3D space of the scene. Thus, the first of the intermediate buffers to be created are two geometry buffers into which we store the world space location of each texel as well as the surface normal. These buffers allow all following stages to operate without needing any access to the original triangle mesh. We also simultaneously produce a mask image for the parameterization so that stages further down the pipeline can quickly discard texels which do not map onto the mesh.

Cell Formation: Central to our texturing process is the division of the target surface into smaller fragments whose texture can be derived from the same finite set of source photographs. We reference these fragments using the term *cells* as in our system we derive these fragments from a structure which is very nearly an nth-order voronoi diagram of the scene partitioned by the euclidean distances of its cameras. Where n is the number of cameras we use to texture an individual cell.

The algorithm starts with a compute shader which launches a single invocation for each texel. Each invocation first reads the world space position of the texel from the previously rendered geometry buffer. It then iterates over the cameras in the scene while a small data structure keeps track of the top n nearest cameras. This structure works as a priority queue, but has been simplified for implementation on the GPU in GLSL. Each camera first has its view frustum and view direction checked for visibility of the texel. If the texel is visible the camera is submitted to the queue. Each time a camera is submitted to the queue, it linearly checks the distances of the cameras currently stored, and inserts the new camera if appropriate. It is assumed that the size of the array will be small enough to make losses in efficiency negligible when compared to a typical implementation. The result of this computation is a tuple of n camera identification associated with each texel.

This information is then condensed into the set of all unique tuples that were found in the prior computation. To do so the algorithm iterates over every texel from the prior step and extracts its tuple. Each unique tuple is added into a contiguous array to enable random access later in the algorithm. Likewise, a new integer valued image map is created such that each texel holds an index into this array. Individual tuples characterize a cell, and so the array in combination with the image map form a partitioning of the mesh into cells. A visualization of this cell index mapping can be seen in both Figs. 3 and 4 labelled as *Cell Index Map*. This organization of pixels by their tuples is the single step of the algorithm done on the CPU, however it is still relatively inexpensive when compared to other stages of the system.

Final Texture: To compute the final texture, the texture caches are appropriately sized based on the maximum number of source photographs the algorithm can concurrently store and access on the GPU and a *batch size* is computed as the maximum number of cells to be processed at once without exceeding space limitations. The set of all cells is then split into batches, and each execute the following steps individually.

First, the source photographs as well as additional reference images needed by the cells in the batch are loaded. At this time the algorithm loads high dynamic range images which store both a pre-rendered depth map from the perspective of a given camera, as well as a sobel filtered copy of the source image. A separate cache handles these reference images, and when they are requested attempts to load them from disk, or renders them anew if needed. Once all assets are loaded onto the GPU, the algorithm dispatches a compute job for this batch of cells. Again each invocation operates on a single texel and its logic is summarized in Fig. 4. Each texel in the final texture is colored from the closest n cameras that can 'see' that texel, resulting in a final texture with higher frequency details as shown in Fig. 5.

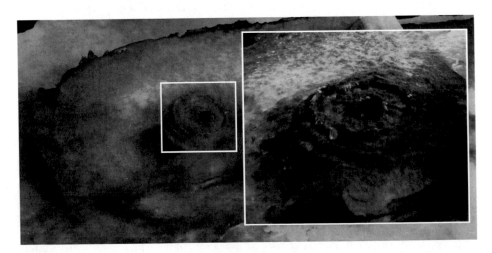

Fig. 5. A close up view of the gun mount on the Maori using our view dependent texture blending (right inset). Contrasted against the gun mount as scene in the Agisoft generated texture.

Color Correction. One of the final challenges our system must address is that fact that all the textures created by default from the underwater camera frames exhibit an overly blue tint. For color correction, two separate FFmpeg command line filtergraphs are used. The first is a simple S-curve used to increase contrast on images being used for photogrammetry. In the second FFmpeg filter, a midway equalization filter is applied to the video clip which attempts to match its histogram against a reference clip which was chosen during setup of the pipeline. Next, a color curve filter is applied which is configured using one or more frames from the reference clip. The corrected images can then be used during texture generation to create a model that is more visually distinct allowing a viewer to better distinguish plant matter in an ocean environment. Figure 7 shows our color correction along with a recent commercial alternative we explored [2].

4 Results

We present results from our system for the reconstruction of underwater archaeology sites of interest. Our system is tuned for video data captured from a goPro camera mounted on an AUV. We propose specific system processes to manage the limitations of the AUV trajectory and most importantly an algorithm that utilizes the graphics pipeline and hardware to create view dependent textures to minimize distortion from underwater frames and create an overall clearer final texture. We demonstrate the system and algorithms on data of a known shipwreck in Malta, including a close up of the gun mount on the Maori, Fig. 5 and a rendering of the full wreck in Fig. 7, with more high frequency image data preserved.

Our texturing system takes advantage of graphics hardware parallelism by utilizing our novel data structures, many GPU computations, and LRU caching. The acceleration achieved as a result of this system is such that most computation times are trivial when compared to the mostly unavoidable cost of loading resources from disk. When operating on a sufficiently small number of images (≤ 256) our system eventually loads all resources needed into memory concurrently, at which point the complete rendering of a 4096×4096 texture image is typically completed in less than 3 seconds. When operating on a much larger set of images (≈ 2700) the time needed to generate a texture of the same size increases to the order of between 450 and 750 hundred seconds, however GPU computation typically represents less than a tenth of a percent of the total time while resource loading occupies above 99%. Similarly the majority of the cell computation stage of our system is computation time on the CPU during organization of camera tuples. Even when each of over 16 million invocations of the computation shader must find the nearest cameras out of the (≈ 2700), the computation is typically completed in under a second. All timings were tested on a system containing Intel® Core™ i7-8700 CPU, 16 GB physical memory, and an NVIDIA Titan V. As a result we are able to process a scene with over 2700 virtual cameras and over 5400 total images to produce a texture preserving high frequency information without human intervention. Our system attains a final reconstruction mesh which captures both remarkable geometric and textural detail as seen in Fig. 7.

One way to measure the improvement provided by our texturing algorithm is to measure the overall blurriness from the original texture and our final texture, measured in texture space using the variance of the laplacian of each texture. The resulting scalar value is higher for sharper images as they are characterized by more rapid information change. We compare using a basis image formed by first applying a 3×3 guassian blur to both our textures and the Photoscan textures, then equally blending these blurred images together. As shown by Fig. 6 the variance of the laplacian for our textures are consistently higher than those produced by Agisoft Photoscan.

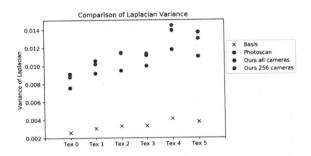

Fig. 6. Graph of the variance of the Laplacian of our textures, Photoscan's, and our basis image.

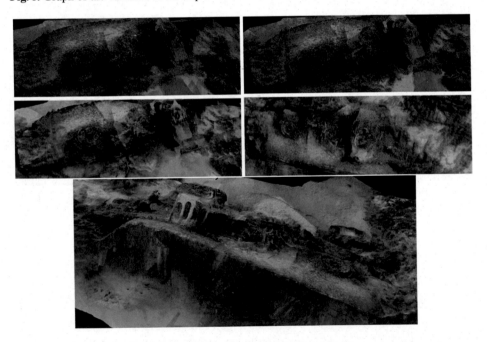

Fig. 7. Our Final result textures. Top: left was generated from 256 cameras, right uses the complete set of approximately 2700 images. The middle two images shows two alternative color correction methods. The final image shows a side view using the second color correction method.

4.1   Limitations and Future Work

One stage of our pipeline which could benefit from further research is the alignment of regions during the reconstruction of the archaeological site. Due to the constrained mobility of an AUV, it is not possible to get full coverage of most sites with a continuous shot. Instead many regions must be reconstructed separately then merged. Improved global region alignment, or aligning cameras in image space prior to projection to maximize overlap are areas of future work.

In addition, our method for color correction fits well within our tool-chain, but is rudimentary when compared to some related work. Finally, the abrupt transitions in exposure and color seen in our textures could be improved with a more adaptive blending algorithm within the final stage of our texturing system (of particular interest is multi-band blending [4,5,9]).

Acknowledgements. We would like to acknowledge the entire 2018 ICEX team. This material is based upon work supported by the National Science Foundation under Grant No. 1460153.

References

1. Ffmpeg 4.1. fFmpeg Team (2018)
2. Dive+ world's diving community app, life Plus Tech (Shenzhen) Co., Ltd. (2019)
3. Agisoft-LLC: Agisoft photoscan (2010)
4. Allène, C., Pons, J.P., Keriven, R.: Seamless image-based texture atlases using multi-band blending. In: 19th International Conference on Pattern Recognition (ICPR 2008), France, p. 10, no. 1 (2008)
5. Baumberg, A.: Blending images for texturing 3D models. In: Proceedings of the British Machine Vision Conference (2002)
6. Bazeille, S., Quidu, I., Jaulin, L., Malkasse, J.P.: Automatic underwater image preprocessing. In: CMM 2006 (2006)
7. Callieri, M., Cignoni, P., Corsini, M., Scopigno, R.: Masked photo blending: mapping dense photographic dataset on high-resolution 3D models. Comput. Graph. **32**, 464–473 (2008)
8. Candeloro, M., Mosciaro, F., Srensen, A.J., Ippoliti, G., Ludvigsen, M.: Sensor-based autonomous path-planner for sea-bottom exploration and mosaicking. In: IFAC Conference on Manoeuvring and Control of Marine Craft, pp. 31–36 (2015)
9. Chen, Z., Zhou, J., Chen, Y., Wang, G.: 3D texture mapping in multi-view reconstruction. In: Bebis, G., et al. (eds.) ISVC 2012. LNCS, vol. 7431, pp. 359–371. Springer, Heidelberg (2012). https://doi.org/10.1007/978-3-642-33179-4_35
10. Dale, L.K., Amato, N.M.: Probabilistic roadmaps-putting it all together. In: Proceedings 2001 ICRA. IEEE International Conference on Robotics and Automation (Cat. No. 01CH37164), vol. 2, pp. 1940–1947, May 2001. https://doi.org/10.1109/ROBOT.2001.932892
11. Debevec, P.E.: Modeling and rendering architecture from photographs. Ph.D. thesis, University of California at Berkeley, Computer Science Division, Berkeley CA (1996)
12. Fallon, M.F., Kaess, M., Johannsson, H., Leonard, J.J.: Efficient AUV navigation fusing acoustic ranging and side-scan sonar. In: 2011 IEEE International Conference on Robotics and Automation (ICRA). IEEE Computer Society (2011)
13. von Fock, S.M.T.S., et al.: Pipeline for reconstruction and visualization of underwater archaeology sites using photogrammetry. In: Proceedings of the 2017 ISCA International Conference on Computers and Their Applications, March 2017

14. Iqbal, K., Odetayo, M.O., James, A.E., Salam, R.A., Talib, A.Z.: Enhancing the low quality images using unsupervised colour correction method. In: SMC, pp. 1703–1709 (2010)
15. Li, T.Y., Shie, Y.C.: An incremental learning approach to motion planning with roadmap management. In: Proceedings 2002 IEEE International Conference on Robotics and Automation (Cat. No. 02CH37292), vol. 4, pp. 3411–3416, May 2002
16. McCarthy, J., Benjamin, J.: Multi-image photogrammetry for underwater archaeological site recording: an accessible, diver-based approach. J. Marit. Archaeol. 9(1), 95–114 (2014)
17. Paull, L., Saeedi, S., Seto, M., Li, H.: AUV navigation and localization: a review. IEEE J. Oceanic Eng. 39(1), 131–149 (2014)
18. Petit, F., Capelle-Laize, A.S., Carre, P.: Underwater image enhancement by attenuation inversionwith quaternions (2009)
19. Poppinga, J., Birk, A., Pathak, K., Vaskevicius, N.: Fast 6-DOF path planning for autonomous underwater vehicles (AUV) based on 3D plane mapping. In: IEEE International Symposium on Safety, Security, and Rescue Robotics (SSRR), pp. 1–6. IEEE Press (2011)
20. Rantanen, M.: Improving probabilistic roadmap methods for fast motion planning. Ph.D. thesis, School of Information Sciences, University of Tampere, August 2014
21. Ruiz, I.T., De Raucourt, S., Petillot, Y., Lane, D.M.: Concurrent mapping and localization using sidescan sonar. IEEE J. Oceanic Eng. 29(2), 442–456 (2004)
22. Van Damme, T.: Computer vision photogrammetry for underwater archaeological site recording in a low-visibility environment. Remote Sensing & Spatial Information Sciences, International Archives of the Photogrammetry (2015)
23. Viswanathan, V.K., et al.: AUV motion-planning for photogrammetric reconstruction of marine archaeological sites. In: IEEE International Conference on Robotics and Automation (2017)
24. Waechter, M., Moehrle, N., Goesele, M.: Let there be color! large-scale texturing of 3D reconstructions. In: Fleet, D., Pajdla, T., Schiele, B., Tuytelaars, T. (eds.) ECCV 2014. LNCS, vol. 8693, pp. 836–850. Springer, Cham (2014). https://doi.org/10.1007/978-3-319-10602-1_54
25. Wu, J., et al.: Multi-AUV motion planning for archeological site mapping and photogrammetric reconstruction. J. Field Robot. 36, 1250–1269 (2019)
26. Yamafune, K., Torres, R., Castro, F.: Multi-image photogrammetry to record and reconstruct underwater shipwreck sites. J. Archaeol. Method Theory 24, 703–725 (2016)

Segmentation/Recognition

Adaptive Attention Model for Lidar Instance Segmentation

Peixi Xiong[1(✉)], Xuetao Hao[2], Yunming Shao[3], and Jerry Yu[3]

[1] Northwestern University, Evanston, IL 60208, USA
peixixiong2018@u.nortwestern.edu
[2] University of Southern California, Los Angeles, CA 90089, USA
xuetaoha@usc.edu
[3] SAIC Innovation Center, San Jose, CA 95134, USA
{yshao,jyu}@saicusa.com

Abstract. Detecting and categorizing the instances of objects using Lidar scans are of critical importance for highly autonomous vehicles, which are expected to safely and swiftly maneuver through complex urban streets without the intervention of human drivers. In contrast to recent detection-based approaches [6, 10], we formulate the problem as a point-wise segmentation problem and focus on improving the recognition of small objects, which is very challenging due to the low resolution of commercial Lidar systems. Specifically, we propose a novel end-to-end convolutional neural network (CNN) that encapsulates adaptive attention information, and achieve instance segmentation by fusing multiple auxiliary tasks. We examined our algorithms on the 2D projection data derived from KITTI 3D object detection dataset [8] and achieved at least 14.6% improvement in Intersection over Union (IoU) with faster inference time (25.3 ms per Lidar scan) than the state-of-the-art algorithms.

Keywords: Segmentation · CNN · Lidar · Autonomous driving

1 Introduction

Autonomous driving has long been considered as holding the promises of revolutionizing transportation in efficiency and safety. To handle complex and dynamic urban driving scenarios, most highly automated vehicles (SAE[1] Level 4 and 5) are equipped with Lidar sensors, which provide precise 3D point clouds of surrounding environment. One of key challenges in autonomous driving system is to extract the locations and categories for multiple objects from each Lidar scan in real-time. In contrast to rich visual information in images, the low resolution of commercial Lidar systems poses additional challenges in recognizing small and faraway objects.

In this paper, we focus on instance segmentation of 3D point clouds using Bird's Eye View encoder (i.e., top-down view), shown as Fig. 1. Concretely, we propose a novel

---

[1] Society of Automotive Engineers.

P. Xiong and X. Hao—Both authors contributed equally to this research.

G. Bebis et al. (Eds.): ISVC 2019, LNCS 11844, pp. 141–155, 2019.
https://doi.org/10.1007/978-3-030-33720-9_11

Fig. 1. An example of Lidar scan and our segmentation results. The upper figure is the color stereo image. The bottom left one is the 3D instance segmentation in point cloud, and the bottom right image is Bird's Eye View instance segmentation, where cars are marked as green and pedestrians are marked as pink. (Color figure online)

end-to-end network with location-sensitive and adaptive error map to jointly enhance the semantic segmentation performance. To achieve further instance segmentation, we utilize multi-task architecture with two additional headers of center offset and contour template map, and then merge intermediate outputs by a shallow fusion network to yield the final prediction.

The rest of this paper is organized as follows: Sect. 2 reviews works that are most related to the proposed method; Sect. 3 describes the proposed method in details; Sect. 4 analyzes the experimental results and comparisons with state-of-the-art approach. Section 5 summarizes our contributions and indicates potential advantageous applications.

2   Related Work

2.1   Segmentation for 3D Point Clouds

With the booming of autonomous driving, many works have been proposed in 3D point clouds segmentation. Basically, they are mainly divided into two branches [14]. The first one focuses on mathematics and geometric reasoning techniques [7, 17]. However, it is inaccurate to deal with complex scenarios and brings about expensive computations. The other one is based on extracting feature information from point clouds and feeding them into a neural network [1, 21]. The latter one preserves the capacity to handle most occasions, but there is still potential for improvements.

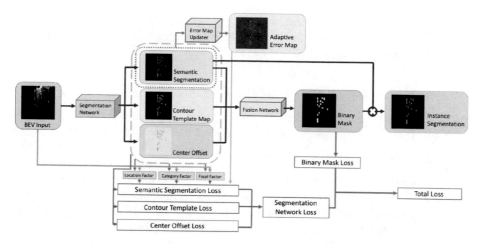

Fig. 2. Framework diagram. The BEV representation is fed into the Segmentation Network, which generates three intermediate features as semantic segmentation, contour template map, and center offset. Later, the fusion network fuses these three features and yields final instance segmentation. The total loss mainly consists of two parts: the segmentation network loss and the binary mask loss.

2.2 Bird's Eye View and Front View Methods

Two kinds of encoders are applied to point clouds for convenient adaptation of existing deep neural network structures. The first is Front View representation [15,22], while the second is Bird's Eye View (BEV) representation [3]. Both of them are to project the original 3D point clouds into corresponding 2D cells. The Front View encoder is suitable for merging with RGB image, however, it has less powerful feature representation due to dense point clouds projected into the same cell and occlusion in faraway objects, which results in lost information. The BEV representation is free from such issue. Even though the BEV may project some points vertically into the same cell, it can be relieved by encoding a few binary maps as occupancy along height range [6, 13, 24]. Meanwhile, BEV will get rid of issues from occlusion and multi-scale shapes of the object.

2.3 Detection-Based and Segmentation-Based Model

Recent literature focuses on two main patterns to recognize the object of interest in Lidar scans. The first one is detection model [3,6,10] which generates detection bounding box, and the second one is segmentation model [16,19,22] which classifies each point. However, each of these existing methods has weakness in different cases. For the detection based approach, it is quite common to miss small objects, e.g. the pedestrians and cyclists, in bird's eye view than segmentation based approach. The reason is that segmentation makes point-wise predictions under higher resolution. Besides, regressing distinct variance, between region proposal anchor and ground truth from detection model, becomes a challenging task during training. However segmentation based methods are hard to achieve instance-level segmentation that is required to separate nearby or occluded objects. To alleviate that problem, [18] leverages a fully convolutional neural networks to predict multiple information, and then integrates multi-task outputs to obtain final instance segmentation.

2.4   Contour Information and Center Direction

Contour information is of significant importance in the segmentation of medical images and geographic information maps. It can be regarded as the edge detection and also preserve distance information, representing how close each pixel gets to boundary of the building [4].

Even though contour information can be used to define the object outline, contour boundary usually occupies very few pixels, thus its representation is a delicate signal compared with region-based representation [2]. To address this issue, [18] proposes instance center direction, which is defined as each pixel's direction towards its corresponding instance center. Masklab [5] also relies on the instance center direction to separate instances under the same semantic label, and shows state-of-the-art performance on COCO segmentation benchmark. Inspired by these works, we propose the concept of center offset which is represented by a 2D vector per pixel, demonstrating both the magnitude and direction towards the instance center. Our proposal is different from them in two aspects: (1) the center offset is predicted by regression instead of classification; (2) our representation is more explicit in terms of combination of boundary and center information.

2.5   Fusion Network

To improve segmentation performance, some previous works focus on post-processing methods such as clustering [11]. Although it is conductive to refine segmentation, complex computation makes real-time detection infeasible. Inspired by [23], the end-to-end learning strategy effectively achieves instance segmentation, which is designed by fusing multi-channel information in a shallow convolution neural network. This fusion network architecture [9] plays a vital role in exploiting interactions among intermediate outputs, and then generates new features for decoder.

3   Approach

3.1   Approach Overview

In the following sections, we will explain our approach, which is displayed in Fig. 2. The segmentation network takes BEV representation from 3D points cloud as input, training with multi-task strategy to generates semantic segmentation, center offset and contour template map. Simultaneously, to achieve attention adaptation, three factors and adaptive error maps contribute to calculate semantic segmentation loss. Then the semantic segmentation, center offset and contour template map, regarded as internal features, will be fed into fusion network to extract foreground by a shallow convolution neural network. The foreground information combined with semantic segmentation produces the final instance segmentation.

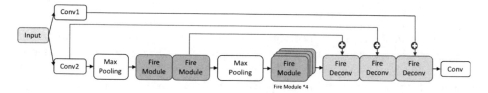

Fig. 3. Segmentation backbone network.

3.2 Input Representation

Lidar point cloud consists of a set of cartesian coordinates (x, y, z) along with corresponding reflectivity. We project the original point clouds into BEV representation with 0.1 m resolution like [6,20]. The region of interest for the point cloud is set to $[0, 60] \times [-30, 30] \times [-2.5, 1.0]$ m in KITTI Lidar coordinates. Within this region, the input representation contains three layers, the maximum height, density and reflectivity feature map, which are calculated by points inside the 0.1×0.1 grid.

3.3 Segmentation Network

For this part, we derive a segmentation network from SqueezeNet [6], and the architectural diagram is shown in Fig. 3. The input tensor is $600 \times 600 \times 3$ BEV representation. This tensor is passed into two paths. The first path is $Conv1$ with stride 1 to keeps same resolution as input. For the second path, it down-samples input by $Conv2$ layer with stride 2, following max pooling layer. After that, *Fire Modules* [22] are used to extract features. In order to keep output with the same resolution as input, three *Fire Deconvs* [22] take responsibility to up-sample the features. Additionally, skip connections are built between the low-level and high-level features with same dimension to further improves performance.

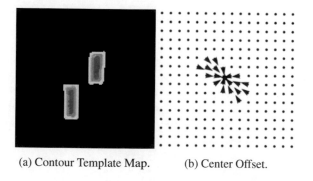

(a) Contour Template Map.   (b) Center Offset.

Fig. 4. (a) Contour Template Map of Car Object. The lighter areas have the higher probability to be the instance contour. (b) Center Offset of Car Object. Each arrow points toward its neighbor closest to the direction between current pixel and instance centroid.

3.4   Contour Template Map

The primary challenge of instance segmentation is to distinguish two close instances. In other words, it cannot make very accurate prediction for the contour of instance. To solve this issue, we propose a Contour Template Map as one of our multi-task branches. It predicts the probability of pixels to be the instance contour, which is shown in Fig. 4(a). The ground truth of probability is calculated based on the distance between the pixel inside instance and this instance boundary. To normalize it, the values in background template are set to be 0, while the values of boundary are set to be 1. As the pixel gets closer to the center of instance, the template value will decrease. After normalization and quantization, it becomes a classification problem to predict the boundary level for each pixel using cross entropy loss.

3.5   Center Offset

To further improve capacity of distinctly separating instances, we propose another multi-task branch as center offset to predict clustering direction. Our model generates a normalized center offset vector (x_i, y_i) for each pixel as Fig. 4(b), which represents the center direction pointing from each pixel inside instance to its corresponding instance centroid. The points outside instance should be represented as vector $(0, 0)$.

$$(x_i, y_i) = \begin{cases} (\frac{x_i - x_c}{\| x_i - x_c, y_i - y_c \|}, \frac{y_i - y_c}{\| x_i - x_c, y_i - y_c \|}), & \text{if } (x_i, y_i) \in \text{ instance} \\ (0, 0), & \text{otherwise} \end{cases} \quad (1)$$

Here, $\|\cdot\|$ is the Euclidean distance between the point (x_i, y_i) inside ground truth and the instance center (x_c, y_c). We formulate the prediction of center direction as a regression problem using the smooth-L1 loss during training.

3.6   Loss Function

We adopt multi-task loss [10] to train the full network (Eq. 2).

$$Loss = w_1 \, L_{seg} + w_2 \, L_{mask} \quad (2)$$

Here, L_{mask} is the classification loss in the fusion network, while L_{seg} is the loss summed by semantic segmentation loss L_{sem}, contour prediction loss L_{ct} and center offset regression loss L_{co}. w_1 and w_2 are loss weights for these two stages. In the experiment we set 2.0 and 1.0 respectively. For L_{sem}, it is modified from the original cross entropy loss to multiplication of the following four factors, the location factor F_{loc}, object category factor F_{cat}, focal factor F_{focal}, and adaptive error map E demonstrating where the model made wrong classification in last iteration.

$$L_{sem} = F_{loc} * F_{cat} * F_{focal} * E \quad (3)$$

The first two factors are determined by the input representation. The last two are adjustable during the training process, so that they will make the segmentation loss to achieve adaptive attention based on the previous performances. In the following four parts, we will explain them in details.

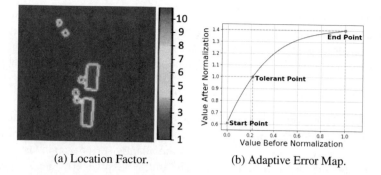

(a) Location Factor.   (b) Adaptive Error Map.

Fig. 5. (a) Location Factor. This example includes pedestrian and car objects. The higher value means on those pixels the model puts more attention and has higher penalties when making wrong prediction. The penalties are not only set on the instance edge, but also set on the connectivity area among different instances. (b) Adaptive Error Map Normalization.

A. **Location Factor**

To further separate adjacent objects, location-sensitive strategy is applied on loss function. Like Fig. 5(a), this factor makes the model care about the edge area in foreground and connectivity area in background among different instances. It will force model to pay more attention on the key pixels which need to be made correct classification.

B. **Category Factor**

In this part, it mainly focuses on the class imbalance issue. First, for the small object like pedestrian and cyclist, they obtain fewer training samples which leads to slower and unstable convergence compared with car. Second, there are many small shrubs, bushes or even road signs which have similar shapes with vehicle or human in BEV representation. Those two potential reasons make multi-class segmentation task even harder. To alleviate those issues, there should be an incremental point-wise weight for small object and relevant decrement on car object. Need to mention that, it will not have a fair good performance if setting too low weight for the background, since it may cause false positives from our experiments.

C. **Focal Factor**

To further relieve the class imbalance issue and lower the dominance of easy-classified samples, a factor reflecting the probability of prediction is added. This factor is similar with [12]. Here the probability p_i is for each pixel i in feature maps.

$$F_{focal}(i) = -\alpha(1 - p_i)^\gamma \log(p_i) \qquad (4)$$

γ is the focusing parameter which smoothly gives the easy examples lower weight, and α is a class-balanced parameter. In practice, we set γ as 2 and α as 0.25.

D. **Adaptive Error Map**

For some areas, the segmentation model always has trouble to make correct predictions, so that it is in need to supervise such consistent errors during training. We introduce a concept named adaptive error map, which monitors and records incorrect prediction for each pixel in semantic segmentation.

The adaptive error map is updated every epoch following Eq. 5. During updating, the previous adaptive error map will not be discarded, but be merged with the current adaptive error map by a decay weight. Such mechanism helps model put more attention on high error incidence region, which adaptively monitors our training process.

$$E_i(m,n) = w_d\, E_{i-1}(m,n) + (1 - w_d)\, V_i(m,n) \tag{5}$$

Here V_i represents point-wise differences between ground truth and prediction in the i epoch. If the prediction is correct for point (m,n), $V_i(m,n)$ is equal to 0. Otherwise, it is equal to 1. E_{i-1} represents the adaptive error map in last epoch, and E_i is the updated one in current epoch. The initial adaptive error map E_0 is an all-one map. To update the adaptive error map, w_d is the decay rate. In our experiments, it is set as 0.6. The smaller E_i gets, the better this point is trained.

With formula 5, E_i will be quickly restricted into a really small value after several continuous correct predictions. For example, if a point is correctly predicted for two sequential times, its value will be 0.36. This value may be below the medium value of the adaptive error map range, meaning the model will not pay much attention to that sample. Apparently, right classification just in two times cannot ensure it reliable. It should be guaranteed for more times. Thus we design the following strategy to relieve such situation. From Fig. 5(b), a nonlinear projection is used on the adaptive error map, mapping the original error map's domain $[0, 1]$ to $[w_d, 1+(1-w_d)]$ along with a $Tolerant\ Point$. Such point is calculated by w_d^n. Here n represents that after how many sequential times of correct prediction, this sample will be confident enough on further prediction regarded as an easily classified one. Then the projection will map that value below 1.0, so that the model does not need to focus on it in further training steps until it makes wrong classification again. In our experiment, we set n as 3 in order to involve more valid samples to train.

To keep the loss converge better, this mechanism is not implemented at the beginning but used in the middle of training, and it is only implemented to record the error of semantic segmentation.

3.7   Fusion Network and Output

A learning-based shallow fusion network is used to integrate multi-channel information from the previous stage as input, then yield a binary mask representing objectness and non-objectness.

We feed intermediate outputs, predicted center offset P_{co}, contour map P_{ct} and semantic segmentation P_{sem}, into fusion network as Fig. 2. Mathematically, final segmentation result is calculated by following equations:

$$P(Y_{cls} = k, Y_{bin} = 1) = P_{sem}\, P_{mask} \tag{6}$$

$$P_{sem} = P(Y_{cls} = k) \tag{7}$$

$$P_{mask} = P(Y_{bin} = 1 | P_{co}, P_{ct}, P_{sem}) \tag{8}$$

where P_{sem} is semantic segmentation result, and P_{mask} is the binary mask generated by fusion network. In the first term, Y_{cls} is the classification from semantic segmentation, and $k = 1, 2, 3$ means three classification classes which respectively are car, pedestrian and cyclist. Here, car represents all vehicles in KITTI dataset, including car, van and truck. In the second term, $Y_{bin} = 1$ represents the points belonging to the foreground.

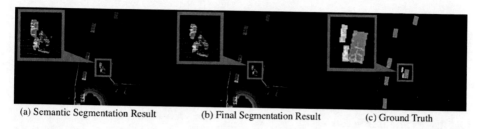

(a) Semantic Segmentation Result   (b) Final Segmentation Result   (c) Ground Truth

Fig. 6. Semantic Segmentation Result and Final Segmentation Result. With fusion network, cyclist objects (the blue area) are separated well. Green area represents car object. (Color figure online)

After fusion network, pixels for each category are located more accurately shown as Fig. 6, and detection bounding box based on final segmentation can be generated easily by minimum area rectangular algorithm.

4 Experiments

4.1 Evaluation Criteria

For point-wise segmentation evaluation, we use precision, recall and intersection over union (IoU) to evaluate the performance. They are defined by following:

$$Precision = \frac{|Pred \cap GT|}{|Pred|} \tag{9}$$

$$Recall = \frac{|Pred \cap GT|}{|GT|} \tag{10}$$

$$IoU = \frac{|Pred \cap GT|}{|Pred \cup GT|} \tag{11}$$

Here $Pred$ and GT respectively represent prediction and ground-truth points, and $|\cdot|$ denotes the size of the set. From Eqs. 9, 10 and 11, IoU can represents both precision and recall to some extent. Thus, IoU is primary accuracy metric in our experiments.

For instance segmentation evaluation, we generate detection bounding boxes for unconnected instances, based on final segmentation map with different confidence thresholds which are set from 0.0 to 1.0 with $step = 0.01$. This evaluation metrics are similar with standard object detection evaluation. It is based on all labeled objects, without limitation in difficulty levels: easy, medium and hard as KITTI benchmark [8].

The precision and recall for object detection are defined by Eqs. 12 and 13:

$$Precision = \frac{TP}{TP + FP} \qquad (12)$$

$$Recall = \frac{TP}{TP + FN} \qquad (13)$$

Here TP, FP and FN represent True Positives, False Positives, and False Negatives of bounding boxes respectively. Average Precision is calculated from precision-recall curve.

4.2   Experimental Setup

We randomly split the original KITTI dataset into two groups. The first one consisting of 6481 frames is used for training; the second one consisting of 1000 frames is used for validation. To guarantee that the validation set can truly reflect the performance of the model, we ensured the similar frames would not appear in the training and validation set at the same time.

4.3   Experimental Results

The result of segmentation is shown in Table 1. We tested our methods on two types of BEV representation. The first one is encoded with 3 layers' feature map: reflectivity, density and maximum height, the other one is exactly same as AVOD [10] with 6 layers' feature map. The first 5 layers are encoded with maximum height of 5 equal slices along Z axis and the last layer is density information.

Table 1. Segmentation performance with different layers.

		Car	Pedestrian	Cyclist
IoU	3 layers	71.5	43.4	51.9
	6 layers	72.5	45.2	52.7
Precision	3 Layers	87.1	50.1	68.1
	6 layers	89.4	53.3	68.5
Recall	3 Layers	80.0	76.4	68.5
	6 layers	79.2	74.8	69.7

With different encoded features, our method obtains a relatively high performance on recall, which prevents missing detection problems in common situations during autonomous driving. Here the small objects (e.g. cyclist and pedestrian) do not perform well as the larger one (e.g. car), because of the class imbalance and less information for encoded small objects.

Table 2. Ablation study on IoU performance for segmentation network.

	Car	Pedestrians	Cyclist
w/o Adaptive Error Map	69.7	41.7	48.2
w/o Contour Template	67.7	39.3	41.6
w/o Location Factor	68.0	40.6	42.8
w/o Center Offset	71.0	41.5	48.8
Baseline [22]	56.9	31.4	22.5
Full segmentation	**71.5**	**43.4**	**51.9**

Table 3. Average precision for small and large objects in KITTI validation set.

	AVOD	Ours 3 layers	Ours 6 layers
Large Objs	71.1	75.2	79.8
Small Objs	60.8	60.6	67.1

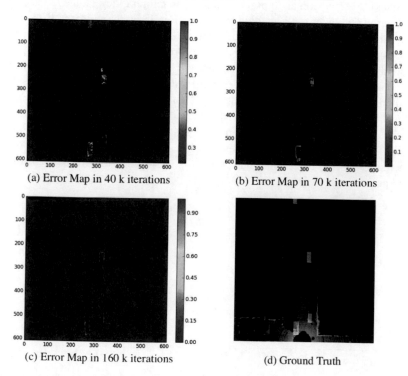

(a) Error Map in 40 k iterations   (b) Error Map in 70 k iterations

(c) Error Map in 160 k iterations   (d) Ground Truth

Fig. 7. Error maps in different iterations.

We also discover that the IoU performance will get better with more feature layers' version, however, the inference time will increase. We tested average inference time on Tesla P100-PCIE GPU. The 3 layers version is 25.3 ms and the 6 layers version is 38.1 ms, while AVOD inference time is 69 ms per Lidar frame. It becomes a trade-off between the performance and speed. For later experiments, we prefer to use the 3 layers version to present our model performance.

Table 2 demonstrates the effect of each innovation in the framework. The comparisons are using 3 layers version under those four variations. We build SqueezeSeg-like [22] baseline model with our 3 layers BEV inputs, instead of its original Front View encoder. Here, these four variables do make contributions to our full segmentation, since the performance of IoU will drop without any of them. Figure 7 shows alterations of error maps in different iterations. With training step increasing, wrong classified points highly occur at the edge of objects. Figure 6 demonstrates that after fusion network, some small objects, which are connected in semantic segmentation, will be separated in final result.

Based on large object's 0.5 IoU threshold and small object's 0.25 IoU threshold, the Average Precision (AP) comparison is shown in Table 3, and the recall-precision curve is shown in Fig. 8. Since the setting of easy, medium, hard for KITTI dataset is determined by occlusion and observation level in camera view, some labeled objects may be filtered out under such standard for evaluation. In our experiment, the evaluation is based on all labeled objects, without limit to easy, medium and hard objects. We compare our both 3-layers and 6-layers detection results with 6-layers AVOD [10].

From the detection comparison, our method still obtains better performance on recall, even with 3-layers feature. Besides, with the same input feature layers as AVOD, our method can get a even better result on AP and Precision-Recall Curve. While if only considering precision, AVOD indeed gets high performance.

Figure 9 represents our final segmentation results, which successfully segment all instances. The detection bounding boxes are also shown in red color. Figure 9(d) indicates there are missing detection issues, which is mostly due to severe occlusion or no observed point cloud.

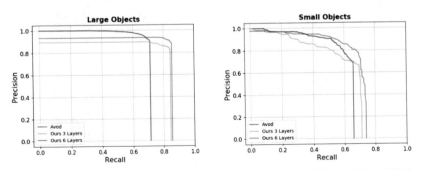

(a) Precision Recall Curve of Large Object. (b) Precision Recall Curve of Small Object.

Fig. 8. Detection performance comparisons with AVOD.

Fig. 9. (a) (b) (c) Success mode. (d) Failure mode. (Color figure online)

5   Conclusion

In this paper we propose a novel end-to-end network that significantly improves instance segmentation performance for autonomous driving system. Our architecture explicitly models several critical factors such as object contour, location, category and center offset. In addition, our method designs a new attention mechanism that is adaptive to learning errors, which leads to a faster and better convergence. Combining these factors, our architecture outperforms the state-of-the-art algorithms in both segmentation and detection tasks, and efficiently processes Lidar frames in real-time. Experimental results further indicate that our method is especially suitable for recognizing small objects, such as pedestrian and cyclist, with promising IoU and recall.

References

1. Anguelov, D., et al.: Discriminative learning of Markov random fields for segmentation of 3D scan data. In: 2005 IEEE Computer Society Conference on Computer Vision and Pattern Recognition (CVPR 2005), vol. 2, pp. 169–176, June 2005. https://doi.org/10.1109/CVPR. 2005.133
2. Arbelaez, P., Maire, M., Fowlkes, C., Malik, J.: Contour detection and hierarchical image segmentation. IEEE Trans. Pattern Anal. Mach. Intell. **33**(5), 898–916 (2011). https://doi. org/10.1109/TPAMI.2010.161
3. Beltran, J., Guindel, C., Moreno, F.M., Cruzado, D., Garcia, F., de la Escalera, A.: BirdNet: a 3D object detection framework from LiDAR information. arXiv preprint arXiv:1805.01195, May 2018
4. Bischke, B., Helber, P., Folz, J., Borth, D., Dengel, A.: Multi-task learning for segmentation of building footprints with deep neural networks. CoRR abs/1709.05932 (2017). http://arxiv. org/abs/1709.05932
5. Chen, L., Hermans, A., Papandreou, G., Schroff, F., Wang, P., Adam, H.: Masklab: instance segmentation by refining object detection with semantic and direction features. CoRR abs/1712.04837 (2017)
6. Chen, X., Ma, H., Wan, J., Li, B., Xia, T.: Multi-view 3D object detection network for autonomous driving. In: IEEE CVPR, vol. 1, p. 3 (2017)
7. Fischler, M.A., Bolles, R.C.: Random sample consensus: a paradigm for model fitting with applications to image analysis and automated cartography. Commun. ACM **24**(6), 381–395 (1981). https://doi.org/10.1145/358669.358692. http://doi.acm.org/10.1145/358669.358692
8. Geiger, A., Lenz, P., Urtasun, R.: Are we ready for autonomous driving? The KITTI vision benchmark suite. In: Conference on Computer Vision and Pattern Recognition (CVPR) (2012)
9. Jiang, W., Ma, L., Jiang, Y., Liu, W., Zhang, T.: Recurrent fusion network for image captioning. CoRR abs/1807.09986 (2018)
10. Ku, J., Mozifian, M., Lee, J., Harakeh, A., Waslander, S.: Joint 3D proposal generation and object detection from view aggregation. In: IROS (2018)
11. Liang, X., Wei, Y., Shen, X., Yang, J., Lin, L., Yan, S.: Proposal-free network for instance-level object segmentation. CoRR abs/1509.02636 (2015)
12. Lin, T., Goyal, P., Girshick, R.B., He, K., Dollár, P.: Focal loss for dense object detection. In: IEEE International Conference on Computer Vision, ICCV 2017, Venice, Italy, 22–29 October 2017, pp. 2999–3007 (2017). https://doi.org/10.1109/ICCV.2017.324
13. Luo, W., Yang, B., Urtasun, R.: Fast and furious: real time end-to-end 3D detection, tracking and motion forecasting with a single convolutional net. In: The IEEE Conference on Computer Vision and Pattern Recognition (CVPR), June 2018
14. Nguyen, A., Le, B.: 3D point cloud segmentation: a survey. In: RAM, pp. 225–230. IEEE (2013)
15. Qi, C.R., Liu, W., Wu, C., Su, H., Guibas, L.J.: Frustum pointnets for 3D object detection from RGB-D data. arXiv preprint arXiv:1711.08488 (2017)
16. Shin, M., Oh, G., Kim, S., Seo, S.: Real-time and accurate segmentation of 3-D point clouds based on Gaussian process regression. IEEE Trans. Intell. Transp. Syst. **18**(12), 3363–3377 (2017)
17. Tarsha-Kurdi, F., Landes, T., Grussenmeyer, P.: Hough-transform and extended RANSAC algorithms for automatic detection of 3D building roof planes from LiDAR data. In: ISPRS Workshop on Laser Scanning 2007 and SilviLaser 2007, Espoo, Finland, vol. XXXVI, pp. 407–412, September 2007. https://halshs.archives-ouvertes.fr/halshs-00264843

18. Uhrig, J., Cordts, M., Franke, U., Brox, T.: Pixel-level encoding and depth layering for instance-level semantic labeling. In: Rosenhahn, B., Andres, B. (eds.) GCPR 2016. LNCS, vol. 9796, pp. 14–25. Springer, Cham (2016). https://doi.org/10.1007/978-3-319-45886-1_2

19. Wang, D.Z., Posner, I., Newman, P.: What could move? Finding cars, pedestrians and bicyclists in 3D laser data. In: ICRA, pp. 4038–4044. IEEE (2012)

20. Wang, W., Yu, R., Huang, Q., Neumann, U.: SGPN: similarity group proposal network for 3D point cloud instance segmentation. In: CVPR (2018)

21. Wu, B., Wan, A., Yue, X., Keutzer, K.: SqueezeSeg: convolutional neural nets with recurrent CRF for real-time road-object segmentation from 3D LiDAR point cloud. arXiv preprint arXiv:1710.07368 (2017)

22. Wu, B., Wan, A., Yue, X., Keutzer, K.: SqueezeSeg: convolutional neural nets with recurrent CRF for real-time road-object segmentation from 3D LiDAR point cloud. CoRR abs/1710.07368 (2017). http://arxiv.org/abs/1710.07368

23. Xu, Y., et al.: Gland instance segmentation using deep multichannel neural networks. CoRR abs/1611.06661 (2016)

24. Yang, B., Luo, W., Urtasun, R.: PIXOR: real-time 3D object detection from point clouds. In: The IEEE Conference on Computer Vision and Pattern Recognition (CVPR), June 2018

View Dependent Surface Material Recognition

Stanislav Mikeš and Michal Haindl[(✉)] [iD]

The Institute of Information Theory and Automation
of the Czech Academy of Sciences, Prague, Czechia
{xaos,haindl}@utia.cz
http://www.utia.cz/

Abstract. The paper presents a detailed study of surface material recognition dependence on the illumination and viewing conditions which is a hard challenge in a realistic scene interpretation. The results document sharp classification accuracy decrease when using usual texture recognition approach, i.e., small learning set size and the vertical viewing and illumination angle which is a very inadequate representation of the enormous material appearance variability. The visual appearance of materials is considered in the state-of-the-art Bidirectional Texture Function (BTF) representation and measured using the upper-end BTF gonioreflectometer. The materials in this study are sixty-five different wood species. The supervised material recognition uses the shallow convolutional neural network (CNN) for the error analysis of angular dependency. We propose a Gaussian mixture model-based method for robust material segmentation.

1 Introduction

The visual appearance of surface materials and object shapes are crucial for visual scene understanding or interpretation. Visual aspects of surface materials which manifest themselves as visual textures even if there is still missing a rigorous definition of the texture [6]. Thus reliable visual scene interpretation cannot avoid a sound texture recognition quality. The correct recognition is hindered by the considerable variability of a material appearance and thus its corresponding textural representation based on changing observation conditions. Numerous texture recognition methods were published but we are not aware of a method which accounts for simultaneously variable illumination and viewing angle.

Most materials classification methods which respect illumination and view changes are restricted to BRDF (Bidirectional Reflectance Distribution Function) material representation [10, 15, 17] which neglects not only self-occlusion and inter-reflection material properties but also the essential spatial material features. The per-pixel SVM (Support Vector Machine) classification [15] is based on spectral BRDF and detects from training samples a discriminative illumination. The paper [10] is restricted to 5 steel classes, BRDF, and illumination changes only. [25] demonstrate the usefulness of several images of a material sample with different view-light conditions for material identification. [11] studies nine fabric classes with 2000 samples recognition using SIFT (Scale Invariant Feature Transform) and CNN (Convolutional Neural Network) features from albedo images and three concatenated normals into a single image. The authors

G. Bebis et al. (Eds.): ISVC 2019, LNCS 11844, pp. 156–167, 2019.
https://doi.org/10.1007/978-3-030-33720-9_12

[23] used convolutional neural network for 12 material classes (with 100 images per class) recognition represented in 4D light-field measurements and achieved 7% accuracy improvement compared to single view images only. Material BRDF estimation from the 4D light-field using a convolutional neural network is also studied in [17]. The BTF classification exceptions are the papers [16] which studies the effects of illumination patterns, rotation, moreover, the scale for bag-of-words classification and [24] which uses an SVM classifier for synthetically generated material samples in the BTF representation. For detailed evaluation of ten previously published texture segmenters on BTF dataset see mosaic.utia.cas.cz [5].

Real surface material visual appearance is a very complex physical phenomenon which intricately depends on the incident and reflected spherical angles, time, and light spectrum among other physical quantities. The general and physically correct material reflectance function should be at least sixteen dimensional [6] which is recently unmeasurable, and even if some simplifying assumptions have to be inevitably accepted, the essential dependencies have to be respected. Among them, these are spectral, illumination, and viewing parameters.

Our main contributions are:

- Introduction of a new large BTF wood database measurement with 65 wood species.
- A first detailed evaluation of material recognition accuracy dependent on view and illumination angles.
- A detailed recognition accuracy evaluation of the BTF wooden mosaics mapped on generated 3D surfaces and using different viewing and illumination learning subsets.

1.1 Bidirectional Texture Function

The seven-dimensional bidirectional texture function (BTF) reflectance model is currently the state-of-the-art general reflectance function model approximation which can be simultaneously measured and modeled [3,6].

Multispectral BTF is a seven-dimensional function, which considers measurement dependency on color spectrum, planar material position, as well as its dependence on illumination (i) and viewing (v) angles: $BTF(r, \theta_i, \phi_i, \theta_v, \phi_v)$, where the multiindex $r = [r_1, r_2, r_3]$ specifies planar horizontal and vertical position in material sample image, r_3 is the spectral index and θ, ϕ are elevation and azimuthal angles of the illumination and view direction vectors. The BTF measurements comprise a whole hemisphere of light and camera positions in observed material sample coordinates according to selected quantization steps.

2   BTF Wood Measurement Database

Since the accurate and reliable BTF acquisition is not a trivial task, only a few BTF measurement systems exist [3,6,12,18,19,21,22]. Several material databases were already published [2,9]. A BTF database of 84 measured materials in seven categories, each containing 12 different material samples, was presented in [24]. [16] measured in 150 lighting conditions eight categories with 90 samples in total in their dome system.

Table 1. Measured illumination and viewing elevation (θ) and azimuthal ϕ angles for six viewing angular sets A–F, the number of directions in each set and their relative weights in the whole BTF space.

Set	$\theta_{i,v}$	$\triangle\phi_{i,v}$	♯directions	Weight [%]
A	0	–	1	1
B	15	60	6	7
C	30	30	12	15
D	45	20	18	22
E	60	18	20	25
F	75	15	24	30

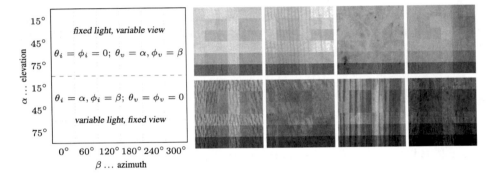

Fig. 1. Selected combinations (right) of illumination and viewing elevation (θ) and azimuthal ϕ measurement cutouts arranged as denoted in the left table from (rightwards, top-down) maple, spruce, oak, plum, sycamore, bubinga pomele, zebrano, and macassar, respectively.

We used a high precision robotic gonioreflectometer. The setup consists of independently controlled arms with camera and light. Its parameters such as angular precision 0.03°, spatial resolution 1000 DPI, or selective spatial measurement, classify this gonioreflectometer to the state-of-the-art devices. The typical resolution of the area of interest is around 2000×2000 pixels, sample size 7×7 [cm], sensor distance ≈ 2 [m] with field of view angle 8.25° and each of them is represented using at least 16-bit floating point value for a reasonable representation of high-dynamic-range visual information. Illumination source are eleven LED array, each having flux 280 lm at 0.7 A, spectral wavelength $450-700$ [nm], and have its optics. The memory requirements for storage of single material sample amount to 360 gigabytes per color channel but can be much more for a more precise spectral measurement.

We measured each wood sample in 81 viewing positions n_v and 81 illumination positions n_i resulting in 6561 images per sample (4 tera-bytes of data). Table 1 summarizes for each combination of elevation and azimuthal angle the number of measurements (♯) and the corresponding angular difference steps ($\triangle\phi_{i,v}$). The spatial resolution of the rectified original measurements was $M \times N \approx 1800 \times 1800$ pixels (Fig. 1).

The BTF wood database, used in this study, contains veneers from sixty-five varied European, African, and American wood species. The wood species are acacia tree, afzelia, alder, anigre, apple tree, ayous, cedar, elm, etimoe, eucalyptus, fir, gabon, hornbeam, iroko, jatoba, larch, limba, linden, macassar, mahogany, mansonia, meranti, merbau, movingui, olive tree, ovangkol, padouk, pear, pine, plane tree, plum, satin, teak, tineo, tulipwood, wenge, zebrawood; two species of cherry trees, birchs, ash trees, bamboo, bubingas, palisanders, spruces, and beeches; three species of oaks and walnuts; four species of maple trees.

3   Convolutional Neural Network

We use the open source TensorFlow library [1] for implementation of the convolutional neural network (CNN) for our experiments either as the classifier or as the source of features [13, 14, 20]. We used the shallow network with three convolution layers, 64 5×5 kernels, ReLU (rectified linear unit) activation functions, max pooling with stride 2, and local response normalization (for details see [14]). Another two fully connected layers (384 and 192 units) use the rectified linear activation, and finally, the linear transformation is applied to produce logits. CNN accept input image of the size with 48×48 in three spectral bands (RGB pixels). The images (64×64 patches) are processed as follows: they are cropped to 48×48 pixels, centrally for evaluation or randomly for training; they are per image standardized to make the model insensitive to dynamic range. For training, we additionally apply a series of random distortions to increase the dataset size artificially. These are image flip from left to right (H), image flip from up to down (V), rotation about $90°$ (R), and distortion of brightness and contrast. The model marking ($\mathbf{X}_{HVR}^{d}$) shows these training options (V, H, R). The network is trained to perform N-way classification using multinomial logistic regression. For regularization, we apply the common l_2 loss losses to all learned variables. The objective function for the model is the cross-entropy loss plus L_2 loss. For training this model we use the standard gradient descent optimizer with a learning rate (starting from 0.1) that exponential decay (0.1) over time (350 epochs), and random weights initialization.

4   Mixture-Based Segmenter

We propose the segmenter based on the Gaussian mixture model similar to the unsupervised algorithm in [4], but their original Markovian textural features we have replaced with the parameters (Θ) obtained from the learned CNN model on the floating window. Thus the segmenter is invariant to both illumination and viewing angles changes and benefits from strong noise suppression property of the Gaussian mixture model. The number of components (K) is variable based on the Kullback Leibler divergence estimation. The Gaussian mixture model for CNN parametric representation is

$$p(\Theta_{x,y}) = \sum_{i=1}^{K} p_i\, p(\Theta_{x,y} \mid \mu_i, \Sigma_i), \tag{1}$$

$$p(\Theta_{x,y} \mid \mu_i, \Sigma_i) = (2\pi)^{\frac{-n}{2}} |\Sigma_i|^{-\frac{1}{2}} \exp\left\{ -\frac{(\Theta_{x,y} - \mu_i)^T \Sigma_i^{-1} (\Theta_{x,y} - \mu_i)}{2} \right\}, \tag{2}$$

where x, y spatial coordinates, μ, Σ the Gaussian data model parameters, and $n = 66+3+2$ the number of features (CNN parameters, local color, and spatial coordinates). The mixture model Eqs. (1), (2) are solved using the EM algorithm and the parametric vectors representing texture mosaic pixels are assigned to the classes according to the highest component probabilities.

5   Results

All our experiments were provided on two BTF wooden sets. The first set contains $426465 = 65 \times 81^2$ measured wooden textures from 65 different wood species, while the second set contains ten synthetic BTF wooden mosaics from the Prague texture segmentation data-generator and benchmark [5, 7].

5.1   Learning from the Complete BTF Space

Each measured BTF space image was divided into four quadrants. From each quadrant randomly selected 64×64 cutouts for every single combination of an illumination and viewing angle were chosen, i.e., **a** from left upper, **b** from lower left, **c** from upper right, and **d** from lower right. Figures 2 and 3 show how the CNN recognition accuracy depends on the viewing elevation angle for different learning scenarios averaged over all wooden species and all illumination angles. The short line segments in right in these graphs (Figs. 2 and 3) highlight the corresponding weighted average value between angles $0°-75°$.

Viewing Angle Dependence and Horizontal Learning Flip. The CNN model $(\mathbf{X}_H^b)$ was learned on the cutout **b** in all classification experiments in cutouts **a–d**. The accuracy curves (Fig. 2) show the similar ranking in all eleven angle combination experiments the best hold out results are on the **a** cutous (always in the direction along the grain) then **d** (close parallel with **b**) and finally **c** (distant parallel with **b**). The best classification accuracy is reached if all sets are used for learning $(\mathbf{A}\text{-}\mathbf{F}_H^b)$. Table 2-left show the weighted (Table 1) averaged accuracy for all four possible cutouts and viewing elevation ranges from $0°$ until $0°-75°$. This table confirms the best possible results for the resubstitution accuracy estimates (**b**) for every angular range and the overall best accuracy (85.6) for the A–F range, followed with results on the **a** cutout. The worst accuracy has the most distant cutout **c** with the exception on the range A.

Table 2. Weighted averaged accuracy for the **a–d** cutouts over viewing elevation (θ) and azimuthal (ϕ) angles. CNN learning cutout is **b/d**.

	$\mathbf{X}_H^b$						$\mathbf{X}_{HVR}^d$					
θ_v [°]	0	0–15	0–30	0–45	0–60	0–75	0	0–15	0–30	0–45	0–60	0–75
a	36.3	51.7	59.9	67.9	75.1	79.8	27.4	43.3	51.8	58.6	64.0	68.5
b	38.2	54.5	63.6	72.6	80.2	85.6	27.9	43.0	51.9	58.8	64.2	68.8
c	29.2	44.0	50.9	57.2	63.5	67.5	33.8	52.1	61.7	69.5	76.4	81.8
d	29.1	44.7	52.4	58.8	65.1	69.4	35.4	53.5	63.8	72.0	79.2	85.0

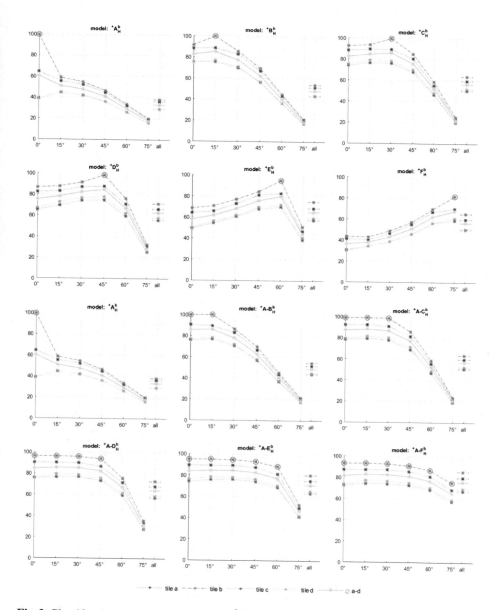

Fig. 2. Classification accuracy of the model $\mathbf{X}_H^b$ for cutouts a, b, c, d, a–d after learning from the b cutouts ($\circledast$) with the horizontal flip obtained from the set $X \in \{A, B, C, D, E, F\}$ (see Table 1). The vertical axes show accuracy in %, while the horizontal axes show the viewing elevation angles.

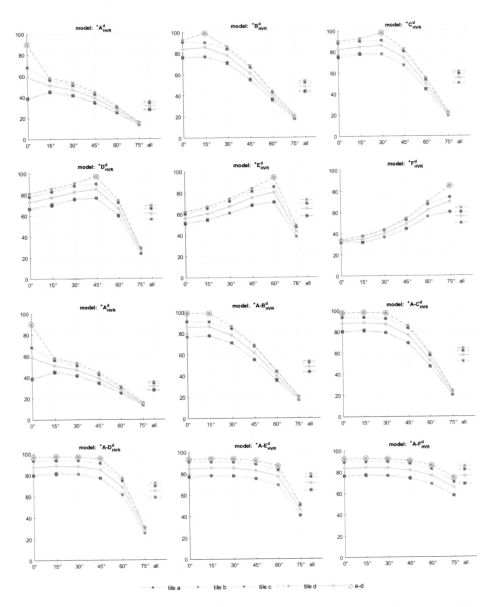

Fig. 3. Classification accuracy of the model $\mathbf{X}_{HVR}^d$ for cutouts a, b, c, d, a–d after learning from the d cuts (⊛) with the horizontal, vertical flips and 90° rotation. The vertical axes show accuracy in %, while the horizontal axes show the viewing elevation angles.

Viewing Angle Dependence with Horizontal, Vertical Flip and Sample Rotation Learning. The CNN model ($\mathbf{X}_{HVR}^{d}$) was learned on the cutout **d** in all classification experiments in Fig. 3. The accuracy curves show the similar ranking again in all eleven experiments the best results are on the **c** cutous (in the direction along the grain), effects on **a, b** cutouts are very similar. The best classification accuracy is reached if all sets are used for learning ($\mathbf{A}$-$\mathbf{F}_{HVR}^{d}$). Table 2-right show the weighted averaged accuracy for all four possible cutouts and viewing elevation ranges from $0°$ until $0°-75°$. As expected, also in this table the best possible results are the resubstitution estimates (**d**) for every angular range and the overall best accuracy is 85.0 for the A–F range, very similar with the corresponding result in the Table 2-left. The results on the cutouts **a, b** are very similar for all tested angular ranges. This is the consequence of the additional learning data (vertical flip and rotation). Comparing the results in both tables, it is possible to see that the additional flip and rotation learning data are advantageous only for the closest cutout (**c**) for $\mathbf{X}_{HVR}^{d}$ and larger angular ranges $> \langle 0; 30 \rangle$ but not for all ranges in the more distant cutouts (**a**) and all experiments on the A set only. However, the accuracy difference is very small for comparable cutouts and angles mostly in the range of 1%. Poor performance on the A set in both part of Table 2 illustrates inadequate learning set size (one image only) and the perpendicular viewing and illumination angle which is the standard but a very insufficient representation of the huge material appearance variability. The difference between the best and the worst accuracy in each angular range is gradually increasing from set A until A–F for both tables. This accuracy difference is between 38.3% (Table 2-left-**c**) and 49.6% (Table 2-right-**d**).

5.2 Synthetic BTF Wooden Mosaic

This experiment used the synthetic BTF wooden mosaic scenes from the Prague texture segmentation data-generator and benchmark [5, 7] as well as the online evaluation capability (Table 3) of this web-based (http://mosaic.utia.cas.cz) service. The benchmark ranks segmentation experiments or algorithms results according to a chosen criterion. The benchmark has implemented twenty-seven frequented evaluation criteria (see [5] for their detailed explanation) categorized into region-based, pixel-wise, clustering comparison criteria, and consistency measures criteria sub-groups.

The benchmark test 1024×1024 mosaics layouts and each cell texture membership are randomly generated and filled with the measured BTF wooden textures from the large UTIA BTF database [8]. The BTF wood measurements are mapped on the randomly generated 3D spline surfaces. Each surface region is mapped with a physically correct wood material measurement which precisely corresponds to the local illumination and viewing conditions, and as such it represents the state-of-the-art realistic material visual representation [6] and also the best available current texture segmentation benchmark. The benchmark allows generating an unlimited number of experimental physically correct mosaics with exactly known segmentation ground truth. All benchmark mosaic experiments were carried out with the Gaussian mixture-based supervised classifier (Sect. 4) applied to CNN learned features. Table 3 illustrates the differences between classification accuracy between models learned on different viewing angle training subsets.

Table 3. BTF wood benchmark results; (Benchmark criteria: CS = correct segmentation; OS = over-segmentation; US = under-segmentation; ME = missed error; NE = noise error; O = omission error; C = commission error; CA = class accuracy; CO = recall - correct assignment; CC = precision - object accuracy; I. = type I error; II. = type II error; EA = mean class accuracy estimate; MS = mapping score; RM = root mean square proportion estimation error; CI = comparison index; GCE = Global Consistency Error; LCE = Local Consistency Error; dD = Van Dongen metric; dM = Mirkin metric; dVI = variation of information; $\bar{f}$ are the performance curves integrals); small numbers are the corresponding measure rank over the listed methods.

Benchmark – BTF wood

	A-D$^{d}_{HVR}$ (2.90)	B$^{d}_{HVR}$ (3.05)	E$^{d}_{HVR}$ (3.90)	A-C$^{d}_{HVR}$ (3.95)	F$^{d}_{HVR}$ (5.90)	C$^{d}_{HVR}$ (6.00)	D$^{d}_{HVR}$ (6.71)	A$^{d}_{HVR}$ (7.48)	A-F$^{d}_{HVR}$ (8.33)	A-B$^{d}_{HVR}$ (8.48)	A-E$^{d}_{HVR}$ (9.24)
↑CS	80.20^{2}	**81.02**^{1}	80.13^{3}	77.87^{5}	78.72^{4}	71.83^{8}	72.97^{7}	77.01^{6}	70.27^{10}	*69.70*^{11}	71.30^{9}
↓OS	50.63^{3}	56.30^{5}	58.36^{8}	47.98^{2}	51.44^{4}	58.80^{9}	**45.02**^{1}	57.20^{6}	59.59^{10}	*63.16*^{11}	57.65^{7}
↓US	1.28^{2}	4.72^{5}	3.31^{3}	7.19^{9}	4.18^{4}	5.13^{7}	5.23^{8}	*7.74*^{11}	**1.05**^{1}	7.26^{10}	4.98^{6}
↓ME	2.23^{9}	0.66^{2}	1.46^{4}	**0.58**^{1}	2.74^{10}	1.16^{3}	1.90^{7}	*4.44*^{11}	2.23^{8}	1.89^{6}	1.76^{5}
↓NE	3.80^{9}	**0.87**^{1}	2.94^{5}	1.21^{2}	3.80^{8}	2.00^{4}	1.40^{3}	*4.69*^{11}	4.50^{10}	3.01^{6}	3.75^{7}
↓O	4.39^{3}	3.06^{2}	5.88^{7}	5.10^{6}	10.39^{10}	4.41^{4}	**2.95**^{1}	4.46^{5}	*12.11*^{11}	7.87^{8}	9.78^{9}
↓C	**61.71**^{1}	81.13^{3}	90.15^{7}	80.40^{2}	83.16^{4}	84.01^{5}	86.64^{6}	100.00^{10}	91.20^{9}	*100.00*^{11}	90.30^{8}
↑CA	**87.12**^{1}	86.75^{3}	86.82^{2}	85.96^{4}	84.47^{5}	83.24^{7}	82.60^{8}	83.79^{6}	81.47^{10}	81.48^{9}	*80.54*^{11}
↑CO	**88.88**^{1}	88.61^{3}	88.69^{2}	88.43^{4}	87.25^{5}	85.23^{8}	85.31^{7}	86.98^{6}	83.04^{10}	83.97^{9}	*82.72*^{11}
↑CC	97.76^{2}	97.19^{4}	97.19^{5}	96.59^{7}	96.07^{9}	97.21^{3}	95.71^{10}	*94.79*^{11}	**97.77**^{1}	96.70^{6}	96.56^{8}
↓I.	**11.12**^{1}	11.39^{3}	11.31^{2}	11.57^{4}	12.75^{5}	14.77^{8}	14.69^{7}	13.02^{6}	16.96^{9}	16.03^{10}	*17.28*^{11}
↓II.	**0.25**^{1}	0.32^{4}	0.38^{5}	0.44^{7}	0.48^{10}	0.32^{3}	0.47^{8}	*0.67*^{11}	0.28^{2}	0.47^{9}	0.38^{6}
↑EA	91.74^{2}	91.35^{3}	**91.78**^{1}	90.74^{4}	89.62^{5}	88.83^{7}	88.29^{8}	89.17^{6}	88.05^{9}	87.44^{10}	*86.84*^{11}
↑MS	**87.63**^{1}	87.26^{3}	87.42^{2}	86.65^{4}	85.17^{5}	83.83^{7}	83.46^{8}	84.56^{6}	81.89^{10}	82.08^{9}	*81.01*^{11}
↓RM	1.77^{4}	1.94^{6}	1.52^{2}	1.71^{3}	**1.41**^{1}	2.05^{8}	*2.73*^{11}	1.99^{7}	2.09^{9}	1.80^{5}	2.29^{10}
↑CI	**92.47**^{1}	92.07^{3}	92.32^{2}	91.39^{4}	90.43^{5}	89.85^{7}	89.33^{8}	89.93^{6}	89.17^{9}	88.66^{10}	*88.12*^{11}
↓GCE	4.31^{2}	**4.27**^{1}	4.67^{3}	5.00^{7}	6.62^{10}	4.75^{4}	4.78^{5}	*6.90*^{11}	4.98^{6}	5.17^{8}	6.03^{9}
↓LCE	3.11^{5}	**2.38**^{1}	3.42^{8}	2.78^{3}	3.39^{7}	2.74^{2}	2.82^{4}	3.59^{9}	3.81^{10}	3.18^{6}	*4.00*^{11}
↓dD	6.70^{2}	**6.54**^{1}	6.90^{4}	6.70^{3}	7.57^{5}	8.40^{7}	8.53^{8}	7.97^{6}	9.92^{10}	9.12^{9}	*10.27*^{11}
↓dM	4.29^{3}	4.54^{6}	4.24^{2}	**3.94**^{1}	4.47^{5}	5.18^{7}	6.20^{9}	4.41^{4}	6.80^{10}	5.90^{8}	*6.97*^{11}
↓dVI	15.97^{6}	15.82^{4}	15.91^{5}	**15.61**^{1}	15.81^{3}	16.39^{8}	16.03^{7}	15.70^{2}	16.73^{10}	16.48^{9}	*16.74*^{11}
↑$\overline{CS}$	**74.65**^{1}	74.11^{2}	72.42^{3}	72.37^{4}	70.53^{5}	68.17^{7}	68.05^{8}	69.03^{6}	*63.00*^{11}	65.24^{9}	63.07^{10}
↓$\overline{OS}$	48.46^{3}	53.41^{6}	55.03^{8}	43.91^{2}	49.88^{4}	56.36^{10}	**43.00**^{1}	53.48^{7}	56.35^{9}	*58.68*^{11}	53.10^{5}
↓$\overline{US}$	**1.09**^{1}	3.74^{4}	1.87^{3}	6.12^{10}	4.89^{7}	4.64^{6}	5.33^{8}	*6.38*^{11}	1.34^{2}	6.03^{9}	3.87^{5}
↓$\overline{ME}$	8.01^{5}	**5.91**^{1}	9.16^{7}	6.87^{2}	9.76^{8}	7.67^{3}	7.87^{4}	10.60^{9}	10.73^{10}	8.94^{6}	*11.63*^{11}
↓$\overline{NE}$	8.73^{5}	**6.06**^{1}	10.13^{7}	7.39^{2}	10.50^{8}	8.19^{4}	7.90^{3}	11.17^{9}	12.37^{10}	9.72^{6}	*13.29*^{11}
↑$\overline{F}$	**92.27**^{1}	91.87^{3}	92.17^{2}	91.21^{4}	90.20^{5}	89.56^{7}	89.04^{8}	89.71^{6}	88.85^{9}	88.31^{10}	*87.75*^{11}

The first row shows various view angle ranges (A, B, C, D, E, F, A–B, A–C, A–D, A–E, A–F) used for CNN learning as explained in Table 1. Small numbers are the corresponding criteria rank value in this table and the second row in Table 3 lists the average rank for the corresponding learning set. The best learning set is A–D (2×10^{5} learning images with elevation angles $0° - 45°$) with ten best performing criteria. This set is the best compromise between the learning variability and recognition accuracy.

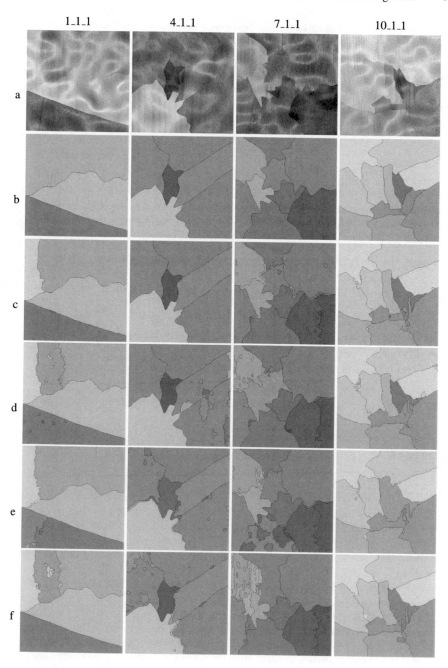

Fig. 4. Selected BTF benchmark mosaics (a), ground-truth (b), **A-D**$_{HVR}^{d}$ (c), **B**$_{HVR}^{d}$ (d), **E**$_{HVR}^{d}$ (e), **A-C**$_{HVR}^{d}$ (f) segmentation results, respectively.

The learning sets ordering in Table 3 is based on the best average rank over all segmentation criteria rightwards. The worst segmenter performance (eleven worst criteria) is learned from the set AE. This learning variant has the worst class accuracy, recall, and nine other criteria values, and none winning criterion.

The best-fixed learning elevation angle is 15° - the B set from the region-based criteria point of view, while the A set (0°) has the worst average rank and only the variation of information being the second best (Fig. 4).

6 Conclusions

This study presented two experiments of view and illumination-dependent material recognition analysis. The sixty-five wood species measured in the state-of-the-art bidirectional texture function representation is classified using the convolutional neural network. The novel Gaussian mixture based segmenter with CNN learned features is favourably evaluated on eleven different angular combinations. The results document sharp classification accuracy decrease when using standard texture recognition approach, i.e., small learning set size and the vertical viewing and illumination angle which is a very inadequate representation of the enormous material appearance variability. The ideal learning is to use the whole possible viewing angle range. The benchmark experiments suggest 15° to be the best single elevation angle and $0° - 45°$ the best range of elevation angles. The mosaic surfaces are smooth without sharp declinations thus they possibly prefer narrower elevation ranges than an object in real visual scenes.

Acknowledgments. The Czech Science Foundation project GAČR 19-12340S supported this research.

References

1. TensorFlow. Technical report, Google AI. http://www.tensorflow.org/
2. Dana, K.J., van Ginneken, B., Nayar, S.K., Koenderink, J.J.: Reflectance and texture of real world surfaces. Technical report CUCS-048-96, Columbia University, December 1996
3. Dana, K.J., Nayar, S.K., van Ginneken, B., Koenderink, J.J.: Reflectance and texture of real-world surfaces. In: CVPR, pp. 151–157. IEEE Computer Society (1997)
4. Haindl, M., Mikeš, S.: Unsupervised texture segmentation using multispectral modelling approach. In: Tang, Y., Wang, S., Yeung, D., Yan, H., Lorette, G. (eds.) Proceedings of the 18th International Conference on Pattern Recognition, ICPR 2006, vol. II, pp. 203–206. IEEE Computer Society, Los Alamitos, August 2006
5. Haindl, M., Mikeš, S.: Texture segmentation benchmark. In: Lovell, B., Laurendeau, D., Duin, R. (eds.) Proceedings of the 19th International Conference on Pattern Recognition, ICPR 2008, pp. 1–4. IEEE Computer Society, Los Alamitos, December 2008
6. Haindl, M., Filip, J.: Visual Texture. ACVPR. Springer, London (2013). https://doi.org/10.1007/978-1-4471-4902-6
7. Haindl, M., Mikeš, S.: A competition in unsupervised color image segmentation. Pattern Recogn. **57**(9), 136–151 (2016)
8. Haindl, M., Mikeš, S., Kudo, M.: Unsupervised surface reflectance field multi-segmenter. In: Azzopardi, G., Petkov, N. (eds.) CAIP 2015. LNCS, vol. 9256, pp. 261–273. Springer, Cham (2015). https://doi.org/10.1007/978-3-319-23192-1_22

9. Hayman, E., Caputo, B., Fritz, M., Eklundh, J.-O.: On the significance of real-world conditions for material classification. In: Pajdla, T., Matas, J. (eds.) ECCV 2004. LNCS, vol. 3024, pp. 253–266. Springer, Heidelberg (2004). https://doi.org/10.1007/978-3-540-24673-2_21

10. Jehle, M., Sommer, C., Jähne, B.: Learning of optimal illumination for material classification. In: Goesele, M., Roth, S., Kuijper, A., Schiele, B., Schindler, K. (eds.) DAGM 2010. LNCS, vol. 6376, pp. 563–572. Springer, Heidelberg (2010). https://doi.org/10.1007/978-3-642-15986-2_57

11. Kampouris, C., Zafeiriou, S., Ghosh, A., Malassiotis, S.: Fine-grained material classification using micro-geometry and reflectance. In: Leibe, B., Matas, J., Sebe, N., Welling, M. (eds.) ECCV 2016. LNCS, vol. 9909, pp. 778–792. Springer, Cham (2016). https://doi.org/10.1007/978-3-319-46454-1_47

12. Koudelka, M.L., Magda, S., Belhumeur, P.N., Kriegman, D.J.: Acquisition, compression, and synthesis of bidirectional texture functions. In: Texture 2003: Third International Workshop on Texture Analysis and Synthesis, Nice, France, pp. 59–64, October 2003

13. Krizhevsky, A.: Learning multiple layers of features from tiny images. Master's thesis, University of Toronto, Canada (2009)

14. Krizhevsky, A., Sutskever, I., Hinton, G.E.: ImageNet classification with deep convolutional neural networks. In: Advances in Neural Information Processing Systems, pp. 1097–1105 (2012)

15. Liu, C., Gu, J.: Discriminative illumination: per-pixel classification of raw materials based on optimal projections of spectral BRDF. IEEE Trans. Pattern Anal. Mach. Intell. **36**(1), 86–98 (2014)

16. Liu, C., Yang, G., Gu, J.: Learning discriminative illumination and filters for raw material classification with optimal projections of bidirectional texture functions. In: The IEEE Conference on Computer Vision and Pattern Recognition (CVPR), June 2013

17. Lu, F., He, L., You, S., Chen, X., Hao, Z.: Identifying surface BRDF from a single 4-D light field image via deep neural network. IEEE J. Sel. Top. Sig. Process. **11**(7), 1047–1057 (2017)

18. Müller, G., Meseth, J., Sattler, M., Sarlette, R., Klein, R.: Acquisition, synthesis and rendering of bidirectional texture functions. In: Eurographics 2004, STAR - State of The Art Report, pp. 69–94. Eurographics Association (2004)

19. Ngan, A., Durand, F.: Statistical acquisition of texture appearance. In: Eurographics Symposium on Rendering. Eurographics (2006)

20. Pattanayak, S.: Pro Deep Learning with TensorFlow. Apress, New York (2017)

21. Sattler, M., Sarlette, R., Klein, R.: Efficient and realistic visualization of cloth. In: Eurographics Symposium on Rendering, June 2003

22. Wang, J., Dana, K.: Relief texture from specularities. IEEE Trans. Pattern Anal. Mach. Intell. **28**(3), 446–457 (2006)

23. Wang, T.-C., Zhu, J.-Y., Hiroaki, E., Chandraker, M., Efros, A.A., Ramamoorthi, R.: A 4D light-field dataset and CNN architectures for material recognition. In: Leibe, B., Matas, J., Sebe, N., Welling, M. (eds.) ECCV 2016. LNCS, vol. 9907, pp. 121–138. Springer, Cham (2016). https://doi.org/10.1007/978-3-319-46487-9_8

24. Weinmann, M., Gall, J., Klein, R.: Material classification based on training data synthesized using a BTF database. In: Fleet, D., Pajdla, T., Schiele, B., Tuytelaars, T. (eds.) ECCV 2014. LNCS, vol. 8691, pp. 156–171. Springer, Cham (2014). https://doi.org/10.1007/978-3-319-10578-9_11

25. Weinmann, M., Klein, R.: Material recognition for efficient acquisition of geometry and reflectance. In: Agapito, L., Bronstein, M.M., Rother, C. (eds.) ECCV 2014. LNCS, vol. 8927, pp. 321–333. Springer, Cham (2015). https://doi.org/10.1007/978-3-319-16199-0_23

3D Visual Object Detection from Monocular Images

Qiaosong Wang$^{(\boxtimes)}$ and Christopher Rasmussen

Department of Computer and Information Sciences, University of Delaware,
Newark, DE, USA
{qiaosong,ras}@udel.edu

Abstract. 3D visual object detection is a fundamental requirement for autonomous vehicles. However, accurately detecting 3D objects was until recently a quality unique to expensive LiDAR ranging devices. Approaches based on cheaper monocular imagery are typically incapable of identifying 3D objects. In this paper, we propose a novel approach to predict accurate 3D bounding box locations on monocular images. We first train a generative adversarial network (GAN) to perform monocular depth estimation. The ground truth training depth data is obtained via depth completion on LiDAR scans. Next, we combine both depth and appearance data into a birds-eye-view representation with height, density and grayscale intensity as the three feature channels. Finally, We train a convolutional neural network (CNN) on our feature map leveraging bounding boxes annotated on corresponding LiDAR scans. Experiments show that our method performs favorably against baselines.

Keywords: 3D object detection · Depth estimation · Monocular vision

1 Introduction

In the past few years, new types of LiDAR (Light Detection And Ranging) sensors have been developed for autonomous vehicles. These sensors provide an accurate 3D perception of the surrounding environment in real-time. As a result, several LiDAR-based classification, detection, and segmentation datasets are made available to public [10]. LiDAR is popular and advantageous compared to traditional stereo or multi-camera ranging devices for a variety of reasons. Firstly, LiDAR is able to give accurate measurements invariant of the ego car distance, while camera based ranging algorithms typically give a degraded performance on distant objects. This is because the object size reduces quadratically with distance to the camera for most imaging sensors. Secondly, LiDAR is an active time-of-flight (ToF) sensing device which works on a variety of objects including specular/metallic surfaces and textureless regions. Also, depending on the wavelength, LiDAR devices have certain levels of see-through capability on transparent objects (e.g. cloud, rain, snow). On the contrary, computer vision algorithms operating on camera sensors will start to fail when reflective/textureless/transparent regions increase. Finally, most LiDAR devices give 360-degree surrounding scans and immediate reading of orientation and distance to the object, whereas camera sensors usually

© Springer Nature Switzerland AG 2019
G. Bebis et al. (Eds.): ISVC 2019, LNCS 11844, pp. 168–180, 2019.
https://doi.org/10.1007/978-3-030-33720-9_13

have limited field-of-view (FOV) and multi-camera calibration issues, plus additional computation overheads to produce depth maps from raw input images. In the 2007 DARPA Urban Challenge, a team [20] finished in the second place using LiDAR alone with no camera sensors involved. Despite its advantages, there are a few major drawbacks of LiDAR sensors. Firstly, they are typically bulky and expensive for wide use and deployment. Secondly, even top-of-the-line LiDAR sensors only provide 64 or 128 sparse scanlines across the 3D space, while camera sensors operate at a much higher resolution (typically ranging from 5 to 20 megapixels). Finally, LiDAR signals are inherently limited to spatial information and do not provide what cameras can typically see, such as words on the traffic sign, color, and pattern of the vehicle, etc. Therefore, it is still important to keep the camera sensors as a supplementary/fall-back option.

Fig. 1. Sample output and intermediate results from our pipeline (Best viewed electronically). Top left: Our predicted 3D bounding boxes (red) *vs.* ground-truth annotations on the KITTI dataset (green). Top middle: predicted depth map. Top right: 2D detection results on our depth map projected to the birds-eye-view (BEV) map. Bottom: Our transformed point cloud aligned with LiDAR scanlines. The intensity values on our point cloud are calculated using grayscale intensity values from the input RGB image. (Color figure online)

Intuitively, depth data provide more useful descriptions of spatial information, while appearance data provide more visual cues to identify objects into different categories. Therefore, when combining semantically rich appearance data with depth information, one can improve the performance of both locating and categorizing objects in an image. Early research attempts to combine simple depth cues with image features for richer representation [25]. However, due to difficulty in propagating gradients in the model, simply stacking features from different modalities could not give satisfactory performance. Gupta *et al.* proposed to use horizontal disparity, height above ground, and angle with the direction of gravity to form another 3 channel image for training [13].

Due to difficulty on training these type of feature maps, it is a common practice to finetune on existing models trained on RGB images [26]. However, it is questionable whether this way of inter-model fusion is reasonable as depth features seldom resemble shape, color, and appearance from the visible light spectrum. Lenz *et al.* proposes to learn features from RGB and depth images separately and then fuse at a higher level [17]. This method is termed *Late Fusion* by Eitel *et al.* [7]. Most work on 3D detection, on the other hand, are either purely based on LiDAR data [4,24] or simply use visual cues to supplement LiDAR data [18,21].

In this paper, we propose a novel approach to leverage both depth and visual cues for 3D object detection on monocular images. At the core of our technique is to integrate appearance and structural cues for better object detection. Our method contains three stages. Firstly, we use an unpaired image to image translation network to learn bi-directional transformations from RGB images to depth maps. Secondly, we calculate height, density and grayscale intensity as 3 feature channels and project the feature map to a birds-eye-view representation. Finally, we take advantage of 3D bounding box annotations on LiDAR data and train our object detection model on the feature map (See Fig. 1). The overall architecture of our network is shown in Fig. 2. The rest of this paper is organized as follows. In Sect. 2 we discuss related work. In Sect. 3 we demonstrate different components of the proposed method. We show experimental results and analysis in Sects. 4, 5 and draw conclusions in Sect. 6.

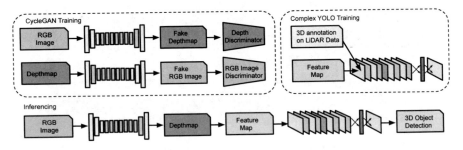

Fig. 2. Architecture of our network. Top left: our CycleGAN based depth prediction network. Top right: our 3D detection network based on Complex YOLO. Bottom: our network for inference. Note that for training our method requires both monocular images and aligned LiDAR scans. However, for inference we only need monocular images to predict 3D object locations and categories. See Sect. 3 for details.

2   Related Work

Dual Learning. The idea of using forward and backward consistency to improve training has a long history [5]. Recently, He *et al.* [14] proposed the concept of dual learning to improve the performance of machine translation systems. The proposed mechanism can be viewed as a two-agent communication game. The two agents may not be able to translate one language to another, but are still able to evaluate and collectively improve the quality of the two translation models by going through the full forward-backward translation cycle. This procedure can be performed by an arbitrary number of rounds until the two models are fully converged. This idea inspired conditional GANs based cross-domain translation tasks [29] and improves performance in image-based depth/shape estimation tasks. [11,28]. In this paper, we choose to use GAN for depth prediction because it allows unpaired image domain transfer, while other depth prediction models are usually dependent on LiDAR input guidance.

Image-to-Image Translation. The idea of learning from a pair of images and then apply the model at inference time to produce an analogous target image from the input image dates back to [15]. More recently, Isola *et al.* [16] proposed a method which exploits conditional adversarial networks as a unified framework for image to image translation. It uses the L1 loss function to enforce generated synthetic images to be similar to ground truth training images while letting GANs to only hallucinate high-frequency details in the image. This is because the L1 loss can already guarantee similarity at low frequencies. Therefore, instead of processing the whole image, the discriminator only attempts to classify if a $N \times N$ image patch is correct or not. This method produces remarkable results on a variety of tasks, including photographs from sketches, automatic colonization of black and white images, raw images to label maps, thermal to visible light images, and so on.

3D Object Detection on LiDAR Data. Recent advance in sensor and computing technology enables 3D object detection on structural data. Due to the difficulty in processing large-scale point cloud data, most works preprocess the raw input data into either voxels or birds-eye-view maps (BEV). Chen *et al.* converts LiDAR data to a BEV representation for 3D object detection in the road scene [6]. Liang *et al.* develop a 3D object detector that reasons in BEV space and integrates visual cues by learning to project camera-based features into the BEV space [18]. YOLO3D [4] extends the 2D YOLOv2 object detector [22] to the BEV map and achieves real-time performance on the KITTI dataset. Complex-YOLO [24] also operates on the BEV map by running an E-RPN that estimates object orientations by both imaginary and real numbers.

3D Object Detection on RGB Images. More recent publication [27] introduces the concept of *pseudo LiDAR*, arguing that by converting the image-based depth maps to a representation that closely mimics the LiDAR signal, one could obtain state-of-the-art results on stereo vision based 3D object detection. Our method is along the lines of performing 3D object detection on RGB images. However, our method differs from the pseudo-LiDAR approach in a few aspects. Firstly, our detection is performed on a feature map consists of height, density, and grayscale intensity information. This feature map combines both depth and visual cues and is not intended to mimic the LiDAR signal. Secondly, our method leverages unpaired adversarial learning to predict the depth map, eliminating the need for collecting pairwise-aligned RGB and depth data, thus making it much easier to apply to use cases other than autonomous driving (*e.g.* indoor scenes, close-up scenes, top-down surveillance videos, etc.)

3   Approach

3.1   Depth Estimation

We adopt the CycleGAN [29] for depth estimation from monocular images. We use the sparse to dense [19] depth completion results on KITTI LiDAR scans as groudtruth for training. The learning objective contains 2 terms: an adversarial loss and a cycle consistency loss:

$$
\begin{aligned}
&\mathcal{L}(G, F, D_X, D_Y) \\
&= \gamma_{adv}\mathcal{L}_{adv}(G, D_X, D_Y, X, Y) + \gamma_{cyc}\mathcal{L}_{cyc}(G, F)
\end{aligned}
\tag{1}
$$

Where γ_{adv}, γ_{cyc} are the hyper-parameters to adjust loss on each term and are empirically set during the experiment. $\{x_i \in X\}_{i=1}^N$ and $\{y_i \in Y\}_{i=1}^N$ are N training images from the RGB dataset and depth dataset, respectively. G and F are mapping functions $G : X \rightarrow Y$ and $F : Y \rightarrow X$ to transform RGB images to depth maps or vice versa. D_X and D_Y are adversarial discriminators to distinguish between real images $\{x\}$ and synthetic images $\{F(y)\}$, or $\{y\}$ with $\{F(x)\}$. The cycle consistency loss is defined as:

$$
\begin{aligned}
\mathcal{L}_{cyc}(G, F) = &\mathbb{E}_x \sim p_{data}(x)[\|F(G(x)) - x\|] \\
&+ \mathbb{E}_y \sim p_{data}(y)[\|G(F(y)) - y\|]
\end{aligned}
\tag{2}
$$

It can be viewed as translating an RGB image into a depth image and then translate it back to compare with the original using L1 norm. Based on the cycle consistency loss, two discriminators D_X and D_Y are introduced to calculate the adversarial loss [12]. This term enforces the distribution of translated images to be as close to the training images as possible. The adversarial loss is defined as:

$$
\begin{aligned}
&\mathcal{L}_{adv}(G, F, D_X, D_Y, X, Y) \\
&= \mathbb{E}_y \sim p_{data}(y)[logD_Y(y)] + \mathbb{E}_x \sim p_{data}(x)[logD_X(x)] \\
&+ \mathbb{E}_x \sim p_{data}(x)[log(1 - D_Y G(x))] \\
&+ \mathbb{E}_y \sim p_{data}(y)[log(1 - D_X G(y))]
\end{aligned}
\tag{3}
$$

By using the above two loss terms we aim to minimize adversarial discriminator errors of both visual and structural cues, as well as L1 error of predicted images *vs.* original images.

3.2   Feature Map Generation

Once we obtained the trained GAN model for depth prediction, we would like to transform the depth map from camera coordinate system to the LiDAR coordinate system for alignment with ground-truth bounding box annotations. In order to do this, we first transform the depth map to the rectified (rotated) camera coordinate system:

$$
\begin{aligned}
z_{rect} &= D(u, v) \\
x_{rect} &= \frac{(u - c_u) \times z_{rect}}{f_u} + b_x \\
y_{rect} &= \frac{(v - c_v) \times z_{rect}}{f_v} + b_y
\end{aligned}
\tag{4}
$$

Fig. 3. Bidirectional transforms between LiDAR and camera coordinates (Best viewed electronically). Top left: LiDAR scans provided by the KITTI dataset projected to the camera imaging plane, color-coded by depth. Middle left: LiDAR scans projected to the corresponding RGB image. Bottom left: predicted depth map with one-to-one mappings to the input image. Top right: predicted depth map transformed to the LiDAR coordinates, color-coded by one channel grayscale intensity. Middle right: LiDAR scan color-coded by intensity/reflectivity. Bottom right: our transformed point cloud aligned with the LiDAR scan. Note the LiDAR has a much wider field of view (FOV).

Where $(x_{rect}, y_{rect}, z_{rect})$ is the 3D point coordinate in the rectified camera coordinates. (u, v) denotes a pixel location in the predicted depth map. (c_u, c_v) is the pixel location corresponding to the imaging center, f_u, f_v are the horizontal and vertical focal length and b_x, b_y are the baselines with respect to reference camera. The camera intrinsic can be obtained from the projection matrix provided by [10]:

$$\mathbf{P}_{rect} = \begin{pmatrix} f_u & 0 & c_u & -f_u b_x \\ 0 & f_v & c_v & -f_v b_y \\ 0 & 0 & 1 & 0 \end{pmatrix} \tag{5}$$

Next, we transform the 3D point cloud from rectified camera coordinates to reference camera coordinates and then to the LiDAR coordinates by calling the KITTI utility library [2]. Let $\mathbf{T}_{cam}^{velo}$ be the 4×4 transformation matrix from the camera coordinate system to the LiDAR coordinates, $\mathbf{R}_{rect}$ be the 4×4 rectifying rotation matrix converted from Cartesian to homogeneous coordinates by adding a fourth zero row and setting $\mathbf{R}_{rect}(4, 4) = 1$, $\mathcal{P}_{velo}$ and $\mathcal{P}_{rect} \in \mathbb{R}^3$ be the 3D point coordinates in the LiDAR and rectified camera coordinates, we can write the transformation as:

$$\mathcal{P}_{velo} = \mathbf{T}_{cam}^{velo} \mathbf{R}_{rect}^{-1} \mathcal{P}_{rect} \tag{6}$$

Note that we also store the RGB value and index of each point in another table to obtain the RGBXYZ representation of $\mathcal{P}_{velo}$. Next, we perform preprocessing in a fashion similar to Complex YOLO [24] to transform $\mathcal{P}_{velo}$ into the BEV feature map. The only difference between Complex YOLO and our method is that we are using grayscale intensity (visual) as the blue channel of the image while Complex YOLO sets the blue channel to LiDAR intensity (reflectivity). More formally, let $\mathcal{S}$ be the mapping function to map each point in $\mathcal{P}_{velo}$ to a grid cell $\mathcal{S}_{bev}$ [24], we can formulate the transformation as:

$$f_g\left(\mathcal{S}_{bev}^j\right) = \max\left(\mathcal{P}_{velo \rightarrow bev}^i \cdot [0,0,1]^T\right)$$
$$f_b\left(\mathcal{S}_{bev}^j\right) = \max\left(I\left(\mathcal{P}_{velo \rightarrow bev}^i\right)\right) \qquad (7)$$
$$f_r\left(\mathcal{S}_{bev}^j\right) = \min(1.0, \log(\left|\mathcal{P}_{velo \rightarrow bev}^i\right| + 1)/64)$$

Where f is the resulting 3-channel feature map. f_g, f_b, f_r denotes height map, grayscale intensity map and density map, respectively. I is the grayscale intensity of $\mathcal{P}_{velo}$ calculated from the RGB values. $\mathcal{P}_{velo \rightarrow bev}$ denotes the 3D points mapped to the grid cell $\mathcal{S}_{bev}$. To this end, we have constructed the feature map which is aligned with LiDAR 3D object bounding box annotations ready for training. We visualize the height, density and intensity maps of both LiDAR data and predicted depth data in Fig. 5. We also show the alignment of LiDAR data *vs.* our transformed point cloud in Fig. 3. As can be seen from Fig. 3, the LiDAR scanlines are accurately projected onto the camera coordinates. Also, the transformed point cloud is well-aligned with LiDAR data. It is worth-noting that the field of view (FOV) of LiDAR is much larger than the camera. This is reflected in both Fig. 3 (row 1 column 2 *vs.* row 2 column 2) and Fig. 5 (first row *vs.* second row). Therefore, unlike other methods, during mAP evaluation we only compare with ground-truth bounding box annotations that falls within the camera FOV.

3.3   3D Object Detection

We follow the Complex YOLO model architecture put forth by [24] to train the 3D object detector. This detector takes the BEV feature map mentioned in Sect. 3.2 as input, and extends the YOLOv2 detector [22] by a complex angle regression and a Euler region proposal networks (E-RPN). The E-RPN is a direct extension of the region proposal networks (RPN) proposed by Ren *et al.* [23]. Specifically, consider (x, y, w, l, ϕ)

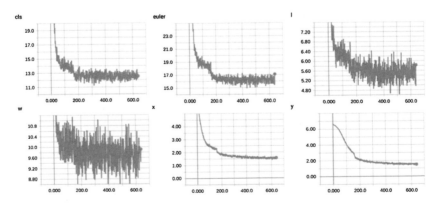

Fig. 4. Training loss visualization using TensorBoard [3]. Top: training loss on class labels, Euler region proposals and object length. Bottom: training loss on object width, horizontal and vertical locations. See Sect. 4 for details.

as a vector describing 2D locations, size and orientations of 3D objects in the BEV coordinates, the parameterizations of the 5 coordinates can be obtained as [23,24]:

$$b_x = \sigma(t_x) + c_x, b_y = \sigma(t_x) + c_y$$
$$b_w = p_w e^{t_w}, b_l = p_l e^{t_l} \tag{8}$$
$$b_\phi = \arg\left(|z|e^{ib_\phi}\right) = \arctan_2\left(t_{Im}, t_{Re}\right)$$

The loss function of Complex YOLO is defined as a multi-part loss. The first part is the YOLOv2 loss [22] and the second part is an Euler regression loss:

$$L_{\text{Total}} = L_{\text{YOLO}} + L_{\text{Euler}}$$
$$L_{\text{Euler}} = \lambda_{\text{coord}} \sum_{i=0}^{S^2} \Sigma_{j=0}^{B} 1_{ij}^{obj} \left| e^{ib_\phi} - e^{i\hat{b}_\phi} \right| \tag{9}$$

According to the authors, the Euler loss leads to a closed-form space eliminating singularities. This leads to state-of-the-arts results on the KITTI 3D object detection dataset, while achieving real-time performance on the embedded NVIDIA TX2 platform [24].

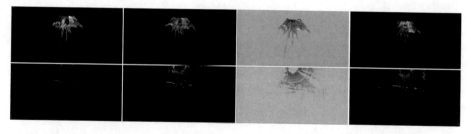

Fig. 5. Feature map visualization (Best viewed electronically). Top: Our combined BEV feature map, density map, height map and grayscale intensity map. Bottom: Feature map, density map, height map and intensity map on corresponding LiDAR scans used by Complex YOLO [24]. See Sect. 3.2 for details.

4   Experiments

We use the KITTI 3D object detection benchmark suite for training and evaluation. The KITTI 3D object detection benchmark consists of 7481 training images as well as the corresponding point clouds, training labels and camera calibration files. We first use the supervised model [19] provided by the author to obtain depth maps for all training images. We subsequently perform a random train (60%)/validation (25%)/test (15%) split and use the code provided by the author [29] for training the CycleGAN model. The model is trained from scratch with random weight initialization. We set base learning rate = 0.0002, gamma = 0.5, momentum = 0.5. We train for 200 epochs and use the CycleGAN model for constructing BEV feature maps.

Next, we modify the Complex YOLO framework by constructing feature maps on-the-fly during training. We still use the same train/validation sets and construct the BEV feature map for every image. We run CycleGAN inference on every image to obtain the depth map, then follow the transformations outlined in Sect. 3.2 to obtain the 3-channel feature map as input for the Complex YOLO framework. Our implementation is based on the open source code provided by [1]. The ground-truth labels are obtained by converting 3D bounding box labels to 2D bounding boxes in the BEV coordinates. We set the base learning rate = 0.0001, gamma = 0.5, momentum = 0.9 and batch size = 32. We train for 700 epochs with four NVIDIA Titan V GPUs. The training losses mentioned in Sect. 3.3 are visualized in Fig. 4 using TensorBoard [3] until the 600th step (∼4 epochs).

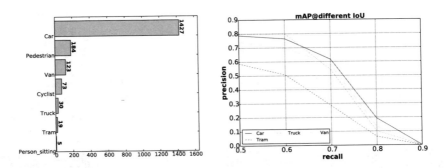

Fig. 6. Dataset statistics and precision-recall curve. Left: Number of objects per class in the KITTI dataset. Right: mean Average Precision (mAP) values on the car, truck, van and tram classes across varying Intersection-over-Union (IoU) values. Note that the performance of our model is robust to stricter IoU criterias and the performance only begins to significantly degrade when IoU is bigger than 0.6.

Similar to [24] which perform PASCAL VOC [9] style mean Average Precision (mAP) evaluation on its own test set split, we run mAP on 2D bounding boxes in the BEV space. There is one difference from our evaluation scheme *vs.* LiDAR-based methods: since LiDAR data has much wider FOV, we only evaluate against ground-truth bounding boxes that fall within our camera FOV. This means that we are not considering ground-truth labels that are too far away, or outside of our camera view frustum.

Table 1. Quantitative mAP results. Note that we only evaluate within the visible range of the predicted depth map/point cloud, whereas all other methods evaluate on the full LiDAR scan. Also, our method and ComplexYOLO report scores on the random test split while MV3D evaluate on the test set. Both MV3D and ComplexYOLO scores are reported under the easy category of the BEV evaluation task. See Sect. 4 for details.

Method	Train	Test	Car	Tram	Truck	Van
MV3D [6]	LiDAR+RGB	LiDAR+RGB	86.02	N/A	N/A	N/A
C-YOLO [24]	LiDAR	LiDAR	85.89	N/A	N/A	N/A
Ours	LiDAR+RGB	RGB	78.78	58.70	80.00	74.14

Also, since our predicted depth map is not able to capture fine structures of small objects like LiDARs do, we only evaluate on four categories including car, tram, truck and van. As shown in Fig. 6, these four (out of seven) categories consist of more than 85% of objects in the KITTI 3D object detection dataset. We also vary the IoU threshold from 0.5 to 0.9 with a 0.1 interval and recalculate the mAP scores. We show the mAP scores at different IoU thresholds in Fig. 6. Compared to existing methods, our framework is one of the few that directly performs inference on RGB images. We compare with MV3D [6] and Complex YOLO [24] results in Table 1. The scores of MV3D and Complex YOLO are adopted from the original paper in the BEV category with easy difficulty. Easy difficulty is defined according to the bounding box height and occlusion/truncation levels. In general, the easy task corresponds to cars within 30 m of the ego-car distance, according to [27]. Note that the effective range of our transformed point cloud is shorter than this 30-meter range. Also, the Complex YOLO scores are reported on the test split (similar to our evaluation) whereas the MV3D reports on the KITTI test set.

5 Discussion

We show quantitative PR-curve evaluations in Fig. 6 and compare with other methods in Table 1. As can be seen from Fig. 6, our method achieves satisfactory results on car, truck, van and tram categories, and the car category demonstrates the highest mAP scores across varying IoUs. This may due to the fact that cars are more common in real-life scenes and thus easier to recognize. Also, because the categories in the KITTI dataset is highly imbalanced, it is possible that the car class is over-represented and the classifier is biased towards this single class. In the future, we plan to test our approach on an evenly sampled 3D object detection dataset with more diverse examples. According to Fig. 6, the mAP starts to dramatically decrease only when the IoU value is more than 0.6. This shows that our detector is robust to stricter evaluation criteria, which is generally more desirable for complex real-life scenes. Also, according to Table 1, our method is competitive when compared to other LiDAR-based methods, even though our network only uses RGB images as input to perform forward inference. We visualize the qualitative results in Fig. 7. Our approach works well in cluttered scenes (*e.g.* row 1 and 2). It might be difficult for appearance-based methods to separate vehicles parked closely together (row 2 column 1), but our method makes accurate depth predictions and the BEV map (row 2 column 2) makes it much easier to learn the relative locations of the vehicles. However, for small objects and thin structures (*e.g.* pedestrian in row 3 and 4), our network is not able to capture, as the predicted depth maps are not as accurate as LiDAR scans. Also, our method takes both structural (*e.g.* height) and visual cues for inference. For example, in the last row, the closest and farthest objects are wrongly classified as vans while the middle object is correctly classified as a car. This is because our feature map also contains the height map. The SUV and MPV in the front and back are taller than the sedan in the middle, which possibly leads to the wrong classification result. In general, Fig. 7 demonstrates that the bounding box predictions (structural) are more accurate than class predictions (visual appearance). This implies that our network is good at localizing objects but is still having difficulties learning

Fig. 7. Qualitative results on the KITTI dataset. Left: our 3D bounding box predictions (red) *vs.* ground-truth (green) annotations projected to the camera imaging plane. Right: our 2D bounding box predictions (red) on the BEV map vs ground-truth (green) annotations. Note that the camera optical axis is facing down on the BEV map for better visualization. See Sect. 5 for details. (Color figure online)

visual features of an object. This can also be observed in Fig. 4, where the classification loss curve shows more oscillations than bounding box coordinates (x and y). Although the learning objective is designed to minimize both classification and localization errors, it is interesting to see what roles the structural and visual cues play, and when one overwhelms the other. In the future, we plan to train and test on more datasets and visualize neuron activation heatmaps in each channel (height, density and color intensity).

6   Conclusion

In this paper, we have presented a framework to detect and classify 3D objects from monocular images. Experiments show that our approach performs favorably against competitive methods trained on LiDAR data. Our method leverages generative adversarial networks to perform monocular depth estimation. The training groudtruth are obtained by completing LiDAR scans. The GAN approach is more flexible in terms of extending to other computer vision tasks. On the contrary, traditional monocular depth prediction networks are heavily dependent on pair-wise color-to-depth alignment and LiDAR input. Also, we integrate both visual and structural cues into the feature map representation, which distinguishes our method from those purely operating on LiDAR data, and those who learn depth from a monocular image but still perform detection on the pseudo LiDAR data (ignoring visual information). Our system can be used to add visual intelligence to smart vehicles, which is particularly useful for improving camera-based advanced driver-assistance systems (ADAS) for L3 level autonomy. Also, our system could be used as a supplementary or fall-back option to LiDAR sensors. In the future, we plan to include spatiotemporal data to improve both depth prediction (*e.g.* optical flow) and object detection (*e.g.* YOLO4D [8]).

References

1. Complex yolo with uncertainty. https://github.com/wl5/complex_yolo_3d
2. pykitti open source utility library. https://github.com/utiasSTARS/pykitti
3. Abadi, M., et al.: TensorFlow: a system for large-scale machine learning. In: USENIX Symposium, pp. 265–283 (2016)
4. Ali, W., Abdelkarim, S., Zidan, M., Zahran, M., Sallab, A.E.: YOLO3D: end-to-end real-time 3D oriented object bounding box detection from LiDAR point cloud. In: Leal-Taixé, L., Roth, S. (eds.) ECCV 2018. LNCS, vol. 11131, pp. 716–728. Springer, Cham (2019). https://doi.org/10.1007/978-3-030-11015-4_54
5. Blum, A., Mitchell, T.: Combining labeled and unlabeled data with co-training. In: Proceedings Annual Conference on Computational Learning Theory, pp. 92–100. ACM (1998)
6. Chen, X., Ma, H., Wan, J., Li, B., Xia, T.: Multi-view 3D object detection network for autonomous driving. In: CVPR, pp. 1907–1915 (2017)
7. Eitel, A., Springenberg, J.T., Spinello, L., Riedmiller, M., Burgard, W.: Multimodal deep learning for robust RGB-D object recognition. In: IROS, pp. 681–687. IEEE (2015)
8. El Sallab, A., Sobh, I., Zidan, M., Zahran, M., Abdelkarim, S.: YOLO4D: a spatio-temporal approach for real-time multi-object detection and classification from LiDAR point clouds (2018)
9. Everingham, M., Van Gool, L., Williams, C.K., Winn, J., Zisserman, A.: The PASCAL visual object classes (VOC) challenge. IJCV **88**(2), 303–338 (2010)
10. Geiger, A., Lenz, P., Stiller, C., Urtasun, R.: Vision meets robotics: the KITTI dataset. IJRR **32**(11), 1231–1237 (2013)
11. Godard, C., Mac Aodha, O., Brostow, G.J.: Unsupervised monocular depth estimation with left-right consistency. In: CVPR, vol. 2, p. 7 (2017)
12. Goodfellow, I., et al.: Generative adversarial nets. In: NIPS, pp. 2672–2680 (2014)
13. Gupta, S., Girshick, R., Arbeláez, P., Malik, J.: Learning rich features from RGB-D images for object detection and segmentation. In: Fleet, D., Pajdla, T., Schiele, B., Tuytelaars, T. (eds.) ECCV 2014. LNCS, vol. 8695, pp. 345–360. Springer, Cham (2014). https://doi.org/10.1007/978-3-319-10584-0_23

14. He, D., et al.: Dual learning for machine translation. In: NIPS, pp. 820–828 (2016)
15. Hertzmann, A., Jacobs, C.E., Oliver, N., Curless, B., Salesin, D.H.: Image analogies. In: Conference on Computer Graphics and Interactive Techniques. ACM (2001)
16. Isola, P., Zhu, J.Y., Zhou, T., Efros, A.A.: Image-to-image translation with conditional adversarial networks. arXiv preprint (2017)
17. Lenz, I., Lee, H., Saxena, A.: Deep learning for detecting robotic grasps. IJRR **34**(4–5), 705–724 (2015)
18. Liang, M., Yang, B., Wang, S., Urtasun, R.: Deep continuous fusion for multi-sensor 3D object detection. In: Ferrari, V., Hebert, M., Sminchisescu, C., Weiss, Y. (eds.) ECCV 2018. LNCS, vol. 11220, pp. 663–678. Springer, Cham (2018). https://doi.org/10.1007/978-3-030-01270-0_39
19. Mal, F., Karaman, S.: Sparse-to-dense: depth prediction from sparse depth samples and a single image. In: ICRA, pp. 1–8. IEEE (2018)
20. Montemerlo, M., et al.: Junior: the stanford entry in the urban challenge. J. Field Robot. **25**(9), 569–597 (2008)
21. Qi, C.R., Liu, W., Wu, C., Su, H., Guibas, L.J.: Frustum PointNets for 3D object detection from RGB-D data. In: CVPR, pp. 918–927 (2018)
22. Redmon, J., Farhadi, A.: YOLO9000: better, faster, stronger. In: CVPR, pp. 7263–7271 (2017)
23. Ren, S., He, K., Girshick, R., Sun, J.: Faster R-CNN: towards real-time object detection with region proposal networks. In: NIPS, pp. 91–99 (2015)
24. Simon, M., Milz, S., Amende, K., Gross, H.-M.: Complex-YOLO: an Euler-region-proposal for real-time 3D object detection on point clouds. In: Leal-Taixé, L., Roth, S. (eds.) ECCV 2018. LNCS, vol. 11129, pp. 197–209. Springer, Cham (2019). https://doi.org/10.1007/978-3-030-11009-3_11
25. Socher, R., Huval, B., Bath, B., Manning, C.D., Ng, A.Y.: Convolutional-recursive deep learning for 3D object classification. In: NIPS, pp. 656–664 (2012)
26. Song, S., Lichtenberg, S.P., Xiao, J.: SUN RGB-D: a RGB-D scene understanding benchmark suite. In: CVPR, vol. 5, p. 6 (2015)
27. Wang, Y., Chao, W.L., Garg, D., Hariharan, B., Campbell, M., Weinberger, K.: Pseudo-LiDAR from visual depth estimation: bridging the gap in 3D object detection for autonomous driving. arXiv preprint arXiv:1812.07179 (2018)
28. Zhou, T., Krahenbuhl, P., Aubry, M., Huang, Q., Efros, A.A.: Learning dense correspondence via 3D-guided cycle consistency. In: CVPR, pp. 117–126 (2016)
29. Zhu, J.Y., Park, T., Isola, P., Efros, A.A.: Unpaired image-to-image translation using cycle-consistent adversarial networks. In: ICCV (2017)

Skin Identification Using Deep Convolutional Neural Network

Mahdi Maktab Dar Oghaz[1(✉)], Vasileios Argyriou[1], Dorothy Monekosso[2], and Paolo Remagnino[1]

[1] Kingston University London, London, UK
{m.maktabdaroghaz,vasileios.argyriou,p.remagnino}@kingston.ac.uk
[2] Leeds Beckett University, Leeds, UK
d.n.monekosso@leedsbeckett.ac.uk

Abstract. Skin identification can be used in several security applications such as border's security checkpoints and facial recognition in biometric systems. Traditional skin identification techniques were unable to deal with the high complexity and uncertainty of human skin in uncontrolled environments. To address this gap, this research proposes a new skin identification technique using deep convolutional neural network. The proposed sequential deep model consists of three blocks of convolutional layers, followed by a series of fully connected layers, optimized to maximize skin texture classification accuracy. The proposed model performance has been compared with some of the well-known texture-based skin identification techniques and delivered superior results in terms of overall accuracy. The experiments were carried out over two datasets including FSD Benchmark dataset as well as an in-house skin texture patch dataset. Results show that the proposed deep skin identification model with highest reported accuracy of 0.932 and minimum loss of 0.224 delivers reliable and robust skin identification.

Keywords: Skin texture analysis · Convolutional Neural Networks · Deep learning · Segmentation

1 Introduction

Traditionally, skin identification approaches used color information to discriminate between skin and non-skin regions. Due to the high amount of overlap between skin and non-skin color clusters, color information solely is not capable to effectively classify between skin and non-skin image segments. Another limitation of color-based skin identification techniques is their vulnerability to variations in illumination [2]. Texture based techniques skin identification techniques emerged to address the short comings of color-based techniques by incorporating the spatial properties of pixels with their intensities. Textural features portray the intensities and color deviations that usually originate from the object surface roughness. Unlike color-based techniques which only utilizing the colors of

© Springer Nature Switzerland AG 2019
G. Bebis et al. (Eds.): ISVC 2019, LNCS 11844, pp. 181–193, 2019.
https://doi.org/10.1007/978-3-030-33720-9_14

the individual pixels as discriminant features, texture based approaches utilize the spatial and statistical relations of a group of neighboring pixels to segment image. This allows texture-based skin identifiers to be robust to variations in illumination and improving skin identification in uncontrolled lighting conditions such as border's security checkpoints and facial recognition in bio-metric systems [8].

Numerous texture analysis techniques have been proposed for skin identification and segmentation. These techniques can be categorized into five major groups: statistical, spectral, structural, model-based and deep neural network approaches. Structural texture analysis approaches, interpret skin texture patterns by means of repetitive pattern primitives along with a specific placement rules to identify skin regions. These approaches shine in analysis of predictable and deterministic texture patterns (ordered textures) like man made objects; nevertheless, most of the textural patterns in nature, including human skin, have high levels of randomness and uncertainty and they do not exhibit repetitive and constant texture pattern [7,17].

Spectral texture analysis approaches employ frequency transformations to analyze and identify skin texture patterns, as do structural texture analysis approaches. These perform better in the analysis of deterministic and predictable texture patterns (ordered textures). Fourier transformation, Gabor filters, DCT, autocorrelation and wavelets are some notable examples of spectral skin texture analysis methods [9,15].

Statistical texture analysis approaches analyze the spatial distribution of intensities, by computing local features at each point in the image, and deriving a set of statistics from the distributions of the local features. These approaches, which yield characterizations of textures such as smooth, coarse and grainy, are appropriate for analysis of disordered or weakly ordered textures such as human skin. Grey level co-occurrence matrix (GLCM), local binary patterns (LBP) and histogram of oriented gradients (HOG) are some prominent examples of statistical texture analysis approaches [11,12,19,21].

Model-based texture analysis is basically a mathematical procedure capable of producing and describing a textured image. Models can be used either to describe the observed image texture or to generate synthetic texture according to given parameters. Markov random field and Stochastic and Fractal models are the most prevalent model-based approaches for texture analysis of natural objects [14,18].

Deep learning and in particular Convolutional Neural Network (CNN) are well suited to address computer vision problems such as skin identification. The majority of the classic computer vision techniques have been overshadowed by CNN. Deep learning eliminates the need for domain expertise and hard-core feature extraction, instead a series of consecutive convolution operations between the input image and convolutional filters, form the feature map and extracts the discriminative skin patterns. In recent years several studies [3,5,20,22] attempted to use deep convolutional neural networks for skin identification and segmentation. However their focus were the detection of skin lesion, disorder and cancer only.

In this regard, this research presents a novel deep convolutional neural network model with the aim to identify skin regions in image. The proposed sequential deep model consists of three blocks of convolutional layers, each have two convolutions, two batch normalization and one drop-out layers. Convolutional layers output will be flattened and fed into a block of fully connected layers that aimed to classify skin texture. Our network architecture was devised to decompose the intrinsic textural features of the skin and identify skin texture patterns. Major deep neural network parameters such as learning and decay rate, loss function, optimizer, weight decay rate and drop-out rates have been investigated and optimized empirically to maximize skin identification accuracy. The experiments in this study were carried using two dataset including FSD Benchmark dataset [13] as well as an in-house skin texture dataset. The main contribution of this research is a novel deep convolutional model which optimized for skin identification. The rest of this paper is organized as following: Sect. 2 describes the proposed deep convolutional neural network model, Sect. 3.1 describes the datasets used in this study, Sect. 3.3 presents the evaluation results, analysis and comparison and finally Sect. 4 concludes the findings of this research.

2 Deep Skin Identifier Model

The proposed sequential deep skin identifier model consists of three blocks of convolutional layers followed by a series of dense fully connected layers. The network structure is inspired by the VGG [16] network. However, it was modified to handle finer grades of micro structures that usually exist in skin texture. The input layer takes texture patches at fixed resolution of (128×128) pixels. The model uses all three color channels (Red, Green, Blue) to infer textural features of input patches. Other color spaces such as YC_bC_r and LAB were also being investigated. However, experiments showed there is no correlation between the model performance and the color space. The input texture patches undergo several augmentation operations including horizontal and vertical flip, rotation and shift that significantly increase the number as well as diversity of the inputs patches. Aside from the last dense fully connected layer which uses *Softmax* activation function, all other Convolutional and dense layers feature the *Relu* activation function. All convolutional layers in our model feature a L2 kernel regularizer with fixed weight decay ratio of 0.001 which helps to control overfitting. Each block of convolutional layers includes two batch normalization layers which help to prevent internal covariate shift of gradients. The network also includes three (2×2) Max-pooling layers across three convolutional block layers which helps to resolve higher level textural features from the low level patterns and also reduce the number of parameters in the network. Three dropout layers with respective dropout ratio of 0.3, 0.35 and 0.4 intended to reduce overfitting. Dropout ratios are set empirically. The number of convolutional filters across the network doubles at each block, starting with 32 filter for the first block and

64 and 128 for the second and third block respectively. After convolutional layers, there are three fully connected dense layers with 4096, 1024 and 2 neurons respectively; the first two, include a *relu* activation function and the last layer uses the *softmax* activation function to facilitate texture classification. Categorical cross-entropy (CCE) and binary cross-entropy (BCE) loss functions are investigated and compared. This study also investigates the Stochastic Gradient Descent, RMSprop and ADAM optimizers with learning rate of 0.001, and decay rate of 1e-5. Figure 1 shows the overall deep skin identifier network architecture.

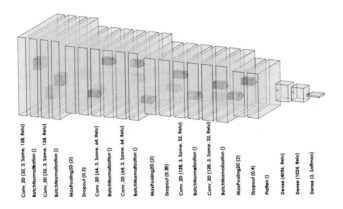

Fig. 1. Network architecture

3   Results and Discussion

3.1   Dataset Setup

The experiments in this study were carried out using two datasets. The first dataset is an in-house 2-class dataset consisting of 1,000 texture patches, 500 of which represent human skin texture were acquired from real world photographic images of over 100 different individuals. The remaining 500 texture patches denote the texture of objects with high degree of color and texture similarity with human skin. This allows us to evaluate the effectiveness and performance of the texture model in challenging scenarios. This study also uses FSD [13], a benchmark face and skin detection dataset, comprising 4000 images of human face and skin regions. FSD images were acquired in uncontrolled lighting conditions and environment which mimics the skin texture patterns in real world images. The positive skin texture class in the FSD dataset taken from the sub blocks fall into skin/face region while the negative non-skin class taken from the complementary background regions. Figure 2 shows some example of FSD and in-house skin texture dataset. Datasets statistics can be observed in Table 1.

Table 1. Datasets statistics

Dataset	Training set		Validation set	
	Skin texture	None-skin texture	Skin texture	None-skin texture
Skin texture dataset	350	350	150	150
FSD dataset	1500	1500	500	500

Fig. 2. Examples of FSD dataset (up) and in-house skin texture dataset (down)

3.2 Experimental Setup

Training and validation datasets were formed by splitting both dataset into two distinct complementary subsets with ratio of 0.3 and 0.25 for skin texture and FSD dataset respectively (refer to Table 1). In order to facilitate skin segmentation in FSD dataset we have devised a block-wised sliding windows approach where detection happens in a block of 128 by 128 pixels which over-sampled from an 8 by 8 sub-block from the original image. To recreate the original image all blocks will be down-sampled to the original image size. This method allows us to perform skin segmentation using a much faster classifier network with minimum loss in accuracy. The proposed model was trained for 100 epochs, with a batch size of 20 images and 35 step per epochs for the texture patch dataset and batch size of 50 images and 60 steps per epochs for FSD dataset. All experiments in this study were carried out on a workstation machine powered by Intel Xeon E5-2623 processors, 128 GB of memory and dual Nvidia GeForce RTX 2080Ti graphics card. Validation accuracy and validation loss were used as the figure of merit in this study.

3.3 Results

Performance of the proposed deep skin identifier model was tested with three popular optimizers: Adam optimizer, RMSProp and Stochastic Gradient Descent (SGD). We have paired each optimizer with both categorical cross-entropy and binary cross-entropy to find the most suitable combination for skin identification. Experiment results of both datasets show that in general, the Adam optimizer and the RMSProp (adaptive optimizers) fall behind the traditional SGD optimizer, regardless of the acquired loss function. Although in theory, adaptive optimizers allow faster convergence of the network but due to overparameterization of the proposed network and dense nature of the texture data, these optimizers failed to perform as expected. Du *et al.* [4] investigate a very similar issue with adaptive optimizers. Our observations show that, due to dense nature of our data, large per-parameter learning rate in adaptive optimizers behave similar to a large global learning rate which causes the model to stops learning and acquiring new additional knowledge entirely. This issue is more pronounced for highly isolated and dense skin texture patch dataset. Table 2 summarizes the optimal accuracy and loss in both texture patch and FSD dataset, show the superiority of SGD over two other optimizers across both the skin texture patch and the FSD dataset. The highest observed accuracy of 0.932 and minimum loss of 0.224 was achieved with the SGD optimizer and CCE loss function.

Table 2. Optimal validation accuracy and loss of the proposed deep skin texture model across various optimizers and loss function using skin texture patch and FSD dataset

		Categorical cross entropy		Binary cross entropy	
		Acc	Loss	Acc	Loss
Texture patch dataset	SGD	**0.932**	**0.224**	0.900	0.241
	RMSProp	0.772	0.311	0.768	0.334
	Adam	0.725	0.354	0.718	0.362
FSD dataset	SGD	0.875	0.292	0.862	0.288
	RMSProp	0.764	0.329	0.755	0.349
	Adam	0.709	0.375	0.689	0.370

In terms of loss, both categorical cross entropy and binary cross entropy showed similar performance in the experiments. However, with the texture patch dataset, categorical cross entropy seems to marginally outperform binary cross entropy. This is mainly due to a softmax function applied to the last fully connected layer. A sigmoid function in the last fully connected layer can probably work in favor of the binary cross entropy. Figure 3 illustrates the average loss per epoch using texture patch and FSD datasets respectively. Results show a very similar Trend across both datasets. However, the proposed network performed relatively better on texture patch dataset regardless of the loss function used. We believe this might be due to extremely diverse contents in the FSD dataset which challenge convergence.

In terms of accuracy, the proposed model has similar behavior to what we have observed with the loss measures. In the FSD dataset, both loss functions performed nearly indistinguishably. However, categorical cross entropy outperformed binary cross entropy in the texture patch dataset. Figure 4 illustrates the average accuracy per epoch of the proposed model using texture the patch and the FSD datasets respectively. In general, the accuracy and loss curves across both datasets indicate the model learns and acquires knowledge across epochs. The proposed model achieved highest accuracy of 0.932 and minimum loss of 0.224 using stochastic gradient descent optimizer with learning rate of 0.001 and decay rate of 1e-5 paired with categorical cross entropy loss function.

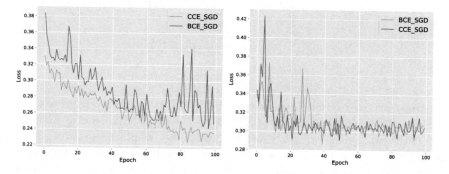

Fig. 3. The average loss per epoch of BCE and CCE loss functions using texture patch dataset

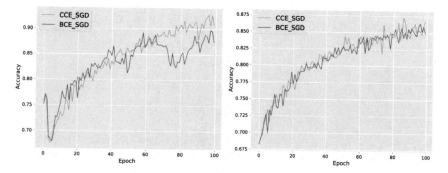

Fig. 4. The average accuracy per epoch of BCE and CCE loss functions using texture patch dataset

3.4   Comparison

The proposed deep skin identifier model performance has been compared with some of the well-known classic texture analysis techniques, including Fourier Power Spectrum, Gray Level Co-occurrence Matrix, Multi-Block Local Binary Patterns, Gabor Filters, Discrete Cosine Transform and delivered superior results in terms of overall accuracy. Both FSD and texture patch datasets have been used to conduct this comparison. The classic texture-based skin identifiers have been trained through 10-fold stratified cross validation using the SVM classifier.

The Fourier Power Spectrum decomposes an image into the sum of complex exponential functions of varying magnitudes, frequencies and phases. The Discrete Fourier transform (DFT) is the sampled Fourier Transform and therefore does not contain all frequencies forming an image, but only a set of samples which is large enough to fully describe the spatial domain image. For a square image of size $N * N$, the two-dimensional DFT is given by Eq. (1):

$$F(K, I) = \sum_{i=0}^{N-1} \sum_{i=0}^{N-1} f(i, j) e^{-i2\pi(\frac{Ki}{N} + \frac{Ij}{N})} \tag{1}$$

where $f(i, j)$ is the image in the spatial domain and the exponential term is the basis function corresponding to each point $F(K, I)$ in the Fourier space. The value of each point $F(K, I)$ is obtained by multiplying the spatial image with the corresponding base function and summing the result. The power spectrum of Fourier transform represents the frequency and direction of the pattern. The strength of each spatial frequency can be obtained by computing the complex modulus (magnitude) of the Fourier transform as shown in Eq. (2):

$$P(K, I) = |F(K, I)|^2 \tag{2}$$

In polar coordinates, the distributions of the power spectrum $P(r, e)$ can be represented as Eqs. (3) and (4):

$$P(r) = 2 \sum_{\theta=0}^{\pi} P(r, \theta) \tag{3}$$

$$P(\theta) = \sum_{r=0}^{\pi/2} P(r, \theta) \tag{4}$$

where $P(r)$ and $P(\theta)$ are the sum of the powers in ring and sector regions of the power spectrum space, respectively. The peak in $P(r)$ indicates the size of the dominant texture elements or the texture coarseness. The peak in $P(\theta)$ indicates the texture direction. Power spectrum analysis is useful to identify textures which have regular wave patterns with a constant interval. The radial distribution of energy in the power spectrum reflects the coarseness of the texture, and the angular distribution relates to the direction. Various texture features can be derived from the distribution of energy in the Fourier power spectrum. The Fourier power spectrum is partitioned into circular rings and sectors to measure the energy present in these segments. The ring energy band distribution shown in Eq. (5) can be used to assess the coarseness of a texture, whereas the sector energy distribution shown in Eq. (6) describes its direction. To construct the feature vector from the energy spectrum, we measured the integral of the energy spectrum for five annular logarithmically decreasing frequency bands and eight sectors with offset of $45°$ (0, 45, 90, 135, 180, 225, 270 and 315), which generates a feature vector of 40 features, each representing a specific frequency band.

GLCM characterizes the texture of an image by calculating how often pairs of pixels with specific values and in a specified spatial relationship co-occur in an image. The number of gray levels (quantization level) is one of the most important parameters in the GLCM. Having more gray levels roughly provides more information about the textural features of a region; however, this might increase the noise frequency and slows down the texture analysis process exponentially. The displacement magnitude and direction of the co-occurring pixels provide another important parameter in the GLCM. Coarse surfaces require relatively large displacement magnitudes, while fine surfaces demand smaller displacement magnitudes. The choice of displacement direction is very dependent on the orientation of the surface textures. Several numeric features and statistics such as Entropy, Energy, Contrast, Correlation and Homogeneity can be derived from the co-occurrence matrix. These statistical features initiate the feature vector of the GLCM in our comparison. This study employs optimized GLCM skin texture parameter used by [10].

Multi-Block Local Binary Pattern (MB-LBP) is a variant of LBP which applies LBP operations to blocks of pixels instead of a single pixel and uses the block mean value for its computations. This study employed three different block sizes, $3 * 3$, $5 * 5$ and $7 * 7$, to construct the MB-LBP array and generate the histogram and feature vector.

Gabor filters decompose the input skin texture patch into feature maps using a bank of filters. These feature maps then form a feature vector which is used for skin texture classification and segmentation. Gabor filters use local Fourier analysis to generate sine and cosine functions modulated by a Gaussian window. Gabor filters are defined in Eq. (5):

$$G_{x,y} = exp(\frac{-(x\cos\theta + y\sin\theta)^2 + \gamma^2(-x\sin\theta + y\cos\theta)^2}{2\sigma^2})*$$
$$cos(2\pi\frac{1}{\lambda}(x\cos\theta + y\sin\theta) + \phi) \qquad (5)$$

where x and y represent the spatial coordinates, λ is the wavelength of the cosine, θ is the orientation of the Gabor filter, ϕ is the phase offset, σ is the Gaussian blur factor and γ is the spatial aspect ratio. Choice of the appropriate filter parameters is a complex problem, which has been analyzed in many publications. This study employs a similar Gabor filter parameter to that used by Han and Lee [6] to identify skin texture frequencies. The Gabor transform of an image $R_{x,y}$ is defined as the convolution of a Gabor filter $G_{x,y}$ with image $I_{x,y}$ as shown in Eq. (6):

$$R_{x,y} = G_{x,y} * I_{x,y} = \sum_{m=0}^{M-1}\sum_{n=0}^{N-1} g(m,n) \cdot I(x-m, y-m) \qquad (6)$$

where $\cdot$ indicates two-dimensional linear convolution and M and N are the sizes of the Gabor filters. The local texture energy of the filtered image can be obtained by computing the absolute average deviation of the transformed values of the filtered image from the mean μ within a window W of size M_x, M_y. Thus, the filtered images have zero mean. The texture energy $E_{x,y}$ can be measured through Eq. (7):

$$E_{x,y} = \frac{1}{M} \sum_{(a,b) \in W} |R(a,b) - \mu| \tag{7}$$

The histogram of these local energy maps of the filtered image will be used to construct the feature vector.

DCT decomposes an image as a sum of sinusoids of varying magnitudes and frequencies which have different importance with respect to the visual quality of the image. For a typical image, most of the visually significant information about the image is concentrated in just a few coefficients of the DCT. For this reason, the DCT is often used in image compression. The DCT coefficients of an image are able to represent the regularity, complexity and some textural features of an image. Given an image $F(x,y)$ and block size of $N * N$, the corresponding two dimensional DCT coefficients are defined in Eq. (8):

$$C(u,v) = \frac{1}{4} C_v C_u \sum_{x=0}^{N-1} \sum_{y=0}^{N-1} F(x,y) \cos[\frac{(2x+1)u\pi}{2N}] \cos[\frac{(2y+1)v\pi}{2N}] \tag{8}$$

$$C_u = \begin{cases} \frac{1}{\sqrt{2}} & if \ u = 0 \\ 1 & else \end{cases} \tag{9}$$

$$C_v = \begin{cases} \frac{1}{\sqrt{2}} & if \ v = 0 \\ 1 & else \end{cases} \tag{10}$$

In order to represent the textural features of the human skin in form of DCT coefficients, the input skin texture patch is divided into blocks of 8 by 8 pixels and two-dimensional DCT is measured for each block. This study adopts the feature vector extraction technique of [1] where a feature vector of nine features was measured for each DCT coefficient. These features include the DC coefficient of each block which represents the average energy of the block, the coefficients groups representing frequency band characteristic and the coefficients groups representing spatial characteristics such as vertical, horizontal and diagonal patterns. Each feature is computed from the summation of the each group coefficients. Table 3 summarizes the comparison results in terms of accuracy. The comparison results in FSD dataset shows that Multi-Block Local Binary Patterns with reported accuracy of 0.893 marginally outperformed the proposed model with accuracy of 0.875. On skin texture patch dataset the proposed deep skin identifier model with accuracy of 0.932 outperformed all other texture-based algorithms in this comparison and achieved highest reported accuracy.

Table 3. Comparison of the proposed deep skin identifier model with classic texture-based techniques in terms of average accuracy

	FSD dataset	Texture patch dataset
Fourier Power Spectrum	0.741	0.783
Gabor Filters	0.796	0.831
Gray Level Co-occurrence Matrix	0.829	0.848
Multi-Block Local Binary Patterns	0.893	0.926
Discrete Cosine Transform	0.810	0.822
Proposed deep texture model	**0.875**	**0.932**

4   Conclusion

To address the shortcoming of classic texture-based skin identifiers, this research proposes a new skin identification model using deep convolutional neural networks. The proposed sequential deep model consists of three blocks of convolutional layers, followed by a series of fully connected layers, optimized to maximize the skin identification accuracy. The experiments were carried out over two datasets: FSD Benchmark dataset as well as an in-house skin texture dataset. The proposed deep skin identifier model performance was compared with classic texture-based techniques, including Fourier Power Spectrum, Gabor Filters, Gray Level Co-occurrence Matrix, Multi-Block Local Binary Patterns and Discrete Cosine Transform and delivered superior results in terms of overall accuracy. Results show that the proposed deep skin identifier delivers highest accuracy of 0.932 and minimum loss of 0.224 and outperformed existing texture-based methods.

Acknowledgments. This research is supported by the MIDAS project (agreement G5381), under the NATO Science for Peace and Security Programme. The Titan X Pascal GPU used for this research was donated by NVIDIA.

References

1. Bae, H.J., Jung, S.H.: Image retrieval using texture based on DCT. In: Proceedings of 1997 International Conference on Information, Communications and Signal Processing, ICICS 1997, vol. 2, pp. 1065–1068. IEEE (1997)
2. Bargo, P.R., Kollias, N.: Measurement of skin texture through polarization imaging. Br. J. Dermatol. **162**(4), 724–731 (2010)
3. Chaichulee, S., et al.: Multi-task convolutional neural network for patient detection and skin segmentation in continuous non-contact vital sign monitoring. In: 2017 12th IEEE International Conference on Automatic Face & Gesture Recognition (FG 2017), pp. 266–272. IEEE (2017)
4. Du, S.S., Zhai, X., Poczos, B., Singh, A.: Gradient descent provably optimizes over-parameterized neural networks. arXiv preprint arXiv:1810.02054 (2018)

5. Esteva, A., et al.: Dermatologist-level classification of skin cancer with deep neural networks. Nature **542**(7639), 115 (2017)
6. Han, W.Y., Lee, J.C.: Palm vein recognition using adaptive Gabor filter. Expert Syst. Appl. **39**(18), 13225–13234 (2012)
7. Haralick, R.M.: Statistical and structural approaches to texture. Proc. IEEE **67**(5), 786–804 (1979)
8. Lloyd, K., Marshall, D., Moore, S.C., Rosin, P.L.: Detecting violent crowds using temporal analysis of GLCM texture. arXiv preprint arXiv 1605 (2016)
9. Mahmoud, M.K.A., Al-Jumaily, A.: A hybrid system for skin lesion detection: based on Gabor wavelet and support vector machine. In: Information Technology: Proceedings of the 2014 International Symposium on Information Technology (ISIT 2014), Dalian, China, 14–16 October 2014, p. 39. CRC Press (2015)
10. Oghaz, M.M., Maarof, M.A., Rohani, M.F., Zainal, A., Shaid, S.Z.M.: An optimized skin texture model using gray-level co-occurrence matrix. Neural Comput. Appl. **31**(6), 1835–1853 (2019)
11. Oghaz, M.M., Maarof, M.A., Zainal, A., Rohani, M.F., Yaghoubyan, S.H.: A hybrid color space for skin detection using genetic algorithm heuristic search and principal component analysis technique. PLoS ONE **10**(8), e0134828 (2015)
12. Pang, H., Chen, T., Wang, X., Chang, Z., Shao, S., Zhao, J.: Quantitative evaluation methods of skin condition based on texture feature parameters. Saudi J. Biol. Sci. **24**(3), 514–518 (2017)
13. Phung, S.L., Bouzerdoum, A., Chai, D.: Skin segmentation using color pixel classification: analysis and comparison. IEEE Trans. Pattern Anal. Mach. Intell. **27**(1), 148–154 (2005)
14. Raupov, D.S., Myakinin, O.O., Bratchenko, I.A., Zakharov, V.P., Khramov, A.G.: Skin cancer texture analysis of OCT images based on Haralick, fractal dimension, Markov random field features, and the complex directional field features. In: Optics in Health Care and Biomedical Optics VII, vol. 10024, p. 100244I. International Society for Optics and Photonics (2016)
15. Rubel, A., Lukin, V., Uss, M., Vozel, B., Pogrebnyak, O., Egiazarian, K.: Efficiency of texture image enhancement by DCT-based filtering. Neurocomputing **175**, 948–965 (2016)
16. Simonyan, K., Zisserman, A.: Very deep convolutional networks for large-scale image recognition. arXiv preprint arXiv:1409.1556 (2014)
17. Sun, Y., Tistarelli, M., Maltoni, D.: Structural similarity based image quality map for face recognition across plastic surgery. In: 2013 IEEE Sixth International Conference on Biometrics: Theory, Applications and Systems (BTAS), pp. 1–8. IEEE (2013)
18. Torkashvand, F., Fartash, M.: Automatic segmentation of skin lesion using Markov random field. Can. J. Basic Appl. Sci. **3**(3), 93–107 (2015)
19. Yaghoubyan, S.H., Maarof, M.A., Zainal, A., Foâ, M., Oghaz, M.M., et al.: Fast and effective bag-of-visual-word model to pornographic images recognition using the freak descriptor. J. Soft Comput. Decis. Support Syst. **2**(6), 27–33 (2015)
20. Yuan, Y., Chao, M., Lo, Y.C.: Automatic skin lesion segmentation using deep fully convolutional networks with jaccard distance. IEEE Trans. Med. Imaging **36**(9), 1876–1886 (2017)

21. Zhang, X., Weng, C., Yu, B., Li, H.: In-vivo differentiation of photo-aged epidermis skin by texture-based classification. In: Optics in Health Care and Biomedical Optics VI, vol. 9268, p. 92682G. International Society for Optics and Photonics (2014)
22. Zuo, H., Fan, H., Blasch, E., Ling, H.: Combining convolutional and recurrent neural networks for human skin detection. IEEE Signal Process. Lett. **24**(3), 289–293 (2017)

Resolution-Independent Meshes
of Superpixels

Vitaliy Kurlin$^{(\boxtimes)}$ and Philip Smith

Department of Computer Science, University of Liverpool, Liverpool, UK
`vitaliy.kurlin@gmail.com`

Abstract. The over-segmentation into superpixels is an important pre-processing step to smartly compress the input size and speed up higher level tasks. A superpixel was traditionally considered as a small cluster of square-based pixels that have similar color intensities and are closely located to each other. In this discrete model the boundaries of superpixels often have irregular zigzags consisting of horizontal or vertical edges from a given pixel grid. However digital images represent a continuous world, hence the following continuous model in the resolution-independent formulation can be more suitable for the reconstruction problem.

Instead of uniting squares in a grid, a resolution-independent superpixel is defined as a polygon that has straight edges with any possible slope at subpixel resolution. The harder continuous version of the over-segmentation problem is to split an image into polygons and find a best (say, constant) color of each polygon so that the resulting colored mesh well approximates the given image. Such a mesh of polygons can be rendered at any higher resolution with all edges kept straight.

We propose a fast conversion of any traditional superpixels into polygons and guarantees that their straight edges do not intersect. The meshes based on the superpixels SEEDS (Superpixels Extracted via Energy-Driven Sampling) and SLIC (Simple Linear Iterative Clustering) are compared with past meshes based on the Line Segment Detector. The experiments on the Berkeley Segmentation Database confirm that the new superpixels have more compact shapes than pixel-based superpixels.

1 Introduction

1.1 Over-Segmentation for Low-Level Vision

The important problem in low-level vision is to quickly detect key structures such as corners and edges where color intensities substantially change. The over-segmentation problem is to split an image into *superpixels*, which are small patches of square-based pixels having similar colors and positions.

Electronic supplementary material The online version of this chapter (https://doi.org/10.1007/978-3-030-33720-9_15) contains supplementary material, which is available to authorized users.

G. Bebis et al. (Eds.): ISVC 2019, LNCS 11844, pp. 194–205, 2019.
https://doi.org/10.1007/978-3-030-33720-9_15

Traditional superpixels often have irregular shapes with zigzag boundaries of only horizontal or vertical short edges. This rigid discretization can be avoided if we allow edges of any length and direction, because continuous objects are much better represented by polygons not restricted to a given pixel grid.

The color intensity in real images always changes gradually over 2–3 pixels without jumps, see [18, Fig. 1]. Hence an edge between different objects can be inside a square pixel, not along its sides. These hurdles disappear if we look for *continuous objects* represented by pixel values discretely sample on a grid.

Fig. 1. SLIC superpixels (left) with zigzag boundaries of pixel-based superpixels are converted into a resolution-independent mesh (right) of polygons with straight edges that can be rendered at any higher resolution for better and smoother animations.

1.2 Resolution-Independent Polygonal Superpixels

Digital images represent a continuous world around us, but are restricted to a fixed pixel grid. We consider the over-segmentation problem in the following *resolution-independent* formulation introduced by Viola et al. [18].
We split an image into a fixed number of possibly non-convex polygons so that

- all polygons have straight edges and vertices with any real coordinates (not restricted to a given pixel grid, so independent of an initial image resolution);
- the resulting colored mesh (with a best constant color over each polygon) approximates the original image, e.g. by minimizing an energy in Sect. 4.

Such a polygonal mesh can be rendered at any higher resolution and is called *resolution-independent*. In general, a *mesh* for a rectangular image $I \subset \mathbb{R}^2$ is a graph $G \subset \mathbb{R}^2$ that contains the boundary of I and consists of non-intersecting line segments that split I into possibly non-convex polygons. Figure 2 shows long thin superpixels for the tripod legs in the famous cameraman image.

1.3 Key Contributions to the State-of-the-Art for Superpixels

- We solve the over-segmentation problem for polygonal *resolution-independent* superpixels that have few straight edges with infinitely many possible slopes.

- The algorithm RIMe in Sect. 3 can convert any pixel-based superpixels into a resolution-independent mesh with quality guarantees in Theorem 3.
- The experiments in Sect. 4 confirm that the resolution-independent meshes based on SEEDS and SLIC superpixels, achieve better results on objective measures, perform similarly to SEEDS and SLIC on the BSD benchmarks.
- RIMe beats all other resolution-independent superpixels on the objective reconstruction error and benchmarks of the Berkeley Segmentation Database [2].

Fig. 2. The pixel-based superpixels on the left (SEEDS and SLIC) have irregular zigzag boundaries, which are straightened by the algorithm RIMe on the right.

2   Review of the Past Work on Superpixels

We review the widely used algorithms for pixel-based and resolution-independent superpixels for the harder reconstruction problem of continuous real-life objects.

2.1   Pixel-Based Superpixel Algorithms

The first successful algorithms were based on the graph of the 4-connected pixel grid [5, 11, 16]. The *Lattice Cut* algorithm by Moore et al. [15] guarantees that the final mesh of superpixels is regular as the original grid of pixels. The best quality in this category is achieved by Entropy Rate Superpixels (ERS) of Lie et al. [13] minimizing the entropy rate of a random walk on a graph. Based on *Compact Superpixels* by Veksler and Boykov [17], the fastest algorithm is by Zhang et al. [20] processing an average image from BSD500 in 0.5 s. Our experiments will use the algorithms SEEDS, SLIC from OpenCV, VLFeat libraries.

The *Simple Linear Iterative Clustering* (SLIC) algorithm by Achanta et al. [1] forms superpixels by k-means clustering in a 5-dimensional space using 3 colors and 2 coordinates per pixel. Because the search is restricted to a neighborhood of a given size, the complexity is $O(kmn)$, where n and m are the numbers of pixels and iterations. The later *Linear Spectral Clustering* (LSC) by Li et al. [12] is based on a weighted k-means clustering in a 10-dimensional space. The SMURF algorithm by Luengo et al. [14] obtains superpixels in a parallelized way within larger super-regions and alternates split/merge steps at several levels.

SEEDS (Superpixels Extracted via Energy-Driven Sampling) by Van den Bergh et al. [3] seems the first superpixel algorithm to use a *coarse-to-fine opti-mization* that progressively refines superpixels. At the initial coarse level, each superpixel consists of large rectangular blocks of pixels. At the next level, all blocks are subdivided into four rectangles and any boundary block can move to an adjacent superpixel, an so on until all blocks become pixels. SEEDS puts the colors of all pixels within each fixed superpixel are put in bins (five for each color channel) and iteratively maximizes the sum of deviations of all bins from an average bin within every superpixel. The color deviation is maximal for a superpixel whose pixels have colors in one bin.

The similar Coarse-to-Fine (CtF) algorithm by Yao et al. [19] minimizes the discrete Reconstruction Error from Sect. 4. The recent improvement of this Coarse-to-Fine approach [9] allows the user to make shapes of superpixels more round by giving more weight to an isoperimetric quotient.

2.2   Edge Detection at Subpixel Resolution

Both past algorithms for resolution-independent superpixels (Voronoi and CCM: Convex Constrained Meshes) are based on the Line Segment Detector algorithm (LSDA), which outputs line segments at subpixel resolution [8]. The parameters are a tolerance τ for angles between gradients and a threshold ϵ for false alarms. For the values $\tau = 22.5°$, $\epsilon = 1$ and the random model of a uniformly distributed gradient field, the LSDA outputs on average at most one false positive.

The LSDA edges have endpoints and gradients with any real coordinates, but the use has no control over a number of line segments in the output. The recent persistence-based line segment detector [10] guarantees edges without intersections and small angles.

2.3   Resolution-Independent Polygonal Superpixels

The *Voronoi superpixels* by Duan and Lafarge [4] split an image into polygons not restricted to a pixel grid. For points $p_1, \ldots, p_k$ (called *centers*), the *Voronoi cell* $V(p_i)$ is the polygonal neighborhood of the center p_i consisting of all points closer (in the Euclidean distance) to p_i than to other centers. These centers are chosen on both sides of each LSDA edge so that all LSDA edges are covered by the boundaries of Voronoi cells, though no guarantees were proved. The main advantage of Voronoi superpixels is their almost "round" shape, see Sect. 4.

The CCM superpixels (Convex Constrained Meshes) by Forsythe et al. [6] directly include LSDA edges as hard constraints, which improves the Boundary Recall, see Sect. 4. After post-processing LSDA edges to get a straight line graph without self-intersections, this graph is converted into a full mesh of convex polygons that are guaranteed to have no angles smaller than $20°$. The boundaries of CCM superpixels are always in a small offset of LSDA edges.

Both Voronoi and CCM superpixels crucially depend on the quality of LSDA, which may not output a desired number of strongest edges. Pixel-based superpixels are better optimised for the Boundary Recall. The goal of the paper is to transfer this advantage to new resolution-independent superpixels.

3   RIMe: A Resolution-Independent Mesh of Polygons

3.1   RIMe Algorithm: Pipeline, Input, Parameters and Output

The algorithm RIMe converts any pixel-based superpixels into a mesh of polygons whose straight edges approximate boundaries with guarantees in Theorem 3. The *input* is the matrix $s(p)$ of superpixel indices for every pixel $p = (i, j)$.

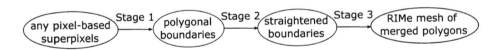

Fig. 3. Pipeline of the RIMe algorithm through 3 stages in Subsect. 3.2.

RIMe essentially uses the OpenMesh library and saves the final mesh to a .off file. One can find the most optimal color for every polygon and output the colored mesh as a small representation for further processing, see Sect. 4.

3.2   Conversion Algorithm RIMe Step-by-Step

Stage 1: Convert any traditional superpixels into a proper pixel-based mesh by extracting polygonal boundaries of any given pixel-based superpixels. All past algorithms output a matrix $s(p)$ of superpixel labels (integer indices) over all pixels p. Unfortunately, the union of pixels having the same label s is often

disconnected (as a subset in the 4-connected or 8-connected grid). Even if connected, one superpixel can be surrounded by another superpixel (in this case the surrounding superpixel can be better split into two smaller superpixels). We convert any output into a mesh whose polygons are connected unions of pixels.
Step 1.1. Starting from an initial position at a corner of an image, we follow the boundary of a current polygon within the pixel grid and check at every pixel corner whether we should turn left/right or go forward as shown in Fig. 4.

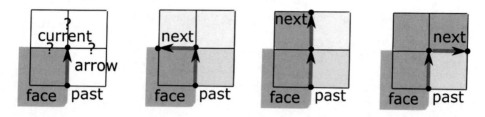

Fig. 4. Choosing the next point at a corner (colors indicate different superpixels).

Step 1.2. When we meet a new superpixel, we save an initial arrow (a directed edge between pixels) to make sure that we later go around the new superpixel.
Step 1.3. After we have returned to the initial position, a closed boundary of a superpixel was traced and we check if there are any unexplored superpixels.
Step 1.4. Check that all found superpixels have the expected areas, otherwise we find more connected components by looking at unexplored boundary pixels from the matrix of superpixel labels, so the number of superpixels can increase.
Step 1.5. If a found polygon still does not have the expected area, it must surround another polygon. We add a straight edge (say, D_1) between two closest vertices on the boundaries of the superpixels to split the surrounding superpixel into two. This edge D_1 cannot intersect another edge (say, D_2), which would contradict Lemma 1 for the quadrangle with the intersecting diagonals D_1, D_2.

Lemma 1. *In any convex quadrilateral with all sides longer than the shortest diagonal, the longest diagonal is longer than any side.*

Proof. Triangle inequality implies that the sum of the two diagonals is greater than the sum of either pair of opposite sides. Assuming that the shortest diagonal is shorter than any side, the longest diagonal should be longer than any side. $\square$

Stage 2: Straighten all boundaries of a mesh from Stage 1. The key advantage of RIMe is the possibility to *run Stage 2 in parallel* for different pairs of polygons.
Step 2.1: Find the edge chain (a sequence of successive non-boundary edges) between any two adjacent polygons.
Step 2.2: Given a chain between vertices A, B, find the maximum Euclidean distance d_C from an intermediate vertex C to the straight line AB, see Fig. 5.

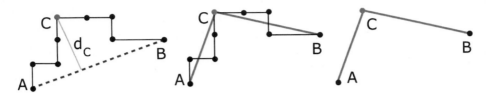

Fig. 5. Straightening polygonal chains of edges recursively in Step 2.3 when d_C is small.

Step 2.3: We replace the whole chain by the segment AB if

(1)   the max distance $d_C < 1$ or $d_C < \dfrac{\text{Color\_Offset}}{\text{Color\_difference}}$,

where Color_difference is the absolute difference between *average intensities* (estimated from pixel-based superpixels in Stage 1) of the polygons F_1, F_2 on both sides of the chain.

Step 2.4: For $d_C \geq 1$, we check that the new potential edge AB does not intersect any existing edges of the polygons F_1, F_2 sharing the chain. We check if AB has angles more than Min_Angle all incident edges in the current mesh.

Step 2.5: If any condition in Steps 2.3–2.4 fails, we recursively straighten the subchains AC, CB as above.

Stage 3: Merge adjacent polygons whose average intensities differ by less than Max_Color_Dif. Many images have uniform backgrounds and superpixels consisting of pixels with the same intensity. Hence merging the resulting polygonal superpixels keeps important edges from a given image.

3.3   Theoretical Guarantees (Proved in Appendices)

We assume that pixel-based superpixels are given with their average intensities, otherwise these averages can be quickly computed for Step 2.3. Apart from these averages, the algorithm RIMe accesses only a smaller number m of *boundary pixels* that have at least one neighboring pixel from a different superpixel.

Proposition 2. *The algorithm RIMe in Sect. 3 has the* linear running time *in the number m of boundary pixels that are not strictly inside one superpixel.*

Let d be the Euclidean distance between points in $\mathbb{R}^2$. The *r-offset* (dilation with a disk of radius r) of any $S \subset \mathbb{R}^2$ is its thickened neighborhood $\{p \in \mathbb{R}^2 : d(p, S) \leq r\}$, where $d(p, S) = \min\{d(p, q) : q \in S\}$ is the distance from p to S.

Theorem 3. *The inequality $d_C < 1$ in (1) implies that*
(3a) for any pixel-based superpixels, the edges of a resolution-independent mesh can meet only at endpoints.
Moreover, the conversion algorithm RIMe guarantees that
(3b) all angles between incident edges in a final resolution-independent mesh are at least Min_Angle,

(3c) any chain of edges between original superpixels with Color_difference *is replaced by a polygonal line within the* $\dfrac{\text{Color\_Offset}}{\text{Color\_difference}}$ *-offset of the original chain.*

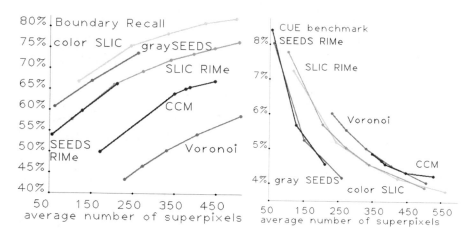

Fig. 6. Boundary Recall (↑ better). Corrected Undersegmentation Error (↓ better).

The value Color_Offset = 30 means that any chain between polygons whose average intensities differ by 10 is straightened within a 3-pixel neighborhood.

4   Experimental Comparison of Six Algorithms on BSD

The *Berkeley Segmentation Database* BSD [2] has 500 images widely used for evaluating segmentation algorithms due to (sometimes imperfect) human-sketched ground truth boundaries. For an image I, let $I = \cup G_j$ be a segmentation into ground truth regions and $I = \cup_{i=1}^{k} S_i$ be an oversegmentation into superpixels produced by an algorithm. Each quality measure below compares the superpixels $S_1, \ldots, S_k$ with the best suitable ground truth for every image from the BSD.

Let $G(I) = \cup G_j$ be the union of ground truth boundary pixels and $B(I)$ be the set of boundary pixels produced by a superpixel algorithm. For a distance ε in pixels, the *Boundary Recall* $BR(\varepsilon)$ is the ratio of ground truth boundary pixels $p \in G(I)$ within 2 pixels from the superpixel boundary $B(I)$.

Van den Bergh et al. [3] suggested the *Corrected Undersegmentation Error*
$$CUE = \frac{1}{k} \sum_i |S_i - G_{max}(S_i)|,$$ where $G_{max}(S_i)$ is the ground truth region having the largest overlap with S_i. The *Achievable Segmentation Accuracy* is $ASA = \frac{1}{k} \sum_i \max_j |S_i \cap G_j|$. If a superpixel S_i is covered by a ground truth region G_j, then $|S_i \cap G_j| = |S_i|$ is the maximum value. Otherwise $\max_j |S_i \cap G_j|$ is the maximum

area of S_i covered by the most overlapping region G_j. If we use superpixels for the higher level task of semantic segmentation, then *ASA* is the upper bound on the number of pixels that are wrongly assigned to final semantic regions. All values of BR, CUE, ASA are in [0,1] and can be measured in percents.

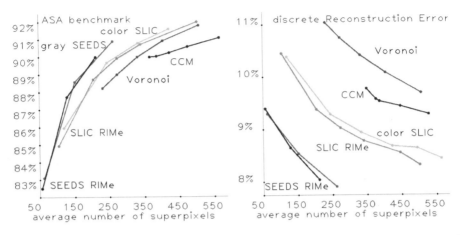

Fig. 7. Achievable Segm. Accuracy (↑ better). Discrete Reconstruction Error (↓ better).

The BSD benchmarks above involve some parameters, *e.g.* the 2-pixel offset for the Boundary Recall, which can be hard to justify. That is why several objective cost functions were proposed in an energy minimization framework. The main energy term for CtF superpixels [19] depends only on pixel intensities as follows and can be called the *discrete Reconstruction Error*:

$$dRE = \sum_{\text{pixels } p} \left|\left|\text{Intensity}_p - \text{average intensity of } S(p)\right|\right|^2, \text{ where}$$

$S(p)$ is the pixel-based superpixel containing a pixel p. For colored images, the intensity can be considered as a vector of 3 colors with any (say, Euclidean) norm. So *dRE objectively measures* how well the colored mesh (with average intensities over all superpixels) approximates the original image over all pixels.

Compactness measures for superpixels were used as regularizers by different authors [17,19]. We propose the simplest version based on the isoperimetric quotient $Q(S) = \dfrac{4\pi \text{ area}(S)}{\text{perimeter}^2(S)}$, which has the maximum value 1 for a round disk S. The *Compactness* is the average $Comp = \sum\limits_{\text{superpixels } S} \dfrac{Q(S)}{\#\text{superpixels}}$.

Here are the parameters of the RIMe superpixels for benchmarking below.

- Color_Offset = 30 is used for straightening in Step 2.3 and controls approximation guarantees in Theorem 3.

- Max_Color_Dif = 2 is the maximum (grayscale) intensity difference for merging adjacent polygons in Stage 3 (larger values will lead to larger superpixels).
- Min_Angle = 30° (can be 0) is the minimum angle between adjacent edges (only to avoid narrow triangles).

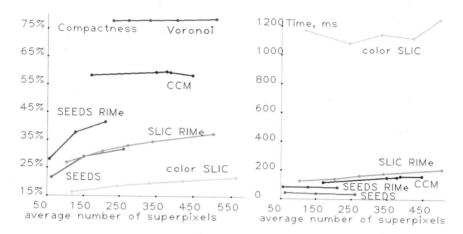

Fig. 8. Compactness (↑ better). Time on 8G RAM 2.6 GHz Intel Core i5 (↓ better).

Figures 6, 7 and 8 show 6 benchmarks for 6 superpixel algorithms. Each dot on the curves corresponds to a single run on 500 images and has the coordinates (average number of superpixels, average benchmark value over BSD).

The SLIC algorithm crucially uses 3 color values (converted to a Lab space) and we marked its curve as color SLIC. We ran SEEDS on grayscale version of BSD images and marked the curve by gray SEEDS, because both Voronoi and CCM algorithms accept only a grayscale input needed for LSDA edges. The corresponding outputs of RIMe are marked by SLIC RIMe, SEEDS RIMe.

The two remaining curves are for Voronoi [4] and CCM meshes [7]. Figure 9 shows that RIMe conversions lead to visually better reconstructions than the only other resolution-independent superpixels on Voronoi and CCM meshes.

5 Conclusions, Applications and Further Problems

Starting from any pixel-based superpixels, the RIMe conversion produces polygonal superpixels with almost the same BSD benchmarks BR, CUE, ASA and the objective error dRE in Figs. 6 and 7. In comparison with any pixel-based superpixels, polygonal superpixels have much fewer edges (no long zigzags in boundaries) with slopes of any potential direction (not only horizontal or vertical).

The RIMe superpixels have twice better compactness (more "round") shapes than their original pixel-based superpixels such as SEEDS and SLIC in Fig. 8.

The RIMe conversions of SLIC, SEEDS outperform other polygonal resolution-independent superpixels (Voronoi and CCM) on BR, CUE, ASA, dRE.

When a resolution of the cameraman image is decreased as in the last figure of supplementary materials, pixel-based superpixels include more and more visible zigzags, while corresponding RIMe superpixels keep nice straight boundaries.

The key advantage of polygonal resolution-independent superpixels is the possibility to render a polygonal mesh at any higher resolution. This up-scaling can convert low resolution photos into high-resolution images. In Computer Graphics, polygonal meshes with few edges can be easily manipulated to improve animations converted from traditional videos by cheap cameras.

The next step is to optimize positions of branched vertices, for example by minimizing an energy containing the exact reconstruction error and compactness.

Acknowledgments. The work has been supported by the EPSRC grant "Application-driven Topological Data Analysis" (2018-2023), EP/R018472/1.

References

1. Achanta, R., Shaji, A., Smith, K., Lucchi, A., Fua, P., Süsstrunk, S.: Slic superpixels compared to state-of-the-art superpixel methods. T-PAMI **34**(11), 2274–2282 (2012)
2. Arbelaez, P., Maire, M., Fowlkes, C., Malik, J.: Contour detection and hierarchical image segmentation. Trans. PAMI **33**, 898–916 (2011)
3. Van de Bergh, M., Boix, X., Roig, G., Van Gool, L.: Seeds: superpixels extracted via energy-driven sampling. Int. J. Comput. Vision **111**, 298–314 (2015)
4. Duan, L., Lafarge, F.: Image partitioning into convex polygons. In: Proceedings of CVPR (Computer Vision and Pattern Recognition), pp. 3119–3127 (2015)
5. Felzenszwalb, P., Huttenlocher, D.: Efficient graph-based image segmentation. Int. J. Comput. Vision **59**, 167–181 (2004)
6. Forsythe, J., Kurlin, V.: Convex constrained meshes for superpixel segmentations of images. J. Electron. Imaging **26**(6), 061609 (2017)
7. Forsythe, J., Kurlin, V., Fitzgibbon, A.: Resolution-independent superpixels based on convex constrained meshes. In: Proceedings of ISVC (2016)
8. Von Gioi, R.G., Jakubowicz, J., Morel, J.M., Randall, G.: LSD: a line segment detector. Image Process. Line **2**, 35–55 (2012)
9. Kurlin, V., Harvey, D.: Superpixels optimized by color and shape. In: Pelillo, M., Hancock, E. (eds.) EMMCVPR 2017. LNCS, vol. 10746, pp. 297–311. Springer, Cham (2018). https://doi.org/10.1007/978-3-319-78199-0_20
10. Kurlin, V., Muszynski, G.: A persistence-based approach to automatic detection of line segments in images. In: Proceedings of CTIC, pp. 137–150 (2019)
11. Levinshtein, A., Stere, A., Kutulakos, K., Fleet, D., Siddiqi, K.: Turbopixels: fast superpixels using geometric flows. Trans. PAMI **31**, 2290–2297 (2009)
12. Li, Z., Chen, J.: Superpixel segmentation using linear spectral clustering. In: Proceedings of CVPR, pp. 1356–1363 (2015)
13. Liu, M.Y., Tuzel, O., Ramalingam, S., Chellappa, R.: Entropy rate superpixel segmentation. In: Proceedings of CVPR, pp. 2097–2104 (2011)
14. Luengo, I., Basham, M., French, A.: Smurfs: Superpixels from multi-scale refinement of super-regions. In: Proceedings of BMVC (2016)

15. Moore, A., Prince, S., Warrell, J.: Lattice cut - constructing superpixels using layer constraints. In: Proceedings of CVPR, pp. 2117–2124 (2010)
16. Shi, J., Malik, J.: Normalized cuts and image segmentation. Trans. PAMI **22**, 888–905 (2000)
17. Veksler, O., Boykov, Y., Mehrani, P.: Superpixels and supervoxels in an energy optimization framework. In: Proceedings of ECCV, pp. 211–224 (2010)
18. Viola, F., Fitzgibbon, A., Cipolla, R.: A unifying resolution-independent formulation for early vision. In: Proceedings of CVPR, pp. 494–501 (2012)
19. Yao, J., Boben, M., Fidler, S., Urtasun, R.: Real-time coarse-to-fine topologically preserving segmentation. In: Proceedings of CVPR, pp. 216–225 (2015)
20. Zhang, Y., Hartley, R., Mashford, J., Burn, S.: Superpixels via pseudo-boolean optimization. In: Proceedings of ICCV, pp. 211–224 (2011)

Video Analysis and Event Recognition

Automatic Video Colorization Using 3D Conditional Generative Adversarial Networks

Panagiotis Kouzouglidis[1], Giorgos Sfikas[1,2(✉)], and Christophoros Nikou[1]

[1] Department of Computer Science and Engineering,
University of Ioannina, 45110 Ioannina, Greece
`sfikas@cs.uoi.gr`
[2] Information Technologies Institute, CERTH, 57001 Thessaloniki, Greece

Abstract. In this work, we present a method for automatic colorization of grayscale videos. The core of the method is a Generative Adversarial Network that is trained and tested on sequences of frames in a sliding window manner. Network convolutional and deconvolutional layers are three-dimensional, with frame height, width and time as the dimensions taken into account. Multiple chrominance estimates per frame are aggregated and combined with available luminance information to recreate a colored sequence. Colorization trials are run successfully on a dataset of old black-and-white films. The usefulness of our method is also validated with numerical results, computed with a newly proposed metric that measures colorization consistency over a frame sequence.

Keywords: Video colorization · Generative Adversarial Networks · Three-dimensional convolution · Black-and-white films

1 Introduction

In this paper, we address the problem of automatic colorization of monochrome digitized videos [8,9,13,15,16]. Perhaps the most straightforward practical application is to colorizing black-and-white footage from old films or documentaries. Video compression is another possible application of note [16].

Video colorization methods can be categorized according to the level of user interaction required. A group of methods assume that a partially colored frame exists in the video, where color has been manually annotated in the form of color seeds [7,12,16]. The method must then propagate color from these seeds to the rest of the frame, then to other frames in the video. Other methods assume instead that a reference colored image exists that is similar in content and structure to the target monochrome video frames [1,13,15]. These methods may or may not require user intervention; for example, in [14] the user can specify matching areas between the reference and the target frames. In reference image-based methods, the problem of video colorization is hence converted to

© Springer Nature Switzerland AG 2019
G. Bebis et al. (Eds.): ISVC 2019, LNCS 11844, pp. 209–218, 2019.
https://doi.org/10.1007/978-3-030-33720-9_16

the problem of how to propagate color from the reference frame to other frames and/or from frame to frame. Optical flow estimation has been used to guide frame-to-frame color propagation [9,13]. In [12], Gabor feature flow is used as alternative to standard optical flow as a more robust guide to color propagation. Naturally, methods of this vein work best for coloring short videos or frames coming from the same scene [13].

In the present work, we propose a learning-based method for video colorization. As such, we assume that a collection of colored frames exist, that will be used to train the model. In particular, the proposed method is based on an appropriately designed Generative Adversarial Network (GAN) [4]. GANs have gained a fair amount of traction in the last few years. Despite their being harder to train even more than standard neural networks, requiring the employment of various heuristics and careful choosing of hyperparameters to attain convergence to a Nash equilibrium [3,11], they have proven to be excellent generative models. The proposed model employs a conditional GAN (cGAN) architecture, popularized by the pix2pix model [5]. In the current work, convolutional and deconvolutional layers are 3D (height, width, time dimensions) to accomodate for the sequential nature of video data.

The main novel points of the current paper are as follows: (a) we present a model for learning-based automatic video colorization that can take advantage of the sequential nature of video, while avoiding the use of frame-by-frame color propagation techniques that come with their own inherent limitations (typically they require existing colored key frames and/or are practically applicable within a single shot). Other recent works use learning methods to color video via propagation [8], or via frame-by-frame image colorization, with each frame processed separately [6]; (b) we elaborate on the issue of video colorization evaluation and propose a quantitative colorization metric specifically for video; (c) we show that the proposed method creates colorization models that are transferable, in the sense that learning over a particular frame sequence produces a plausible output usable on a sequence of different content.

The rest of the paper is organized as follows. In Sect. 2, we briefly discuss preliminaries on adversarial nets and present the architecture and processing pipeline of the proposed video colorization method. In Sect. 3, we elaborate on existing numerical evaluation methods and propose a new metric to evaluate video colorization. In Sect. 4, we show numerical and qualitative results of our method, tested on a collection of old films. We close the paper with Sect. 5, where we discuss conclusions and future work.

2 Proposed Method

The proposed method assumes the existence of a training set consisting of a sequence of N_{train} colored frames, and a test set consisting of a sequence of N_{test} monochrome frames that are to be colorized. During the training phase, a cGAN model is used to learn how to color batches of C ordered frames. Hyperparameter C is fixed beforehand with $C << min\{N_{train}, N_{test}\}$. During the

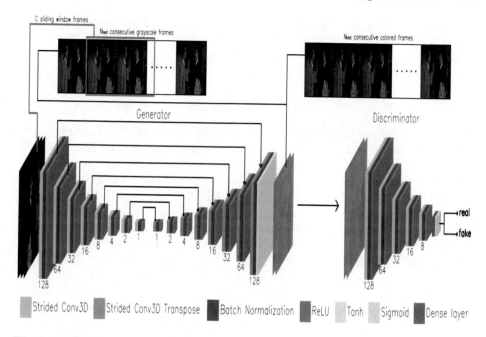

Fig. 1. Architecture of the proposed model. Sequences of luminance frames ('L' channels) are fed to the generator network, which creates chrominance channels for the corresponding frames ('a', 'b' channels). The discriminator network quantifies to what extend the generated chrominance sequence corresponds to a plausible colorization. As inputs and outputs are frame sequences, all convolutions are three-dimensional. During training, model weights are estimated through optimization of a GAN loss that effectively combines these constraints: how plausible the generated colorization is per frame *and as a sequence*, and how close the chrominance estimate is to the ground truth. In test time, the video is processed in a sliding window manner, producing C colorization estimates (the size of the sliding window) for each frame, which are then aggregated to obtain a single estimate per frame. The output chrominance is finally combined with the luminance input in order to recreate a sequence of colorized frames.

testing phase, the model is run on the input monochrome video in a sliding window manner. Windows are overlapping and move by a single frame at a time, thereby producing a set of C colorization estimates *for each* monochrome frame, hence C video colorization proposals. These C estimates are then combined to produce a single colorized output. In what follows we discuss the details of this process.

A GAN is a generative, neural network-based model that consists of two components, the generator network and the discriminator network. The cGAN architecture [5] that is employed as part of the proposed method, is a supervised variant of the original unsupervised GAN [4]. A cGAN learns a mapping from observed input x to target output y^1.

Formally, the objective to be optimized is:

$$\arg \min_G \max_D [\mathbb{E}_y[logD(y)] \\ + \mathbb{E}_x[log(1 - D(G(x)))]] + \lambda \mathbb{E}_{x,y}[\|y - G(x)\|_1], \tag{1}$$

with hyperparameter λ controlling the trade-off between the GAN (discriminator) loss and the L_1 loss. $D(\cdot)$ and $G(\cdot)$ correspond to the discriminator and generator respectively. The GAN loss quantifies how plausible the colorization output, while the L_1 loss forces the colorization to be close to the ground truth. We use representations in the CIE Lab color space (following e.g. [17]). For a monochrome frame sequence, only luminance is known beforehand. Input is a sequence of luminance channels (channel L) of C consecutive frames $x \in \mathbb{R}^{H \times W \times C \times 1}$, and the objective is to learn a mapping from luminance to chrominance (channels a,b) $y \in \mathbb{R}^{H \times W \times C \times 2}$ where H, W are frame dimensions.

The generator network is comprised of a series of convolutional and deconvolutional layers. Skip connections are added in the manner introduced by UNet [10]. As inputs and outputs are sequences of fixed-size frames, all convolutions and deconvolutions are three-dimensional (frame height, width and time dimensions). The encoder and decoder stacks comprise 8 strided convolutional/deconvolutional layers each (stride = 2), followed iteratively by batch normalization (BN) and rectified linear unit (ReLU) activation layers. Following [2], outputs are forced to lie in the $(-1, 1)$ range with a tanh activation layer at the end of the generator network, and only later renormalized to valid a, b chrominance values. The discriminator network is a 3D convolutional network comprising 5 convolutional layers iteratively followed by BN and ReLU layers. The discriminator is topped by a fully connected ("dense") layer and a sigmoid activation unit in order to map the image to a real/fake probability figure.

At test time, we use the generator in a sliding window fashion over the footage to be colorized. Hence, each frame is given as input to the generator at a total of C times, since C is the size of the sliding window. The produced C chrominance estimates $\chi_1, \chi_2, \cdots, \chi_C{}^2$ then need to be used to produce a single estimate $\hat{\chi}$. We can write $\hat{\chi}$ as a maximum-a-posteriori (MAP) estimate as:

$$\hat{\chi} = \arg \max_\chi p(\chi|\chi_1, \cdots, \chi_C) \tag{2}$$

where a prior distribution $p(\chi)$ can be assumed over possible a, b values in order to favor a particular chrominance setup. If identical distributions centered around each χ_i and an uninformative prior is used, the above formula simplifies as an average over all chrominance values per frame pixel: $\hat{\chi} = 1/c \sum_{i=1}^{C} \chi_i$.

---

[1] Other variants of a cGAN are possible; for example, a noise variable z could be added to produce a non-deterministic output [5]. We employ a deterministic cGAN variant in this work.

[2] χ_i denotes the ith colorization estimate for a frame. y denotes a colorization estimate for a sequence of C frames.

2D cGAN   Proposed

Fig. 2. Comparison of proposed model vs non-sequential 2D cGAN model. The proposed model produces better results than the non-sequential variant, as the former can take advantage of optical flow information, with its 3D convolution/deconvolution layers and estimate aggregation scheme. (Note for example how each method colorizes the hand of the standing actor on the top frame, or the color of the suit on the bottom frame). Depicted frames are samples from the film "Dial M for Murder".

Finally, the chrominance estimate is recombined with input luminance to recreate colored RGB frames for the input video. The architecture of the proposed model is summarized in Fig. 1.

Grayscale   Ground Truth   Proposed

Fig. 3. Colorization results using our method. Depicted frames are samples from films: "Et Dieu..créa la femme" and "Tzéni, Tzéni" (2 top and 2 bottom rows respectively).

3   Metrics for Numerical Evaluation of Video Colorization

In this section we describe the metrics we use for numerical evaluation of video colorization. We use two metrics that measure per-frame colorization quality, also usable in single-image colorization. Furthermore, we propose a new metric suitable for video colorization in particular.

Peak Signal-to-Noise Ratio (PSNR): PSNR is calculated per each test frame in the RGB colorspace, and their mean is reported as a benchmark over the whole video.

Raw Accuracy (RA): Raw Accuracy, used in [17] to evaluate image colorization, is defined in terms of accuracy of predicted colors over a varying threshold. Colors are classified as correctly predicted if their Euclidean distance in the *ab* space is lower than a threshold. Accuracy is computed over color values for every pixel position and frame. Integrating over the curve that is produced by taking into account varying threshold yields the RA metric. We integrated from 0 to 150 distance units as in [17].

Color Consistency (CC): The aforementioned metrics measure strictly the quality of colorization of each frame separately. We propose and use a metric to measure both per-frame quality and also the consistency of the choice of colors between consecutive frames. Such a metric can, for example, penalize erratic differences in colorization from frame to frame, that would otherwise be "invisible" to the other metrics, borrowed from single image restoration/colorization. We define color consistency over sets of two consecutive colorization predictions $\hat{\chi}^{(t)}, \hat{\chi}^{(t+1)}$ and corresponding ground truth values $\chi^{(t)}, \chi^{(t+1)}$ as

$$CC^{(t,t+1)} = 1/HW \sum_{i=1}^{H} \sum_{j=1}^{W} 1/2[A_{ij}^{(t)} + A_{ij}^{(t+1)}]A_{ij}^{(t \times t+1)} \tag{3}$$

where affinity matrices $A^{(t)}$ and $A^{(t \times t+1)}$ are defined as

$$A_{ij}^{(t)} = \phi(||\chi_{ij}^{(t)} - \hat{\chi}_{ij}^{(t)}||),$$
$$A_{ij}^{(t \times t+1)} = \phi(\left|||\chi_{ij}^{(t)} - \chi_{ij}^{(t+1)}|| - ||\hat{\chi}_{ij}^{(t)} - \hat{\chi}_{ij}^{(t+1)}||\right|),$$

with function $\phi(\cdot)$ a positive, strictly decreasing function that is used to convert distances to similarities. We use $\phi_{ij}(X) = \lfloor 60X_{ij}/(\max(X) + \epsilon) + 1 \rfloor^{-1}$. Total CC over a video sequence is calculated as the average CC over all consecutive frames. Higher values correspond to better results.

4   Experiments

We have tested our method over a collection of old films: (*a*) "Dial M for Murder" (USA, 1954; 63,243 frames) [18] (*b*) "Et Dieu..créa la femme" (France, 1956; 54,922 frames) [19] (*c*) "Tzéni, Tzéni" (Greece, 1965; 58,932 frames) [20] (*d*) "A streetcar named desire" (USA, 1951; 18,002 frames) [21] (*e*) "Twelve angry men" (USA, 1957; 12,000 frames) [22]. Frames were sampled off these films at 10 fps. Films (*a*), (*b*), (*c*) are colored, while (*d*) and (*e*) are originally black-and-white. Consequently, only the colored films could be used for training, while the black-and-white ones could be used only for testing with a colorizer trained on another film.

We have first experimented with training and testing on different parts of the same (colored) film. For training/testing we have used the first 75%/last 25%

from each of the colored films. The proposed 3D cGAN model was used, with model parameters set to $C = 3$ (sliding window size), $\lambda = 100$ (GAN-L_1 loss tradeoff), and compared against a 2D cGAN model that learned to colorize each frame separately. We have also use data augmentation on our training set, with random horizontal flips (50% chance to use a flipped input during training) and gaussian additive noise ($\sim \mathcal{N}(0, 1.2e - 3)$). For estimate aggregation (Eq. 2) we present results with an uninformative prior (preliminary tests with priors learned over data statistics did not give any definite improvement). We also compare with a greyscale baseline, i.e. the case where the "colorized" video estimate uses only luminance information. Numerical results can be examined in Table 1.

Table 1. Numerical results for colorization evaluation. Training and testing is performed on different clips of the same film. PSNR is measured in dB; RA and CC values are percentages. Higher values are better. The proposed model performs best, in all cases.

	PSNR	RA	CC
(a) "Dial M for Murder"			
Grayscale	32.69	96.55	73.09
2D cGAN	34.97	96.67	82.07
Proposed	**35.66**	**96.73**	**85.59**
(b) "Et Dieu..créa la femme"			
Grayscale	30.23	94.07	47.82
2D cGAN	32.08	95.17	56.67
Proposed	**32.32**	**95.31**	**58.80**
(c) "Tzéni, Tzéni"			
Grayscale	29.83	92.85	39.17
2D cGAN	31.44	93.87	50.81
Proposed	**31.77**	**94.14**	**55.16**

Qualititative results can be examined in Figs. 2 and 3. While in general both models fare satisfactorily, the proposed model can avoid erroneous colorizations in several cases (cf. Fig. 2). This point is validated by our numerical results, where we calculate the metrics presented in Sect. 3. While w.r.t. to PSNR and RA the proposed model still is better, it could be argued that the difference in the result is statistically insignificant. This is not the case with the proposed CC metric however, where the performance of the proposed model is markedly better. These results validate our expectation, as the 3D structure of the proposed model can take into account the sequential structure of the video, in contrast to its 2D counterpart.

We have also run tests for training and testing on different films. The case that is perhaps closest to a practical application of the current model is using

Fig. 4. Colorization results where color ground-truth is unavailable. Depicted are samples from "A streetcar named desire" and "Twelve angry men" (2 leftmost, 2 rightmost columns respectively), colorized with the proposed model trained on "Dial M for Murder".

trained models on one of the colored films to color black-and-white footage, i.e. in our case films (d) and (e). Results for this case can be examined at Fig. 4 (training performed on film (a)). Video colorization demos are available online[3].

5   Conclusion and Future Work

We have presented a method for automatic video colorization, based on a novel cGAN-based model with 3D convolutional and deconvolutional layers and an estimate aggregation scheme. The usefulness of our model has been validated with tests on colorizing old black-and-white film footage. Model performance has also been evaluated with single-image based metrics as well as a newly proposed metric that measures sequential color consistency. As future work, we envisage exploring the uses of the color prior in our aggregation scheme.

Acknowledgements. We gratefully acknowledge the support of NVIDIA Corporation with the donation of the Titan XP GPU used for this research.

References

1. Ben-Zrihem, N., Zelnik-Manor, L.: Approximate nearest neighbor fields in video. In: IEEE International Conference on Computer Vision and Pattern Recognition (CVPR), pp. 5233–5242 (2015)

---

[3] http://www.cs.uoi.gr/~sfikas/video_colorization.

2. Chintala, S., Denton, E., Arjovsky, M., Mathieu, M.: How to train a GAN? Tips and tricks to make GANs work (2016). http://github.com/soumith/ganhacks. Accessed 25 January 2018
3. Daskalakis, C., Ilyas, A., Syrgkanis, V., Zeng, H.: Training GANs with optimism. CoRR abs/1711.00141 (2017). http://arxiv.org/abs/1711.00141
4. Goodfellow, I., et al.: Generative adversarial nets. In: Advances in Neural Information Processing Systems (NIPS), pp. 2672–2680 (2014)
5. Isola, P., Zhu, J.Y., Zhou, T., Efros, A.A.: Image-to-image translation with conditional adversarial networks. arXiv preprint arXiv:1611.07004 (2016)
6. Juliani, A.: Pix2Pix-Film (2017). http://github.com/awjuliani/Pix2Pix-Film. Accessed 2 January 2018
7. Levin, A., Lischinski, D., Weiss, Y.: Colorization using optimization. ACM Trans. Graph. (TOG) **23**, 689–694 (2004)
8. Meyer, S., Cornillère, V., Djelouah, A., Schroers, C., Gross, M.: Deep video color propagation. arXiv preprint arXiv:1808.03232 (2018)
9. Otani, M., Hioki, H.: Video colorization based on optical flow and edge-oriented color propagation. In: Computational Imaging XII. vol. 9020, p. 902002. International Society for Optics and Photonics (2014)
10. Ronneberger, O., Fischer, P., Brox, T.: U-Net: convolutional networks for biomedical image segmentation. In: Navab, N., Hornegger, J., Wells, W.M., Frangi, A.F. (eds.) MICCAI 2015. LNCS, vol. 9351, pp. 234–241. Springer, Cham (2015). https://doi.org/10.1007/978-3-319-24574-4_28
11. Salimans, T., Goodfellow, I., Zaremba, W., Cheung, V., Radford, A., Chen, X.: Improved techniques for training GANs. In: Advances in neural information processing systems (NIPS), pp. 2234–2242 (2016)
12. Sheng, B., Sun, H., Magnor, M., Li, P.: Video colorization using parallel optimization in feature space. IEEE Trans. Circuits Syst. Video Technol. **24**(3), 407–417 (2014)
13. Veeravasarapu, V.R., Sivaswamy, J.: Fast and fully automated video colorization. In: 2012 International Conference on Signal Processing and Communications (SPCOM), pp. 1–5. IEEE (2012)
14. Welsh, T., Ashikhmin, M., Mueller, K.: Transferring color to greyscale images. ACM Trans. Graph. (TOG) **21**, 277–280 (2002)
15. Xia, S., Liu, J., Fang, Y., Yang, W., Guo, Z.: Robust and automatic video colorization via multiframe reordering refinement. In: IEEE International Conference on Image Processing, pp. 4017–4021. IEEE (2016)
16. Yatziv, L., Sapiro, G.: Fast image and video colorization using chrominance blending. IEEE Trans. Image Process. **15**(5), 1120–1129 (2006)
17. Zhang, R., Isola, P., Efros, A.A.: Colorful image colorization. In: Leibe, B., Matas, J., Sebe, N., Welling, M. (eds.) ECCV 2016. LNCS, vol. 9907, pp. 649–666. Springer, Cham (2016). https://doi.org/10.1007/978-3-319-46487-9_40
18. Dial M for murder. https://www.imdb.com/title/tt0046912/ (1954)
19. Et Dieu.créa la femme. https://www.imdb.com/title/tt0049189/ (1956)
20. Tzéni, tzéni. https://www.imdb.com/title/tt0145006/ (1966)
21. A streetcar named desire. https://www.imdb.com/title/tt0044081/ (1951)
22. Twelve angry men. https://www.imdb.com/title/tt0050083/ (1957)

Improving Visual Reasoning
with Attention Alignment

Komal Sharan[✉], Ashwinkumar Ganesan, and Tim Oates

University Of Maryland Baltimore County (UMBC), Baltimore, MD, USA
{ksharan1,gashwin1}@umbc.edu, oates@cs.umbc.edu

Abstract. Since attention mechanisms were introduced, they have become an important component of neural network architectures. This is because they mimic how humans reason about visual stimuli by focusing on important parts of the input. In visual tasks like image captioning and visual question answering (VQA), networks can generate the correct answer or a comprehensible caption despite attending to wrong part of an image or text. This lack of synchronization between human and network attention hinders the model's ability to generalize. To improve human-like reasoning capabilities of the model, it is necessary to align what the network and a human will focus on, given the same input. We propose a mechanism to correct visual attention in the network by explicitly training the model to learn the salient parts of an image available in the VQA-HAT dataset. The results show an improvement in the visual question answering task across different types of questions.

Keywords: Neural attention · Neural networks · Visual Question Answering (VQA) · Supervised learning · Artificial intelligence

1 Introduction

For any real world learning task, certain parts of inputs are more relevant than others. Attention mechanisms are an attempt to identify those interesting or useful parts of an input [7]. Attention mechanisms (AM) are a way to differentially weight portions of the input based on contextual information (like a question given with the image) and interpret a model's behavior [7]. AI tasks such as machine translation [3], object detection [2] and image captioning [18] use the attention methods to improve the model's interpretability. When inputs are images, one may understand attention mechanisms as replicating the steps taken by a human brain to reason about an image. Independent of the task that could be answering a question about an image or giving a caption to an image, it is essential that the model learns to look at the right parts of the image. This is because in our visual process we tend to selectively focus on certain parts of the image and ignore other parts which improve our perception. Visual question answering models are augmented with attention mechanisms [7]. Two types of visual question answering systems augmented with an AM are Stacked

© Springer Nature Switzerland AG 2019
G. Bebis et al. (Eds.): ISVC 2019, LNCS 11844, pp. 219–230, 2019.
https://doi.org/10.1007/978-3-030-33720-9_17

attention networks [19] and Hierarchical Co-attention networks [11]. Although AM has greatly increased their accuracy, the attention maps generated by them are very different from human generated attention maps [8].

Das et al. [8] evaluate whether humans and deep neural networks look at the same parts of an image and found that salient parts of an image that people focus on while answering a question about an image are quite different from machine generated attention maps. Although machine generated attention maps have a positive correlation with the regions chosen by humans, there is still a significant difference between the two [8]. Our work reduces the gap between the human and machine generated attentions by augmenting the training of a VQA model with additional supervised training to generate attention maps that closely mirror human attention using the VQA-HAT dataset that contains the annotations of regions of the image people focus on while answering questions from the VQA dataset. This helps in learning dynamic weightings of input vectors using the human annotated attentions to act as an additional input to the attention mechanisms. Using these human generated attention maps as an input we add a KL divergence loss to the VQA models so that the attention is more aligned with the human generated attention.

2   Related Work

2.1   Visual Question Answering

A visual question answering system (VQA) can be described as one which takes an image and a question as input and provides an answer to the question [1]. There are diverse set of questions about each image, thus providing the model with different contexts. For example, to answer a "how many" question, there needs to be an object detector while a binary "yes/no" question need a scene to be classified. The reasoning about the image is the most critical part of such a system that may require a knowledge graph to reason. Most VQA systems have three building blocks: a visual computation block (typically a convolutional neural network) that is used to extract features from images, a recurrent neural network (RNN) to model sequences of text and word embeddings that initialize the word representations used in the RNN. VGGNet is one such visual computing architecture that is used in VQA tasks [15]. Pre-trained word embeddings modeled using methods like FastText [5] are used to initialize the embedding layer. Generally, the word vectors are of fixed length.

2.2   Attention Mechanisms

The goal of attention mechanisms are to bias the model to focus on relevant parts of the an input sample while optimizing it. In soft attention [4], the next hidden state of the decoder in an encoder-decoder architecture is computed as a combination of its previous state and the context vector which is weighted sum of hidden states of the encoder. In self-attention, Vaswani et al. [17] replace the encoder-decoder network with a purely attention based model to generate text.

Attention mechanism make the model interpretable too. Visual question answering systems also use attention mechanisms to generate a probability distribution over the image to highlight the part of the image that is relevant for answering the question [19].

Two popular attention mechanisms for VQA systems are explained as follows:

Stacked Attention Network (SAN). For a visual question answering system a SAN optimizes the system by identifying the regions important for answering a question [19]. Instead, reasoning via multiple attention layers progressively, the SAN is able to gradually filter out noise and pinpoint regions that are highly relevant to the answer [19].

Hierarchical Co-Attention Network (HAN). A co-attention model jointly reasons about the visual attention and the question attention. There are two co attention mechanisms namely parallel co-attention and alternating co-attention [11].

2.3   Attention Correction

One way to correct the attention of a model when it misaligned in comparison what a human attends to, is to explicitly collect annotations about which regions of the input are salient for a given sample. Das et al. [8] ask people to annotate which part of the image is salient for the given image-question pair. Qiao et al. [14] create a human attention network (HAN) learns to predict the salient portions of an image given the image-question pair. The network is trained on the VQA-HAT dataset. This trained model is then utilized to generate the saliency maps for the VQA 2.0 dataset so as to produce the human-like attention dataset (HLAT). As a final step, this new dataset is used to train an attention network while showcasing an improvement in accuracy. This validates the intuition behind our experiments. As there is a large variation in possible image-question pairs (even for a limited set of images) and their subsequent human attention maps, this work further incorporates a human-in-the-loop mechanism by adding a loss in a standard Multilinear Low-Rank Bilinear Attention Network [9].

Image captioning systems have also been optimized using attention mechanisms. Image captioning models attend to different areas of the image to generate words. To correct the generated maps human supervision and annotations are used as ground truth to optimize the image captioning models [18].

2.4   Image Saliency

Saliency has been explored by carrying out various studies on the shifting of the human gaze over images and videos to capture context [6,12]. The VQA-HAT (Human attention) dataset is one such example. This dataset consists of image-question-answer triplets from the VQA dataset. Initially the images are blurred annotators are asked to deblur the portion of the image which, according to them, is relevant to answer the question. Das et al. [8] collect dataset in three scenarios. In the first scenario, the human subjects are given the image-question pair and asked to sharpen the regions they felt are useful for answering the question about the image. The answer is hidden from them. In the second scenario, the human subjects are given a blurred image, the question and also its answer. They are then asked to sharpen precisely enough regions needed to answer the question. In the third scenario, the human subjects are given the question, the answer, and the high-resolution image. The humans are then asked to imagine a scenario where someone has to answer the question without looking at the original image. This enables them to provide accurate attention maps. Das et al. [8] observe that the regions marked differ when the amount of contextual information provided (from giving the answer to the high resolution image).

2.5   Saliency Based Optimization

Correcting the attention can also improve a video captioning system [20]. This dataset collected for this purpose (VAS) has a set of video clips with captions along with human gaze regions that are associated with those captions. This network is known as the Gaze Encoding Attention Network which uses the human gaze tracking data for generating spatial and temporal information [20].

Park et al. [13] design a model that learns to correct its attention and improve the model's interpretability by generating textual explanations for the model's answer when given a question-image pair and aligning them with the ground truth explanations collected from people.

3   Architecture and Methodology

3.1   Attention Loss Function

The attention over an image is represented in the form of a probability distribution over the image, highlighting portions of the image that are important with high probability.

We modify attention weights more effectively by training the network on the VQA-HAT dataset. The VQA-HAT dataset contains 3 channel png images having attention in the form of pixel values with brighter areas denoting attended regions which are then converted into a target probability distribution that denotes the expected attention.

To get the probability distributions from these values we use a L_1 normalization. After getting a probability distribution in the form of an attention map we now have two probability distributions. The first distribution is the probability generated by the second attention layer in our pipeline and the second distribution which we get by normalizing the VQA-HAT images. As there are two distributions, we use a Kullback-Leibler (KL) divergence loss between these two distributions and add it to the cross-entropy loss used to train the decoder.

If we have two distributions p and q, then we can define KL divergence between them as:

$$D(p||q) = -\sum_{i=1}^{N} p_i.(log(p_i/q_i))$$ (1)

We treat this as an auxiliary loss with the standard loss of the base model in a multi-task learning pipeline and learn from two tasks.

3.2   Multitask Learning with VQA-HAT

As described before, the model learns from two tasks. If we only use one of the models, there is a possibility of ignoring the information learned from a large set of images and questions while refining the attentions using the model with the new loss. Hence to optimize the model we train on the VQA images on the original stacked attention model and the new model which includes the loss calculated from the VQA-HAT images as ground truth in alternate batches as shown in Fig. 1.

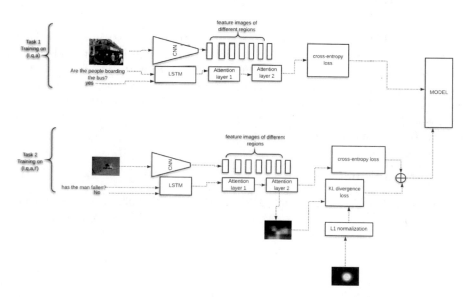

Fig. 1. Multitask Learning in an attention network. In the above diagram the two tasks of a MTL pipeline are shown. The first task learns from the (I,q,a) tuple which denotes the image(I), question(q) and answer(a) while the second task learns from the (I,q,a,I') which denotes the Image(I), question(q), answer(a) and the expected attention on the image(I').

The dataset used by the first model is VQA version 1 and the dataset used by the second model is VQA-HAT, which is a version of the VQA 1.0 dataset along with the corresponding human annotations. Figure 1 also shows the difference in losses between the two tasks. The task which uses only the VQA data has a only a cross entropy loss. Let p' be the predicted probability and p be the probability of the class. The cross entropy can be mathematically written as:

$$H(p, p') = -\sum_{i=1}^{n} p_i.log(p_i')$$ (2)

and the KL loss when q is the second probability which is calculated from the VQA-HAT dataset for the corresponding question ID is denoted by Eq. 3. We also multiply a parameter to boost the KL loss for our experiments. The value of the parameter is determined empirically (we use 25 in our experiments).

Hence for the first task where we only have the VQA dataset, the loss is described by Eq. 2 and for the second task the loss is given as:

$$TotalLoss = D(p||q) + H(p, p')$$ (3)

or

$$TotalLoss = (\alpha * (-\sum_{i=1}^{N} p_i.(log(p_i/q_i))) + (-\sum_{i=1}^{N} p_i.log(p_i'))$$ (4)

The VQA-HAT images are converted into probability distributions using L_1 normalization as explained in Sect. 3.1. For each question ID that is present in the VQA-HAT dataset, we create the dataset which contains the image feature, question and answer vector along with the VQA-HAT image converted into a probability distribution. After getting the probability distribution we need to process the result to create a mask that can be overlayed on the original image to show the attention areas on the image.

3.3   System Configuration

The model is trained with an initial learning rate of 0.0003 with a decay factor of 0.999. The optimizer used is Adam optimizer [10]. To carry out multitask learning as described in Sect. 3.2 we add an auxiliary loss. We alternate the learning with one batch with a standard cross entropy as loss and the other with an additional KL loss. The training is done with a batch size of a 100 data points over 75000 iterations. We have approximately 50,000 data points, so we train our model over 150 epochs.

4   Experiment and Analysis

4.1   Dataset

The images used for this study are a subset of the COCO dataset. The training set has 58,475 attention maps, and the validation set has 4,122 attention maps with multiple attention maps for a single image [8].

Evaluation of this pipeline is a complicated process as in many cases the quality of answers is greatly affected by the category of questions and images used in the VQA-HAT images. The test set of the VQA version 1 dataset has a variety of images and questions. The questions are categorized into 64 categories based on the words they start with[1].

4.2   Evaluation

Quantitative Evaluation. Training with the VQA-HAT dataset is carried out excluding a set of 3000 attention masks for learning from the auxiliary loss which we use in the analysis on the improvement of visual attention. The mechanism used to evaluate the improvement in visual attention is called intersection over union (IoU). Since we have the 3000 VQA-HAT images which are human annotations, we treat them as the ground truth. We also have the generated attention maps from both the initial base model and the new model.

Let X be the attention mask generated by any of the models, and the ground truth is G, then the measure of performance of the map generated the model can be written as the intersection over union(IoU):

$$IoU = X \cap G / X \cup G \tag{5}$$

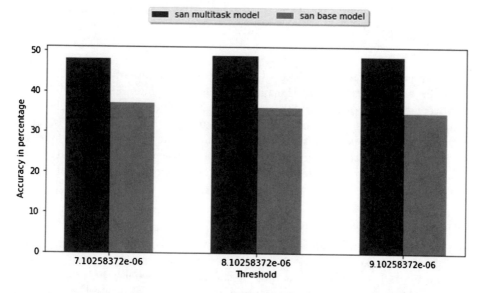

Fig. 2. The X-axis depicts the various thresholds taken in order to convert the probability distribution into a binary format from the generated attention masks in increasing order and the Y-axis denotes the accuracy in percentage of the intersection over union for the models. The color red represents the base model and the color blue represents the new model. (Color figure online)

---

[1] The code repository for the base model has been referred from TingAnChien [16].

The IoU calculated from the attention maps generated by the two models have been plotted in the bar graph given in the Fig. 4 for three different thresholds used to convert probability distribution into a binary image.

As we can see in Fig. 2 there is a clear difference between the IoU calculated using the attention maps generated by the multi-task model (denoted by blue color) and the IoU calculated using the attention maps generated by the base-task model (denoted by red color). The difference also increases as we increase the threshold value. The overlap of the generated probability with the ground truth generated by the multi-task model is better than the overlap of the generated probability with the ground truth generated by the base model. Hence there is a clear improvement in the visual attention.

Overall Language Attention. The next part is the overall quantitative evaluation over the complete VQA test set with the two models shown in Table 1. There are three categories of questions for which the accuracy has been calculated namely "Binary(Yes/No)", the "number questions" and the "other" category which are basically the Multiple choice answers.

Table 1. Accuracy of models for different question types vs overall performance.

Model Type	Binary (Yes/ No)	Numerical	Other	Overall
SAN Multitask model	78.08	32.56	40.03	53.33
SAN Base Model	78.38	33.46	41.70	54.39

As we analyze Fig. 2 and Table 1, we can see that one of the challenges of improving visual attention in the model is that the gains do not translate to improvement in the quality of language generated. The model accurately learns to attend to regions in the image but the same shift of focus is not observed in the answering hence pointing to a hypothesis that the reasoning capability of a model is not directly correlated with the improvement in visual attention. Figure 3 shows some examples of the generated attention for images and questions from the VQA test set.

4.3   Qualitative Evaluation

The multitask trained model has been evaluated based on the accuracy in percentage of the type of question being answered based on the first 3–4 words in the questions. Figure 4 shows a plot of the accuracy where the labels on the x-axis denote a number that represents a specific types of a question out of 64 categories for which our model did better. Table 2 below gives a mapping of the numbers and the actual question type to give further clarity.

Figure 4 shows the categories of questions where our model has performed better which are [0, 3, 13, 26, 28, 29, 34, 40, 41, 47, 48, 50, 53 and 61 in the Table 2]. Orange represents the baseline accuracy and the black represents the new model accuracy.

Original Image: SAN Base Attention image: SAN New attention image:

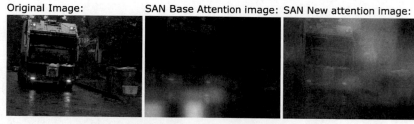

Question asked: What is the weather like?
Answer generated by base SAN: rainy
Answer generated by new SAN: rainy

Original Image: SAN Base Attention image: SAN New attention image:

Question asked: How many elephants are there?
Answer generated by base SAN: 2
Answer generated by new SAN: 2

Fig. 3. Different attention maps overlayed onto the the original image. In each example, the SAN model with attention correction has a better attention map as compared to the baseline SAN model.

Table 2. The x-axis values for different question types. **X** represents the X-label while **Q** represents the question-type. The table is a key for the graph in Fig. 4.

X:Q	X:Q	X:Q	X:Q
0: are there	3: what color is	13: is there a	26: how many
28: has	29: was	34: which	40: can you
41: what time	47: how many people are in	48: do you	50: why is the
53: could	61: is there		

Statistical Significance. In order to see how well the new model has performed over some categories we compute the statistical significance between the outcomes for each model. In this test we take lists of scores per question for each category and calculate the difference in the confidence values in both the lists and sum of those values. After this we calculate the difference 100000 times in a randomized manner assuming that the score is equally likely to come from either models and create another list of differences. Then we calculate number of elements in the list which are greater than the sum of differences of the confidence scores from the new and the original list. Essentially, we try to calculate if we can reject the null hypothesis that there is no difference between the algorithms. The result is the percentage of samples for which the difference of confidence

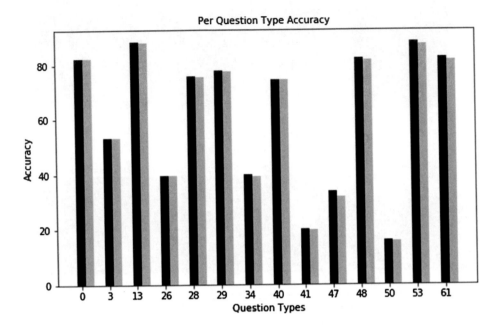

Fig. 4. Accuracy of the baseline SAN model and the MTL trained SAN model for different types of questions. (Color figure online)

Table 3. Accuracy for different percentage of samples from the randomization test.

Category	SAN Base Model	SAN MTL Model	%samples
are there	82.23%	82.422%	33.000%
what color is	53.291%	53.319%	49.000%
is there a	88.133%	88.468%	8.000%
how many people are in	39.435%	39.566%	43.000%
has	75.388%	75.939%	29.000%
was	77.515%	77.912%	32.000%
which	39.408%	39.824%	26.000%
can you	74.371%	74.556%	43.000%
what time	19.712%	20.069%	19.000%
how many people are in	31.577%	33.901%	5.000%
do you	81.777%	82.444%	27.000%
why is the	15.734%	16.109%	33.0000%
is there	81.751%	82.782%	0.0%
could	87.448%	88.486%	11.0%

values is smaller as compared to the sum of all the differences for that category (Table 3).

5 Conclusion

The experiments show a superior performance of an ensemble learning method like multitask learning with one or more tasks based on human generated input serving as low-level representation. By sharing of weights/information between the two models we observe an improvement in the visual understanding of scenes as compared to a standard attention network. There is also an improvement in answering certain types of questions which brings us to the conclusion that multi-task method of training was effective in bringing up the performance of the model for a certain type of questions which indicates increased correlation between language and visual attention.

References

1. Antol, S., et al.: Vqa: visual question answering. In: Proceedings of the IEEE International Conference on Computer Vision, pp. 2425–2433 (2015)
2. Ba, J., Mnih, V., Kavukcuoglu, K.: Multiple object recognition with visual attention (2014)
3. Bahdanau, D., Cho, K., Bengio, Y.: Neural machine translation by jointly learning to align and translate (2014)
4. Bahdanau, D., Cho, K., Bengio, Y.: Neural machine translation by jointly learning to align and translate. arXiv preprint arXiv:1409.0473 (2014)
5. Bojanowski, P., Grave, E., Joulin, A., Mikolov, T.: Enriching word vectors with subword information. Trans. Assoc. Comput. Linguist. **5**, 135–146 (2017)
6. Cerf, M., Frady, E.P., Koch, C.: Faces and text attract gaze independent of the task: experimental data and computer model. J. Vis. **9**(12), 10 (2009)
7. Chaudhari, S., Polatkan, G., Ramanath, R., Mithal, V.: An attentive survey of attention models (2019)
8. Das, A., Agrawal, H., Zitnick, L., Parikh, D., Batra, D.: Human attention in visual question answering: do humans and deep networks look at the same regions? Comput. Vis. Image Underst. **163**, 90–100 (2017)
9. Kim, J.H., On, K.W., Lim, W., Kim, J., Ha, J.W., Zhang, B.T.: Hadamard product for low-rank bilinear pooling (2016)
10. Kingma, D.P., Ba, J.: Adam: a method for stochastic optimization. arXiv preprint arXiv:1412.6980 (2014)
11. Lu, J., Yang, J., Batra, D., Parikh, D.: Hierarchical question-image co-attention for visual question answering. In: Advances In Neural Information Processing Systems, pp. 289–297 (2016)
12. Papadopoulos, D.P., Clarke, A.D.F., Keller, F., Ferrari, V.: Training object class detectors from eye tracking data. In: Fleet, D., Pajdla, T., Schiele, B., Tuytelaars, T. (eds.) ECCV 2014. LNCS, vol. 8693, pp. 361–376. Springer, Cham (2014). https://doi.org/10.1007/978-3-319-10602-1_24
13. Park, D.H., Hendricks, L.A., Akata, Z., Schiele, B., Darrell, T., Rohrbach, M.: Attentive explanations: Justifying decisions and pointing to the evidence (2016)

14. Qiao, T., Dong, J., Xu, D.: Exploring human-like attention supervision in visual question answering. In: Thirty-Second AAAI Conference on Artificial Intelligence (2018)
15. Simonyan, K., Zisserman, A.: Very deep convolutional networks for large-scale image recognition. arXiv preprint arXiv:1409.1556 (2014)
16. TingAnChien: san-vqa-tensorflow. https://github.com/TingAnChien/san-vqa-tensorflow (2016)
17. Vaswani, A., et al.: Attention is all you need. In: Advances in Neural Information Processing Systems, pp. 5998–6008 (2017)
18. Xu, K., et al.: Show, attend and tell: neural image caption generation with visual attention. In: International Conference on Machine Learning, pp. 2048–2057 (2015)
19. Yang, Z., He, X., Gao, J., Deng, L., Smola, A.: Stacked attention networks for image question answering. In: Proceedings of the IEEE Conference on Computer Vision and Pattern Recognition, pp. 21–29 (2016)
20. Yu, Y., Choi, J., Kim, Y., Yoo, K., Lee, S.H., Kim, G.: Supervising neural attention models for video captioning by human gaze data. In: Proceedings of the IEEE Conference on Computer Vision and Pattern Recognition, pp. 490–498 (2017)

Multi-camera Temporal Grouping for Play/Break Event Detection in Soccer Games

Chunbo Song$^{(\boxtimes)}$ and Christopher Rasmussen

Department of Computer & Information Sciences,
University of Delaware, Newark, DE 19716, USA
{songcb,ras}@udel.edu

Abstract. Many current deep learning approaches to action recognition focus on recognizing concrete (e.g., single actor) actions in trimmed videos from datasets such as *UCF-101 and HMDB-51*. However, high-level semantic analysis of sports videos often requires recognizing more abstract events or situations involving multiple players with longer time-scale context. This paper builds upon inflated 3D (I3D) ConvNets for video action recognition to detect and differentiate six abstract categories of events in untrimmed videos of soccer games from multiple fixed cameras: normal play, plus breaks in play due to kick-offs, free kicks, throw-ins, and goal and corner kicks. Raw video unit classifications by variants of the basic I3D network are post-processed by two novel and efficient grouping methods for localizing the boundaries of events. Our experiments show that the proposed methods can achieve 84.2% weighted precision for event categories at the level of video units, and boost event temporal localization mean average precision at 0.5 tIoU (mAP@0.5) to 62.0%.

Keywords: Event classification · Event localization · I3D

1 Introduction

Computer vision is fast becoming a powerful tool for sports video analysis. All kinds of vision-based tasks traditionally performed by the players themselves, spectators, referees, camera operators, and expert commentators can potentially be automated or enhanced for a myriad of applications. These include training and coaching feedback, enhanced rule enforcement accuracy, replay annotation and explanation for broadcasters, measuring detailed player and team statistics, and even serving as perception modules for robotic sports participants. While the exact purpose of the analysis may vary, as well as the sensors employed, there are certain visual skills such as ball tracking [22,30], player segmentation [3,14,21], recognition [11], and pose estimation [17], and recognition of formations, plays, and situations [1,12,31,32] that many sports vision systems have in common.

© Springer Nature Switzerland AG 2019
G. Bebis et al. (Eds.): ISVC 2019, LNCS 11844, pp. 231–243, 2019.
https://doi.org/10.1007/978-3-030-33720-9_18

One of the most basic forms of sports video understanding, at a high level, is *play/break* categories classification [7,28,38]. That is, can one infer whether a particular video sequence depicting part of a game is showing actual game *play*, or is there a *break* in the action? We follow the event definition introduced by Giancola, *et al.* [12] to represent *play/breaks* in videos of soccer games, who defined an event as an action that is anchored in a single time instance, defined within a specific context respecting a specific set of rules. Distinguishing between these two game states is not trivial, because during breaks the players (as well as the ball) may still be visible, and still moving. Events like shots, passes, and fouls that occur in the course of play are understandably popular subjects of study for game analysis [3,28,31]. However, here we investigate break events, which may be due to a timeout, a foul, halftime, an injury, a ball out of bounds, or any number of sports-specific events[1].

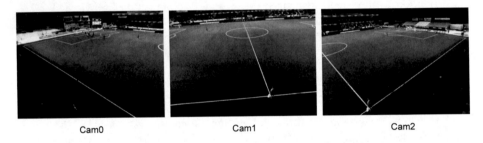

Cam0   Cam1   Cam2

Fig. 1. Example frames of a *corner kick* event defined in the rule of soccer games. In the SVPP dataset, three fixed cameras capture different regions of the field.

Rather than recognizing events or actions in the long untrimmed video either from one camera or from a broadcast feed (in this case, a video contains camera panning and zooming, shot boundaries and subjects and scenes selected of the action), in this paper we aim to differentiate and localize *play* and *break* events using the Soccer Video and Player Position Dataset (SVPP) [25] which has two complete soccer games from three fixed cameras, like Fig. 1 shows. This dataset doesn't have event categories, we manually annotate them in a frame level. Therefore, the event segment can be extracted. We first consider the Two-Stream Inflated 3D ConvNet (I3D) [4] trained on three cameras be the one worthy for the comparison since it is one of state-of-the-art architectures. The I3D, which takes several seconds of video context or a sequence of frames in a

---

[1] In particular, we study soccer *break* event categories as defined in the FIFA rule book [8]: (1) kick-offs (to start each half or after a goal), (2) free kicks (after a foul), (3) penalty kicks, (4) throw-ins (touch line out of bounds), (5) goal kicks (end line out of bounds caused by offensive team), (6) corner kicks (end line out of bounds caused by defensive team), and (7) dropped balls (all other situations), Detecting these *break* event segments in the soccer game video is a difficult task due to the sparsity within a video, but also they have different duration.

fixed length (which we call video unit for differentiating with the event segment), is able to recognize play and different break categories fairly reliably. Because of multi-camera, an assistant neural network (AN) is then utilized to combine all I3D's predictions on synchronous units from all cameras. We also extend I3D to our C-I3Ds by integrating observations from multiple cameras, even those not directly viewing the action, are able to boost performance non-trivially. In C-I3Ds, each camera corresponds to one I3D with two-stream (RGBs and Optical Flows). The integration of these I3Ds takes synchronous video units from all cameras as inputs. Outputs are combined to generate predictions.

Here is an assumption: if a classifier performs well with unit inputs, boundaries will be localized easily and efficiently. Unlike recent methods [9,10,42] feed by trained deep features for localizing actions or generating action proposals in untrimmed videos, we propose two efficient methods to group adjacent video units for the event localization: probability-based grouping (PBG) and class-based grouping (CBG). Both grouping methods build upon predicted probabilities and classes by our I3D-based model. They and their combination achieve promising performance on our testing.

In summary, our contribution are three-fold: (1) We extend the I3D network to be suitable for the multi-camera case to classify video units. (2) We propose probability-based and class-based grouping methods to facilitate C-I3Ds for event localization. (3) The combination of both grouping methods boosts performance on both classification and localization during testing.

2   Related Work

Deep learning architectures for video classification and action recognition in videos have also shown great promise recently [16,33,34], including LSTM networks for human action classification [13] and recognizing pass, shoot, dribble actions from multi-camera video with player and ball trajectories [31]. Strategies for fusing optical flow with spatial information have also achieved considerable success [4,26,36,37], as well as 3D convolutional neural networks which extract features from the spatial and the temporal domains jointly by performing 3D convolutions to capture the motion information encoded in multiple adjacent frames [15]. Based on an Inception module [29], I3D expands 2D filters and pooling kernels to 3D to make it possible to learn seamless spatio-temporal features from video and applied on two-stream (RGB and Optical Flow). The optical flow input may provide some sense of recurrence [4]. The I3D network trained on optical flows carries optimized, smooth flow information. Experimentally it is valuable to classify actions. After pre-training on the Kinetics dataset [6], I3D models have reached 80.9% on HMDB-51 and 98.0% on UCF-101 [4,18,27] which is the most state-of-the-art method to our best knowledge.

Despite these advances, localizing action boundaries in a long, untrimmed video is still a difficult problem. Applying temporal sliding window is a typical scheme after classification [24,35]. The feature extracted from deep neural networks is globally pooled within each window for generating SVM inputs. Yuan *et al.* [39] proposed an approach to address the uncertainty of action occurrence and utilization of information from different scales. Although these works have shown promising performance in their task, the efficiency is still unresolved. Many recent methods have examined this problem as analogous to object detection but in the temporal dimension, they utilize features from deep neural networks to localize action boundaries, including temporal action proposals [5,9,10].

In the work which is similar with ours, Giancola, *et al.* [12] try to "spot" three soccer event categories: (*goal, card,* and *substitution*). However, they didn't try to identify the boundaries of an action within a video, but simply the anchor time that identifies an event with one-minute resolution.

Some other soccer datasets include ISSIA [19], which contains player, referee, and ball positions as seen from multiple fixed cameras; and SoccerNet [12]. But, ISSIA is very short – only 2-min sequences, and while SoccerNet is huge (764 hours of video), it only contains very sparse yellow/red card, goal, and substitution events at essentially 1-min label resolution. AZADI [2] has play/break labels and Soccer 152-A [20] has a number of actions, including those of referees, coaches, and spectators, but neither of these could be obtained for this work.

3   Dataset and Annotation

The Soccer Video and Player Position Dataset [25] (SVPP) is used in our work. The portion of the dataset that we use consists of two complete soccer game videos captured at 30 fps by three fixed cameras whose overlapping fields of view each roughly cover one-third of the length of the field. These two games are TromsoIL vs. Anzhi (*TvA*) and TromsoIL vs. Stromsgodset (*TvS*). The original resolution of each frame in the video is 1280×960. The video of the games are untrimmed, and no broadcast content. 324,284 frames of each camera are annotated with *play* occupying about 65.9% and *break* 34.1%. There are no instances of penalty kicks or drop balls in the videos, so we remove these two break categories. Of the break frames, 0.4% are kick-off (only at the beginning of the game or after the half, as there are no goals), 32.4% free kick, 24.4% throw-in, 14.7% corner kick, and 28.1% goal kick. And different event categories have various time duration.

4   Methods

4.1   Classification

I3D, Assistant Neural Network (AN) and C-I3Ds. Because deep neural networks have displayed good ability of generalization [23,41], we firstly train one I3D network on units from all cameras. And assign one trained I3D model to a related camera during testing. It implies that different I3D networks share weights with each other. Thus, synchronous units from different cameras are sent to their corresponding I3D networks. Their outputs (confidence scores or logits) are concatenated to feed into AN, which is, in our work, a fully-connected

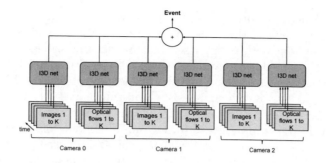

Fig. 2. C-I3Ds: the combination for multiple two-stream I3D framework.

network for outputting event classification results by combining confidence scores from different cameras' related I3D models.

However, in the multi-camera case, both machine and human may be error-prone on pointing out the event when some cameras are unavailable. Training one I3D network on units from all cameras may result in bad recognition. Like the right frame showed in Fig. 1, people cannot tell the exact event. Therefore, deploying several I3D networks for different cameras on training is an alternative way. Unlike the previous way we used, these I3D networks don't share weights with each other. Figure 2 shows its architecture. Each pair of two-stream I3D networks corresponds to a camera. And the output of these separate I3D networks are combined lately, without applying AN. We call this C-I3Ds. Because synchronous video units have the same categories, we trained these separate I3D networks jointly and averaged their predictions at both training and testing time.

4.2   Event Boundaries Localization

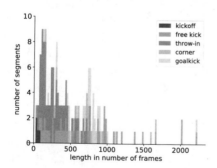

Fig. 3. The distribution of different *break* categories in length on our training set.

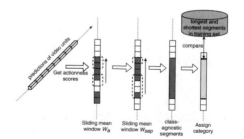

Fig. 4. Probability-based grouping

Probability-Based Grouping (PBG). A temporal sequence of predicted probabilities may indicate the transition from one state to another. Ideally, such transition would be smooth and precise. But, in videos, classifiers may not always achieve perfect results due to several reasons such as subjective labelling, restrictions of the classifier, limited data and etc. Using good classifiers, false classification on frames/units still commonly exists, and thus makes localization difficult. To address this problem, we applied a sliding window manner on predicted probabilities from deep neural networks to not only filter out some errors, but also can group adjacent segments together. The probability-based grouping has two steps: actionness scores grouping and break categories assigning. Figure 4 illustrated the full pipeline of PBG.

We extend the definition of actionness scores in [42] and use it to describe the probability of a given video unit is a break event. For an unit k, we get its actionness score by $prob_{k,a} = 1 - prob_{k,p}$, where $prob_{k,a}$ is the actionness score and $prob_{k,p}$ is the probability of 'play' of k. If $\forall k \in [i,j], prob_{k,a} \geq t_a$, we will be able to get a class-agnostic segment $S_{i,j}$, t_a is a threshold of differentiating 'break' with 'play', and i, j are the boundary of a segment. Based on observations, the beginning of any break event is usually very similar with 'play' and the beginning of any play is also very similar with its previous neighbor 'break'. Therefore, for each break segment $S_{i,j}$, we utilize $l_{aw} - 1$ units before i. And apply a mean window W_a with size l_{aw} and stride st from $i - l_{aw} + 1$ to $j - l_{aw} + 1$. It will adjust $S_{i,j}$ to $S_{p,j}$ given t_a. After that, an adjusted segment may overlap or too close with its neighbor segments. We collect these averaged actionness scores from m to n and apply another mean window W_{sep} to determine if separate or group them. We define l_{sep} be the size of W_{sep}. l_{sep} also implies the minimum length (i.e. if the distance between two adjacent segments is less than l_{sep}, we think they are too close). We densely slide W_{sep} across $[m, n]$ with stride 1, and compare every scores with a threshold t_{ma}. If the number of consecutive steps for W_{sep} is more than l_{sep} and the mean scores are less than t_{ma}, then separate them. It is worth noticing that we shrink the size of W_{sep} if $n - t + 1 < l_{sep}$ for outputting $n - m + 1$ mean scores, where t is the index of the current unit.

For assigning break categories, we average probabilities of all categories for all units within the refined segment, denoted by $P_{i',j'}$. Because, for each category c, the shortest and the longest lengths $G_{c,short}$ and $G_{c,long}$ can be obtained from the training set, we iteratively check and assign the most possible category to the segment based on the its length $l_{i',j'}$, if $l_{i',j'} \geq G_{c,short}$ and $l_{i',j'} \leq G_{c,long}$. If no category can satisfy this segment, 'play' will be assigned to it.

Class-Based Grouping (CBG). The drawback of PBG is, l_{aw} and l_{sep} might not be very large because large window size will eliminate some short but true predictions. Therefore, many false positives are retained. Based on the rule of professional soccer games, we observed facts that any break category must start at the end of 'play', rather than other break categories, except 'kickoff'. And, any break category will usually not takes too short, similar as what we mentioned in assigning break categories in PBG. So based on these facts, we utilize predicted classes to further adjust both boundaries and categories. For each input segment $S_{i,j}$ (including 'play') with length is $l_{i,j}$, its two neighbor segments $S_{x,i-1}$ and $S_{j+1,y}$ are extracted if $l_{i,j} < t_{len}$, where t_{len} is a threshold for indicating small segments. Then, group $S_{j+1,y}$ with $S_{i,j}$ and assign its category to $S_{i,j}$ if $l_{x,i-1} < l_{j+1,y}$. Otherwise, combine $S_{x,i-1}$ to it. This step is processed iteratively until all lengths are greater than t_{len}. After that, if any adjacent segment all belong to any 'break' category (except 'kickoff'), we merge the short segment with the adjacent longer one and assign the category to it.

5 Experiment and Analysis

Data Preparation. We randomly extract synchronous video units from three halves' videos and all cameras to generate the training set. The three halves are: the 2nd half of *TvA* and the 1st and 2nd half of *TvS*. In our work, each video unit has 64 frames with 1 frame of unit's stride. Figure 3 displays the distribution of length of event segments in different break categories in our training set. We assign the label of the last frame in an unit to be the category of this video unit. Due to highly imbalanced number of categories in our dataset, we over-sampled video units which are break categories. Thus, for each category (include play), 9,000 synchronous video units from 3 cameras are in the training set. Data augmentation is necessary to improve the ability of generalization of models because of limited instances of some categories. For each frame, we randomly cropped with size 1160×921. Frames in the same video unit are cropped at the same place, as well as the corresponding optical flows images. These frames are re-sized to 224×224 for feeding into I3D and C-I3Ds. We also applied random right-left flipping, frames and corresponding optical flows images in the same video unit do have the same flipping direction. For the test set, we use the 1st half of *TvA* with unit's stride 1 frame as well for both the event classification and boundary detection. There are 81,471 units in our test set.

Implementation Details of Training. We train the I3D network in an end-to-end manner, with units of video frames as the input. The optical flows are calculated by Dual TV_L^1 method [40]. The I3D network is trained on randomly selected units from all cameras. For both I3D and C-I3Ds, we use SGD to learn parameters. The learning rates are set to 0.01. And dropout of both I3D and C-I3Ds is 0.5 during training. We make AN have 2 layers of 20 hidden nodes. We deploy the same I3D models to predict confidence scores on different camera units. The input of AN is the confidence score from I3D models on synchronous units. The optimization of AN is launched by Adam optimizer with learning rate 0.0001. The training iterations of both I3D and C-I3Ds are 240K, and they are all trained from scratch. The batch size is 4 because of the memory issue. AN is trained for 20 K iterations with batch size 64.

Evaluation Metrics. For event classification, we calculate Precision for different event categories (include 'play'). The Weighted Precision is calculated as well

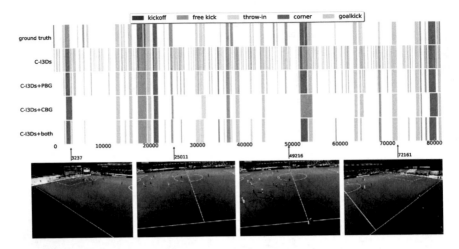

Fig. 5. This is the demonstration of our methods' prediction on the test set. Applying both PBG and CBG after C-I3Ds, precise event boundaries are localized. We sampled four images that are the last frames of their corresponding segments in the ground truth to illustrate some categories are hard to be recognized.

for indicating the overall classification performance. For event localization, we report mean Average Precision (mAP) and Average Recall (AR) using temporal Intersection over Union (tIoU) threshold of 0.5. Because none of the 'kickoff' units is recognized, it is not included in the analysis of the results.

Classification. Table 1 displays the precision of the different model on testing. I3D network trained on units from all cameras doesn't perform really well, even AN is applied. The C-I3Ds perform better than the I3D with AN on almost all categories, except 'free kick'. Without any grouping method, its weighted precision achieves 78.7%. Units can obtain labels after applying grouping methods with the C-I3Ds. If both l_{aw} and l_{sep} are 46, the weighted precision reaches 83.5%. If the CBG is applied with t_{len} is 125, the weighted precision (80.9%) is lower than using PBG, but still higher than C-I3Ds'. We also combine PBG and CBG to adjust predicted categories of units and it achieves relatively good weighted precision performance (84.2%).

The classification result indicates that different levels of difficulty of these event categories. This may be caused by limited number of events in our training set, even though we over-sample frames with this category to make the training set balance. Moreover, owing to diversities, the 'free kick' is also hard to be differentiated from other categories.

Event Localization. We use C-I3Ds as the baseline to evaluate performance on the localization by making input video units be in the chronological order and

Table 1. Per-unit (stride 1) classification precision (%)

method	play	free kick	throw-in	corner	goalkick	weighted precision
I3D	88.4	15.8	18.9	51.1	37.6	73.3
I3D+AN	85.4	29.4	31.8	63.4	44.4	74.0
C-I3Ds without grouping	88.7	16.5	50.5	66.8	61.2	78.7
C-I3Ds+PBG($l_{aw}, l_{sep} = 33$)	90.6	17.8	65.5	68.5	72.1	82.2
C-I3Ds+PBG($l_{aw}, l_{sep} = 46$)	91.3	20.3	71.2	72.6	**73.8**	83.5
C-I3Ds+CBG($t_{len} = 65$)	89.5	**29.9**	77.5	**73.3**	**73.8**	83.2
C-I3Ds+CBG($t_{len} = 125$)	88.7	18.3	77.3	58.5	72.6	80.9
C-I3Ds+both($l_{aw}, l_{sep} = 33, t_{len} = 65$)	91.0	19.2	76.2	65.0	72.6	82.9
C-I3Ds+both($l_{aw}, l_{sep} = 33, t_{len} = 125$)	91.2	21.3	76.6	65.0	73.1	83.3
C-I3Ds+both($l_{aw}, l_{sep} = 46, t_{len} = 65$)	91.3	22.0	**79.6**	72.6	72.3	84.0
C-I3Ds+both($l_{aw}, l_{sep} = 46, t_{len} = 125$)	**91.6**	27.7	75.7	72.6	71.6	**84.2**

localizing boundaries because of its decent classification performance. Tables 2 and 3 display the precision and the recall on the event localization.

While the C-I3Ds achieves a decent performance on the classification, the result of event localization is bad. Given tIoU threshold as 0.5, the mAP is less than 1%, and AR is 14.0%. After applying PBG after C-I3Ds with l_{aw} and l_{sep} are 33, the mAP@0.5 and AP@0.5 have reached 33.4% and 41.9%, respectively. If l_{aw} and l_{sep} are all 46, the mAP@0.5 is 39.3% and the AR@0.5 is 46.5%. Because some segments are pretty short in the training set, it appears both window sizes l_{aw} and l_{sep} is small to maintain these correct segments as many as possible.

C-I3Ds with CBG performs well, which achieves 41.3% mAP@0.5 when set t_{len} to be around the unit size (i.e. 65). Assigning it a larger value for t_{len}, some short but true segments will be merged into their neighbors. When t_{len} is much larger (e.g. 125), both mAP and AR will be low (30.2% and 25.6%) due to the incorrect merging. C-I3Ds with PBG achieves higher recalls than CBP (46.5% vs. 34.9%). The PBG will still leave too many short segments because of its short window sizes. In these segments, the number of false positives is far more than true positives'. And, CBG with relatively larger t_{len} can be applied for eliminating them. Thus, we test the combination of these two grouping methods after C-I3Ds. The combination boosts mAP@0.5 up to 62.0% without sacrificing AR much as Tables 2 and 3 showed. Figure 5 shows qualitative examples on testing. The four frames display some correct and incorrect recognition. Besides 'kickoff', 'free kick' is the most difficult category for recognition, like the first frame with the number 3237. The corresponding segment of the third frame with the number 49216 is eliminated by the grouping since C-I3Ds only predicts a few short segments. 'goalkick' is the easiest category to be detected in the testing, as the rightmost frame shows. From the Fig. 5, although some short segments in the ground truth are hardly detected by C-I3Ds, the predicted boundary can be adjusted accurately by applying our grouping methods. Both PBG and CBG are efficient. Running both after C-I3Ds only spends less than 1 s on testing.

Table 2. Results for event localization in precision(%) and mAP(%)@0.5 tIoU

method	free kick	throw-in	corner	goalkick	mAP
C-I3Ds without grouping	0.3	0.0	0.0	1.0	0.3
C-I3Ds+PBG($l_{aw}, l_{sep} = 33$)	5.3	38.5	50.0	44.4	33.4
C-I3Ds+PBG($l_{aw}, l_{sep} = 46$)	9.4	41.7	60.0	56.3	39.3
C-I3Ds+CBG($t_{len} = 65$)	22.2	50.0	50.0	44.4	41.3
C-I3Ds+CBG($t_{len} = 125$)	33.3	0.0	**66.7**	**70.0**	30.2
C-I3Ds+both($l_{aw}, l_{sep} = 33, t_{len} = 65$)	10.0	55.6	50.0	47.1	41.9
C-I3Ds+both($l_{aw}, l_{sep} = 33, t_{len} = 125$)	20.0	**83.3**	50.0	53.3	56.7
C-I3Ds+both($l_{aw}, l_{sep} = 46, t_{len} = 65$)	13.6	62.5	60.0	56.3	48.9
C-I3Ds+both($l_{aw}, l_{sep} = 46, t_{len} = 125$)	**37.5**	**83.3**	60.0	56.3	**62.0**

Table 3. Results for event localization in recall(%) and AR(%)@0.5 tIoU

method	free kick	throw-in	corner	goalkick	AR
C-I3Ds without grouping	12.5	0.0	0.0	55.6	14.0
C-I3Ds+PBG($l_{aw}, l_{sep} = 33$)	25.0	**27.8**	**50.0**	88.9	41.9
C-I3Ds+PBG($l_{aw}, l_{sep} = 46$)	**37.5**	**27.8**	**50.0**	**100.0**	**46.5**
C-I3Ds+CBG($t_{len} = 65$)	25.0	11.1	**50.0**	88.9	34.9
C-I3Ds+CBG($t_{len} = 125$)	25.0	0.0	33.3	77.8	25.6
C-I3Ds+both($l_{aw}, l_{sep} = 33, t_{len} = 65$)	25.0	**27.8**	33.3	88.9	39.5
C-I3Ds+both($l_{aw}, l_{sep} = 33, t_{len} = 125$)	25.0	**27.8**	33.3	88.9	39.5
C-I3Ds+both($l_{aw}, l_{sep} = 46, t_{len} = 65$)	**37.5**	**27.8**	**50.0**	**100.0**	**46.5**
C-I3Ds+both($l_{aw}, l_{sep} = 46, t_{len} = 125$)	**37.5**	**27.8**	**50.0**	**100.0**	**46.5**

6   Conclusion and Future Work

In this paper, we firstly introduce our construction upon the I3D network to make it be suitable with multi-camera in the soccer game and apply it to classify soccer game event rather than actions from individuals. We also propose PBG and CBG to localize/adjust event boundaries in the video of the soccer game. The performance demonstrates the combination of these two grouping methods can achieve a promising result. In the future, we will test our methods on the event classification and localization in more general scenarios. And, due to our grouping methods are not in a learning manner, we are still interested in inferring event boundaries by machine learning approaches.

References

1. Assfalg, J., Bertini, M., Colombo, C., Bimbo, A.D., Nunziati, W.: Semantic annotation of soccer videos: automatic highlights detection. Comput. Vis. Image Underst. **92**(2), 285–305 (2003)

2. Bozorgpour, A., Fotouhi, M., Kasaei, S.: Robust homography optimization in soccer scenes. In: Iranian Conference on Electrical Engineering (2015)
3. Canales, F.: Automated semantic annotation of football games from TV broadcast. Ph.D. thesis, Department of Informatics, TUM Munich (2013)
4. Carreira, J., Zisserman, A.: Quo vadis, action recognition? a new model and the Kinetics dataset. In: IEEE Conference on Computer Vision and Pattern Recognition (2017)
5. Chao, Y.W., Vijayanarasimhan, S., Seybold, B., Ross, D.A., Deng, J., Sukthankar, R.: Rethinking the faster R-CNN architecture for temporal action localization. In: Proceedings of the IEEE Conference on Computer Vision and Pattern Recognition, pp. 1130–1139 (2018)
6. DeepMind: Convolutional neural network model for video classification trained on the Kinetics dataset (2017). https://github.com/deepmind/kinetics-i3d
7. Fani, M., Yazdi, M., Clausi, D., Wong, A.: Soccer video structure analysis by parallel feature fusion network and hidden-to-observable transferring markov model. IEEE Access **5**, 27322–27336 (2017)
8. Fédération Internationale de Football Association (FIFA): Laws of the game (2015). https://img.fifa.com/image/upload/datdz0pms85gbnqy4j3k.pdf
9. Gao, J., Chen, K., Nevatia, R.: Ctap: Complementary temporal action proposal generation. In: Proceedings of the European Conference on Computer Vision (ECCV), pp. 68–83 (2018)
10. Gao, J., Yang, Z., Chen, K., Sun, C., Nevatia, R.: Turn tap: temporal unit regression network for temporal action proposals. In: Proceedings of the IEEE International Conference on Computer Vision, pp. 3628–3636 (2017)
11. Gerke, S., Muller, K., Schafer, R.: Soccer jersey number recognition using convolutional neural networks. In: IEEE International Conference on Computer Vision Workshop (2015)
12. Giancola, S., Amine, M., Dghaily, T., Ghanem, B.: Soccernet: a scalable dataset for action spotting in soccer videos. In: CVPR Workshop on Computer Vision in Sports (2018)
13. Grushin, A., Monner, D.D., Reggia, J.A., Mishra, A.: Robust human action recognition via long short-term memory. In: The 2013 International Joint Conference on Neural Networks (IJCNN), pp. 1–8. IEEE (2013)
14. Huda, N., Jensen, K., Gade, R., Moeslund, T.: Estimating the number of soccer players using simulation-based occlusion handling. In: CVPR Workshop on Computer Vision in Sports (2018)
15. Ji, S., Xu, W., Yang, M., Yu, K.: 3D convolutional neural networks for human action recognition. IEEE Trans. Pattern Anal. Mach. Intell. **35**(1), 221–231 (2013)
16. Karpathy, A., Toderici, G., Shetty, S., Leung, T., Sukthankar, R., Fei-Fei, L.: Large-scale video classification with convolutional neural networks. In: Proceedings of the IEEE conference on Computer Vision and Pattern Recognition, pp. 1725–1732 (2014)
17. Kazemi, V., Sullivan, J.: Using richer models for articulated pose estimation of footballers. In: British Machine Vision Conference (2012)
18. Kuehne, H., Jhuang, H., Garrote, E., Poggio, T., Serre, T.: HMDB: a large video database for human motion recognition. In: IEEE International Conference on Computer Vision (2011)
19. Leo, M., Mosca, N., Spagnolo, P., Mazzeo, P., et al.: A semi-automatic system for ground truth generation of soccer video sequences. In: Advanced Video and Signal Based Surveillance (2009)

20. Liu, T., et al.: Soccer video event detection using 3D convolutional networks and shot boundary detection via deep feature distance. In: International Conference on Neural Information Processing (2017)

21. Lu, K., Chen, J., Little, J.J., He, H.: Light cascaded convolutional neural networks for accurate player detection. In: British Machine Vision Conference (2017)

22. Maksai, A., Wang, X., Fua, P.: What players do with the ball: A physically constrained interaction modeling. In: Proceedings of the IEEE conference on computer vision and pattern recognition (2016)

23. Neyshabur, B., Bhojanapalli, S., McAllester, D., Srebro, N.: Exploring generalization in deep learning. In: Advances in Neural Information Processing Systems, pp. 5947–5956 (2017)

24. Ni, B., Yang, X., Gao, S.: Progressively parsing interactional objects for fine grained action detection. In: Proceedings of the IEEE Conference on Computer Vision and Pattern Recognition, pp. 1020–1028 (2016)

25. Pettersen, S.A., et al.: Soccer video and player position dataset. In: ACM Multimedia Systems Conference (2014)

26. Simonyan, K., Zisserman, A.: Two-stream convolutional networks for action recognition in videos. In: Advances in neural information processing systems, pp. 568–576 (2014)

27. Soomro, K., Zamir, A.R., Shah, M.: UCF101: a dataset of 101 human actions classes from videos in the wild. Technical report CRCV-TR-12-01, University of Central Florida (2012)

28. Sozykin, K., Khan, A.M., Protasov, S., Hussain, R.: Multi-label class-imbalanced action recognition in hockey videos via 3D convolutional neural networks. In: IEEE/ACIS International Conference on Software Engineering, Artificial Intelligence, Networking and Parallel/Distributed Computing (2018)

29. Szegedy, C., et al.: Going deeper with convolutions. In: Proceedings of the IEEE conference on computer vision and pattern recognition, pp. 1–9 (2015)

30. Tong, X., Lu, H., Liu, Q.: An effective and fast soccer ball detection and tracking method. In: International Conference on Pattern Recognition (2004)

31. Tsunoda, T., Komori, Y., Matsugu, M., Harada, T.: Football action recognition using hierarchical LSTM. In: CVPR Workshop on Computer Vision in Sports (2017)

32. Wagenaar, M., Okafor, E., Frencken, W., Wiering, M.: Using deep convolutional neural networks to predict goal-scoring opportunities in soccer. In: International Conference on Pattern Recognition Applications and Methods (2017)

33. Wang, H., Schmid, C.: Action recognition with improved trajectories. In: Proceedings of the IEEE international conference on computer vision, pp. 3551–3558 (2013)

34. Wang, L., Li, W., Li, W., Van Gool, L.: Appearance-and-relation networks for video classification. arXiv preprint arXiv:1711.09125 (2017)

35. Wang, L., Xiong, Y., Lin, D., Van Gool, L.: Untrimmednets for weakly supervised action recognition and detection. In: Proceedings of the IEEE conference on Computer Vision and Pattern Recognition, pp. 4325–4334 (2017)

36. Wang, L., et al.: Temporal segment networks: towards good practices for deep action recognition. In: Leibe, B., Matas, J., Sebe, N., Welling, M. (eds.) ECCV 2016. LNCS, vol. 9912, pp. 20–36. Springer, Cham (2016). https://doi.org/10.1007/978-3-319-46484-8_2

37. Wang, Y., Song, J., Wang, L., Van Gool, L., Hilliges, O.: Two-stream SR-CNNs for action recognition in videos. In: BMVC (2016)

38. Xie, L., Xu, P., Chang, S.F., Divakaran, A., Sun, H.: Structure analysis of soccer video with domain knowledge and hidden markov models. Pattern Recogn. Lett. **25**(7), 767–775 (2004)
39. Yuan, J., Ni, B., Yang, X., Kassim, A.A.: Temporal action localization with pyramid of score distribution features. In: Proceedings of the IEEE Conference on Computer Vision and Pattern Recognition, pp. 3093–3102 (2016)
40. Zach, C., Pock, T., Bischof, H.: A duality based approach for realtime TV-L^1 optical flow. In: Hamprecht, F.A., Schnörr, C., Jähne, B. (eds.) DAGM 2007. LNCS, vol. 4713, pp. 214–223. Springer, Heidelberg (2007). https://doi.org/10.1007/978-3-540-74936-3_22
41. Zhang, C., Bengio, S., Hardt, M., Recht, B., Vinyals, O.: Understanding deep learning requires rethinking generalization. arXiv preprint arXiv:1611.03530 (2016)
42. Zhao, Y., Xiong, Y., Wang, L., Wu, Z., Tang, X., Lin, D.: Temporal action detection with structured segment networks. In: Proceedings of the IEEE International Conference on Computer Vision, pp. 2914–2923 (2017)

Trajectory Prediction by Coupling Scene-LSTM with Human Movement LSTM

Manh Huynh[✉] and Gita Alaghband

Department of Computer Science and Engineering,
University of Colorado Denver, Denver, USA
{manh.huynh,gita.alaghband}@ucdenver.edu

Abstract. We develop a novel human trajectory prediction system that incorporates the scene information (Scene-LSTM) as well as individual pedestrian movement (Pedestrian-LSTM) trained simultaneously within static crowded scenes. We superimpose a two-level grid structure (grid cells and subgrids) on the scene to encode spatial granularity plus common human movements. The Scene-LSTM captures the commonly traveled paths that can be used to significantly influence the accuracy of human trajectory prediction in local areas (i.e. grid cells). We further design scene data filters, consisting of a hard filter and a soft filter, to select the relevant scene information in a local region when necessary and combine it with Pedestrian-LSTM for forecasting a pedestrian's future locations. The experimental results on several publicly available datasets demonstrate that our method outperforms related works and can produce more accurate predicted trajectories in different scene contexts.

Keywords: Human movement · Scene information · LSTM network

1 Introduction

Human movement trajectory prediction is an essential task in computer vision with applications in autonomous driving cars [11], robotic navigation systems [14,19], and intelligent human tracking systems [9,12]. Given the past movement trajectories of pedestrians in a video sequence, the goal is to predict their near future trajectories (lists of continuous two-dimensional locations) (Fig. 1). For the most part, predicting future human trajectories is challenging due to: **(i)** existence of many possible future trajectories, especially in open areas where people move and change directions freely at any time (multi-modal problem); **(ii)** social interactions (e.g. grouping, avoiding, etc.) can impact decisions of the next movements; **(iii)** structures within scenes can impose certain paths.

To deal with these challenges, several social-interaction methods [1,7,14–16,18,20] have been proposed. The traditional methods [14,16,22] use hand-crafted features to characterize the social interactions. Recently, several social-interaction methods [1,7,18,20] leverage the power of LSTM (Long Short-Term

© Springer Nature Switzerland AG 2019
G. Bebis et al. (Eds.): ISVC 2019, LNCS 11844, pp. 244–259, 2019.
https://doi.org/10.1007/978-3-030-33720-9_19

Memory) networks for modeling the individual movement behaviors and social interactions. Although social interaction has been shown to be effective in predicting future human locations in some scenarios, it does not perform well in multi-modal environments. For example, to avoid collisions with other people while walking, one can choose to go left or right.

To partially handle this multi-modal problem, the contexts of a scene can be used. Several proposed methods [2,3,17,21] have gained improvements by extracting the scene's visual features from video images and use them in combination with social-interaction features. They hypothesize that people may move in the same directions under similar scene contexts. The main limitation is that the low-level visual features cannot fully explain the human movements. Given the same scene layouts, there is still a high probability that people will choose different paths. Furthermore, generating similar visual

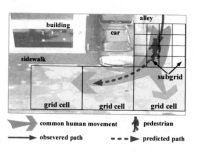

Fig. 1. Scene-LSTM learns common human movements on a two-level grid structure. The common human movement is filtered and used in combination with individual movement (Pedestrian-LSTM) to predict a pedestrian's future locations.

features for similar scene contexts is difficult due to camera positions, angles, etc. Thus, these visual features are often used in combination with the social-interaction features to achieve the desired accuracy.

In this paper, we propose and develop a novel scene model, called Scene-LSTM, to learn common human movement features in each grid cell (and at finer subgrid level when necessary) as shown in Fig. 1, which can be used in combination with individual movement (Pedestrian-LSTM) to predict a pedestrian's future locations. A Scene Data Filter (SDF) is further designed to select the relevant scene information to predict the pedestrians' next locations, based on their current locations and walking behaviors. The key components of the SDF are a "hard filter" and a "soft filter." The hard filter makes decisions on whether the scene information should be used in predicting pedestrians' future trajectories based on their current locations on the two-level grid structures (grid cells and subgrids). The filtered scene information from the hard filter is used by the soft filter for further processing. The soft filter selects the relevant scene information for each pedestrian, based on their movement behaviors, to predict future locations.

In summary, the contributions of this paper are threefold: **(1)** A new Scene-LSTM model is learned simultaneously with a LSTM-based human walking model; **(2)** a SDF selects relevant scene information to predict pedestrians' trajectories with the help of hard filer and soft filter; **(3)** Evaluations on public datasets show that Scene-LSTM outperforms several related methods in terms of human trajectory prediction accuracy. Ablation studies are conducted to show the relevance and impact of each system component.

2   Related Works

Research in predicting future human trajectories has been focused on modeling human-human interactions [1,7,14–16,18,20]. There have been very few studies related to human-scene interactions [2,3,17,21].

Human-Human Methods. To model human-to-human interactions, some researchers [14,16,22] characterize their social interactions as features and calculate the next locations of each pedestrian by minimizing some function of these features. For example, Pellegrini et al. [14] calculates the desired velocities of each pedestrian by minimizing the energy function of collision avoidance, speed, and direction towards the pedestrians' final destinations. Yamaguchi et al. [22] broadens the model [14] with social group behaviors such as attractions and groupings using energy functions which are minimized using gradient descent [8]. Trautman et al. [16] characterizes human movements and collision potentials using Gaussian processes with multiple particles and apply maximum a posteriori (MAP) to minimize the collision potentials to yield the best next locations. Although utilizing these social-interaction features helps predict future human movements, they are built upon specific social-interaction rules; thus, they do not apply well to all possible scenarios.

Recently, several LSTM based methods [1,7,18,20] have been proposed to learn individual human movement behaviors and social interactions by leveraging the memorizing power of LSTM. For example, Social-LSTM [1] uses a social pooling layer to learn the social interactions of the main target and nearby pedestrians. Other methods [7,18,20] model the social interactions in the entire scene, where people far-away from the main target may also have social impacts on this target's movements. These methods use different types of network architectures such as structural recurrent neural network [18], generative neural network [6], and deep neural network [20].

Human-Scene Methods. A relatively small body of recent work have studied the impact of scene structures (e.g. buildings, static obstacles, etc.) on human trajectory prediction. These methods [2,3,17,21] combine scene features with social interactions to predict human movement trajectories. Some methods [17,21] extract feature of the scene layouts using Convolutional Neural Network. Ballan et al. [2] utilizes several techniques (e.g. color histograms, scale-invariant feature transform (SIFT), etc.) to calculate scene visual descriptors in local (patch) and global (image) context. Bartoli et al. [3] measures the distances between the targets and obstacles in the scene and combines them with Social-LSTM [1]. These human-scene methods have made gains in improving prediction accuracy. However, the limitation is that the low-level scene visual features cannot fully capture the high-level scene contexts (e.g. common human movements), which can significantly improve the accuracy of human trajectory prediction as we will present in this paper.

3   System Design

Problem Definition: The problem under consideration is prediction of human movement trajectories in static crowded scenes. Let's define $X_i^t = (x_i^t, y_i^t)$ as the spatial location of target i at time t, and N as the number of pedestrians in the number of observed frames, T_{obs}. The problem is stated as: given the trajectories of all pedestrians in observed frames (x_i^t, y_i^t), where $t = 1, ..., T_{obs}$ and $i = 1, ..., N$, predict the next locations for each pedestrian in the predicted frames T_{pred}. [Time t corresponds to frame number.]

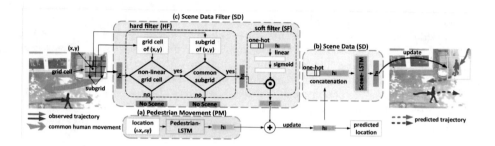

Fig. 2. The system consists of three main modules: Pedestrian Movement (PM), Scene Data (SD) and Scene Data Filter (SDF). PM models the individual movement of pedestrians. SD encodes common human movements in each grid cell. SDF selects relevant scene data to update the Pedestrian-LSTM, which is used to predict the future locations. $\otimes$ denotes elementwise multiplication. $\oplus$ denotes vector addition. h_i and h_s are the hidden states of Pedestrian-LSTM and Scene-LSTM, respectively.

Our system design, depicted in Fig. 2, consists of three main modules: Pedestrian Movement (PM), Scene Data (SD), and Scene Data Filter. The description of each module is explained below:

(a) Pedestrian Movements (PM) module models the individual pedestrian's movement behavior using a LSTM (Pedestrian-LSTM) (one LSTM/pedestrian). Pedestrian-LSTM utilizes its memory cell to remember the past movements of a pedestrian. For better adaptability across scenes, pedestrian's relative locations with respect to the previous locations are used as inputs to the Pedestrian-LSTM network at each training step.

(b) Although the PM is responsible for modeling the individual pedestrian's movement behavior, there will be scenarios where the pedestrian model alone does not have adequate information to predict trajectories. In such cases, data from scene can help steer the prediction trajectories the right way. The Scene Data (SD) module models all human movements within the entire scene identifying commonly travelled paths at various movement granularities. The scene is superimposed with a two-level grid structure: grid cells which are further divided into subgrids. The SD uses a LSTM (Scene-LSTM) (one/grid cell) to

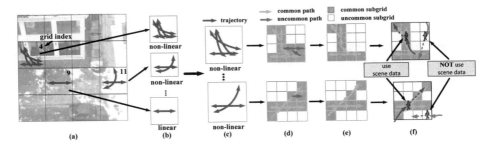

Fig. 3. Illustrations of the hard filter, which determines whether the scene data should be applied in predicting the future locations of a pedestrian. (a) the frame image is first divided into $n \times n$ grid cells ($n = 4$ in this example) to capture all human movements in each grid cell; (b) & (c) only non-linear grid cells are selected for further processing at the subgrid level; the scene data is not applied for pedestrians in the linear grid cell; (d) a non-linear grid cell is further divided into $m \times m$ subgrids ($m = 4$) and each trajectory is parsed into subgrid paths; (e) the common subgrids, occupied by common subgrid paths; (f) at prediction time, the decision of use/not use scene data depends on the current location of each pedestrian. If the pedestrian's current location is in the common subgrids, the scene data is used (red pedestrian); otherwise, it is not used (green pedestrian). (Color figure online)

encode the pedestrians' movements in each grid cell. The absolute location (x, y) of each pedestrian is used to locate them in the scene at the subgrid level. This is represented in the form of a one-hot vector described in the next section. The combination (i.e. concatenation) of the one-hot vector and the hidden state h of Pedestrian-LSTM is used as an input to Scene-LSTM. Although Scene-LSTMs are able to encode all human movements in each grid cell of a scene during the training process, we must recognize that using the combined scene and pedestrian data will not work well for all cases. The following two scenarios describe when the scene data should not be used to influence next prediction: **(1)** The scene data is not needed for predicting the future locations of the pedestrians whose movements are linear and therefore not impacted by the scene structures. For example, the pedestrians in open areas (e.g. grid cell 9, Fig. 3a) mostly walk linearly without any scene structure constraints. The scene information has no effect on the pedestrians' movements in these areas. **(2)** The scene information in the grid cells where various past trajectories coincide may be unhelpful in predicting the human future locations. This is because the memories of these grid cells, encoding all different types of trajectories, do not learn any specific common movements and worsen the prediction accuracy.

(c) To handle the aforementioned challenges, we propose the Scene Data Filter (SDF) which consists of two filters: a hard filter (HF) and a soft filter (SF). The HF helps us decide whether the scene data of a grid cell should be applied to predict a given pedestrian's next location based on this pedestrian's current grid cell and subgrid locations. This is done based on whether the grid cell is labeled as linear or non-linear during training/observation period; Fig. 3b shows.

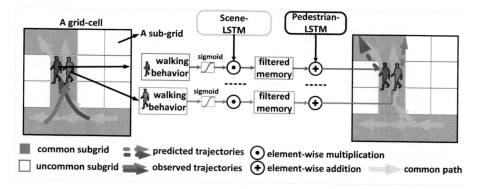

Fig. 4. Illustrations of the soft filter. The relevant information of scene data (i.e. Scene-LSTM) is selected using each pedestrians' walking behavior. The filtered grid-cell memory of each pedestrian is then used in combination with pedestrian movements (Pedestrian-LSTM) to predict the future trajectories. (Color figure online)

A grid cell is characterized as "linear" if all human trajectories in this grid cell are linear. In other words, people always make linear movements in this cell. Prediction of future trajectory of a pedestrian that travels in a linear grid cell is simple and can rely on Pedestrian-LSTM only. However, pedestrians travelling in a non-linear grid cell which contains non-linear trajectories, may have varying paths caused by social interactions and/or scene structures. This scenario can be captured by the subgrid structure of the non-linear grid cells. The HF in this case is used to enforce the coupling of the scene data with the pedestrian model to predict a pedestrian's next location based on this person's current subgrid location and common path.

The intuition of the HF at the subgrid level granularity is based on the observation that if pedestrians walk in the common subgrid paths, there is a high probability that they tend to follow the same path. In this case, the scene data will be used in conjunction with the pedestrian data. A common subgrid path, as shown in Fig. 3d, is a path between two subgrids commonly travelled by a number of pedestrians greater than a pre-defined threshold $p = 3$. The subgrids travelled by common paths are called common subgrids (Fig. 3e). If the pedestrian's current location is in a common subgrid, the scene information will be applied; otherwise, only the PM is used (Fig. 3f). It is important to note that once the common subgrids are selected, the HF not only will capture the common movements caused by the scene constraints or social interactions, but also implicitly excludes all uncommon movements that can degrade the prediction. The selections of non-linear/linear grid cells and common paths is done by processing the training data only once at the pre-processing step, while the hidden states h and memory cells c in Pedestrians-LSTMs and Scene-LSTMs are updated at every training step.

Lastly, the soft filter (SF) processes the scene data (obtained from HF) for each pedestrian based on their movement behaviors. As shown in Fig. 4, although two pedestrians (red and green) step on the same common subgrids at the same time, they travel in different paths in the future. Thus, the relevant scene data should be selected for each pedestrian depending on their past movements. The relevant scene data is then used to update the hidden state h of Pedestrian-LSTM and predict the next locations. The updated hidden state h of a pedestrian is also used to update the scene data of the non-linear grid cell where this person walks in.

4   Implementation Details

Pedestrian Movement Module (PM). In this paper, we adopt a LSTM network similar to the one proposed in Social-LSTM [1] to model each pedestrian's movement behavior. Given the relative location $(\Delta x_i^t, \Delta y_i^t) = (x_i^t, y_i^t) - (x_i^{t-1}, y_i^{t-1})$ of person i at time t, we embed it to get a fixed length vector e_i^t and use it as an input to learn this person's LSTM state (h_i^t, c_i^t):

$$e_i^t = \phi(W_{ie}, [\Delta x_i^t, \Delta y_i^t]) \tag{1}$$

$$(h_i^t, c_i^t) = \text{LSTM}((h_i^{t-1}, c_i^{t-1}), e_i^t; W_{pm}) \tag{2}$$

where $\phi(\cdot)$ is embedding function with ReLU non-linearity. W_{ie} denotes embedding weights. W_{pm} denotes LSTM weights and are shared among all pedestrians.

Scene Data Module (SD). The Scene-LSTM (h_g^t, c_g^t) of grid cell g at time t is updated as:

$$V_i^t = O(x_i^t, y_i^t) \tag{3}$$

$$(h_g^t, c_g^t) = \text{LSTM}((h_g^{t-1}, c_g^{t-1}), [V_i^t, h_i^t]; W_g) \tag{4}$$

where W_g denotes LSTM weight matrices, $O(\cdot)$ is a function to convert the absolute location (x_i^t, y_i^t) of pedestrian i to a one-hot vector V_i^t. The one-hot vector V_i^t represents the relative location of this person corresponding to a subgrid within the grid cell g. In order to calculate V_i^t, each grid cell is further divided into $m \times m$ subgrids; thus, V_i^t has size $m \times m$ with values $[0, \ldots 1, \ldots 0]$, where 1 indicates the subgrid that this target occupies. The concatenation of V_i^t and h_i^t, $([V_i^t, h_i^t])$, represents the current walking behavior and location of pedestrian i in grid cell g. Thus, the grid cell's memory, encoding this information, captures all human movements, which can be used to predict the human future locations.

Hard Filter. The illustrations of the hard filter (HF) at the grid cell and the subgrid level for various scenarios are shown in Fig. 3. The trajectories in each grid cell of a scene are collected at pre-processing step for training data (Fig. 3a). Each grid cell is classified as "linear" or "non-linear" (Fig. 3b). The linear grid cell indicates that the scene data will not be applied to predict human future locations in this grid cell while the non-linear grid cells are selected (Fig. 3c) to be processed at the subgrid level. At the subgrid level, each trajectory in a non-linear grid cell is parsed into subgrid paths, which are then classified as common and uncommon subgrid paths (Fig. 3d). The common subgrid paths define the common subgrids (Fig. 3e). At prediction time, if a pedestrian steps in the common subgrids (e.g. red pedestrian, Fig. 3f), the scene data will be applied to predict this person's next location; otherwise, no scene data will be used (green pedestrian).

Soft Filter (SF). The final filtered scene data F_i^t for pedestrian i at time t is calculated as:

$$S_i = \sigma(linear([V_i^t, h_i^t])) \tag{5}$$

$$F_i^t = S_i \odot h_g^t \tag{6}$$

where h_g^t and h_i^t are the hidden states of the Scene-LSTM of the non-linear grid cell and Pedestrian-LSTM, respectively. S_i, the soft-filter vector of pedestrian i, is calculated by first concatenating one-hot vector V_i^t and h_i^t. It is further processed using a linear layer, followed by a sigmoid function to convert S_i within range $[0, 1]$. The final filtered scene data F_i^t is a result of element-wise multiplication ($\odot$) between S_i and the scene data from hard filter h_s^t.

Finally, F_i^t is used to update hidden state h_i^t (obtained from the Pedestrian-LSTM) of pedestrian i. h_i^t is then used to predict the next location of this person:

$$h_i^t = h_i^t + F_i^t \tag{7}$$

$$(\mu_i^{t+1}, \sigma_i^{t+1}, p_i^{t+1}) = W_{of} h_i^t \tag{8}$$

$$(\Delta\hat{x}_i^{t+1}, \Delta\hat{y}_i^{t+1}) \sim \aleph(\mu_i^{t+1}, \sigma_i^{t+1}, p_i^{t+1}) \tag{9}$$

$$(\hat{x}_i^{t+1}, \hat{y}_i^{t+1}) = (\hat{x}_i^t + \Delta\hat{x}_i^{t+1}, \hat{y}_i^t + \Delta\hat{y}_i^{t+1}) \tag{10}$$

where W_{of} is a weight matrix. Similar as [1], the bivariate Gaussian distribution $\aleph(\mu_i^{t+1}, \sigma_i^{t+1}, p_i^{t+1})$ is used to predict the next locations. model is trained by minimizing the negative log-likelihood loss L [8]:

$$L(W) = -\Sigma_{i=0}^N \Sigma_{t=0}^T \log(P(x_i^t, y_i^t | \mu_i^t, \sigma_i^t, p_i^t)) \tag{11}$$

where W is the set of weight matrices. N is number of targets, $T = T_{obs} + T_{pred}$ is the number of frames used for training. (x_i^t, y_i^t) is the true location of target i at time t. By minimizing $L(W)$, the likelihood that the predicted location $(\hat{x}_i^t, \hat{y}_i^t)$ is closer to the true location (x_i^t, y_i^t) is maximized.

5 Evaluation

Datasets: As with the related prior research [1,7,18,21], we first evaluate our model on two publicly available datasets: ETH [10] and UCY [14]. These datasets contain 5 video sequences (ETH-Hotel, ETH-Univ, UCY-Univ, ZARA-01, and ZARA-02) consisting of 1536 pedestrians in total with different movement patterns and social interactions: people crossing each other, avoiding collisions, or moving in groups. These sequences are recorded in 25 frames/second (fps) and contain 4 different scene backgrounds. To present the generalizability of our method on other datasets, we further evaluate on: Town Center [4] (1 video) and PETS09S2 [5] (3 videos), and Grand Central [23] (1 video). The Town Center and the PETS09S2 datasets consist of short-duration videos, originally used for human tracking, and consist of considerable amounts of social interactions (e.g. collision avoidings and group walkings). We also test our model on a long-duration video (33:20 mins) of Grand Central dataset, which consists of densely social interactions and was originally used for crowd behavior analysis.

Metrics: we evaluate our system using three metrics, introduced by Pellegrini et al. [14]:

(a) Average displacement error (ADE): The mean square error (MSE) (Euclidean distance) over all locations of predicted trajectories and the true trajectories.
(b) Average non-linear displacement error (NDE): The MSE over all locations of non-linear predicted trajectories and true trajectories.
(c) Average final displacement error (FDE): The mean square error at the final predicted location and the final true location of all human trajectories.

Comparison with Existing Methods: We compare our results with two baselines (Linear [1,7], LSTM [1]) and two state-of-the-art methods (Social-LSTM [[1], SGAN [7]):

- Linear model Linear [1,7] (non-LSTM) uses a linear regressor to estimate the linear parameters, minimizes the mean square error; assumes pedestrians move linearly.
- LSTM [1] models a LSTM for each pedestrian without considering social interactions or scene information.
- Social-LSTM [1] models the human social interactions using "social" pooling layers. We use the publicly available code given by the authors.
- SGAN [7] models social interactions by using GAN. We use two models SGAN-20V-1 and SGAN-20VP-1, where 20 V denotes that models are trained using variety loss with 20 predicted trajectories, P denotes social pooling layer. Both models generate one predicted trajectory for each pedestrian in testing phase. We used released code given in SGAN [7] to report their results.

Since the goal is to generate the best predicted trajectory, closest in L_2 norm with the ground truth trajectory, we do not compare with the model SGAN-20VP-20 because this model generates 20 predicted trajectories for each pedestrian in testing phase and selects the best predicted one (the lowest ADE score compared to ground truth trajectory) which is not feasible under the problem constrains. Hence, SGAN-20VP-20 is out-of-context for our comparisons.

Implementation Details: The implementation is done using the PyTorch framework [13]. The size of all memory cells and hidden state vectors is set to 128. The network is trained with Adam optimizer [8], an extension to stochastic gradient descent, to update network weights during the training process. The learning rate is 0.003, and the dropout value is 0.2. The value of the global norm of gradients is clipped at 10 to ensure stable training. The model is trained on GPU Tesla P100-SXM2.

Training. The training is conducted in two stages:

Stage 1: A similar "leave-one-out" approach used in [1,7] is adopted. In details, indexing the five video sequences (ETH-Univ, UCY-Univ, UCY-Zara01, and UCY-Zara02) as (i, j, k, l, m), we train (100 epochs) and validate four video sequences (V_i, V_j, V_k, V_l), select the best trained model to be used in stage 2 for the remaining (unseen) video sequence V_m. This process is repeated for each permutation. The data ratio for training/validation is 80/20.

Stage 2: Since the scene information of each video scene is needed, the best model is further trained (in 10 epochs) on the 50% video frames of the fifth video V_m. The remaining video frames are used for testing.

Testing: The scene data of each grid cell in a scene and the trained network weights are fixed. We use the best trained model (weights from stage 2) and observe trajectory of each person for 8 time-steps and predict the next 12 time-steps.

We note that the social-interaction methods only use the stage-1 training (as reported in original papers [1,7]) to learn the social interactions. However, for reasonable comparisons we apply the same training and testing procedures for all methods. The implementation of our method will be made available.

5.1   Quantitative Results

We compare our model (Scene-LSTM) with the five models described above in Table 1. The results confirm that our method significantly outperforms all other methods on the three metrics: ADE, NDE, and FDE. Especially, our method predicts the final destinations (FDE) with much higher accuracy (by 0.5 m) than the state-of-the-art SGAN-20V-1. We notice that the two models SGAN-20V-1 and SGAN-20VP-1 perform slightly better than our method in predicting non-linear trajectories (NDE) on the two video sequences ETH-Univ, UCY-Zara02. This is because our method does not capture the uncommon social interactions as they do not form common paths in these video scenes. However, the overall results validate the importance of our common human movement features in predicting future trajectories.

Table 1. Quantitive results on ETH and UCY datasets (5 video sequences). All methods predict human trajectories in 12 frames using 8 observed frames. Error metrics are reported in meters (lower is better).

Metrics	Sequences	Linear	LSTM	Social-LSTM	SGAN-20V-1	SGAN-20VP-1	Scene-LSTM
ADE	ETH-Hotel	1.49	1.35	1.14	0.76	0.75	**0.36**
	ETH-Univ	2.04	1.97	2.28	1.26	1.18	**0.95**
	UCY-Univ	1.68	1.83	2.02	0.79	1.08	**0.63**
	UCY-Zara01	2.60	2.30	3.14	0.61	0.62	**0.45**
	UCY-Zara02	1.11	1.23	2.05	0.52	0.57	**0.40**
	Average	1.78	1.74	2.13	0.79	0.84	**0.56**
NDE	ETH-Hotel	3.30	1.71	2.01	1.66	1.48	**0.76**
	ETH-Univ	3.45	3.16	3.64	**1.55**	1.57	1.88
	UCY-Univ	2.22	2.08	2.36	1.00	1.21	**0.92**
	UCY-Zara01	2.40	1.75	2.75	0.71	0.78	**0.65**
	UCY-Zara02	2.67	2.40	2.87	0.88	**0.81**	0.93
	Average	2.81	2.22	2.73	1.36	1.17	**1.00**
FDE	ETH-Hotel	2.67	2.45	2.11	1.64	1.58	**0.67**
	ETH-Univ	3.41	3.60	4.03	2.44	2.42	**1.77**
	UCY-Univ	3.03	3.49	3.78	1.73	2.21	**1.41**
	UCY-Zara01	4.77	3.98	5.69	1.32	1.36	**1.00**
	UCY-Zara02	2.05	2.34	4.14	1.14	1.20	**0.90**
	Average	3.19	3.17	3.95	1.65	1.75	**1.15**

5.2 Ablation Study

In this section, we present the impact of several system components (Table 2): Pedestrian Movement module using absolute locations (PM_{abs}) vs. relative locations (PM_{rel}), Scene Data module (SD), hard filter at the grid level (HF_{grid}) and the subgrid level ($HF_{subgrid}$), and soft filter (SF).

Impact of Using Relative Locations. PM_{rel} produces significantly lower errors compared to PM_{abs}. This is because PM_{abs} is strongly biased to a specific scene layout, while PM_{rel} models individual target's relative movement behavior regardless of the scene layouts; thus, PM_{rel} allows for better transfer learning to new scenes.

Impact of Scene Data (SD). As expected, using SD without the filters (the third row) worsens most of individual movement predictions.

Impact of Hard Filter at the Grid Cell Level (HF_{grid}). At this level (without subgrid), the hard filter allows the Scene-LSTMs of the non-linear grid cells learn all human movements, which significantly helpful to predict the non-linear movements (lower NDE) in these cells. We also observed that the ADE is slightly increased because the scene data has a negative impact on predicting linear trajectories in the non-linear grid cells.

Impact of Hard Filter at the Subgrid Level ($HF_{subgrid}$). The $HF_{subgrid}$ resolves the issue of predicting linear trajectories in HF_{grid} and further reduces the prediction errors in all three metrics. This demonstrates the effectiveness of

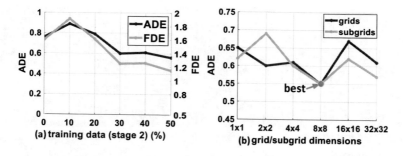

Fig. 5. The impact of (a) training data amount at stage-2 and (b) finding grid/subgrid sizes to optimize prediction accuracy. The results (ADE and FDE) are calculated on average of 5 videos. (Color figure online)

Table 2. Ablation study. PM_{abs} and PM_{rel}: PM module with absolute and relative locations, respectively. SD: Scene Data module. HF_{grid}: hard filter at the grid level. $HF_{subgrid}$: hard filter at the subgrid level. SF: soft filter. The results (in meters) are averaged on ETH and UCY datasets (5 videos) (lower is better).

Components used	ADE	NDE	FDE
PM_{abs}	1.89	2.72	3.53
PM_{rel}	0.66	1.11	1.36
PM_{rel}, SD	0.69	1.34	1.41
PM_{rel}, SD, HF_{grid}	0.72	0.91	1.41
PM_{rel}, SD, HF_{grid}, $HF_{subgrid}$	0.57	0.90	1.19
PM_{rel}, SD, HF_{grid}, SF	0.62	**0.86**	1.30
PM_{rel}, SD, HF_{grid}, $HF_{subgrid}$, SF	**0.56**	1.00	**1.15**

using the subgrid common paths as it removes uncommon paths caused by the social interactions and implicitly captures the common paths, caused by either social interactions or scene structures.

Impact of Soft Filter (SF). Using SF at the grid cell level (the sixth row) produces more accurate non-linear trajectory predictions (lower NDE) than at the subgrid level (the last row). This is because predicting the non-linear trajectories requires more scene data obtained at grid cell level. However, considering different trajectory types (e.g. linear and non-linear) and long-term predictions, the full model (last row) still achieves the best ADE/FDE results.

Impact of Training Data Amount in Stage 2. To see the impact of stage 2 training data in learning common movement patterns of a new scene, an experiment is conducted by ranging the training data amounts in stage 2 from 0% to 50% of video frames and using the remaining 50% data for testing (Fig. 5a). As expected, both ADE and FDE continue to decrease when more training data is used and reach the best results at 50% video frames training.

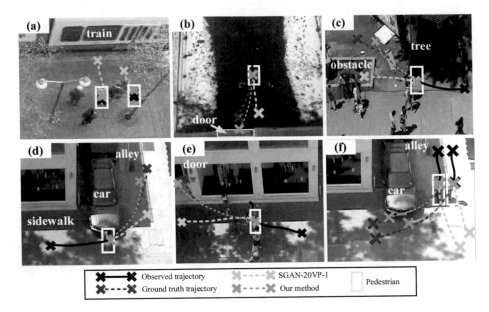

Fig. 6. Qualitative comparison between our method with SGAN-20VP-1 in different scenarios: (a) pedestrians are standing still and waiting for trains, (b) a pedestrian is entering the door, (c) a pedestrian is finding a path between obstacle and trees, (d) a pedestrian makes a left-turn to the alley, (e) a pedestrian turns right to enter the building, (f) a couple turn right from the alley.

Impact of Grid and Sub-grid Sizes. The grid and subgrid sizes should be selected to best capture common human movements in each video scene. The experiment is done in two steps: (1) we first train our model on ETH and UCY datasets (5 videos) with a fixed grid size 8×8 and different subgrid sizes: 1×1, 2×2, 4×4, 8×8, 16×16, and 32×32. The best selected subgrid size is 8×8 (red line, Fig. 5b) (2) We run the model again by fixing the subgrid size to 8×8 while varying grid sizes. The result, as shown in blue line, confirms that the best selected grid and subgrid sizes are 8×8. The size 8×8 indicates that the grid/subgrid size should not be too big or small; otherwise, it would not capture common human movements impacted by the scene layouts.

5.3 Qualitative Results

We present qualitative comparisons with the social model SGAN-20VP-1 (Fig. 6). SGAN-20VP-1 considers the social interactions that are meaningful and socially acceptable while SGAN-20V-1 does not consider social interactions. The visualizations show that our method generates more accurate trajectories (closer to ground truth trajectory) compared to SGAN-20VP-1 in different scene-contexts. This demonstrates the importance of learning common movements and using them to predict human movements in highly structural constrained areas.

Table 3. The quantitative results (ADE/FDE in meters) on Town Center (1 short video sequence) and PETS09S2 (3 short videos) and Grand Central (1 long video) datasets.

Datasets	T_{pred} (s)	SGAN-20V-1 [7]	SGAN-20VP-1 [7]	Scene-LSTM
Town	4.8	0.22/0.46	0.21/0.42	**0.09/0.18**
Center	6.4	0.37/0.80	0.38/0.81	**0.14/0.27**
PETS09	4.8	0.23/0.51	0.30/0.66	**0.06/0.15**
S2	6.4	0.43/0.93	0.53/1.21	**0.11/0.23**
Grand	4.8	0.21/0.45	0.40/0.74	**0.11/0.17**
Central	6.4	0.32/0.62	0.79/1.50	**0.14/0.25**

5.4 Generalization: Evaluations on Town Center, PETS09, and Grand Central

To present the generalizability, we further conduct experiments on new (unseen) datasets: Town Center [4], PETS09S2 [5], and Grand Central [23]. **Setup.** We use the pre-trained network on ETH and UCY datasets from the previous section and further train it on 50% of frame data of each video in this experiment (this process is similar as training stage 2 in previous experiment). The remaining frames of each video is used for testing. We generate trajectory predictions for $T_{pred} = 4.8$ and 6.4 s. **Results.** We compare our method with two variants of SGAN [7] as shown in Table 3. We confirm that our method outperforms them on three datasets in ADE and FDE. For Town Center and PETS09S2 datasets, where the scenes are crowded but people mostly move linearly, the SGAN [7] method often over-predicts by considering all interactions among all pedestrians, thus fails to predict the linearity. The Grand Central dataset consists of lots of complex local social interactions, however, the common movements are paths from one train station to another, thus our method performs better by capturing these common motions. The results indicate our method can be applied to achieve the state-of-the-art results in new video sequences.

6 Conclusion

The novel Scene-LSTM model presented in this paper enables us to consider common human movements in localities within the scene. We have demonstrated substantial improvement in predicting trajectories using the resulting scene information, outperforming related methods. We plan to investigate fusing the scene model with social model to improve prediction quality and further explore the social interactions not only among humans but also between human and other static or moving objects.

References

1. Alahi, A., Goel, K., Ramanathan, V., Robicquet, A., Fei-Fei, L., Savarese, S.: Social LSTM: human trajectory prediction in crowded spaces. In: Proceedings of the IEEE Conference on Computer Vision and Pattern Recognition, pp. 961–971 (2016)
2. Ballan, L., Castaldo, F., Alahi, A., Palmieri, F., Savarese, S.: Knowledge transfer for scene-specific motion prediction. In: Leibe, B., Matas, J., Sebe, N., Welling, M. (eds.) ECCV 2016, Part I. LNCS, vol. 9905, pp. 697–713. Springer, Cham (2016). https://doi.org/10.1007/978-3-319-46448-0_42
3. Bartoli, F., Lisanti, G., Ballan, L., Del Bimbo, A.: Context-aware trajectory prediction. In: International Conference on Pattern Recognition, pp. 1941–1946. IEEE (2018)
4. Benfold, B., Reid, I.: Stable multi-target tracking in real-time surveillance video. In: CVPR, pp. 3457–3464. IEEE (2011)
5. Ferryman, J., Shahrokni, A.: PETS 2009: dataset and challenge. In: Twelfth IEEE International Workshop on Performance Evaluation of Tracking and Surveillance, pp. 1–6. IEEE (2009)
6. Goodfellow, I., et al.: Generative adversarial nets. In: Advances in Neural Information Processing Systems, pp. 2672–2680 (2014)
7. Gupta, A., Johnson, J., Fei-Fei, L., Savarese, S., Alahi, A.: Social GAN: socially acceptable trajectories with generative adversarial networks. In: Proceedings of the IEEE Conference on Computer Vision and Pattern Recognition, pp. 2255–2264 (2018)
8. Kingma, D.P., Ba, J.: Adam: a method for stochastic optimization. arXiv preprint: arXiv:1412.6980 (2014)
9. Leonard, J.J., Durrant-Whyte, H.F.: Application of multi-target tracking to sonar-based mobile robot navigation. In: 29th IEEE Conference on Decision and Control, pp. 3118–3123. IEEE (1990)
10. Lerner, A., Chrysanthou, Y., Lischinski, D.: Crowds by example. In: Computer Graphics Forum, vol. 26, pp. 655–664. Wiley Online Library (2007)
11. Levinson, J., et al.: Towards fully autonomous driving: systems and algorithms. In: 2011 IEEE Intelligent Vehicles Symposium (IV), pp. 163–168. IEEE (2011)
12. Manh, H., Alaghband, G.: Spatiotemporal KSVD dictionary learning for online multi-target tracking. In: 2018 15th Conference on Computer and Robot Vision (CRV), pp. 150–157. IEEE (2018)
13. Paszke, A., Gross, S., Chintala, S., Chanan, G.: PyTorch: tensors and dynamic neural networks in python with strong GPU acceleration 6 (2017)
14. Pellegrini, S., Ess, A., Schindler, K., Van Gool, L.: You'll never walk alone: modeling social behavior for multi-target tracking. In: 2009 IEEE 12th International Conference on Computer Vision, pp. 261–268. IEEE (2009)
15. Robicquet, A., Sadeghian, A., Alahi, A., Savarese, S.: Learning social etiquette: human trajectory understanding in crowded scenes. In: Leibe, B., Matas, J., Sebe, N., Welling, M. (eds.) ECCV 2016, Part VIII. LNCS, vol. 9912, pp. 549–565. Springer, Cham (2016). https://doi.org/10.1007/978-3-319-46484-8_33
16. Trautman, P., Krause, A.: Unfreezing the robot: navigation in dense, interacting crowds. In: 2010 IEEE/RSJ International Conference on Intelligent Robots and Systems, pp. 797–803. IEEE (2010)
17. Varshneya, D., Srinivasaraghavan, G.: Human trajectory prediction using spatially aware deep attention models. arXiv preprint: arXiv:1705.09436 (2017)

18. Vemula, A., Muelling, K., Oh, J.: Social attention: modeling attention in human crowds. In: IEEE International Conference on Robotics and Automation (ICRA), pp. 1–7. IEEE (2018)
19. Vivacqua, R.P.D., Bertozzi, M., Cerri, P., Martins, F.N., Vassallo, R.F.: Self-localization based on visual lane marking maps: an accurate low-cost approach for autonomous driving. IEEE Trans. Intell. Transp. Syst. **19**(2), 582–597 (2017)
20. Xu, Y., Piao, Z., Gao, S.: Encoding crowd interaction with deep neural network for pedestrian trajectory prediction. In: Proceedings of the IEEE Conference on Computer Vision and Pattern Recognition, pp. 5275–5284 (2018)
21. Xue, H., Huynh, D.Q., Reynolds, M.: SS-LSTM: a hierarchical LSTM model for pedestrian trajectory prediction. In: 2018 IEEE Winter Conference on Applications of Computer Vision (WACV), pp. 1186–1194. IEEE (2018)
22. Yamaguchi, K., Berg, A.C., Ortiz, L.E., Berg, T.L.: Who are you with and where are you going? In: CVPR 2011, pp. 1345–1352. IEEE (2011)
23. Zhou, B., Wang, X., Tang, X.: Understanding collective crowd behaviors: learning a mixture model of dynamic pedestrian-agents. In: 2012 IEEE Conference on Computer Vision and Pattern Recognition, pp. 2871–2878. IEEE (2012)

Augmented Curiosity: Depth and Optical Flow Prediction for Efficient Exploration

Juan Carvajal[✉], Thomas Molnar, Lukasz Burzawa, and Eugenio Culurciello

Purdue University, West Lafayette, IN 47907, USA
{carvajaj,tmolnar,lburzawa,euge}@purdue.edu

Abstract. Exploring novel environments for a specific target poses the challenge of how to adequately provide positive external rewards to an artificial agent. In scenarios with sparse external rewards, a reinforcement learning algorithm often cannot develop a successful policy function to govern an agent's behavior. However, intrinsic rewards can provide feedback on an agent's actions and enable updates towards a proper policy function in sparse scenarios. Our approaches called the Optical Flow-Augmented Curiosity Module (OF-ACM) and Depth-Augmented Curiosity Module (D-ACM) extend the Intrinsic Curiosity Model (ICM) by Pathak et al. The ICM forms an intrinsic reward signal from the error between a prediction and the ground truth of the next state. Shown with experiments in visually rich and sparse feature scenarios in ViZDoom, our predictive modules exhibit improved exploration capabilities and learning of an ideal policy function. Our modules leverage additional sources of information, such as depth images and optical flow, to generate superior embeddings that serve as inputs for next state prediction. With D-ACM we show a 63.3% average improvement in time to convergence of a policy over ICM in "My Way Home" scenarios.

Keywords: Reinforcement Learning · Exploration · Curiosity · Self supervision

1 Introduction

At a fundamental level, humans learn from their interactions with the environment. Reinforcement Learning (RL) algorithms emulate this behavior by learning a policy function that maximizes the rewards an agent obtains in an environment. These rewards are specific to the environment and goal at hand. In Deep Reinforcement Learning, neural networks are used to approximate the policy functions by mapping input states to actions.

Different variants of RL algorithms have been used for exploration and navigation problems [11]. To assess RL algorithms, scenarios are set up for an agent to explore an environment and find a desired target. Traditionally, RL algorithms expect dense and well-shaped reward functions to continuously update

---

J. Carvajal, T. Molnar and L. Burzawa—Equal Contribution.

© Springer Nature Switzerland AG 2019
G. Bebis et al. (Eds.): ISVC 2019, LNCS 11844, pp. 260–271, 2019.
https://doi.org/10.1007/978-3-030-33720-9_20

their policy while interacting with the environment. However in general navigation and exploration tasks, positive feedback is received only when a target is reached. While "shaping" dense rewards for each specific environment is a possibility, this is not a scalable approach [3]. A viable alternative is to generate rewards "intrinsic" to the agent which complement external rewards. Intrinsic rewards help incentivize an agent to explore new states and provide feedback for an agent to better predict the outcomes of its actions.

Our work is based on the Intrinsic Curiosity Model (ICM) by [8]. This approach proposes an intrinsic reward generator that supplements external rewards found in an environment. The ICM receives three inputs, an agent's current state, its next state and the action taken by the agent to move from the current state to the next state. In the inverse model, the ICM uses the current state feature embedding and the next state feature embedding to predict the agent's sampled action. The embeddings are outputs from shared weight neural networks which transform the original input state space into a feature space. Given that the labels for training are the actions sampled from the function policy at each step, this process falls under the self-supervision paradigm. As the only incentive is to predict the action leading to the next state, the training process ensures that the feature space only encodes information influencing the specific actions.

Given the current state embedding and an agent's sampled action as inputs, the ICM trains a forward dynamics model to predict a feature space embedding of the next state. An intrinsic reward is generated from the error between the forward model's prediction of the next state embedding and the actual next state ground truth embedding. The intrinsic reward factor for example then grows large whenever the agent explores previously unvisited areas. In turn, an agent experiences a rewarding sense of "curiosity" by visiting new and unfamiliar areas. An Asynchronous Advantage Actor Critic (A3C) [7] algorithm strives to maximize the sum of an extrinsic reward provided by the environment and the intrinsic reward signal provided by the ICM.

In our approach to reward sparsity, we leverage Pathak et al.'s use of intrinsic reward signals. However, we also provide our modules, named the Optical Flow-Augmented Curiosity Module (OF-ACM) and Depth-Augmented Curiosity Module (D-ACM), with depth and optical flow inputs to develop superior embeddings for exploration. Optical flow describes the motion of elements in a visual scene caused by the relative motion between an observer and the given scene. Optical flow offers knowledge on how pixels change position in subsequent frames, and in static scenarios, optical flow gives information on how the agent's position changes. Depth images also provide a better sense of relationships between objects than standard RGB images [9]. By using optical flow and depth information rather than only pixels from RGB images, the OF-ACM and D-ACM utilize localization information and higher level representations of a given scene. While the ICM inverse model predicts the action relating two consecutive states, our modules' modified inverse models predict either a depth image or the optical flow between two states. In the combined variant of our architecture module, two different curiosity-based predictive modules are initialized to generate depth and optical flow predictions.

We used several scenarios in ViZDoom to evaluate the scalability, performance and generalizability of our predictive network relative to Pathak et al.'s ICM, which served as a baseline. These are all maze-like scenarios, where the agent is spawned at a location with the goal of locating a piece of armor at another location. In addition to the ViZDoom scenarios used by [8], we created more complex and variant scenarios. These different scenarios show how well the architectures perform in more challenging environments and transfer knowledge between environments.

After evaluation across several scenarios, we demonstrate how the combined use of intrinsic rewards systems and supplementary input data results in a capable system, even in scenarios with sparse external rewards. Through utilizing readily available information in depth and optical flow in addition to standard RGB image data, we developed a more efficient system.

2 Methodology

2.1 Experiment Environments

Environments in ViZDoom, a Doom-based AI research platform [5] were set-up to evaluate our modules' abilities to explore and search for objectives in environments with sparse external rewards. In these scenarios, the agent's goal was to locate a piece of armor. The simulations would restart after the agent reached its goal, therefore receiving a terminal reward of +1, or after exceeding 2100 time steps without finding the target. The base scenario used for evaluations was "MyWayHome-v0" (MWH), a part of the OpenAIGym [1]. MWH is composed of 8 different rooms, each room having its own distinct wall texture. To add variability and robustness to the testing process, we also created two new scenarios. The first, "My Way Home Mirrored" (MWH-M), is a re-oriented version of MWH. Besides providing an additional testbed for the various networks, MWH-M tests how well networks' learned knowledge applies between scenarios. To evaluate the modules' limitations in complex scenarios, we created "My Way Home Giant" (MWH-G) with 19 rooms. These scenarios are shown in Fig. 1.

For each scenario, we add variability in two more ways through **Variability in Reward Sparsity** and **Variability in Visual Texture Features** [8]. For reward sparsity, a scenario has either a sparse or dense setup, offering different degrees of complexity for exploration. In both cases, the target location remains constant, while the agent's start location may vary. With the dense setting, the agent starts randomly at 1 of 17 uniformly distributed locations to begin exploring from. Some start locations are far away from the target, while others are close to the target. These diverse positions allow the agent to reach the target even by random actions. Conversely with sparse, the start location is far from the target and does not vary. This requires the agent to take several directed actions to reach its goal.

(a) My Way Home   (b) My Way Home Mirror   (c) My Way Home Giant

Fig. 1. ViZDoom Scenarios. The target is the green circle at the rightmost part of each image. The purple circles indicate possible agent start locations for the dense case. For the sparse case, an agent spawns at the location indicated by the green circle situated at the left of each scenario. (Color figure online)

With visual features in scenarios, we developed two variants of the texture of the maze walls. While the layout of the environment remains the same, the texture, or pattern, of the walls is modified to either be uniform or vary across every room in the environment. The variants are referred to as either **uniform texture scenarios** or **varied texture scenarios**, respectively, as shown in Fig. 2. In uniform scenarios, a model must have a high-level and abstract understanding of the environment to adequately explore and locate the target without information from rich visual features in the environment. Each scenario then has 4 variations. For example, the MWH scenario has the following setups: MWH Dense Texture, MWH Dense Uniform, MWH Sparse Texture and MWH Sparse Uniform.

(a) Varied Texture   (b) Uniform Texture

Fig. 2. Variability in Visual Texture Features. (a) Shows a frame from the agent's point of view in a uniform texture scenario. (b) Agent's view of a varied texture scenario.

2.2   Advantage Actor Critic

RL algorithms enable an artificial agent to learn tasks by maximizing cumulative rewards provided within an environment. Pathak et al. train an A3C agent to perform navigation. For this, the agent only receives a terminal reward after reaching the target. However, when combining the ICM with A3C, an intrinsic curiosity signal is added as a reward.

Actor-critic methods output a policy and a value function. Given input state s_t and an action a, the policy $\pi_\theta(a|s_t)$, parameterized by network parameters θ, outputs probabilities for each available action. In our environments, the agent has a discrete action space with four possible movements: move forward, move left, move right and no action. Sampling an action, a_t, from the policy, results in transitioning to next state s_{t+1} and receiving reward r_{t+1}. The value function $V_v(s_{t+1})$, with network parameters v, returns an estimate of the expected final total reward obtainable by the agent from that state. This function serves as a "critic" to the policy function, judging the resulting state of the previously taken action. Advantage Actor Critic methods offer a variant for the value estimate, the advantage function $A(s_t, a_t) = r_{t+1} + \gamma V_v(s_{t+1}) - V_v(s_t)$ with γ the discount factor, to account for future rewards losing value. This function estimates how a specific action is better than other actions at a given state. The gradient of the loss function is $\nabla_\theta J(\theta) \sim \sum_{t=0}^{T-1} \nabla_\theta \log \pi_\theta(a_t|s_t) A(s_t, a_t)$. The set of network parameters θ and v are updated in the gradient's direction.

The A3C algorithm [8] implements multiple agents that interact with different copies of an environment in parallel [7]. A global network hosts the shared parameters. At each time step, the agents have copies of the shared network. If an independent agent reaches t_{max} time steps or a terminal state, that network copy's gradient is computed from its own interaction. Independently of the other agents, the global network's parameters are then asynchronously updated by the independent agent's experience. In our experiments, we use a similar implementation but with synchronous (A2C) update of global parameters [10]. The global update then waits until all agents have finished their current interaction. This allows for efficient use of graphics processing units (GPUs).

2.3 Augmented Curiosity Models

We replicated and evaluated the ICM proposed by Pathak et al. in each scenario as a baseline against our model variants. The ICM generates a feature representation of the input states by predicting the action that connects two subsequent states. However, our approach extends this framework to support prediction of depth, optical flow and a combination of the two when creating feature embedding representations. These network architectures are described in Fig. 3, and we demonstrate improved navigation and exploration capabilities using depth over the baseline ICM.

The original ICM module assumes two key arguments with regards to the curiosity reward. First, predictions of a future state in the forward model using a feature space instead of pixel space is more advantageous than previous approaches. When the dimension of predictions is lower, the predictions are simpler. More importantly, changes in pixels themselves might not be the real objective, as these changes may or may not be influenced by an agent's actions. Secondly, to model only changes in an environment that are direct outcomes of an agent's actions, the inverse model prediction must provide a proper embedding in the feature space. The ICM's embeddings of the current and next state, ϕ_t and ϕ_{t+1}, are obtained from predicting an action when given the successive

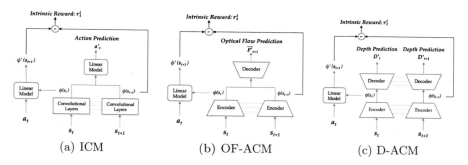

(a) ICM   (b) OF-ACM   (c) D-ACM

Fig. 3. (a) The ICM [8] encodes RGB frames from the agent's point of view at states s_t and s_{t+1} into ϕ_t and ϕ_{t+1} by a Convolutional Layer block. Embeddings are concatenated and passed to linear layers block to predict action a'_t. Through a linear block, ϕ_t and label a'_t are used to predict ϕ'_{t+1}. The difference between ϕ'_{t+1} and ϕ_{t+1} is used as intrinsic reward r^i_t. (b) OF-ACM leverages latent space in an encoder-decoder as ϕ_t and ϕ_{t+1} embeddings. (c) D-ACM predicts a depth image from each input frame. Convolutional Layer blocks consist of four convolutional layers, each with 32 filters and kernel size 3×3. Each layer is followed by batch normalization and an ELU as an activation function. Linear Model blocks are defined as two fully connected layers with an ELU activation between them. Encoder and Decoder blocks consist of four layers of 32 filters with 3×3 kernels followed by equal numbers of filters and kernel size deconvolutions. Dashed lines represent shared weights between networks.

states, s_t and s_{t+1}, as inputs. This encodes information from the input state to the embeddings that is related to an agent's actions in the environment.

As a result, the quality of the curiosity reward depends on the embeddings. Predicting only actions a'_t with the inverse model does provide an adequate embedding for a curious agent. However by using additional information in the prediction, the embeddings can better summarize changes in pixels and interpret textural and structural aspects of an environment.

Optical Flow-Augmented Curiosity Module (OF-ACM). The first variant of the ICM we propose uses the inverse model to predict optical flow instead of the action between frame inputs. We use OpenCV library's implementation of dense optical flow with Gunnar Farneback's algorithm [2]. The output $\overrightarrow{F}_{t+1}$ consists of a 2D matrix measuring the displacement of each pixel in a frame when compared to its predecessor. OpenCV's implementation provides a real-time optical flow output that is used as the ground-truth for training the modified inverse model's prediction. The network architecture changes considerably given that our approach reconstructs a 2D pixel displacement matrix from image inputs. We use an autoencoder architecture for the inverse model. States s_t and s_{t+1} are input frames and are transformed through convolutional layers into features in a latent space. After concatenating these features, the result is passed through deconvolution layers to generate the desired output matrix. During training, the autoencoder's latent space learns to encode the key information relevant to reconstructing the optical flow prediction $\overrightarrow{F'}_{t+1}$ from input images. This is due to how network loss only depends on creating an accurate optical flow reconstruction. This latent space serves as the new feature space for embeddings ϕ_t and ϕ_{t+1}. The action a_t and embedding ϕ_t are inputs to the forward model, which outputs the predicted next state's embedding ϕ'_{t+1}.

While the ICM's action prediction process accounts for pixel information, the OF-ACM enables embeddings to contain information on the displacement of tracked pixels. Even if pixels are redundant in predictions, the constraint of predicting dense sets of pixels provides embeddings a better awareness of the changes in the perceived environment correlated to the agent's movement.

Depth-Augmented Curiosity Module (D-ACM). We also extend the principles from the OF-ACM with depth images. The inverse model uses an autoencoder to obtain embeddings from the latent space features. The autoencoder predicts the depth images D'_t and D'_{t+1} corresponding to the RGB inputs. The ViZDoom platform provides ground-truth depth images that are used as labels. While this approach does not necessarily encode the influence of an agent's actions in embeddings, it provides embeddings with structural information of the environment. From previous work on localization and navigation tasks [4,6], we contend that 3D information provides a better representation of environments than 2D texture information. These depth-based embeddings contain important information regarding how agents' movement affects its perceived 3D environment. Therefore, they offer advantageous representations and more efficiently inform the agent when venturing to a new area.

Depth+Optical Flow Combined Curiosity Module (C-ACM). Two independent curiosity-based modules generate separate depth and optical flow predictions, each generating an intrinsic reward. The final intrinsic reward signal is a scaled value obtained from the two prediction errors.

Curriculum Training. To evaluate how our approach transfers knowledge to different scenarios, we transfer network parameters from a trained module to use as a starting point for the new testing environment. To validate our arguments, we evaluated ICM and our proposed modules in the environments and setups discussed in Sect. 2.

3   Results

Table 1 below illustrates differences in the size and performance of each model. The percent difference columns compare our model variants to the ICM. The ICM consists of fewer trainable parameters than our model variants, however the discrepancy is marginal. Also noted is the comparison in model performance with respect to timing, where the ICM completes a single training step fastest. Our model variations with depth and optical flow are comparable with respect to timing and parameters. These standardized timing parameters were obtained from testing each model type individually in MWH with varied texture while utilizing 20 parallel workers on the GeForce GTX 1080 GPU with 8114 MiB

Table 1. Model size and timing comparisons.

Model type	# Trainable parameters	% Difference	Time to complete 1 step (ms)	% Difference
ICM	915,945	Baseline	1.13	Baseline
D-ACM	944,170	3%	1.36	18.5%
OF-ACM	953,675	4.1%	1.63	36.2%
Combined	1,308,560	35.3%	2.46	74.1%

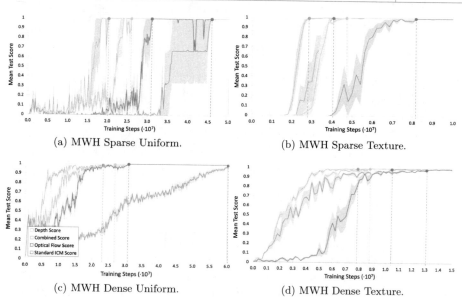

(a) MWH Sparse Uniform.   (b) MWH Sparse Texture.

(c) MWH Dense Uniform.   (d) MWH Dense Texture.

Fig. 4. My Way Home Results. Across evaluation scenarios, a minimum of five instances of each module variant were setup and averaged for the score trend line. The shaded area around each trend line indicates the one standard error range. The ovals roughly indicate where a module has completely converged to a policy function.

Table 2. My Way Home Scenario Time Performance Results. Time required to converge to an optimal training policy is in seconds. The percent difference columns compare models' performance to the ICM, either a positive speedup or decline in performance.

Scenario	Model type						
	ICM (s)	D-ACM (s)	% Difference	OF-ACM (s)	% Difference	Combined (s)	% Difference
Dense, Varied Texture	1.24E+04	1.02E+04	+21.9%	2.14E+04	−41.8%	2.10E+04	−40.9%
Dense, Uniform Texture	6.78E+04	3.06E+04	+121.6%	4.89E+04	+38.7%	6.64E+04	+2.1%
Sparse, Varied Texture	4.52E+03	3.74E+03	+20.9%	1.32E+04	−65.8%	1.13E+04	−60.1%
Sparse, Uniform Texture	5.14E+04	2.72E+04	+89.0%	5.05E+04	+1.8%	6.27E+04	−18.0%

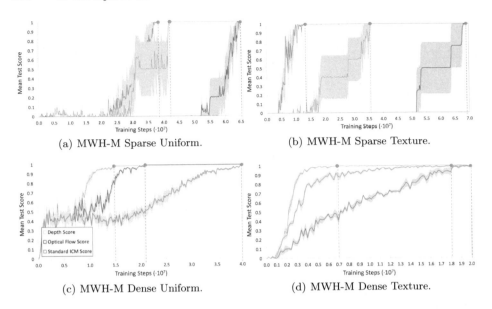

(a) MWH-M Sparse Uniform.

(b) MWH-M Sparse Texture.

(c) MWH-M Dense Uniform.

(d) MWH-M Dense Texture.

Fig. 5. My Way Home Mirrored results.

of memory. We use this information below to standardize results of the models from training steps in terms of relative time.

Figure 4(a–d) shows the performance of the ICM relative to our predictive modules in the MWH dense and sparse scenarios. The results of Fig. 4 are summarized in Table 2. The ICM performance lags behind that of the depth network but is comparable to the optical flow module. The uniformity in maze texture proves to be significantly challenging to the different modules, as the modules converge to optimal policies faster in the varied texture scenarios. These evaluations demonstrate the superior performance of the depth-based module over the others. In initial tests, the combined network fails to outperform the D-ACM, typically matching the OF-ACM or ICM performance. Thus, the combined module was not included in the subsequent evaluations.

Figures 5(a–d) and 6(a–d) show results from testing in the MWH-M scenarios, with and without use of curriculum training. Results for these plots are summarized below in Table 3. From the results, one is able to gauge how well the ICM, D-ACM and OF-ACM are able to apply previously learned knowledge.

As the table depicts, each of the modules is able to leverage curriculum training to obtain time improvements with converging to an optimal policy. The OF-ACM variant benefited the most from using curriculum training, followed by the D-ACM and lastly ICM. The ICM and D-ACM prove fairly comparable overall in the scenarios, while the ICM performs slightly better in sparse scenarios, whereas depth moreso in the dense cases.

Following evaluations in the MWH-M scenarios, the models were tested in the MWH-G to determine their ability to perform in larger and more complex

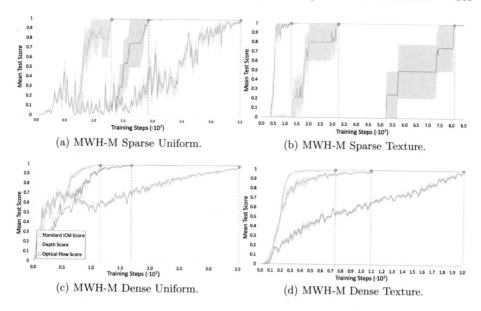

(a) MWH-M Sparse Uniform.   (b) MWH-M Sparse Texture.

(c) MWH-M Dense Uniform.   (d) MWH-M Dense Texture.

Fig. 6. My Way Home Mirrored with curriculum training results.

Table 3. My Way Home mirrored scenario time performance results, with and without curriculum training.

Scenario	Model type				
w/o Curriculum Training	ICM (s)	D-ACM (s)	% Difference	OF-ACM (s)	% Difference
Dense, Varied Texture	2.03E+04	8.84E+03	+130.1%	3.23E+04	−37.0%
Dense, Uniform Texture	4.52E+04	2.04E+04	+121.6%	3.42E+04	+32.1%
Sparse, Varied Texture	1.70E+03	4.83E+03	−64.9%	1.11E+05	−84.7%
Sparse, Uniform Texture	4.29E+04	5.78E+04	−25.7%	1.06E+05	−59.5%
Scenario	Model type				
w/ Curriculum Training	ICM (s)	D-ACM (s)	% Difference	OF-ACM (s)	% Difference
Dense, Varied Texture	1.24E+04	1.02E+03	+21.9%	3.26E+04	−61.9%
Dense, Uniform Texture	3.96E+04	1.50E+04	+164.4%	2.69E+04	+47.1%
Sparse, Varied Texture	1.41E+03	4.22E+03	−66.5%	1.32E+05	−89.3%
Sparse, Uniform Texture	3.96E+04	1.70E+04	+132.7%	3.26E+0e	+21.3%

environments. Shown below in Figs. 7(a–b) and 8(a–b) are the results for performance in MWH-G, without and with use of curriculum training respectively.

The results of MWH-G are summarized in Table 4. In this scenario, all models failed to achieve any form of an ideal policy when operating in the sparse scenario variants. Although the instances were allowed to run for 20E+7 training steps, they never reached the target in the training phase, regardless of the use of curriculum training. The D-ACM significantly outperformed the ICM and OF-ACM in the giant scenario as well, while the ICM benefits the most from

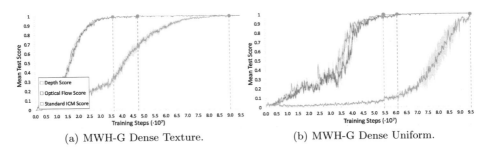

(a) MWH-G Dense Texture.   (b) MWH-G Dense Uniform.

Fig. 7. My Way Home Giant results.

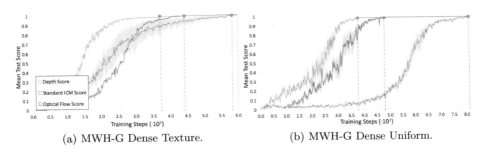

(a) MWH-G Dense Texture.   (b) MWH-G Dense Uniform.

Fig. 8. My Way Home Giant with curriculum training results.

Table 4. My Way Home giant scenario time performance results, with and without curriculum training.

Scenario	Model type				
w/o Curriculum Training	ICM (s)	D-ACM (s)	% Difference	OF-ACM (s)	% Difference
Dense, Varied Texture	1.02E+05	5.92E+04	+71.9%	7.82E+04	+30.0%
Dense, Uniform Texture	1.07E+05	7.55E+04	+42.2%	1.02E+05	+5.4%
Scenario	Model type				
w/ Curriculum Training	ICM (s)	D-ACM (s)	% Difference	OF-ACM (s)	% Difference
Dense, Varied Texture	6.55E+04	5.10E+04	+28.5%	7.12E+04	−8.0%
Dense, Uniform Texture	9.15E+04	5.17E+04	+77.1%	7.82E+04	+17.0%

use of curriculum training in this high complexity scenario. The modules did successfully manage to develop an optimal policy in the dense scenario variants, even given uniform textures.

4   Conclusions

Given the results, the D-ACM improves upon the ICM with an average 63.3% time speedup in MWH scenarios, 40.3% in MWH-M and 57.1% in MWH-G. This approach develops more generalized network embeddings across different scenarios and converges faster in environments with sparse external rewards. OF-ACM seems promising in larger scenarios, as shown in MWH-G. The D-ACM and OF-ACM perform similar to the ICM in MWH and MWH-M but drastically outperform it in the more complex MWH-G. This highlights how depth and optical flow inputs allow better environment representations for exploration. However, when dealing when simpler scenarios, the representations do not offer a significant advantage. Our work illustrates how by leveraging additional inputs, rather than solely pixels from RGB images, a RL agent can improve performance and scalability across scenarios to better handle the issue of reward sparsity. Future work will focus on evaluations in dynamic scenarios with moving elements independent of an agent. Additionally, performance may be improved by refining the combination of depth and optical flow inputs, such as with a combined loss function. While our work on combining OF-ACM and D-ACM has not produced a module more effective than depth alone, this subject still presents an area of interest.

References

1. Brockman, G., et al.: OpenAI gym. CoRR abs/1606.01540 (2016)
2. Farnebäck, G.: Two-frame motion estimation based on polynomial expansion. In: Bigun, J., Gustavsson, T. (eds.) SCIA 2003. LNCS, vol. 2749, pp. 363–370. Springer, Heidelberg (2003). https://doi.org/10.1007/3-540-45103-X_50
3. Grześ, M.: Reward shaping in episodic reinforcement learning. In: Proceedings of the 16th Conference on Autonomous Agents and MultiAgent Systems, AAMAS 2017, pp. 565–573. International Foundation for Autonomous Agents and Multiagent Systems, Richland (2017)
4. He, Y., Chen, S.: Advances in sensing and processing methods for three-dimensional robot vision. Int. J. Adv. Robot. Syst. **15**(2) (2018). https://doi.org/10.1177/1729881418760623
5. Kempka, M., Wydmuch, M., Runc, G., Toczek, J., Jaskowski, W.: ViZDoom: a doom-based AI research platform for visual reinforcement learning. CoRR abs/1605.02097 (2016)
6. Lu, F., Milios, E.: Globally consistent range scan alignment for environment mapping. Auton. Robots **4**(4), 333–349 (1997)
7. Mnih, V., et al.: Asynchronous methods for deep reinforcement learning. CoRR abs/1602.01783 (2016)
8. Pathak, D., Agrawal, P., Efros, A.A., Darrell, T.: Curiosity-driven exploration by self-supervised prediction. In: ICML (2017)
9. Tai, L., Liu, M.: Towards cognitive exploration through deep reinforcement learning for mobile robots. CoRR abs/1610.01733 (2016)
10. Wu, Y., Mansimov, E., Liao, S., Grosse, R.B., Ba, J.: Scalable trust-region method for deep reinforcement learning using Kronecker-factored approximation. CoRR abs/1708.05144 (2017)
11. Zhang, M., Levine, S., McCarthy, Z., Finn, C., Abbeel, P.: Policy learning with continuous memory states for partially observed robotic control. CoRR abs/1507.01273 (2015)

Visualization

Information Visualization for Highlighting Conflicts in Educational Timetabling Problems

Wanderley de Souza Alencar[1]([⊠]) [iD], Hugo Alexandre Dantas do Nascimento[1] [iD],
Walid Abdala Rfaei Jradi[1] [iD], Fabrizzio Alphonsus A. M. N. Soares[2] [iD],
and Juliana Paula Felix[1] [iD]

[1] Instituto de Informática, Universidade Federal de Goiás, Goiânia, GO, Brazil
{wanderley,hadn,julianafelix}@inf.ufg.br,
walid.jradi@gmail.com
[2] Department of Computer Science,
Southern Oregon University, Ashland, OR, USA
soaresf@sou.edu
http://www.inf.ufg.br, http://www.sou.edu

Abstract. Scheduling is a very important problem in many organizations, such as hospitals, transportation companies, sports confederations and educational institutions. Obtaining a *good schedule* results in the maximization of some desired benefit. In particular, in educational institutions (from elementary school to universities) this problem is periodically experienced, either during the preparation of class-teacher or examination timetabling. When a *solution proposal* is being elaborated (manual, semi-automatic or automatic processes), it is common the occurrence of the phenomenon called *conflict, clash* or *collision*. It is characterized by the simultaneous use of a resource (human or material) that can not be shared and, therefore, its occurrence makes that proposal impracticable for adoption. In semi-automatic systems, it is common the identification of such problems and, through user interaction, its resolution. Automatic systems, on the other hand, try to identify/solve conflicts without user intervention. Despite this, conflicts are not easy to resolve. This article proposes the use of information visualization techniques as an approach to highlight the occurrence of conflicts and, using user hints, contribute to its resolution, aiming at obtaining better quality timetables for practical adoption. The proposed visualizations were evaluated in order to determine its expressiveness and effectiveness, considering four aspects: coverage of the research questions, efficiency of the adopted visual mapping, supported level of human interaction and scalability. A conceptual qualitative study showed that the use of these techniques can aim users, mainly non-specialized, to identify conflicts and improve the desired educational timetables.

Keywords: Timetabling Problem · Scheduling Problem ·
Educational · Conflict · Clash · Collision · Violation · Information
Visualization · User Hints · User-driven · Interactive application

© Springer Nature Switzerland AG 2019
G. Bebis et al. (Eds.): ISVC 2019, LNCS 11844, pp. 275–288, 2019.
https://doi.org/10.1007/978-3-030-33720-9_21

1   Introduction

Timetabling Problems (TTPs) consists of allocating resources that are needed for carrying out a predefined set of tasks in a certain period of time. The allocation must satisfy, as much as possible, a list of desired goals [20]. *Resources* can vary from tools and/or machines, water, energy to even people (workers). A *task* can be defined as an activity or piece of work that must be done. The time period available to fulfill these tasks can vary from a few minutes to years. As can be noted, TTPs occur daily in a large amount of scenarios such as in hospitals, transportation companies, hotels, schools, among many others.

It is of particular interest of the present article the TTPs in educational institutions, when it is necessary to schedule classes for a certain period of time (a semester or a school year) and to organize the application of final exams. In this context, TTPs are called Educational Timetabling Problems (Ed-TTPs) or Academic Scheduling Problems, with their specifications having huge variations according to the intrinsic needs of each institution [10,12].

In educational institutions the approaches for defining timetabling vary from completely *handmade* to made using semi-automatic or automatic computer systems [6], in response to factors such as the type of institution, the education level, the size of the problem in terms of time slots, allocation demands and resources, geographic location and cultural aspects, among others.

During the process of defining a timetabling solution, a recurring phenomenon is the existence of *conflicts*, *clashes* or *collisions*. It represent a situation in which one or more not shareable resources are scheduled to be used at the same time by two or more distinct events. Three examples are: (1) a teacher who has to be at two different places at the same moment; (2) a student who needs to attend two lectures, in different places, at time intervals for which there is a overlap; and (3) an equipment required at the same time at two different physical locations. A number of scientific works highlight the importance of managing conflicts, which occurs much often than one might imagine at first glance [4,17].

In general, popular Ed-TTPs pieces of software detect conflicts and help to manage them, generating a viable solution. However, it is common that such computer generated solutions will not be considered completely suitable for practical usage by its users. One of the reasons for this is that the nature of many Ed-TTPs are subjective and depends on many human conditions and preferences that are difficult to predict and to model. Therefore, the *modeling process* of a timetabling problem may fail in capturing all its nuances.

In addition, the Mathematics and Computer Science theoretical foundations of this class of problems insert them into the so-called $\mathcal{NP}$-Complete or $\mathcal{NP}$-Hard problems, according to the way they are formulated as decision or optimization problems, as presented by several works [3,5]. Thus, currently, it is unknown a method that efficiently solves any kind of Ed-TTPs [10].

Semi-automatic approaches are much better options for solving Ed-TTPs since, through human-computer interaction, domain knowledge can be inserted into the problem representation and actions can be carried out by the users in order to solve conflicts. Nevertheless, this is not a simple task [4,8,13] and the use of Information Visualization (IV) techniques is essential, since it can help the users to understand the complexity of a timetabling and to perceive what needs to be done for improving the quality of the current solution.

Nowadays, the amount of research dedicated to the use of IV for Ed-TTPs is still small as shown by [2,13]. Therefore, the present article contributes to its enrichment by proposing and discussing two visualizations for Ed-TTPs.

This remainder of the article is organized as follows: Sect. 2 presents the main works that apply IV to Ed-TTPs. Section 3 explains the visualizations here proposed. They help to identify and highlight *conflicts* in Ed-TTPs. Then, in Sect. 3.4, a qualitative evaluation of conceived visualizations is detailed, highlighting their advantages over typical methods of characterizing such conflicts. Finally, the Sect. 4 synthesizes the conclusions obtained by this work and points out potential future research, some of them already under development by the authors of this text.

2   Literature Review

The first use of IV techniques for Ed-TTPs is in the form of a 2D-table representation. This is still the most common visual format, showed in many papers and timetabling systems, that we called here as *traditional* or *grid* presentation [19]. Typically, in the table representation, the days of the week and time periods are related to rows and events (for examples, classes) are distributed in columns. Figure 1 illustrates this representation, where there are different alternative configurations for column and row content.

DAY OF WEEK	TIME	CLASS-1	CLASS-2	CLASS-3	CLASS-4
MON	09am - 10am	Math Smith, T.	English Jones, C.	Sciences Jackson, B.	Biology Moore, C.
	10am - 11am	English Jones, C.	Biology Moore, C.	Sciences Jackson, B.	Math Smith, T.
TUE	09am - 10am	English Jones, C.	Math Smith, T.	Biology Moore, C.	Sciences Jackson, B.
	10am - 11am	Biology Moore, C.	Sciences Jackson, B.	English Jones, C.	Math Smith, T.
WED	09am - 10am	Math Smith, T.	English Jones, C.	--	–
	10am - 11am	Math Smith, T.	Biology Moore, C.	English Jones, C.	Sciences Jackson, B.

Fig. 1. Extract of a morning timetable of a fictitious elementary school (mon–wed).

It is possible to identify in Fig. 1 that, on Tuesday, from 09 am to 10 am, *Jones, C.* teaches *English* for *Class-1* and, from 10 am to 11 am, he teaches the same subject in *Class-3*. In this visualization, to identify conflicts is not trivial, as it requires visual inspection of all timetable cells. In spite of this, as stated, the 2D-table representation is widely used as the *final form* of visualizing a solution.

In [11] is proposed an interactive decision support system for the analysis and solution elaboration for Ed-TTPs. The system has a visualization module with an interface customized according to the user profile (designers, analyzers and consultants) that employs both 2D-tables and time charts (resources × time) for user interactions. A solution is built manually with a constraint-based reasoning engine assisting the user to obtain a solution to a problem instance, including detection of *hard* and *soft* constraint violation in a semi-automatic way.

In [14], the authors focus on solving Examination TTPs (Exam-TTPs) and propose a *visual framework* that operates on three interrelated phases: (1) pre-processing: visualizing raw data inserted by user; (2) processing: solving the optimization problem and visualizing the produced solution; and (3) post-processing: improving the current timetabling solution.

A visual model is used as an instrument to clarify the problem complexity and to provide an integrated visualization of the phases that can contribute to its understanding and satisfactory resolution. The article details the use of IV for the pre-processing phase, in which, for example, directed graph drawings indicate the relationship between enrolled students with the courses for a particular semester. Courses are represented by nodes and constraints are modelled as edges.

Further studies of the same group [16,18] added a tool – *VizSolution* – for the processing phase of the conceived *visual framework*. An interactive visualization approach is adopted, in which a user and a machine (a scheduler implemented as a constraint satisfaction program) operate in a symbiotic way trying to solve an Exam-TTP instance, including the allocation of classrooms. The tool allows to define the problem by means of an element called *Filter*, which employs graph drawing to represent constraints and to indicate conflicts and/or preferences.

Regarding the uncapacitated Exam-TTP, in [15] *parallel coordinates* (PCs) were used for answering the question: "How hard is this problem to solve?". The PCs are constructed using the following sets: dates (day/time), exams, students and rooms. A tool called *ParExaViz* was conceived in order to simplify the exploration of raw data in a problem instance and to highlight conflicts.

With the goal of helping the user to more easily identify/solve time conflicts in teachers and courses schedules, in [4], a system named CORECTS is proposed to model a timetabling solution through a graph. A modified version of a standard graph drawing algorithm is employed for visually presenting the solution and to highlight conflicts. Via "simple stroke gestures" on the visualization, using a touch screen monitor, it is possible to do operations that affect the conflicts.

In the work [1], addressing the university timetabling problem, it is introduced a *visual graphic* communication tool that lets the users to specify their problem in an abstract manner, involving human resources (students/teachers), events (lectures) and meta-events (courses). These elements are represented by nodes in a graph, while edges indicate their relationships (teaching, attending).

A system called *ExamViz* [17] was conceived with an *integrated problem solving environment* (PSE) to the Exam-TTP. It works as a computational mechanism with automated steering interactions and/or with a user-driven process. Through the user interface, it is possible to perform conflict analysis in the timetable and to apply a reconciliation process based on evolutionary algorithms. The analysis can be done visually using parallel coordinates as well 2D-tables and graph drawings.

Treating the Exam-TTP for an university, the work [13] conceived a tool called *Visual Analytics*, that integrates the key component of scientific visualization and search based heuristics in the same optimization model, with local search algorithm. The data is then visualized and interpreted by the user in order to perform problem solving with direct interactions. The visualization highlights the conflicts by means of parallel coordinates and 2D-table views.

Finally, in a review work, [2] shows the existence of research opportunities for the application of IV techniques to the Ed-TTPs, calling attention to the fact that there are a small number of scientific research dedicated to this theme over the last twenty years.

3   Proposed Visualizations

This section presents two interactive visualization proposals for the Ed-TTP conflicts, but first it conceptualizes what an Ed-TTP is, having as guideline that the definition should be able to accommodate its many specifications, from elementary level schools to universities.

3.1   Concepts and Definitions

In the context of the present work, a *timetable* is a set of events ($\{e_1, e_2, e_3, \ldots, e_n\}$), where $1 \leq i \leq n$ and $n \in \mathbb{N}^*$. Each event e_i, in turn, is defined by the following ordered set of elements:

$$e = (d, T, S, V, F, R) \tag{1}$$

where:

d is the date/time of the event, being expressed by day, day of week, start and finish times;

T is the set of *teachers* that attend the event;

S is the group of *students* participating in the event (lectures, typically);

V is the set of *venues* that are used by the event (rooms, typically);

F is the set of people who form the technical-administrative staff that supports the event;

R is the set of *resources*, concrete or abstract, necessary for the accomplishment of the event, except venues, which because of their relevance receive a special treatment, characterized by a specific category of resources.

A *conflict* consists of two distinct events (e_1 and e_2) that overlap in time, partially or completely, and have, in common, at least one of their not shareable elements of the sets T, S, V, F or R – a *real* conflict. However, there are cases where, even when this condition is satisfied, this does not characterize a conflict – an *apparent* conflict. That happens, for example, when a single professor teaches a lecture to two or more groups of students simultaneously in the same room or when multiple professors teach for a group of students separated into subgroups. The user can, previously, define which conflicting situations should be treated as *apparent* conflicts. This is done by creating *exception* for conflicts.

3.2 Visualizations

As previously highlighted, the purpose of all IV techniques is to present answers, quickly and clearly, to a given set of questions *that can not be easily inferred* from the simple reading and/or observation of raw/textual data. The knowledge gained through such visualizations can solve the problem under analysis or lead to the raising of new inquiries. In the specific case of conflicts, the proposed visualizations seek to answer to the following questions, which are often formulated within the scope of the Ed-TTPs: (Q.1) Where do conflicts occur? That is, at what intervals of time are there conflicts? (Q.2) What resources are involved in a conflict? (Q.3) How can a timetable that has conflicts be solved with as few changes as possible? (Q.4) In the case of several concomitant conflicts, is it possible to categorize them according to a set of criteria in order to facilitate the resolution process? (Q.5) In the case of several concomitant conflicts, is it possible to categorize them according to a set of criteria in order to produce a lower cost solution (according to the objective function defined for the problem)?

The first visualization, called the *Enhanced Tabular Visualization* (ETV) and showed in Fig. 2, displays a column to represent the days of the week, another for the possible event times and one column per group of involved students. Thus, each row refers to events occurring on a certain day of the week and time, where the row/column intersection, a *cell*, contains information about an event e, as defined in Eq. 1. One can select which attributes of e will be visible in the cell and, when the information is presented in light gray, this indicates the absence of any conflict. For example, on Monday *Jones, C* teaches only for *Class 1-A* from 07:10 to 08:00.

Two cells can be connected through a colored pair of points and a bidirectional arc, pointing the existence of a *real/apparent* conflict between them, as described in Subsect. 3.1. The color of the points/arc makes the distinction between: (1) a single teacher attending two or more groups of students that form a *super group* (purple points/arc) points that there is "no conflict here", as showed by *Davis, A.* in classes *1-A* and *2-A* on Monday, from 09:10 to 10:00; (2) two or more professors, teaching a lecture to a group of students who are divided into *subgroups* (orange points/arc), means "no conflict here", as depicted by *Davis, A./Anderson, P.* in classes *1-A* and *2-A* on Tuesday, from 09:10 to 10:00; and (3) conflicting groups (red points/arc), since some of its resources (material or human) are being used simultaneously in two different lectures, as indicated by teacher *Smith, T.* in classes *1-A* and *3-A* on Monday, from 08:00 to 08:50, since these classes are in rooms *106-A* and *108-A*, as can be seen in the Fig. 4.

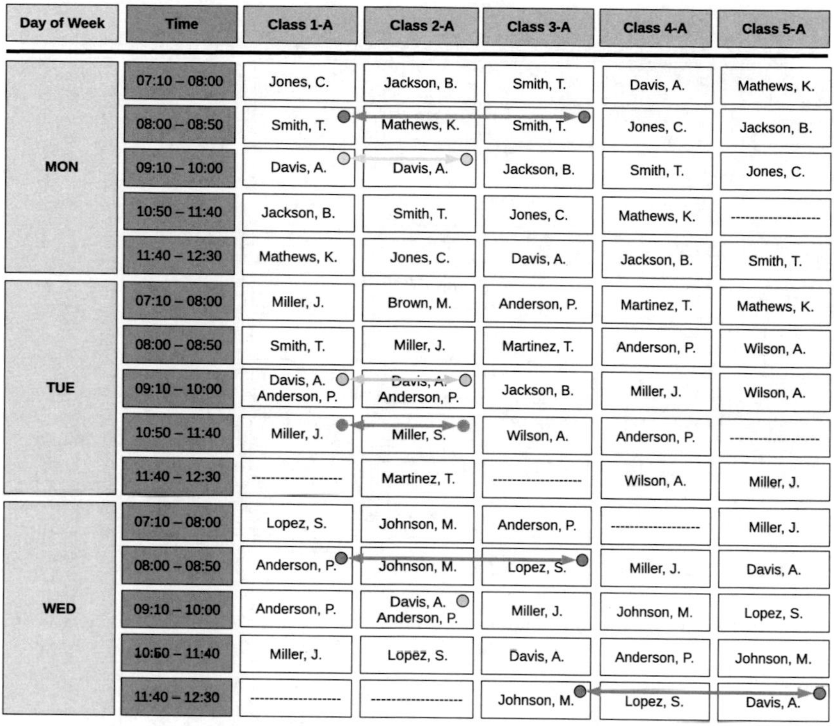

Day of Week	Time	Class 1-A	Class 2-A	Class 3-A	Class 4-A	Class 5-A
MON	07:10 – 08:00	Jones, C.	Jackson, B.	Smith, T.	Davis, A.	Mathews, K.
	08:00 – 08:50	Smith, T.	Mathews, K.	Smith, T.	Jones, C.	Jackson, B.
	09:10 – 10:00	Davis, A.	Davis, A.	Jackson, B.	Smith, T.	Jones, C.
	10:50 – 11:40	Jackson, B.	Smith, T.	Jones, C.	Mathews, K.	------------------
	11:40 – 12:30	Mathews, K.	Jones, C.	Davis, A.	Jackson, B.	Smith, T.
TUE	07:10 – 08:00	Miller, J.	Brown, M.	Anderson, P.	Martinez, T.	Mathews, K.
	08:00 – 08:50	Smith, T.	Miller, J.	Martinez, T.	Anderson, P.	Wilson, A.
	09:10 – 10:00	Davis, A. Anderson, P.	Davis, A. Anderson, P.	Jackson, B.	Miller, J.	Wilson, A.
	10:50 – 11:40	Miller, J.	Miller, S.	Wilson, A.	Anderson, P.	------------------
	11:40 – 12:30	------------------	Martinez, T.	------------------	Wilson, A.	Miller, J.
WED	07:10 – 08:00	Lopez, S.	Johnson, M.	Anderson, P.	------------------	Miller, J.
	08:00 – 08:50	Anderson, P.	Johnson, M.	Lopez, S.	Miller, J.	Davis, A.
	09:10 – 10:00	Anderson, P.	Davis, A. Anderson, P.	Miller, J.	Johnson, M.	Lopez, S.
	10:50 – 11:40	Miller, J.	Lopez, S.	Davis, A.	Anderson, P.	Johnson, M.
	11:40 – 12:30	------------------	------------------	Johnson, M.	Lopez, S.	Davis, A.

Fig. 2. The distinction between a *real* and an *apparent* conflict. (Color figure online)

In ETV, when the user hovers over the points/arc of a conflict, general information about it is shown by using some *icons*. A *teacher*, a *door*, a *technical staff member* and a *datashow* represent, respectively, a conflict in: (1) the teacher's timetable; (2) a room, being used simultaneously by two or more groups of students; (3) a technical staff member's timetable; and (4) a material resource. The Fig. 3 shows the obtained visualization.

Another option for the user in ETV is to click on the points/arc. This action will popup a menu detailing the conflict and also providing a functionality to solve it in the form of a button – as depicted in Fig. 4. By pressing that button, another window, called *Conflict Resolution Window*, is presented showing possible options for solving the conflict. It is adapted for each conflict situation (teacher, room, etc.).

For example, if the conflict problem involves only one teacher, then other teachers that may give their classes at the same date/time are showed. Next, the user may choose one of the suggested teachers/subjects to replace the original one. If no other teacher/subject is available, still yet the interface may offer options for combining multiple changes.

The Fig. 5 shows the *Conflict Resolution Window*. In the header and on the left side is detailed the type of conflict, ie, there is a single teacher involved, in

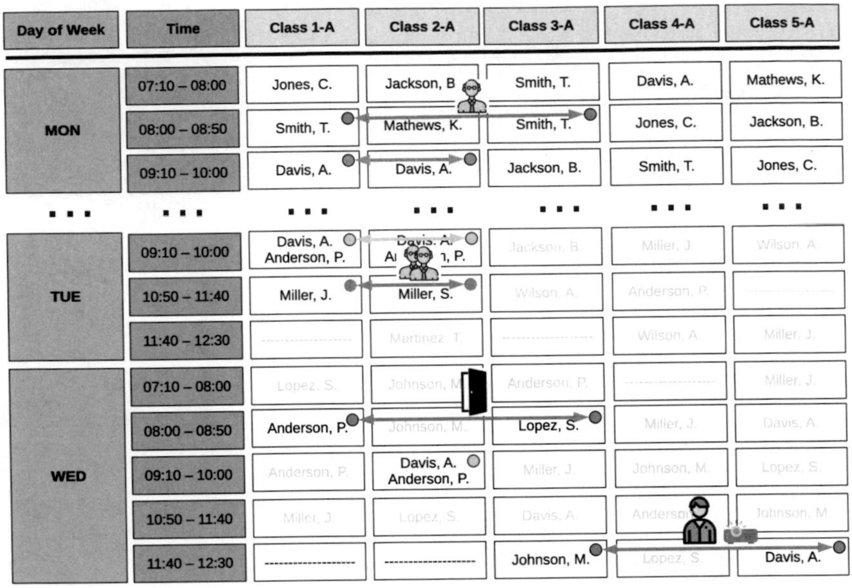

Day of Week	Time	Class 1-A	Class 2-A	Class 3-A	Class 4-A	Class 5-A
MON	07:10 – 08:00	Jones, C.	Jackson, B	Smith, T.	Davis, A.	Mathews, K.
	08:00 – 08:50	Smith, T.	Mathews, K.	Smith, T.	Jones, C.	Jackson, B.
	09:10 – 10:00	Davis, A.	Davis, A.	Jackson, B.	Smith, T.	Jones, C.
	...	...	...	...	...	...
TUE	09:10 – 10:00	Davis, A. Anderson, P.	Davis, A. An n, P.	Jackson, B	Miller, J.	Wilson, A.
	10:50 – 11:40	Miller, J.	Miller, S.	Wilson, A.	Anderson, P.	
	11:40 – 12:30	-----------------	Martinez, T.	-----------------	Wilson, A.	Miller, J.
WED	07:10 – 08:00	Lopez, S.	Johnson, M.	Anderson, P.	-----------------	Miller, J.
	08:00 – 08:50	Anderson, P.	Johnson, M.	Lopez, S.	Miller, J.	Davis, A.
	09:10 – 10:00	Anderson, P.	Davis, A. Anderson, P.	Miller, J.	Johnson, M.	Lopez, S.
	10:50 – 11:40	Miller, J.	Lopez, S.	Davis, A.	Anderson	Johnson, M.
	11:40 – 12:30	-----------------	-----------------	Johnson, M.	Lopez, S.	Davis, A.

Fig. 3. Example of general information about conflicts in events. (Color figure online)

this case. Here, three forms of resolution are presented: (1) ignore the conflict occurrence; (2) manually choose a teacher to be used as substitute from a list of options, presented in descending order of availability (ranging from available, already allocated to the unavailable ones); (3) select one solving algorithm and a set of teachers, where several selection filters are available. Regardless the chosen method, a preliminary timetable with the proposed changes is presented and the user can accept it or not.

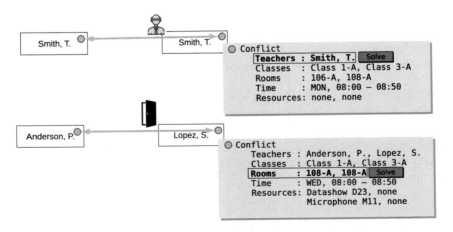

Fig. 4. Example of detailed information about conflicts showed by ETV. (Color figure online)

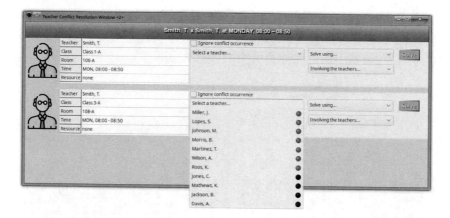

Fig. 5. Conflict Resolution Window for a single teacher conflict.

This work also proposes an alternative to tabular visualization, named *Multi-layer Diagram Visualization* (MDV). It resembles the well-known *Venn Diagram*, although it is distinct because it considers that the sets involved are in *different layers* in the visualization, since each one is associated to one of the categories of resources involved in a conflict: staff and material resources. As a result, the intersection of sets is reinterpreted: instead of indicating elements in common to two sets, it means that a conflict involves elements associated with those two categories. The rooms are considered a special subcategory of the material resources that deserve differentiated treatment and, therefore, appear as a separated subset. This visualization, showed in the Fig. 6, illustrates the same conflicts listed in Fig. 2. The user, clicking a conflict icon, opens an equivalent popup menu showed in Fig. 4, which is an artistic representation that, in order to avoid visual pollution and due to space constraints, omits the *technical staff member* and *material resource* conflict popup menus.

In MDV, the size of each set can be proportional to the total number of its compounding elements or, at the user's choice, only to its conflicting elements. This makes it easier for the user to perceive the relationship between the number of conflicts and the total number of entities involved. Duplicated icons indicate a temporal conflict between different entities. This conflict usually arises from a restriction imposed on the elements (not having simultaneous events), such as a couple of teachers *Miller, J.* and *Miller, S.*, who need to care for their children.

The presented visualizations, as well as the other concepts introduced in this subsection, were used in the definition of the architecture of the application of analysis and resolution of conflicts in Ed-TTP, described next.

3.3   Application Architecture

The proposed interactive IV application (IIV-App) follows the concept presented by [7], which classifies the paradigms for graphical-object modelling into six cate-

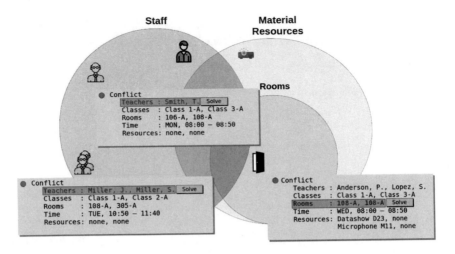

Fig. 6. The multilayer diagram visualization (MDV) showing conflicts.

gories (fully manual, constrained-based, critic-based, improver-based, fully automated and cooperative CAD), each one representing different levels of automation in which design decisions are made and implementation details are defined. In the last categories, the degree of automation is more flexible, as the user can dynamically adjust the system to have a higher, or lower, control of the design process. The IIV-App is suitable for all categories that involves human interaction in order to understand and improve an optimization solution, particularly for the cooperative CAD paradigm.

The IIV-App architecture also employs the concepts of the framework named *User Hints* [9], and it is illustrated by Fig. 7. The IIV-App is able to, by employing optimization methods, generate one or more initial solutions for the specified Ed-TTP. Right after, through the visual interface, the user can manipulate it, changing it through tools like *selection, focus* and *context, drag-and-drop, zoom in/out*, etc. In response to user actions, a new solution is generated, always observing the constraints applied to the problem. There is an agent responsible for storing, among others, the best generated solution. The *optimization objective* and *constraints* can also be dynamically adjusted by the user. After changed, a solution can be resubmitted to optimization methods, creating a new solution, restarting the cycle. It is important to mention that, in Fig. 7, although the *change* functionality is directly connected to the solution, highlighting its effect, it is carried out through the IIV-App. In an analogous way, the user can *choose* one of several visualizations available.

The Fig. 8 shows the *main screen* of the IIV-App, with four elements: (1) *main menu*, that allows registration and maintenance of the institution's academic structure (campus, buildings, rooms, institutes, departments, etc.), constraints, events and system configuration options (such as color assignment for conflicts and other elements of the GUI); (2) *toolbars*, that enable easy access to

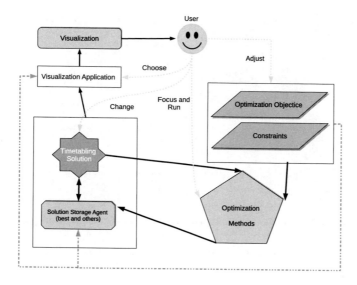

Fig. 7. The architecture of proposed interactive IV application.

most functionalities present in the main menu and its sub-items; (3) *work area*, divided into two interactive subareas: the *global view* (left side) and the *detail view* (right side). The former shows the visualizations generated by the application, with horizontal and vertical scrolling features. The detail view presents and allows changes of the properties of objects selected in the global view; (4) a *message and status area*, that continuously presents information about the quality of the current and best solutions and aspects that demand user actions. The employment of this area avoids having some popup windows appearing over the work area.

3.4   Qualitative Evaluation

At the current stage of the research, a conceptual qualitative study has been carried out in order to evaluated aspects of expressiveness and effectiveness of the two proposed visualizations. It has involved professors who work in the administration of an university and are routinely involved in defining up timetables of several academic departments. An extensive qualitative evaluation, with controlled experiments and the participation of users with different profiles, is yet to be done.

In this scenario, it is presented now an analysis of some aspects of the visualizations that help to infer about their quality. In particular, four aspects were considered:

(1) *coverage of the questions regarding a solution*: both visualizations allow the user to answer the questions listed in Sect. 3.2;

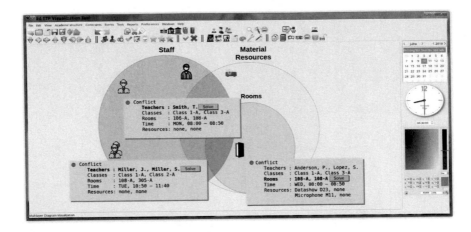

Fig. 8. Proposed interactive IV application main screen.

(2) *efficiency of the adopted visual mapping*: ETV is based on the traditional 2D-table approach, but extends it to highlight the elements of the optimization problem that are involved in the conflicts. Thanks to this, it is expected that it is easy to use, fast, because it benefits from the previous knowledge that users usually have when dealing with tables, needing only to understand the new visual elements that have been added. MDV represents a different proposal than usual, which should require a longer learning time for the user. However, unlike displaying all of Ed-TTP, it presents only on items that are involved in conflicts, allowing the user to focus only on solving these problems;

(3) *supported level of human interaction*: both proposals explore an additional approach in relation to those commonly found in the area of interactive timetabling, which is to click on one of the visual interface items and thus obtain detailed information about that specific conflict and, additionally, trigger a solving functionality that presents the possible ways for its resolution or, when possible, solves it by an optimization method;

(4) *scalability*: ETV has the possibility to resize the work area by zooming in/out, using scrollbars and, in some cases, applying filters to add/remove row and column information. In MDV, scalability is more natural, since it only shows the elements involved in the conflicts, although it also has the possibility of applying filters to only present conflicts involving certain entities (teachers, for example).

4   Conclusions and Future Works

The identification of resources allocation *conflicts* is a challenge for those who need to prepare solutions for an Ed-TTP. Many computer systems, semi-automatic or automatic ones, are capable of identifying and, in some cases, solving conflicts with or without the aid of human interaction. Nevertheless, the way in which conflicts are presented to the user is not always the most convenient and/or easier to understand, especially when the user has no formal knowledge about the intrinsic difficulties of the timetabling problem.

In this described scenario, the design and/or use of interactive IV techniques that can highlight conflicts and help to solve them is an essential tool for producing better timetables. The present work reported the design, prototypical implementation and conceptual qualitative evaluation of two interactive visualizations for conflict analysis and resolution. The evaluation showed that the use of these techniques can aim users, mainly non-specialized, to identify conflicts and improve the desired educational timetables.

As future works, we intend to develop other visualizations that: (1) shows a comparison between the total available workload of the person (teacher, mainly) and the one that has already been used. The purpose is to enable the user to more easily recognize people who can be used to solve conflicts by comparing them; (2) compares the timetable of a group of teachers (typically between two people like: husband and wife, brothers, and so on); and (3) displays conflicts as a colored, directed and interactive graph, which allows improvements through user interventions. Approaches already exists on this line, but they is still space for improving visual perception and human interaction. The first author is a PhD candidate and thanks the Brazilian research supporting agency FAPEG (Fundação de Amparo à Pesquisa do Estado de Goiás) for scholarships. The others authors thanks CAPES (Comissão de Aperfeiçoamento de Pessoal do Nível Superior).

References

1. Abdelraouf, I., Abdennadher, S., Gervet, C.: A visual entity-relationship model for constraint-based university timetabling. In: Abreu, S., et al. (eds.) Proceedings of the 19th International Conference on Applications of Declarative Programming and Knowledge Management (INAP 2011), pp. 183–194, September 2011
2. Alencar, W.S., Nascimento, H.D., Soares, F.A.A.M.N., Longo, H.J.: Visualization methods for educational timetabling problems: a systematic review of literature. In: Proceedings of the 14th International Joint Conference on Computer Vision, Imaging and Computer Graphics Theory and Applications (IVAPP), vol. 3, pp. 275–281. INSTICC, SciTePress, February 2019. https://doi.org/10.5220/0007375802750281
3. Elloumi, A., Kamoun, H., Jarboui, B., Dammak, A.: The classroom assignment problem: complexity, size reduction and heuristics. Appl. Soft Comput. **14**, 677–686 (2014). https://doi.org/10.1016/j.asoc.2013.09.003
4. Fui, Y.T., Onn, C.W., Yeen, C.W., Meian, K.H.: Graph-based conflict rectification using stroke gesture approach in timetabling system (corects). In: Baharom, F., Mahmuddin, M., Yusof, Y., Ishak, W.H.W., Saip, M.A. (eds.) Proceedings of the 5th Knowledge Management International Conference (KMICE 2010), Kuala Terengganu, Malaysia, pp. 618–623, May 2010
5. Garey, M.R., Johnson, D.S., Stockmeyer, L.: Some simplified NP-complete problems. In: Proceedings of the Sixth Annual ACM Symposium on Theory of Computing, STOC 1974, pp. 47–63. ACM, New York (1974). https://doi.org/10.1145/800119.803884

6. Houhamdi, Z., Athamena, B., Abuzaineddin, R., Muhairat, M.: A multi-agent system for course timetable generation. TEM J. **8**, 211–221 (2019). https://doi.org/10.18421/TEM81-30

7. Kochhar, S., Marks, J., Friedell, M.: Interaction paradigms for human-computer cooperation in graphical-object modeling. In: Proceedings of Graph Interface 1991, GI 1991, pp. 180–191. Morgan Kaufmann (1991). https://doi.org/10.20380/GI1991.24

8. Leite, N., Melicio, F., Rosa, A.C.: A fast simulated annealing algorithm for the examination timetabling problem. Expert Syst. Appl. **122**, 137–151 (2019). https://doi.org/10.1016/j.eswa.2018.12.048

9. Nascimento, H.A.D., Eades, P.: User hints: a framework for interactive optimization. Future Gener. Comp. Syst. **21**(7), 1177–1191 (2005). https://doi.org/10.1016/j.future.2004.04.005

10. Oude Vrielink, R.A., Jansen, E.A., Hans, E.W., van Hillegersberg, J.: Practices in timetabling in higher education institutions: a systematic review. Ann. Oper. Res. **275**(1), 145–160 (2019). https://doi.org/10.1007/s10479-017-2688-8

11. Piechowiak, S., Ma, J., Mandiau, R.: An open interactive timetabling tool. In: Burke, E., Trick, M. (eds.) PATAT 2004. LNCS, vol. 3616, pp. 34–50. Springer, Heidelberg (2005). https://doi.org/10.1007/11593577_3

12. Pillay, N.: A survey of school timetabling research. Ann. Oper. Res. **218**(1), 261–293 (2014). https://doi.org/10.1007/s10479-013-1321-8

13. Thomas, J.J., Belaton, B., Khader, A.T., Justtina: Visual analytics solution for scheduling processing phases. In: Vasant, P., Zelinka, I., Weber, G.W. (eds.) ICO 2018. AISC, vol. 866, pp. 395–408. Springer, Cham (2019). https://doi.org/10.1007/978-3-030-00979-3_42

14. Thomas, J.J., Khader, A.T., Belaton, B.: A visual analytics framework for the examination timetabling problem. In: Fifth International Conference on Computer Graphics, Imaging and Visualisation, pp. 305–310, August 2008. https://doi.org/10.1109/CGIV.2008.16

15. Thomas, J.J., Khader, A.T., Belaton, B.: A parallel coordinates visualization for the uncapaciated examination timetabling problem. In: Badioze Zaman, H., et al. (eds.) IVIC 2011, Part I. LNCS, vol. 7066, pp. 87–98. Springer, Heidelberg (2011). https://doi.org/10.1007/978-3-642-25191-7_10

16. Thomas, J.J., Khader, A.T., Belaton, B., Christy, E.: Visual interface tools to solve real-world examination timetabling problem. In: Seventh International Conference on Computer Graph, Imaging and Visualization, pp. 167–172 (2010). https://doi.org/10.1109/CGIV.2010.36

17. Thomas, J.J., Khader, A.T., Belaton, B., Ken, C.C.: Integrated problem solving steering framework on clash reconciliation strategies for university examination timetabling problem. In: Huang, T., Zeng, Z., Li, C., Leung, C.S. (eds.) ICONIP 2012, Part IV. LNCS, vol. 7666, pp. 297–304. Springer, Heidelberg (2012). https://doi.org/10.1007/978-3-642-34478-7_37

18. Thomas, J.J., Khader, A.T., Belaton, B., Leow, J.: VIZSolution: an interface tool to solve real-world examination timetabling problem. Int. J. Adv. Comp. Tech. **2**(5), 80–88 (2010). https://doi.org/10.4156/ijact.vol2.issue5.9

19. Wehrer, A., Yellen, J.: The design and implementation of an interactive course-timetabling system. Ann. Oper. Res. **218**(1), 327–345 (2014). https://doi.org/10.1007/s10479-013-1384-6

20. Wren, A.: Scheduling, timetabling and rostering — a special relationship? In: Burke, E., Ross, P. (eds.) PATAT 1995. LNCS, vol. 1153, pp. 46–75. Springer, Heidelberg (1996). https://doi.org/10.1007/3-540-61794-9_51

ContourNet: Salient Local Contour Identification for Blob Detection in Plasma Fusion Simulation Data

Martin Imre[1(✉)], Jun Han[1], Julien Dominski[3], Michael Churchill[3], Ralph Kube[3], Choong-Seock Chang[3], Tom Peterka[2], Hanqi Guo[2], and Chaoli Wang[1]

[1] University of Notre Dame, Notre Dame, USA
mimre@nd.edu
[2] Argonne National Laboratory, Lemont, USA
[3] Princeton Plasma Physics Laboratory, Princeton, USA

Abstract. We present ContourNet, a deep learning approach to identify salient local isocontours as blobs in large-scale 5D gyrokinetic tokamak simulation data. Blobs—regions of high turbulence that run along the edge wall down toward the diverter and can damage the tokamak—are non-well-defined features but have been empirically localized by isocontours in 2D normalized fluctuating density fields. The key of our study is to train ContourNet to follow the empirical rules to detect blobs over the time-varying simulation data. The architecture of ContourNet is a convolutional neural segmentation network: the inputs are the density field and a rasterized isocontour; the output is a set of isocontour encircling blobs. At the training stage, we feed the network with manually identified isocontours and propagated labels. At the inference stage, we extract isocontours from the segmented blob regions. Results show that our approach can achieve both high accuracy and performance, which enables scientists to understand the blob dynamics influencing the confinement of the plasma.

Keywords: XGC plasma fusion · Blob detection · Local isocontour selection · Segmentation

1 Introduction

Fusion energy is a promising future source of energy with the minimal ecological footprint. A leading candidate for controlled fusion technique is to use a *tokamak*, which confines hot plasma in a torus-shaped reactor with a strong magnetic field. The edge of the plasma plays a dominant role in the confinement of the plasma, but needs to be managed to ensure high confinement without ruining the tokamak walls. Scientists conduct large-scale 5D gyrokinetic fusion plasma simulations using XGC [7,8] in order to study the edge and improve the tokamak design. XGC is a particle-in-cell simulation with the output consisting of

© Springer Nature Switzerland AG 2019
G. Bebis et al. (Eds.): ISVC 2019, LNCS 11844, pp. 289–301, 2019.
https://doi.org/10.1007/978-3-030-33720-9_22

scalar fields that characterize the fluctuating level. The output is on a number of discrete 2D planes around the tokamak, with each poloidal plane representing a 2D cross-section of the simulated tokamak reactor.

The focus of this paper is the detection of *blobs*—regions of high turbulence that are thought to be a major cause of lost confinement at the edge—in fusion simulation data. Blob detection is challenging because blobs are *non-well-defined features*. While experienced scientists are able to empirically identify blobs, defining these features mathematically remains an open challenge [6, 9]. Scientists urge the need for reliable detection methods to better understand the formation and impact of these blobs.

In practice, scientists empirically encircle a blob as a simply-connected and closed isocontour [11], or a *local contour*, in the output 2D scalar field. An example of a blob can be seen in Fig. 1(a). Scientists have been using simple heuristics to find proper local contours based on their intuitions of blobs. In general, blobs have a certain size, shape, value ranges, and could only appear in certain areas of the domain. To this end, Davis et al. [11] and Zweben et al. [29] use half-maximum levels as isovalues to compute local contours for blob detection. In Wu et al. [28], the isovalue is determined by the statistical distribution of the input data in a region of interest. However, all existing methods are based on arbitrary choices that involve manual selections and thus hard to generalize to the time-varying simulation output data.

Based on the discussion with scientists, we transform the problem of *blob detection* to *salient local isocontour detection*. Such a local treatment allows identifying each blob's isovalue independently instead of finding a universally valid heuristic for blob identification. Furthermore, such an isovalue-based detection meets the need of domain scientists. Isovalue selection has been widely studied. However, to the best of our knowledge, there exists no approach to select local, independent isovalues. Current methods for isovalue selection either analyze the entire volume and suggest global values, or perform local isovalue selection using topological analysis while still relying on a universal rule.

We instead propose a new deep-learning-based approach for detecting salient isocontours for blob identification. We present *ContourNet*, a framework that tackles the aforementioned problems using a *convolutional neural network (CNN)* to identify blobs in the XGC plasma fusion simulation data. We inspect 2D cross-sections of the reactor at a given time step. Scientists help us label blobs in these cross-sections so that we can obtain the training data used by ContourNet for training. ContourNet is a CNN that uses a combination of a 2D cross-section with a contour mask to segment blob regions in the cross-section. To avoid the enormous labeling effort, we introduce a label propagation strategy that heuristically extends the labeled data to neighboring time steps. In summary, the contributions of this work are the following:

- a salient local contour identification algorithm based on deep neural network for blob detection in the fusion plasma simulation;
- a label propagation strategy that augments labeled local contours for ContourNet training to overcome the lack of training data;

– a baseline for using CNN in blob detection with minimal labeling effort[1].

2   Background and Related Work

In this section, we formalize the blob detection problem in fusion sciences, and then review the literature on salient isovalue selection and image segmentation.

Blob Detection in Fusion Sciences. Blob detection is regarded as an ill-posed problem in fusion sciences, because there exists no clear definition for blobs. D'Ippolito et al. [13] characterized blobs as higher-than-background density filaments propagating outwards and lower-than-background density filaments propagating inwards [13], and thus blobs have certain shapes, sizes, value ranges, and could only appear in certain areas of the domain.

Formally, the input of blob detection is the scalar field $f_{t,s} : \mathbb{D} \to \mathbb{R}$ on the sth 2D cross-section of the tokamak at time step t, where $\mathbb{D} \subset \mathbb{R}^2$ is the domain for a 2D cross-section, and the output is a number of regions $\{B_{t,s}^i\}$ that represent blobs. Depending on the context of different experimental and simulation studies, the input scalar field can be temperature, electron densities, scalar derivative of electrostatic potential, and normalized fluctuating density that characterize the fluctuating level. Without loss of generality, we only study blobs that are associated with local maxima. Assuming the smoothness of the input scalar field $F_{t,p}(\mathbf{x})$, we define

$$L(f_{t,s}, \theta) = \{\mathbf{x} \mid F_{t,s}(\mathbf{x}) \geq \theta\} = \bigcup_{k \in \mathbb{I}} R_{t,s}^k(\theta) \tag{1}$$

as the *super-levelset* of $f_{t,s}(\mathbf{x})$ with respect to the threshold θ; $\{R_{t,s}^k(\theta)\}$ are disjoint connected components $(R_{t,s}^k(\theta) \cap R_{t,s}^l(\theta) = \emptyset$, for any $k \neq l \in \mathbb{I})$ of the super-levelset and $\mathbb{I}$ is the index set. We further define a *blob candidate*

$$C(f_{t,s}, \theta, \mathbf{x}) = \{R_{t,s}^k \mid \mathbf{x} \in R_{t,s}^k\} \tag{2}$$

as the simply connected component that contains $\mathbf{x}$ in the super-levelset $L(f_{t,s}, \theta)$. The blobs $\{B_{t,s}^j\}$ are a subset of blob candidates that meet the empirical rules defined by scientists, where j is the index of the blob.

In practice, scientists define empirical rules to filter the candidates that connected to a few selected local maxima locations $\{\mathbf{m}_{t,s}^j\}$ $(\mathbf{m}_{t,s}^j \in \mathbb{D})$ with different super-levelset thresholds $\{\theta_{t,s}^j\}$, that is,

$$B_{t,s}^j = C(N, \theta_{t,s}^j, \mathbf{m}_{t,s}^j). \tag{3}$$

In Kube et al. [16], the threshold $\theta_{t,s}^j$ was set to 60% of the selected maximum value $f_{t,s}(\mathbf{x}_j)$. Davis et al. [11] first found large local maxima in $f_{t,s}(\mathbf{x})$ by thresholding, and then fitted an ellipse to the contour at the 50% maximum

---

[1] A PyTorch implementation can be found at https://github.com/mimre25/ContourNet.

level. The same technique was used by Zweben et al. [29] and Churchill et al. [9], but the selection of local maxima is nontrivial and subject to small perturbations of $f_{t,s}(\mathbf{x})$. Based on the statistics of $f_{t,s}(\mathbf{x})$ in a small region of interest, Wu et al. [28] determined the local contour level to only incorporate regions with significantly higher temperatures and densities than the surroundings. A two-phase algorithm was proposed that first selects candidate points and then extracts blobs as the connected components of the candidates.

In this paper, we follow the convention to localize blobs by contouring. Although it is possible to approach blob detection as an object detection problem by segmenting a 2D cross-section into blob and non-blob areas, a local contour has clearer physical meaning than an arbitrary segmentation does. In general, the output segmentation is not necessarily local isocontours and thus could be misleading. Therefore, we aim to segment the image into areas that can be encircled with local isocontours.

For ease of description in terms of image input data, we define $v_{t,s}(i)$ as the $W \times H$ regular 2D image that represents $f_{t,s}(\mathbf{x})$, where $0 \le i < W \times H$ is the the the pixel index. The blob candidate $c_{t,s}(i)$ is defined as the binary (0 or 1) image of the connected component $C(f_{t,s}, f_{t,s}(\mathbf{x}_i), \mathbf{x}_i)$ that contains $\mathbf{x}_i$, the physical coordinates of i. We also define the Boolean function $b_{t,s}(i)$ to denote if the blob candidate $c_{t,s}(i)$ is a blob. The purpose of ContourNet is to learn *blob labels* $\widetilde{b}_{t,s}(i)$, in order to predict $b_{t,s}(i)$ for arbitrary t, s, and i, as detailed in further sections.

Salient Isovalue Selection. Our study is related to the problem of salient isovalue selection, which aims at highlighting key materials or structures in scalar field data. Salient isovalue selection algorithms can be categorized into *statistics-*, *topology-* and *similarity-*based methods.

For statistics-based analysis, Bajaj et al. [1] introduced the contour spectrum to facilitate an easier choice of isovalue by displaying several statistics in a 2D curve in relation to the isovalue. Pekar et al. [22] proposed a fast one-pass algorithm to analyze volumetric datasets and find intensity transitions between different surface materials based on gray-value histograms. Carr et al. [3] showed that histogram is inferior to statistics like area, or approximation of those, e.g., triangle count, in terms of representing the underlying function distribution. Scheidegger et al. [19] revisited the relationship between histograms and the underlying geometric structure of a volume dataset. They used geometric measure theory to establish a convergence between the area statics and the histogram.

For topology-based analysis, a prominent technique is using contour trees to inspect the development of underlying geometry based on the change of isovalue. Carr et al. [4] showed that contour trees can be computed in all dimensions, while Pascucci et al. [21] introduced branch decomposition to simplify the analysis of contour trees. Later on, Carr et al. [5] introduced simplification based on local geometric measures of feature importance to allow an interactive and flexible selection of isovalues.

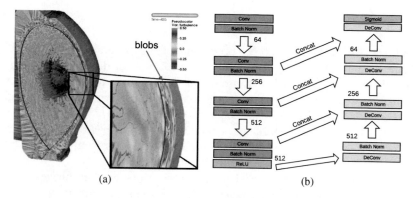

(a)   (b)

Fig. 1. (a) shows a zoomed view of a blob. The dark red area corresponds to the blob. (b) shows the architecture of ContourNet. Similar to U-Net, ContourNet has two phases. However, there is no change of the image size. The numbers in the figure show the number of channels after a given batch normalization. (Color figure online)

For similarity-based analysis, Bruckner and Möller [2] introduced isosurface similarity maps. These maps are based on the distance fields of the analyzed volume and show the inverse of the mutual information obtained from pair-wise joint histograms. They further introduced a priority-ranking algorithm based on the similarity maps. Other works have extended their approach to multi-modal analysis [14,25] or to identify nearly equally-distanced isosurfaces [15]. A shortcoming of these methods is that they all limit their selection to a single or multiple isovalues for the whole volume.

The purpose of salient isovalue selection is different from our application, because the outputs of salient isovalue selection are a levelset of a given threshold θ in the entire scalar field. We instead need to identify salient local contours defined by different levels $\{\theta^i_{t,p}\}$ locally using deep learning approaches.

Image Segmentation Using Neural Networks. Our method is inspired by U-Net [23], a deep CNN for medical image segmentation. U-Net detects cells in light microscopy images by downsampling and upsampling an input image while copying over features between the downward and upward phases. It was later adapted to work in 3D [10,20]. Other approaches use hierarchical cascaded models [24] or create semantic segmentation of objects [17]. Nabla-net [18] uses an encoder-decoder framework or biomedical image segmentation. Other researchers proposed interactive segmentation using CNNs [26,27] to guide users during a segmentation task.

For blob detection, we cannot directly use a segmentation technique to identify salient local contours. The typical output in such a task is a pixel-wise segmentation mask which often does not encompass additional information. In our case, we need super-levelsets that are encircled by closed isocontours, which is not necessarily the case in the output of a straightforward segmentation. However, adopting such an approach to extract isocontours instead of regions with different values can overcome this.

3   Overview

Blob Detection Workflow. The input data of our blob detection workflow is the scalar field $f_{t,s}(\mathbf{x})$, and the outputs are a number of detected blobs $\{B_{t,s}^j\}$. The core of our approach is ContourNet, a deep neural network that takes a single slice as input and returns a segmentation for blob and non-blob regions. In this study, ContourNet is based on a modified U-Net [23], which is a CNN originally designed for medical image segmentation. For the ease of data handling using ContourNet, we transform the scalar field $f_{t,s}(\mathbf{x})$ into an image and the ground truth blob candidates into a binary mask.

We tailor both the training and inference routines of ContourNet, in order to detect blobs accurately and efficiently. At the training stage, we gather as many labeled blobs as possible through expert labeling and label propagation. We worked closely with scientists on the user interface design for expert labeling, and co-designed the automatic label propagation strategy, in order to minimize the burden of manual labeling and to maximize the blob detection accuracy.

ContourNet Architecture. The original U-Net is designed for image segmentation: the input is a fixed-size image and the output is a mask that segments the different areas of the image. U-Net contains a downward phase and an upward phase. At each level of the downward phase, a convolutional layer halves the size of the image and doubles the size of the feature maps. Within each level of the upward phase, the exact opposite happens by applying deconvolution operations. Additionally, the features in a given level of the downward phase are copied over as additional input into the same level of the upward phase.

The modified U-Net design for ContourNet is illustrated in Fig. 1(b). ContourNet consists of four levels in both the downward and upward phases. The biggest difference to the original U-Net architecture is that ContourNet does not perform any downscaling of the input. We do this as blobs are small-scale features in comparison to the image, which could get missed in an early layer and not be recovered later. The input to each (de-)convolutional layer varies depending on its position in the network. The ith level has the same size as the input image but with a different number of features in the feature map. To copy over the features from the downward to the upward phase, we concatenate them to the already existing feature map.

The last layer produces a binary segmentation mask that we then perform the following to further transform into a mask of isocontours. First, we compute the connected components for every blob in a segmentation mask. Second, we generate a super-levelset for every point of a given connected component. Third, we compare the given super-levelset to the area from the segmentation using the Dice coefficient and pick the best fit. Finally, we extract the isocontour from the super-levelset and store the seed point for future use.

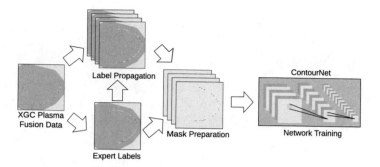

Fig. 2. The training stage for ContourNet. Expert labels are first propagated to increase the amount of training data. The data slice is then combined with a blob mask as input for network training.

4   ContourNet Training

The training stage of ContourNet is shown in Fig. 2. During training, we preprocess the simulation data into input image $v_{t,s}(i)$ and obtain labeled samples $\tilde{b}_{t,s}(i)$ from scientists. We further improve the accuracy of ContourNet by introducing propagated labels.

Data Preprocessing. Because the input image $v_{t,s}(i)$ is not directly available from the simulation, we need to preprocess the simulation data. Based on the instructions from scientists, we first derive $f_{t,s}(\mathbf{x})$ by normalizing the electrostatic potential field with the plasma temperature. The field data, which are defined on a 2D unstructured mesh, are stored in multiple HDF5 files. Because the current CNN implementations do not inherently support unstructured mesh data, we interpolate and convert the data into a 400×400 regular mesh, which is fine enough to capture blobs for this study. During mask preparation, we collect all the labeled blobs for a time step and slice combination and generate another regular 400×400 grid with blob areas set to 1 and the rest to 0.

Label Propagation. We propagate the blob labels $\tilde{b}_{t,s}(i)$ to a few neighboring time steps to increase the amount of training data and ease the amount of time that scientists need to spend on labeling. Although the propagation is an approximation and cannot be used to detect newly appeared or disappeared blobs, based on the verification from scientists, the propagated blobs are acceptable for the training purpose. A set of propagated labels can be seen in Fig. 3. In each image, we show blobs as filled regions rather than contours as we used a region-based coefficient to select the best matches. In the figure, (a) shows the expert labels at time step 60, (b) is the propagation to time step 59 which shows very good quality. The propagation to time step 65 is shown in (c). Here we can already see the quality deteriorating as fewer blobs are propagated, but the output is still acceptable. In (d), we can see that the propagation to time step 70 showing even fewer blobs, resulting in a misleading training sample.

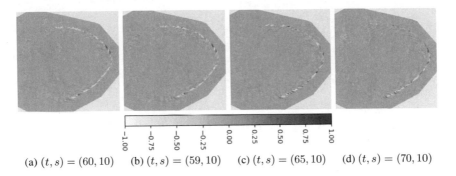

(a) $(t, s) = (60, 10)$ (b) $(t, s) = (59, 10)$ (c) $(t, s) = (65, 10)$ (d) $(t, s) = (70, 10)$

Fig. 3. Four different time steps showing the same slice with the expert-labeled (a) or propagated (b–d) blobs. (t, s) are for time step ID and slice ID, respectively. We use the underlying density values $\rho_{t,s}$ as the background and overlay them with the blobs in yellow. The density values are clamped to $[-1, 1]$. The background is light gray. The images use a 400×400 pixel resolution. (Color figure online)

Formally, we propagate the labels $\widetilde{b}_{t,s}(i)$ to the next n time steps $\{t+1, \ldots, t+n\}$. The propagation to preceding time steps can be done similarly. Based on the verification from scientists, we set $n = 5$ to achieve a balance between the propagation precision and the number of propagated labels. With this setting, the propagation enables us to generate ten times the labeled blobs that we obtained from the scientists.

The propagation is an iterative process over the consequent time steps. In the kth iteration, we find all blob candidates $c_{t+k,s}(i)$ that are already labeled as blobs, that is, $\widetilde{b}_{t+k,s}(i) = 1$ for all i. We then compare each $c_{t+k,s}(i)$ with all possible blob candidates $c_{t+k+1,s}(i')$ using the Dice coefficient [12]. The Dice coefficient for two binary images is defined as

$$\mathrm{dice}(I_1, I_2) = \frac{2 \times |V(I_1) \cap V(I_2)|}{|V(I_1)| + |V(I_2)|}, \tag{4}$$

where I_1 and I_2 are the two blob candidates being compared, and $V(\cdot)$ is the number of nonzero elements in the image. We then find the blob candidate $c_{t+k+1,s}(i')$ with the max Dice coefficient

$$\arg \max_{i'} \mathrm{dice}\left(c_{t+k,s}(i), c_{t+k+1,s}(i')\right), \tag{5}$$

and label $\widetilde{b}_{t+k+1,s}(i')$ as 1. If there is no overlap found, we disregard all candidates.

To generate possible blob candidates, we exhaustively sample the area close to the outer wall at a given slice s at time step t. To do so, we first filter the ring-like structure of the cross-section. Starting from the remaining area, we inspect every pixel and use it as a seed point to compute an isocontour with its corresponding value and fill the area for propagation.

Training Process. We use all labels $\widetilde{b}_{t,s}(i)$ including both expert labels and propagated labels to train ContourNet. Domain scientists labeled every slice for time step 60, yielding a total of 225 labeled blobs for 15 slices. We extend this set with our label propagation strategy to obtain a total of 165 slices label with about 15 blobs for each slice. We then train ContourNet for 100 epochs on these sets of training data. One epoch took about 52 s on a server with an Intel Core i7-7700K 4.2 GHz quad-core processor, 32 GB main memory, and an NVIDIA Titan Xp GPU. Every input slice comes with a ground-truth mask which is used to compare the weighted cross-entropy loss defined as follows

$$L = -\left(\delta B \log\left(p\right) + \gamma(1 - B)\log\left(1 - p\right)\right), \tag{6}$$

where B is the ground truth segmentation mask, p is the predicted likelihood for each pixel to be part of a blob, and δ and γ are, respectively, the weighting factors for the blob and non-blob classes. For the results shown in Sect. 5, we set δ to 5 and γ to 1.

5   Results and Discussion

We used 90% of our data for training and 10% for inference. Among the testing set, the prediction yields a Dice score of 0.628. A commonly acceptable Dice score for segmentation tasks is ≥ 0.7. However, in our scenario, we lower the requirement to a score of ≥ 0.6 for two reasons. First, we compare inferred results to heuristically generated and noisy "ground truth" (propagated results). Second, small-scale blobs are very difficult to segment and jointly, they only account for a fraction of the image. The average prediction time was 7.56 s (segmentation 0.52 s, contour extraction 7.04 s). In the following, we discuss selective results in detail.

Comparison to the Ground Truth. Figure 4 shows the comparison of our prediction and the ground truth at time step 60. Note that we show the images side by side to avoid the overlap of contours. In (a), we can see that the overall prediction for slice 6 is very good. While some of the blobs differ in the shape or position from the ones shown in (b), the differences are relatively low. In (c), we can see that ContourNet detects more blobs than shown in the ground truth for slice 7. Besides that, some of the blobs have different shapes (bottom right) and there are a few missing ones (top center and right). These results are mostly false positives. We point out that the goal of ContourNet is to assist scientists in identifying blobs, and therefore, false positives are better than a false negatives.

Figure 5 shows a comparison of our prediction and the propagated labels at time step 56. (a) and (b) show slice 8 with ContourNet predicting some false positives (center right, bottom). However, the shapes of the detected blobs seem fairly accurate. In (c) and (d), we can see that the prediction for slice 12 is more accurate but misses some of the blobs (top center, right middle).

Expert Evaluation. We conduct an expert evaluation of ContourNet with fusion scientists. Their feedback is as follows. All in all, ContourNet correctly

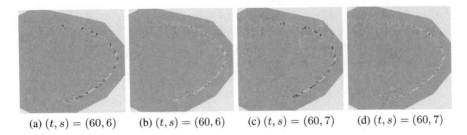

(a) $(t, s) = (60, 6)$ (b) $(t, s) = (60, 6)$ (c) $(t, s) = (60, 7)$ (d) $(t, s) = (60, 7)$

Fig. 4. Comparing ContourNet's segmentation results to the ground truth. (a) and (c) show the predictions (red), whereas (b) and (d) show the ground truth (yellow). (Color figure online)

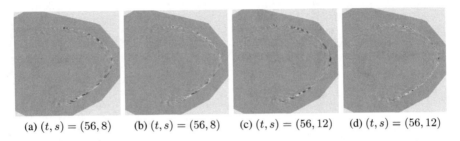

(a) $(t, s) = (56, 8)$ (b) $(t, s) = (56, 8)$ (c) $(t, s) = (56, 12)$ (d) $(t, s) = (56, 12)$

Fig. 5. Comparing ContourNet's segmentation results to the propagated ground truth. (a) and (c) show the predictions (red), whereas (b) and (d) show the ground truth (yellow). (Color figure online)

identifies relevant potential blob candidates across a large spectrum of different simulation data. Figure 6 shows toroidal slices of the simulation data at four different time steps. These instances show a variety of situations that typically occur in simulations. In (a), a large number of potential blobs can be seen at the magnetic separatrix. ContourNet identifies the relevant large-amplitude regions in the data and visually, no other region would be a blob candidate. The situation in (b) is more difficult. Again, ContourNet correctly identifies the relevant large-amplitude regions of the image. Note that these regions appear more stretched out along the poloidal direction than in (a). On the other hand, the negative regions in the outboard mid-plane region might be relevant for the physics of the system. In (c), perturbations of the electric potential can be seen all along the separatrix. Here ContourNet identifies contour regions only on the rightmost half, the region where blob dynamics are most relevant to plasma confinement. This inference result is significantly better than the corresponding propagated result shown in Fig. 3(d). The simulation data shown in (d) are a difficult test case. Again, small-scale perturbations of the potential appear all along the magnetic separatrix. These stretch out over an X-shaped region at the bottom of the simulation domain. ContourNet identifies multiple blob instances, two of them in the X-shaped bottom region. This area is relevant for the physics underlying

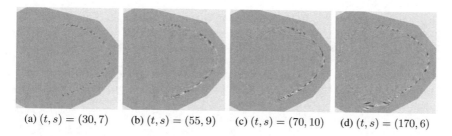

(a) $(t, s) = (30, 7)$ (b) $(t, s) = (55, 9)$ (c) $(t, s) = (70, 10)$ (d) $(t, s) = (170, 6)$

Fig. 6. ContourNet segmentation results where contours are highlighted in red. (Color figure online)

blob motion. There are no regions identified in the left half of the image, a region that is not very relevant for blob motion.

6 Conclusions and Future Work

We have presented ContourNet, a deep CNN to detect blobs as local isocontours in the XGC plasma fusion simulation. ContourNet learns from expert labeled data and profits from a label propagation strategy that allows us to heuristically label neighboring time steps from the ones labeled by experts. We further present expert evaluation agreeing with the performance of ContourNet. Our work provides a baseline for future improvement that uses only minimal labeling effort.

For future work, an interesting addition to ContourNet would be semi-supervised learning, or better, an active learning concept. Using ContourNet to detect blobs and incorporating the feedback from domain experts during training could be beneficial for the performance, especially when considering that it mostly produces false positives and suffers from a low amount of training data. A further extension would be the discrimination between different kinds of blobs. In fusion sciences, there are distinctions among different kinds of turbulent eddies, such as blobs and streamers. Finally, using ContourNet for in-situ blob detection in coupled simulation codes would be beneficial for scientists to gain better insights into the underlying physics of blobs.

Acknowledgments. This research was supported in part by the U.S. National Science Foundation through grants IIS-1455886, CNS-1629914, and DUE-1833129, and the U.S. Department of Energy through grant DE-AC02-06CH11357 and the Exascale Computing Project (17-SC-20-SC).

References

1. Bajaj, C.L., Pascucci, V., Schikore, D.R.: The contour spectrum. In: Proceedings of IEEE Visualization Conference, pp. 167–173 (1997)

2. Bruckner, S., Möller, T.: Isosurface similarity maps. Comput. Graph. Forum **29**(3), 773–782 (2010)
3. Carr, H., Brian, D., Brian, D.: On histograms and isosurface statistics. IEEE Trans. Vis. Comput. Graph. **12**(5), 1259–1266 (2006)
4. Carr, H., Snoeyink, J., Axen, U.: Computing contour trees in all dimensions. In: Proceedings of ACM Symposium on Discrete Algorithms, pp. 918–926 (2000)
5. Carr, H., Snoeyink, J., Van De Panne, M.: Flexible isosurfaces: simplifying and displaying scalar topology using the contour tree. Comput. Geom. **43**(1), 42–58 (2010)
6. Chang, C.S., et al.: Fast low-to-high confinement mode bifurcation dynamics in a tokamak edge plasma gyrokinetic simulation. Phys. Rev. Lett. **118**(17), 1–6 (2017)
7. Chang, C.S., Ku, S.: Spontaneous rotation sources in a quiescent tokamak edge plasma. Phys. Plasmas **15**(6), 062510 (2008)
8. Chang, C.S., et al.: Compressed ion temperature gradient turbulence in diverted tokamak edge. Phys. Plasmas **16**(5), 056108 (2009)
9. Churchill, R.M., Chang, C.S., Ku, S., Dominski, J.: Pedestal and edge electrostatic turbulence characteristics from an XGC1 gyrokinetic simulation. Plasma Phys. Control. Fusion **59**(10), 105014 (2017)
10. Çiçek, Ö., Abdulkadir, A., Lienkamp, S.S., Brox, T., Ronneberger, O.: 3D U-Net: learning dense volumetric segmentation from sparse annotation. In: Ourselin, S., Joskowicz, L., Sabuncu, M.R., Unal, G., Wells, W. (eds.) MICCAI 2016, Part II. LNCS, vol. 9901, pp. 424–432. Springer, Cham (2016). https://doi.org/10.1007/978-3-319-46723-8_49
11. Davis, W.M., Ko, M.K., Maqueda, R.J., Roquemore, A.L., Scotti, F., Zweben, S.J.: Fast 2-D camera control, data acquisition, and database techniques for edge studies on NSTX. Fusion Eng. Des. **89**(5), 717–720 (2014)
12. Dice, L.R.: Measures of the amount of ecologic association between species. Ecology **26**(3), 297–302 (1945)
13. D'Ippolito, D., Myra, J., Zweben, S.: Convective transport by intermittent blob-filaments: comparison of theory and experiment. Phys. Plasmas **18**(6), 060501 (2011)
14. Haidacher, M., Bruckner, S., Groller, E.: Volume analysis using multimodal surface similarity. IEEE Trans. Vis. Comput. Graph. **17**(12), 1969–1978 (2011)
15. Imre, M., Tao, J., Wang, C.: Identifying nearly equally spaced isosurfaces for volumetric data sets. Comput. Graph. **72**, 82–97 (2018)
16. Kube, R., Garcia, O.E., LaBombard, B., Terry, J., Zweben, S.: Blob sizes and velocities in the alcator c-mod scrape-off layer. J. Nucl. Mater. **438**, S505–S508 (2013)
17. Long, J., Shelhamer, E., Darrell, T.: Fully convolutional networks for semantic segmentation. In: Proceedings of IEEE Conference on Computer Vision and Pattern Recognition, pp. 3431–3440 (2015)
18. McKinley, R., et al.: Nabla-net: a deep dag-like convolutional architecture for biomedical image segmentation. In: Crimi, A., Menze, B., Maier, O., Reyes, M., Winzeck, S., Handels, H. (eds.) BrainLes 2016. LNCS, vol. 10154, pp. 119–128. Springer, Cham (2016). https://doi.org/10.1007/978-3-319-55524-9_12
19. Meyer, M., Scheidegger, C.E., Schreiner, J.M., Duffy, B., Carr, H., Silva, C.T.: Revisiting histograms and isosurface statistics. IEEE Trans. Vis. Comput. Graph. **14**(6), 1659–1666 (2008)
20. Milletari, F., Navab, N., Ahmadi, S.A.: V-Net: fully convolutional neural networks for volumetric medical image segmentation. In: Proceedings of International Conference on 3D Vision, pp. 565–571 (2016)

21. Pascucci, V., Cole-McLaughin, K., Scorzelli, G.: Multi-resolution computation and presentation of contour trees. LLNL Technical report number UCRL-PROC-208680. Lawrence Livermore National Laboratory, Livermore (2004)
22. Pekar, V., Wiemker, R., Hempel, D.: Fast detection of meaningful isosurfaces for volume data visualization. In: Proceedings of IEEE Visualization Conference, pp. 223–230 (2001)
23. Ronneberger, O., Fischer, P., Brox, T.: U-Net: convolutional networks for biomedical image segmentation. In: Navab, N., Hornegger, J., Wells, W.M., Frangi, A.F. (eds.) MICCAI 2015, Part III. LNCS, vol. 9351, pp. 234–241. Springer, Cham (2015). https://doi.org/10.1007/978-3-319-24574-4_28
24. Seyedhosseini, M., Sajjadi, M., Tasdizen, T.: Image segmentation with cascaded hierarchical models and logistic disjunctive normal networks. In: Proceedings of IEEE International Conference on Computer Vision, pp. 2168–2175 (2013)
25. Tao, J., et al.: Exploring time-varying multivariate volume data using matrix of isosurface similarity maps. IEEE Trans. Vis. Comput. Graph. 25(1), 1236–1245 (2019)
26. Wang, G., et al.: DeepIGeoS: a deep interactive geodesic framework for medical image segmentation. arXiv preprint: arXiv:1707.00652 (2017)
27. Wang, G., et al.: Interactive medical image segmentation using deep learning with image-specific fine tuning. IEEE Trans. Med. Imaging 37(7), 1562–1573 (2018)
28. Wu, L., et al.: Towards real-time detection and tracking of spatio-temporal features: blob-filaments in fusion plasma. IEEE Trans. Big Data 2(3), 262–275 (2016)
29. Zweben, S., et al.: Edge and SOL turbulence and blob variations over a large database in NSTX. Nucl. Fusion 55(9), 093035 (2015)

Mutual Information-Based Texture Spectral Similarity Criterion

Michal Haindl$^{(\boxtimes)}$ (iD) and Michal Havlíček

The Institute of Information Theory and Automation of the Czech Academy
of Sciences, Prague, Czechia
{haindl,havlimi2}@utia.cz
http://www.utia.cz/

Abstract. Fast novel texture spectral similarity criterion, capable of assessing spectral modeling resemblance of color and Bidirectional Texture Functions (BTF) textures, is presented. The criterion reliably compares the multi-spectral pixel values of two textures, and thus it allows to assist an optimal modeling or acquisition setup development by comparing the original data with its synthetic simulations. The suggested criterion, together with existing alternatives, is extensively tested in a long series of thousands specially designed monotonically degrading experiments moreover, successfully compared on a wide variety of color and BTF textures.

1 Introduction

A reliable mathematical criterion which would allow to an automatic assessment and mutual-similarity evaluation of two or more visual textures is important but still unsolved difficult image understanding problem. Recent validation of the state-of-the-art image and texture fidelity criteria [5] on the web-based benchmark (http://tfa.utia.cas.cz) has demonstrated that none of published criteria (CW-SSIM [24], STSIM-1, STSIM-2, STSIM-M) [27], ζ [13]) can be reliably used for this task at all.

However, the development of visually correct mathematical texture models and the estimation of their optimal parameters requires a reliable criterion for comparison of the original texture with a synthesized or reconstructed one. Such similarity metrics is also needed for spectral content-based image retrieval. Various textural features developed for texture classification applications such as Haralick's features [8], Run-Length features [4], Laws's filters [14], Gabor features [15], LBP [17], and so forth are not descriptive (except for Markovian features [6]), and thus, they can be used for identity but not a degree of similarity decisions. Furthermore, most advanced textural features are limited to mono-spectral images, which neglects color is arguably the most significant visual feature.

The psychophysical evaluations [7,22], i.e., quality assessments performed by humans, currently represent the only reliable but awkward option. The psychophysical texture similarity assessment requires strictly controlled laboratory

© Springer Nature Switzerland AG 2019
G. Bebis et al. (Eds.): ISVC 2019, LNCS 11844, pp. 302–314, 2019.
https://doi.org/10.1007/978-3-030-33720-9_23

conditions experiment design setup, representative and sufficient numbers of testers who are naive concerning the purpose and design of the experiment. Thus it is extremely impractical, expensive, generally demanding, and hence nontransferable into daily routine practice.

In this article, the visual textures or general images, we compare as independent sets of pixels irrespectively of their location. We will investigate this restricted problem of texture spectral similarity in the rest of the paper which is organized as follows: Sect. 2 briefly presents existing possibilities to solve the problem of image spectral composition comparison, including some criteria based on modifications of techniques developed for slightly different purposes. Section 3 explains in detail the proposed approach and Sect. 4 describes the performed criteria, validation experiments, and test data. Section 5 shows the achieved results. The conclusion summarizes the paper with a discussion and compares the proposed criterion with the existing alternatives.

2   Related Criteria

In this section, we briefly survey existing methods capable of comparing image spectral composition. The symbols $\downarrow, \uparrow$ indicate the increasing similarity direction for the corresponding criterion. Most methods deal with color images, i.e., three spectral channels only. The straightforward option is to use a three-dimensional (3-D) histogram or local histogram [25], which approximates the image color distribution. Let us denote by a_ϱ and b_ϱ the ϱ-th bin of the 3-D histogram of the images A and B respectively, where A is the template image and similarly B is the image to be compared. The range of the histogram multi-index $\varrho = [i, j, k]$ depends on a color space C in which the image is represented, e.g., in case of the standard 24-bit RGB color space, the range of all three components of the multi-index is an integer from 0 to 255.

The histogram based criteria often use the Minkowski distance:

$$\downarrow \, \Delta_p H(A, B) = \left(\sum_{\varrho \in C} |a_\varrho - b_\varrho|^p \right)^{1/p} \geq 0. \tag{1}$$

either in the most intuitive the 3-D histograms difference version $p = 1$ (ΔH also known as the block or Manhattan distance), or the Euclidean distance $p = 2$, a fractional dissimilarity $p = \frac{1}{2}$, alternatively, the maximum distance also called Chebyshev distance and known as chessboard distance ($p = \infty$):

$$\downarrow \, \Delta_\infty H(A, B) = \sum_{\varrho \in C} \max \{|a_i - b_i|, |a_j - b_j|, |a_k - b_k|\} \geq 0, \tag{2}$$

where a_i, a_j, a_k represents 1st, 2nd and 3rd components of vector a_ϱ and similarly for b_i, b_j, b_k. Let us mention that for $0 < p < 1$ so-called fractional dissimilarity, the Minkowski distance is not a metric because it violates the triangle inequality [10].

Several other possibilities for 3-D histogram comparison have been suggested, such as the histogram intersection [21]:

$$\downarrow \cap H(A, B) = 1 - \frac{\sum_{\varrho \in C} \min\{a_\varrho, b_\varrho\}}{\sum_{\varrho \in C} b_\varrho} \geq 0, \tag{3}$$

the squared chord [12]:

$$\downarrow d_{sc}(A, B) = \sum_{\varrho \in C} \left(\sqrt{a_\varrho} - \sqrt{b_\varrho}\right)^2 \geq 0, \tag{4}$$

the Canberra metric [12]:

$$\downarrow d_{can} = \sum_{C_0} \frac{|a_\varrho - b_\varrho|}{a_\varrho + b_\varrho} \geq 0, \tag{5}$$

where $C_0 = \{\varrho : a_\varrho + b_\varrho \neq 0\} \subset C$.

The information theoretic measures can also be considered for evaluating the histogram difference. One possible option is the Kullback-Leibler divergence:

$$\downarrow KL(A, B) = \sum_{C^0} a_\varrho \log \frac{a_\varrho}{b_\varrho}, \tag{6}$$

where $C^0 = \{\varrho : a_\varrho b_\varrho \neq 0\} \subset C$ and $\log$ denotes common logarithm. Another possible option is the symmetric modification of the Kullback-Leibler divergence – a variant of the empirical Jeffrey divergence:

$$\downarrow J(A, B) = \sum_{C^0} a_\varrho \log \frac{2a_\varrho}{a_\varrho + b_\varrho} + b_\varrho \log \frac{2b_\varrho}{a_\varrho + b_\varrho} \geq 0. \tag{7}$$

The Jeffrey divergence is numerically stable, symmetric and robust concerning noise and the size of histogram bins [18]. Another measure, based on χ^2 statistic was suggested in [26]:

$$\downarrow \chi^2(A, B) = \sum_{C_0} \frac{2\left(a_\varrho - \frac{a_\varrho + b_\varrho}{2}\right)^2}{a_\varrho + b_\varrho} \geq 0. \tag{8}$$

The Earth Mover's Distance (EMD) or Wasserstein [19] is a method to evaluate dissimilarity between two multidimensional distributions in some feature space. It is based on the minimal cost that must be paid to transform one distribution into another where the cost for moving a single feature unit in the feature space is defined by the Euclidean distance, and the total cost is the sum of such single feature moving costs. The measure in its smoothed dual solution [1] is too time-consuming for any practical application (see Table 2).

The generalized color moments (GCM) [16] suits well to the image spectral composition comparison problem. The GCM of the $(p + q)$-th order and the $(\alpha + \beta + \gamma)$-th degree is defined as [16]:

$$\downarrow \Delta GCM_{pq}^{\alpha\beta\gamma}(A,B) = \left| \int\int_{\langle A \rangle} r_1^p r_2^q \, [Y_{r_1,r_2,1}^A]^\alpha \, [Y_{r_1,r_2,2}^A]^\beta \, [Y_{r_1,r_2,3}^A]^\gamma \, dr_1 dr_2 \right.$$

$$\left. - \int\int_{\langle B \rangle} r_1^p r_2^q \, [Y_{r_1,r_2,1}^B]^\alpha \, [Y_{r_1,r_2,2}^B]^\beta \, [Y_{r_1,r_2,3}^B]^\gamma \, dr_1 dr_2 \right|, \tag{9}$$

where $[r_1, r_2] \in \langle A \rangle$ represents planar coordinates of the image pixel Y_r^A, $Y_{r_1,r_2,i}^A$ denotes a pixel intensity in the i-th spectral plane of the image A, similarly $Y_{r_1,r_2,r_3=i}^B$ where $[r_1, r_2] \in \langle B \rangle$. In the case of using GCM for spectral composition comparison, neither of the terms r_1^p and r_2^q is useful and therefore both might be put equal to one, using those GCMs for which $p = q = 0$ holds. Moreover, it has been observed that the best results are achieved if $\alpha = \beta = \gamma$, specifically using GCMs for $\alpha = \beta = \gamma < 4$. Thus, GCM directly compares image pixels not using their 3-D histograms like methods (1), (3)–(8), similar to the cosine-function-based dissimilarity, which computes an angle between two vectors. Both images A, B must have an identical number of pixels which is a significant drawback of this criterion. This criterion is the only one mentioned in this article suffering from this. All values of corresponding image spectral channels are arranged into vectors V_A and V_B and the difference is computed as [26]:

$$\uparrow d_{cos}(A,B) = \frac{V_A^T \cdot V_B}{\|V_A\| \|V_B\|} \quad \in \langle 0; 1 \rangle, \tag{10}$$

where $\| \ \|$ denotes the vector magnitude.

Various set-theoretic measures can serve as criteria as well. Let sets S_A and S_B denote the sets of unique multi-dimensional vectors representing pixels occurring in the images A and B, respectively. Spectral composition comparison criteria can be based on methods developed for comparing the similarity and diversity of the sample sets, such as the Jaccard index [11]:

$$\uparrow JI(A,B) = \frac{|S_A \cap S_B|}{|S_A \cup S_B|} \quad \in \langle 0; 1 \rangle, \tag{11}$$

or the Sørensen-Dice index [3]:

$$\uparrow SDI(A,B) = \frac{2\,|S_A \cap S_B|}{|S_A| + |S_B|} \quad \in \langle 0; 1 \rangle, \tag{12}$$

where $\| \ $ denotes the cardinality of the set. Since SDI does not satisfy the triangle inequality, it can be considered a semi-metric version of JI.

Another alternative may be a modified criterion developed for texture comparison as the texture spectral composition comparison might be considered a very special case of this task. It is possible to modify the structural similarity metric (SSIM) [23] for example. SSIM compares local statistics in corresponding sliding windows in two images in either the spatial or wavelet domain. Its form consists of three terms that reflect luminance, contrast, and structure of the textures. In the case of the spectral composition comparison the structure term is irrelevant so that we define a reduced SSIM:

$$\downarrow rSSIM(A,B) = \frac{1}{\#\{r_3\}} \sum_{\forall r_3} \frac{2\mu_{A,r_3}\mu_{B,r_3}}{\mu_{A,r_3}^2 + \mu_{B,r_3}^2} \frac{2\sigma_{A,r_3}\sigma_{B,r_3}}{\sigma_{A,r_3}^2 + \sigma_{B,r_3}^2}, \tag{13}$$

where $\#\{r_3\}$ is the spectral index cardinality, i.e., the number of spectral channels, μ_{A,r_3} is the mean of r_3-th spectral plane of A and σ_{A,r_3} is the standard deviation of r_3-th spectral plane of A; similarly for μ_{B,r_3} and σ_{B,r_3}. $rSSIM(A,B) = 1$ for spectrally equal textures.

A MEMD criterion was proposed in [9]

$$\downarrow \zeta(A,B) = \frac{1}{M} \sum_{(r_1,r_2)\in\langle A\rangle} \min_{(s_1,s_2)\in U} \{\rho\left(Y_{r_1,r_2,\bullet}^A, Y_{s_1,s_2,\bullet}^B\right)\} \quad \geq 0, \tag{14}$$

where $Y_{r_1,r_2,\bullet}^A$ represents the pixel at location (r_1,r_2) in the image A, $\bullet$ denotes all the corresponding spectral indices, and similarly for $Y_{s_1,s_2,\bullet}^B$. Further, ρ is an arbitrary vector metric.

3 Proposed Criterion

The proposed texture spectral similarity criterion is based on the mutual information:

$$\uparrow \varepsilon(A,B) = \log_2 n - \frac{1}{n}\sum_{i=1}^{n_A} {}^A n_i \log_2 {}^A n_i - \frac{1}{n}\sum_{j=1}^{n_B} {}^B n_j \log_2 {}^B n_j$$

$$+\frac{1}{n}\sum_{i=1,j=1}^{n_A,n_B} n_{i,j} \log_2 n_{i,j} \quad \geq 0, \tag{15}$$

$$n = \sum_{i=1,j=1}^{n_A,n_B} n_{i,j},$$

where ${}^A n_i$ is the number of color x_i appearances in A, ${}^B n_j$ is the number of color y_j appearances in B, n_{ij} is the number of pixels with identical color $x_i = y_j$, and n_A, n_B are the number of the corresponding color histogram cells. $\varepsilon(A,B) = 0$ if both textures have independent colors. The criterion is non-negative and symmetric $\varepsilon(A,B) = \varepsilon(B,A)$.

3.1 Evaluation Meta-Criterion

The tested criteria are applied to quantify spectral composition differences between the template image, i.e., the first member of the degradation sequence and the remaining members. As all those sequences are created to guarantee a monotonic degradation of the original image, i.e., the similarity of the members of the sequence and the original image is decreasing with the order. A good criterion should preserve this monotonicity.

The meta-criterion is the number of monotonicity violations of the criterion τ in the experiment X:

$$\Xi^{X,\tau} = \sum_{i=1}^{l} \left[1 - \delta \left(o_i^X - o_i^{X,\tau} \right) \right],$$

(16)

where τ is a tested criterion, o_i^X is the rank of a degraded image and $o_i^{X,\tau}$ its corresponding correct ordering of the τ-criterion-based ranking, and δ is the Kronecker delta function.

4 Criteria Evaluation

We proposed the set of six controllable degradation experiments described in detail below with the aim to investigate how the individual previously published (1)–(14) criteria as well as the novel proposed criterion are affected by the spectral composition changes comparing the image with its modified versions. In the following sections, we describe the performed experiments as well as used test data.

4.1 Controlled Degradation of the Test Data

A sequence of gradually degraded textural images is generated from the original test one. The original image serves as the first member of the sequence, i.e., $A_1^X = A$ and each member, except for the first one, is generated from its predecessor in the sequence as: $A_t^X = f_X \left(A_{t-1}^X \right)$, $t = 1, \ldots, l$, where l equals the length of the sequence and X is the label identifying the experiment (individual experiments described below). Further $Y_{r,t}^A$ denotes the multi-spectral pixel from the experimental image A_t^X at $r = [r_1, r_2, r_3]$ which is a multi-index with image row, column, and spectral components, respectively. X is the corresponding label of one of following six degradation experiments we established for validation tests:

A Replacing spectral intensity values of pixels with the maximal or minimal value in the used color space with the probability $p = \frac{1}{l}$:

$$Y_{r,t}^A \overset{p=\frac{1}{l}}{\longleftrightarrow} \begin{cases} [255, 255, 255]^T : \text{with } p = 0.5 \\ [0, 0, 0]^T : \text{otherwise} \end{cases}$$

B Adding a constant $c = \frac{255}{l}$ to spectral intensities of the pixels:
$$Y_{r,t}^B \overset{p}{\longleftrightarrow} Y_{r,t-1}^B + [c, c, c]^T$$

C Replacing spectral intensity values of pixels with the minimal value in the used color space ($[0,0,0]^T$) with randomly driven propagating with 50% probability with 8-connected pixels from $I_r^{(8)}$:

1. $Y_{r,t}^C \overset{p}{\leftrightarrow} [0,0,0]^T$
2. $Y_{s,t}^C \overset{0.5}{=} Y_{r,t}^C, \ \forall s \in \ I_r^{(8)}$

D,E   Randomly driven propagating with 50% probability with 8-connected (D) or 4-connected (E) pixels from $I_r^{(8)}$:

$$Y_{s,t}^D \overset{0.5}{=} Y_{r,t}^D, \ \forall s \in \ I_r^{(8)}/I_r^{(4)}$$

F Adding a constant $c = \frac{255}{l}$ to the spectral intensities of the pixel and randomly driven propagating with 50% probability with 8-connected pixels from $I_r^{(8)}$:

1. $Y_{r,t}^F \overset{p}{\leftrightarrow} Y_{r,t-1}^F + [c,c,c]^T$
2. $Y_{s,t}^F \overset{0.5}{=} Y_{r,t}^F, \ \forall s \in \ I_r^{(8)}$

Several selected members of the degradation sequences generated during the experiments are shown in Fig. 1.

4.2   Test Data

The proposed criterion was validated and compared with the alternative criteria on two types of visual data - color textures and BTF textures.

Color Textures. The tested criteria were validated using 250 color textures of 64×64 pixels saved as 24-bit RGB PNG files (Fig. 2). The textures were selected from a large collection of both natural and man-made materials. Each material category was represented by several examples. All used textures were downloaded from free internet texture databases[1,2]. The obtained results are summarized in Table 1-left.

Bidirectional Texture Functions. Simple color textures cannot represent physically correct visual appearance of the corresponding surface materials under variable observation conditions. Recent most advanced visual representation of such surfaces, Bidirectional Texture Function (BTF) [2], which is a seven-dimensional function describing surface appearance variations due to varying spatial position and illumination and viewing angles are the state-of-the-art replacement of static color textures. A static BTF texture representation requires complex seven-dimensional models, which have not yet been developed [7]. Thus,

---

[1] http://texturer.com/.
[2] http://www.mayang.com/textures/.

their measurement or mathematical modeling use a BTF space factorization into a large set of less dimensional factors. The measured BTF data usually consist of several thousand color images per material which are analyzed for their intrinsic dimensionality [7] and then subsequently approximated by a smaller number of BTF subspaces. It is not possible to run all experiments for all infinite number images, i.e., for any combination of the continuous spherical illumination and viewing angles, of synthetic BTF space texture components. Tested BTF measurements are represented by 20 subspace clusters, which subsequently can serve for building the BTF mathematical model. Subspace cluster were images of 32×32 pixels saved as 24-bit RGB PNG files. We used ten BTF data sets (one example of subspace is shown in Fig. 3) and therefore 200 textures obtained from the University of Bonn database[3] [20]. The achieved results are presented in Table 1-right.

5   Results

In this section, we present and summarize all achieved results during the experiments described in Sect. 4.1 performed on color and BTF textures and compared and comment on the performance of the criteria.

5.1   Color Textures

Achieved results of experiments with color textures in the RGB space (Fig. 2) are summarized in Table 1-left. The criterion ζ achieves the best results on average without any monotonicity violation and $\Delta_2 H$ (1) achieves the second best results, although the difference between the best criterion and the second best criterion is only 4% in average. The proposed criterion ε (15) is he third best with only 5% monotonicity violation in average. $\Delta_2 H$ is $\leq 2\%$ more correct than ε in cases **A–E** but 4% less correct in case of **F**. $rSSIM$ (13) is the second most correct criterion in case of **B** and **C** and its average error is 6% but worsen it performance in cases **D** and **E**. Other criteria fail on average more than 15% and cannot be considered reliable, although in some cases they work well, e.g., ΔGCM_{00}^{111} in case of **F**, ΔH, $\Delta_{1/2} H$, $\cap H$, d_{sc}, d_{can}, χ^2 in case of **A**. The criteria were on average the most successful in case of **A** with average failure only 4% and the least successful in case of **F** with average failure 53%.

5.2   Bidirectional Texture Functions

The achieved results are summarized in the right part of Table 1. Both criteria ε and ζ are the only criteria that reached zero average error in all experiments. The second most successful criterion $\Delta_2 H$ achieved 1% worse result in average. The ε, ζ can be considered as absolutely reliable for BTF textures. $rSSIM$ achieved 5% average error and it is quite successful in most experiments but

---

[3] http://cg.cs.uni-bonn.de/en/projects/btfdbb/download/ubo2003/.

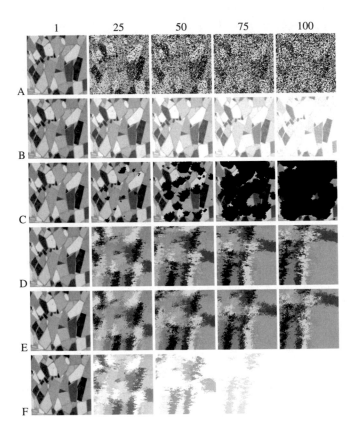

Fig. 1. The figure illustrates selected members of the degradation sequence generated during the experiments, **A-F** top-down. The leftmost column represents the original image, and the degradation intensifies in the rightward direction, where the column number indicates the order of the image in the sequence.

Fig. 2. Selected examples of the color textures used in our experiments.

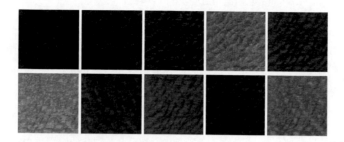

Fig. 3. Textures representing BTF subspace clusters approximating original BTF data acquired by measuring the wood material. Original data were taken from BTF database of the University of Bonn [20]. BTF subspace textures were used in our experiments.

Table 1. The average strict monotonicity violation (in percent) for 250 test color texture sequences (left) 200 test BTF data sequences (right) per experiment performed in the RGB color space, average over all experiments and the rank for the tested criteria.

Color textures									BTF textures							
	A	B	C	D	E	F	$\oslash$	Rank	A	B	C	D	E	F	$\oslash$	Rank
ΔH	0	14	14	35	22	86	29	9	0	3	3	0	1	67	12	5
$\Delta_2 H$	0	7	7	2	2	7	4	2	0	1	1	0	0	3	1	2
$\Delta_\infty H$	5	12	12	97	97	98	54	14	1	4	4	96	96	98	50	10
$\Delta_{1/2} H$	0	31	31	49	48	9	28	8	0	18	18	73	70	6	31	9
$\cap H$	0	14	14	35	22	86	29	9	0	3	3	0	1	67	12	5
d_{sc}	0	16	16	3	3	86	21	6	0	3	3	0	0	64	12	5
d_{can}	0	33	33	29	28	55	30	10	0	20	20	23	23	8	16	6
KL	19	37	36	20	23	86	37	12	18	32	32	17	20	65	31	9
J	19	38	38	4	4	86	32	11	17	32	32	1	1	65	25	8
χ^2	0	16	16	4	4	86	21	6	0	3	3	1	1	64	12	5
ΔGCM_{00}^{111}	14	13	13	23	24	0	15	5	4	4	4	23	24	0	10	4
d_{cos}	13	13	13	43	43	20	24	7	2	2	2	45	46	37	22	7
JI	1	31	31	54	49	98	44	13	0	16	16	0	0	98	22	7
SDI	1	32	32	54	49	98	44	13	0	17	17	0	0	98	22	7
$rSSIM$	3	3	3	12	13	3	6	4	0	0	0	13	14	1	5	3
ζ	0	0	0	0	0	0	0	1	0	0	0	0	0	0	0	1
ε	1	9	9	3	4	3	5	3	0	0	0	0	0	0	0	1
$\oslash$	4	19	19	27	26	53	25		2	9	9	17	17	44	17	

Table 2. The average evaluation time, on Pentium-2.8 GHz-equivalent CPU, depending on the size of compared images for individual criteria.

	8×8	16×16	32×32	64×64
$\Delta H, \cap H, d_{sc}, d_{can}, J, \chi^2$	0.7 s	0.7 s	0.7 s	0.7 s
EMD	1.8 ms	85.6 ms	5.7 s	7.6 min
ΔGCM_{00}^{111}	67.0 μs	0.1 ms	0.2 ms	0.5 ms
d_{cos}	32.0 μs	88.0 μs	93.0 μs	0.6 ms
JI, SDI	0.3 ms	4.0 ms	9.0 ms	48.0 ms
$rSSIM$	31.0 μs	0.1 ms	0.2 ms	1.4 ms
ζ	0.1 ms	2.0 ms	18.0 ms	0.2 s
ε	0.1 ms	0.2 ms	0.7 ms	2.2 ms

it fails again in cases **D** and **E**. ΔGCM_{00}^{111} achieved better results like the other criteria in **A**–**C** but its average error in case of **D** and **E** stayed the same. In average, all criteria, except $\Delta_{1/2}H$, achieved better results (with average improvement 8%), which may be due to the lower amount of distinct colors of BTF textures compared to the data described in Sect. 4.2.

6   Conclusions

We introduced the mutual information based criterion for comparing the spectral similarity of the color textures and bidirectional texture functions. Although the criterion neglects spatial pixels arrangement and thus it represents only a partial solution for the quality assessment of the multi-spectral textured images and also for the most advanced visual representation of material surfaces - the bidirectional texture function, it can assist in numerous texture-analytic or synthesis applications. The performance quality of the proposed criterion is demonstrated on the extensive series of specially designed monotonically image degrading experiments, which also serve for the comparison with the existing alternative methods.

Similarly to several other existing approaches (1)–(8), the criterion (15) is based on 3-D histograms, thus it cannot be efficiently used for hyperspectral images. Although it has slightly worse performance than the best ζ (14) spectral similarity criterion, it is symmetric, can be easily modified to a metric, and is much faster.

The presented criterion proposes a reliable fully automatic alternative to psychophysical experiments, which are, moreover, extremely impractical due to their cost and strict demands on design setup, conditions control, human resources, and time.

Acknowledgments. The Czech Science Foundation project GAČR 19-12340S supported this research.

References

1. Cuturi, M., Peyré, G.: A smoothed dual approach for variational wasserstein problems. SIAM J. Imaging Sci. **9**(1), 320–343 (2016)
2. Dana, K.J., Nayar, S.K., van Ginneken, B., Koenderink, J.J.: Reflectance and texture of real-world surfaces. In: CVPR, pp. 151–157. IEEE Computer Society (1997)
3. Dice, L.R.: Measures of the amount of ecologic association between species. Ecology **26**(3), 297–302 (1945)
4. Galloway, M.: Texture analysis using gray level run lengths. Comput. Graph. Image Process. **4**(2), 172–179 (1975)
5. Haindl, M., Kudělka, M.: Texture fidelity benchmark. In: 2014 International Workshop on Computational Intelligence for Multimedia Understanding (IWCIM), pp. 1–5. IEEE Computer Society CPS, Los Alamitos, November 2014. https://doi.org/10.1109/IWCIM.2014.7008812, http://ieeexplore.ieee.org/stamp/stamp.jsp?tp=&arnumber=7008812&isnumber=7008791
6. Haindl, M., Mikeš, S.: Unsupervised texture segmentation using multispectral modelling approach. In: Tang, Y., Wang, S., Yeung, D., Yan, H., Lorette, G. (eds.) Proceedings of the 18th International Conference on Pattern Recognition, ICPR 2006. vol. II, pp. 203–206. IEEE Computer Society, Los Alamitos, August 2006. https://doi.org/10.1109/ICPR.2006.1148
7. Haindl, M., Filip, J.: Visual Texture. Advances in Computer Vision and Pattern Recognition. Springer, London (2012). https://doi.org/10.1007/978-1-4471-4902-6
8. Haralick, R.M., Shanmugam, K., Dinstein, I.: Textural features for image classification. IEEE Trans. Syst. Man Cybern. **3**(6), 610–621 (1973)
9. Havlíček, M., Haindl, M.: Texture spectral similarity criteria. IET Image Process. **13** (2019). https://doi.org/10.1049/iet-ipr.2019.0250
10. Howarth, P., Rüger, S.: Fractional distance measures for content-based image retrieval. In: Losada, D.E., Fernández-Luna, J.M. (eds.) ECIR 2005. LNCS, vol. 3408, pp. 447–456. Springer, Heidelberg (2005). https://doi.org/10.1007/978-3-540-31865-1_32
11. Jaccard, P.: Etude comparative de la distribution florale dans une portion des Alpes et du Jura. Impr. Corbaz (1901)
12. Kokare, M., Chatterji, B., Biswas, P.: Comparison of similarity metrics for texture image retrieval. In: TENCON 2003. Conference on Convergent Technologies for the Asia-Pacific Region, vol. 2, pp. 571–575. IEEE (2003)
13. Kudělka, M., Haindl, M.: Texture fidelity criterion. In: 2016 IEEE International Conference on Image Processing (ICIP), pp. 2062–2066. IEEE, September 2016. https://doi.org/10.1109/ICIP.2016.7532721, http://2016.ieeeicip.org/
14. Laws, K.: Rapid texture identification. In: Proceedings of SPIE Conference on Image Processing for Missile Guidance, pp. 376–380 (1980)
15. Manjunath, B.S., Ma, W.Y.: Texture features for browsing and retrieval of image data. IEEE Trans. Pattern Anal. Mach. Intell. **18**(8), 837–842 (1996). https://doi.org/10.1109/34.531803
16. Mindru, F., Moons, T., Van Gool, L.: Color-based moment invariants for viewpoint and illumination independent recognition of planar color patterns. In: Singh, S. (ed.) International Conference on Advances in Pattern Recognition, pp. 113–122. Springer, London (1998). https://doi.org/10.1007/978-1-4471-0833-7_12
17. Ojala, T., Pietikäinen, M., Mäenpää, T.: Multiresolution gray-scale and rotation invariant texture classification with local binary patterns. IEEE Trans. Pattern Anal. Mach. Intell **24**(7), 971–987 (2002)

18. Puzicha, J., Hofmann, T., Buhmann, J.M.: Non-parametric similarity measures for unsupervised texture segmentation and image retrieval. In: Proceedings of the IEEE International Conference on Computer Vision and Pattern Recognition, pp. 267–272. IEEE (1997)
19. Rubner, Y., Tomasi, C., Guibas, L.J.: The earth mover's distance as a metric for image retrieval. Int. J. Comput. Vis. **40**(2), 99–121 (2000). https://doi.org/10.1023/A:1026543900054
20. Sattler, M., Sarlette, R., Klein, R.: Efficient and realistic visualization of cloth. In: Eurographics Symposium on Rendering 2003, June 2003
21. Swain, M.J., Ballard, D.H.: Color indexing. Int. J. Comput. Vis. **7**(1), 11–32 (1991)
22. Viethen, J., van Vessem, T., Goudbeek, M., Krahmer, E.: Color in reference production: the role of color similarity and color codability. Cogn. Sci. **41**, 1493–1514 (2017)
23. Wang, Z., Bovik, A.C., Sheikh, H.R., Simoncelli, E.P.: Image quality assessment: from error visibility to structural similarity. IEEE Trans. Image Process. **13**(4), 600–612 (2004). https://doi.org/10.1109/TIP.2003.819861
24. Wang, Z., Simoncelli, E.P.: Translation insensitive image similarity in complex wavelet domain. In: IEEE International Conference on Acoustics, Speech, and Signal Processing, 2005. Proceedings. (ICASSP 05), pp. 573–576 (2005)
25. Yuan, J., Wang, D., Cheriyadat, A.M.: Factorization-based texture segmentation. IEEE Trans. Image Process. **24**(11), 3488–3497 (2015). https://doi.org/10.1109/TIP.2015.2446948
26. Zhang, D., Lu, G.: Evaluation of similarity measurement for image retrieval. In: Proceedings of the 2003 International Conference on Neural Networks and Signal Processing, 2003, vol. 2, pp. 928–931. IEEE (2003)
27. Zujovic, J., Pappas, T., Neuhoff, D.: Structural texture similarity metrics for image analysis and retrieval. IEEE Trans. Image Process. **22**(7), 2545–2558 (2013). https://doi.org/10.1109/TIP.2013.2251645

Accurate Computation of Interval Volume Measures for Improving Histograms

Cuilan Wang[✉]

School of Science and Technology, Georgia Gwinnett College, Lawrenceville, USA
cwang@ggc.edu

Abstract. The interval volume measure is defined as the volume of the space occupied by a range of isosurfaces corresponding to an interval of isovalues. The interval volume measures are very useful since they can be taken as an alternative way of producing a smooth noise-suppressing histogram. This paper proposes two new methods (i.e., the subdividing method and the slicing method) that can calculate interval volume measures with very high accuracy for scalar regular-grid volumetric datasets. It is assumed that the underlying function inside the grid cell is defined by trilinear interpolation. A refined histogram method that can produce accurate interval volume measures is also presented in the paper. All three methods are compared against one another in terms of accuracy and performance. Their improvement for computing global and local histograms is demonstrated by comparing against the previous methods.

Keywords: Isosurface · Interval volume · Histogram · Trilinear interpolation · Marching Cubes

1 Introduction

The interval volume region (i.e., interval region) is defined as the region between two isosurfaces [4,6]. It is the space that is occupied by a range of isosurfaces corresponding to an interval of isovalues. The interval volume measure is the volume of the interval region. For this search work, the input datasets are scalar regular-grid volumetric datasets where each grid cell is a unit cube and the data value at each grid vertex is an integer. The histogram is the number of the grid vertices with each given scalar value in a scalar dataset [17]. Histograms are important statistics in scientific visualization. It has been used for transfer function design [7] and significant isovalue detection [10,12]. However, histograms are often noisy, which make it difficult to use [3]. Local histograms, i.e., the histograms collected in local neighborhoods, allows users to examine subregions of the volume in greater detail. However, since local histograms have less available data, they are usually much noisier than global histograms. Therefore, making smoother substitutes for global and local histograms is very useful. For scalar regular-grid volumetric datasets, as the sampling resolution increases, the histogram has been proven to converge to a sequence of the interval volume

© Springer Nature Switzerland AG 2019
G. Bebis et al. (Eds.): ISVC 2019, LNCS 11844, pp. 315–329, 2019.
https://doi.org/10.1007/978-3-030-33720-9_24

measures where each bin of the histogram corresponds to the isovalue interval of an interval volume measure in the sequence [3]. Therefore, interval volume measures can be taken as an alternative effective way of producing a smooth noise-suppressing histogram.

This paper proposes two new methods for accurate computation of interval volume measures for scalar regular-grid volumetric datasets. One is called the subdividing method and one is called the slicing method. The subdividing method recursively subdivides each cube into 8 equal-sized subcubes until certain termination conditions are met. The slicing method slices the cube and integrates the cross-sectional areas of the interval region on all slices to generate volume. Although the two methods use very different strategies, both of them converge to the same set of values. Similar methods have been used to calculate the volume between the triangular mesh isosurface and the isosurface given by trilinear interpolation for estimating the accuracy of the isosurface extraction algorithms or generating adaptive isosurfaces with better accuracy and not excessive triangle count [14–16]. This paper also gives a refined version of the histogram method that increases the accuracy of interval volume measures by sampling the data inside a cube. All three methods presented in this paper are compared against one another in terms of accuracy and performance. They are also compared against the previous methods to show their improvement for generating global and local histograms.

2   Related Work

The histogram method is a well-known method to display the statistics of the grid vertices and measure the importance of an isovalue. This method counts the number of grid vertices with each scalar value σ in a scalar grid, which represents the frequency of the scalar value σ in the grid. Let $g(\sigma)$ denote this frequency. The histogram can be represented by a bar graph or a polygonal line with vertices $(\sigma, g(\sigma))$. In this paper, the histogram is represented by a polyline. However, many datasets' sampling resolution is not high enough for the histogram method to produce smooth and useful results.

Some methods have been developed to measure interval volumes [17]. Scheidegger et al. proposed a measure, called the weighted isosurface area, that approximates the interval volume measure by multiplying the area of the isosurface with the inverse gradient magnitude [11]. This is like replacing the isosurface with a thin shell of non-uniform thickness and compute the volume of this thin shell. Also, they used the cube span to approximate the gradient magnitude and the area of the triangular mesh extracted by the Marching Cubes algorithm to approximate the area of the isosurface. Their method is based on the Coarea Formula by Federer [9]. This formula relates an integral over a range of isosurfaces to an integral over the volume where this range of isosurfaces is defined. They also proposed to use cheap alternatives, such as active edge count, active cube count, and triangle count, to approximate the isosurface area in their formula. When active cube count is used as the alternative, the measure is called the weighted cube count. However, this method doesn't consider the existence of homogenous cells (i.e., all 8 vertices of the cell have the same value) which do not intersect the isosurface. Moreover, if the isovalue interval of the interval volume is larger than 1, it may miss non-homogenous cells as well since those cells may be entirely within the interval region.

Duffy et al. made an adjustment to Scheidegger et al.'s weighted isosurface area measure by including the volume of the homogenous cells [3]. In this paper, this measure is called adjusted weighted isosurface area. However, when this measure is used to approximate the interval volume measure, it doesn't guarantee that the sum of the measures for all isovalue intervals equals the volume of the whole dataset, which it should be for the true interval volume measures. This is mainly because the cube span is only a very coarse approximation of the gradient magnitude. Duffy et al. also modified Scheidegger et al.'s weighted cell count measure to include the volume of the homogenous cells. Here, this measure is called adjusted weighted cell count. This measure can guarantee that the total of all the interval volume measures is equal to the volume of the dataset.

Local histograms also have been used in many data analysis and visualization applications, such as transfer function design [8], identifying material interfaces [12,13], and tracking features in time-varying data [5]. Besides directly counting each scalar value in a local region, there are other methods for computing local histograms for rectilinear grids [2], and for tetrahedral meshes and curvilinear grids [18].

3   Accurate Interval Volume Measure Computation

In this section, two new methods, i.e., the subdividing and slicing methods, and a refined histogram method that can calculate interval volume measures with high accuracy are presented. Here, it is assumed that data inside each cube of the volumetric dataset is modeled by trilinear interpolation. The trilinear interpolation function is commonly used when the underlying data function is unknown. It is also the basis of Marching Cubes and its related algorithms. It is also assumed that the volume of each cube in the dataset is 1, therefore, the volume of the whole dataset is the number of cubes in the dataset.

The data range of the whole dataset is evenly divided into N intervals. The interval length can be greater than, equal to, or less than 1. The subdividing and slicing methods only require one pass through the volumetric dataset to generate all the interval volume measures. When a cube is processed, its contributions to all the interval regions that it intersects with are determined, i.e., the volume of the cube is split among all those isovalue intervals. After all cubes are processed, all N interval volume measures are generated. The refined histogram method also needs a single pass through the dataset.

3.1 Subdividing Method

To calculate the volume of an interval region, the subdividing method recursively subdivides each cube in the grid into 8 equal-sized subcubes until certain termination conditions are met or the subdivision limit is reached. Then, each subcube's contribution to the interval volume is determined. Summing up their contributions yields the cube's contribution to the interval volume. The interval volume for the whole dataset is just the sum of all cubes' contribution to the interval volume. This idea is illustrated in Fig. 1. In this figure, the small subcube (red) is located inside the interval region between the grey and green isosurfaces. Therefore, its volume contributes to the interval volume measure. In this method, the subdivision depth determines the size of the final subcube, and thus determines the precision of the method. The higher the subdivision depth, the more accurate the results generated.

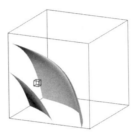

Fig. 1. Illustration of the subdividing method (Color figure online)

Let R be the interval region between two isosurfaces associated with isovalues σ_1 and σ_2. Assume $\sigma_1 < \sigma_2$. Let K be a cube or a subcube. Let p and q be the smallest and largest vertex values of K, respectively. The span of K is $span(K) = q - p$. The size of K, $size(K)$, is the volume of K. If the subdivision depth is D, then the size of the subcube is $(1/8)^D$. Based on the trilinear interpolation function, it is easy to verify that if $[p, q] \subseteq [\sigma_1, \sigma_2]$, then K is entirely inside R and its contribution to the interval volume measure is its volume. Or, if $[p, q] \cap [\sigma_1, \sigma_2] = \emptyset$, then K is entirely outside R and it has zero contribution to the interval volume measure. In these two situations, there is no need to further subdivide K. This early termination condition is especially useful when the span of K is small. If it is not one of these two situations, then K should be kept subdivided until the subdivision limit is reached. When K is the final subcube, the following approximation is used to determine the contribution of K to the interval volume measure of R:

$$T(K) = size(K) \cdot t(K), \tag{1}$$

where

$$t(K) = \begin{cases} 0, & R \cap K = \emptyset \\[2mm] 1, & R \cap K = K,\ [p,q] \subseteq [\sigma_1, \sigma_2] \\[2mm] \dfrac{\sigma_2 - \sigma_1}{span(K)}, & R \cap K \neq \emptyset,\ [\sigma_1, \sigma_2] \subset [p,q] \\[2mm] \dfrac{\sigma_2 - p}{span(K)}, & R \cap K \neq \emptyset,\ \sigma_1 \leq p \leq \sigma_2\ and\ q > \sigma_2 \\[2mm] \dfrac{q - \sigma_1}{span(K)}, & R \cap K \neq \emptyset,\ p < \sigma_1\ and\ \sigma_1 \leq q \leq \sigma_2 \end{cases} \qquad (2)$$

When the subdivision depth is zero, which means no cube is subdivided, and $\sigma_1 = i - 0.5$, $\sigma_2 = i + 0.5$, where i is an integer, this method is just Duffy et al.'s adjusted weighted cube count method [3]. Note that all three methods presented in this paper, i.e., the subdividing, slicing, and refined histogram methods, are general methods. They don't require the interval length to be 1 and an interval region to center at an integer.

3.2 Slicing Method

In this method, each cube is evenly sliced along a major axis. The cross-sectional area of the interval region on each slice is calculated analytically. Then, a numerical approach that is similar to integrating areas to find volume is applied to generate the approximation of the interval volume inside the cube. The more slices the cube is sliced into, the more accurate the result is.

The main idea of this method is illustrated in Fig. 2. In (a), the interval region is the region between the grey and green isosurfaces. The intersections of the slice (light blue and semi-transparent) with the grey and green isosurfaces are shown as the red and yellow curves, respectively. The area between the yellow and red curves is the cross section of the interval region on the slice. (b) shows the 2D view of the cross section (darker blue). The interval region's volume can be calculated based on its cross-sectional areas on all the slices.

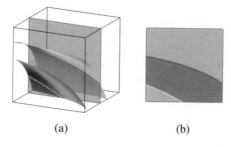

(a)   (b)

Fig. 2. Illustration of the slicing method. (Color figure online)

Suppose the cube is evenly sliced along the y-axis. This divides the range of the cube's side $[0, 1]$ into n subranges with the width $\Delta d = 1/n$. The ith slice is located at $y_i = (i - 1)\Delta d$. The cross-sectional area of the interval region on the ith slice is denoted as $A(y_i)$. Assuming that the cross-sectional area between two adjacent slices is a constant, the interval volume inside the cube can be approximated by

$$\sum_{i=1}^{n} A(y_i)\Delta d \tag{3}$$

Analytical Calculation of the Cross-sectional Area. The intersection of the trilinear interpolation isosurface with a slice is a hyperbola, which represents the bilinear interpolation's isocontour on the slice. This hyperbola is denoted as an isocontour hyperbola. On each slice, the cross section of the interval region is enclosed by the isocontour hyperbolas of the two isosurfaces and slice edges.

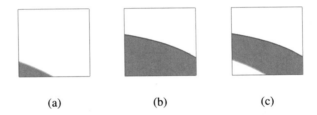

(a)   (b)   (c)

Fig. 3. The inside region (shown in blue) of the red isocontour (b) subtracting the inside region of the yellow isocontour (a) yields the cross section of the interval region (c). (Color figure online)

The region in the volumetric dataset that only contains values greater than or equal to the isovalue is denoted as the inside region and the rest of the dataset is denoted as the outside region. Let $S1$ and $S2$ be the isosurfaces associated with isovalues σ_1 and σ_2, respectively. Assume $\sigma_1 < \sigma_2$. Each isosurface separates the whole $3D$ volumetric dataset into inside and outside regions. It is obvious that $S1$ and $S2$ don't intersect with each other and the inside region of $S2$ is always within the inside region of $S1$. Let $C1$ and $C2$ be the isocontours on a cube slice that are associated with isovalues σ_1 and σ_2, respectively. Similarly, on a slice, an isocontour C splits the $2D$ slice into the inside region C_{in} and the outside region C_{out}. It is easy to prove that $C2_{in} \subset C1_{in}$. Therefore, the region in between $C1$ and $C2$ is $C1_{in} - C2_{in}$. This region is just the cross section of the interval region enclosed by S_1 and S_2 on the slice. Figure 3 uses the instance given in Fig. 2 to illustrate this idea. Therefore, the cross-sectional area on the ith slice, $A(y_i)$, can be calculated as

$$A(y_i) = C_{in}(\sigma_1, y_i) - C_{in}(\sigma_2, y_i), \tag{4}$$

where the function $C_{in}(\sigma, y)$ denotes the inside area (i.e., the area of the inside region) of the isocontour with isovalue σ on the slice at y. Next, how to calculate $C_{in}(\sigma, y)$ is explained.

Area Under Hyperbola. The bilinear interpolation function over a slice of the cube parallel to the XZ plane is defined as:

$$B(x, z) = B_{00}(1 - x)(1 - z) + B_{10}x(1 - z) + B_{01}(1 - x)z + B_{11}xz, \quad (5)$$

where B_{00}, B_{10}, B_{01}, and B_{11} are the values of the 4 corners of the slice located at $(0, 0)$, $(1, 0)$, $(0, 1)$ and $(1, 1)$, and (x, z) represents a location in the slice with $0 \le x \le 1$ and $0 \le z \le 1$. Here, a slice is considered as a unit square. An alternative representation of the bilinear interpolation function is

$$B(x, z) = axz + bx + cz + d, \quad (6)$$

where $a = B_{00} - B_{10} - B_{01} + B_{11}$, $b = B_{10} - B_{00}$, $c = B_{01} - B_{00}$, and $d = B_{00}$. The bilinear interpolation isocontour is defined as

$$C_B \equiv \{(x, z) : B(x, z) = \sigma\}, \quad (7)$$

where σ is the isovalue of the isocontour. It is easy to verify that this isocontour curve is a hyperbola. The isocontour function can also be expressed as z being a function of x:

$$z = f(x) = \frac{-bx - d + \sigma}{ax + c} \quad (8)$$

Let $H(x_1, x_2)$ be the area under the isocontour hyperbola $z = f(x)$ and above the x-axis between $x = x_1$ and $x = x_2$ (shown as the shaded area in Fig. 4). This area can be found by integrating $z = f(x)$ between the limits of x_1 and x_2:

$$H(x_1, x_2) = \int_{x_1}^{x_2} f(x)dx$$
$$= v(x_2 - x_1) + w \ln \left| \frac{x_2 - u}{x_1 - u} \right|. \quad (9)$$

where $u = -\dfrac{c}{a}$, $v = -\dfrac{b}{a}$, and $w = \dfrac{bc - ad + a\sigma}{a^2}$.

If a in Eq. 6 is zero, then the isocontour on the slice is a line segment. In this case, the area under the isocontour must be calculated as the area under the line segment and above the x-axis, which can be easily computed.

Inside Area Calculation. Given the y location of a slice, first, the slice vertex values are determined using linear interpolation on the cube edges. Then, the intersection points of the isocontour and slice edges parallel to the x axis are calculated using linear interpolation on the slice edges. Let x_1 and x_2 be the x values of the bottom and top slice edge intersection points, respectively. If a slice vertex value is greater than or equal to the isovalue, it is labeled as an inside vertex, otherwise, it is labeled as an outside vertex.

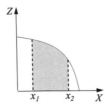

Fig. 4. Area under the isocontour hyperbola.

Slices are classified into different configurations (i.e., cases). For each case, x_1 and/or x_2 are used to divide the x value range of the slice, $[0, 1]$, into some sub-ranges so that the area under hyperbola function can be applied to the subranges. Figure 5 summarizes all cases and their corresponding inside area calculation formulas. For each case, the inside area calculation formula is listed below the case diagram. In the case diagram, the inside and outside vertices are shown in red and yellow, respectively. The isocontour hyperbola is shown as the red curves. The inside region on the slice is shown in blue. In the case notation, the first label number means the number of inside vertices of the slice, the second is the subcase number.

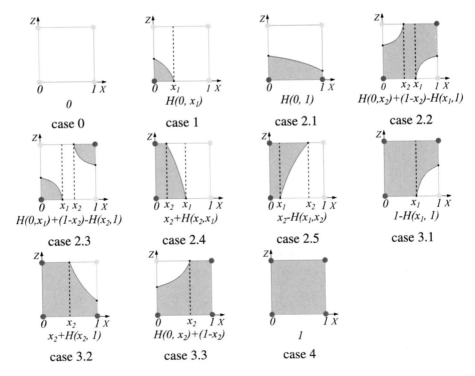

Fig. 5. Inside area calculation formulas for all cases (Color figure online)

To reduce the number of cases, the slice is rotated so that the bottom left vertex always has the largest value among 4 slice vertices. Although the number of cases can be further reduced by rotation or reflection, this is chosen not to do in order to keep the coefficients of the bilinear interpolation function given in Eq. 6 the same for all isovalues. This is for the computational performance consideration.

3.3   Refined Histogram Method

In the refined histogram method, a cube is repeatedly subdivided into 8 equal-sized subcubes and the vertex values of the subcubes are determined based on trilinear interpolation. When the subdivision limit is reached, 8 vertices of each final subcube are visited and the corresponding bin of each vertex value is increased by 1.

To convert number of vertices to volume, the number of vertices needs to multiply by $1/8$ of the final subcube volume. The usage of the factor $1/8$ is because that a final subcube has 8 vertices and each vertex should contribute the equal proportion of the final subcube's volume to its bin. It also solves the problem that when a vertex is on the boundary of the volume, the total amount of volume that it contributes to its bin should not be one final subcube's volume, but $1/8$ of the final subcube's volume if it is at a volume corner (since it is visited only once) and $1/4$ of the final subcube's volume if it is on a volume edge (since it is visited 2 times) and $1/2$ of the final subcube's volume if it is on a volume face (since it is shared by 4 final subcubes).

4   Results and Discussions

Here, a CT scan engine dataset with size $256 \times 256 \times 256$ and a tooth dataset with size $256 \times 256 \times 161$ were used to test and compare different interval volume calculation methods. Both datasets are from Roettger's Volume Library [1]. Let R_i, $0 \leq i \leq M$, be the interval region associated with the isovalue range $[i - 0.5, i + 0.5)$, where i is an integer and M is the largest data value of the dataset. The experiments here use this way of dividing the data range of the volumetric dataset in order to compare the methods presented in this paper against the previous methods.

4.1   Subdividing vs. Slicing vs. Refined Histogram

In this section, the three methods presented in this paper: the subdividing, slicing, and refined histogram methods are compared. In the subdividing method, higher subdivision depth means smaller final subcubes, and thus higher accuracy of the interval volume measures computed. Since the subdividing method is relatively straightforward and its correctness can be proved by a Riemann sum approach similar to the one used in [3] to prove the convergence of the histogram to the interval volume measures when the sampling rate increases, the measures generated by the subdividing method with subdivision depth 5 are used as the baseline for comparison.

For the engine dataset, the average and maximum absolute relative errors of the interval volume measures of all R_i, $0 \leq i \leq 255$ were computed for the subdividing method with subdivision depths 0–5, the refined histogram method with subdivision depths 0–5, and the slicing method with the numbers of slices 1, 2, 4, 8, 16, and 32. The errors are reported in Table 1. The table also reports the execution time of each run. Similarly, Tables 2 shows the results of comparing the three methods for the tooth dataset. Here, the highest 20 isovalue intervals are excluded since they have very small true interval volume values and their relative errors are much larger than other isovalue intervals. Also, those highest isovalues are not significant for this dataset.

Table 1. Accuracy and performance comparison for the engine dataset.

Subdividing method				Slicing method				Refined histogram method			
Subdiv. depth	Avg. Abs. relative error	Max. Abs. relative error	Time (sec.)	Number of slices	Avg. Abs. relative error	Max. Abs. relative error	Time (sec.)	Subdiv depth	Avg. Abs. relative error	Max. Abs. relative error	Time (sec.)
0	4.89%	16.55%	0.6	1	2.85%	32.99%	1.7	0	24.73%	474.05%	1.0
1	1.30%	5.87%	2.5	2	0.82%	14.16%	3.4	1	16.80%	332.55%	3.8
2	0.42%	2.13%	13.2	4	0.26%	5.64%	6.2	2	12.10%	182.75%	26.7
3	0.12%	0.84%	64.3	8	0.09%	3.37%	11.9	3	8.23%	100.35%	215.9
4	0.04%	0.28%	313.6	16	0.03%	1.48%	22.8	4	5.14%	44.37%	1722.1
5	0.00%	0.00%	1623.8	32	0.02%	0.22%	44.3	5	2.73%	15.44%	13475.1

Table 2. Accuracy and performance comparison for the tooth dataset.

Subdividing method				Slicing method				Refined histogram method			
Subdiv. depth	Avg. Abs. relative error	Max. Abs. relative error	Time (sec.)	Number of slices	Avg. Abs. relative error	Max. Abs. relative error	Time (sec.)	Subdiv depth	Avg. Abs. relative error	Max. Abs. relative error	Time (sec.)
0	11.43%	667.01%	0.6	1	3.79%	150.00%	4.7	0	15.29%	1528.74%	0.8
1	3.02%	170.33%	3.0	2	1.04%	54.03%	8.7	1	3.87%	292.62%	2.5
2	0.74%	43.75%	17.5	4	0.29%	14.84%	17.0	2	1.11%	56.33%	16.2
3	0.17%	8.69%	116.5	8	0.09%	2.79%	33.6	3	0.36%	11.34%	127.9
4	0.04%	1.83%	707.0	16	0.03%	0.45%	67.0	4	0.12%	3.56%	1022.2
5	0.00%	0.00%	4546.1	32	0.02%	0.38%	133.6	5	0.04%	0.61%	9191.3

The results show that the subdividing and slicing methods converge to the same set of values, although they use very different strategies to compute the interval volume measures. The slicing method takes much less time to converge than the subdividing method. This is because the cross-sectional area of the interval region is computed analytically. Although the subdividing and refined histogram methods both use the subdivision strategy, the subdividing method converges faster and is more accurate than the refined histogram method at the same subdivision level. This is because the early termination conditions in the subdividing method help improve the computational performance of the method. Also, the subdividing method evenly split a final subcube's volume among all isovalue intervals that the final subcube intersects with, while the refined histogram method only split the final subcube's volume into the bins corresponding to the values of the final subcube's 8 vertices. Although the refined histogram method can converge to the same set of values as the other two methods, for some datasets, such as the engine dataset, it requires a lot more subdivision iterations to converge and even after several times of subdivision, the histograms are still very noisy.

The results suggest that for the applications where high accuracy of interval volume measures is required, the slicing method is a best choice since it is faster than the other two methods to achieve the same level of accuracy; if the execution speed is the main concern, then the subdividing method with no subdivision or subdivision depth 1 is a good choice.

4.2   Comparison with Previous Methods

Improvement for Global Histograms. In this set of experiments, the slicing method with 32 slices (called slicing 32) is compared with the original histogram, adjusted weighted isosurface area [3], and adjusted weighted cube count [3] methods. Here, the whole volumetric dataset is processed to produce the global histograms or global histogram substitutes, i.e., interval volume measures. The results generated by all four methods are plotted in Figs. 6 and 7 for the engine and tooth datasets, respectively. In those two figures, the interval volume axis is plotted on a log scale.

The results show that the interval volume measures produced by the adjusted weighted isosurface area method are about 0.7%–47.9% less than true interval volume measures and this factor is not a constant across all isovalue intervals.

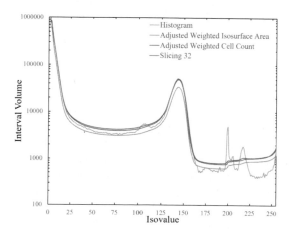

Fig. 6. Comparison of the slicing 32 method with the three existing methods for the engine dataset.

In addition, the sum of the true interval volume measures of all R_i should equal the volume of the whole volumetric dataset. This is true for the histogram, adjusted weighted cube count, and slicing 32 methods. However, for the adjusted weighted isosurface area method, this sum is only 82% of the whole dataset's volume for the tooth dataset and 90% for the engine dataset. This is because the adjusted weighted isosurface area method multiplies the isosurface area and inverse gradient magnitude to produce the interval volume for non-homogeneous cells and it uses the cube span to approximate the gradient magnitude. However, the cube span usually overestimates the gradient magnitude [11], thus, the inverse of the cube span is usually smaller than the inverse of the gradient magnitude.

The results also show that the global histograms generated by the histogram method is very noisy. The interval volume measures generated by the adjusted weighted cell count and slicing 32 methods are both smooth and close to each other, but there are still minor visible differences between the two.

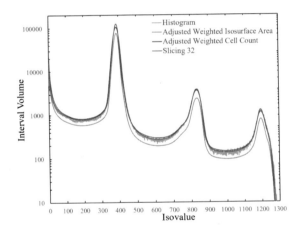

Fig. 7. Comparison of the slicing 32 method with the three existing methods for the tooth dataset.

Improvement for Local Histograms. In this set of experiments, multiple local regions in the engine and tooth datasets were tested. Due to the page limit of this paper, only the results of testing two local regions in the tooth dataset are reported. Similar results are obtained from the engine dataset experiments. The size of each region is $8 \times 8 \times 8$ cubes, which is the size of the local regions used in [8]. In Fig. 8, the local region is the region inside the black box; the local region in (a) contains the background and the dentin; the local region in (b) crosses the background and the enamel.

Figure 9 shows the local histogram generated by the histogram method and the local interval volume measures generated by the adjusted weighted isosurface area, adjusted weighted cell count, and slicing 32 methods for the neighborhood

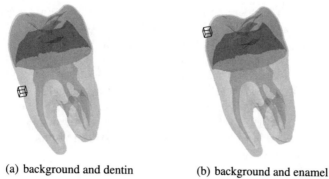

(a) background and dentin   (b) background and enamel

Fig. 8. Two local regions.

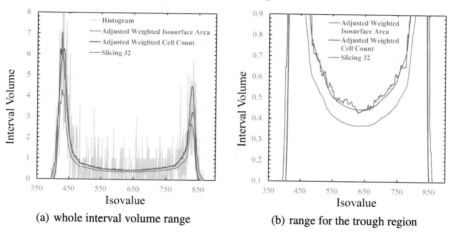

(a) whole interval volume range   (b) range for the trough region

Fig. 9. Comparison of slicing 32 with previous methods for the local region in Fig. 8 (a).

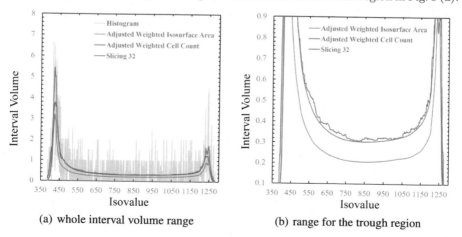

(a) whole interval volume range   (b) range for the trough region

Fig. 10. Comparison of slicing 32 with previous methods for the local region in Fig. 8 (b).

region in Fig. 8 (a). Here, only the cubes in the neighborhood region is processed. Figure 9(a) shows the whole interval volume range for the local region. In (a), the left and right peaks in the plot indicate the background itself and the dentin itself, respectively. The trough between the two peaks corresponds to the boundary between the two materials. Figure 9(b) shows the interval volume range for the trough region, which allows the trough region to be seen in more detail. In (b), since the histogram plot is very noisy, it is not shown to make the comparison of the other three methods clear. Similar results are shown in Fig. 10 for the local region in Fig. 8 (b). In Fig. 10(a), the two peaks indicate the background and the enamel.

The results show that the histogram method produces even noisier local histograms than global histograms, which makes them hard to use. The local interval volume measures generated by the adjusted weighted isosurface area method are smooth, but still have the same problem as the global measures produced by this method.

Figures 9(a) and 10(a) show that there are obvious differences between the interval volume measures generated by the adjusted weighted cell count and slicing 32 methods in the peak regions. From Figs. 9(b) and 10(b) we can see that the interval volume measures generated by the slicing 32 method is smooth, while the measures generated by the adjusted weighted cell count method is very noisy. This is because that the approximation of the interval volume in a cube involving the cube span used by the adjusted weighted cell count method is coarse. This problem becomes more severe for computing local interval volume measures where there is less data available than computing global measures. Therefore, the slicing 32 method is better than the adjusted weighted isosurface area and adjusted weighted cell count methods for producing local histogram substitutes in terms of smoothness and accuracy.

The run times of the slicing 32, adjusted weighted isosurface area, adjusted weighted cube count, and original histogram methods are 0.02958, 0.00759, 0.00006, and 0.00005 s, respectively, for the background/dentin local region, and 0.07204, 0.01717, 0.00010, and 0.00007 s, respectively, for the background/enamel local region.

5   Conclusions and Future Work

In this paper, two new methods and a refined histogram method for accurate computation of interval volume measures are presented. All three method can accurately compute interval volume measures to improve histograms. They converge to the same set of values. However, their execution times to achieve the same level of accuracy are different. The slicing method is the method of choice among the three methods and it can produce smoother and more accurate global and local histogram substitutes than the previous methods. Future research work may result in a pure analytical method to compute interval volume measures, which can be both fast and accurate. The accurate interval volume measures may also be used in detecting significant isovalues and designing transfer functions for direct volume rendering.

References

1. Roettger's volume library. http://schorsch.efi.fh-nuernberg.de/data/volume/. Accessed June 2018
2. Chaudhuri, A., et al.: Scalable computation of distributions from large scale data sets. In: IEEE Symposium on Large Data Analysis and Visualization (LDAV), pp. 113–120 (2012)
3. Duffy, B., Carr, H., Möller, T.: Integrating isosurface statistics and histograms. IEEE Trans. Vis. Comput. Graph. **19**(2), 263–277 (2013)
4. Fujishiro, I., Maeda, Y., Sato, H.: Interval volume: a solid fitting technique for volumetric data display and analysis. In: Proceedings of Visualization 1995, Atlanta, USA, pp. 151–158 (1995)
5. Gu, Y., Wang, C.: Transgraph: hierarchical exploration of transition relationships in time-varying volumetric data. IEEE Trans. Vis. Comput. Graph. **17**, 2015–2024 (2011)
6. Guo, B.: Interval set: a volume rendering technique generalizing isosurface extraction. In: Proceedings of Visualization 1995, Atlanta, USA, pp. 3–10 (1995)
7. Kniss, J., Kindlmann, G., Hansen, C.: Interactive volume rendering using multi-dimensional transfer functions and direct manipulation widgets. In: Proceedings Visualization, 2001. VIS 2001, pp. 255–562 (2001)
8. Lundström, C., Ljung, P., Ynnerman, A.: Local histograms for design of transfer functions in direct volume rendering. IEEE Trans. Vis. Comput. Graph. **12**(6), 1570–1579 (2006)
9. Morgan, F.: Geometric Measure Theory: A Beginner's Guide. Academic Press, Boston (2016)
10. Pekar, V., Wiemker, R., Bystrov, D.: Fast detection of meaningful isosurfaces for volume data visualization. In: Proceedings Visualization, 2001. VIS 2001, pp. 223–230 (2001)
11. Scheidegger, C., Schreiner, J., Duffy, B., Carr, H., Silva, C.: Revisiting histograms and isosurface statistics. IEEE Trans. Vis. Comput. Graph. **14**(6), 1659–1666 (2008)
12. Tenginakai, S., Lee, J., Machiraju, R.: Salient iso-surface detection with model-independent statistical signatures. In: Proceedings Visualization, 2001. VIS 2001, pp. 231–238 (2001)
13. Thompson, D., et al.: Analysis of large-scale scalar data using hixels. In: 2011 IEEE Symposium on Large Data Analysis and Visualization, pp. 23–30 (2011)
14. Wang, C., Lai, S.: Adaptive isosurface reconstruction using a volumetric-divergence-based metric. In: Bebis, G., et al. (eds.) ISVC 2016. LNCS, vol. 10072, pp. 367–378. Springer, Cham (2016). https://doi.org/10.1007/978-3-319-50835-1_34
15. Wang, C., Newman, T., Lee, J.: On accuracy of marching isosurfacing methods. In: Proceedings of the Eurographics/IEEE VGTC Workshop on Volume Graphics 2008, Los Angeles, pp. 49–56 (2008)
16. Wang, C.: A fast method to calculate the volumetric divergence metric for evaluating the accuracy of the extracted isosurface. Proc. ACM Comput. Graph. Interact. Techn. **1**(2), 27:1–27:19 (2018)
17. Wenger, R.: Isosurfaces: Geometry, Topology, and Algorithms. CRC Press, Hoboken (2013)
18. Zhou, B., Chiang, Y.J., Wang, C.: Efficient local statistical analysis via point-wise histograms in tetrahedral meshes and curvilinear grids. IEEE Trans. Vis. Comput. Graph. **25**, 1392–1406 (2019)

Ant-SNE: Tracking Community Evolution via Animated t-SNE

Ngan V. T. Nguyen[✉] and Tommy Dang

Texas Tech University, Lubbock, TX 79409, USA
{Ngan.V.T.Nguyen,tommy.dang}@ttu.edu

Abstract. We introduce a method for tracking the community evolution and a prototype (*Ant-SNE*) for analyzing multivariate time series and guiding interactive exploration through high-dimensional data. The method is based on t-distributed Stochastic Neighbor Embedding (t-SNE), a machine learning algorithm for nonlinear dimension reduction well-suited for embedding high-dimensional data for visualization in a low-dimensional space of two or three dimensions. By tracking the evolution of temporal multivariate data points, we are able to locate unusual behaviors (outliers) and interesting sub-series for further analysis. In the experiments, we conducted two case studies with the US employment dataset and the HPC health status dataset in order to confirm the effectiveness of the proposed system.

Keywords: Multivariate time series analysis · Radar charts · Scatterplot matrix · Parallel coordinates · High-dimensional data analysis · t-distributed stochastic neighbor embedding

1 Introduction

Detecting latent community in networks is a fundamental research area in visual analytics as many systems in nature can be modeled as networks [45]. Members can be grouped in such a way they share common features among group members while the similarity between members in different groups is less common [31,39]. Finding the latent community structure is challenging, especially when community structure change over time [34]. This yields the definition of "dynamic network" as opposed to a "static network." Keeping track of community evolution is vital in understanding the dynamics of the system, i.e., characterizing the trends/patterns as well as locating anomalous. For example, authors in the same papers often come from the same institute or laboratory forming co-authorship networks, an author breaks out his cluster to join a new one might be due to accepting his/her new position at another university, or suddenly increasing phone calls/credit card transactions between a group of employee within a specific day might be a sign of a financial crime. Quickly identifying emerging patterns in latent communities is critical for early warnings in many application domains, such as crime prevention [11].

© Springer Nature Switzerland AG 2019
G. Bebis et al. (Eds.): ISVC 2019, LNCS 11844, pp. 330–341, 2019.
https://doi.org/10.1007/978-3-030-33720-9_25

The paper proposes a new approach to highlight the "switches" in community formations for multivariate time series which can not be simply captured by traditional time series visualizations (such as line charts [13] or stream graphs) or multidimensional visualizations (such as radar charts or parallel coordinates). Our contributions in this paper thus are:

- We present an approach for community tracking via t-SNE of high-dimensional data points represented in a customized radar chart which allows users to spot the data patterns quickly and to mitigate overplotting a large number of instances on a limited display.
- We develop a prototype, *Ant-SNE*, to guide users on interactively visualizing and exploring high dimensional time series datasets focusing on community evolutions. The visual interface supports a full range of non-blocking interactions (via multithreading), such as lensing and zooming, brushing and linking, ordering, and filtering.
- We highlight the benefits of our approach by using *Ant-SNE* on real-world datasets. We conduct an informal study with three industry experts on real-time monitoring and detecting unusual events in a High-Performance Computing Center.

The paper is structured as follows: We describe related work in the following section. Then we introduce the motivation and design of our *Ant-SNE* prototype. Then we present use cases and results of our informal study. Finally, we conclude our work and provide the future direction in the last section.

2   Related Work

2.1   High-Dimensional Data Visualization

Visualization of high-dimensional data is an essential task in many application domains, and hence there are many researches have been proposed in this research domain. Finding ways to represent multidimensional data and reducing them to a lower number of dimensions are two main strategies in this field. Examples of the first strategy include geometric projection technique like parallel coordinates [24], iconographic technique such as using faces to represent data points [12], pixel-oriented technique which maps data values to pixels (pixel color and positions on the screen) [25], hierarchical techniques like using dimensional stacking [28] and treemap [37], and graph-based techniques [5]. These techniques often involve complex visualization plots which lead to low interpretability [32].

Dimension reduction techniques are roughly categorized as linear and non-linear techniques. Two important techniques in the first category are Principle Component Analysis (PCA) [23] and classical Multidimensional Scaling (MDS) [41]. These techniques tend to keep dissimilar data points far-apart and not the similar data close together [42]. This makes them not suitable for clustering application as it requires to optimize both inter-cluster and intra-cluster distances. To keep the local structure of the data, non-linear techniques are used, these include

Sammon mapping [36], curvilinear component analysis [18], Stochastic Neighbor Embedding (SNE) [22], Isomap [40], Maximum Variance Unfolding (MVU) [46], Locally Linear Embedding (LLE) [35], Laplacian Eigenmaps [6], and t-SNE [42]. In the non-linear category, t-SNE is superior to other techniques as it could preserve both global and local structures of the data when transforming them from high-dimensional space to the low-dimensional space.

2.2   t-SNE for Multivariate Time Series Data

The advantages of t-SNE comparing to other non-linear dimensional reduction techniques make it widely used in many application domains, including visualization of high-dimensional time series data. Using Euclidean distance to calculate similarities in multivariate time series data is not suitable, so Nguyen et al. [32] proposed to use Extended Frobenius norm (EROS) [47] as the distance metric in this case. However, this deals with the time series as a whole and in many cases, we need to keep track of the movement of points from one time step to another. Applying t-SNE to individual data set at a specific time step introduces a random sequence of projections. This leads to the loss of the fluid movement of the t-SNE result from one time-step to another (i.e., the change in the mapping positions doesn't reflect the temporal change). To deal with this issue, Rauber et al. [33] proposed Dynamic t-SNE approach which allows controlling the trade-off between temporal coherence and projection reliability by adding to the cost for unnecessary movement of points between time steps.

2.3   Dynamic Network Visualization

In the 2016 survey, Beck et al. [4] provide a high-level categorization of dynamic graph visualizations as animated node-link diagrams, timeline-based static charts [14], or hybrids. Greilich et al. [20] propose a technique to organize a dynamic compound digraph by drawing a sequence of node-link diagrams vertically by the hierarchical structure. In *Parallel edge splatting* [9], a sequence of narrow stripes is placed perpendicular to the horizontal timeline making the final graph similar to parallel coordinates. *Parallel edge splatting* encounters the problem of visual clutter that occurs when drawing many lines onto a small screen portion. Rapid Serial Visual Presentation [3] is a hybrid approach of animated and timeline-based diagrams. Its radial variance [10] achieves shorter links but harder to follow.

Matrices are becoming more popular for visualizing dynamic networks [30,48], particularly dense graphs [15,21] since they resolves the edge-crossing issue in node-link diagrams [19,26]. *TimeMatrix* [48] displays a small bar chart to show the changes of edge weights for the two vertices within each cell of the matrix. *gestaltmatrix* [8] uses *gestaltlines*, intra-cell lines that encode different metrics using the angle and length. Individual time slices can be difficult to extract from matrix representations, but *Matrix Cubes* [2] stacks adjacency matrices at each time step to form a space-time cube that can be decomposed into different 2D time slices or vertex slices. *MultiPiles* [1] piles similar consecutive snapshots together to provide a more compressed view of large time series. The main drawback of matrix representations is that temporal connections between nodes are difficult to trace [16,17].

3   *Ant-SNE* Visualization

This section will start with the design motivations of *Ant-SNE* and then describe its components in detail with visual examples.

3.1   Motivation and Design Considerations

Tracking the communities evolution is challenging due to the large number of entries, time steps, and the highly dynamic nature of the network. The top row of Fig. 1 shows an example of tracking health status (10 dimensions, such as CPU temperature, fan speeds, and power consumption) of 467 computers in a high-performance computing center using storyline visualizations. The bottom row of Fig. 1 shows unemployment rates of five major economic factor (including construction, nonfarm, government, leisure and hospitality, and transportation), each polyline is a state in the US. The red curves in these examples depict how these attributes change over time, leading to different cluster structures of these data entries (computed based on their metrics).

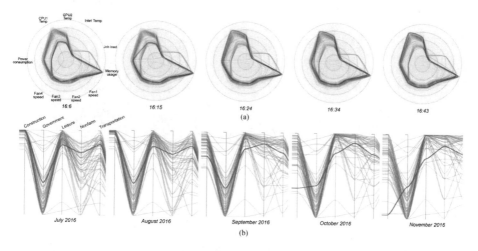

Fig. 1. The dynamic nature of multivariate data: (a) The health status of 467 computers at six different time stamps on October 4, 2018, and (b) The monthly unemployment rate on five economic factors of 50 states in the US. The red curves are example data entries to show how they vary over time. Tracking multivariate dynamics for long time series is a daunting task. (Color figure online)

While storyline visualizations [29] is an appealing visual solution where each entity is represented as a line/curve and relationships between entities are encoded according to the relative distances between the associated lines over time [27], it usually runs into the issues of overplotting as the number of entries and communities increases [38].

In this paper, we adopt the animated approach where only the t-SNE projection (on all dimensions) of a single timestamp is presented at a time. One limitation of this approach is that it requires more mental efforts, such as memorizing and visual mapping, in order to link multiple snapshots for comparisons. To mitigate this issue, we keep track the trajectory of neighborhood projects and rank them by travel distance, as shown in Box B of Fig. 2. We hypothesize that the highly dynamic multivariate data points are connected to emerging features of the model.

3.2 *Ant-SNE* Interface

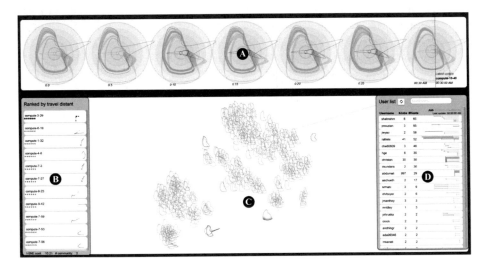

Fig. 2. The main interface of our *Ant-SNE* for real-time monitoring computer communities defined by their multivariate behaviors.

Figure 2 shows the main interface of our *Ant-SNE* for real-time tracking the health status of the high-performance computing (HPC) center. Box A is the overview panel: each radar chart summarizes 467 computer status at a timestamp. The main view (Box C) contains the animated t-SNE projection of all computer in the system. As the computer status is iteratively updated (one at a time), new t-SNE projection is smoothly transformed from its previous positions. The HPC admin can use a time slider to roll back any particular time for system tracking and debugging. Box B contains the ranked list of computers and their trajectories which will also be updated as the new status is retrieved.

In particular, the top of this list is highly dynamic computers that vary significantly (possibly changing community) in the projected display. Box D displays the current list of HPC users and their job scheduling.

The Customized Radar Chart: Due to the limited screen display and a large number of data entries, we revise the radar chart to embed the transformed color scale directly into the inside area of the radar. This allows users to quickly spot the multivariate values on small thumbnails and make sense the cluster formation as depicted in Fig. 2. Notice that parallel coordinates depicted in the lower row of Fig. 1 are not suited for this purpose, especially with the increasing number of dimensions. Figure 3 shows an enlarged version of our customized radar chart for a computer which has high memory usage, power consumption, and CPU1 temperature.

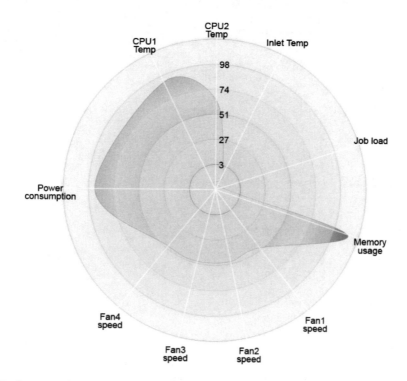

Fig. 3. Our new design embeds the color scale into the radar: red indicates high score on the associated dimension. (Color figure online)

3.3 Implementation

Ant-SNE is implemented using D3.js [7]. The demo video, online application, more examples, and source code of the visualization can be found at the Github page https://idatavisualizationlab.github.io/N/Ant-SNE.

4   Experiments

4.1   Use Case 1: US Unemployment

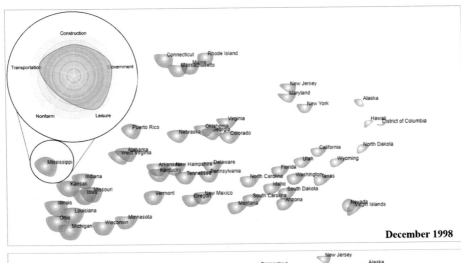

Fig. 4. State unemployment status on five economic factors are significant different in two consecutive months (Color figure online).

Data for the first use-case is the monthly unemployment rate of 50 states over 27 years (1990–2016). Among the top of the ranked list, we can easily splot several states with similar trends toward the end of 1998. Figure 4 shows this transition of the US unemployment rates from December 1998 to January 1999 of t-SNE projections based on five major economic dimensions (including construction, nonfarm, government, leisure and hospitality, and transportation) organized in

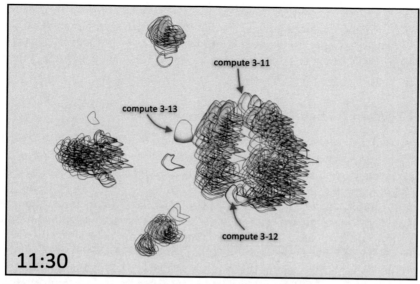

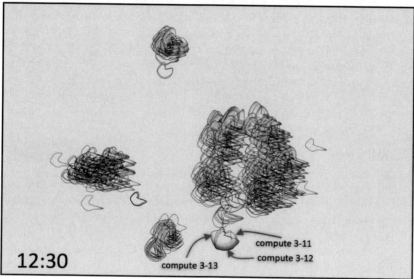

Fig. 5. The health status of 467 computers in a HPC center at Texas Tech University.

our customized radar charts. The top panel highlights many states with high unemployment rates (bigger and hotter radars) such as Louisiana, Mississippi, Michigan. This is due to the disastrous 1998 Atlantic hurricane with the highest number of fatalities (began on June 1 and ended on November 30). The recovery only starts in January 1999 (bottom panel) as the yellowish area sink, and the cluster structure begins to transform back its regular layout.

An enlarged radar (with axis labels) of Mississippi is presented on the top left corner. Rainbow colormaps are suitable for categorization, or to show some abrupt changes on specific range values. Otherwise, it is ineffective [44]. As depicted in Fig. 4, users can select a blue to green to yellow colormap, entitled "viridis" [43].

4.2   Use Case 2: High-Performance Computing

In the second use case, we use *Ant-SNE* to monitor the health status of an HPC Center at a university. Figure 5 shows an event when the CPU2 on *computer-3-13* suddenly became over-heated. The top panel summarizes the system at 11:30: The fans of *computer-3-13* starts to speeds while its CPUs are normal (only the low portion is red). At 12:30, the CPU2 of *computer-3-13* suddenly burn up cause fan speeds on neighboring *computer-3-11* and *computer-3-12* to pump the rate as they sensed the heat. Notice that these computers automatically form an "overheat" cluster lead by *computer-3-13* and they all share high fan speeds. Our web interface was able to pick up this event and alerted the system administrator to replace the defected CPU on *computer-3-13* before it could harm others.

We discussed this thermal excursion through an informal interview with three Dell experts and the HPC director. They mentioned that "The rainbow radar design did a good job in capturing the morphology of high-dimensional curves". The t-SNE projections provide an unsupervised mechanism to summarize the systems of hundreds/thousands of computers. These clusters might be responsible for different types of jobs/users/configurations which is suitable for applying machine learning techniques to characterize, cluster, and classify the shapes.

5   Conclusion

This paper proposes a technique applying animated t-SNE to track community evolution of multivariate time series. This approach relies on the hypothesis that important events happen to cause the significant changes in the data attributes and therefore to lead to the community "switches" in the projected t-NSE space. We verified this hypothesis through the use case of US unemployment and the HPC health status data. The developed prototype not only demonstrate a visual tool for users to track communities and to locate communities and outliers but also provide real-time monitoring HPC system as a whole and raise early warnings of unusual behavior. In future work, we will apply our approach to more complex and higher-dimensional data. Moreover, we would like to integrate the pattern recognition and predictive analysis to our system.

References

1. Bach, B., Henry-Riche, N., Dwyer, T., Madhyastha, T., Fekete, J.D., Grabowski, T.: Small MultiPiles: piling time to explore temporal patterns in dynamic networks. Comput. Graph. Forum. **34**, 31–40 (2015)

2. Bach, B., Pietriga, E., Fekete, J.D.: Visualizing dynamic networks with matrix cubes. In: Proceedings of ACM Conference on Human Factors in Computing Systems, pp. 877–886 (2014)
3. Beck, F., Burch, M., Vehlow, C., Diehl, S., Weiskopf, D.: Rapid serial visual presentation in dynamic graph visualization. In: Proceedings of IEEE Symposium on Visual Languages and Human-Centric Computing, pp. 185–192 (2012)
4. Beck, F., Burch, M., Diehl, S., Weiskopf, D.: A taxonomy and survey of dynamic graph visualization. Comput. Graph. Forum **36**, 133–159 (2016)
5. Becker, R.A., Eick, S.G., Wilks, A.R.: Visualizing network data. IEEE Trans. Visual. Comput. Graph. **1**(1), 16–28 (1995)
6. Belkin, M., Niyogi, P.: Laplacian eigenmaps and spectral techniques for embedding and clustering. In: Advances in Neural Information Processing Systems, pp. 585–591 (2002)
7. Bostock, M., Ogievetsky, V., Heer, J.: D3 data-driven documents. IEEE Trans. Vis. Comput. Graph. **17**(12), 2301–2309 (2011)
8. Brandes, U., Nick, B.: Asymmetric relations in longitudinal social networks. IEEE Trans. Vis. Comput. Graph. **17**(12), 2283–2290 (2011). https://doi.org/10.1109/TVCG.2011.169
9. Burch, M., Vehlow, C., Beck, F., Diehl, S., Weiskopf, D.: Parallel edge splatting for scalable dynamic graph visualization. IEEE Trans. Vis. Comput. Graph. **17**(12), 2344–2353 (2011). https://doi.org/10.1109/TVCG.2011.226
10. Burch, M., Beck, F., Weiskopf, D.: Radial edge splatting for visualizing dynamic directed graphs. In: Proceedings of International Conference on Information Visualization and Applications, pp. 603–612 (2012)
11. Cai, Z., Jermaine, C.: The latent community model for detecting sybils in social networks. In: NDSS (2012)
12. Chernoff, H., Association, S., Jun, N.: The Use of Faces to Represent Points in K-Dimensional Space Graphically **68**(342), 361–368 (2007)
13. Dang, T.N., Wilkinson, L.: TimeExplorer: similarity search time series by their signatures. In: Bebis, G., et al. (eds.) ISVC 2013. LNCS, vol. 8033, pp. 280–289. Springer, Heidelberg (2013). https://doi.org/10.1007/978-3-642-41914-0_28
14. Dang, T.N., Anand, A., Wilkinson, L.: TimeSeer: scagnostics for high-dimensional time series. IEEE Trans. Vis. Comput. Graph. **19**(3), 470–483 (2013). https://doi.org/10.1109/TVCG.2012.128
15. Dang, T.N., Cui, H., Forbes, A.G.: MultiLayerMatrix: visualizing large taxonomic datasets. In: Andrienko, N., Sedlmair, M. (eds.) EuroVis Workshop on Visual Analytics (EuroVA). The Eurographics Association (2016). https://doi.org/10.2312/eurova.20161125
16. Dang, T.N., Franz, N., Ludäscher, B., Forbes, A.G.: ProvenanceMatrix: a visualization tool for multi-taxonomy alignments. In: Proceedings of the ISWC Workshop on Visualization and User Interfaces for Ontologies and Linked Data (VOILA), vol. 1456, pp. 13–24. CEUR Workshop Proceedings (2015)
17. Dang, T.N., Murray, P., Forbes, A.G.: PathwayMatrix: visualizing binary relationships between proteins in biological pathways. BMC Proc. **9**(6), S3 (2015)
18. Demartines, P., Hérault, J.: Curvilinear component analysis: a self-organizing neural network for nonlinear mapping of data sets. IEEE Trans. Neural Networks **8**(1), 148–154 (1997)
19. Ghoniem, M., Fekete, J.D., Castagliola, P.: On the readability of graphs using node-link and matrix-based representations: a controlled experiment and statistical analysis. Inf. Vis. **4**(2), 114–135 (2005). https://doi.org/10.1057/palgrave.ivs.9500092

20. Greilich, M., Burch, M., Diehl, S.: Visualizing the evolution of compound digraphs with TimeArcTrees. In: Proceedings of Eurographics Conference on Visualization, pp. 975–990 (2009). https://doi.org/10.1111/j.1467-8659.2009.01451.x
21. Henry, N., Fekete, J.D.: MatrixExplorer: a dual-representation system to explore social networks. IEEE Trans. Vis. Comput. Graph. **12**(5), 677–684 (2006). https://doi.org/10.1109/TVCG.2006.160
22. Hinton, G.E., Roweis, S.T.: Stochastic neighbor embedding. In: Advances in Neural Information Processing Systems, pp. 857–864 (2003)
23. Hotelling, H.: Analysis of a complex of statistical variables into principal components. J. Educ. Psychol. **24**(6), 417 (1933)
24. Inselberg, A., Dimsdale, B.: Parallel coordinates: a tool for visualizing multi-dimensional geometry. In: Proceedings of the 1st Conference on Visualization 1990, pp. 361–378. IEEE Computer Society Press (1990)
25. Keim, D.A.: Designing Pixel-Oriented Visualization Techniques: Theory and Applications **6**(1), 59–78 (2000)
26. Keller, R., Eckert, C.M., Clarkson, P.J.: Matrices or node-link diagrams: which visual representation is better for visualising connectivity models? Inf. Vis. **5**(1), 62–76 (2006). https://doi.org/10.1057/palgrave.ivs.9500116
27. Kim, N.W., Card, S.K., Heer, J.: Tracing genealogical data with timenets. In: Proceedings of International Conference on Advanced Visual Interfaces, pp. 241–248 (2010). https://doi.org/10.1145/1842993.1843035
28. LeBlanc, J., Ward, M.O., Wittels, N.: Exploring n-dimensional databases. In: Proceedings of the 1st Conference on Visualization 1990, pp. 230–237. IEEE Computer Society Press (1990)
29. Liu, S., Wu, Y., Wei, E., Liu, M., Liu, Y.: StoryFlow: tracking the evolution of stories. IEEE Trans. Vis. Comput. Graph. **19**(12), 2436–2445 (2013). https://doi.org/10.1109/TVCG.2013.196
30. Ma, C., Kenyon, R.V., Forbes, A.G., Berger-Wolf, T., Slater, B.J., Llano, D.A.: Visualizing dynamic brain networks using an animated dual-representation. In: Proceedings of Eurographics Conference on Visualization, pp. 73–77 (2015)
31. Newman, M.E.J., Girvan, M.: Finding and evaluating community structure in networks. Phys. Rev. E **69**, 026113 (2004). https://doi.org/10.1103/PhysRevE.69.026113
32. Nguyen, M., Purushotham, S., To, H., Shahabi, C., Angeles, L.: m-TSNE : A Framework for Visualizing High-Dimensional Multivariate Time Series (2017)
33. Rauber, P.E., Falcão, A.X., Telea, A.C.: Visualizing time-dependent data using dynamic t-SNE. In: Proceedings of the Eurographics/IEEE VGTC Conference on Visualization: Short Papers, EuroVis 2016, Eurographics Association, Goslar Germany, pp. 73–77 (2016). https://doi.org/10.2312/eurovisshort.20161164
34. Reda, K., Tantipathananandh, C., Johnson, A., Leigh, J., Berger-Wolf, T.: Visualizing the evolution of community structures in dynamic social networks. In: Proceedings of Eurographics Conference on Visualization, pp. 1061–1070 (2011)
35. Roweis, S.T., Saul, L.K.: Nonlinear dimensionality reduction by locally linear embedding. Science **290**(5500), 2323–2326 (2000)
36. Sammon, J.W.: A nonlinear mapping for data structure analysis. IEEE Trans. Comput. **100**(5), 401–409 (1969)
37. Shneiderman, B.: Tree Visualization with Tree-Maps : 2-d Space-Filling Approach **11**(1), 92–99 (1992)
38. Tanahashi, Y., Ma, K.L.: Design considerations for optimizing storyline visualizations. IEEE Trans. Vis. Comput. Graph. **18**(12), 2679–2688 (2012). https://doi.org/10.1109/TVCG.2012.212

39. Tantipathananandh, C., Berger-Wolf, T.Y.: Finding communities in dynamic social networks. In: 2011 IEEE 11th International Conference on Data Mining, pp. 1236–1241, December 2011. https://doi.org/10.1109/ICDM.2011.67

40. Tenenbaum, J.B., De Silva, V., Langford, J.C.: A global geometric framework for nonlinear dimensionality reduction. Science **290**(5500), 2319–2323 (2000)

41. Torgerson, W.S.: Multidimensional scaling: I. theory and method. Psychometrika **17**(4), 401–419 (1952)

42. Van Der Maaten, L., Hinton, G.: Visualizing Data using t-SNE **9**, 2579–2605 (2008)

43. Van der Walt, S., Smith, N.: mpl colormaps (2015). http://bids.github.io/colormap

44. Ward, M., Grinstein, G., Keim, D.: Interactive Data Visualization: Foundations, Techniques, and Applications. A. K. Peters, Ltd., Natick (2010)

45. Wasserman, S., Faust, K.: Social Network Analysis: Methods and Applications. Structural Analysis in the Social Sciences. Cambridge University Press, New York (1994). https://doi.org/10.1017/CBO9780511815478

46. Weinberger, K.Q., Sha, F., Saul, L.K.: Learning a kernel matrix for nonlinear dimensionality reduction. In: Proceedings of The Twenty-first International Conference on Machine Learning, p. 106. ACM (2004)

47. Yang, K., Shahabi, C.: A PCA-based similarity measure for multivariate time series. In: Proceedings of the 2nd ACM International Workshop on Multimedia Databases, pp. 65–74. ACM (2004)

48. Yi, J.S., Elmqvist, N., Seungyoon, L.: TimeMatrix: analyzing temporal social networks using interactive matrix-based visualizations. Int. J. Hum. Comput. Int. **26**(11–12), 1031–1051 (2010)

ST: Computational Vision, AI and Mathematical Methods for Biomedical and Biological Image Analysis

Automated Segmentation of the Pectoral Muscle in Axial Breast MR Images

Sahar Zafari[1,2]([⊠]), Mazen Diab[3,4,5], Tuomas Eerola[1], Summer E. Hanson[5], Gregory P. Reece[5], Gary J. Whitman[7], Mia K. Markey[4,6], Krishnaswamy Ravi-Chandar[3,6], Alan Bovik[2], and Heikki Kälviäinen[1]

[1] Department of Computational and Process Engineering, School of Engineering Science, Lappeenranta-Lahti University of Technology LUT, Lappeenranta, Finland
sahar.zafari@lut.fi

[2] Department of Electrical and Computer Engineering, The University of Texas at Austin, Austin, TX, USA

[3] Department of Aerospace Engineering and Engineering Mechanics, The University of Texas at Austin, Austin, TX, USA

[4] Department of Biomedical Engineering, The University of Texas at Austin, Austin, TX, USA

[5] Department of Plastic Surgery, The University of Texas MD Anderson Cancer Center, Houston, TX, USA

[6] Department of Imaging Physics, The University of Texas MD Anderson Cancer Center, Houston, TX, USA

[7] Department of Diagnostic Radiology, Division of Diagnostic Imaging, The University of Texas MD Anderson Cancer Center, Houston, TX, USA

Abstract. Pectoral muscle segmentation is a crucial step in various computer-aided applications of breast Magnetic Resonance Imaging (MRI). Due to imaging artifact and homogeneity between the pectoral and breast regions, the pectoral muscle boundary estimation is not a trivial task. In this paper, a fully automatic segmentation method based on deep learning is proposed for accurate delineation of the pectoral muscle boundary in axial breast MR images. The proposed method involves two main steps: pectoral muscle segmentation and boundary estimation. For pectoral muscle segmentation, a model based on the U-Net architecture is used to segment the pectoral muscle from the input image. Next, the pectoral muscle boundary is estimated through candidate points detection and contour segmentation. The proposed method was evaluated quantitatively with two real-world datasets, our own private dataset, and a publicly available dataset. The first dataset includes 12 patients breast MR images and the second dataset consists of 80 patients breast MR images. The proposed method achieved a Dice score of 95% in the first dataset and 89% in the second dataset. The high segmentation performance of the proposed method when evaluated on large scale quantitative breast MR images confirms its potential applicability in future breast cancer clinical applications.

© Springer Nature Switzerland AG 2019
G. Bebis et al. (Eds.): ISVC 2019, LNCS 11844, pp. 345–356, 2019.
https://doi.org/10.1007/978-3-030-33720-9_26

1   Introduction

Several studies in the literature have established the potential of patient specific biomechanical models in computing deformation of the female breast under different loading conditions, predicting outcomes of reconstructive surgeries of female breast, and serving as a surgical tool for image-guided lesion detection [1–3]. The basis of the biomechanical model is a patient-specific 3D geometry of the female breast that is often reconstructed from in vivo medical imaging procedures such as Magnetic Resonance Imaging (MRI). This requires segmentation of MR images to construct the 3D geometry of the female breast that is located between the front surface of the breast skin and the posterior boundary of the pectoral muscle that serves as the boundary between the breast and the rest of the body as shown in Fig. 1.

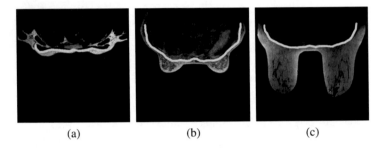

(a)   (b)   (c)

Fig. 1. Examples of breast MR images and the corresponding pectoral muscle boundaries.

Different techniques have been reported in the literature for the segmentation of the pectoral muscle and estimating its boundary [4–6]. Image thresholding is one of the most prominent approaches for pectoral muscle segmentation. Czaplicka *et al.* [7] applied an iterative Otsu's thresholding procedure with specific criteria to find the pectoral region. Mustra *et al.* [8] employed thresholding with image enhancement followed by polynomial curvature estimation to detect the pectoral muscle boundary. Twellmann *et al.* [9] used a combination of contrast enhancement, median filter, and Otsu's thresholding to extract the pectoral muscle region. The pectoral and the breast regions usually have similar image intensities, making the thresholding methods a less ideal candidate for pectoral muscle segmentation.

Gradient-based techniques are the alternative approaches for segmentation of the pectoral muscle. These methods incorporate the gradient information to estimate the boundary of the pectoral muscle. Giannini *et al.* [10] developed a method for detection of the upper border of the pectoral muscle using the gradient information. Chakraborty *et al.* [11] exploited the gradient information with curve smoothing to approximate the pectoral muscle boundary. Ferrari *et al.* [12] employed Gabor filters to capture pectoral muscle edges within limited orientations and computed the magnitude and phase images from each of the Gabor filter responses through a vector-summation procedure. The resulting image was used to estimate the initial pectoral boundary by Sobel edge detection. Despite all the improvements introduced by gradient-based methods, they may still experience difficulties with the segmentation of low image contrast and dense breasts.

Line fitting is another group of methods that have been applied for the estimation of the pectoral muscle boundary. Kwok et al. [13] proposed a method that uses line fitting to highlight the pectoral muscle boundary. The estimated straight line is then refined through an iterative cliff detection [14] to estimate the actual boundary. Karssemeijer [15] combined the global thresholding and gradient information to extract the pectoral muscle region. The method utilizes Hough transform on the gradient image to represent the pectoral muscle boundary. Yam et al. [16], combined Hough transform with a dynamic programming method to approximate the pectoral muscle boundary. Nie et al. [17] proposed a method based on the B-spline curve fitting to extract and remove the pectoral muscle from the breast region. The approaches based on line fitting strongly rely on the linearity assumption of the pectoral muscle boundary, and therefore they run into difficulties when estimating the curved boundary regions of the pectoral muscle.

Atlas-based segmentation a commonly used method in medical image analysis has been also employed for the segmentation of the pectoral muscles [18]. To perform the segmentation, these methods use prior information such as shape, size, and orientation of the object. A specific model (atlas) is constructed from the prelabeled images [19]. Using an image registration technique, a coordinate mapping between an image and an atlas is computed. The end segmentation results are obtained by fusing the most similar atlases. Gubern et al. [5] developed a probabilistic atlas in a Bayesian framework for breast segmentation. Khalvati et al. [20] employed a multi-atlas segmentation algorithm that is robust to intensity variations using phase congruency maps. Fooladivanda et al. [21] introduced an atlas segmentation algorithm that uses both the pectoral muscle and the chest region. Accurate image registration and computation complexity limit the efficiency of the atlas-based methods for segmentation of the pectoral muscle.

Although the aforementioned segmentation techniques have been shown to provide satisfactory results for the segmentation of the pectoral muscle, their performance is not optimal and comes with certain limitations due to their implicit assumptions. The intensity operation-based methods (thresholding and gradient) requires accurate delineation between the pectoral muscle and the breast tissue. These methods do not work when the pectoral and the breast regions are homogeneous. Line fitting-based methods make a specific assumption about the linearity of the pectoral muscle, so, they fail to work on pectoral muscle with a curved shape. Atlas-based methods require an accurate registration algorithm and are not sufficient to provide accurate results for a wide range of datasets. In order to overcome the aforementioned challenges in pectoral muscle segmentation, a deep learning-based segmentation method is introduced in this paper that provides a more general solution for pectoral muscle segmentation in breast MR axial images.

This work makes two main contributions to the study of breast MR image segmentation. The first contribution of this work is the annotation of the pectoral muscles on MR images. To the extent of our knowledge, there is not any publicly available human-annotated dataset of the pectorals muscle on breast MR axial images. To this end, we first annotated 1100 images of 92 subjects from two different sources, 80 subjects from The Cancer Imaging Archive (TCIA) [22,23] and 12 subjects from our own private dataset, to construct a dataset for pectoral muscle segmentation. The TCIA annotation is publicly available at [24]. The second contribution is a segmentation method based on convolutional neural networks. The segmentation is formulated as a semantic segmentation task in which each pixel in the image is assigned to an object class, the pectoral muscle, and the background, and is implemented based on the well-known U-Net architecture [25].

After segmentation, the pectoral muscle boundary is estimated through candidate points detection and contour segmentation. Moreover, validation of existing methods is usually limited to their small private dataset of breast MRI. This work presents the first effort to expand the validation to include datasets of MR images of 92 different subjects.

2   Proposed Method

The proposed method automatically estimates the pectoral muscle boundary from MR axial images in two steps. First, the region of interest (ROI) i.e., pectoral muscle, is extracted from the image through a deep learning framework. Second, the pectoral muscle boundary is identified by finding the candidate points and segmenting the boundary.

Pectoral Muscle Segmentation: Due to heterogeneous tissues densities, neighborhood complexities and breast shape variability, segmentation of the pectoral muscle is a challenging task. In this work, pectoral muscle segmentation is formulated as a pixel classification problem that is performed by a convolutional encoding-decoding framework. In particular, it is implemented by the U-Net architecture proposed in [25]. The U-Net (see Fig. 2) contains several layers of convolutional encoders and decoders, followed by the final pixelwise classification layer. Each encoder layer is composed of duplicated 3×3 convolution operations followed by a rectified linear unit (ReLU). Following that, the encoder layers downsample the feature maps using a 2×2 max pooling operation with stride 2. To avoid loss of spatial information during downsampling, the encoder feature maps are up-sampled and summed to the corresponding decoder feature maps and passed to the next layer after rectification in the decoder layers. To reduce the complexity and dimensionality of feature maps, the bottleneck is built from 2 convolutional layers between the encoder and decoder paths. The final layer is 1×1 convolution to map each feature vector to the desired classes. To classify each pixel and to ensure that all predicted pixels are in the range $[0, 1]$ the

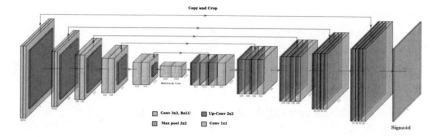

Fig. 2. U-Net architecture.

sigmoid activation function is applied at the output layer. The loss function for training the network is based on the Dice coefficient [26]. Given the prediction O_p and the ground truth O_g the Dice Similarity Coefficient (DSC) measures the similarity as follows:

$$\text{DSC} = \frac{2|O_p \cap Og|}{|O_p| + |Og|}. \tag{1}$$

The higher the DSC value, the greater the similarity. Since the training aims to minimize the loss function, we instead used the negative dice coefficient (–DSC).

Pectoral Muscle Boundary Estimation: Once the pectoral muscle is segmented and its boundary is obtained by the Canny edge detection, the minimum and maximum points are identified along with the X coordinates of the pectoral muscle boundary. These points divide the boundary into two segments, upper and lower, as shown in Fig. 3(b). The pectoral muscle boundary points can be found by probing the Y coordinate values of the boundary points. The pectoral muscle boundary of interest is the boundary segments with the lower average Y values.

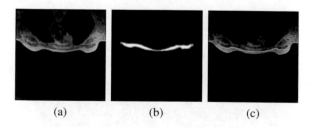

(a)   (b)   (c)

Fig. 3. Proposed method workflow: (a) Original image; (b) Segmented pectoral muscle; (c) Estimated pectoral muscle boundary.

3   Experiments

3.1   Data

The experiments were carried out on the breast MR images obtained from two sources:

The University of Texas MD Anderson Cancer Center: MR images were collected and deidentified for patients who provided informed consent in accordance with the institutional review board-approved protocol (2015-1117). This dataset contains the T1-Weighted MR images of 12 female patients, each of 512 × 512 pixels. The images were acquired on different GE Medical systems including Signa HDxt, Discovery MR 450 and Discovery MR750w with TR/TE ≈ 5.3/2.1 ms and bandwidth per pixel fixed at 244.1 HZ (T1-Weighted). In total 780 images, were annotated from this dataset for training purpose.

The Cancer Imaging Archive (TCIA): Publicly available MR image datasets were obtained from the TCIA website [23]. This dataset contains the T2-Weighted MR images of 80 patients. The images were acquired using Phillips Achieva 1.5 T with TR/TE ≈ 4000/120 ms and bandwidth per pixel in the range 146–245 HZ (T2-Weighted). In total 320 images, 4 from each subject, were annotated from this dataset for testing purposes only.

The in-plane pixel resolution for the complete datasets varies between 0.48 mm and 0.71 mm and the slice thickness between 1.8 mm and 2.2 mm. The weight of subjects varies from 50 to 140 kg with mean value of 80 kg. To generate the binary mask and to annotate the images the Liablabel tool [27] was used. It is a polygon annotation tool that allows the user to specify semantic classes and to export these polygon files to semantic and instance label maps. This information was further used to generate the ground truth pectoral muscle boundary. A sample image and the corresponding annotation of the pectoral muscle is shown Fig. 4.

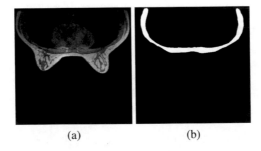

(a)   (b)

Fig. 4. An example of image and annotation mask: (a) Original image; (b) Annotation mask.

3.2   Training

We trained and evaluated our network on 780 images of the MD Anderson dataset. The training images were zero-centered and normalized to unit variance. The network was trained for 50 epochs using the Adam optimization algorithm with a fixed initial rate of 1e-4 and a mini-batch size of 16 patches in Keras.

3.3   Performance Metrics

To evaluate the performance of the proposed segmentation method, the following metrics were used:

$$\text{Recall} = \frac{TP}{TP + FN}, \tag{2}$$

$$\text{Precision} = \frac{TP}{TP + FP}, \tag{3}$$

$$\text{F-measure} = \frac{2 \cdot (\text{Recall} \cdot \text{Precision})}{(\text{Recall} + \text{Precision})}, \tag{4}$$

where true positive (TP) is the number of pixels correctly segmented as pectoral muscle, false positive (FP) is the number of pixels falsely segmented as pectoral muscle, and false negative (FN) is the number of pixels falsely detected as background. To quantitatively validate the segmentation results, the Dice similarity coefficient defined in Eq. 1 was also used. DSC was chosen since it interprets the similarity by the ratio of overlap between the ground truth pectoral muscle and the segmented pectoral muscle.

To precisely evaluate the performance of automated pectoral muscle boundary detection, the average distance (AD) between the detected boundary points and their corresponding closest points on the ground truth boundary was measured and used as the boundary estimation performance metric.

3.4   Results

The proposed segmentation method was applied to estimate the pectoral muscle boundary in both the MD Anderson and the TCIA datasets.

To ensure the robustness and accuracy of the method, we performed 10-fold cross-validation where the best performing model was recorded on each epoch.

The results of 10-fold cross validation for the pectoral muscle segmentation applied to the MD Anderson dataset is presented in Table 1. The results show

Table 1. Average performance via 10-fold cross-validation on the MD Anderson dataset.

Dataset	Recall [%]	Precision [%]	F-measure [%]	DSC [%]	AD [pixel]
MD Anderson	96 ± 0.003	94 ± 0.001	95 ± 0.002	95 ± 0.002	0.01 ± 0.03

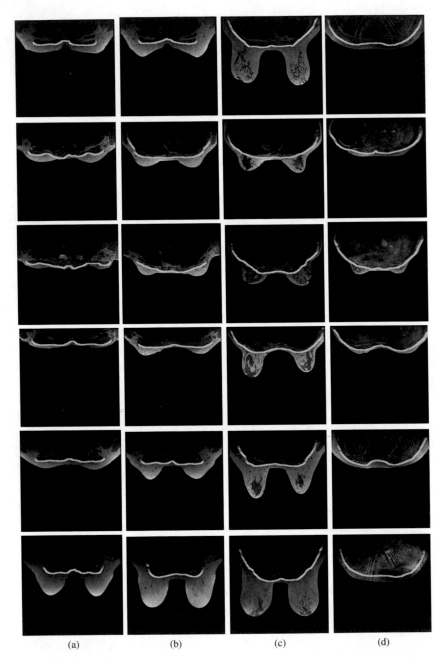

Fig. 5. Exemplar pectoral muscle boundary estimation results for six different subjects in the MD Anderson dataset having different ranges of size, shape, and weight. Each row represent the results for one subject: (a) Upper breast; (b) Superior upper breast; (c) Middle breast; (d) Lower breast.

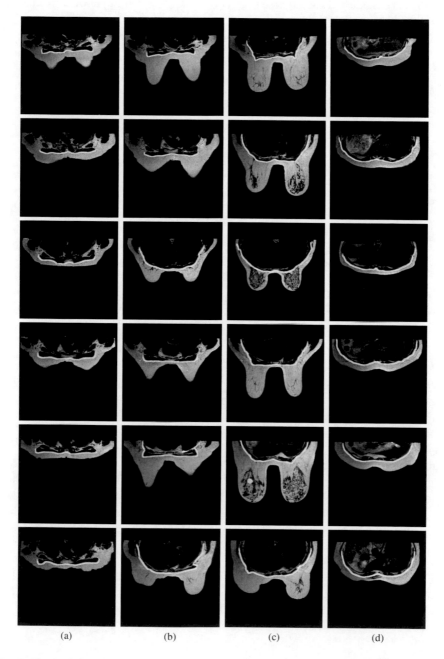

Fig. 6. Exemplar pectoral muscle boundary estimation results for six different subjects in the TCIA dataset having different ranges of size, shape, and weight. Each row represent the results for one subject: (a) Upper breast; (b) Superior upper breast; (c) Middle breast; (d) Lower breast.

Table 2. Performance of the proposed method on the TCIA dataset when trained on the MD Anderson dataset.

Dataset	Recall [%]	Precision [%]	F-measure [%]	DSC [%]	AD [pixel]
TCIA	90 ± 0.01	89 ± 0.01	89 ± 0.01	89 ± 0.04	0.05 ± 0.03

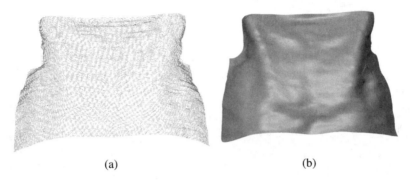

(a)   (b)

Fig. 7. A representative example of a 3D model constructed using the segmented boundary of the pectoral muscle: (a) Point cloud; (b) The corresponding 3D surface.

that the proposed method achieved a Dice score of 95%, precision of 94%, recall of 96%, and F-measure of 95%.

We further evaluated the generality of the proposed method by applying it to the TCIA dataset. As it can bee seen from Table 2, the proposed method achieved a Dice score of 89%, precision of 89%, recall of 90%, and F-measure of 89%.

From Tables 1 and 2, it can be seen that the average distance between the ground truth boundary and the segmented boundary was 0.01 pixel in the MD Anderson dataset and 0.05 pixel in the TCIA dataset. This confirms the high efficiency of the proposed method in estimation of the pectoral muscle boundary.

Figures 5 and 6 demonstrate the results of the pectoral muscle boundary detection applied to six subjects from the MD Anderson and the TCIA datasets respectively. As it can be seen, the proposed method detects the pectoral boundaries in the both datasets accurately.

Figure 7 represents an example of a 3D point cloud and its corresponding 3D surface constructed using the segmented boundary of the pectoral muscle of 256 slices of MR images of one subject. The 3D surface is constructed using the commercial software SOLIDWORKS.

4   Conclusions

This paper presents a novel method for automated segmentation and boundary delineation of the pectoral muscle in breast MR images. The proposed method consists of two steps: the pectoral muscle segmentation to segment the pectoral muscle region from the image and the pectoral muscle boundary estimation to detect the actual pectoral muscle boundary. The pectoral muscle segmentation was performed using the well known U-Net deep encoder-decoder framework. The boundary estimation was performed by detecting candidate points and contour segmentation. The proposed method was extensively evaluated on a large and challenging dataset and was shown to achieve a high segmentation accuracy.

Acknowledgments. This project was supported in part by the Academy of Finland (Cell vision project, Decision No. 313598); and The National Institutes of Health (R01CA143190 and R01CA203984). This study was approved by The University of Texas MD Anderson Cancer Center (protocol number 2015-1117). The authors would like to acknowledge the help received from Mary Catherine Bordes at The University of Texas MD Anderson Cancer Center for collecting the MRI datasets.

References

1. Del Palomar, A.P., Calvo, B., Herrero, J., López, J., Doblaré, M.: A finite element model to accurately predict real deformations of the breast. Med. Eng. Phys. **30**, 1089–1097 (2008)
2. Vavourakis, V., Eiben, B., Hipwell, J.H., Williams, N.R., Keshtgar, M., Hawkes, D.J.: Multiscale mechano-biological finite element modelling of oncoplastic breast surgery—numerical study towards surgical planning and cosmetic outcome prediction. PLoS ONE **11**, e0159766 (2016)
3. Conley, R.H., et al.: Realization of a biomechanical model-assisted image guidance system for breast cancer surgery using supine MRI. Int. J. Comput. Assist. Radiol. Surg. **10**, 1985–1996 (2015)
4. Wang, L., Filippatos, K., Friman, O., Hahn, H.K.: Fully automated segmentation of the pectoralis muscle boundary in breast MR images (2011)
5. Gubern-Mérida, A., Kallenberg, M., Martí, R., Karssemeijer, N.: Segmentation of the pectoral muscle in breast MRI using atlas-based approaches. In: Ayache, N., Delingette, H., Golland, P., Mori, K. (eds.) MICCAI 2012. LNCS, vol. 7511, pp. 371–378. Springer, Heidelberg (2012). https://doi.org/10.1007/978-3-642-33418-4_46
6. Pandey, D., et al.: Automatic and fast segmentation of breast region-of-interest (ROI) and density in MRIs. Heliyon **4**, e01042 (2018)
7. Czaplicka, K., Włodarczyk, H., et al.: Automatic breast-line and pectoral muscle segmentation. Schedae Informaticae **2011**, 195–209 (2012)
8. Mustra, M., Grgic, M.: Robust automatic breast and pectoral muscle segmentation from scanned mammograms. Sig. Process. **93**, 2817–2827 (2013)
9. Twellmann, T., Lichte, O., Nattkemper, T.W.: An adaptive tissue characterization network for model-free visualization of dynamic contrast-enhanced magnetic resonance image data. IEEE Trans. Med. Imaging **24**, 1256–1266 (2005)
10. Giannini, V., et al.: A fully automatic algorithm for segmentation of the breasts in DCE-MR images. In: 2010 Annual International Conference of the IEEE Engineering in Medicine and Biology Society, EMBC 2010, pp. 3146–3149 (2010)
11. Chakraborty, J., Mukhopadhyay, S., Singla, V., Khandelwal, N., Bhattacharyya, P.: Automatic detection of pectoral muscle using average gradient and shape based feature. J. Digit. Imaging **25**, 387–399 (2012)

12. Ferrari, R.J., Rangayyan, R.M., Desautels, J.E.L., Borges, R.A., Frere, A.F.: Automatic identification of the pectoral muscle in mammograms. IEEE Trans. Med. Imaging **23**, 232–245 (2004)
13. Kwok, S.M., Chandrasekhar, R., Attikiouzel, Y., Rickard, M.T.: Automatic pectoral muscle segmentation on mediolateral oblique view mammograms. IEEE Trans. Med. Imaging **23**, 1129–1140 (2004)
14. Kwok, S.M., Chandrasekhar, R., Attikiouzel, Y.: Automatic pectoral muscle segmentation on mammograms by straight line estimation and cliff detection. In: The Seventh Australian and New Zealand Intelligent Information Systems Conference, pp. 67–72 (2001)
15. Karssemeijer, N.: Automated classification of parenchymal patterns in mammograms. Phys. Med. Biol. **43**, 365–378 (1998)
16. Yam, M., Brady, M., Highnam, R., Behrenbruch, C., English, R., Kita, Y.: Three-dimensional reconstruction of microcalcification clusters from two mammographic views. IEEE Trans. Med. Imaging **20**, 479–489 (2001)
17. Nie, K., et al.: Development of a quantitative method for analysis of breast density based on three-dimensional breast MRI. Med. Phys. **35**(12), 5253–5262 (2008)
18. Gubern-Mérida, A., Wang, L., Kallenberg, M., Martí, R., Hahn, H.K., Karssemeijer, N.: Breast segmentation in MRI: quantitative evaluation of three methods. In: Medical Imaging 2013: Image Processing, pp. 86693g–86693g-7 (2013)
19. Cabezas, M., Oliver, A., Lladó, X., Freixenet, J., Cuadra, M.B.: A review of atlas-based segmentation for magnetic resonance brain images. Comput. Methods Programs Biomed. **104**, e158–e177 (2011)
20. Khalvati, F., Gallego-Ortiz, C., Balasingham, S., Martel, A.L.: Automated segmentation of breast in 3-D MR images using a robust atlas. IEEE Trans. Med. Imaging **34**, 116–125 (2015)
21. Fooladivanda, A., Shokouhi, S.B., Mosavi, M.R., Ahmadinejad, N.: Atlas-based automatic breast MRI segmentation using pectoral muscle and chest region model. In: 2014 21st Iranian Conference on Biomedical Engineering (ICBME), pp. 258–262 (2014)
22. Clark, K., et al.: The cancer imaging archive (TCIA): maintaining and operating a public information repository. J. Digit. Imaging **26**, 1045–1057 (2013)
23. Bloch, B.N., Jain, A., Jaffe, C.C.: Data from breast-diagnosis. The Cancer Imaging Archive (2015). https://doi.org/10.7937/K9/TCIA.2015.SDNRQXXR
24. Zafari, S., Eerola, T., Kälviäinen, H.: Cellvision - automatic segmentation of overlapping objects for cell image analysis, the cell vision project web page. http://www2.it.lut.fi/project/cellvision/index.shtml
25. Ronneberger, O., Fischer, P., Brox, T.: U-Net: convolutional networks for biomedical image segmentation. In: Navab, N., Hornegger, J., Wells, W.M., Frangi, A.F. (eds.) MICCAI 2015. LNCS, vol. 9351, pp. 234–241. Springer, Cham (2015). https://doi.org/10.1007/978-3-319-24574-4_28
26. Zhang, W., et al.: Deep convolutional neural networks for multi-modality isointense infant brain image segmentation. NeuroImage **108**, 214–224 (2015)
27. Geiger, A., Lauer, M., Wojek, C., Stiller, C., Urtasun, R.: 3D traffic scene understanding from movable platforms. IEEE Trans. Pattern Anal. Mach. Intell. **36**(5), 1012–1025 (2013)

Angio-AI: Cerebral Perfusion Angiography with Machine Learning

Ebrahim Feghhi, Yinsheng Zhou, John Tran, David S. Liebeskind,
and Fabien Scalzo$^{(\boxtimes)}$

Department of Neurology, University of California,
Los Angeles (UCLA), Los Angeles, CA 90095, USA
`fscalzo@mednet.ucla.edu`

Abstract. Angiography is a medical imaging technique used to visualize blood vessels. Perfusion angiography, where perfusion is defined as the passage of blood through the vasculature and tissue, is a computational tool created to quantify blood flow from angiography images. Perfusion angiography is critical in areas such as stroke diagnosis, where identification of areas with low blood flow and where assessment of revascularization are essential. Currently, perfusion angiography is performed through deconvolution methods that are susceptible to noise present in angiographic imaging. This paper introduces a machine learning-based formulation to perfusion angiography that can greatly speed-up the process. Specifically, kernel spectral regression (KSR) is used to learn the function mapping between digital subtraction angiography (DSA) frames and blood flow parameters. Model performance is evaluated by examining the similarity of the parametric maps produced by the model as compared those obtained via deconvolution. Our experiments on 15 patients show that the proposed Angio-AI framework can reliably compute parametric cerebral perfusion characterization in terms of cerebral blood volume (CBV), cerebral blood flow (CBF), arterial cerebral blood volume, and time-to-peak (TTP).

Keywords: Perfusion angiography · Machine learning · Digital Subtraction Angiography · Stroke

1 Introduction

Every year, roughly 800,000 Americans experience strokes, with the majority (about 87%) being acute ischemic strokes. This specific type of stroke is caused by a blood vessel in the brain narrowing or being blocked, restricting blood flow and energy supply to brain tissue. During an acute ischemic stroke, the tissue immediately surrounding the area with low blood flow is irreversibly damaged and referred to as infarct core. This core is surrounded by an outer layer of tissue, termed ischemic penumbra [4], which is hypoperfused and in danger of permanent damage. However, ischemic penumbra can be salvaged if blood flow is restored in time. People who arrive at the hospital within three hours of a

© Springer Nature Switzerland AG 2019
G. Bebis et al. (Eds.): ISVC 2019, LNCS 11844, pp. 357–367, 2019.
https://doi.org/10.1007/978-3-030-33720-9_27

stroke are more likely to reduce disability compared to those who receive delayed care [11].

Therefore, a primary concern in stroke treatment is effectively restoring blood flow in a timely manner. This presents a need for imaging technologies which can examine blood flow through the brain and accurately identify areas affected by the stroke, allowing doctors to target these areas in treatment. The three main imaging technologies currently in use are CT and MRI perfusion, and Digital Subtraction Angiography (DSA) [9]. All three typically involve injecting a dye into blood vessels to allow for imaging of blood flow. DSA uses X-ray technology and image subtraction methods to remove unwanted elements (i.e. the skull). It is currently the gold-standard approach because of its high spatio-temporal resolution, lower cost, and ability to be used in operating rooms.

One pitfall of DSA is that it is susceptible to noise due to electronic components and random distribution of X-rays [4]. This noise is further amplified by image subtraction methods. Algorithms to reduce the noise are challenging to access or customize as they are typically coded in the hardware. This leads to issues when implementing perfusion angiography [13], a tool which uses deconvolution methods to compute blood flow parameters from DSA images. The calculation of these parameters through deconvolution, which include cerebral blood volume (CBV), cerebral blood flow (CBF), arterial cerebral blood flow volume, and time-to-peak (TTP); each of those parameters can be affected by noise. Parametric images computed using deconvolution are shown in Fig. 1. Blue pixels indicate low intensity values and red pixels indicate high intensity values, with colors in between such as yellow and orange represent pixel intensity values in the middle.

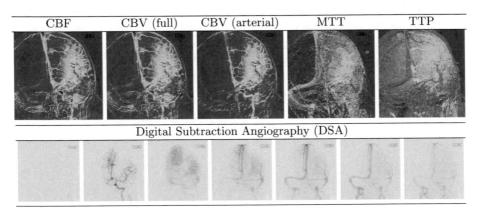

Fig. 1. Parametric perfusion maps (including cerebral blood flow (CBF), blood volume (CBV), mean transit time (MTT), and time-to-peak (TTP)) computed from digital subtraction angiography (DSA) using Perfusion Angiography [13] using deconvolution. (Color figure online)

One solution to address the noise issue is to leverage machine learning so that they are trained to compute the parameters in presence of noise. Whereas deconvolution methods compute parameter values per pixel, machine learning models are able to take in and learn from a large amount of data, averaging over and reducing noise. This approach has been successfully applied in the context of MR perfusion [8] and is viable because of the existing labeled dataset created through deconvolution methods. A model can be trained to learn the function mapping between a pixel vector and one of the four parameters. An additional benefit of this is that it removes the need to design specific computing heuristics for each output parameter. We hypothesize that machine learning could provide a generalized framework for perfusion angiography.

The aim of this project is to evaluate the effectiveness of a machine learning model trained to establish the mapping between temporal pixel values from the angiogram and each parametric blood perfusion value. In order to accomplish this, we sample time-intensity curves across spatial location from the dataset and use them as our training set. Pixels from background are not informative and were eliminated using the Otsu's threshold method [10]. Models were then trained to predict parameter values based on the sampled pixels. Performance was then analyzed by computing the difference between predicted values and values given from deconvolution methods used as groundtruth.

2   Methods

2.1   Dataset Overview

The original imaging dataset for this study was obtained from a Comprehensive Stroke Center located in the United States (US), and was approved for use by the local Institutional Review Board (IRB). The dataset consisted of time-series X-ray DSA scans from 15 patients with symptoms of acute ischemic stroke within the past 6 h. Images were obtained after a thrombectomy procedure. All images have 1024×1024 pixel values and a total number of 20 frames (temporally resampled using bilinear interpolation), leading to a $1024 \times 1024 \times 20$ matrix. DSA frames were captured from two angles: anterior-posterior and lateral.

2.2   Groundtruth

The groundtruth was established using Perfusion Angiography [13] which uses deconvolution to compute blood flow parameters for each patient, including cerebral blood flow (CBF), blood volume (CBV), mean transit time (MTT), and time-to-peak (TTP). This resulted in a 1024×1024 image for each parameter. Low CBV and CBF values indicate areas where blood flow is impaired [3]. TTP gives the time until maximum pixel intensity, and higher values indicate blood flow impairment. These parameters can be visualized by charting the contrast concentration value over time as observed in Fig. 2.

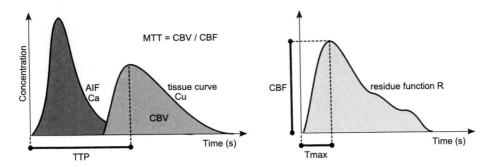

Fig. 2. Illustration of a time-intensity curve C_u (yellow) with respect to an arterial input function (AIF) C_a (blue). The deconvolution of the tissue curve C_u with C_a removes the dependence on the AIF and produces the residue function R (right). CBF is extracted at the maximum value reached at Tmax, while MTT is calculated as CBV/CBF, where CBV is determined as the area under the tissue curve (yellow). Because of the presence of arterial delays in stroke patients, the residue function is not always maximal at $t = 0$, but might be maximal after a delay (Tmax). (Color figure online)

2.3   Data Sampling and Pre-processing

The machine learning task is posed such that each pixel is predicted independently using the time-intensity curve obtained from the digital subtraction angiography (DSA). The goal of the model is to learn the function mapping between the value of a pixel $DSA(i, j)$ over the 20 successive frames, leading to a 1×20 vector, and its corresponding scalar parameter value (obtained via perfusion angiography). Normalization of the dataset was performed between the 1st and 99th percentile so that outliers do not contribute to the model.

Moreover, the four parameters (CBF, CBV, arterial CBV, TTP) we are aiming for are only affected by the presence of contrast represented by each frame. Meanwhile, the large amount of background does not hold useful information for the models. We segment the background using Otzu's method applied to the imaging representing the total contrast observed at each pixel (which corresponds to the blood volume, CBV).

The uniform sampling is performed on the foreground pixel locations, ensuring the area of interest consists of only pixels that received some contrast. This intensity range was then uniformly divided into 5 bins using the (20, 40, 60, 80) percentiles. Pixels were then randomly sampled for each bin from a given parameter image until each bin contained 100 pixel locations, a total of 500 pixels had been sampled, per patient. The rationale behind this sampling method versus an unconstrained random sampling method was to limit over-selection of pixel intensities that occur frequently, ensuring a relatively uniform pool of pixel intensities. The coordinates of these pixels were then stored and used to access pixel intensity values across the 20 DSA frames, creating a 500×20 vector for each individual.

An additional step was performed by concatenating the intensity time-curve of the arterial input function (AIF); which is located on the main feeding artery (internal carotid artery, ICA). This additional set of 1×20 vectors is concatenated to every of the 500 time curves extracted of the patient, leading to a 500×40 set of input vectors. The processing steps detailed above describe data generation for one patient. In summary, for each patient 500 pixels, or less if a bin was not filled up, were selected from each of the four parametric images.

2.4 SR-KDA Model

The machine learning model used as part of our framework is based on the SR-DA algorithm [2]; a method introduced to solve discriminant analysis (DA) as a regularized regression problem,

$$\alpha = \mathrm{argmin}_\alpha \sum_{i=1}^{n} (\alpha^T x_i - y_i)^2 + \delta ||\alpha||^2 \tag{1}$$

where x_i is the input vector (i.e. histogram), y_i the corresponding HT outcome, α is the eigenvector, and δ is the regularization parameter.

To solve this problem (Eq. (1)), the main idea behind SR-DA is to find vectors α that map the input features x to the output y so that samples that are close also produce similar outputs. SR-DA formulates the regularization as follows,

$$\alpha = (XX^T + \delta I)^{-1} X^T y \tag{2}$$

where I is the identity matrix, α is the eigenvector, and $\delta > 0$ the regularization parameter. Interestingly, this formulation can be solved efficiently using a Cholesky decomposition,

$$r = \mathrm{chol}(XX^T + \delta I) \tag{3}$$
$$\alpha = r\backslash(r^T\backslash(X^T y)). \tag{4}$$

SR-KDA [2] generalizes SR-DA to utilize a kernel projection of the data and obtain nonlinearity. Input data samples $x \in X$ are projected onto a high-dimensional space via a Gaussian kernel K,

$$K(i,j) = \exp{-||x_i - x_j||^2/2\sigma^2} \tag{5}$$

where σ is the standard deviation of the kernel.

Similarly to SR-DA, SR-KDA uses a Cholesky decomposition from the regularized positive definite matrix K and class labels y to obtain vectors α,

$$r = \mathrm{chol}(K + \delta I) \tag{6}$$
$$\alpha = r\backslash(r^T\backslash y). \tag{7}$$

When a new input feature vector, x_{new}, is extracted from a new patient, the likelihood for HT, $\hat{y}_{new}$, is computed using

$$k(i) = \exp{-||x_i - x_{new}||^2/2\sigma^2}, i = 1 \ldots n \tag{8}$$
$$\hat{y}_{new} = \hat{\alpha}^T k \tag{9}$$

where k is the vector resulting from the kernel projection of x_{new} into the kernel space using training data X.

2.5   Evaluation

After initialization, models were fit using the training dataset generated. A separate model was trained for each parameter. Performance was evaluated using a leave-one-out crossvalidation at the patient level. This ensures that we use the full potential of our dataset which contains 15 patients, with 500 points of each patient in the testing set. The difference between predicted values and values generated through deconvolution was represented using the bland altman plot [1]. The models learned as part of the crossvalidation were also used to predict parameter values for an entire image (1024 × 1024) on each patient, allowing us to reproduce the whole image.

3   Results

The results of the crossvalidation are illustrated in Figs. 3, 4, 5 and 6, for CBF, CBV, arterial CBV, and TTP respectively. The left plot shows the correlation between the predicted values and the groundtruth, with a r-squared of [.85, .76, .7, .55], while the Bland-Altman plots are shown on the right side with a reproducibility coefficient (RPC) of [.17, .2, .25, .4] for CBF, CBV, arterial CBV, and TTP respectively.

As is shown in the images generated in Fig. 7, the model achieved a high degree of similarity to the original deconvolution based perfusion angiography for both the calculation of CBF and CBV. This is supported by the high correlation coefficient and low RPC values for these two blood flow parameters. One important observation to note is that as the intensity of a parameter value increases, our machine learning model tends to diverge from the deconvolution based method.

Machine learning based perfusion angiography differed from the deconvolution based method to a greater extent for TTP calculation. This is evident from the lower correlation coefficient value and higher RPC value, as well as the stark visual difference between the TTP images generated from the two methods. We believe this is due to two reasons. First, unlike CBF and CBV, TTP is a discrete value and another machine learning model may have served better. Second, TTP does not incorporate AIF in its calculation, so including AIF in the input data may have further complicated the function mapping for TTP.

4   Discussion

The implementation of the SR-KDA model proves to be a solid method for the prediction of perfusion angiography parameters in presence of a small sample size (15 patients). One important upside is its increase in efficiency. Results can be generated within seconds, while the deconvolution-based method may take several minutes. Compared to deconvolution-based methods, this property can increase its clinical value since results are often needed rapidly.

Bland-Altman Plot

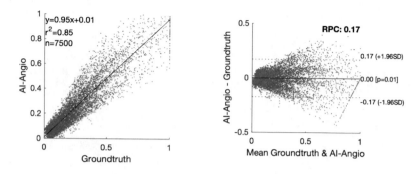

Fig. 3. Bland-Altman graph for CBF.

Bland-Altman Plot

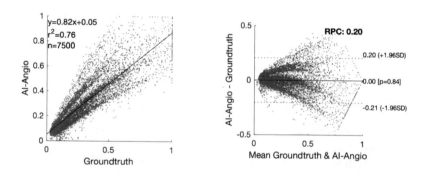

Fig. 4. Bland-Altman graph for CBV.

Bland-Altman Plot

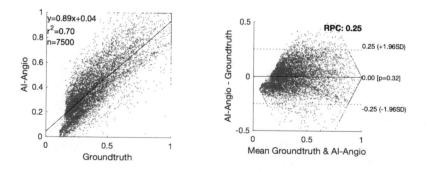

Fig. 5. Bland-Altman graph for arterial CBV.

Bland-Altman Plot

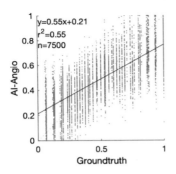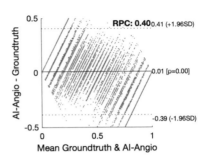

Fig. 6. Bland-Altman graph for arterial TTP.

It is unclear whether differences from the deconvolution based method are positive or negative. Parameters generated from deconvolution methods are susceptible to noise from DSA images, and are therefore are not truly ground-truth labels. Differences from these noisy labels may therefore be positive as it may indicate reduction in noise. In order to investigate this, we hope to create noise-free ground truth labels using computational fluid dynamics and compare machine learning and deconvolution methods in their ability to match this phantom dataset.

One limitation of the current implementation is the small size of the dataset, having only 15 patients in total. We ensured that the patients included in this study were free of significant motion artifacts that would produce a visualization of the skull, which is undesirable. The current model uses the time-intensity curve of individual pixels to infer the parameter values. The use of regional information, for example using local patches [12], could provide additional robustness to noise and artifacts and add discriminatory power to better capture subtle patterns in the source DSA associated with specific parameter values. Moreover, another weakness of the current dataset which largely impacts the training process is that neither the DSA images were acquired with different settings in terms of the pose, and strength of the X-ray tube. Additional normalization strategies (such as normalization with respect to specific vessels in the brain) could be considered to ensure equivalence of the DSA intensities across patients.

There is a promising trend in the medical imaging community to apply machine learning to source (i.e. native) data, such as MRI to predict clinically relevant variables such as tissue fate [5], time from stroke onset [6], and hemorrhagic transformation [14], for example.

Finally, in this case our model only predicts CBF, CBV, arterial CBV and TTP. However, in clinical situation, more parameters such as MTT, Tmax, K-Trans may also be needed. Hence, one final way of improvement would be to train on additional parameters. A potential additional evaluation is to compare

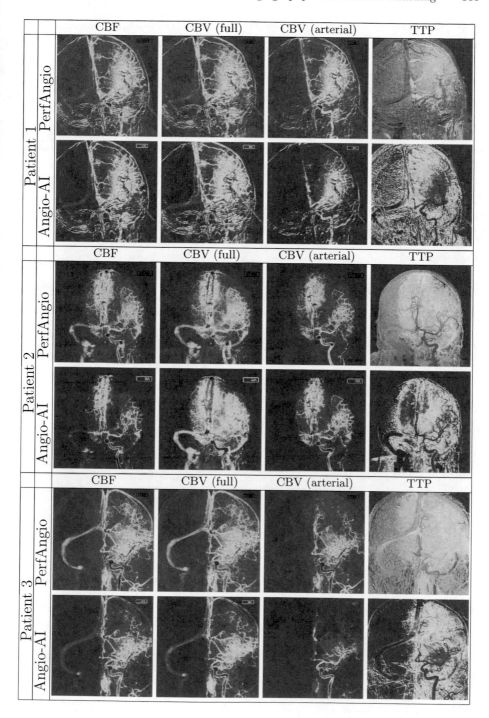

Fig. 7. Comparison of parametric perfusion maps computed from digital subtraction angiography (DSA) using Perfusion Angiography [13] and Angio-AI.

parametric CBF values to TICI scores [7]. Parameter values should indicate low blood flow in areas affected by stroke in patients with low TICI scores.

5   Conclusion

This paper introduces a machine learning formulation for the estimation of blood perfusion in the brain from angiography. Such framework can robustly and efficiently produce CBF, CBV, TTP perfusion maps as compared to the conventional deconvolutional methods. The promising results obtained on a small set of 15 acute ischemic stroke patients can serve as a strong indicator of potential success on large cohorts and more advanced machine learning models such as Deep Learning.

References

1. Altman, D.G., Bland, J.M.: Measurement in medicine: the analysis of method comparison studies. J. R. Stat. Soc. Ser. D (Stat.) **32**(3), 307–317 (1983). http://www.jstor.org/stable/2987937
2. Cai, D., He, X., Han, J.: Spectral regression for efficient regularized subspace learning. In: ICCV (2007). https://doi.org/10.1109/ICCV.2007.4408855
3. Cunli, Y., Khoo, L.S., Lim, P.J., Lim, E.H.: CT angiography versus digital subtraction angiography for intracranial vascular pathology in a clinical setting. Med. J. Malays. **68**(5), 415 (2013)
4. Hanley, M., Zenzen, W., Brown, M., Gaughen, J., Evans, A.: Comparing the accuracy of digital subtraction angiography, CT angiography and MR angiography at estimating the volume of cerebral aneurysms. Interv. Neuroradiol. **14**(2), 173–177 (2008)
5. Ho, K.C., Scalzo, F., Sarma, K.V., Speier, W., El-Saden, S., Arnold, C.: Predicting ischemic stroke tissue fate using a deep convolutional neural network on source magnetic resonance perfusion images. J. Med. Imaging (Bellingham) **6**(2), 026001 (2019)
6. Ho, K.C., Speier, W., Zhang, H., Scalzo, F., El-Saden, S., Arnold, C.W.: A machine learning approach for classifying ischemic stroke onset time from imaging. IEEE Trans. Med. Imaging **38**(7), 1666–1676 (2019)
7. Liebeskind, D.S., et al.: Abstract WP39: perfusion angiography in TREVO2: quantitative reperfusion after endovascular therapy in acute stroke. Stroke **44**, AWP39 (2013)
8. McKinley, R., Hung, F., Wiest, R., Liebeskind, D.S., Scalzo, F.: A machine learning approach to perfusion imaging with dynamic susceptibility contrast MR. Front. Neurol. **9**, 717 (2018)
9. Musuka, T.D., Wilton, S.B., Traboulsi, M., Hill, M.D.: Diagnosis and management of acute ischemic stroke: speed is critical. CMAJ **187**(12), 887–893 (2015)
10. Otsu, N.: A threshold selection method from gray-level histograms. IEEE Trans. Syst. Man Cybern. **9**(1), 62–66 (1979). https://doi.org/10.1109/TSMC.1979.4310076
11. Prabhakaran, S., Ruff, I., Bernstein, R.A.: Acute stroke intervention: a systematic review. JAMA **313**(14), 1451–1462 (2015)

12. Scalzo, F., Hao, Q., Alger, J.R., Hu, X., Liebeskind, D.S.: Regional prediction of tissue fate in acute ischemic stroke. Ann. Biomed. Eng. **40**(10), 2177–2187 (2012)
13. Scalzo, F., Liebeskind, D.S.: Perfusion angiography in acute ischemic stroke. Comput. Math. Methods Med. **2016**, 14 (2016)
14. Yu, Y., Guo, D., Lou, M., Liebeskind, D., Scalzo, F.: Prediction of hemorrhagic transformation severity in acute stroke from source perfusion MRI. IEEE Trans. Biomed. Eng. **65**(9), 2058–2065 (2018)

Conformal Welding for Brain-Intelligence Analysis

Liqun Yang[1], Muhammad Razib[1], Kenia Chang He[1], Tianren Yang[1],
Zhong-Lin Lu[2,3], Xianfeng Gu[4], and Wei Zeng[1(✉)]

[1] Florida International University, Miami, FL 33199, USA
wzeng@cs.fiu.edu
[2] New York University Shanghai, Shanghai 200122, China
[3] New York University, New York, NY 10003, USA
[4] Stony Brook University, Stony Brook, NY 11794, USA

Abstract. In this work, we present a geometric method to explore the relationship between brain anatomical structure and human intelligence based on conformal welding theory. We *first* generate the anatomical atlas on the structural MRI data; *then*, compute the signature for each cortical region by welding the conformal maps of the region and its complement domain along the common boundary, and combine all the region signature as that for the whole brain; and *finally*, use the signatures for shape visualization and classification using the learning methods. The signature is global, intrinsic to surface and curve geometry, and invariant to conformal transformations; and the computation is efficient through solving sparse linear systems. Experiments on real data set with 243 subjects demonstrate the efficacy of the proposed method and concluded that the conformal welding signature of cortical surface can classify human intelligence with a competitive accuracy rate compared with traditional features.

Keywords: Conformal welding · Brain structure · Human intelligence

1 Introduction

One of the large scientific challenges identified for the 21st century concerns how brain, body and mind interact to produce thought, feeling and behavior. The way in which differences in brain structure and function contribute to differences in social and cognitive behavior is central to this endeavor. Methods with theoretical rigor, numerical accuracy, and processing efficiency to translate pictorial descriptions of cortical surfaces into quantitative mathematical descriptions are urgently needed in the human brain mapping research. This work aims to explore this direction through the innovations in computational conformal geometry that quantify the relationship between the shape of the brain and its functionality, here with the focus of *human intelligence*.

© Springer Nature Switzerland AG 2019
G. Bebis et al. (Eds.): ISVC 2019, LNCS 11844, pp. 368–380, 2019.
https://doi.org/10.1007/978-3-030-33720-9_28

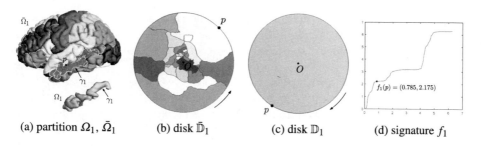

(a) partition $\Omega_1, \bar{\Omega}_1$ (b) disk $\bar{\mathbb{D}}_1$ (c) disk $\mathbb{D}_1$ (d) signature f_1

Fig. 1. Conformal welding signature for a cortical region.

Previous Methods. A wide number of studies have been done to correlate human intelligence with brain structure in recent decades [4, 23]. Most commonly used properties to represent brain structure include *density, area, thickness,* and *curvature,* computed based on voxel-based morphometry (VBM) analysis methods (see [1] for a review). In detail, Jung et al. [8] linked differences in grey matter density to human intelligence quotient (IQ). Haier et al. [5] showed an inverse correlation between IQ based on Raven's advanced progressive matrices (RAPM) and glucose metabolism in areas around the cortex. Shaw et al. [21] showed that IQ is most closely related to the trajectory of change in the thickness of the cerebral cortex. Narr et al. [14] suggested that variation in the thickness of prefrontal and temporal association cortices is specifically relevant to IQ based on Wechsler adult intelligence scale (WAIS). Luders et al. [12] found significant positive correlation between intelligence and the corpus callosum thickness, corresponding to posterior body, isthmus, and anterior sections of the splenium. Im et al. [7] found that IQ (WAIS) was correlated with fractal dimension positively which represents the cortical complexity and that the correlation is significantly positive in right hemisphere. Karama et al. [9] reported the relation between the cortical thickness of multi modal association areas and cognitive ability factor (an estimate of general intelligence, derived from adjusted WAIS). Luders et al. [11] found the correlation of IQ (WAIS) with cortical convolution based on mean curvature of lateral and medial surfaces of each individual cortical model. They found IQ positively associated with the degree of folding in the temporo-occipital lobe, particularly in the outermost section of the posterior cingulate gyrus. In addition, Yang et al. [23] proposed the combination of different morphometric properties of complex cortical surface with cortical thickness, surface area, sulcal depth, and absolute mean curvature using partial least squares regression can be used to predict 30% of IQ (WAIS). Shape-based morphometry analysis is another category, where, instead of curvatures, shape descriptors of surface geometry can be applied. Su et al. [22] used the Wasserstein distance based on the optimal mass transport theory to classify IQ (RAPM).

Our Method. With the advancement of computational conformal geometry, we can explicitly compute the shape of the brain by rigorous and effective methods to quantitatively measure the similarities, and classify and differentiate the complicated cortical shapes. In this work, we propose a geometric representation, *Conformal Welding Signature*, to describe the global structure of the 3D cortical surface and characterize shape differences between 3D cortical surfaces; and then based on this, we explore how the brain shape differences contribute to the differences of intelligence. Discrete conformal welding theory was initially proposed in [20] for 2D simply-connected domain for shape analysis in computer vision, and later was generalized to multiply-connected domains [13,24] for shape classification. The corresponding conformal welding signatures were computed for the non-intersecting regions of interest (ROIs) on a domain. In our method, we extract a signature for every cortical region and combine all region signatures as the signature for the whole cortical surface.

As shown in Fig. 1, one cortical surface can be partitioned into different anatomical regions. The boundary of a cortical region is a closed loop, which separates the cortical surface into two connected components: the region and its complement. The region can be mapped onto the planar unit disk by a Riemann mapping, so is its complement. The boundary loop of the region is mapped to the circular boundary of both disks. This induces a mapping between the two circles, which is the conformal welding signature. The conformal welding signature for a region is determined by the geometry of the region, the geometry of the complement on the cortical surface, and the relative geometric relationship between the region and its complement; and vice versa, the contour of the region can be recovered by its conformal welding signature. We compute all region signatures and combine them. By comparing the conformal welding signatures, we can determine the shape distance of regions or whole surfaces across different brains, and further use that to discover its relationship to human intelligence.

Contribution. This work presents a theoretically sound geometric approach to discovering brain structure-function relationship. The *novelty* of this work is to compute the conformal welding signature for a closed genus zero surface with atlas graph by combining all atlas region signatures, and apply the conformal welding signature to analyze how brain structure correlates to human intelligence. We found that the conformal welding signature can classify human intelligence (IQ) through the experiments on real data set, with a more competitive classification accuracy rate than traditional features.

2   Our Conformal Welding Signature

Here we describe the major concepts and theorem for the proposed method. Readers may refer to [3] for more details.

Given a genus zero closed surface S with an atlas graph. Suppose the graph regions have the boundaries, $\Gamma = \{\gamma_0, \gamma_1, \cdots, \gamma_n\}$, which is a set of simple closed curves on S. γ_i segments the surface to two connected components, Ω_k (the foreground domain, contoured by γ_k) and $\bar{\Omega}_k$ (the complement background domain), $0 \leq k \leq n$. Construct the uniformization mapping $\varphi_k : \Omega_k \rightarrow \mathbb{D}_k$ to map the foreground segment Ω_k to a circle domain $\mathbb{D}_k$, and similarly, $\bar{\varphi}_k :$

$\bar{\Omega}_k \to \bar{\mathbb{D}}_k$ map the background segment $\bar{\Omega}_k$ to a disk domain $\bar{\mathbb{D}}_k$. Let $f_k|_{\mathbb{S}^1} :=$ $\varphi_k \circ \bar{\varphi}_k^{-1}|_{\mathbb{S}^1} : \mathbb{S}^1 \to \mathbb{S}^1$ be the diffeomorphism from the circle to itself, and $f_k : [0, 2\pi] \to [0, 2\pi]$. We call the diffeomorphism f_k the *signature of* γ_k. The *conformal welding signature* of the family of non-intersecting closed curves Γ on a genus zero closed surface can be defined as:

$$\mathcal{W}(\Gamma) := \{f_0, \cdots, f_k\}.$$

The conformal welding theory [3] guarantees that the signature is determined by a family of curves unique up to a Möbius transformation, and inversely that the curves can be uniquely recovered by the signature unique up to a conformal transformation.

As shown in Fig. 1, the contour γ_1 in (a) is mapped to the circles of $\bar{\mathbb{D}}_1, \mathbb{D}_1$ in (b-c). The diffeomorphism $f_1 : \partial\bar{\mathbb{D}}_1 \to \partial\mathbb{D}_1$ induces the signature for the region, plotted as a monotonically increasing curve in (d). For example, given a point p on the boundary and compute the angles from that. Note that because two domains are obtained by slicing the common boundary open on the original surface, the boundaries of the two disk domains has opposite orientation, as shown in (b-c).

Concept Novelty. Existing conformal welding signatures [13, 20, 24] considers a closed genus zero surface with a family of non-intersecting closed curves $\Gamma = \{\gamma_0, \gamma_1, \cdots, \gamma_n\}$. They include not only the diffeomorphisms f_k generated by all curves and also the conformal module of the complement background domain $\bar{\mathbb{D}}$, which is a poly-annulus obtained by cutting all non-intersecting regions off the closed surface. The uniformization mapping result of the $\bar{\mathbb{D}}$ is a circle domain, i.e., a disk domain with circular holes. The conformal module of $\bar{\mathbb{D}}$ is defined as the combination of the circle centers and radii of the circle domain. The signature is then defined as $\mathcal{W}(\Gamma) := \{f_0, \cdots, f_k\} \cup \{Mod(\bar{\mathbb{D}})\}$, where Mod denotes the conformal module of $\bar{\mathbb{D}}$. In our case, we propose a novel way to compute the signature for a genus zero closed surface associated with atlas graph on that. We consider the contours of all atlas regions. For each region, its complement background domain is a topological disk and mapped to a unit disk, where the conformal module is ignored. Our conformal welding signature describes the shape and the correlation of the whole atlas structure and the surface.

Geometric Intuition. The conformal welding signature of a cortical region is intrinsically determined by its geometry, its complement, and their relationship. Intuitively, one can glue two planar unit disks to get a closed surface, the gluing pattern along the disk boundaries is specified by the conformal welding signature. If the glued shape can be conformally mapped to the original cortical surface, then the glued circles are mapped to the original region boundary. This shows that the conformal welding signature can determine the position and shape of the loop. In order to compare the shapes of different regions, or the corresponding regions on different cortical surfaces, or the whole cortical surfaces, one can just compare their signatures, which are in the same space of the diffeomorphisms of the unit circle and much easier to compare and manipulate.

This signature is *global* and captures the difference of *intrinsic* conformal structures. It is *rigorous, unique* and *accurate*, and is *invariant* under Möbius transformation (angle preserving); area distortions in the conformal mappings won't change the signature. Moreover, conformal mappings are robust to geometry noise, so the signature is *stable*.

3   Computational Pipeline

The pipeline includes the following 4 steps: (1) reconstruct cortical surfaces from MRI data and generate atlas parcellation; (2) partition anatomical regions one by one from a cortical surface; (3) compute the Riemann mappings for each region (foreground) and the corresponding complement surface (background); and (4) extract the conformal welding signature for each region and combine them to build the final signature. Details are as follows. Figure 2 shows the pipeline for computing the signature for one region.

1. Reconstruction and Parcellation. First of all, we reconstruct the 3D meshes from the MRI brain scans. This can be done in various ways. Here, we employed FreeSurfer automated pipeline (www.freesurfer.net). It gives the desired cortical surface and the anatomical atlas parcellation encoded by different colors. Each brain hemisphere has 35 anatomical regions, indexed by integer 1, 2, 3, ..., 35. Besides all of these regions, there is a black region with the id 0 which is the part connecting the left and right hemispheres. Through our experimental analysis, region 4 is totally in the interior and has no exposure on the cortical surface, therefore not considered. So there are totally 34 regions to be computed for each

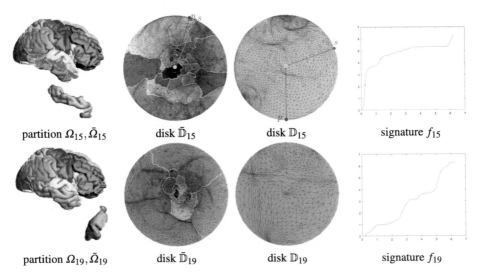

partition $\Omega_{15}, \bar{\Omega}_{15}$ disk $\bar{\mathbb{D}}_{15}$ disk $\mathbb{D}_{15}$ signature f_{15}

partition $\Omega_{19}, \bar{\Omega}_{19}$ disk $\bar{\mathbb{D}}_{19}$ disk $\mathbb{D}_{19}$ signature f_{19}

Fig. 2. Illustration of the signature computation for two regions 15 and 19 with triangular meshes. Red point is the starting point to compute angles. (Color figure online)

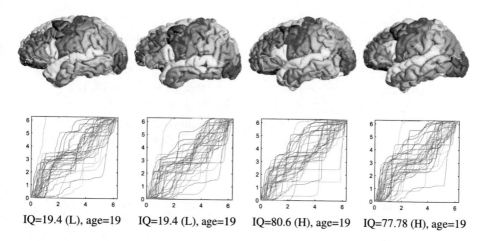

IQ=19.4 (L), age=19   IQ=19.4 (L), age=19   IQ=80.6 (H), age=19   IQ=77.78 (H), age=19

Fig. 3. The left brain hemispheres and their cofnormal welding signatures with different IQ levels.

cortical hemisphere. Note that we only need the cortical surfaces with the atlas under the same atlas protocol and don't need register them. Other software tools such as BrainSuite can also work for this purpose.

2. Partition. For computing the conformal mappings of the regions, we extract 34 regions from the cortical surface one by one. The cortical surface is a genus zero surface. By slicing the cortical surface open along a region, we obtain the region surface (foreground) and the cortical surface without the region (background). Note that their boundaries are a copy of the contour of the region.

3. Mapping Brains. We run the Reimann mapping on both the foreground and the background surfaces. The computation is based on the discrete holomorphic 1-forms [13]. With the puncture, each patch is a topological annulus with an exterior boundary γ_0 and an interior boundary γ_1. In practice, the surface is tessellated as a triangle mesh $M = (V, E, F)$, where V, E, F denote the set of vertex, edge and face, respectively.

We first compute a *harmonic function*, $f : M \to \mathbb{R}$, such that $\Delta f(v_i) = 0, \forall v_i \notin \partial M, f|_{\gamma_0} = 1, f|_{\gamma_1} = 0$. The discrete Laplace-Beltrami operator Δ acts on a function f,

$$\Delta f(v_i) = \sum_{[v_i, v_j] \in M} w_{ij}[f(v_i) - f(v_j)],$$

where the weight w_{ij} is chosen to be the mean value coordinates which guarantees to be positive for any triangulation cases. Then $\omega_1 = df$ is a closed 1-form. We further find the shortest path γ from γ_0 to γ_1. We slice the mesh along γ to get an open mesh $\bar{M}$, γ becomes two boundary segments γ^+ and γ^- on $\bar{M}$. We randomly assign a function $g : \bar{M} \to \mathbb{R}$, such that $g|_{\gamma^+} = 1, g|_{\gamma^-} = 0$. Then $\omega_2 = dg$ is a closed 1-form. We then find another function h, such that $\omega_2 + dh$

is harmonic for all vertices, $\sum_{[v_i,v_j]\in M} w_{ij}[\omega_2([v_i,v_j]) + h(v_i) - h(v_j)] = 0$, and update $\omega_2 = \omega_2 + dh$. Finally, we compute a constant λ, such that $\lambda\omega_2$ is as close to $*\omega_1$ as possible. The discrete holomorphic 1-form $\omega = \omega_1 + i\omega_2$ is obtained.

We then integrate ω over M, $\phi(v_k) = \int_{\gamma(v_0,v_k)\in M} \omega$, $\forall v_k \in V$, where γ_k is an arbitrary path from the base vertex v_0 to the current vertex v_k and $\phi(v_0) = (0,0)$, and compute the map $v_k \rightarrow exp(\frac{1}{T}\int_{\gamma_k} \omega)$, where T is the period $T = \frac{2\pi}{\int_{\gamma_0} \omega_2}$. Thus we obtain the conformal map, which maps the annulus M to a canonical annulus with the unit exterior radius and is independent of the choice of the path γ_k. The computation of harmonic functions is equivalent to solving linear systems, and therefore is efficient.

4. Extracting Signatures. The contour of each region is a loop embedded in 3D space, and is mapped twice to be the unit circles in the two Riemann mappings of both the foreground and background domains. Therefore we can form a diffeomorphism between the two circles since they share the same chain of vertices but in reverse order. We represent the diffeomorphism $f : \theta_0 \rightarrow \theta_1$ (θ_i is the radial angle of $\phi(\gamma_i)$) using the pair of radial angles (θ_0, θ_1), which can recover the two circles exactly. In detail, we fix one vertex on the boundary as the starting point which corresponds the curve endpoints, $(0,0)$ and $(2\pi, 2\pi)$ (see Figs. 1 and 2). For the consistency of the starting point on each contour over various brains, we utilize the branching vertex of common regions along the contour as the starting point. Figure 3 gives the examples for the brains with various IQ scores. We observe that the signatures are similar for brains with the same IQ level; moreover, there are visible differences between two groups, showing the promising ability for IQ classification.

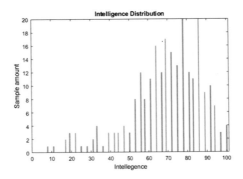

Fig. 4. The IQ distribution in the data set.

4   Experiments and Discussion

We performed our analysis on a real data set which consists of 243 subjects, 146 females and 97 males aging from 18 to 30 (mean 20.8). MRI recording was performed using a standard 12-channel head coil on a Siemens 3T Trio MRI system with TIM. The collection of IQ is based on the online questionnaire of Raven's Advanced Progressive Matrices (RAPM) [15] in Qualtrics (www.qualtrics.com). The range of IQ is [0,100], taking the value as the rate of the correct answers multiplied by 100, which is different from the traditional IQ scores using the median score of the norming sample as IQ 100.

In this application, due to the size limit of the training data set, it won't be practical to predict the exact value of IQ from a brain. So we take it as a classification problem and then try to label the brains by IQ. Earlier study [6] states that young human IQ has a normal distribution $N(\mu, \sigma^2)$ (μ - mean value, σ - standard deviation) and ($\mu - 0.5\sigma$) is the segmentation line for low IQ. As shown in Fig. 4, our data set admits that and has corresponding IQ score 60 as segmentation line. We used that to group subjects (63 subjects of Low and 180 subjects of High).

Evaluation Plan. To evaluate the efficiency and the efficacy of the proposed method, two experiments were performed: (1) feature visualization, to illustrate the distribution of the features of this data set (see Sect. 4.1); and (2) classification, to demonstrate the ability of the features to differentiate IQs (see Sect. 4.2).

We used FreeSurfer automated pipeline with Desikan Killiany atlas template for parcellation. As we described in Sect. 3, we computed signatures for 34 regions for each hemisphere, totaling $34(regions) \times 2(hemispheres) = 68$ signature curves for each brain (see Fig. 3). All regions can be handled in parallel and the running time for a cortical mesh with $270k$ triangles is 30 s. In our experiments, we used the area under curve (AUC) to build feature vector to feed the classifier. In detail, the area under f_i is computed as $AUC(f_i) = \Sigma_0^{2\pi} f_i(x_k)$, where x_k are the uniform samples on x-axis. Therefore, the feature vector for a brain has dimension 68.

At the same time, we compared the performance of our geometric signature with that of the FreeSurfer features for all regions [16,17]. They include *CurvInd* (Curvature index), *FoldInd* (Folding index), *GausCurv* (Gaussian curvature), *GrayVol* (Volume of gray matter (surface-based)), *MeanCurv* (Mean curvature), *NumVert* (Number of vertices), *SurfArea* (Surface area), *ThickAvg* (Average of thickness), and *ThickStd* (Standard deviation of thickness in ROI). Each feature is a single value, then the feature vector for a brain has dimension 68. If combing all features, then the total feature vector for a brain has dimension $68 \times 9 = 612$. All experiments were conducted on a workstation with 3.7 GHz CPU and 16 GB RAM. The computation is automatic, stable and robust without human intervention.

4.1 Feature Visualization

We first visually test the distribution of the signatures and the relation to IQ. We employ the variational autoencoder (VAE) [10] method to compress the conformal welding signature and FreeSurfer feature to the same dimension. VAE is a kind of unsupervised neural network, and there is no need to provide label of IQ to it. Because the input is composed of continuous values, we define the loss function of VAE as

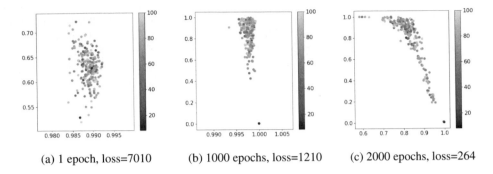

(a) 1 epoch, loss=7010   (b) 1000 epochs, loss=1210   (c) 2000 epochs, loss=264

Fig. 5. The IQ distribution based on encoded conformal welding signature.

$$loss = \sum_{i=1}^{n} (x^{(i)} - \hat{x}^{(i)})^2 + \frac{1}{2}\sum_{j=1}^{J}(1 + \log((\sigma_j^{(i)})^2) - (\mu_j^{(i)})^2 - (\sigma_j^{(i)})^2),$$

where $x^{(i)}$ is the ith real data for each batch and the $\hat{x}^{(i)}$ is the ith output result of the decoder for each batch, μ_j is the jth elements in output of z_{mean} layer for each samples and σ_j is the jth elements in output of z_{log} layer for each samples. In practice, we only use the z_{mean} as the code of the original data. For the training process, all samples are trained in one batch, which can avoid the random error in loss decreasing process of neural network. The VAE is trained with 100 iterations each epoch and the learning rate is 0.00001. Figure 5 shows the distribution of the conformal welding signatures of the whole brain data set with different epochs. Each point in the plot represents a sample, the position is the encoded feature value, and the color encodes the IQ value of the sample as shown in the color bar. We can see that as the loss decreases, the encoding result shows a gradually clustered distribution.

Comparison with FreeSurfer Features. We applied the same method to visualizae the distribution of the traditional features provided by FreeSurfer. Figure 6 demonstrates that the combination of the 9 FreeSurfer features could not give obvious clusters compared to the conformal welding feature. These visualization experiments imply that our geometric features are more closely related to the IQ than those traditional features. To analyze the output of VAE numerically, we used IQ as the group mark to calculate the silhouettes scores [19] of VAEs' outputs, which is a useful metric to evaluate the cluster result. The silhouettes score is defined as

$$s(i) = \frac{a(i) - b(i)}{max\{a(i), b(i)\}},$$

where $a(i)$ is the average distance among samples in the ith group, $b(i)$ is the average distance between samples in the ith group and samples out of the ith group. And here, we use IQ as the group mark, the silhouetes score has the range $[-1, 1]$. The greater silhouettes score denotes the better clustering effect.

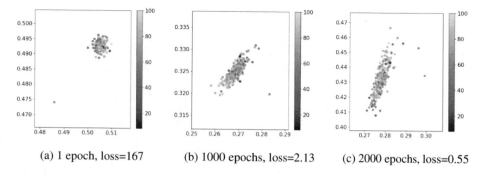

(a) 1 epoch, loss=167   (b) 1000 epochs, loss=2.13   (c) 2000 epochs, loss=0.55

Fig. 6. The IQ distribution based on encoded region features provided by FreeSurfer.

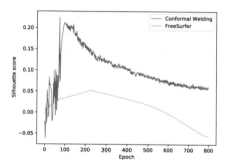

Fig. 7. Silhouette Coefficient comparison between features based on conformal welding signature curves and features provided by FreeSurfer.

Figure 7 shows that as the loss decreases, more unrelated information are involved and the silhouette score drops gradually; the silhouettes score of conformal welding signature becomes higher than FreeSurfer's, which means that the clustering effect of conformal welding signature is stronger. Therefore, conformal welding signature is more suitable than FreeSurfer's feature to classify IQ.

4.2   IQ Classification

We numerically tested the ability of our method to classify the IQs to two groups. In our experiments, to balance the data set and increase the sensitivity of a classifier to the minority class, we used the Synthetic Minority Over-Sampling Technique (SMOTE) [2] for data argumentation. We applied the support vector machine (SVM) with linear kernel function (using LIBSVM, www.csie.ntu.edu. tw/~cjlin/libsvm/) as classifier and the 5-fold cross validation. For all tests, 70% of the whole data set is randomly chosen as the training set to prevent bias (the resting as the testing set). We also computed the receiver operating characteristic curve (ROC) to evaluate the classifier. The classification accuracy rate is 81.44% and the AUC of ROC is 0.86926 (see Fig. 8). This result demonstrates that our signature is effective for IQ classification.

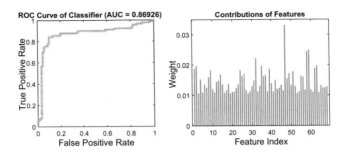

Fig. 8. Classification results. Left: The receiver operating characteristic curve of our classifier; Right: The contribution of each entry (region) in the feature vector.

Biological Finding for IQ. We further tested the contribution of each region to the classification result using the infinite latent feature selection method in [18]. We found that the correlation is significantly positive in right hemisphere (see Fig. 8), which is consistent to the finding in [7]. The summation of the weights for left vs. right hemisphere are 0.47 vs. 0.53. The top three significantly positive features are entries 47 (the medial orbitofrontal, region 14), 58 (the precuneus, region 25) and 59 (the rostral anterior cingulate, region 26), with weights 0.033, 0.025 and 0.026, respectively.

Comparison with Literature. In computation, we compared our method with the existing methods for intelligence classification in terms of the accuracy rate given in Table 1. With the same experimental configuration and data set, our method performs better than the others. In theory, our method based on conformal welding theory has the advantages of theoretic rigor and computational efficiency. The conformal welding signature is achieved by solving *sparse linear* systems, much more efficient than the nonlinear Wasserstein distance method based on optimal mass transport theory [22]. It is invariant to conformal transformations (subsuming rigid motions, scalings and isometry); the Wasserstein distance is invariant under rigid motions and scalings. The current work computes a novel conformal welding signature specially for all atlas regions covering the whole surface and for analyzing intelligence, while the works [13, 24] computed non-intersecting regions of interest for medical image analysis and disease diagnosis.

Applicability and Impact. The conformal welding representation of the brain is fundamental, which can be used to discover the correlations of brain structure with other functionalities, such as well-being, personality, and autism spectrum disorder. It can be explored on other human organs in medical imaging and cognitive neuroscience, such as human faces and colon walls with interest of regions (e.g., abnormality areas).

Table 1. Classification rates of our signature and traditional features.

Method	Rate%
Conformal Welding (ours)	**81.44**
CurvInd	49.31
FoldInd	46.15
GausCurv	48.89
GrayVol	53.11
MeanCurv	60.71
NumVert	48.12
SurfArea	48.55
ThickAvg	73.11
ThickStd	61.20
All 9 above	70.10

5   Conclusion and Future Work

In this work, we proposed to apply conformal welding theory to quantify brain structure and explore its correlation to human intelligence. The conformal welding signature was introduced to represent the cortical structure intrinsically and globally. Experiments on real data set demonstrated the efficiency and efficacy of our method to differentiate brains and discovered more correlation of the brain structure (especially right hemisphere) to intelligence than traditional features. In the future, we will investigate more geometric approaches for brain structure and function correlation analysis along with more other attributes such as age, sex, education, and so on, and explore large data sets by combining deep learning techniques.

References

1. Ashburner, J., Friston, K.J.: Voxel-based morphometry–the methods. NeuroImage **11**(6), 805–821 (2000)
2. Chawla, N.V., Bowyer, K.W., Hall, L.O., Kegelmeyer, W.P.: SMOTE: synthetic minority over-sampling technique. J. Artif. Intell. Res. **16**, 321–357 (2002)
3. Gardiner, F., Lakic, N.: Quasiconformal Teichmüler Theory. American Mathematical Society, Providence (1999)
4. Haier, R.J.: Neuro-intelligence, neuro-metrics and the next phase of brain imaging studies. Intelligence **37**, 121–123 (2009)
5. Haier, R.J., Siegel, B., Tang, C., Abel, L., Buchsbaum, M.S.: Intelligence and changes in regional cerebral glucose metabolic rate following learning. Intelligence **16**(3–4), 415–426 (1992)
6. Hunt, E.: Human Intelligence. Cambridge University Press, Cambridge (2010)
7. Im, K., et al.: Fractal dimension in human cortical surface: multiple regression analysis with cortical thickness, sulcal depth, and folding area. Hum. Brain Mapp. **27**(12), 994–1003 (2006)

8. Jung, R.E., Haier, R.J.: The Parieto-frontal Integration Theory (P-FIT) of intelligence: converging neuroimaging evidence. Behav. Brain Sci. **30**(2), 135–154 (2007). discussion 154–187

9. Karama, S., et al.: Erratum to "positive association between cognitive ability and cortical thickness in a representative us sample of healthy 6 to 18 year-olds". Intelligence **37**(4), 432–442 (2009)

10. Kingma, D.P., Welling, M.: Auto-encoding variational Bayes. arXiv preprint: arXiv:1312.6114 (2013)

11. Luders, E., et al.: Mapping the relationship between cortical convolution and intelligence: effects of gender. Cereb. Cortex **18**(9), 2019–2026 (2007)

12. Luders, E., et al.: Positive correlations between corpus callosum thickness and intelligence. Neuroimage **37**(4), 1457–1464 (2007)

13. Lui, L.M., Zeng, W., Yau, S.-T., Gu, X.: Shape analysis of planar multiply-connected objects using conformal welding. IEEE Trans. Pattern Anal. Mach. Intell. (TPAMI) **36**(7), 1384–1401 (2014)

14. Narr, K.L., et al.: Relationships between IQ and regional cortical gray matter thickness in healthy adults. Cereb. Cortex **17**(9), 2163–2171 (2006)

15. Raven, J., Raven, J.C., Court, J.H.: Raven Manual: Section 4, Advanced Progressive Matrices. Oxford Psychologists Press Ltd., Oxford (1998)

16. Reuter, M., Rosas, H.D., Fischl, B.: Highly accurate inverse consistent registration: a robust approach. NeuroImage **53**(4), 1181–1196 (2010)

17. Reuter, M., Schmansky, N.J., Rosas, H.D., Fischl, B.: Within-subject template estimation for unbiased longitudinal image analysis. NeuroImage **61**(4), 1402–1418 (2012)

18. Roffo, G., Melzi, S., Castellani, U., Vinciarelli, A.: Infinite latent feature selection: a probabilistic latent graph-based ranking approach. In: The IEEE International Conference on Computer Vision (ICCV), October 2017

19. Rousseeuw, P.J.: Silhouettes: a graphical aid to the interpretation and validation of cluster analysis. J. Comput. Appl. Math. **20**, 53–65 (1987)

20. Sharon, E., Mumford, D.: 2D-shape analysis using conformal mapping. In: Proceedings of the IEEE Conference on Computer Vision and Pattern Recognition, pp. 350–357 (2004)

21. Shaw, P., et al.: Intellectual ability and cortical development in children and adolescents. Nature **440**(7084), 676 (2006)

22. Su, Z., Zeng, W., Wang, Y., Lu, Z.-L., Gu, X.: Shape classification using Wasserstein distance for brain morphometry analysis. In: Ourselin, S., Alexander, D.C., Westin, C.-F., Cardoso, M.J. (eds.) IPMI 2015. LNCS, vol. 9123, pp. 411–423. Springer, Cham (2015). https://doi.org/10.1007/978-3-319-19992-4_32

23. Yang, J.-J., et al.: Prediction for human intelligence using morphometric characteristics of cortical surface: partial least square analysis. Neuroscience **246**, 351–361 (2013)

24. Zeng, W., Shi, R., Wang, Y., Yau, S.-T., Gu, X.: Teichmüller shape descriptor and its application to Alzheimer's disease study. Int. J. Comput. Vis. **105**(2), 155–170 (2013)

Learning Graph Cut Class Prototypes for Thigh CT Tissue Identification

Taposh Biswas and Sokratis Makrogiannis$^{(\boxtimes)}$ (iD)

Delaware State University, Dover, DE 19901, USA
tbiswas16@students.desu.edu, smakrogiannis@desu.edu
http://www.miviclab.org

Abstract. Perceptual grouping remains a challenging topic in the fields of image analysis and computer vision. Image segmentation is often formulated as an optimization problem that may be solved by graph partitioning, or variational approaches. The graph cut method has shown wide applicability in various segmentation and object recognition tasks. It approaches image segmentation as a graph partitioning problem. To find the optimal graph partition, graph cut methods minimize an energy function that consists of data and smoothness terms. An advantage of this method is that it can combine local and global visual information to obtain semantic segmentation of objects in the visual scene. In this work, we introduce unsupervised and supervised learning techniques for generating the class prototypes used by graph cuts. Our hypothesis is that computation of accurate statistical priors improves the accuracy of the graph cut solution. We utilize these techniques for tissue identification in the mid-thigh using CT scans. We evaluate the performance of the compared approaches against reference data. Our results show that inclusion of accurate statistical priors produces better delineation than unsupervised learning of the prototypes. In addition, these methods are suitable for tissue identification as they can model multiple tissue types to perform simultaneous segmentation and identification.

1 Introduction

Image segmentation aims to localize objects or other relevant information of an image and produce a meaningful representation. It is a popular research topic of image analysis with many applications in the computer vision and medical imaging domains, such as object recognition and delineation of anatomical structures and tissues. The image segmentation literature is vast, mainly because it is a challenging problem and no universal solution has been found yet. Image segmentation techniques may vary from fundamental gradient-, intensity- and region-based techniques, to advanced modeling, graph-based or statistical learning approaches.

In more recent years, the concept of superpixels has been frequently employed for computing image features in computer vision applications [1, 14, 17]. A superpixel is a cluster of connected pixels with similar features such as color, brightness, texture and proximity. Superpixel methods group pixels according to their

© Springer Nature Switzerland AG 2019
G. Bebis et al. (Eds.): ISVC 2019, LNCS 11844, pp. 381–392, 2019.
https://doi.org/10.1007/978-3-030-33720-9_29

degree of similarity, which can help to reduce the redundancy of visual information and the computational complexity in subsequent image analysis operations
to a significant extent [1]. In graph-based segmentation, an image is represented
by a graphical model. The goal is to find a graph partition, which will optimize
an objective function, or energy that expresses content localization [7–9,12,15].
The normalized cuts method defined a global criterion for partitioning the graph
and the solution was determined using linear algebra techniques. The proposed
criterion expresses similarity within groups and dissimilarity between the different groups [15]. Graph cut (GC) techniques seek a globally optimal result by
energy minimization using Markov Random Field (MRF) modeling and min-
cut/max-flow algorithms [3]. In the recent years these methods have become
very popular and have been applied to computer vision and biomedical imaging applications [5,6,13]. Graph cut segmentation techniques detect objects or
anatomical structures using prototypes of object classes corresponding to the terminal nodes [6,13]. Graph cut methods are not limited to image processing and
computer vision, but they are also well suited for minimizing discrete functions
and could be applied to several optimization problems with certain properties.

In this work, we investigate and evaluate techniques for incorporation of
statistical priors into graph cut-based segmentation and their application to
object detection in generic images and tissue identification in medical images.
We hypothesize that the use of more accurate statistical priors will improve the
segmentation accuracy of graph cuts compared to generic terminal node prototyping techniques such as K-Means clustering [10]. We first describe the graph
cut segmentation. Then we investigate supervised learning techniques using normal distribution models. Finally, we describe the applications of object detection
in generic images and tissue identification in CT scans and evaluate the performance of the developed segmentation methods in these two domains.

Graph cut methods define an appropriate discrete energy function for the
given problem. This is a function of the labels assigned to the graph that determine the segmentation. The energy function includes a term for the smoothness
of the labeling and a term for matching with object prototypes. A graph structure is constructed to represent the image content and the relationships between
the image elements and between each image element and objects. The object
prototypes may be learned by unsupervised or supervised techniques. The goal
is to find the graph labeling that minimizes the energy function. These methods
seek cuts that optimize a graph partition function. The main stages of this model
are outlined in Fig. 1.

1.1   Energy Minimization Using Graph Cuts

In [4], the authors use min-cut/max-flow algorithms to find a binary labeling
that is globally optimal. An energy minimization framework has been used for
finding an estimate of the maximum a posteriori probability of a generalized
Potts model Markov Random Field for binary labeling.

$$E(L) = \sum_{p \in I} D_p(L_p^i) + \lambda \sum_{p,q \in Nb} v_{p,q}(f_p, f_q) \tag{1}$$

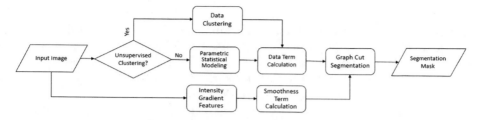

Fig. 1. Flowchart of the graph cut method with supervised or unsupervised learning of the data term.

In the above formula, L is a labeling of the image I, $D_p(L_p^i)$ is a function that calculates the cost of assigning tissue label i to pixel p, $v_{p,q}(f_p, f_q)$ is a smoothness function that calculates the intensity or feature vector dissimilarity between f_p and f_q, and Nb is the set of neighboring pixel pairs in the image I. The data penalty indicates a likelihood function and the interaction potentials force spatial coherence. The partition of the set of vertices of a graph is a graph cut into two disjoint subsets and that is known as s-t cut or source-sink separation.

The min-cut of the weighted graph represents the segmentation that best separates the object from its background. Typical applications of graph cuts to image segmentation differ only in the definitions of $D_p(L_p^i)$ and $v_{p,q}(f_p, f_q)$. The data term costs correspond to the penalty associated to assigning the corresponding label to that pixel. The data term is also known as regional term. In a log-likelihood framework this is given by:

$$D(L_p^i) = -log P(f_p|L_p^i), \tag{2}$$

where p is the pixel index, L_p^i is the class label at p, and $P(f_p|L_p^i)$ is the probability mass function of the observed class. The cost of the smoothness term represents the penalty for not assigning the two neighboring pixels to the same label. It connects each pairwise combination of neighboring pixels (p, q) with a non-negative edge weight determined by a penalty for boundary discontinuity, $V(p, q)$. A frequent selection for the smoothness function is

$$V(p, q) = \exp\left(-\frac{\|f_p - f_q\|_2^2}{2\sigma^2}\right) \frac{1}{\|p - q\|}, \tag{3}$$

where σ is a user-defined parameter and $\|f_p - f_q\|_2$ is the L2 distance of intensity, or other types of feature vectors. An s-t cut partitions the nodes into two subsets. The cost of a cut is equal to the cost of the edges in the cut and no path can be established between source and sink.

2   Learning Parametric Models for Object Detection and Labeling

One of the main advantages of the graph cut method is that it incorporates prior knowledge about the objects of the scene into the energy function that enables it to use global and local information for segmentation. Also, the terminal vertices are used for embedding object information that can be used for identification of an object. This feature is particularly applicable to biomedical image analysis tasks such as delineation of anatomical structures. For the successful delineation of such structures, it is critical to find a good estimate of $P(f_p|L_p^i)$, $i = 1, ..., n$, where n is the number of objects/classes. We estimate the likelihood for a pixel value fitting into a class distribution by use of parametric normal probability model

$$P(f_p|L_p^i) = \frac{1}{2\pi||\sum_i||^{\frac{1}{2}}} exp[-\frac{1}{2}(f_p - M_i)^t \Sigma_i^{-1}(f_p - M_i)]. \tag{4}$$

where $i \in \mathcal{T}$ is the index of tissue type, M_i, C_i are the mean vector and covariance matrix of the tissue type i in the employed domain with dimensionality D. One may use unsupervised or supervised techniques to learn the parameters (M_i, Σ_i). Early techniques utilized unsupervised clustering for automated segmentation or some user input for supervised learning.

In this work, we introduce approaches to learning the parametric models for multiple classes that correspond to object classes, or tissue types.

In the first approach, given only the number of classes, unsupervised learning is used for determining the terminal node prototypes [4]. This approach requires minimal user interaction, as it employs unsupervised learning on the test image to learn the distribution parameters. We employed centroid clustering using K-Means denoted by GC-KMPL, probabilistic estimation of gaussian mixtures denoted by GC-GMPL, and hierarchical clustering using complete linkage criteria denoted by GC-LKPL. A post-labeling step is still required for identifying the class objects using prior knowledge for the centroids. Then the data term is calculated using Eqs. 2 and 4 and graph cuts are applied to minimize the total energy in Eq. 1.

Another approach is to initialize the cluster prototypes using prior class information obtained by reference data and employ unsupervised learners on the test image for convergence to the class prototype. The next step is to calculate the probability distribution parameters and the data term. We denote these approaches by GC-KMCSP (when using K-Means) and GC-GMCSP (when using Gaussian Mixtures).

In our third approach we estimate the normal distribution model parameters $N(M_i, \Sigma_i)$ for each class directly from a training dataset. During training, we calculate the normal distribution model parameters $N(M_i, \Sigma_i)$ for each object type based on the images, the reference masks of the training dataset, or lines drawn by the user. In the testing stage, we use the learned models to segment the test samples. Then we use these priors to calculate the class likelihood values utilizing Eq. 4. This is a maximum likelihood estimation approach to learning the distribution parameters for each class. We denote this approach as graph cuts with statistical priors, GC-SP.

2.1   Centroid Clustering Using K-Means (GC-KM)

This algorithm that seeks to partition the data samples into K disjoint groups by minimizing distances within each cluster, and maximizing pairwise distances between the clusters. The centroid of each cluster in the employed feature space is used for representing the cluster prototype. Assuming a data set with N samples $y_1, y_2, \ldots, y_N$ of dimensionality D, our goal is to assign the samples to K clusters with centroids μ_k, where $k = 1, \ldots, K$. We also use a set of binary indicator variables $r_{(n,k)} \in \{0,1\}$, where $k = 1, \ldots, K$ and $n = 1, \ldots, N$ so that y_n is assigned to the k-th cluster, if and only if $r_{(n,k)} = 1$. The clustering objective is to find the sets $r_{(n,k)}$ and $\{\mu_k\}$, such that a squared error function J is minimized. In K-Means J is defined as:

$$J = \sum_{n=1}^{N} \sum_{k=1}^{K} r_{(n,k)} \|y_n - \mu_k\|^2 \tag{5}$$

The objective function is minimized in two steps: (1) assign samples y_n to the closest centroids μ_k to define $r_{(n,k)}$, then (2) calculate the new centroids by

$$\mu_k = \frac{\sum\limits_{n} r_{(n,k)} y_n}{\sum\limits_{n} r_{(n,k)}}. \tag{6}$$

We applied clustering to the feature space of Hounsfield Unit (HU) samples (pixel intensities). This method groups the unlabeled samples given a pre-defined number of clusters K, and optionally the initial values of μ_k, without requiring a training stage. Each region is assigned to the closest matching tissue by use of the maximum likelihood rule.

2.2   Probabilistic Learning Using Gaussian Mixture Models (GC-GM)

We model the HU samples by a K-component model of Gaussian Mixture Model (GMM) corresponding to the object classes [2]. The normal probability mass parametric model of a voxel intensity sample X in the HU domain for each tissue type denoted by $P(f_p|L_p^i)$ was defined in Eq. 4. The tissue type sample distributions produce the observed Gaussian mixture

$$P(f_p) = \sum_{i \in \mathcal{T}} [a_i \cdot P(f_p|L_p^i, M_i, C_i)]. \tag{7}$$

We used the Expectation-Maximization (E-M) algorithm to fit the Gaussian mixture model and find $P(f_p|L_p^i, M_i, C_i)$ and $a_i, \forall\, i \in \mathcal{T}$. We note that $a_i = P(\omega_i)$, where $P(\omega_i)$ denotes the prior probability of each tissue. Given the tissue probability mass models and the priors, we classified each voxel into a tissue type using likelihood ratio-based discriminant functions.

2.3   Hierarchical Clustering Using Agglomerative Linkage (GC-LK)

We employed hierarchical clustering methods [2] to learn the tissue prototypes that will be used to calculate the data term of the graph cut energy. This method first calculates all pairwise distances between the samples and sorts them in ascending order. It merges the clusters iteratively and recalculates the pairwise distances between the formed clusters at each similarity level. Linkage methods build nested graphs that represent the connectivity of the samples at each similarity level. The final partition is formed by cutting the dendrogram at a specific level of the similarity, or by setting the number of required clusters. The inter-cluster distance function can be single-link, complete-link, or minimum-variance.

In this work we utilized the complete-link distance function that tends to form compact clusters corresponding to the tissue prototypes. We then calculated summary statistics of the tissue prototypes to determine the components of $P(f_p|L_p^i, M_i, C_i)$.

3   Experiments and Discussion

We hypothesize that the use of more accurate statistical priors will improve the segmentation accuracy of graph cuts compared to generic terminal node proto-typing techniques such as centroid clustering [10]. In this section, we evaluate techniques for building and introducing priors into the graph cut optimization method. We compare the performance of graph cuts for segmentation using (i) unsupervised and (ii) supervised learning of statistical priors. We apply these techniques to object segmentation and detection, and tissue identification in the mid-thigh using CT images.

We measure the segmentation accuracy by the Dice similarity coefficient denoted by DSC. DSC quantifies the similarity between two sets of points X, Y:

$$DSC = \frac{2|X \cap Y|}{|X| + |Y|}. \tag{8}$$

3.1   Application: Thigh CT Tissue Identification

The goal of this application is to delineate and identify tissue types from CT scans of the mid-thigh. We randomly sampled a subset of the subjects of Baltimore Longitudinal Study of Aging (BLSA), which is an ongoing, prospective study of longitudinal physical and cognitive changes associated with aging and age-related diseases [16]. Automated tissue identification is a key element in studying anatomical changes of large populations in BLSA and other epidemiological studies [11].

Our subset consists of 66 CT scans and the tissue types to be delineated are muscle, total adipose tissue (TAT), cortical bone, trabecular bone and the air. We segmented these scans using GC with statistical priors (GC-SP), GC cuts with K-Means posterior labeling (GC-KMPL), GC using K-Means with centroid supervised priors (GC-KMCSP), GC with Gaussian mixture modeling and post labeling (GC-GMPL), GC using Gaussian mixture modeling with centroid supervised priors (GC-KMCSP), and GC with linkage and post labeling (GC-LKPL). Then, we compared the segmentation masks produced by the tested algorithms to reference segmentations from the database using the Dice Similarity Coefficient. For every image in the thigh BLSA CT images database there is a reference tissue label map that corresponds to the original image. In Fig. 2 we display an example of the training procedure using reference masks and the statistical distributions that we built for each tissue using the reference data in the training stage. We estimated the tissue log likelihood functions in Eq. 2 from these distributions.

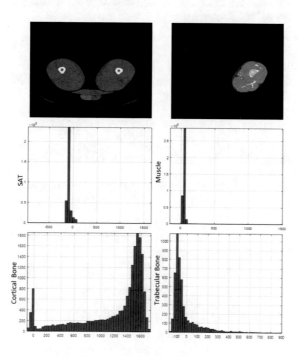

Fig. 2. Tissue intensity distributions (in Hounsfield units) utilized for learning the statistical priors using input images (one example displayed in first row, left side) and reference images (one example displayed in first row, right side).

To evaluate the performance of these methods, we followed a cross-validation approach. We randomly selected 50% of the CT scans for training, and the remaining scans for testing. We calculated the DSC measure for each tissue label to evaluate the delineation accuracy. We repeated this process 10 times to reduce any bias that may originate from the selection of samples.

We show examples of tissue identification results produced by the compared approaches on four test images in Fig. 3. Table 1 contains the DSC summary statistics for each tissue and over all tissues produced by the compared techniques. The DSC over all tissues is the average of the individual-tissue DSC

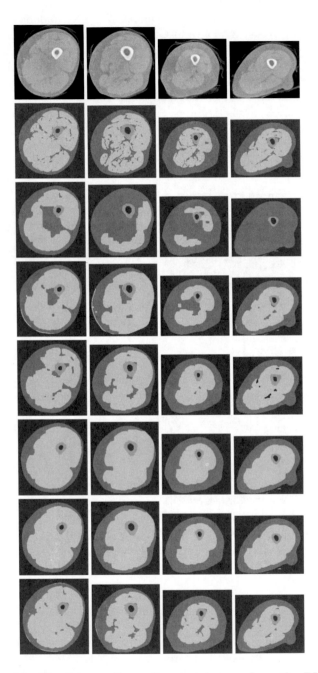

Fig. 3. Tissue identification results on four test images from the BLSA thigh CT dataset. First row: thigh CT scans. Second row: reference tissue label maps. Third to eighth row: results produced by GC-LKPL, GC-GMPL, GC-GMCSP, GC-KMPL, GC-KMCSP, and GC-SP.

Table 1. Summary of tissue-specific and overall DSC scores produced by the evaluated techniques.

Method	Tissue type	DSC Mean %	DSC Std. Dev. %
GC-LKPL	TAT	68.75	2.06
	Muscle	49.58	5.47
	Cortical bone	91.28	1.07
	Trabecular bone	87.09	2.21
	Over all tissues	74.17	2.29
GC-GMPL	TAT	79.96	1.37
	Muscle	89.27	0.44
	Cortical bone	93.01	0.88
	Trabecular bone	93.10	0.51
	Over all tissues	88.84	0.42
GC-GMCSP	TAT	83.00	2.64
	Muscle	84.70	3.42
	Cortical bone	80.39	2.44
	Trabecular bone	71.95	5.21
	Over all tissues	80.01	3.43
GC-KMPL	TAT	85.85	0.93
	Muscle	93.37	0.31
	Cortical bone	93.75	0.69
	Trabecular bone	95.02	0.18
	Over all tissues	92.00	0.52
GC-KMCSP	TAT	85.15	1.28
	Muscle	93.45	0.28
	Cortical bone	93.77	0.95
	Trabecular bone	94.93	0.24
	Over all tissues	91.83	0.42
GC-SP	TAT	90.43	0.76
	Muscle	96.06	0.08
	Cortical bone	92.37	1.03
	Trabecular bone	93.78	0.42
	Over all tissues	93.16	0.27

values and expresses a general criterion for the segmentation accuracy. The quantitative results show that GC-SP produces the highest DSC estimate averaged over all tissues at 93.16%. It also produces the top DSC values for TAT at 90.43% and muscle at 96.06%. GC-KMPL and GC-KMCSP produce almost equal overall DSC scores. GC-KMPL yields the top DSC of 95.02% for trabecular bone, and GC-KMCSP produces the top DSC for cortical bone at 93.77%. GC-LKPL

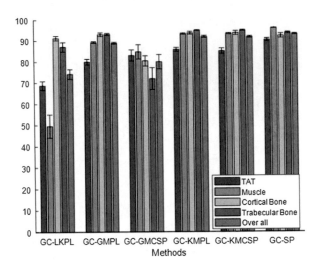

Fig. 4. Segmentation performance chart measured by DSC rates for each tissue and over all tissues.

produced high false positive rate for TAT and muscle, but was able to identify the bone components. Figure 4 illustrates bar graphs of the DSC indices grouped by tissue type. The bar graphs also illustrate the very good overall performance of the above methods.

In Fig. 3, we observe that the delineations produced by GC-SP and GC-GMCSP look more accurate than the others. GC-SP was able to detect inter-muscular adipose tissue with good specificity, i.e. few false positives. However, inter-muscular adipose tissue is difficult to be identified in CT scans, even by semi-manual methods. So, it is difficult to evaluate the detection rate for this tissue. GC-SP also produces more accurate delineation of the TAT-muscle interface than GC-KMPL and GC-KMCSP. Clustering performance was hindered by the significant inequalities of tissue region cardinalities combined with tissue intensity distributions that were statistically difficult to identify. To address these difficulties, we applied piecewise histogram equalization to the test image for all methods that do not use prior knowledge for initialization (GC-LKPL, GC-KMPL and GC-GMPL). At the pre-processing stage, we applied denoising by median filtering to address limitations of SNR originating from the low radiation dose of CT. These operations improved the convergence of the unsupervised learning methods to more accurate solutions. A noteworthy characteristic of these learning approaches is that they may generalize well, even for a limited amount of training data. Therefore, they may be useful for applications with limited training data availability, in contrast to more complex learning methods such as deep networks, for example.

4 Conclusion

In this work, we explored graph cut methods using statistical priors for image segmentation and tissue identification. We proposed methods for introducing supervised learning priors into the energy cost function. We evaluated the segmentation accuracy over 66 mid-thigh CT scans from the clinical BLSA database. The criterion used for evaluating segmentation accuracy was the Dice similarity coefficient. Graph cuts with supervised prior learning, denoted by GC-SP, produced very good segmentation results for generic and medical images. This work can be extended in the following ways: include region-based texture and color features in object and background prototypes, segment different organs and anatomical structures in medical imaging data, develop different objective functions for optimization, and apply graph cuts to region entities instead of pixels to improve segmentation accuracy. Among future plans is a comparison to convolutional neural network approaches.

Acknowledgments. This research was supported by the National Institute of General Medical Sciences of the National Institutes of Health (NIH) under Award Number SC3-GM113754 and by the Intramural Research Program of National Institute on Aging, NIH.

References

1. Achanta, R., Shaji, A., Smith, K., Lucchi, A., Fua, P., Susstrunk, S.: Slic superpixels. IEEE Trans. Pattern Anal. Mach. Intell. **34**(11), 2274–2281 (2012)
2. Bishop, C.M.: Pattern Recognition and Machine Learning. Springer, New York (2006)
3. Boykov, Y., Jolly, M.P.: Interactive graph cuts for optimal boundary & region segmentation of objects in n-d images. In: International Conference on Computer Vision, vol. 1, pp. 105–112 (2001)
4. Boykov, Y., Veksler, O., Zabih, R.: Fast approximate energy minimization via graph cuts. IEEE Trans. Pattern Anal. Mach. Intell. **23**(11), 1222–1239 (2001)
5. Chen, X., Udupa, J.K., Bagci, U., Zhuge, Y., Yao, J.: Medical image segmentation by combining graph cuts and oriented active appearance models. IEEE Trans. Image Process. **21**(4), 2035–2046 (2012)
6. Danek, O., Matula, P.: Graph cuts and approximation of the Euclidean metric on anisotropic grids. In: VISAPP International Conference on Computer Vision Theory and Applications (2010)
7. Felzenszwalb, P.F., Huttenlocher, D.P.: Efficient graph-based image segmentation. Int. J. Comput. Vision **59**(2), 167–181 (2004). https://doi.org/10.1023/B:VISI. 0000022288.19776.77
8. Grady, L.: Random walks for image segmentation. IEEE Trans. Pattern Anal. Mach. Intell. **28**(11), 1768–1783 (2006)
9. Jalled, F.: Object detection using image processing. Moscow Institute of Physics & Technology, Department of Radio Engineering & Cybernetics (2016). Moscow Institute of Physics & Technology, Department of Radio Engineering & Cybernetics Ilia Voronkov, Moscow Institute of Physics & Technology, Department of Radio Engineering & Cybernetics

10. Kanungo, T., Mount, D., Netanyahu, N., Piatko, C., Silverman, R., Wu, A.: An efficient k-means clustering algorithm: analysis and implementation. IEEE Trans. Pattern Anal. Mach. Intell. **24**(7), 881–892 (2002)
11. Makrogiannis, S., Boukari, F., Ferrucci, L.: Automated skeletal tissue quantification in the lower leg using peripheral quantitative computed tomography. Physiol. Meas. **39**(3), 035011 (2018). http://stacks.iop.org/0967-3334/39/i=3/a=035011
12. Makrogiannis, S., Economou, G., Fotopoulos, S., Bourbakis, N.G.: Segmentation of color images using multiscale clustering and graph theoretic region synthesis. IEEE Trans. Syst. Man Cybern. Part A **35**(2), 224–238 (2005)
13. Pednekar, A., Bandekar, A.N., Kakadiaris, I.A., Naghavi, M.: Abdominal fat segmentation using graph cut methods. In: 2005 Seventh IEEE Workshops on Applications of Computer Vision (WACV/MOTION 2005) - Volume 1, vol. 1, pp. 308–315 (2005)
14. Ren, X., Malik, J.: Learning a classification model for segmentation. In: Proceedings of the 9th IEEE International Conference on Computer Vision, pp. 10–17 (2003)
15. Shi, J., Malik, J.: Normalized cuts and image segmentation. IEEE Trans. Pattern Anal. Mach. Intell. **22**(8), 888–905 (2000)
16. Shock, N.W., et al.: Normal Human Aging: The Baltimore Longitudinal Study on Aging. NIH Publication, Washington, D.C. (1984). http://health-equity.pitt.edu/2557/
17. Stutz, D., Hermans, A., Leibe, B.: Superpixels: an evaluation of the state-of-the-art. Comput. Vis. Image Underst. **166**, 1–27 (2017)

Automatic Estimation of Arterial Input Function in Digital Subtraction Angiography

Alexander Liebeskind[2], Adit Deshpande[1], Julie Murakami[1],
and Fabien Scalzo[1(✉)]

[1] Department of Neurology, University of California, Los Angeles (UCLA),
Los Angeles, CA 90095, USA
`fscalzo@mednet.ucla.edu`
[2] Department of Computer Engineering, Columbia University,
New York, NY 10025, USA

Abstract. Estimation of cerebral blood flow (CBF) from digital subtraction angiogram (DSA) is typically obtained through deconvolution of the contrast concentration time-curve with the arterial input function (AIF). Automatic detection of the AIF through analysis of angiograms could expedite this computation and improve its accuracy by allowing fully automated angiogram processing. This optimization is decisive given the significance of CBF modeling in diagnosing and treating cases of acute ischemic stroke, arteriovenous malformation, brain tumor, and other deviations in cerebral or renal perfusion, for example. This study presents an AIF detection model that relies on the identification of the intracranial carotid artery (ICA) through image segmentation. A contrast agent is used to detect the presence of blood flow in the angiogram, which facilitates signal intensity monitoring throughout 20 frames, ultimately allowing us to compute the AIF. When compared to the manually outlined AIF, the predicted model reached an AUROC value of 98.54%. Automatic AIF detection using machine learning methods could therefore provide consistent, reproducible, and accurate results that could quantify CBF and allow physicians to expedite more informed diagnoses to a wide variety of conditions altering cerebral blood flow.

1 Introduction

Digital subtraction angiography (DSA) is the most commonly used imaging technique to assess blood flow characteristics on wide range of vascular diseases. DSA requires injection of a paramagnetic contrast agent, which delineates vessel boundaries by highlighting blood flow. In DSA, the magnitude of the signal intensity at a particular voxel drops in the presence of the paramagnetic contrast agent and thus provides a quantitative measurement of the contrast agent concentration in any given region. However, cerebral blood flow (CBF) in a specific region of brain tissue cannot be estimated based on the contrast agent

© Springer Nature Switzerland AG 2019
G. Bebis et al. (Eds.): ISVC 2019, LNCS 11844, pp. 393–402, 2019.
https://doi.org/10.1007/978-3-030-33720-9_30

concentration curve alone. Instead, this concentration curve must be considered in conjunction with the arterial input function (AIF), a time-dependent curve that characterizes the rate at which the contrast agent enters or leaves the tissue. This study focuses on the ICA as a region of interest, while presenting a machine learning approach to automatically detect the area of interest and compute the arterial input function by monitoring image intensity over time.

CBF is one of the most important parameters related to brain function. Delays in diagnosis of abnormal cerebral blood flow can lead to irreversible neuronal injury, cerebral disfunction [1], and subsequent tissue damage [2]. Accurate estimation of the AIF, a fundamental factor in quantification of CBF, is hence vitally important [3]. Precision in AIF detection (as illustrated in Fig. 1) is also pivotal in assessing CBF: wide AIF selection often results in an artificially high measured CBF, while narrow AIF selection commonly results in an artificially low CBF value, even if the concentration curve is accurate. This significance further stresses the importance of accurate AIF modeling.

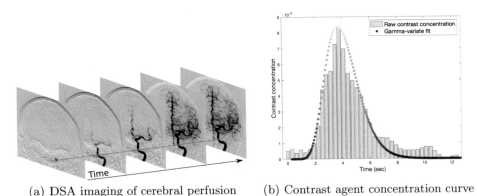

(a) DSA imaging of cerebral perfusion   (b) Contrast agent concentration curve

Fig. 1. Timescaled imaging of the intracranial carotid artery using DSA.

There are numerous factors which characterize a desirable region for AIF measurement. From a general standpoint, a global AIF is commonly computed since the AIF can differ at every region of the brain. More specifically, a particular region favorable for AIF measurement features an early contrast arrival time, strong amplitude, narrow width, and good approximation to the Gaussian gamma-variate function [4]. Early contrast arrival time helps to prevent the selection of a venous circulation. Strong AIF amplitude encourages selection of a major feeding vessel, which is desirable since pixels with small amplitudes may show decreased average pixel resolutions (as compared to the true values) due to the partial volume effect. Narrow width selection, meanwhile, eliminates AIFs that have a wide width due to convolution or dispersion effects, which could prolong the presence of the contrast agent in the pixel. The consideration of gamma-variate fit reduces the presence of noisy spikes.

Beyond estimating the AIF and CBF, machine learning techniques have been applied to a wide variety of biomedical imaging problems, including the detection of cancer cells [5], the prediction of hemorrhage transformation [6] and tissue outcome [7] for stroke victims. If incorporated properly, similar methodologies could improve the AIF detection process, providing valuable automatic inputs to physicians. Currently, manual methods such as Independent Component Analysis [8,9] are tedious and time-consuming, demanding extensive investigation of several pixels within a selected region of interest until a desirable AIF is found. This manual method requires the investigator to be highly trained in AIF identification, and does not have results that are easily reproducible since the selection is subjectively partial to the investigator's bias and prior training. Automated AIF detection would produce consistent and reproducible results that take an average of 72 s less than manual AIF detection according to a study done by the Stanford Stroke Center [10]. This difference is critical given the limited time window available to salvage damaged neurons following alterations in cerebral blood flow, as evidenced by the rapidity of ischemic stroke. In addition to improving time demand, automated AIF detection has been shown to successfully avoid detection of pixels with venous activity, while reliably selecting AIF pixels from major feeding vessels where the global AIF is desirable such as the middle cerebral artery, anterior communicating artery, and posterior communicating artery [11].

This paper introduces a machine learning model for the automatic estimation of the arterial input function using segmentation of the DSA timeseries (2D + time). By creating a model from a number of training examples, computing an estimated AIF, and comparing it to that resulting from a manually generated mask, we are able to analyze the accuracy of the system.

2 Methods

2.1 Overview

The dataset used in this study was comprised of digital subtraction angiograms taken from patients treated for acute ischemic stroke. After the data were acquired, individual mask images specifying the boundaries of the intracranial carotid artery were manually annotated by neurologists. These masks were used to train the initial model on the training set. AIF input curves were shifted in time with respect to the arrival time of the contrast agent in the image, in order to normalize the curves to the same time frame. Following pre-processing, discriminant analysis was performed using the SR-DA algorithm, which mapped input feature vectors to the output space using the training data. This process was repeated for angiograms from each new test patient, which provided predicted characteristic values that were compared to the ground truth values. The accuracy of the model was given by the area under the respective ROC curve.

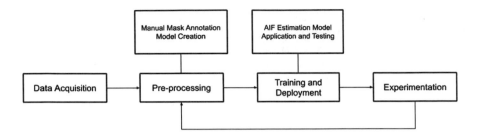

Fig. 2. Machine learning processing pipeline for automatically quantified CBF.

2.2   Dataset

The imaging dataset used in this study to evaluate our framework was collected from patients evaluated at a single, academic comprehensive stroke center and identified with symptoms of acute ischemic stroke. The use of this dataset was approved by the local Institutional Review Board (IRB). Inclusion criteria for this study included: (1) presenting symptoms suggestive of acute stroke, (2) last known well time within six hours at admission, (3) Digital Subtraction Angiography (DSA) of the brain performed at the end of a thrombectomy procedure, (4) final diagnosis of ischemic stroke. A total of 92 patients (median age, 68 years (IQR 53, 79), including 57 males and 35 females, satisfied the above criteria. All patients underwent thrombectomy with various success in revascularization which was determined using the Thrombolysis in Cerebral Infarction (TICI) score. The distribution of TICI scores is as follows: TICI 0 (4 patients), 1 (1 patients), 2a (17 patients), 2b (35 patients), 3 (9 patients). Mechanical clot-retrieval devices include Trevo® (7 patients), MERCI® (17 patients), and Solitaire® (32 patients). The median NIH stroke scale (NIHSS) is 18, IQR 13, 21. The DSA scanning was performed on a Philips Allura Xper FD20® Biplane using a routine timed contrast-bolus passage technique. A manual injection of omnipaque 300 was performed at a dilution of 70% (30% saline) such that 10cc of contrast was administered intravenously at an approximate rate of $5\,\mathrm{cm}^3/\mathrm{s}$. Image acquisition parameters vary across subjects. In the biplane acquisition setting, frames are acquired in an interleaved fashion at two standard viewpoints; anterior-posterior (ap) and lateral. The median number of frames acquired is 20 frames, IQR 17, 22, and the median peak voltage output of 95 Kv, IQR 86, 104. Image size was uniformly 1024 × 1024, though field of view varied (Fig. 2).

2.3   Pre-processing

Manual Annotation. A DSA angiogram was acquired for each patient. Each DSA comprises a series of 20 frames taken over a few seconds. A 2D binary image was established based on the annotation of a clinical researcher in neurology. This mask image was constructed to highlight the intracranial carotid artery (ICA);

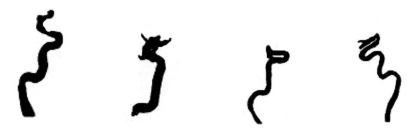

Fig. 3. Illustration of the sample masks that have been created by clinical researchers.

which is the ideal location of the target AIF. A mask image was created for each of the 92 patients. Figure 3 illustrates some examples of masks that were delinated by the clinical researchers and used as part of the training data.

Creating the Model. For each set of patient angiograms, the constructed mask image contained only the intracranial carotid artery. The mask was used to identify the location of data points inside and outside the intracranial carotid artery. Using the location of these set number of points inside and outside the mask, intensity values were obtained for the points in the input training set of DSA images X_{train}. These values were used to train the model on the characteristics of the AIF. Every point had 20 intensity values, each associated with one of the 20 frames of the area taken over time. To account for time as a confounding variable, timing was normalized by shifting all scans according to the contrast agent arrival time. Since the mask explicitly identifies whether the point is within or outside the artery, the learning was supervised by feeding the corresponding Y_{train} value of [0, 1] depending on location inside or outside the mask. Prior to training, 3×3 median filters were also applied to remove the noise and artifacts from each frame of the DSAs.

For each angiogram, a set of image locations were randomly sampled from the image. The first half of these points were located within the ICA, while the latter half were located outside the ICA. In order to better represent the variability in the background to cover both the uniform values and the motion/bone artifacts, points were selected from pre-determined groups based on average intensity. The groups were obtained by dividing the intensity of each DSA into 5 groups based on the following percentile intervals of the non-ICA pixels $[0, 20], [21, 40], [41, 60], [61, 80], [81, 100]$. Uniform, random selection from these groups helped to ensure a balanced and representative dataset of the background class. Information about the x and y coordinates for each point was used and concatenated to the input features. Using this information, a K_{test} kernel was constructed from the training data. The K_{test} kernel was then multiplied by the model of eigenvectors and predicted characteristic values for each test point were derived.

2.4 Training and Deployment

AIF Estimation Model. The SR-DA algorithm [12] has been developed to solve discriminant analysis as a regularized regression problem and was used to classify pixels based on their temporal contrast curve,

$$\alpha = \text{argmin}_\alpha \sum_{i=1}^{n} (\alpha^T x_i - y_i)^2 + \beta ||\alpha||^2 \tag{1}$$

where x_i is the input vector (i.e. histogram), y_i the corresponding HT outcome, α is the eigenvector, and β is the regularization parameter.

To solve this problem (Eq. (1)), the main idea behind SR-DA is to find vectors α that map the input features x to the output y so that samples that are close also produce similar outputs. SR-DA formulates the regularization as follows,

$$\alpha = (XX^T + \delta I)^{-1} X^T y \tag{2}$$

where I is the identity matrix, α is the eigenvector, and $\delta > 0$ the regularization parameter. Interestingly, this formulation can be solved efficiently using a Cholesky decomposition,

$$r = \text{chol}(XX^T + \delta I) \tag{3}$$
$$\alpha = r \backslash (r^T \backslash (X^T y)). \tag{4}$$

SR-KDA [12] generalizes SR-DA to utilize a kernel projection of the data and obtain nonlinearity. Input data samples $x \in X$ are projected onto a high-dimensional space via a Gaussian kernel K,

$$K(i,j) = \exp -||x_i - x_j||^2 / 2\sigma^2 \tag{5}$$

where σ is the standard deviation of the kernel.

Similarly to SR-DA, SR-KDA uses a Cholesky decomposition from the regularized positive definite matrix K and class labels y to obtain vectors α,

$$r = \text{chol}(K + \delta I) \tag{6}$$
$$\alpha = r \backslash (r^T \backslash y). \tag{7}$$

When a new input feature vector, x_{new}, is extracted from a new patient, the likelihood for HT, $\hat{y}_{\text{new}}$, is computed using

$$k(i) = \exp -||x_i - x_{\text{new}}||^2 / 2\sigma^2, i = 1 \ldots n \tag{8}$$
$$\hat{y}_{\text{new}} = \hat{\alpha}^T k \tag{9}$$

where k is the vector resulting from the kernel projection of x_{new} into the kernel space using training data X.

3   Experiments

In order to assess the accuracy of the model, the predicted label values for each point was compared to its respective groundtruth value, using the area under the ROC curve as a measurement of the model's accuracy. ROC curves are typically used to analyze the performance of a binary classifier, taking into account the relationship between the rates of false positives and true positives, as it was the case in this study. The calculated area under the curve therefore yielded an indication of the accuracy of the model. In addition to the ROC curve, we report the prediction-recall curve to ensure the results are not biased due to the possible class imbalance, difference in complexity between the classes in the dataset.

4   Results

Validity of Machine Learning Model. The 10-fold cross validation method was used to test the accuracy of artery detection, by iteratively creating a model from 9/10th of the patients' data. 100 points inside the mask and 100 points outside (total of 200 points per patient) were selected and employed to train the model. Using the resulting data set after cross validation, a set of 16,600 points from the model was compared the results from the known results, using the mask to obtain the labels of the tested points. The most accurate model used Kernel ridge regularization and a Gaussian kernel. A standard threshold-based method was used as baseline method such that 20 thresholds were uniformly generated between the minimum and maximum of the DSA intensity and applied on the first 10 frames of the DSA. From the ROC curves generated, the model's capacity for prediction was concluded functional given an AUROC of 98.54 with a 95% confidence interval of [97.76, 99.32], and area under the precision recall curve of 98.63 with a 95% confidence interval of [97.95, 99.31] (Fig. 4). These results

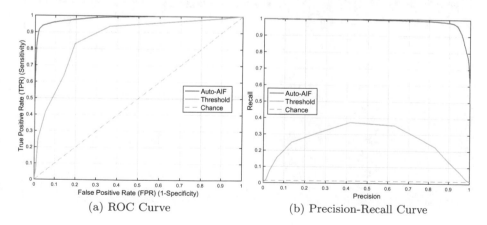

(a) ROC Curve   (b) Precision-Recall Curve

Fig. 4. Results depicting the ability of the Auto-AIF model in detecting the AIF on our dataset.

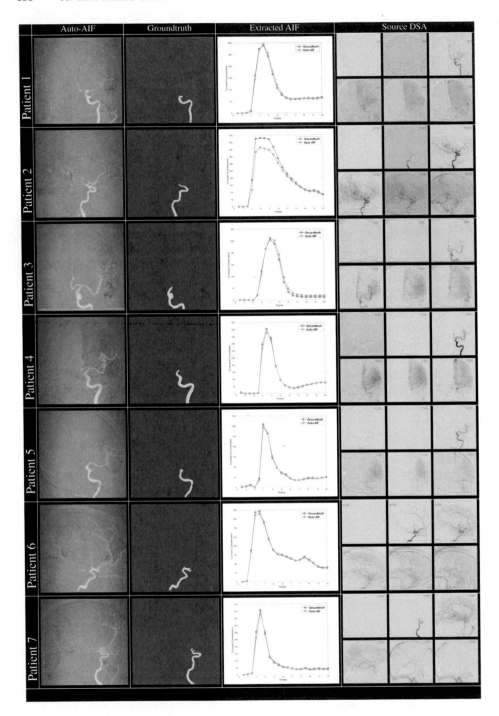

Fig. 5. Illustration of the predictions of our automatic AIF detector (Auto-AIF), groundtruth, the extracted AIF curves, and the source DSA used for the segmentation.

validate the model as a means of accurate arterial detection and highlight the significant improvement when compared to the baseline method (AUC-ROC: 86% and AUC-PR: 26%). As demonstrated by Fig. 5, the machine learning approach successfully automated the AIF selection and ICA detection processes.

5   Discussion

There are a number of upsides to applying machine learning to medical imaging, which is demonstrated by recent growth in novel uses [13]. Machine learning models create a rare reproducibility and consistency in analysis, unparalleled by manual human methods. Given an appropriate dataset and a sufficient number of examples for the system to train under, successful models could easily improve treatment and diagnosis methods. There are a number of considerations in generating these models.

To create such a machine learning model for prediction, the size of the data set is among the first considerations. This study used the data from all but 1/10th of the 92 patients, excluding them for evaluation and repeating the process 10 times. This allowed for a sufficiently large amount of data to create a well-trained model, while simultaneously ensuring proper accuracy validation. Generating the models with such a dataset of training data was fast and took less than 10 min; and is much faster than Deep Learning-based models. Since the model only has to be generated once to use for prediction of AIF in new images, the time to create a model may be disregarded. However, the size of the model also increases when more training data is used. A larger model presents a trade-off between well-fit the data and runtime since a larger dataset improves the accuracy of prediction but also increases the computation time to run prediction on a new model. The well known machine learning problem of overfitting can also arise if the model becomes so well tuned to training set that it fails to generalize.

It is also essential to note that the framework described in this study is able to capture the spatio-temporal signature associated with the location of the AIF. Although the characteristics associated with a good AIF are known (early arrival time, high amplitude, narrow width), and could be used to design heuristics to detect them, our framework demonstrates that they can be learned automatically, and with reasonable efficiency in a data drive fashion. If combined with automatic image registration methods [14,15], the resulting framework could lead to a useful pipeline for the processing of serial changes observed on DSA.

Finally, Deep Learning-based segmentation methods such as spatial transformer networks and fully convolutional neural networks could be considered to improve the results of the framework. These methods will, however, require a much larger number of training data samples.

6   Conclusion

We introduced a machine learning-based model for the automatic extraction of AIF on digital subtraction angiograms. Overall, the use of machine learning models in automating the previously tedious task of generating an arterial input function has been proven to be a viable alternative to manual annotation. This study concluded that automated AIF selection simultaneously improves accuracy and time demand, which could consistently inform physicians on a variety of conditions altering cerebral perfusion. Such improvements to AIF selection could monumentally facilitate estimation of blood flow from angiography.

References

1. Khandelwal, N.: CT perfusion in acute stroke. Indian J. Radiol. Imaging **18**, 281 (2008)
2. Markus, H.: Cerebral perfusion and stroke. J. Neurol. Neurosurg. Psychiatry **75**, 353–361 (2004)
3. Scalzo, F., Liebeskind, D.S.: Perfusion angiography in acute ischemic stroke. Comput. Math. Methods Med. **2016**, 1–14 (2016)
4. Kim, Y.J., et al.: New parametric imaging method with fluorescein angiograms for detecting areas of capillary nonperfusion. Healthc. Inform. Res. **20**, 191–198 (2014)
5. Chen, C., et al.: Deep learning in label-free cell classification. Sci. Rep. **6**, 21471 (2016)
6. Yu, Y., Guo, D., Lou, M., Liebeskind, D., Scalzo, F.: Prediction of hemorrhagic transformation severity in acute stroke from source perfusion MRI. IEEE Trans. Biomed. Eng. **65**, 2058–2065 (2018)
7. Stier, N., Vincent, N., Liebeskind, D., Scalzo, F.: Deep learning of tissue fate features in acute ischemic stroke. In: IEEE BIBM, pp. 1316–1321 (2015)
8. Calamante, F., Mørup, M., Hansen, L.K.: Defining a local arterial input function for perfusion MRI using independent component analysis. Magn. Reson. Med. **52**, 789–797 (2004)
9. Calamante, F.: Arterial input function in perfusion MRI: a comprehensive review. Prog. Nucl. Magn. Reson. Spectrosc. **74**, 1–32 (2013)
10. Mlynash, M., Eyngorn, I., Bammer, R., Moseley, M., Tong, D.C.: Automated method for generating the arterial input function on perfusion-weighted MR imaging: validation in patients with stroke. Am. J. Neuroradiol. **26**, 1479–1486 (2005)
11. Carroll, T.J., Rowley, H.A., Haughton, V.M.: Automatic calculation of the arterial input function for cerebral perfusion imaging with MR imaging 1. Radiology **227**, 593–600 (2003)
12. Cai, D., He, X., Han, J.: Spectral regression for efficient regularized subspace learning. In: ICCV (2007)
13. Wernick, M.N., Yang, Y., Brankov, J.G., Yourganov, G., Strother, S.C.: Machine learning in medical imaging. IEEE Signal Process. Mag. **27**, 25–38 (2010)
14. Tang, A., Scalzo, F.: Similarity metric learning for 2D to 3D registration of brain vasculature. In: Bebis, G., et al. (eds.) ISVC 2016. LNCS, vol. 10072, pp. 3–12. Springer, Cham (2016). https://doi.org/10.1007/978-3-319-50835-1_1
15. Tang, A., Zhang, Z., Scalzo, F.: Automatic registration of serial cerebral angiography: a comparative review. In: Bebis, G., et al. (eds.) ISVC 2018. LNCS, vol. 11241, pp. 3–14. Springer, Cham (2018). https://doi.org/10.1007/978-3-030-03801-4_1

Biometrics

One-Shot-Learning for Visual Lip-Based Biometric Authentication

Carrie Wright$^{(\boxtimes)}$ and Darryl Stewart

Queen's University Belfast, Belfast, N. Ireland
cwright32@qub.ac.uk
https://www.qub.ac.uk/schools/eeecs/

Abstract. Lip-based biometric authentication is the process of verifying an individual's identity based on visual information taken from lips whilst speaking. To date research in this area has involved more traditional approaches and inconsistent results that are difficult to compare. This work aims to push the field forward through the application of deep learning. A deep artificial neural network using spatiotemporal convolutional and bidirectional gated recurrent unit layers is trained end-to-end. For the first time one-shot-learning is applied to lip-based biometric authentication by implementing a siamese network architecture, meaning the model only needs a single prior example in order to authenticate new users. This approach sets a new state-of-the-art performance for lip-based biometric authentication on the XM2VTS dataset and Lausanne protocol with an equal error rate of 0.93% on the evaluation set and a false acceptance rate of 1.07% at a 1% false rejection rate.

Keywords: Lip-based · Biometric authentication · One-shot-learning · Siamese network · XM2VTS

1 Introduction

It is widely accepted that single passwords are not a secure means of authentication and this has led to increased attention for biometric authentication. Biometric authentication is the process for verifying the identity of a person based on a unique personal characteristic or trait. Replacing passwords with a biometric has many benefits; it cannot be forgotten, no one can steal your biometrics and it cannot be transferred to another person. Biometric authentication solutions, such as face recognition and fingerprint scanners have already been deployed on many state-of-the-art devices.

Physiological or behavioural data can be used as a biometric, examples of physiological biometrics include face, fingerprint and iris. Behavioural biometrics differ from physiological biometrics as they measure a behaviour or pattern such as voice, signature or gait. When incorporated into a biometric, liveness detection is used to confirm the user is live and present. Naturally, liveness detection is easier to incorporate into a behavioural biometric, making them more desirable.

© Springer Nature Switzerland AG 2019
G. Bebis et al. (Eds.): ISVC 2019, LNCS 11844, pp. 405–417, 2019.
https://doi.org/10.1007/978-3-030-33720-9_31

Behaviours are generally hard to mimic or replicate, however, they are also more difficult to collect, model and authenticate robustly.

Lip-Based Biometric Authentication (LBBA) involves authenticating an individual based on visual information captured from video data of a speaker's lips while they are talking. Lip-movements for authentication on mobile devices have a lot of potential, especially considering the popularity of mobile devices and laptops. It would require no dedicated hardware like with fingerprint and cannot be spoofed using a single image.

Authentication is a 2 stage process involving an enrollment stage, then authentication against the enrollment data. This process is illustrated in Fig. 1. During the enrollment stage it is important to consider usability, a desirable attribute of using facial recognition or fingerprint biometrics is that users do not need to provide large amounts of data to register.

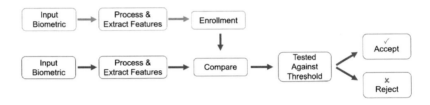

Fig. 1. The 2 stages of biometric authentication. Stage 1, green, is the enrollment phase and stage 2, blue, is the authentication stage. (Color figure online)

To date LBBA has not gained a significant amount of research, especially compared to other biometrics such as face, fingerprint or voice. Section 1.1 reviews the literature in this area, showing that much of the previous research into LBBA is sporadic and inconsistant, with results reported on small or private datasets, and different results metrics making comparison difficult. Section 1.1 also highlights many of the existing approaches require multiple enrollment videos, which could be a potential barrier to adoption.

The aim of this paper is to push the field forward by applying deep learning to improve the performance and usability of LBBA, setting a new state-of-the-art benchmark performance for a large, well known dataset and protocol. A deep Artificial Neural Network (ANN) is trained end-to-end and one-shot-learning applied.

1.1   Existing Publications and Motivation

Previous research into LBBA has stemmed from visual speech recognition and speaker verification. Multiple early publications [3,4,6,9,13,18] on speaker verification included research using visual lip-movements for authentication. These works reported results for the lip-movements as a solo biometric, in addition to their acoustic equivalent and multimodal approaches.

In their speaker verification research [18] explored single and multimodal solutions, using geometric features and dynamic time warping. Results were reported on the XM2VTS dataset. [18] reported an Equal Error Rate (EER) of 14% for lips alone and concluded that information from lips was not competitive with other solo biometrics. However, they also reported that including lip information with other modalities did improve the overall performance in all multimodel combinations investigated.

In [13] they used Hidden Markov Models (HMM) for lip-based speech and speaker recognition. Features were selected from the pixels using Principle Component Analysis (PCA) and Linear Discriminant Analysis (LDA), using the smaller M2VTS dataset. Using only the visual lip-movements, they recorded an EER of 19.7% with the LDA features, which was significantly worse than their acoustic equivalent.

While researching multimodal speaker authentication, [6] also investigated lip-based motion features, created using velocity vectors from 6 regions around the mouth and modelled using Gaussian Mixture Models (GMM). The XM2VTS dataset and Lausanne protocol were used. Results reported a 22% EER on their lip features, and 6% EER on acoustic features. They also reported an improved multimodal result of 2% EER when combining the audio and lip-based features.

Work in [17] used a form of geometric features from visual information for authentication, based on time-series information of points tracked around the lips and the geometric shape of the lips. Results were reported on a 43 person private dataset, achieving a 14.5% False Acceptance Rate (FAR) at a 3% False Rejection Rate (FRR).

All these approaches to LBBA have had limited success, showing that although including visual lip-based information improves performance, lips alone appear weak as a biometric. Results are reported on varying datasets of a wide range of sizes and lack of defined protocols makes comparison difficult.

In [23] they investigated visual lip information as a solo biometric. They used Discrete Cosine Transform (DCT) coefficients and their first and second order derivatives to create features. The features were modelled with GMMs and results reported on the XM2VTS dataset with the Lausanne Protocol. They reported an EER during evaluation of 2.2% and a FAR of 1.7% at a FRR of 3% on the test set. This work showed for the first time that visual information taken from moving lips can achieve comparable accuracy to other single biometric modalities, on a large dataset and known protocol.

LBBA research in [21] divided video data into time steps and categorised it based on the lips at rest, speaking or in transition. The feature representation consisted of 4 different lip properties: (i) shape descriptors calculated from the contour points, (ii) lip texture, (iii) motion vectors of the contour points and (iv) the Local Ordinal Contrast Pattern (LOCP). The features were modelled using HMMs and Support Vector Machines (SVM), and a Universal Background Model (UBM) was used during classification. A private 40 person dataset created for this work was used and a closed-set protocol defined. The small size of the dataset meant during testing there were only 9 registered clients to produce returning client scores. Results were reported separately for the 3 stages (at rest, speaking, transition) and combined, the best reported result was on all stages combined and produced a Half Total Error Rate (HTER) of 1.26%.

Lip information was used when researching identification in [12], where identification differs from authentication as it aims to answer the question 'who out of this dataset is it?'. For this work 20 s RGB video segments containing only the mouth area were used to train an ANN with convolutional and LSTM layers. A 57 person dataset of individuals uttering the digits 0–9 in Chinese was divided into training and testing. The setup mimicked a closed-set protocol and the best reported result was 96.01% accuracy.

[20] proposed fusing face and dynamic visual information from speaker's lips for authentication. For this work they hand engineered features from spatial and temporal information over the frames. The face and lip features were fused using a single layer ANN. For this work the OuluVS corpus was used, which is made up of 20 individuals uttering 10 short phrases 10 times. Results on closed-set tests show, as a single modality, face (83.75%) outperforms lips (71%) but together an improved 93.25% accuracy can be achieved.

From the published literature it can be seen that LBBA using visual information is not a well researched area, which is surprising given the interest in its acoustic equivalent - speaker verification, or its potential for liveness unlike face or fingerprint. Results are still sporadic and frequently reported on evaluation sets, rather than evaluation and test sets. Datasets are often private [11,12,16,17,20,21], making it almost impossible to compare algorithms. Training and reporting results on such small datasets [12,17,20,21] leads to reservations about how scalable the system is, and raises concerns about the possibility of over fitting.

In addition to using a larger, more diverse dataset and defined protocol for comparison of results, there are a number of other considerations for a LBBA solution. Work in [23] currently have the state-of-the-art results on the XM2VTS dataset and Lausanne protocol for LBBA with a 2.2% EER during evaluation and FAR of 1.7% at a FRR of 3% on the test set. In [23] DCT coefficient features were modelled with GMMs. The setup required using 4 videos, each containing 20 digits to create individual GMMs for every individual during the enrollment stage. More recent publications in face recognition [19] and [22], implemented a one-shot-learning solution, where only a single image is required for enrollment during authentication. Both [19] and [22] train deep convolutional neural networks using a siamese network and achieved state-of-the-art results. Results in [19] outperformed human level performance for face recognition.

Drawing from the success of these works, this paper explores the possibility of employing one-shot-learning for LBBA using a siamese network. A one-shot-learning solution would mean authenticating a claimed identity using only one enrollment video. The model trained for this work is referred to as LipAuth. To the best of the authors knowledge, this is the first time one-shot-learning and end-to-end training has been applied to LBBA. In addition this is the first time recurrent convolutional neural networks have been implemented within a siamese network architecture to handle variable length RGB video data for lip-based biometric authentication.

2 Methods

2.1 Siamese Network Overview

A siamese network is used to learn the similarity function between inputs, the architecture consists of two branches, each containing an identical model. See Fig. 2. The similarity function between two inputs is learned by passing each input to one of the branches to obtain a feature embedding for each input. The distance between the feature embeddings is calculated and model weights updated in both arms of the network iden-

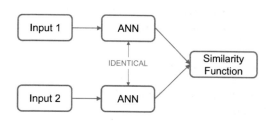

Fig. 2. Siamese Network overview

tically, to minimize the distance between similar inputs and maximise distance between different inputs. The duplicated model weights ensure that if identical inputs are passed to the network they will be mapped to the same feature embedding.

2.2 Artificial Neural Network Layers

STCNN Layers. Spatio-Temporal convolution is a modification of 2D convolution typically used in CNNs. To process video data STCNNs include an additional summation over time. For an input video $\mathbf{x} \in \mathbb{R}^{C \times T \times W \times H}$ and a STCNN layer with C' kernels of size $k_t \times k_w \times k_h$, the output volume is computed as:

$$[stconv\,(\mathbf{x}, \mathbf{w})]_{c'tij} = \sum_{c=1}^{C} \sum_{t'=1}^{T} \sum_{i'=1}^{W} \sum_{j'=1}^{H} w_{c'ct'i'j'} x_{c,t+t',i+i',j+j'} \tag{1}$$

where x_{ctij} is the pixel at location i, j in the cth channel of the video frame at timestep t and $w_{c'ct'i'j'}$ indexes the STCNN layer weights. The equation above ignores the bias and assumes both a stride of 1 and zero padding of frames when $i + i'$ or $j + j'$ are greater than W or H respectively.

Bi-directional Gated Recurrent Units Layer. The RNN portion of the LipNet architecture uses GRU layers [5] formulated as:

$$\Gamma_r \quad = \quad \sigma \left(\mathbf{W}_r \left[\mathbf{c}^{\langle t-1 \rangle}, \quad \mathbf{x}^{\langle t \rangle} \right] + \mathbf{b}_r \right) \tag{2}$$

$$\tilde{\mathbf{c}}^{\langle t \rangle} \quad = \quad \tanh \left(\mathbf{W}_c \left[\Gamma_r \bullet \mathbf{c}^{\langle t-1 \rangle}, \quad \mathbf{x}^t \right] + \mathbf{b}_c \right) \tag{3}$$

$$\Gamma_u \quad = \quad \sigma \left(\mathbf{W}_u \left[\mathbf{c}^{\langle t-1 \rangle}, \quad \mathbf{x}^{\langle t \rangle} \right] + \mathbf{b}_u \right) \tag{4}$$

$$\mathbf{c}^{\langle t \rangle} \quad = \quad \Gamma_u \bullet \tilde{\mathbf{c}}^{\langle t \rangle} + (1 - \Gamma_u) \bullet \mathbf{c}^{\langle t-1 \rangle} \tag{5}$$

where $\mathbf{x}^{\langle t \rangle}$ is the output of the STCNN, $\mathbf{c}^{\langle t-1 \rangle}$ is the previous timestep's activations and $\sigma(\mathbf{z}) = \frac{1}{(1+e^{(-z)})}$. $[\mathbf{W}_r, \mathbf{b}_r]$ and $[\mathbf{W}_u, \mathbf{b}_u]$ denote the parameters of the reset and update gates. A bi-GRU [7] is used to take advantage of information contained in all video frames, not just previous frames.

2.3   Loss Function

There are 2 popular loss functions that are suitable for this task, Binary Cross Entropy Loss (BCE) or Triplet Loss.

Binary Cross Entropy Loss Function. The BCE loss function is used when comparing 2 inputs at a time. When inputs are from the same class the true label will be $y = 1$, else $y = 0$. The loss function $J(y, \hat{y})$ is calculated using:

$$J(y, \hat{y}) \quad = \quad -\frac{1}{m} \sum_{i=1}^{m} (y_i \log(\hat{y}_i) + (1 - y_i) log(1 - \hat{y}_i)) \tag{6}$$

Where the loss is an average of the errors between the predicted labels, $\hat{y}$, and the actual labels y. The predicted labels are represented by the sigmoid of the distance: $\sigma \left(d \left(\mathbf{x}^{(i)}, \mathbf{x}^{(j)} \right) \right)$.

Triplet Loss Function. The triplet loss function differs from the BCE loss function in that the network is passed 3 examples at a time. During training the network described in Fig. 2 has an additional third arm, with another identical copy of the model. Instead of passing the network examples in pairs, the network is trained by passing it triplets where a triplet contains a positive pair and an additional negative example. One of the triplets is the **anchor**, A, and every triplet contains a **positive**, P, and **negative**, N, example. The triplet loss function is defined as:

$$J(y, \hat{y}) = \quad -\frac{1}{m} \sum_{i=1}^{m} \max(d(\mathbf{A}, \mathbf{P}) - d(\mathbf{A}, \mathbf{N}) + \alpha, \quad 0) \tag{7}$$

where a margin α, is the minimum distance between the positive and negative pair that the network tries to satisfy. If the triplet used as a training example is 'too easy', it will have no contribution to the loss and not have any impact on the weight updates, hence the model cannot learn from it. There are 3 groupings of triplets to select from when training:

1. *Easy Triplets*: refers to those which do not contribute to the loss because the positive is very similar to the anchor and the negative is extremely unlike the anchor, therefore: $d(\mathbf{A}, \mathbf{P}) + \alpha < d(\mathbf{A}, \mathbf{N})$ so the loss will be 0.
2. *Semi-Hard Triplets*: are those for which the positive is still closer to the anchor than the negative, but produce a positive loss because the negative falls within the margin: $d(\mathbf{A}, \mathbf{P}) < d(\mathbf{A}, \mathbf{N}) < d(\mathbf{A}, \mathbf{P}) + \alpha$.
3. *Hard Triplets*: refers to triplets where the negative example is more similar to the anchor than the positive example: $d(\mathbf{A}, \mathbf{P}) > d(\mathbf{A}, \mathbf{N})$

2.4   Selecting Training Data

The selection of pairs or triplets used during training has been investigated for both triplet loss and BCE loss. [10] trained a state-of-the-art model for character recognition using randomly sampled triplets, whereas for face recognition [19] trained using only semi-hard triplets. In [19] it was found that when triplets were randomly sampled only a few contributed to the loss and therefore the model took longer to converge, whereas using only the hard triplets caused the model to fail to converge. Work in [1] on person re-identification trained their model using BCE and found a 2:1 ratio of the negative to positive samples, followed by fine tuning the final layers using only hard pairs was optimal.

It is also worth noting when training a siamese network it can be computationally expensive and slow compared to other architectures, because the pairs/triplets need selected each time after updating the network weights as the embeddings of the inputs will have changed with each update.

3   Dataset and Protocol

The XM2VTS dataset [15] was used for the work in this paper. The XM2VTS is a commonly used because of its size, availability and diversity. The dataset contains video data of 295 individuals recorded over 4 months in 4 separate sessions. The time frame between sessions makes the dataset particularly desirable for authentication tasks as it captures general changes in appearance over time. During each session full face audio-visual video data was collected of each individual speaking a 20 digit sequence; '0123456789 5069281374'. Each speaker uttered the sequence 2 times during each session, producing 8 videos per person and 2,360 available videos. Additional video data was captured as part of the XM2VTS but only the digit sequence video data was used in this work. All XM2VTS videos were captured in a well lit up room, with minimal background noise, a blue background and recorded and 25 frames per second.

The XM2VTS is accompanied by the Lausanne Protocol [14]. Configuration II of the protocol was used for this work. The Lausanne protocol is a closed-set protocol because all users are enrolled during training and the protocol does not take new users into consideration during evaluation and testing.

For this work the XM2VTS was cropped to only contain the lips and surrounding mouth area using open-source library, DLib [8].

Training data contains 4 videos per individual, this provided 6 combinations of anchor-positive per person, with $200 \times 6 = 1,200$ postive examples in training. As the pool for choosing negative examples was significantly greater, it was decided to match the number of anchor-positives and use 1,200 anchor-negatives.

During evaluation the anchor videos were selected from the training data, and the positive examples were selected from the evaluation data. With 4 anchors per person and 2 evaluation videos, there were 8 positive videos per individual. This produced $200 \times 8 = 1,600$ positive examples during evaluation. As it is a closed-set evaluation no new anchor videos were added. Imposter tests during evaluation involved testing all 800 anchor videos against all available evaluation videos, where imposters-only contribute $(8 \times 25 \times 800 \text{anchors}) = 160,000$ imposter tests, and returning clients contribute $(2 \times 200 \times 800 \text{anchors}) - 1,600 = 318,400$ imposter tests. This results in **478,400** imposter tests and **1,600** client tests during evaluation.

During testing there are 2 videos per individual. As in evaluation, these 400 videos will produce the same number of anchor-positive examples (1,600) and contribute 318,400 imposter tests. The new imposters-only will contribute an additional $(8 \times 70 \times 800 \text{anchors}) = 448,000$ imposter tests. This results in **761,400** imposter tests and **1,600** client tests during the test stage.

4   Experiments and Discussion

For each branch of the siamese network the model architecture selected was inspired by work in LipNet [2]. LipNet is a deep ANN designed for visual speech recognition. The LipNet model contains $3 \times$ STCNN layers each directly followed with a max pooling layer, and $2 \times$ Bi-GRU layers each with 128 neurons. LipNet's architecture has successfully shown it can handle video data containing only the lips and mouth area, however it was optimised for speaker independant visual lip reading. The aim of the model and optimised weights developed for this work, LipAuth, is to model the uniqueness within the lip movements. Preliminary experiments using only a subset of the available training data were carried out to fine tune the model hyperparameters. This includes dropout, the loss function and initialization. Following the preliminary experiments, LipAuth was trained using all available XM2VTS training data as in the Lausanne protocol.

4.1   Preliminary Experiments

Access was provided to a Nvidia-GPU graphics card, GRID M60-8Q, with 8 GB RAM. The GPU did not provide enough memory for batch training so the model was trained by showing it a single triplet at a time and updating the weights after each triplet. An epoch was considered finished after a full pass of all triplets.

A subsample of the available training and evaluation data was selected and used for preliminary experiments to fine tune the model hyperparameters. If the model struggled to fit the subset of training an evaluation data then it suggests it would not have been suitable for a larger dataset.

For the preliminary experiments the first 30 individuals from the training set were used as a training set, along with the first 10 individuals in the evaluation set. The subset of the data produced 180 anchor-positive pairs for training. The aim of the preliminary experiments was:

- Confirm how LipAuth should be initialized. The LipNet weights might not be useful given LipNet was optimised for a different task.
- Select between the BCE and triplet loss functions.
- Decide if dropout should be removed from the architecture as the aim of LipAuth is to model the uniqueness within individual's lip movements.

Results from the preliminary experiments are shown in Fig. 3. Training data for both loss functions was selected beginning with all 180 anchor-positive pairs, then selecting a negative for each anchor. With BCE the pairs are shown to the model one at a time, and 1 triplet at a time with the triplet loss. Semi-Hard and Easy (SH+E) negative examples were chosen.

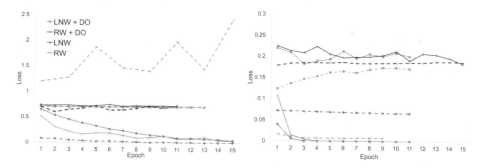

Fig. 3. Loss for the models trained for the preliminary experiments. On the left the figure shows the results from the BCE loss function, and on the right is the triplet loss function. Solid lines show the loss on the training data and dashed lines shows the loss on the evaluation set. LNW = Initialized with LipNet weights, RW = Initialized with Randomised Weights, DO = dropout.

Figure 3 shows the training loss (solid lines) and evaluation loss (dashed lines) for the preliminary experiments. The figure on the left shows models trained with the BCE loss function, and triplet loss function on the right. It can be clearly seen for both loss functions, including dropout prevents the model from making useful updates as the loss remains fairly constant. The model initialized with LipNet weights converged and did not appear to overfit, however, the model initialized with randomised weights overfit the training data. With the triplet loss function the model initialized with LipNet weights overfit the training data and as the training loss dropped to zero it remained overfit. The model trained with the triplet loss, with zero dropout and randomly initialized weights performed the best in the preliminary experiments, the model converged quickly and it did not overfit, these hyperparameters were used to train LipAuth with all available training data.

4.2   Results and Discussions

LipAuth was trained using SH+E triplets with a learning rate of 1×10^{-5}, the triplet loss function, zero dropout, and LipNet architecture. There were 1,600 available anchor-positive pairs for training, all anchor positives were used to generate triplets.

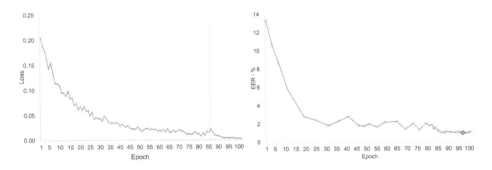

Fig. 4. Training LipAuth. Left figure shows the training loss. The dashed line marks where the learning rate was dropped from 1×10^{-5} to 1×10^{-6}, at epoch 86. The figure on the right shows the EER on the evaluation set. The yellow diamond marks the lowest EER achieved on the evaluation set, 0.93% at epoch 99. (Color figure online)

Figure 4 shows a plot of the training loss on the left, and on the right the evaluation EER set during training. From the figure, the model converged to approximately 2% by epoch 30, after this the model was trained for a further 55 epochs and the evaluation EER did not drop below 1.18%. At epoch 85 the learning rate was reduced to 1×10^{-6} as the training loss appeared to have plateaued. The model was trained for a further 20 epochs at this lower learning rate and achieved a minimum EER of 0.93% at epoch 99. The weights from epoch 99 were used for the LipAuth model to calculate results on the unseen test set.

The LipAuth model produced an EER on the unseen test set of 1.03% and a FAR of 1.07% at a 1% FRR. If the threshold was set to only accept 1% of imposters (FAR=1%), then the FRR=1.09%. This 1.09% FRR equates to 15 returning individual tests that did not successfully log in, 14 of which were from 2 individuals. Each individual had 4 anchor videos and 2 authentication tests, producing 8 attempted logins per person. The 2 problematic individuals: 366 and 369, could not login 7 times each. From reviewing the videos, one individual was male, the other female and there was no facial hair or striking differences between sessions. However, there did appear to be some jitter from the tracking and cropping of these videos caused by the users moving their head while speaking.

Figure 5 shows the FRR against the FAR as the threshold is varied. If the requested authentication application required an extremely secure setup where no imposters could login (0% FAR), then the FRR would be 7.41%.

These results set a new state-of-the-art for lip-based authentication on the XM2VTS dataset. The previous state-of-the-art [23] achieved 2.2% EER on the evaluation set and a FAR = 1.7% at a FRR = 3.0% using the same dataset and protocol. If the LipAuth threshold is set to a FRR = 3% it achieves 0.25% FAR. The LipAuth results also compare very favourably to work in [12], who used an ANN with LSTM layers for lip-based identification and achieved an accuracy of 96.01%. A single layer ANN was trained in [20], where they reported 71% accuracy, and 93.25% accuracy on lips and face combined. In addition, both these works used significantly smaller datasets of 57 and 20 individuals respectively. See Table 1 for comparison of results.

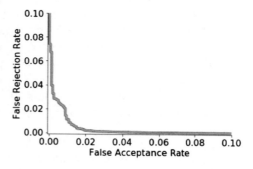

Fig. 5. Results of the LipAuth model on the unseen test set. FRR against the FAR as the threshold for logging in varies.

Table 1. The table shows the results of previous authentication/identification publications using visual lip-based information only and dataset used.

Paper	Dataset	Task	Metric	Result
[18]	XM2VTS, 295	Authentication	EER	14%
[13]	M2VTS, 36	Authentication	EER	19.7%
[6]	private, 43	Authentication	FAR@ 3% FRR	14.5%
[17]	private, 40	Authentication	HTER	1.26%
[23]	XM2VTS, 295	Authentication	FAR@ 3% FRR	1.7%
[12]	private, 57	Identification	Accuracy	96.01%
[20]	OuluVS, 20	Identification	Accuracy	71%
LipAuth	XM2VTS, 295	Authentication	**FAR@ 3% FRR**	**0.25%**
LipAuth	XM2VTS, 295	Authentication	**EER**	**1.03%**

5 Conclusions and Future Work

The work in this paper showed for the first time that ANNs can be successfully applied to LBBA, in particular recurrent convolutional neural networks with

STCNN and Bi-GRU layers. This work explored the application of a siamese network architecture, trained end-to-end for one-shot LBBA at test time. The network trained, LipAuth, and handled variable length RGB video data. Preliminary experiments showed the effects of dropout, pre-trained weights and the training loss function. It was discovered that selecting training data in triplets, where a triplet involves an anchor-positive-negative, and trained with the triplet loss function outperformed training on pairs with the binary cross-entropy loss function. The final LipAuth network was randomly initialized and contained zero dropout.

LipAuth was trained using XM2VTS data. On the Lausanne protocol evaluation and test set LipAuth achieved state-of-the-art performance with an EER = 0.93%, and FAR of 1.07% at a 1% FRR, outperforming the GMM-UBM setup which was previously state-of-the-art for lip-based authentication using the same dataset and protocol. In addition, LipAuth was designed to implement a one-shot-learning approach meaning only one previous example is required for enrollment, whereas the previous state-of-art approach was dependent on multiple videos for each individual.

Although these results show promise, future work is needed to better understand how the performance would be affected with real-world challenges. Future work includes testing with an open-set protocol, exploring real-world datasets with a variety of lighting conditions and diverse content.

References

1. Ahmed, E., Jones, M., Marks, T.K.: An improved deep learning architecture for person re-identification. In: 2015 IEEE Conference on Computer Vision and Pattern Recognition (CVPR), pp. 3908–3916, June 2015. https://doi.org/10.1109/CVPR.2015.7299016
2. Assael, Y.M., Shillingford, B., Whiteson, S., de Freitas, N.: Lipnet: sentence-level lipreading. CoRR abs/1611.01599 (2016). http://arxiv.org/abs/1611.01599
3. Brand, J.: Visual speech for speaker recognition and robust face detection. Ph.D. thesis, University of Wales, Swansea, UK (2001)
4. Cetingul, H.E., Yemez, Y., Erzin, E., Tekalp, A.M.: Discriminative analysis of lip motion features for speaker identification and speech-reading. Trans. Img. Proc. **15**(10), 2879–2891 (2006). https://doi.org/10.1109/TIP.2006.877528
5. Chung, J., Gulcehre, C., Cho, K., Bengio, Y.: Empirical evaluation of gated recurrent neural networks on sequence modeling. CoRR abs/1412.3555 (2014)
6. Faraj, M., Bigun, J.: Motion features from lip movement for person authentication. In: 2006 18th International Conference on Pattern Recognition, ICPR 2006, vol. 3, pp. 1059–1062 (2006). https://doi.org/10.1109/ICPR.2006.814
7. Graves, A., Schmidhuber, J.: Framewise phoneme classification with bidirectional LSTM networks. In: Proceedings 2005 IEEE International Joint Conference on Neural Networks, vol. 4, pp. 2047–2052, July 2005. https://doi.org/10.1109/IJCNN.2005.1556215
8. Kazemi, V., Sullivan, J.: One millisecond face alignment with an ensemble of regression trees. In: 2014 IEEE Conference on Computer Vision and Pattern Recognition, pp. 1867–1874, June 2014

9. Kittler, J., Li, Y.P., Matas, J., Sánchez, M.U.R.: Lip-shape dependent face verification. In: Bigün, J., Chollet, G., Borgefors, G. (eds.) AVBPA 1997. LNCS, vol. 1206, pp. 61–68. Springer, Heidelberg (1997). https://doi.org/10.1007/BFb0015980
10. Koch, G., Zemel, R., Salakhutdinov, R.: Siamese neural networks for one-shot image recognition. In: ICML deep learning workshop, vol. 2 (2015)
11. Lu, L., et al.: Lip reading-based user authentication through acoustic sensing on smartphones. IEEE/ACM Trans. Networking **27**(1), 447–460 (2019). https://doi.org/10.1109/TNET.2019.2891733
12. Lu, Z., Wu, X., He, R.: Person identification from lip texture analysis. In: 2016 IEEE International Conference on Digital Signal Processing (DSP), pp. 472–476, October 2016. https://doi.org/10.1109/ICDSP.2016.7868602
13. Lucey, S.: An evaluation of visual speech features for the tasks of speech and speaker recognition. In: Kittler, J., Nixon, M.S. (eds.) AVBPA 2003. LNCS, vol. 2688, pp. 260–267. Springer, Heidelberg (2003). https://doi.org/10.1007/3-540-44887-X_31
14. Luettin, J., Maître, G.: Evaluation protocol for the extended M2VTS database (XM2VTSDB). Idiap-Com Idiap-Com-05-1998, IDIAP (1998)
15. Messer, K., Matas, J., Kittler, J., Jonsson, K.: Xm2vtsdb: the extended m2vts database. In: In Second International Conference on Audio and Video-based Biometric Person Authentication, pp. 72–77 (1999)
16. Morikawa, S., Ito, S., Ito, M., Fukumi, M.: Personal authentication by lips EMG using dry electrode and CNN. In: 2018 IEEE International Conference on Internet of Things and Intelligence System (IOTAIS), pp. 180–183, November 2018. https://doi.org/10.1109/IOTAIS.2018.8600859
17. Nakata, T., Kashima, M., Sato, K., Watanabe, M.: Lip-sync personal authentication system using movement feature of lip. In: 2013 International Conference on Biometrics and Kansei Engineering (ICBAKE), pp. 273–276, July 2013. https://doi.org/10.1109/ICBAKE.2013.53
18. Sanchez, M.U.R.: Aspects of facial biometrics for verification of personal identity. Ph.D. thesis, University of Surrey, Guilford, UK (2000)
19. Schroff, F., Kalenichenko, D., Philbin, J.: Facenet: a unified embedding for face recognition and clustering. CoRR abs/1503.03832 (2015). http://arxiv.org/abs/1503.03832
20. Shang, D., Zhang, X., Xu, X.: Face and lip-reading authentication system based on android smart phones. In: 2018 Chinese Automation Congress (CAC), pp. 4178–4182, November 2018. https://doi.org/10.1109/CAC.2018.8623298
21. Shi, X., Wang, S., Lai, J.: Visual speaker authentication by ensemble learning over static and dynamic lip details. In: 2016 IEEE International Conference on Image Processing (ICIP), pp. 3942–3946, September 2016. https://doi.org/10.1109/ICIP.2016.7533099
22. Taigman, Y., Yang, M., Ranzato, M., Wolf, L.: Deepface: closing the gap to human-level performance in face verification. In: The IEEE Conference on Computer Vision and Pattern Recognition (CVPR), June 2014
23. Wright, C., Stewart, D., Miller, P., Campbell-West, F.: Investigation into DCT feature selection for visual lip-based biometric authentication. In: Dahyot, R., Lacey, G., Dawson-Howe, K., Pitié, F., Moloney, D. (eds.) Irish Machine Vision & Image Processing Conference Proceedings 2015, pp. 11–18. Irish Pattern Recognition & Classification Society, Dublin, Ireland (2015), winner of Best Student Paper Award

Age Group and Gender Classification of Unconstrained Faces

Olatunbosun Agbo-Ajala and Serestina Viriri[✉]

School of Mathematics, Statistics and Computer, University of KwaZulu-Natal,
Durban, South Africa
viriris@ukzn.ac.za

Abstract. Age and Gender classification of unconstrained imaging conditions has attracted an increased recognition as it is applicable in many real-world applications. Recent deep learning-based methods have shown encouraging performance in this field. We, therefore, propose an end-to-end deep learning-based method for robust age group and gender classification of unconstrained images. Particularly, we address the estimations problem with a classification based model that treats age value as a separate class and an independent label. The proposed deep convolutional neural network model learns the relevant informative age and gender representations directly from the image pixel. Technically, the model is first pre-trained on large-scale IMDb-WIKI facial aging dataset, and then fine-tuned on MORPH-II, another large-scale facial aging dataset to learn, and pick up the bias and particularities of each dataset. Finally, it is fine-tuned on the original dataset (OIU-Adience benchmark) with gender and age group labels. The experimental results when analyzed for estimation accuracy on OIU-Adience dataset, show that our model obtains the state-of-the-art performance in both age group and gender classification with an exact and one-off accuracy of 83.1% and 93.8% on age, and also an exact accuracy of 96.2% on gender.

Keywords: Adience · Age estimation · Face images · Gender classification

1 Introduction

Age and gender classification play a very important role in social interactions [10], and this has attracted more academia and industry attention. It is particularly useful in many real-world applications, such as access control [16], human-computer interaction [2], law enforcement [24], surveillance [8] etc.

The ability to predict age and gender correctly and reliably from unconstrained faces is yet to meet the requirements of commercial applications [19]. Over the past years, a lot of methods have been proposed to solve the classifications problem; many of those methods are handcrafted which manually engineer the facial features from the face. However, those manually-designed features-based methods [4,9,11,14,27], perform unsatisfactorily on recent benchmarks

© Springer Nature Switzerland AG 2019
G. Bebis et al. (Eds.): ISVC 2019, LNCS 11844, pp. 418–429, 2019.
https://doi.org/10.1007/978-3-030-33720-9_32

of unconstrained images (especially from OIU-Adience dataset). Those methods were designed mainly for classifying constrained age and gender tasks, therefore not suitable for real-world and practical applications containing unconstrained images.

In recent years, deep learning with Convolutional Neural Networks (CNN), have proven to be effective in face recognition fields, where it achieved state-of-the-art performance with its good feature extraction technique [12,13,28]. As a result of these achievements, CNN has been introduced to predict the age group and gender of unconstrained real-world faces, and remarkable performance has been obtained with improved classification accuracy. Therefore, in this paper, we propose a deep CNN design with classification-based loss function for age group and gender classification of uncontrained faces. The end-to-end CNN-based architecture, comprises of two stages which include image preprocessing (face detection and face alignment) and CNN-based feature extraction and estimations. Figure 1 displays the pipeline of the proposed model. The contributions of this paper are highlighted as follows:

1. We propose a novel end-to-end CNN-based learning model for age group and gender estimation of uncontrained faces using a classification-based loss function as training targets in deep CNN models.
2. We show that pretraining the model on IMDb-WIKI dataset, to conform to face image contents and then tuned on the training portion of both MORPH-II and OIU-Adience, contributes to the prediction ability of the model.
3. We employ in our design, a robust open-source image preprocessing algorithm that is easily extensible and adaptable, which produce a real-time display on unconstrained real-world images.
4. We evaluate the performance of the proposed design and compare with the current approaches on OIU-Adience benchmark datasets for age and gender classification. Our experimental results demonstrate significant improvement compared with the state-of-the-art.

The remainder of this work is arranged as follows: Sect. 2 briefly reviews the previous works in age and gender classification, while Sect. 3 describes the proposed approach. Experimental results and discussion are described in Sect. 4. Finally, we make a conclusion and present future work in Sect. 5.

2   Related Works

In the past years, several numbers of methods have been proposed to solve age and gender classification problem. Some of the early methods for the estimations were handcrafted, that manually engineer the facial features from the face. Those hand-engineered methods focus more on constrained images that were taken from controlled imaging conditions; only a few of those manually-designed method study age and gender classification of face images from unconstrained real-world environments. To mention a few, Fu and Huang [9] used multiple linear regression on the discriminative aging manifold of facial images. Yan et al. [27]

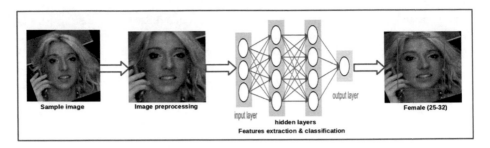

Fig. 1. The pipeline of the proposed method for age group and gender classification.

combined Spatially Flexible Patch (SFP) and Gaussian Mixture Model (GMM) for the estimation task. Gao and Ai [11] proposed a facial age estimation of consumers images with Gabor feature, and Linear Discriminant Analysis (LDA) classifiers. Dib and El-Saban [4] combined Bio-Inspired Features (BIF), and Active Shape Model (ASM) to solve age estimation task. Guowang and Guo [15] used Kernel Partial Least Squares Regression (KPLS) for age, gender, and ethnicity estimation task on MORPH-II dataset. However, all of these methods are only suitable and effective on constrained imaging conditions; they can not handle the unconstrained nature of the real-world images and therefore, cannot be relied on to achieve respectable performance on the in-the-wild images which are common in practical applications.

Recently, CNN has shown remarkable achievement in the face recognition task. It has the ability to learn a discriminative feature representation, especially when the volume of training images is adequately large. To mention a few, in 2015, Levi and Hassncer [19] proposed deep convolutional neural networks that learn the facial features of images. The proposed estimation solution is a simple and sequential convolutional neural network architecture trained and evaluated on Adience benchmark for age and gender estimation. Shaik and Micheal [25] designed a CNN-based model for age and gender estimation with five-layer architecture. In [22], Qawaqneh *et al.* developed a model for age estimation of real-world and unconstrained faces with a deep CNN model. Zhang *et al.* [28] investigated a novel CNN-based method for age group and gender estimation: Residual Networks of Residual Networks (RoR). RoR model is pre-trained on the popular ImageNet dataset before fine-tuned on the IMDb-WIKI-101 dataset. Liu *et al.* [20] also employed a CNN model based on the multi-class focal loss function, for the age and gender classification task. Duan *et al.* [5] also developed age and gender estimation model: CNN2ELM that include a CNN and extreme learning machine (ELM). In [23], Rothe *et al.* used deep learning with VGG-16 CNN to solve age estimation from a single face without the facial landmarks.

Although most of these methods improved classification accuracy on unconstrained images through different CNN model, age group and gender classification can still achieve higher accuracy with a better model. We, therefore, propose a novel end-to-end CNN-based learning model for age group and gender classification of unconstrained real-world faces.

3   Proposed Approach

In this section, we describe the proposed method for age group and gender classification. Our methodology is composed of two steps: image preprocessing (including face detection and face alignment) to prepare and process the unconstrained images before feeding to the network, and 6-layer network architecture of four convolutional and two fully-connected layers for feature extraction and classification task. A detailed description of each step is given as follows:

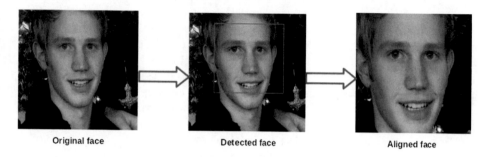

Original face   **Detected face**   **Aligned face**

Fig. 2. Image preprocessing phase.

3.1   Image Preprocessing

Some of the faces in the datasets employed in this work do not show good imaging conditions but rather unconstrained real-world faces, as such, we prepare and preprocess the face images before being fed into the proposed network for both training and testing. The image preprocessing stages is as follows:

Face Detection: For the face detection, we employ a multi-scale model "Head Hunter" face detector developed by Mathias *et al.* [21] to obtain the location of the face and prepare each of the faces for alignment on the original and the rotated faces. The rotated faces are set in the range of −90° and 90° within 5° steps. After which we select the rotated variant of the input face images which produces the best detection score for the face alignment phase.

Face Landmark and Alignment: For the alignment, we implement an open-source multi-view facial landmark detector proposed by [26]. The Deformable Part Models (DPM) based solution, solves the problem of the viewing angle estimation and simultaneous landmark detection in a structured output analysis framework. Diagrammatic presentation of the image preprocessing phase is shown in Fig. 2.

3.2   Network Architecture

Our experiments for age group and gender classification, are implemented using a deep CNN architecture with six layers comprising four convolutional layers

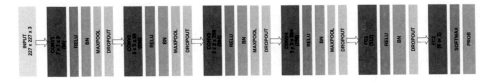

Fig. 3. The detailed CNN architecture for the classification.

and two fully-connected layers. The choice of this network model is defined by the nature of the employed datasets and the peculiarities of the classification problem to solve. We also consider the network as a solution to reduce the problem of overfitting. Unlike the network architecture proposed in [20], we adopt the softmax loss function instead of the multi-class focal loss function, to effectively address the problem as a multi-class, predicting age group of eight classes and gender of two classes. During training, we preprocess the input face images by scaling them into 256×256 pixels and then cropped into 227×227 pixels before being fed to the network. Furthermore, the image is passed through the six-layer CNN-based architecture as follows:

The first convolutional layer learned 96, 7×7 kernels and a stride of 4×4, then followed by an activation layer (rectified linear unit (ReLU)), batch normalization, a max-pooling layer, and a dropout. The second, third and fourth series of convolutional layers applied the same structure only with different filter and filter size. Second convolutional layer learns 256, 5×5 filters, third is near identical to the second convolutional layers but with an increase in the number of filters to 384 and a reduction of the filter size to 3×3. The last and fourth convolutional layer set has a filter of 256 and a filter size of 3×3. All the convolutional layer has a fixed dropout of 0.25 to improve generalization and reduce overfitting.

The composition of the two fully-connected layers is identical, containing 512 neurons, followed by a ReLU, batch normalization and a dropout layer at a dropout ratio of 0.5. In the final fully-connected layer, the output from the previous layer of size 512 features are densely mapped to 8 or 2 neurons for age group or gender classification. A softmax with cross-entropy loss function is adopted to obtain a probability for each class. More details of the network architecture are given in Fig. 3.

3.3 Training Details

The CNN-based model is trained for a multi-class classification problem. We generate the performance when testing for classification (age group and gender of the neuron with the highest probability), and the expected value over the softmax normalized output possibilities. We train two different classifiers; one for predicting the eight age group classes, and the other for classifying the two gender classes.

The six-layer CNN classifiers are initially pre-trained on the IMDb-WIKI, fine-tuned on MORPH-II, and the original (OIU-Adience) datasets. This is necessary for the model to conform to face image contents, and pick-up the peculiarities and the distribution of each dataset. Finally, we evaluate the classifiers on OIU-Adience dataset, to assess the performance accuracy of the two models. Pre-training on IMDb-WIKI, and further fine-tuning on MORPH-II, and OIU-Adience helps in addressing the overfitting problem which improve the performance of the classifiers. For each of the datasets of IMDb-WIKI and MORPH-II, we split into two: 90% for training, and 10% for validation. We also split the original Adience dataset into three: 70% for training, 15% for validation, and 15% for testing.

For the age group classifier, we set the learning rate to an initial value of 0.00001 (to make it train longer), and an L2 weight decay of 0.0005. We employ computationally-efficient Adam optimization algorithm described in [18], to update network weights during training instead of the conventional stochastic gradient descent. The algorithm calculates adaptive learning rates for the parameter and also combines RMSProp, momentum, and learning rate decay. It combines the best features of the RMSProp and AdaGrad algorithms, to provide better performance. The decaying averages of the gradients m_t and m_t (estimates of the mean and uncentered variance of the gradients), are calculated as shown in Eq. (1):

$$m_t = \gamma_1 m_{t-1} + (1 - \gamma_1)g_t$$
$$v_t = \gamma_2 v_{t-1} + (1 - \gamma_2)g_t^2 \tag{1}$$

where γ_1 and γ_2 are the decay rates for the two gradients m_t and v_t respectively and g, the gradient on mini-batch. The bias-corrected of the first and second estimates are also calculated in Eq. (2) as:

$$\hat{m}_t = \frac{m_t}{1 - \gamma_1^t}$$
$$\hat{v}_t = \frac{v_t}{1 - \gamma_2^t} \tag{2}$$

and the update rule of the parameters for the Adam optimizer is as defined in Eq. (3):

$$\beta_{t+1} = \beta_t - \frac{\eta}{\sqrt{\hat{v}_t} + \epsilon}\hat{m}_t \tag{3}$$

where η is the learning rate, β_t as model's parameters at time step t and ϵ as a smoothing term.

For the gender classifier, we set the initial learning rate to 0.001, momentum term to 0.9, and L2 weight decay of 0.0005. We employ Stochastic Gradient Descent (SGD) as the optimization algorithm, to update each training models. The training on the classifiers is terminated when the network begins to overfit on the validation set. SGD produces an update to the parameter of each training input $x^{(i)}$ and label $y^{(i)}$. It performs one update at a time which is always much

Fig. 4. Sample images from IMDb-WIKI, MORPH-II and Adience datasets.

faster. These updates are with a high variation, and this makes the objective function to vary massively. We, therefore, calculate SGD as (see Eq. (4))

$$\beta = \beta - \eta \cdot \nabla_\beta J(\beta; x^{(i)}; y^{(i)}) \tag{4}$$

where η is defined as the learning rate, $\nabla_\beta J$, the gradient of the loss term with respect to the weight vector β.

We also employ a data augmentation (regularization) algorithm to increase the number of altered copies of the face images, and this improves the optimization ability of the model.

Table 1. Description of the Datasets in the Experiment.

Dataset	Samples	Subjects	Age range
IMDb-WIKI [28]	523,051	20,284	0–100
MORPH-II [17]	55,134	13,618	16–77
OIU-Adience [7]	26,580	2284	0–60+

4   Experiments

In this section, we present the results of the experiments when evaluated on the OIU-Adience benchmark for age group and gender classification. We also present the experimental analysis in the discussion section.

4.1   Datasets

We evaluate the proposed method on OIU-Adience [7] taken from uncontrolled environments. IMDb-WIKI dataset [28] is also employed to pre-train our network before fine-tuning on MORPH-II [17] and the original datasets. Summary of these datasets is presented in Table 1, with their sample size, subjects size, and their age range information. Figure 4 shows samples of face images for each dataset. We present below a brief explanation of the datasets.

IMDb-WIKI dataset [28] contains images crawled from IMDb and Wikipedia. It is the largest publicly-available dataset in facial aging with more than half a million images with IMDb contributing 460,723 images of 20,284 celebrities and Wikipedia with 62,328 images.

MORPH-II dataset [17] was collected at the university of north carolina at wilmington by the face aging group. It has attributes labels of age, gender, ethnicity, weight, height, and ancestry. MORPH is divided into Album I and Album II. Album I has a total of 1,724 images of 515 subjects between 27 and 68 years while Album II contains 55,134 face images of about 13,000 subjects.

OIU-Adience dataset [7] is used in studying age and gender classification and contain face images from an ideal real-life and unconstrained scenes, therefore, reflect a high degree of variations in noise, pose, appearance among others.

Table 2. Age group and Gender classification: Performance comparison on Adience.

Methods	Exact Acc (Age)	One-off	Exact Acc (Gender)
Eidinger *et al.* [7]	45.1	79.5	-
Levi and Hassncer [19]	50.7	84.7	86.8
Ekmekji [3]	54.5	84.1	80.8
Anand *et al.* [1]	58.5	-	-
Qawaqneh *et al.* [22]	60.0	90.6	-
Duan *et al.* [5]	52.3	-	-
Liu *et al.* [20]	54.0	88.2	-
Duan *et al.* [6]	66.5	-	88.2
Proposed	**83.1**	**93.8**	**96.2**

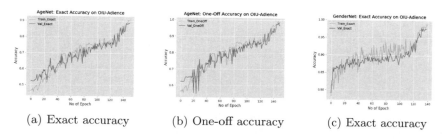

(a) Exact accuracy   (b) One-off accuracy   (c) Exact accuracy

Fig. 5. Graphs of result for the age group and gender classification.

4.2   Evaluation Metrics

To evaluate the performance of the proposed approach in age group and gender classification, we employ two different measures common in the literature: Exact and One-off accuracy.

Exact accuracy calculates the exact age-group and gender results. It measures the percentage of face images that were classified into correct age-group and gender, which is the ratio of the accurate predictions to the total number of the ground-truth label while One-off is off by one adjacent age-group and measures whether the ground-truth class label matches the predicted class label or if the ground-truth label exists in the two adjacent bins.

4.3   Experimental Results

Using the evaluating metrics described above, we, therefore, report the quantitative results of our proposed method on OIU-Adience dataset for age group and gender classification. We present the result for age group estimation using the two criteria while the result for gender classification will only be based on the exact accuracy metric.

Age Group Classification. We report the performance of our method for age group estimation on OIU-Adience dataset, standard benchmark for the existing methods for age group and gender classification. Our model when evaluated on the dataset, achieves an Exact accuracy of 83.1% and One-off accuracy of 93.8%. This improves over best reported state-of-the-art results for Exact accuracy in Duan et al. [6] by 16.6% and an increase of 3.2% on the One-off result reported in Qawaqneh et al. [22]. The graphs in Fig. 5(a) and (b), present the results (Exact and One-off) of the classification on the OIU-Adience dataset.

Gender Classification. We evaluate our method for classifying a person to the correct gender. We evaluate the performance on the same Adience dataset consisting of labels for gender. For this task, we train our network for classification of two classes and report the result on Exact accuracy with pre-training on the three datasets. As presented in Fig. 5(c), we achieve an accuracy of 96.2% compared to the previous state-of-the-art of 88.2% in Duan et al. [6]. Our approach, therefore, achieves the best results not only on the age group estimation but also on gender classification; it outperforms the current state-of-the-art methods. The results are summarized in Table 2.

4.4   Discussion

The proposed CCN-based method achieves state-of-the-art results on OIU-Adience dataset for age group and gender. Training the CNN for classification with a classification-based loss function as training targets, improves the performance of the model. The robust and effective image preprocessing approach handles some of the variability observed in typical unconstrained real-world faces, and this confirms the model applicability for age group and gender classification in-the-wild which help in achieving a better result. Pre-training on the large scale IMDb-WIKI, and finetuning on MORPH-II and original dataset (OIU-Adience), results in a huge boost in performance. Also, data augmentation regularization method on training images seems very efficient and makes an excellent contribution.

In Fig. 6(a), we display the age group and gender predictions of some of the face images from the OIU-Adience dataset using the newly-designed model. In many cases, our solution is able to correctly predict the age-group and gender of faces. Figure 6(b) also shows a few examples of the undetected faces and incorrect estimation that is unsuccessful with our approach on the same benchmark. The error could be as a result of the extremely challenging viewing conditions of the OIU-Adience images including low resolution, non-frontal, lighting conditions, and heavy makeup; this hindered our image preprocessing method to either correctly detect or align the face for the classification process.

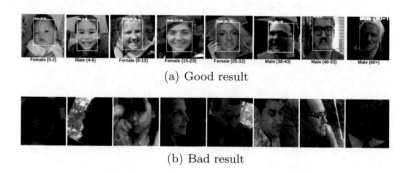

(a) Good result

(b) Bad result

Fig. 6. Visualization of the good and bad estimates for age group and gender.

5   Conclusions and Future Works

In this paper, we proposed a novel deep learning solution for age group and gender classification of uncontrained faces with a classification-based loss function. The method incorporates a robust image preprocessing technique, then a six-layer deep CNN architecture, to solve the classifications problem. First, we show that a suitable image preprocessing algorithm can contribute to the performance of a classifier. Then, we demonstrate that a model pretrained on a very large-scale dataset, fine tuning on another related dataset, and the original dataset, can result in a more accurate estimation. Finally, the evaluation of the original OIU-Adience benchmark for age and gender classification shows that the proposed method obtains state-of-the-art performance. A more robust face detector can lead to better alignment and results in the future. A deeper CNN architecture with sufficient training data might also enhance performance. Apparent age estimation of faces will also be interesting research in the future.

References

1. Anand, A., Labati, R.D., Genovese, A., Munoz, E., Piuri, V., Scotti, F.: Age estimation based on face images and pre-trained convolutional neural networks. In: 2017 IEEE Symposium Series on Computational Intelligence, SSCI 2017 - Proceedings 2017, pp. 1–7 (2017). https://doi.org/10.1109/SSCI.2017.8285381. http://ieeexplore.ieee.org/document/8285381/
2. Badame, V., Jamadagni, M.: Study of approaches for human facial age. Int. J. Innovative Res. Sci. Eng. Technol. **6**(8), 2347–6710 (2017). https://doi.org/10.15680/IJIRSET.2016.0608148
3. Broussely, M., Planchat, J.P., Rigobert, G., Virey, D., Sarre, G.: Lithium-ion batteries for electric vehicles: performances of 100 Ah cells. J. Power Sources **68**(1), 8–12 (1997). https://doi.org/10.1016/S0378-7753(96)02544-X
4. Dib, M.Y.E., El-saban, M.: Human Age Estimation Using Enhanced Bio-inspired Features (EBIF), pp. 1–4. Faculty of Computers and Information, Cairo University, Cairo, Egypt (2010)
5. Duan, M., Li, K., Li, K.: An ensemble CNN2ELM for age estimation. IEEE Trans. Inf. Forensics Secur. **13**(3), 758–772 (2018). https://doi.org/10.1109/TIFS.2017.2766583
6. Duan, M., Li, K., Yang, C., Li, K.: A hybrid deep learning CNN-ELM for age and gender classification. Neurocomputing **275**, 448–461 (2018). https://doi.org/10.1016/j.neucom.2017.08.062
7. Eidinger, E., Enbar, R., Hassner, T.: Age and gender estimation of unfiltered faces. IEEE Trans. Inf. Forensics Secur. **9**(12), 2170–2179 (2014). https://doi.org/10.1109/TIFS.2014.2359646. http://www.adience.com
8. Fu, Y., Guo, G., Huang, T.S.: Age synthesis and estimation via faces: a survey. IEEE Trans. Pattern Anal. Mach. Intell. **32**(11), 1955–1976 (2010). https://doi.org/10.1109/TPAMI.2010.36
9. Fu, Y., Huang, T.S.: Human age estimation with regression on discriminative aging manifold. IEEE Trans. Multimedia **10**(4), 578–584 (2008). https://doi.org/10.1109/TMM.2008.921847
10. Gallagher, A.C., Chen, T.: Estimating age, gender, and identity using first name priors. In: 26th IEEE Conference on Computer Vision and Pattern Recognition, CVPR (Sect. 3) (2008). https://doi.org/10.1109/CVPR.2008.4587609
11. Gao, F., Ai, H.: Face age classification on consumer images with gabor feature and fuzzy LDA method. In: Tistarelli, M., Nixon, M.S. (eds.) ICB 2009. LNCS, vol. 5558, pp. 132–141. Springer, Heidelberg (2009). https://doi.org/10.1007/978-3-642-01793-3_14
12. Guerra, E., de Lara, J., Malizia, A., Díaz, P.: Supporting user-oriented analysis for multi-view domain-specific visual languages. Inf. Soft. Technol. **51**, 769–784 (2015). https://doi.org/10.1016/j.infsof.2008.09.005. http://arxiv.org/abs/1409.1556
13. Günther, J., Pilarski, P.M., Helfrich, G., Shen, H., Diepold, K.: First steps towards an intelligent laser welding architecture using deep neural networks and reinforcement learning. Procedia Technol. **15**, 474–483 (2014). https://doi.org/10.1016/j.protcy.2014.09.007
14. Guo, G., Fu, Y., Dyer, C.R., Huang, T.S.: Image-based human age estimation by manifold learning and locally adjusted robust regression. IEEE Trans. Image Process. **17**(7), 1178–1188 (2008). https://doi.org/10.1109/TIP.2008.924280

15. Guo, G., Mu, G.: Simultaneous dimensionality reduction and human age estimation via kernel partial least squares regression. In: Proceedings of the IEEE Computer Society Conference on Computer Vision and Pattern Recognition, pp. 657–664 (2011). https://doi.org/10.1109/CVPR.2011.5995404

16. Han, H., Jain, A.K.: Age. Gender and race estimation from unconstrained face images, Technical report (2014)

17. Ricanek Jr., K., Tesafaye, T.: MORPH: a longitudinal image age-progression, of normal adult. In: Proceedings of 7th International Conference on Automatic Face Gesture Recognition, pp. 0–4 (2006)

18. Kingma, D.P., Ba, J.: Adam: a method for stochastic optimization. In: ICLR, pp. 1–15 (2014). http://arxiv.org/abs/1412.6980

19. Levi, G., Hassncer, T.: Age and gender classification using convolutional neural networks. IEEE Computer Society Conference on Computer Vision and Pattern Recognition Workshops 2015, pp. 34–42, October 2015. https://doi.org/10.1109/CVPRW.2015.7301352. http://ieeexplore.ieee.org/document/7301352/

20. Liu, W., Chen, L., Chen, Y.: Age classification using convolutional neural networks with the multi-class focal loss. In: IOP Conference Series: Materials Science and Engineering, vol. 428, no. 1 (2018). https://doi.org/10.1088/1757-899X/428/1/012043

21. Mathias, M., Benenson, R., Pedersoli, M., Van Gool, L.: Face detection without bells and whistles. In: Fleet, D., Pajdla, T., Schiele, B., Tuytelaars, T. (eds.) ECCV 2014. LNCS, vol. 8692, pp. 720–735. Springer, Cham (2014). https://doi.org/10.1007/978-3-319-10593-2_47

22. Qawaqneh, Z., Mallouh, A.A., Barkana, B.D.: Deep convolutional neural network for age estimation based on VGG-face model. arXiv, September 2017. http://arxiv.org/abs/1709.01664

23. Rothe, R., Timofte, R., Van Gool, L.: Deep expectation of real and apparent age from a single image without facial landmarks. Int. J. Comput. Vis. **126**(2–4), 144–157 (2018). https://doi.org/10.1007/s11263-016-0940-3

24. Sahoo, T.K., Banka, H.: Multi-feature-based facial age estimation using an incomplete facial aging database. Arab. J. Sci. Eng. **43**(12), 8057–8078 (2018). https://doi.org/10.1007/s13369-018-3293-0. http://link.springer.com/10.1007/s13369-018-3293-0

25. Shaik, S., Micheal, A.A.: Automatic age and gender recognition in human face image dataset using convolutional neural network system. Int. J. Adv. Res. Comput. Sci. Manage. Stud. 4(2), 14–23 (2016)

26. Uřičář, M., Franc, V., Thomas, D., Sugimoto, A., Hlaváč, V.: Multi-view facial landmark detector learned by the structured output SVM. Image Vis. Comput. **47**, 45–59 (2015). https://doi.org/10.1016/j.imavis.2016.02.004

27. Yan, S., Liu, M., Huang, T.S.: Extracting age information from local spatially flexible patches. In: IEEE International Conference on Acoustics, Speech and Signal Processing, ICASSP Proceedings, pp. 737–740 (2008). https://doi.org/10.1109/ICASSP.2008.4517715

28. Zhang, K., et al.: Age group and gender estimation in the wild with deep RoR architecture. IEEE Access **5**(X), 22492–22503 (2017). https://doi.org/10.1109/ACCESS.2017.2761849

Efficient 3D Face Recognition in Uncontrolled Environment

Yuqi Ding[1($\boxtimes$)], Nianyi Li[1], S. Susan Young[2], and Jinwei Ye[1]

[1] Louisiana State University, Baton Rouge, LA 70803, USA
{yding18,nli5,jinweiye}@lsu.edu
[2] U.S. Army Research Laboratory, Adelphi, MD 20783, USA

Abstract. Face recognition in an uncontrolled environment is challenging as body movement and pose variation can result in missing facial features. In this paper, we tackle this problem by fusing multiple RGB-D images with varying poses. In particular, we develop an efficient pose fusion algorithm that frontalizes the faces and combines the multiple inputs. We then introduce a new 3D registration method based on the unified coordinate system (UCS) to compensate for pose and scale variations and normalize the probe and gallery face. To perform 3D face recognition, we train a Support Vector Machine (SVM) with both 2D color and 3D geometric features. Experimental results on a RGB-D dataset show that our method can achieve a high recognition rate and is robust in the presence of pose and expression variations.

Keywords: 3D face recognition · Uncontrolled environment · RGB-D images · Pose fusion · 3D Face registration

1 Introduction

Face recognition (FR) is of great importance as it has numerous applications in access control, surveillance system, and law enforcement. Although the past decade has witnessed tremendous advances in 2D face recognition [5,26], robust recognition in an uncontrolled environment is still challenging as the facial appearance in 2D images is sensitive to illumination, viewpoint, pose, and expression variations. In addition, body movement and/or head motion can cause large occlusions and result in missing facial features. It is urgent to overcome these challenges and provide successful solutions to benefit both civilian and military applications. A viable solution is to apply 3D face models for recognition [27]. As directly associated with the face geometry, a 3D face model is inherently invariant to scene properties (*e.g.*, illumination and viewpoint). However, a complete and accurate 3D face acquisition is often time-consuming and requires expensive devices [22]. Some approaches [2,32] recover 3D face models from one or multiple 2D images by fitting statistical models (*e.g.*, 3DMM [4]). Although no specialized hardware is needed, these methods are usually computationally intensive and the recovered face models are less accurate.

G. Bebis et al. (Eds.): ISVC 2019, LNCS 11844, pp. 430–443, 2019.
https://doi.org/10.1007/978-3-030-33720-9_33

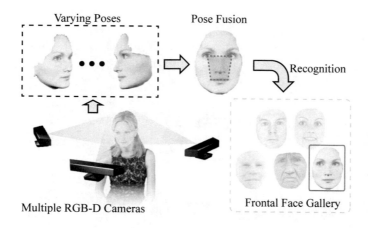

Fig. 1. Schematic illustration of our FR scheme in an uncontrolled environment.

In this paper, we use RGB-D images for 3D face recognition since RGB-D cameras are cheap and easily accessible. However, self-occlusions caused by pose variations result in missing facial features. Most RGB-D image-based methods utilize symmetric filling to complete the 3D face model [16, 20, 25]. Nevertheless, facial asymmetry renders the completion inaccurate. When multiple 3D scans are available, the Iterative Closest Point (ICP) algorithm [3] can be adopted to combine partial 3D face models. But in case of large pose changes where the partial models have small overlap, the ICP algorithm might fail to align them. The seminal work of KinectFusion [33] generated high-quality 3D reconstruction using a moving RGB-D camera. However, this method is not suitable for face recognition with stationary sensors.

To tackle the occlusion problem caused by pose variations, we propose a system consisting of multiple low-cost RGB-D cameras (*e.g.*, Microsoft Kinect) for 3D face recognition (see Fig. 1). The RGB-D cameras surround the subject to capture varying poses. Conceptually, our system can be deployed in various indoor environments (*e.g.*, a building interior and cave) and is able to handle uncontrolled conditions. To fuse face models with varying poses, we develop an efficient fusion algorithm that first frontalizes the faces and then merges the partial face models in a uniform grid. We then introduce a new 3D registration method based on the unified coordinate system (UCS) to compensate for pose and scale variations. We use the UCS to normalize the gallery (frontal face model) and probe (combined model). To perform 3D face recognition, we train a Support Vector Machine (SVM) using both 2D color and 3D depth features. Specifically, we extract 2D features from a normalized canonical color image using a convolutional neural network (CNN) based on a deep feature extractor. We then use the expression-invariant geodesic distances between facial landmarks that are computed on 3D facial meshes as 3D geometric features. We finally concatenate these 2D and 3D features to train the SVM for FR. The processing pipeline of our approach is shown in Fig. 2. Through experiments

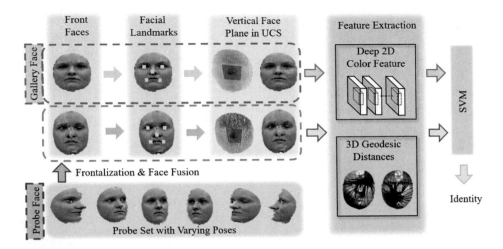

Fig. 2. Processing pipeline of our 3D FR algorithm.

on an RGB-D dataset [16] and comparisons with the state-of-the-art methods, we show that our approach has a high FR accuracy but relatively low computational complexity. More importantly, our approach is robust to pose and expression variations.

2   Related Work

A FR system usually consists of three basic modules [24]: (1) a face detection module for detecting the facial region [31]; (2) a feature detection and alignment module for data normalization [11,35]; and (3) a recognition module applied on the normalized faces [34]. As we present a new pose-invariant FR algorithm in this paper, we briefly review related studies on face registration and 3D FR.

Face Registration. According to [6,13], pose variation is a major factor that leads to reduced FR accuracy. Hence pose-invariant face recognition is of great importance. Face registration aims to align the faces of different poses to a canonical pose. In this way, pose variation is eliminated. Existing face registration methods can be classified into three major categories: (1) one to one registration; (2) all to mean face registration, and 3)registration by coordinate normalization. Given 3D face point clouds, the first-class registers the probe point cloud to each reference face in the gallery by an iterative procedure [23]. The Iterative Closest Point (ICP) algorithm is usually adopted for optimization. However, without good initialization of the parameters, the ICP may fail to converge. Instead of mapping the probe to each face in the gallery, the second class aligns all the face models to a mean face model learned from a training set [9,12]. Each face only needs one-time registration. Therefore, the computational cost is significantly decreased. However, these methods may suffer from large registration errors. The third class aligns faces of different poses by normalizing the coordinates of detected facial landmarks [29]. A set of facial landmarks is first detected and then transformed into a common coordinate system. The resulting transformation is applied to the entire face point cloud for registration. This class of methods is more efficient than the other two in terms of computational cost. However, the accuracy still largely depends on the quality of detected landmarks, which might be missing in the presence of large pose variations. In this paper, we propose to first fuse faces with different poses and then use a unified coordinate system (UCS) to align the 3D face models. Our fused face is more robust to pose variations because it incorporates partial features from each pose to a complete set. Our UCS-based 3D face registration considers the depth information and is, therefore, more accurate than conventional 2D face registration.

3D Face Recognition. We refer readers to [21] for a comprehensive overview of 3D FR. Here, we focus on how 3D FR algorithms handle challenges in pose and expression variations as well as corrupted data. We classify existing 3D FR algorithms into three categories: (1) local descriptor-based; (2) global/model descriptor-based [1]; and (3) learning-based techniques [14,36]. The first category utilizes the characteristics of a small local neighborhood such as curvatures, shape index, and normals for matching. To list a few, Mian *et al.* [18] fused 3D keypoints with 2D Scale Invariant Feature Transform (SIFT) to identify 3D faces. Gupta *et al.* [10] matched the 3D Euclidean and geodesic distances between pairs of facial landmarks for 3D FR. Yet, these approaches are sensitive to facial expressions. The second category usually derives a 3D morphable face model and fits it to all probe faces. The best-matched 3D face is then used for recognition. For example, Gilani *et al.* [8] conducted FR by matching keypoint-based features on a statistical morphable model. However, these methods do not explicitly capture the actual 3D information, with a low-quality depth, they are less accurate, and do not work well on the RGB-D data. Although the third category has achieved great success in 2D FR, its application to 3D FR is still limited due to the absence of massive 3D face datasets. For instance, Kim *et al.* [14] fine-tuned the VGG-Face network on depth images to generate 3D feature descriptors and then used Principal Component Analysis (PCA) for feature matching. Gilani *et al.* [36] developed an end-to-end 3D FR framework by training an augmented 3D face dataset. Although these methods are successful, their datasets and network models are not publicly available. In this paper, we leverage a pre-trained deep neural network for 2D color feature extraction and then integrate expression-invariant 3D features for 3D FR.

3   Pose Fusion Using RGB-D Images

In this section, we describe our pose fusing algorithm using RGB-D images. The goal of the algorithm is to obtain a face model with a complete set of facial landmarks (*i.e.*, four eye corners, nose tip, and two mouth corners, as shown in Fig. 3(a)) by fusing RGB-D images with varying poses.

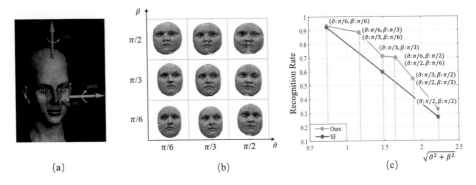

Fig. 3. (a) 3D rotations (yaw, pitch, and roll) with respect to our coordinate axes. (b) Pose fusion results that combine input poses with different rotation angles (α and β refer left and right yaw angles). (c) Recognition rates for using various pose fusion results in (b) as the probe. We compare with the completion results by symmetric filling (SF).

Given RGB-D images as input, we first pre-process the data to recover a point cloud using depth values and crop out the local face region by fitting a sphere centered at the nose tip. The radius of the sphere is determined according to the face scale. The face point cloud is further translated with the nose tip as the origin of coordinates. We then set out to combine the partial face point clouds with varying poses to restore the complete face model. A naïve approach is to directly apply the ICP algorithm to merge the partial point clouds. However, ICP fails easily in case of extreme poses with small overlaps. Instead, we apply 3D rotation to frontalize the faces and merge them into a uniform grid.

In an uncontrolled condition, the 3D face point cloud can exhibit three types of rotations: in-plane, pose, and tilt rotations, which are commonly referred to as roll, yaw, and pitch (see Fig. 3(a)). We use 3D rotation matrices to model these variations and revert the rotations to frontalize the face. To estimate the rotation parameters, we compare the nose region in our 3D face with a nose template from a standard frontal mean face. We compare intensities in the range images instead of the 3D models to reduce the computational cost.

Assuming the range images of our sampled nose region and the mean face nose template to be $N_R(i, j)$ and $N_T(i, j)$, $i, j \in \mathbb{N}$. We use a weighted normalized cross correlation (WNCC) Γ to assess the similarity between N_R and N_T:

$$
\Gamma(N_R, N_T) = w \cdot \frac{\sum\limits_{i,j \in \mathbb{N}} \left(N_R(i, j) - \bar{N}_R\right) \cdot \left(N_T(i, j) - \bar{N}_T\right)}{\sqrt{\sum\limits_{i,j} \left(N_R - \bar{N}_R\right)^2} \cdot \sqrt{\sum\limits_{i,j} \left(N_T - \bar{N}_T\right)^2}} \tag{1}
$$

where $\bar{N}_R$ and $\bar{N}_T$ are the mean values of N_R and N_T. The weight w is introduced to compensate for the missing data in the low-quality RGB-D images and is computed as the percentage of valid range data in the whole grid.

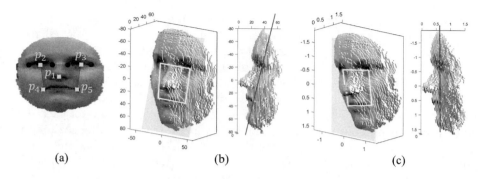

Fig. 4. UCS transformation and the face plane. (a) We illustrate the facial landmarks for constructing the UCS vertical face plane; (b) The initial face plane in the world coordinate system is not vertical due to pose variations; (c) The face plane becomes vertical after UCS transformation.

We then conduct a coarse-to-fine search to find the optimal rotation angle. Firstly, we use a relatively large search step, initialized as $\pi/60$, in the coarse search phase to maximize the Γ and shrink the search space to $\theta_c \pm \pi/30$, where θ_c corresponds to the coarse optimal rotation angle. Then, we implement a more precise search on the refined search space to further optimize Γ. We conduct this search algorithm by reducing the search step iteratively until Γ converges. To speed up our searching process, we employ a bilateral face ratio η that can effectively reduce the initial searching space: $\eta = num(I_l)/(num(I_l) + num(I_r))$, where $num(I_l)$ and $num(I_r)$ are facial pixel counts in the left and right sub-images. If $\eta > 0.5$, we search θ in $[0, \pi/2]$; otherwise, $\theta \in [-\pi/2, 0]$.

Finally, we merge the frontalized point clouds and their corresponding range images by box/grid averaging to generate a resampled face model, denoting the face pre-model. We apply a box filter to the face pre-model to further smooth out the noise. Figure 3(b) illustrates our pose fusion results by combining input poses with various rotation angles. We can see that our method is able to handle large pose variations ($\pm\pi/2$). We also compare our fusion method with symmetric filling in terms of recognition rates (see Fig. 3(c)). We can see that although recognition rates go down as rotation angle increases, our method still works better than the baseline symmetric filling algorithm in all scenarios.

4 Face Normalization Using Unified Coordinate System

In order to normalize the face models for recognition, we introduce a unified coordinate system (UCS) to compensate pose and scale variations. Our UCS is invariant to sensor position with respect to the human subject when the face image is taken (*i.e.*, invariant relative to the head pose).

Our UCS transformation can be viewed as a 3D registration (or 3D stereotactic registration) method. Our method transforms the 3D face pre-model into the UCS to generate a 3D registered face model. The coordinate transformation contains 3D rotation and scaling where the rotation generalizes yaw, pitch, and roll; and scaling normalizes the face size. After UCS transformation, all face models are in a common space and could be fairly compared for recognition.

Now we describe how to construct the UCS. When a human face in 3D is viewed from the side, the depth of the eyes and the mouth are different, which is unique for each person. Thus, when a human head is in a normal position, which is normally termed as a frontal pose, the centers of corners of each eye and the corners of mouth are on two different vertical planes. So the goal of our UCS transformation is to compensate this depth variation such that these four points are on the same vertical plane and we call it the face plane (see Fig. 4). We can see that in order to have the face plane being vertical, the human head is tilted from the normal frontal pose.

To sum up, our UCS is defined with the following steps: (1) we identify five facial landmarks (*i.e.*, nose tip p_1, center of the left eye corners p_2, center of the right eye corners p_3, left mouth corner p_4, and right mouth corner p_5) using the color image; (2) we form a plane use $p_2 \sim p_5$ (if they do not share the same plane, we use the plane in which the distances of the four points are minimal) and estimate the plane's orientation in the world coordinate system; (3) we perform a coordinate transformation such that p_1 is the origin and the face plane is vertical; (4) we scale the coordinate by dividing by a scale factor s, where s is the distance from p_1 to line p_2p_3 such that the sizes of the face models are normalized. The new coordinate system is our UCS where the pose and scale of the face models are normalized. We apply the UCS transformation on both the gallery face and the probe face.

5   RGB-D Face Recognition

In this section, we present a Support Vector Machine (SVM)-based RGB-D face recognition algorithm to identify the probe face in the gallery set. We propose a color and geometric (CG) feature extractor to retrieve the 2D features from the color images and 3D geometric features from the 3D face meshes to describe the face model. Our SVM is trained with CG features from the gallery. Specifically, we leverage a VGG-Face [19] pre-trained convolutional network (CNN) to extract 2D feature vectors from the input color images. To exploit the depth information, we compute the geodesic distances between the facial landmarks on the 3D face meshes and use them as 3D features to allow expression-invariant recognition. By jointly considering the 2D color and 3D depth information, our FR algorithm on the RGB-D images is able to achieve a high recognition rate and is robust under an uncontrolled environment with pose and expression variations. Our FR algorithm is illustrated in Fig. 5. In the following paragraphs, we describe each component in detail.

2D Color Feature. Recent deep networks [19,28] have had great success in 2D face recognition, and the datasets with millions of face images are used to train a robust face classifier. Deep convolutional networks (CNNs) use a cascade of multiple layers of processing units for feature extraction and transformation [30].

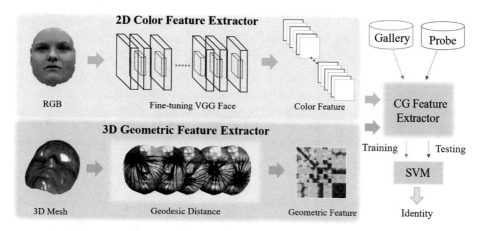

Fig. 5. Our SVM-based face recognition scheme using the Color and Geometric (CG) Feature Extractor.

According to [28], the bottom layers of the CNN typically extract the low-level features of an image, such as Gabor and SIFT. These low-level features can be extracted from an arbitrary generic natural image. In contrast, the outputs of the CNN top layers exhibit high-level characteristics that correspond to facial attributes such as poses and expressions and are thus critical to robust face recognition. Therefore, fine-tuning a pre-trained CNN on a new dataset is an efficient way to achieve high recognition accuracy but with less computational effort. VGG-Face [19] is a CNN-based 2D FR architecture trained on a dataset of 2.6M images and 2622 unique identities. It contains 22 layers, among which there are 13 convolutional layers, 5 max pooling layers, 3 fully connected layers, and a Softmax layer. The expected image resolution of the input layer is 224×224. We therefore take advantage of the VGG-Face to extract 2D color features from our input. To fit the input resolution of VGG-Face, our 2D color face image is resized to 224×224. We then transfer all the weights from VGG-Face to a CNN but remove all fully-connected layers and only keep the embedded $7 \times 7 \times 512$ features maps. We then flatten the feature maps to a 1D array and use it as our 2D color feature.

3D Geometric Feature. To exploit the depth information, we also extract 3D geometric features from our 3D face models. We choose the geodesic distances as our 3D geometric feature because the geodesic distance is the shortest distance between two points on a curved surface and is robust to expression changes [7,17]. To compute geodesic distances, we first construct triangular meshes using the face point cloud by Delaunay triangulation. We then use a smoothing filter to reduce the mesh noise. In our experiment, we implement the fast marching algorithm [15] to compute the geodesic distances on the face mesh from a source point. Facial landmarks are first detected on color images and then transferred to 3D meshes. By assigning k (in our paper, $k = 68$) facial landmarks on each mesh, we generate a $k \times k$ matrix, where the (m, n) element indicates the geodesic distance from the m-th landmark to the n-th landmark. We resize this geodesic distance matrix into a 1D array and use it as our 3D geometric feature.

SVM Training. We finally concatenate the 2D color feature generated by pre-trained CNN and the 3D geometric feature computed with the geodesic distances and use it as our RGB-D face descriptor for classification. To perform face recognition, we train a support vector machine (SVM) as a classifier. Feature descriptors from the gallery set (frontal views) are used for training and the probe face by fusing multiple side views are used as testing input for recognition.

6   Experiments and Results

To validate our approach, we perform the experiment on the CurtinFace dataset [16] in which the RGB-D images are collected by Kinect. The dataset contains 52 subjects (42 males and 10 females), each has different poses, illuminations, and facial expressions. We use the frontal views as the gallery and side-view poses as probes. We use various poses of the same subject to emulate the images captured by our proposed multiple RGB-D camera system.

We compare our method with three state-of-the-art face frontalization algorithms: Li *et al.* [16], Hassner *et al.* [11], and Zhu *et al.* [35]. In order to prove the advantage of our CG feature extractor, we also compared it with a state-of-the-art 3D face recognition method, Emambakhsh *et al.* [7]. We perform both quantitative and qualitative comparisons on pose fusion and face recognition. All experiments are performed on a desktop PC with Intel Core i7-7700T CPU, 64 GB memory and two NVIDIA GeForce GTX 1060 6 GB GPUs. The varying pose fusion, UCS transformation, and geodesic distances are implemented through MATLAB R2018a. The SVM classifier and FR training are implemented with Sklearn, Tensorflow, and Keras.

Pose Fusion. We first demonstrate the effectiveness of our pose fusion algorithm. We perform a comparison with the three state-of-the-art face frontalization algorithms: Li *et al.* [16], Hassner *et al.* [11], and Zhu *et al.* [35]. Hassner *et al.* [11] and Zhu *et al.* [35] are designed for 2D face images. They first frontalize a 2D side-view face by first mapping it to a 3D frontal view average face model and then projecting the matched point cloud to xy-plane. Li *et al.* [16] took 3D face models as input and adopted the ICP algorithm to register the probe face to a mean face model. And they used the symmetric filling (SF) algorithm to obtain the complete face. We also compare it with our multiple pose fusion with SF (*i.e.*, we use our proposed method to frontalize the face and then flip the existing partial face to complete the entire face).

Our experiment is based on three sets of pose fusion: (1) $\pm\pi/2$, (2) $\pm\pi/3$, and (3) $\pm\pi/6$. The fusion results of all methods are shown in Fig. 6. We also use the fused faces of each method as input to our SVM-based face recognition algorithm to further validate the fusion quality. For the recognition task, our method achieves 32.69%, 70.05%, and 93.41% rank-1 accuracy, respectively, as

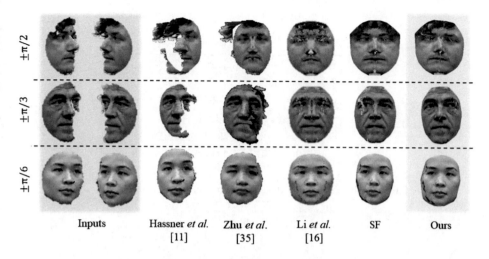

Fig. 6. Qualitative comparisons of the pose fusion results.

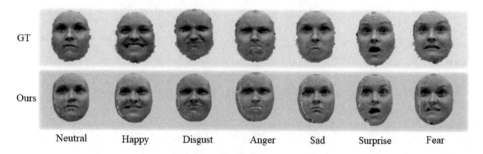

Fig. 7. Our fusion results for various expressions in comparison with the ground-truth (GT) frontal faces.

presented in Table 1. The rank-1 of 93.41% in the third pose set is the highest among all comparisons. It is important to note that 3D frontalization algorithms generally outperform 2D ones, due to the additional depth information and landmark detection failures on 3D faces by 2D approaches. Whereas our approach achieves the best performance especially in cases of large pose changes (for rotation angles larger than $\pi/4$), Li *et al.* [16] suffers from a low recognition rate due to the failure of ICP in presence of large pose variations. The SF results exhibit various artifacts (such as holes and duplicated regions) due to face asymmetry and misalignment. In contrast, our algorithm produces the most visually pleasing and accurate fusion results.

Face Recognition. Next, we show that our pose fusion algorithm and the CG feature representation benefit 3D face recognition. We test face recognition w.r.t. pose and expression variations. For pose variations, our experimental setup is the same as the pose fusion experiments.

Table 1. Recognition rate (%) w.r.t. Pose variations

Modality	Method	$\pm\pi/2$	$\pm\pi/3$	$\pm\pi/6$
2D	Hassner et al. [11]	7.69	23.07	50
	Zhu et al. [35]	7.69	15.38	46.15
	Ours (2D)	**32.69**	67.03	92.86
3D	Li et al. [16]	11.53	28.84	42.30
	SF	26.92	59.61	92.31
	Ours (2D+3D)	**32.69**	**70.05**	**93.41**

Table 2. Recognition rate (%) w.r.t. Expression variations

Modality	Method	Neutral	Happy	Disgust	Anger	Sad	Surprise	Fear
2D	Hassner et al. [11]	50.00	50.00	55.77	51.92	51.92	40.38	55.77
	Zhu et al. [35]	46.15	25.00	32.69	23.84	34.61	26.92	25.00
	Ours (2D)	**100**	88.46	**92.31**	86.54	**98.08**	**90.38**	94.23
3D	Emambakhsh et al. [7]	57.69	63.46	63.46	55.77	59.62	59.62	78.85
	Li et al. [16]	42.31	36.54	34.62	30.77	38.46	30.77	36.54
	SF	92.31	84.82	80.76	75.00	92.31	86.53	90.38
	Ours (2D+3D)	**100**	**92.21**	88.46	**88.46**	**98.08**	**90.38**	**96.15**

Recall that Hassner et al. [11] and Zhu et al. [35] are applied 2D face images as input. For fair comparison, we only use the 2D color features of the gallery faces for SVM training when comparing with these two methods. The recognition rate of all methods are presented in Table 1. We can see that our SVM-based face recognition scheme with 2D color and 3D geometric features achieves a high recognition rate when the input face is of high quality (e.g., when the rotation angles are small). The overall FR performance is improved by taking 3D information into account. In presence of extremely large pose variation (e.g., $\pm\pi/2$), the recognition rate is downgraded due to fusion errors. However, our method still achieves the highest rate in this extreme case.

For expression variations, we pick 7 expression categories: neutral, happy, disgust, anger, sad, surprise, and fear. Recognition is performed in each category with the gallery always being the neutral expression. For each expression category, we use poses of $\pm\pi/6$ for face fusion and then take the fused face as the probe. Our fusion results in comparison to the ground-truth (GT) frontal faces are shown in Fig. 7. To illustrate the robustness of our CG feature extractor with respect to expression variations, we also compare with Emambakhsh et al. [7], which is the state-of-the-art approach for handling various expressions. Emambakhsh et al. [7] use features in the nose region for recognition and is therefore robust to expression variations. However, due to the low-quality of our RGB-D data, high resolution features in the nose region are largely missing. Their FR performance is therefore downgraded. All aforementioned methods are tested in this experiment as well. The recognition rates are presented in Table 2. We can see that our method achieves the highest recognition rate for all expressions and is thus robust to expression variations.

7   Conclusion

In this paper, we presented an efficient 3D face recognition algorithm that is robust in an uncontrolled environment by fusing multiple pose-varying RGB-D images. We first frontalized different poses and then fused them to obtain a front face model with a complete set of facial landmarks. To compensate for the pose and scale variations, we introduced the UCS transformation to normalize the gallery face and probe face. To perform face recognition, we extracted 2D color and 3D geometric features and used them to train a robust SVM classifier. Through experiments and comparisons with the state-of-the-art methods, we showed that our method can achieve the highest face recognition rate and is robust to pose and expression variations. Due to its robustness and efficiency, our technique can be implemented as a practical system for deployment in an uncontrolled environment.

References

1. Abate, A.F., Nappi, M., Riccio, D., Sabatino, G.: 2D and 3D face recognition: a survey. Pattern Recogn. Lett. **28**(14), 1885–1906 (2007)
2. Aldrian, O., Smith, W.A.P.: Inverse rendering of faces with a 3D morphable model. IEEE Trans. Pattern Anal. Mach. Intell. **35**(5), 1080–1093 (2013)
3. Besl, P.J., McKay, N.D.: A method for registration of 3-D shapes. IEEE Trans. Pattern Anal. Mach. Intell. **14**, 239–256 (1992)
4. Blanz, V., Vetter, T.: A morphable model for the synthesis of 3D faces. In: Conference on Computer Graphics and Interactive Techniques. ACM Press (1999)
5. Corneanu, C.A., et al.: Survey on RGB, 3D, thermal, and multimodal approaches for facial expression recognition: history, trends, and affect-related applications. IEEE Trans. Pattern Anal. Mach. Intell. **38**(8), 1548–1568 (2016)
6. Ding, C., Tao, D.: A comprehensive survey on pose-invariant face recognition. ACM Trans. Intell. Syst. Technol. (TIST) **7**(3), 37 (2016)
7. Emambakhsh, M., Evans, A.: Nasal patches and curves for expression-robust 3D face recognition. IEEE Trans. Pattern Anal. Mach. Intell. **39**(5), 995–1007 (2017)
8. Gilani, S.Z., Mian, A., Shafait, F., Reid, I.: Dense 3D face correspondence. IEEE Trans. Pattern Anal. Mach. Intell. **40**(7), 1584–1598 (2017)
9. Gökberk, B., et al.: 3D shape-based face representation and feature extraction for face recognition. Image Vis. Comput. **24**(8), 857–869 (2006)
10. Gupta, S., Markey, M.K., Bovik, A.C.: Anthropometric 3D face recognition. Int. J. Comput. Vis. **90**(3), 331–349 (2010)
11. Hassner, T., Harel, S., Paz, E., Enbar, R.: Effective face frontalization in unconstrained images. In: IEEE Conference on CVPR (2015)
12. Kakadiaris, I.A., et al.: Three-dimensional Face recognition in the presence of facial expressions: an annotated deformable model approach. IEEE Trans. Pattern Anal. Mach. Intell. **29**(4), 640–649 (2007)

13. Kan, M., Shan, S., Chen, X.: Multi-view deep network for cross-view classification. In: IEEE Conference on CVPR, pp. 4847–4855 (2016)
14. Kim, D., Hernandez, M., Choi, J., Medioni, G.: Deep 3D face identification. In: IEEE International Joint Conference on Biometrics (IJCB) (2017)
15. Kimmel, R., Sethian, J.A.: Computing geodesic paths on manifolds. Proc. Nat. Acad. Sci. **95**(15), 8431–8435 (1998)
16. Li, B.Y.L., et al.: Using kinect for face recognition under varying poses, expressions, illumination and disguise. In: IEEE Workshop on Applications of Computer Vision (WACV), pp. 186–192 (2013)
17. Li, X., Zhang, H.: Adapting geometric attributes for expression-invariant 3D face recognition. In: IEEE Conference on Shape Modeling and Applications (2007)
18. Mian, A.S., Bennamoun, M., Owens, R.: Keypoint detection and local feature matching for textured 3D face recognition. Int. J. Comput. Vis. **79**(1), 1–12 (2008)
19. Parkhi, O.M., Vedaldi, A., Zisserman, A., et al.: Deep face recognition. In: British Machine Vision Conference, vol. 1, p. 6 (2015)
20. Passalis, G., et al.: Using facial symmetry to handle pose variations in real-world 3D face recognition. IEEE Trans. Pattern Anal. Mach. Intell. **33**(10), 1938–1951 (2011)
21. Patil, H., Kothari, A., Bhurchandi, K.: 3-D face recognition: features, databases, algorithms and challenges. Artif. Intell. Rev. **44**(3), 393–441 (2015)
22. Phillips, P.J., et al.: Overview of the face recognition grand challenge. In: IEEE Conference on CVPR, vol. 1, pp. 947–954 (2005)
23. Queirolo, C.C., Silva, L., Bellon, O.R., Segundo, M.P.: 3D face recognition using simulated annealing and the surface interpenetration measure. IEEE Trans. Pattern Anal. Mach. Intell. **32**(2), 206–219 (2009)
24. Ranjan, R., et al.: Deep learning for understanding faces: machines may be just as good, or better, than humans. IEEE Signal Process. Mag. **35**(1), 66–83 (2018)
25. Sang, G., Li, J., Zhao, Q.: Pose-invariant face recognition via RGB-D images. Comput. Intell. Neurosci. **2016**, 13 (2016)
26. Sariyanidi, E., Gunes, H., Cavallaro, A.: Automatic analysis of facial affect: a survey of registration, representation, and recognition. IEEE Trans. Pattern Anal. Mach. Intell. **37**(6), 1113–1133 (2015)
27. Soltanpour, S., Boufama, B., Wu, Q.J.: A survey of local feature methods for 3D face recognition. Pattern Recogn. **72**, 391–406 (2017)
28. Taigman, Y., Yang, M., Ranzato, M., Wolf, L.: DeepFace: closing the gap to human-level performance in face verification. In: IEEE Conference on CVPR, pp. 1701–1708 (2014)
29. Tang, X., Chen, J., Moon, Y.S.: Accurate 3D face registration based on the symmetry plane analysis on nose regions. In: European Signal Processing Conference, pp. 1–5 (2008)
30. Wang, M., Deng, W.: Deep face recognition: a survey. arXiv preprint arXiv:1804.06655 (2018)
31. Wang, N., Gao, X., Tao, D., Yang, H., Li, X.: Facial feature point detection: a comprehensive survey. Neurocomputing **275**, 50–65 (2018)
32. Yi, D., Lei, Z., Li, S.Z.: Towards pose robust face recognition. In: IEEE Conference on CVPR (2013)
33. Yu, Y., Mora, K.A.F., Odobez, J.: HeadFusion: 360° head pose tracking combining 3D morphable model and 3D reconstruction. IEEE Trans. Pattern Anal. Mach. Intell. **40**(11), 2653–2667 (2018)
34. Zafeiriou, S., Zhang, C., Zhang, Z.: A survey on face detection in the wild: past, present and future. Comput. Vis. Image Underst. **138**, 1–24 (2015)

35. Zhu, X., Lei, Z., Yan, J., Yi, D., Li, S.Z.: High-fidelity pose and expression normalization for face recognition in the wild. In: IEEE Conference on CVPR, pp. 787–796 (2015)
36. Zulqarnain Gilani, S., Mian, A.: Learning from millions of 3D scans for large-scale 3D face recognition. In: IEEE Conference on CVPR, pp. 1896–1905 (2018)

Pupil Center Localization Using SOMA and CNN

Radovan Fusek$^{(\boxtimes)}$ (iD), Eduard Sojka, and Michael Holusa

Department of Computer Science, FEECS, VSB - Technical University of Ostrava,
17. listopadu 2172/15, 708 00 Ostrava-Poruba, Czech Republic
{radovan.fusek,eduard.sojka,michael.holusa}@vsb.cz

Abstract. We present a new method for eye pupil detection in images.
The algorithm runs in two steps. Firstly, a reasonable number of good
candidates for pupil position are determined quickly by making use of
the self-organizing migrating algorithm. Subsequently, the final position
of pupil, among the preselected candidates, is determined precisely by
making use of a convolutional neural network. The motivation for this
two-step architecture is to create the algorithm that is both precise and
fast. The favorable computational speed follows from the fact that only
the meaningful positions and sizes are checked in the potentially most
time-consuming second step. Moreover, the demands on training and
the training set for the network are lower than if the network is used
exclusively in one step architecture. The algorithm is capable to run on
less powerful computers, e.g. on embedded computers in cars. In our
tests, the algorithm achieved good results.

Keywords: CNN · SOMA · Pupil detection · Iris detection · Deep
learning

1 Introduction

Accurate localization of the pupil (or iris) is a key step in the area of eye movement analysis. Besides the accuracy, the speed of detection is often equally
important, e.g. if the detection should run on embedded devices or on other
less powerful computers. Such a situation can be seen, for example, in vehicles,
where the algorithms for detecting the eye and its parts may become an important component of the systems for detecting the state of driver (they should
determine, for example, gaze direction, blinking frequency, and fatigue of the
driver with the final goal to determine the ability to drive). Naturally, such systems should work with a high precision and quickly although the computational
resources are limited.

In this paper, we propose a fast and accurate method for pupil center localization that can be used in remote eye-tracker systems (i.e. the systems that use
the cameras located away from the user), and that can run on low-performance
computers. In essence, our work improves and extends the method presented in

© Springer Nature Switzerland AG 2019
G. Bebis et al. (Eds.): ISVC 2019, LNCS 11844, pp. 444–453, 2019.
https://doi.org/10.1007/978-3-030-33720-9_34

[6], in which the pupil localization method based on the eye model combined with an evolutionary algorithm called Self-Organizing Migrating Algorithm (SOMA) [16] was proposed. We discovered that this model can be further improved to achieve better performance, which is our first contribution. In addition to this, we propose another improvement consisting in the fact that the final verification of pupil position is done by making use of the convolutional neural network (CNN), which is our second contribution. Thanks to these improvements, our new method outperforms the original method [6] and the state-of-the-art methods in this area.

The rest of the paper is organized as follows. The previously presented papers from the area of eye analysis are mentioned in Sect. 2. In Sect. 3, the main steps of the proposed method are described. In Sect. 4, the results of experiments are presented.

2   Related Work

The detection of pupil and iris is an important task in many areas (e.g. medicine, psychology, bio-metric, auto-motive) and many different approaches have been presented in recent years. A method designed for head-mounted eye-tracking systems for pupil localization was proposed in [13]. The method consists of several steps: removing the corneal reflection, pupil edge detection using a feature-based technique which is followed by ellipse fitting step using RANSAC. Swirski et al. [14] presented the method that is based on a Haar-like feature detector to roughly estimate the pupil location in the first step. In the next step, the potential pupil region is segmented using k-means clustering to find the largest black region. In the final step, the edge pixels of region are used for ellipse fitting using RANSAC. In [2], the authors proposed Exclusive Curve Selector ($ExCuSe$) that is based on the histogram analysis combined with the Canny edge detector and ellipse estimation using the direct least squares method. In [5], the authors presented an approach, known as $ElSe$, that uses edge filtering, ellipse evaluation, and pupil validation. In [8], another pupil detection method known as SET is proposed. This method is based on thresholding, segmentation, border extraction using the convex hull method, and selection of the segment with the best fit. A method for determining the iris centre in low-resolution images is proposed in [7]. In the first step, the coarse location of iris center is determined using a novel hybrid convolution operator. In the second step, the iris location is further refined using boundary tracing and ellipse fitting. In [10], a pupil localization method was proposed that is based on the training process and the Hough regression forest. The method based on a convolutional neural network is proposed in [3,4]. An evaluation of the state-of-the-art pupil detection algorithms is presented in [1].

3   Proposed Method

In this paper, we improve the method presented in [6] in which a certain eye model and a certain fitness function evaluating the quality of matching was introduced. Global optimization using the self-organizing migrating algorithm (SOMA) was used for finding the best value of fitness function, which also gave the position of eye pupil. During extensive experiments and during using the algorithm in practice, we revealed that the precision of algorithm may be improved significantly while its favorable speed is preserved, which is presented in this paper.

To achieve the mentioned better results, the following is done and presented in this paper: A more precise eye model is introduced. The detection itself is done in two steps.

(i) Firstly, the candidates for pupil position are determined by making use of SOMA.
(ii) Subsequently, the final position of pupil, among the candidates, is determined by making use of a convolutional neural network (CNN).

The goal of the first step is to determine a reasonable number of good candidates quickly. In the second step, the final detection is done precisely. In comparison to using one step recognition with CNN only, this two step approach has the following advantages.

(i) It may be faster since only the meaningful positions and sizes are checked in the potentially time-consuming second step by CNN.
(ii) The neural network solves an easier problem now since it is required to decide only certain specific preselected cases, which results in the following: (a) The demands on training and the size of training set are lower than in the case that CNN is used exclusively. (b) Taking into account that the size of training set is practically limited, the two step method may give a better precision (again, simply because the network is required to decide only a less difficult task for which not so big training set is required).

In the next paragraphs, we describe the particular steps of the new method in more details.

The geometrical eye model consists of three areas: pupil, iris, and sclera (Fig. 1(a)). For fast computation, the pupil and iris are considered to be squares, and the sclera consists of two rectangles (Fig. 1(b)). We note that the model slightly differs from the model that was introduced in [6]. The area of sclera is now divided into its left and right part, which obviously better corresponds to the reality if the usual eye images are taken into account (it was also confirmed by our experience with the behavior of the algorithm described in [6]). The fitness function that is used for optimization and determining the candidates now is

$$f = \frac{mean_I}{mean_P} \cdot \frac{mean_{SL}}{mean_P} \cdot \frac{mean_{SR}}{mean_P}, \tag{1}$$

where $mean_P$, $mean_I$, $mean_{SL}$, $mean_{SR}$ stand for the mean value of brightness in the area of pupil, iris, left and right part of sclera, respectively. From the equation, it can be seen that we strive for a big value of contrast between the pupil and iris, and between the pupil and both sides of sclera.

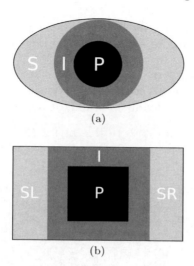

(a)

(b)

Fig. 1. The eye models for determining the fitness functions. The circular model (a) and the simplified rectangular model (b) used in the proposed method.

In order to be able to determine the mentioned mean values and to carry out the optimization, the positions and the sizes of the particular areas must be considered. We use five parameters in total: The position (x, y) of the pupil, i.e. the center point of the whole model, the size of pupil, the size of iris (we remind that the pupil and iris are square shaped), the width of the left and right part of the sclera (both parts have the same width, their height is determined by the size of iris). We note that it is necessary to keep the number of parameters low to achieve a good speed of the SOMA algorithm.

SOMA [16] is a meta-heuristic algorithm which is inspired by the cooperative behavior of intelligent creatures solving a common problem. In essence, the problem that is solved in the first step is to find a certain number of candidates for which the values of the expression from Eq. (1) is either directly equal or is close to its global maximum value. According to our experience, SOMA is able to realize relatively successful searches. The principle of SOMA can be briefly summarized as follows. (We refer the reader to [16] for the details.)

(i) In the first step, an initial population of individuals is generated randomly (Fig. 2(a)). In our case, each individual is characterized by its five randomly generated parameters mentioned before.

(ii) At the beginning of each iterative step, a leader is selected among the individuals in the population, which is the individual with the best value of the fitness function.

(iii) In each iterative step (Fig. 2(b–f)), all the individuals carry out a series of jumps in the direction towards the leader (the number of jumps is a parameter that is chosen a priori). The following is important to note, which ensures that the method does not reduce to a process of finding local maxima only. (a) The jumps may be even substantially longer than is the distance between the individual and the leader. (b) The motion vectors towards the leader are perturbed in such a way that their randomly selected coordinates are set to zero.

(iv) Among all the jumps carried out for each individual in a population, the jump with the best value of the fitness function is selected, which determines the new position of the individual in the next population and next iteration.

These steps are illustrated in Fig. 2. In this figure, the subsequent CNN step is also shown. We note that the iris area image is used as an input for CNN.

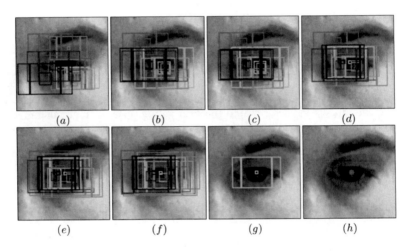

Fig. 2. Steps of the proposed method. The initial population (the size of population is 8 in this particular case) of individuals (a). Examples of five iterative steps in which the jumps of individuals are carried out (b–f). The final eye model that is selected from all possible candidates in (f) using CNN is shown in (g) (the iris area image is used as an input for CNN). The center of the iris area of the selected model represents the final position of pupil (h).

Naturally, the parameters of SOMA must be selected carefully in order to achieve an acceptable compromise between the speed, and the number and quality of candidates for the final evaluation. Their values are discussed in the experiments presented in the next section. The architecture of the network carrying out the final recognition step is not critical. We use the well-known and relatively simple LeNet [12] architecture. According to our experience, the use of more complicated architectures does not improve the detection noticeably.

4   Experiments

In this section, we evaluate the proposed method and we compare it with other state-of-the-art methods for pupil localization, including the method based on SOMA presented in [6]. For the experiments, we used the BioID [9] and GI4E

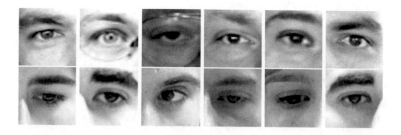

Fig. 3. Examples of eye images used in experiments. The BioID images are in the first row. The GI4E images are in the second row.

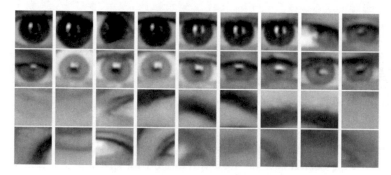

Fig. 4. An example of iris and non-iris images.

[15] public datasets. The BioID dataset contains 1521 gray level images with the resolution of 384 × 286 pixels. Every image shows one of 23 persons with different illumination conditions in different indoor environments. The GI4E database provides 1339 images with the resolution of 800 × 600 pixels along with the manually labeled ground truth consisting of the iris (pupil) center position and eye corners positions. The size of each extracted eye image (from both datasets) is 100 × 100 pixels, and the eye images are purposely extracted with the eyebrow to test the methods in complicated conditions. The examples of eye images from these datasets are shown in Fig. 3. In our experiments, we calculate the error as the Euclidean distance from the ground truth of the pupil center and the center provided by the particular detection method. The average time for processing one eye region was measured on an Intel Core i3 processor (3.7 GHz) with NVIDIA GeForce GTX1050.

As we described in the previous section, the contribution of our new method is in two areas; we presented a more precise eye model used in SOMA, and we applied the convolutional neural network for estimating the final position of pupil. The size of population in SOMA was set to 25, the number of migration steps (i.e. the number of iterative steps mentioned in the previous section) was 6, the number of jumps for each individual in each migration step was set equally to 6. The network consists of two convolutional layers with the depth of 6 and 16, respectively, and a 5 × 5 filter size with a 1 × 1 stride. Each of the layers is

Table 1. The detection results of SOMA-based methods.

	BioID Mean error (pixels)	GI4E Mean error (pixels)	Time per region (ms)
$origSOMA_{25}$	8.15	6.05	2
$newSOMA_{25}$	7.58	5.42	2
$newSOMA_{25} + CNN$	5.74	4.37	4
$newSOMA_{50} + CNN$	5.54	4.06	8

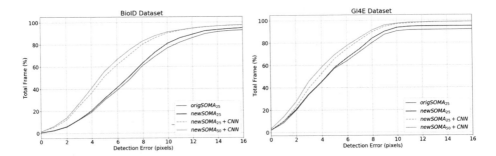

Fig. 5. The cumulative distribution of detection error. The error that is calculated as the Euclidean distance (in pixels) is in the x-axis. The y-axis shows the percentage of frames with the detection error smaller or equal to a specific error. The names of datasets are placed above the pictures.

followed by a rectified linear activation function. Thereafter, a max pooling layer with a window size of 2×2 and with a 2×2 stride is added; the last two layers are fully connected. We used stochastic gradient descent with the learning rate of 0.01 annealed to 0.0001. To compute the recognition score (confidence), we use the soft-max layer, and 32×32 grayscale images are used as an input. The implementation of CNN is based on Dlib [11]. The training set consists of 4600 iris images and 4600 non-iris images that were manually extracted from our eye image data (Fig. 4).

In Table 1, we show the results comparing the method using the new eye model ($newSOMA_{25}$) with the method presented in [6] that uses a simplified eye model ($origSOMA_{25}$). It is seen that a lower mean error is achieved with the proposed eye model, which indicates that this model represents the eye more precisely. If we apply CNN for the final estimation of the pupil position ($newSOMA_{25} + CNN$), which is the second contribution of our method, the mean error is even lower. For comparison, we also increased the size of population in SOMA to 50 and used the new eye model with CNN ($newSOMA_{50} + CNN$). This step slightly decreases the mean error comparing to the population size of 25, on the other hand, the time consumption increases from 4 ms to 8 ms. The diagrams in Fig. 5 show the cumulative distribution of detection error for the mentioned methods.

Table 2. The detection results of methods.

	BioID Mean error (pixels)	GI4E Mean error (pixels)	Time per region (ms)
$newSOMA_{50} + CNN$	**5.54**	**4.06**	**8**
CNN_1	6.41	4.65	240
CNN_2	6.34	4.92	15
$ElSe$	10.50	12.72	16
$ExCuSe$	11.00	7.10	8
$Swirski$	10.43	11.10	10

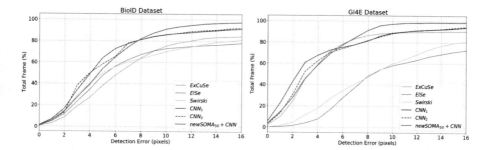

Fig. 6. The cumulative distribution of detection error. The error that is calculated as the Euclidean distance (in pixels) is in the x-axis. The y-axis shows the percentage of frames with the detection error smaller or equal to a specific error. The names of datasets are placed above the pictures.

We also compared the proposed method with the other methods for pupil localization, namely $ElSe$ [5], $ExCuSe$ [2], $Swirski$ [14], and two CNN-based pupil detectors: CNN_1 and CNN_2. In CNN_1, we used a sliding window technique applied to the entire input eye image with one pixel stride. In CNN_2, the stride of four pixels is used. The architecture of CNN is the same as in our method, the size of sliding window is 32×32 pixels in both variants (i.e. 32×32 grayscale images are used as the input). The results are shown in Table 2, the cumulative distribution of detection error is in Fig. 6. Our method (with the population size set to 50) achieved the lowest mean error in both datasets. The speed of our method is the lowest together with the $ExCuSe$ method (8 ms). The results show that the proposed method is faster and more accurate than CNN_1 and CNN_2. It indicates that using SOMA instead of the sliding window is useful. Examples of images in which the proposed method detects the pupil center more precisely than the other compared methods are shown in Fig. 7.

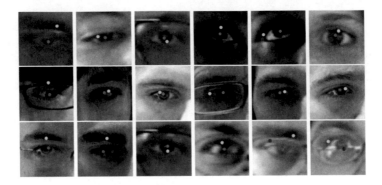

Fig. 7. Examples of images in which the proposed method performs better compared with other tested methods. The results of methods are distinguished by color: $newSOMA_{50} + CNN$ - red, CNN_2 - blue, $origSOMA_{25}$ - cyan. (Color figure online)

5   Conclusion

In this paper, we proposed a new approach for pupil (iris) center localization that can be used in remote eye-tracker systems. The approach consists of two main steps. In the first step, the preliminary candidates for pupil are quickly localized with the use of the self-organizing migrating algorithm. In the second step, the final position is precisely determined by making use of a convolutional neural network. The proposed approach was evaluated and compared with the state-of-the-art methods on two publicly available datasets. Based on the experimental results, we can conclude that the proposed method is faster and more accurate when compared with the existing methods.

Acknowledgments. This work was partially supported by Grant of SGS No. SP2019/71, VŠB - Technical University of Ostrava, Czech Republic.

References

1. Fuhl, W., Geisler, D., Santini, T., Rosenstiel, W., Kasneci, E.: Evaluation of state-of-the-art pupil detection algorithms on remote eye images. In: Proceedings of the 2016 ACM International Joint Conference on Pervasive and Ubiquitous Computing: Adjunct, UbiComp 2016, pp. 1716–1725. ACM, New York, NY, USA (2016). https://doi.org/10.1145/2968219.2968340. https://doi.acm.org/10.1145/2968219.2968340
2. Fuhl, W., Kübler, T., Sippel, K., Rosenstiel, W., Kasneci, E.: ExCuSe: robust pupil detection in real-world scenarios. In: Azzopardi, G., Petkov, N. (eds.) CAIP 2015. LNCS, vol. 9256, pp. 39–51. Springer, Cham (2015). https://doi.org/10.1007/978-3-319-23192-1_4
3. Fuhl, W., Santini, T., Kasneci, G., Kasneci, E.: PupilNet: convolutional neural networks for robust pupil detection. CoRR abs/1601.04902 (2016). http://arxiv.org/abs/1601.04902

4. Fuhl, W., Santini, T., Kasneci, G., Rosenstiel, W., Kasneci, E.: PupilNet v2.0: convolutional neural networks for CPU based real time robust pupil detection. CoRR abs/1711.00112 (2017). http://arxiv.org/abs/1711.00112

5. Fuhl, W., Santini, T.C., Kübler, T.C., Kasneci, E.: Else: ellipse selection for robust pupil detection in real-world environments. CoRR abs/1511.06575 (2015). http://arxiv.org/abs/1511.06575

6. Fusek, R., Dobeš, P.: Pupil localization using self-organizing migrating algorithm. In: Zelinka, I., Brandstetter, P., Trong Dao, T., Hoang Duy, V., Kim, S.B. (eds.) AETA 2018. LNEE, vol. 554, pp. 207–216. Springer, Cham (2020). https://doi.org/10.1007/978-3-030-14907-9_21

7. George, A., Routray, A.: Fast and accurate algorithm for eye localisation for gaze tracking in low-resolution images. IET Comput. Vis. **10**(7), 660–669 (2016). https://doi.org/10.1049/iet-cvi.2015.0316

8. Javadi, A.H., Hakimi, Z., Barati, M., Walsh, V., Tcheang, L.: Set: a pupil detection method using sinusoidal approximation. Front. Neuroeng. **8**, 4 (2015). https://doi.org/10.3389/fneng.2015.00004. https://www.frontiersin.org/article/10.3389/fneng.2015.00004

9. Jesorsky, O., Kirchberg, K.J., Frischholz, R.W.: Robust face detection using the hausdorff distance. In: Bigun, J., Smeraldi, F. (eds.) AVBPA 2001. LNCS, vol. 2091, pp. 90–95. Springer, Heidelberg (2001). https://doi.org/10.1007/3-540-45344-X_14

10. Kacete, A., Royan, J., Seguier, R., Collobert, M., Soladie, C.: Real-time eye pupil localization using hough regression forest. In: 2016 IEEE Winter Conference on Applications of Computer Vision (WACV), pp. 1–8, March 2016. https://doi.org/10.1109/WACV.2016.7477666

11. King, D.E.: Dlib-ml: a machine learning toolkit. J. Mach. Learn. Res. **10**, 1755–1758 (2009)

12. Lecun, Y., Bottou, L., Bengio, Y., Haffner, P.: Gradient-based learning applied to document recognition. Proc. IEEE **86**(11), 2278–2324 (1998). https://doi.org/10.1109/5.726791

13. Li, D., Winfield, D., Parkhurst, D.J.: Starburst: a hybrid algorithm for video-based eye tracking combining feature-based and model-based approaches. In: 2005 IEEE Computer Society Conference on Computer Vision and Pattern Recognition (CVPR 2005) - Workshops, pp. 79–79, June 2005. https://doi.org/10.1109/CVPR.2005.531

14. Świrski, L., Bulling, A., Dodgson, N.: Robust real-time pupil tracking in highly off-axis images. In: Proceedings of the Symposium on Eye Tracking Research and Applications, ETRA 2012, pp. 173–176. ACM, New York, NY, USA (2012). https://doi.org/10.1145/2168556.2168585. https://doi.acm.org/10.1145/2168556.2168585

15. Villanueva, A., Ponz, V., Sesma-Sanchez, L., Ariz, M., Porta, S., Cabeza, R.: Hybrid method based on topography for robust detection of iris center and eye corners. ACM Trans. Multimed. Comput. Commun. Appl. **9**(4), 25:1–25:20 (2013). https://doi.org/10.1145/2501643.2501647

16. Zelinka, I.: SOMA – self-organizing migrating algorithm. In: Onwubolu, G.C., Babu, B.V. (eds.) New Optimization Techniques in Engineering, pp. 167–217. Springer, Heidelberg (2004). https://doi.org/10.1007/978-3-540-39930-8_7

Real-Time Face Features Localization with Recurrent Refined Dense CNN Architectures

Nicolas Livet[✉]

XZIMG Ltd. Research Lab, Kowloon, Hong Kong
nicolas.livet@xzimg.com

Abstract. Based on an innovative, efficient recurrent deep learning architecture, we present a highly stable and robust technique to localize face features on still images, captured and live video sequences. This dense (Fully Convolutional) CNN architecture, referred as the Refined Dense Mobilenet (RDM), is composed of (1) a main encoder-decoder block which aims to approximate face feature locations and, (2) a sequence of refiners which aims to robustly converge at the vicinity of the features. On video sequences, architecture is adapted into a Recurrent RDM where a shape prior component is re-injected in the form of temporal heatmaps obtained at previous frame inference.

Accuracy and stability of RDM/R-RDM architectures are compared with state-of-the-art Random Forest and CNN based approaches. The idea of combining a holistic feature localizer – taking advantage of large receptive fields to minimize large error – and refiners – working at higher resolution to converge at feature vicinities – is proving high accuracy in localizing face features. We demonstrate RDM/R-RDM architectures improve localization scores on 300W and AFLW datasets. Moreover, by relying on modern, efficient convolutional blocks and based on our recurrent architecture, we deliver the first stable and accurate real-time implementation of face feature localization on low-end Mobile devices.

Keywords: Face features localization · Real-time deep learning · Recurrent tracking

1 Introduction

In computer vision, exploring human face features based on sequence of images has been a topic of interest for decades. In particular, Augmented Reality based applications require accurately positioned face features to render perfectly aligned CG layers on top of the user's face. However, accurate positioning can prove difficult due to face non-rigidities, multiple camera viewpoints and other exogenous perturbations like lighting variations, camera noise, etc. Recent Face Identification techniques also rely on accurate localization of face features to produce frontal faces thus improving face description and classification [32]. In

© Springer Nature Switzerland AG 2019
G. Bebis et al. (Eds.): ISVC 2019, LNCS 11844, pp. 454–468, 2019.
https://doi.org/10.1007/978-3-030-33720-9_35

addition, accurate face feature localization has proven usefulness to improve real-time emotions detection accuracy [19].

Several approaches have been carefully engineered in order to try to solve this problem with the highest possible accuracy. However, most manually-crafted approaches appear to become far less efficient when dealing with real life *face-in-the-wild* problems. Important changes in face shape and pose, sensor noise, illumination variations and hard shadows are a few examples of important hurdles that are particularly complex to overcome.

Approaches that attempt to regress face feature locations using multi-stage random forests [2] have proven their efficiency. Such *shape regression* techniques (see [10] for a seminal work) became widely spread in research and industry over the last decade, due to their simplicity and their ability to generalize relatively well on small-scale datasets containing few thousands of images.

More recently, the rise of efficient Deep Neural Network techniques – the reader is referred to the Deep Learning book [12] for a detailed description of modern techniques – has proven that complex vision problems can be solved. Deep learning and more precisely Convolutional Neural Networks (CNNs), have installed themselves as a natural solution to solve Computer Vision most challenging tasks due to their efficiency and their simplicity. Taking advantage of hidden layer architectures – composed of filters separated by non-linearity activations – it is not required to design the filters manually. Instead one can rely on a simple yet efficient learning phase (back-propagation), which minimizes the global loss while updating the model's filters throughout the network.

In contrast with most recent approaches which consist in evaluating ever deeper architectures or averaging several deep models, our main objective is not only robustness but also efficiency and temporal stability. We emphasize real-time solutions, ideally available on low-end devices without having to trade off localization accuracies. Consequently, our research targets recent CNN models which embed separable and efficient convolution layers. We are also studying how we can provide available prior information when learning and inferring models in order to simplify and accelerate the face feature localization process.

In this work, based on recent discoveries on convolutional blocks and CNN architectures, we develop an original refined CNN architecture providing robustness, efficiency and stability. Then, proposed CNN architecture is further improved based on a temporal propagation of previous frame inference outputs (denoted heatmaps hereinafter) in the case of video sequences, thus forming a recurrent version of the architecture. Recurrent Neural Networks are particularly useful for processing (timely ordered) sequential data such as localizing face shapes in a sequence of images.

The remainder is organized as follows: Sect. 2 gives an account of previous work on face feature localization techniques based either on manually-crafted features or on deep learning models. Then Sect. 3 details the main CNN architecture referred as Refined Dense Mobilenet (RDM). Components of the Recurrent RDM (R-RDM) are described in Sect. 4 while optimized low-end Mobile version of the R-RDM is described in Sect. 5. Finally, we present results of the experiments on datasets and discuss implementation details in Sect. 6.

2   Related Work

The quest of computationally analyzing images to retrieve information related to user's faces started several decades ago. A large quantity of manually-designed techniques were first proposed to detect faces and their positions in images. Amongst them, the boosted cascaded classifier approach by Viola and Jones [34] has been one of the most widely adopted technique to detect faces.

Detecting and localizing face features (or landmarks) located around ears, nose, mouth, etc. has proven a harder problem to solve notably due to different face poses, expressions and lighting conditions which change profoundly the face appearance. A large quantity of approaches were designed to fit a deformable shape based on the face geometry and its appearance as in Active Shape Models [6] or in Active Appearance Models [8]. A widely adopted technique and one of the first that has attracted high interests from the community is the Constrain Local Models [9]. Robustness of CLM techniques relies on the joint optimization of the shape error and its appearance discrepancy. CLM techniques were further extended using support vectors [28] or random forests [7] to infer probability maps around features locations and to compute a global fitting.

Multi-stages random forest based localizers then surpassed state-of-the-art CLM approaches. Amongst the number of published work relying on this technique, the authors of [10] and [5] cautiously selected pixel comparisons to form binary features and to regress iteratively a shape. Zhu et al. [38] based their work on composed cascades of shape regressors taking advantage of efficient Local Binary Features (LBF). One main advantage of using simple binary tests in random forest nodes is the efficiency of the approach where a shape can be regressed in a millisecond on a modern CPU as described in [21]. However, most of random forest based approaches suffers from high frequency jitters. Tiny perturbations in the input image space can influence considerably the resulting shape position. Consequently, complex post processing steps such as the use of Kalman filters or recursive template matching become necessary to limit the influence of noise. Because of their efficiency and relative robustness, cascaded regression forests have played, and are still playing, an important role in recent open source [17] and commercial solutions [36].

Since the rise of the Deep Learning, number of proposed solutions to localize face features rely on multi-stage CNN architectures [30]. In [37] authors used a coarse-to-fine cascade of CNNs to improve detection accuracy when compared to existing commercial solutions. More recently [14] and [24] further improved localization accuracies on the 300-W [26] and AFLW [22] competition datasets either by using progressive shape refinement CNNs [14] or by using deeper architectures thus accumulating layers and processing.

In contrast to aforementioned deep learning based regressor architectures, our approach combines a main CNN encoder-decoder block and subsequent CNN blocks to construct dense heatmaps used to extract face feature locations with better accuracies. Such architecture is inspired by the one described in *Convolutional Pose Machines* [35]. In their approach, the authors were using cascaded CNNs to disambiguate belief maps containing multiple peaks at body joints by using larger receptive fields. For face feature localization however, it is not required to enlarge receptive fields, as face features provide less positional ambiguities. Instead, post processing stages are modified to address fine face feature localization.

Only few recent works have studied the benefits of temporality to address and improve face feature localization on video sequences. In [23] authors used a sequence of different type of CNNs to compute a label map which plays the role of temporal shape prior. However, their architecture is computationally expensive and cannot be adapted easily to static images as author target mainly video sequences containing the same face identity.

In [4], authors describe a 2D face alignment process based on several stacked deep networks *Hour-Glass* networks. Their learning process relies a large but slightly inaccurate dataset (containing more than 200,000 images) leading to accurate results on in-the-wild faces. They seem however to miss to locate highly accurate feature position and obtained results are unstable. In [11], different losses, including the *Wing loss*, are presented and compared to improve on AFLW and 300W accuracy scores.

A great quantity of modern work on localizing face features rely on existing CNN models. For example, the VGG architecture (described in [29]) has attracted interest for its simplicity: the VGG architecture is composed of a sequence of 3×3 convolution operators concatenated with some interlaced max pooling operators. Reducing the complexity of deep learning architecture has been address in [3] where author's binarized convolution operators have allowed to maintain higher accuracy while limiting computational resources. Some deep CNN architectures have introduced new blocks to target efficiency, such as Inception [31], Resnet [13] which takes advantage of a particularly robust and efficient net in-the-net modules. Mobilenet CNN architectures [15] rely on separable *pointwise* (also denoted as *pointwise*) and *depthwise* convolutions which are fast, relatively robust and easy to implement. Recently, the Mobilenet v2 architecture [27] further improved efficiency by taking advantage of a new *Inverted Residual Bottleneck Block* that squeezes the depth of the feature maps before applying 3×3 depthwise convolution operator. Our approach relies on those separable filters and on a sequential CNN architecture to achieve state-of-the-art accuracy and maintain high efficiency.

3   Refined Dense Mobilenet Architecture

Designed architecture, loss estimation and corresponding learning strategy are first detailed. It is then described how resulting output heatmaps are used to localizing face features at subpixel accuracy.

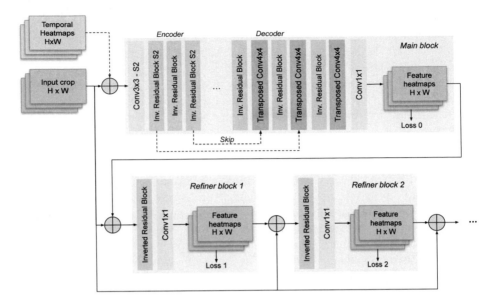

Fig. 1. Main drawing depicting proposed RDM architecture. The *encoder-decoder* part is based on a fully convolutional adaptation of the Google Mobilenet v2. The main block is composed of a first 3×3 convolution operator, Inverted Residual Blocks (IRB), 4×4 transposed convolutions operators and skip layers which connect strided convolutions (noted with the "S2" term) with corresponding up-sampling layers. The last pointwise convolution reduces the depth to obtain the appropriate number of heatmaps. Refiner blocks are composed of an IRB operators and a pointwise operator to construct refined output heatmaps. Each refiner block inputs are built based on previously built feature heatmaps and input image. Each block is used to generate a loss which composes the global architecture loss. Optional *frame-to-frame* recurrent localization is introduced based on the re-injection of previous frame output heatmaps using a concatenation operator which combines these heatmaps with the current RGB input image.

3.1   Architecture Description

Our approach to localize face features is based on the RDM architecture which is an extension of the Mobilenet v2 [27] as illustrated in Fig. 1. A dense CNN (or Fully Convolutional Network denoted as FCN, see [20]) architecture infers a per-pixel prediction instead of a global classification or regression based on an entire image. Dense network outputs produce heatmaps (sometimes called belief maps) expressing, in our case, the level of belief that a pixel is located at a face feature location.

The RDM architecture contains a main block – an encoder-decoder including skip layers similarly to the UNet architecture [25] – and *Refiner* blocks inspired by the post-processing stages in [35]. In contrast with these post-processing stages that aim to disambiguate multiple body features in large complex scene, we operate post-processing CNN blocks at higher resolutions with the objective to refine heatmap responses at face feature vicinities. These *Refiner* blocks have been named to express this idea.

As in Mobilenet v2's approach, main block architecture relies on efficient combinations of 1×1 pointwise and 3×3 depthwise convolution operators grouped as Inverted Residual Blocks. In addition, our model includes a decoder to reconstruct dense outputs matching input resolution. The main block *encoder* is then assigned the task of approximating low resolution heatmaps on the face, limiting large errors. Next, main block *decoder* and later *refiners* are assigned the task of improving local convergence at face feature vicinities considering smaller receptive fields at higher resolution.

Network Depth. The depth of feature maps and the number of architecture layers can be either reduced or expanded according to required performance at inference time. Baseline version matches the setup of the default Mobilenet v2.

Skip Layers. As illustrated in Fig. 1, skip layers connecting each downsampling and upsampling modules can be added to the architecture. However, only very little improvement has been observed when using skip layers on face feature localization problems. As the purpose of skip layers is to achieve better feature maps local positioning, we believe later refiners have played the same role and their effect is thus limited.

Downsampling. Our architecture is composed of three downsampling layers and three corresponding upsampling layers, however, one can control downsampling level according to input resolution and depending on the use-case. For example, image segmentation problems would probably require increased downsampling and *atrous* convolutions which can be added to our architecture.

Heatmaps. In our implementation, heatmaps correspond to rescaled probability density functions, defining the likelihood of a pixel of being located at a certain face feature given an input image and possibly temporal data. Label heatmaps for each face feature l are constructed using a rescaled Gaussian function with the peak centered at face feature ground truth location x_l:

$$H_l(p) = \exp(-\beta \|p - x_l\|_2^2), \tag{1}$$

where p represents heatmap pixels and β controls the spread of the peak.

3.2 Learning and Loss Estimation

To learn the model's parameters, we estimate errors based on the difference between inferred heatmaps and heatmaps generated based on labeled shapes. Huber loss is used to helps avoid the learner being excessively influenced by large errors occurring at first stages of the optimization process.

Per block and per sample losses are then defined as,

$$\mathcal{L}^{(i)} = \frac{1}{PL} \sum_p \sum_l \rho(H_l(p)^{(i)} - \hat{H}_l(p)^{(i)}) \tag{2}$$

With $\hat{H}_l(p)^{(i)}$ indicating the predicted heatmap value at pixel p for face feature indexed l, and where ρ defines how the influence of the error is smoothed and dimmed when it grows (a Huber Loss has been used).

Model loss is then expressed as the summation of the loss over sample errors and over blocks:

$$\mathcal{L} = \alpha_0 \mathcal{L}^{(0)} + \alpha_1 \sum_i \mathcal{L}^{(i)} \tag{3}$$

Model parameters are optimized by minimizing $\mathcal{L}$ iteratively based on batches containing less than 5 samples. The learning process which starts with a learning rate set at 0.005, is separated in phases were each blocks are trained separately. In a final phase, all network weights are optimized jointly.

3.3   Face Features at Sub-pixel Accuracy

The output of the RDM is a set of dense heatmaps containing peaks at pixels located near face feature real locations. Heatmap responses are constructed based on a rescaled probability dense function centered at face feature location. We wish to recover a precise location of each face feature based on CNN dense responses, without having to regress their location by appending yet another fully connected CNN architecture at the end of the RDM.

As output heatmaps already match input image resolution and as small neighborhoods around face feature contain enough data on the shape of the Gaussian peak, sub-pixel locations are calculated using only few neighboring pixels around the maximal response. A quadratic surface $S(x, y) = ax^2 + bxy + cy^2 + dx + ey + f$ around the identified maximal response location is approximated on its neighborhood. The correct location is finally computed by zeroing the x and y derivatives of the quadratic surface.

4   Recurrent Localization

Existing CNN based face feature detectors rarely focus on real-time localization as approaches, trained on datasets images, are designed to run inferences *in-the-cloud*. Other techniques rely on GPU implementation of CNN operations to detect face features on video sequences, but rarely address temporal stability. In contrast, one main objective of this work is to provide a real-time and stable face feature localization technique which can be applied to video sequences. To obtain improved stability and robustness when localizing face features, the RDM architecture is transformed into a Recurrent RDM (R-RDM) by re-injecting previous frame output heatmaps as current frame input.

4.1   Architecture Description

As depicted in Fig. 1, the RDM input data is modified when a shape prior is available based on previous frame results. In this case, a set of heatmap images are generated and stacked with the input RGB image to form a shape prior based on previous frame results. If no shape prior is available, as for the first detected face in a sequence, the temporal heatmap images are constructed based on a centered mean shape.

Instead of learning parameters for the RDM architecture, such that output heatmaps are formed as $\hat{H} = f_{RDM}(X, \phi_{RDM})$, heatmaps construction at time t not only depends on input image X but also on temporal heatmaps at time $t-1$: $\hat{H}_t = f_{R-RDM}(X, \hat{H}_{t-1}, \phi_{R-RDM})$. Learning ϕ_{R-RDM} thus require a tuple (X_t, H_t, H_{t-1}) which can be generate based on annotated video sequences. An inference step simply relies on a concatenation between the current image and the heatmap $\hat{H}_{t-1}$ obtained at previous inference step.

During learning phase, to avoid the tiresome and difficult work of annotating video sequences, we rely on generated virtual temporal heatmaps H_t by using a strategy to simulate frame-to-frame movements, which allows us to avoid the cost of annotating video sequences. Additional parameters in ϕ_{R-RDM} are set to zero as initialization value.

4.2   Temporal Heatmap Generation

We combine a rigid geometric transformation and a non-rigid statistical face model (based on a 3D blendshapes) to estimate the pose of a face $\mathcal{T}$ and corresponding expression state vector b. Fitting rigid and non-rigid parameters on a face is achieved based on a Maximum Likelihood Estimator on the projection error (Fig. 2, step 1):

$$\begin{cases} \min_{w.r.t. \ b, \mathcal{T}} \mathcal{E} = \|s - \hat{s}\|_2^2 \\ s = \mathcal{T}(\Phi b + \bar{x}) \end{cases} \quad (4)$$

where Φ is the matrix of unit eigen vectors, b the vector of non-rigid parameters – comprising both (locked) identity and expression – and $\bar{x}$ the mean shape.

We compute small random perturbation to simulate face rotation, face scale, face translation and face feature movements during the learning phase (Fig. 2,

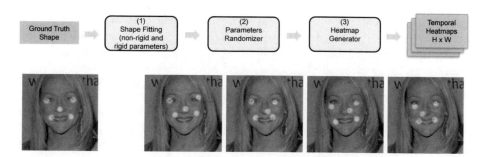

Fig. 2. *First row*: process to generate temporal heatmaps at learning stage. We simulate shape movements from consecutive frames and create a virtual set of heatmaps. *Second row*: an illustration of a ground truth heatmap and examples of generated virtual heatmaps for 5 main face features (combined to ease visualization).

step 2). Random perturbations must cover relatively important temporal *frame-to-frame* displacements. Chosen settings generate shapes with a mean RMSE (see Sect. 6 for details on metrics) of 0.25 with regards to the ground truth shape position. Realistic temporal heatmaps that represent face movements are finally generated using the heatmap generator (Fig. 2, step 3) based on Eq. 1.

5   Optimized Architecture

Inspired by the main architecture, an Optimized Dense Mobilenet (R-ODM) for low-end platforms is introduced. This adapted architecture, which aims to reduce complexity (in terms of MFLOPS) is optimized to run real-time inference on Mobile platforms. As illustrated in Fig. 3, 3×3 transposed convolution are introduced and the total number of IRB components has been reduced.

Importantly, the input temporal heatmap images have been concatenated into a single *fused* temporal heatmap to address the complexity bottleneck introduced by the first layer.

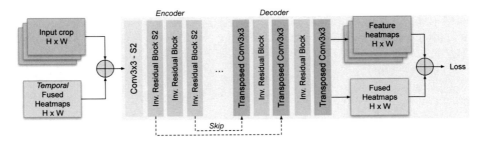

Fig. 3. RDM and R-RDM architectures are optimized for Mobile platforms: the total number of layers has been reduced, input is reduced to a 4-channel image (RGB and fused Temporal Heatmap).

To automatically compute the fused heatmap image, an additional output channel is inferred by the architecture. It is learned as a concatenation of all face feature heatmap images and is built at learning stage by taking per pixel maximum response over all individual face feature heatmaps:

$$H(\mathrm{p}) = \max_l H_l(\mathrm{p}) \tag{5}$$

We take advantage of this fused heatmap channel to perform a learning that considers all the face features in a holistic manner as we included the fused heatmap in the computation of the loss $\mathcal{L}$. A fused heatmap is beneficial during the learning because the model's weights are updated considering positioning of neighboring face features and face features relative positions.

6   Experiments

6.1   Datasets

We followed the protocols defined in [14] (FEC-CNN), [4] (2D-FAN) and [11] (ResNet-50+PDB+Wing) to train and evaluate proposed (R-)RDM, R-ODM architectures. Tests were conducted on two challenging, *in-the-wild* training-validation sets: AFLW [22] and 300W competition [26]. Each set contains face images and corresponding annotated face feature locations.

AFLW Challenge. Dataset comprising 24386 *in-the-wild* face images with large face rotations comprising hidden face parts. Sometimes referred as AFLW-Full, it comprises 19 face features. The training set is built using a shuffled split including 10% of the image.

300W Challenge. The 300W competition [26] employs the indoor and outdoor images (600 images in total). Training rely on a combination of the images from LFPW [1], AFW [39], HELEN [18] and IBUG [26]. 68 face features have been used (including face contour).

Error Estimation. To compare obtained results with state-of-the-art approaches, the (R-)RDM architectures are evaluated using the standard Normalized Mean Error (NME). The normalization term is evaluated using: (1) the face size (using the given face bounding box) on AFLW dataset as described in [11] and, (2) the face size (using computed bounding box) to compare with 2D-FAN on the 300W competition and, (3) eye outer corners to compare with FEC-CNN on the 300W competition.

6.2   Results

Evaluations on AFLW. We compare the performance of (R-)RDM and R-ODM with most accurate techniques of their categories: FEC-CNN [14], Zhu et al. (LBF Shape Regressor [38]) and ResNet-50-Wing [11]. Results, reported in Table 1, demonstrate the ability of our architectures to address in-the-wild faces with difficult pose and various lighting effects. The large amount of available sample has proven beneficial to reach higher accuracies subsequently due to the reasonable amount of weights to train and the nonnecessity to combat overfitting. Additional fused output heatmap was observed beneficial to dim out important positioning errors as face landmarks heatmaps (of a same face) are jointly optimized.

Table 1. Mean error on AFLW (NME normalized using face size)

Zhu et al. [38]	FEC-CNN [14]	ResNet-50-Wing [11]	RDM	R-RDM	R-ODM
0.027	0.017	0.0147	0.01395	0.01325	0.01345

As thousands of resulting shapes have been carefully reviewed, we found only several problematic instances (most incorrectly annotated or presenting hidden, noisy or ambiguous parts).

Evaluations on 300W Competition. Firstly, we evaluate the performance of (R-)RDM, FEC-CNN [14] and MDM [33] in the left-hand side of Fig. 4. RDM, R-RDM outperforms FEC-CNN and MDM significantly. The results also demonstrate the benefit of the fused layer when comparing RDM-REF4-FUSED and RDM-REF4 tests (4 refiners were used for both tests).

In the right-hand side of Fig. 4, we then compare our results with 2D-FAN [4] which has been pre-trained with a dataset containing two orders of magnitude more samples. The recurrent approach R-RDM were able to improve slightly over 2D-FAN as it seems the architecture cope better with larger errors. Refiner blocks demonstrates their usefulness to improve local accuracy.

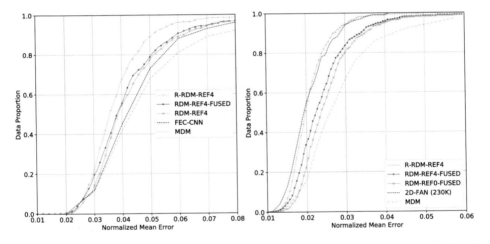

Fig. 4. Comparison on 300W competition, error is normalized using eye corners (left) and using face size (right) to compare with different approaches. *REF* indicates the number of refiner used, while *FUSED* indicates if a final fused loss is used.

Discussions. As illustrated in Table 1 and in Fig. 4, (R-)RDM improved against state-of-the-art approaches for the face features localization task. In one of the most accurate technique, FEC-CNN [14], the CNN cascade is composed of a main initializer to approximate an initial shape along with multiple local multi-stage regressors. We believe that our architecture differs in two aspects: (1) their approach is relatively hard to setup and optimize as author are using multiple branches for each stage and features to locate which contrast with our straight-forward standard architecture. (2) transposed layers and refiners used in our RDM offers better convergence at face feature vicinities.

Temporal propagation of previous frame heatmaps helps to avoid large fitting errors and converge faster to the highly accurate face feature locations. Furthermore, using shape prior proved even better accuracy and stability allowing us to use shallower CNN architectures. The reader is invited to consult the accompanying video material[1].

Moreover, we argue that stacking Hour-Glass networks, like in 2D-FAN [4], haven't proven to be relevant for the face localization use case, as: (1) face feature detection presents only few potential localization ambiguities; (2) both the additional fused heatmap layer and the recurrent architecture are beneficial to address localization of the face features as an ensemble and improves against these ambiguities and larger localization errors; (3) the refiners contributes to improve local responses to get enhanced, stable face feature positions. Accompanying video material comparing RDM with 2D-FAN tends to prove our architecture to be more accurate and more stable.

6.3   Implementation Notes

For the R-RDM architecture, the use of losses after each block is useful to counter vanishing gradients effects. For the optimized version (R-ODM), all weights were learned simultaneously as the architecture is shallower. To combat over-fitting, we employ available augmentations techniques (anisotropic similarities, noise additions, random crops, color distortions, etc.) combined with drop-out layers before the end of each block. However, while training on the ALFW dataset, drop-out and weight decays have been removed as no overfitting was observed and resulting accuracy proved better.

Implementation for iOS is based on efficient GPU CoreML CNN operators. On iPhoneX devices, we have reached 40 fps to compute inference on the R-RDM architecture (with no additional refiner blocks).

Implementation for Android is based on a machine optimized code for the CNN operators. Neon instructions, quantization (as described in [16]), as well as multithreading were used to speed-up processing on the CPU. An Android inference for the R-ODM architecture runs in 25 fps on a Google Pixel 2.

7   Conclusion and Future Work

Based on recent developments in Deep Learning, we introduce an innovative and efficient architecture to robustly localize face features in images and video sequences. Our baseline architecture named RDM is composed of an encoder-decoder main block and a sequence of refiner blocks which is learned efficiently using multiple losses at the end of each block. With the Recurrent RDM architecture, temporal propagation of output heatmap images is a key technique to improve feature localization in live video sequences. Resulting accuracy competes with state-of-the-art approaches on common testing datasets.

---

[1] Accompanying video available at https://vimeo.com/348063383.

In the future, we will complete our work by combining a face emotion detector to the RDM architecture and we will explore 3D blendshape fitting and pose estimation by stacking dedicated CNNs at the end of our architecture.

References

1. Belhumeur, P.N., Jacobs, D.W., Kriegman, D.J., Kumar, N.: Localizing parts of faces using a consensus of exemplars. IEEE Trans. Pattern Anal. Mach. Intell. **35**(12), 2930–2940 (2013)
2. Breiman, L.: Random forests. Mach. Learn. **45**(1), 5–32 (2001)
3. Bulat, A., Tzimiropoulos, G.: Binarized convolutional landmark localizers for human pose estimation and face alignment with limited resources, March 2017
4. Bulat, A., Tzimiropoulos, G.: How far are we from solving the 2D & 3D face alignment problem? (and a dataset of 230, 000 3D facial landmarks). CoRR abs/1703.07332 (2017)
5. Cao, X., Wei, Y., Wen, F., Sun, J.: Face alignment by explicit shape regression. In: 2012 IEEE Conference on Computer Vision and Pattern Recognition, pp. 2887–2894, June 2012
6. Cootes, T.F., Taylor, C.J., Cooper, D.H., Graham, J.: Active shape models: their training and application. Comput. Vis. Image Underst. **61**(1), 38–59 (1995)
7. Cootes, T.F., Ionita, M.C., Lindner, C., Sauer, P.: Robust and accurate shape model fitting using random forest regression voting. In: Fitzgibbon, A., Lazebnik, S., Perona, P., Sato, Y., Schmid, C. (eds.) ECCV 2012. LNCS, vol. 7578, pp. 278–291. Springer, Heidelberg (2012). https://doi.org/10.1007/978-3-642-33786-4_21
8. Cootes, T.F., Edwards, G.J., Taylor, C.J.: Active appearance models. IEEE Trans. Pattern Anal. Mach. Intell. **23**(6), 681–685 (2001)
9. Cristinacce, D., Cootes, T.F.: Feature detection and tracking with constrained local models, vol. 41, pp. 929–938, January 2006
10. Dollár, P., Welinder, P., Perona, P.: Cascaded pose regression. In: CVPR (2010)
11. Feng, Z.H., Kittler, J., Awais, M., Huber, P., Wu, X.J.: Wing loss for robust facial landmark localisation with convolutional neural networks. In: 2018 IEEE Conference on Computer Vision and Pattern Recognition (CVPR), pp. 2235–2245. IEEE (2018)
12. Goodfellow, I., Bengio, Y., Courville, A.: Deep Learning. MIT Press (2016). http://www.deeplearningbook.org
13. He, K., Zhang, X., Ren, S., Sun, J.: Deep residual learning for image recognition. In: 2016 IEEE Conference on Computer Vision and Pattern Recognition (CVPR), pp. 770–778, June 2016
14. He, Z., Kan, M., Zhang, J., Chen, X., Shan, S.: A fully end-to-end cascaded CNN for facial landmark detection. In: 2017 12th IEEE International Conference on Automatic Face Gesture Recognition (FG 2017), pp. 200–207, May 2017
15. Howard, A.G., et al.: MobileNets: efficient convolutional neural networks for mobile vision applications. CoRR abs/1704.04861 (2017)
16. Jacob, B., et al.: Quantization and training of neural networks for efficient integer-arithmetic-only inference. CoRR abs/1712.05877 (2017)
17. King, D.E.: Dlib-ml: a machine learning toolkit. J. Mach. Learn. Res. **10**, 1755–1758 (2009)

18. Le, V., Brandt, J., Lin, Z., Bourdev, L., Huang, T.S.: Interactive facial feature localization. In: Fitzgibbon, A., Lazebnik, S., Perona, P., Sato, Y., Schmid, C. (eds.) ECCV 2012, Part III. LNCS, vol. 7574, pp. 679–692. Springer, Heidelberg (2012). https://doi.org/10.1007/978-3-642-33712-3_49

19. Livet, N., Berkowski, G.: Shape and appearance based sequenced convnets to detect real-time face attributes on mobile devices. In: Perales, F.J., Kittler, J. (eds.) AMDO 2018. LNCS, vol. 10945, pp. 73–84. Springer, Cham (2018). https://doi.org/10.1007/978-3-319-94544-6_8

20. Long, J., Shelhamer, E., Darrell, T.: Fully convolutional networks for semantic segmentation. In: 2015 IEEE Conference on Computer Vision and Pattern Recognition (CVPR), pp. 3431–3440, June 2015

21. Luo, C., Wang, Z., Wang, S., Zhang, J., Yu, J.: Locating facial landmarks using probabilistic random forest. IEEE Signal Process. Lett. **22**(12), 2324–2328 (2015)

22. Koestinger, M., Wohlhart, P., Roth, P.M., Bischof, H.: Annotated facial landmarks in the wild: a large-scale, real-world database for facial landmark localization. In: Proceedings of the First IEEE International Workshop on Benchmarking Facial Image Analysis Technologies (2011)

23. Peng, X., Feris, R.S., Wang, X., Metaxas, D.N.: A recurrent encoder-decoder network for sequential face alignment. In: Leibe, B., Matas, J., Sebe, N., Welling, M. (eds.) ECCV 2016, Part I. LNCS, vol. 9905, pp. 38–56. Springer, Cham (2016). https://doi.org/10.1007/978-3-319-46448-0_3

24. Ranjan, R., Patel, V.M., Chellappa, R.: HyperFace: a deep multi-task learning framework for face detection, landmark localization, pose estimation, and gender recognition. CoRR abs/1603.01249 (2016)

25. Ronneberger, O., Fischer, P., Brox, T.: U-Net: convolutional networks for biomedical image segmentation. In: Navab, N., Hornegger, J., Wells, W.M., Frangi, A.F. (eds.) MICCAI 2015. LNCS, vol. 9351, pp. 234–241. Springer, Cham (2015). https://doi.org/10.1007/978-3-319-24574-4_28. Available on arXiv:1505.04597 [cs.CV]

26. Sagonas, C., Antonakos, E., Tzimiropoulos, G., Zafeiriou, S., Pantic, M.: 300 faces in-the-wild challenge. Image Vision Comput. **47**(C), 3–18 (2016)

27. Sandler, M., Howard, A.G., Zhu, M., Zhmoginov, A., Chen, L.: Inverted residuals and linear bottlenecks: mobile networks for classification, detection and segmentation. CoRR abs/1801.04381 (2018)

28. Saragih, J.M., Lucey, S., Cohn, J.F.: Deformable model fitting by regularized landmark mean-shift. Int. J. Comput. Vision **91**(2), 200–215 (2011)

29. Simonyan, K., Zisserman, A.: Very deep convolutional networks for large-scale image recognition. CoRR abs/1409.1556 (2014)

30. Sun, Y., Wang, X., Tang, X.: Deep convolutional network cascade for facial point detection. In: 2013 IEEE Conference on Computer Vision and Pattern Recognition, pp. 3476–3483, June 2013

31. Szegedy, C., et al.: Going deeper with convolutions. CoRR abs/1409.4842 (2014)

32. Taigman, Y., Yang, M., Ranzato, M., Wolf, L.: DeepFace: closing the gap to human-level performance in face verification. In: 2014 IEEE Conference on Computer Vision and Pattern Recognition, pp. 1701–1708, June 2014

33. Trigeorgis, G., Snape, P., Nicolaou, M., Antonakos, E., Zafeiriou, S.: Mnemonic descent method: a recurrent process applied for end-to-end face alignment, June 2016. https://doi.org/10.1109/CVPR.2016.453

34. Viola, P., Jones, M.: Robust real-time object detection. Int. J. Comput. Vision **4**(34–47), 4 (2001)

35. Wei, S.E., Ramakrishna, V., Kanade, T., Sheikh, Y.: Convolutional pose machines. CoRR abs/1602.00134 (2016)
36. XZIMG: Magic face - face features tracker for augmented reality apps (2016). http://www.xzimg.com
37. Zhou, E., Fan, H., Cao, Z., Jiang, Y., Yin, Q.: Extensive facial landmark localization with coarse-to-fine convolutional network cascade. In: 2013 IEEE International Conference on Computer Vision Workshops, pp. 386–391, December 2013
38. Zhu, S., Li, C., Loy, C.C., Tang, X.: Unconstrained face alignment via cascaded compositional learning, pp. 3409–3417, June 2016
39. Zhu, X., Ramanan, D.: Face detection, pose estimation, and landmark localization in the wild. In: 2012 IEEE Conference on Computer Vision and Pattern Recognition, pp. 2879–2886, June 2012

Virtual Reality I

Estimation of the Distance Between Fingertips Using Silhouette and Texture Information of Dorsal of Hand

Takuma Shimizume$^{(\boxtimes)}$, Takeshi Umezawa, and Noritaka Osawa

Chiba University, Chiba, Japan
simi_saion@chiba-u.jp

Abstract. A three-dimensional virtual object can be manipulated by hand and finger movements with an optical hand tracking device which can recognize the posture of one's hand. Many of the conventional hand posture recognitions are based on three-dimensional coordinates of fingertips and a skeletal model of the hand. It is difficult for the conventional methods to estimate the posture of the hand when a fingertip is hidden from an optical camera, and self-occlusion often hides the fingertip. Our study, therefore, proposes an estimation of the posture of a hand based on a hand dorsal image that can be taken even when the hand occludes its fingertips. Manipulation of a virtual object requires the recognition of movements like pinching, and many of such movements can be recognized based on the distance between the fingertips of the thumb and the forefinger. Therefore, we use a regression model to estimate the distance between the fingertips of the thumb and forefinger using hand dorsal images. The regression model was constructed using Convolution Neural Networks (CNN). Our study proposes Silhouette and Texture methods for estimation of the distance between fingertips using hand dorsal images and aggregates them into two methods: Clipping method and Aggregation method. The Root Mean Squared Error (RMSE) of estimation of the distance between fingertips was 1.98 mm or less by Aggregation method for hand dorsal images which does not contain any fingertips. The RMSE of Aggregation method is smaller than that of other methods. The result shows that the proposed Aggregation method could be an effective method which is robust to self-occlusion.

Keywords: Convolutional neural network · Self-occlusion · 3D user interface

1 Introduction

Estimating the 3D posture of hands is becoming increasingly important due to the central role that hands play. Applications in activity recognition [1], motion control [2], human-computer interaction [3], and virtual/augmented reality (VR/AR) require real-time and accurate hand pose estimation. Many of the conventional methods need to detect the fingertip from the images to estimate the hand posture [4, 17], and self-occlusion of a hand and its fingers hinders estimation of the hand posture. For example, when a finger is bent, the fingertip may not be seen from the outside. It is impossible to detect the position of the hidden fingertip with an optical camera. When no fingertips

© Springer Nature Switzerland AG 2019
G. Bebis et al. (Eds.): ISVC 2019, LNCS 11844, pp. 471–481, 2019.
https://doi.org/10.1007/978-3-030-33720-9_36

are taken in an image, it is difficult to estimate the posture of a hand by the conventional method. Improvement of this situation leads to seamless tracking. For the improvement, it is useful to estimate the hand posture from a hand dorsal image which does not include fingertips. We propose and compare four proposed methods to estimate the distance between the fingertips of the thumb and the forefinger from hand dorsal images where fingertips are occluded. Those methods are Silhouette method, Texture method, Clipping method, and Aggregation method. Silhouette method is based on a silhouette image of a hand. Texture method is based on a skin texture of a hand or a part of a hand image. Clipping method combines Silhouette method and Texture method, and clips the hand texture by the hand silhouette. Aggregation method uses the silhouette image and the texture image as feature maps. Our study demonstrated that the proposed methods could estimate the distance between the fingertips the thumb and forefinger based on a hand dorsal image where the fingertips are not visible and that features of both texture and silhouette are important for accurate estimation of the fingertip distance. Clipping and Aggregation methods could estimate a distance between fingertips with smaller errors than Silhouette and Texture methods.

2   Related Work

This section discusses the related work on hand posture recognition under occlusion.

2.1   Hand Pose Estimation Based on the Position of the Fingertips

Kazuki proposed a method to estimate the coordinates of a fingertip by a fitting glove with markers [4]. The glove has a different color marker on each fingertip and has an AR marker in the center of the back of the hand. The coordinate of the center of the back of the hand is measured based on the AR marker [5]. The three-dimensional position of the fingertip is estimated by solving forward kinematics using the two-dimensional coordinates of the fingertip in the camera image acquired from the color marker, the three-dimensional coordinates and direction of the hand acquired from the AR marker, and the finger constraint conditions [6–8]. When the fingertip is occluded, this method usually estimates the position of the fingertip by assuming that the same motion continues in occlusion [5]. However, if the fingertips are not moving continuously, they may make incorrect estimations. Our method does not estimate from motion but small changes in a silhouette and texture image.

2.2   Pose Estimation Under Occlusion

Several recognition methods of hands explicitly tackle self-occlusions. Mueller et al. [9] reported that many existing methods fail to work under occlusion. Jang et al. [10] and Rogez et al. [11] proposed a robust and accurate freehand tracking system from moving egocentric RGB-D cameras in cluttered real environments. The tracking system can't estimate the hand posture under a large occlusion where the entire finger can hardly be seen. Our method is robust against a large occlusion where the entire finger can hardly be seen because it is estimated based only on the information of the dorsal of hand.

2.3 Recognition Method Using Partial Image

An increasing number of papers have focused on fine-grained object recognition [12, 13]. Many approaches that use partial images trimmed from detailed images [14, 15] have been proposed. Shimizume et al. [16] showed that a touch state of the fingertips of the thumb and the forefinger could be identified based on the MP (metacarpophalangeal joint) joint region of the forefinger in a hand dorsal image. Our new Aggregation method can estimate the distance between the fingertips based on both hand silhouette and skin texture on a hand dorsal image.

3 Proposed Methods

It is not a simple and easy task to map a hand-dorsal image to a distance between fingertips occluded in the image [10]. Figure 1 shows hand-dorsal images where a distance between the fingertips of the thumb and the forefinger is 15 mm. Even if the distance between the fingertips of the thumb and forefinger is fixed, various hand postures can be considered.

We propose four methods to estimate the distance between the fingertips which are based on a hand dorsal image but not fingertip positions. Those methods are Silhouette method, Texture method, Clipping method, and Aggregation method. Each method is explained below.

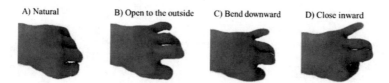

Fig. 1. Various postures of a hand when the fingertips of one's thumb and forefinger are 15 mm apart

3.1 Silhouette Method

Silhouette method is based on a silhouette, that is, a shape, of a hand from a dorsal side of the hand. Silhouette method extracts the region of a hand from a captured image including the hand and converts it to a binary silhouette image in which only the hand part is white and the other part is black (see Fig. 2). This image processing will be referred to as $S(K)$ where S is a contour extraction function and K is an input image.

3.2   Texture Method

Texture method is based on a skin texture of a hand or a part of a hand whose skin is stretched or shrunk as fingers move. Texture method extracts a region on a hand in the image and estimates a distance between the fingertips based on the image of the extracted region. Texture method applies a cropping function to the hand image to extract the texture image region. (see Fig. 2). This image processing will be referred to as $T(K)$ where T is a texture cropping function and K is an input image.

3.3   Clipping Method

Clipping method is based on a skin texture image clipped by the silhouette of a hand. Clipping method applies a masking function to the captured image. The mask is the silhouette image of the hand. The clipping image includes skin textures of the hand and the masked, or white background (see Fig. 2). The output of this image processing will be referred to as $C(K)$ where C is a clipping function and K is an input image.

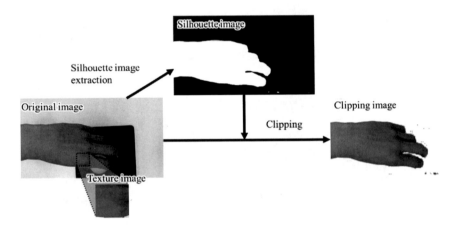

Fig. 2. Flow of Silhouette, Texture, and Clipping method

3.4   Aggregation Method

Aggregation method utilizes the silhouette and texture of a hand as well as the Clipping method but uses them differently. Aggregation method estimates the distance based on two images: a silhouette image and a texture image. Figure 3 shows the flow of creating two images for Aggregation method. The two images are surrounded by a red frame. The output of this image processing will be referred to as A(K) = [S(K); T(K)] where [X; Y] represents a concatenation of X and Y. Aggregation method inputs A(K), that is, both a silhouette image S(K) and a texture image of a region T(K).

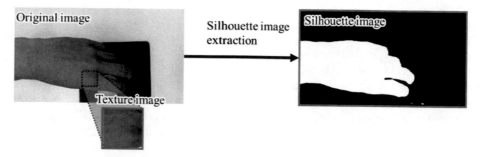

Fig. 3. Flow of creating a silhouette image and a texture image for Aggregation method (Color figure online)

4   Experiment

This study focuses on estimation of the distance between fingertips of the thumb and the forefinger because the distance between the fingertips is essential to identify the knob motion posture although our methods could be applied to the estimation of distances between other fingers.

We evaluate four proposed methods (Silhouette, Texture, Clipping, Aggregation) to show their feasibility and effectiveness in the estimation of the distance between fingertips using Convolution Neural Networks (CNN). The estimation accuracies are compared and discussed. Furthermore, we discuss how a combination of silhouette and texture images affect the estimation of the distance between the thumb and the forefinger.

4.1   Capturing Dorsal Image of Hand

The proposed methods are evaluated under a controlled environment to show their feasibility. We took images of the back of a hand by using the device as shown in Fig. 4. An arm is placed on an arm guide, which is a metal wine glass upside down. The arm guide allows fingertips to move freely. A USB camera with a resolution of 1280 × 720 pixels is placed above the hand. The distance between the camera and the arm was adjusted to 240 mm so that the whole hand fits the image.

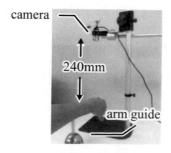

Fig. 4. Device capturing dorsal image of hand

4.2   Distance Control

In the experiment, control of a distance between one's thumb and forefinger is important because ground truth data of the distance should be accurate. It is difficult for one to control the distance by free hands. Since occlusion prevents an optical sensor from measuring the position of the fingertip, it is difficult to measure the distance between the fingertips using the optical sensor. A subject pinches a Styrofoam ball with his thumb and forefinger to control a distance between them. A diameter of the pinched Styrofoam ball is defined as the distance between the fingertips of the thumb and forefinger.

Our study took hand-dorsal images where the distance is 0 mm (the thumb and forefinger are directly touched, not pinching anything), 10 mm, 12 mm, 15 mm, 20 mm, 25 mm, and 40 mm (see Fig. 5).

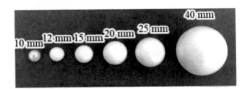

Fig. 5. Polystyrene foam ball to define finger distance

4.3   Procedure for Capturing Images

The hand-dorsal images were photographed consecutively for a relatively short period in a data collection session. The subject was moving his fingers while pinching a Styrofoam ball or touching the fingertips (for 0 mm) during the data collection session. Various hand postures were taken as shown in Fig. 1.

Illumination conditions did not change in one data collecting session. Illumination conditions in sessions on different dates were not controlled.

4.4   Dataset

We collected two datasets on different dates from one subject: Dataset A (dataset created on June 7, 2018) and Dataset B (dataset created on August 17, 2018). Each dataset has 7,000 images. Both datasets were collected within the same facility. However, they were collected in slightly different illumination conditions which is influenced by ambient light from outside on different dates, and in slightly different skin conditions where the health of the hand, skin color and wrinkles may change on different dates.

Each data subset for a distance which has 1,000 images is divided into 800 images for the training, and 200 images for the test. Therefore, each data set (A or B) was divided into training data of 5,600 images (A_t or B_t) and test data of 1,400 images (A_v or B_v). Table 1 summarizes training data and test data. In Table 1, *distance* row shows the distance whose columns show the number of images of corresponding subsets.

Table 1. Summary of data set

distance (mm)		0	10	12	15	20	25	40	Total
Dataset A	A_t	800	800	800	800	800	800	800	5,600
	A_v	200	200	200	200	200	200	200	1,400
Total		1,000	1,000	1,000	1,000	1,000	1,000	1,000	7,000
Dataset B	B_t	800	800	800	800	800	800	800	5,600
	B_v	200	200	200	200	200	200	200	1,400
Total		1,000	1,000	1,000	1,000	1,000	1,000	1,000	7,000

4.5   CNN Models

We use three types of CNN model structures in the experiment. One is a CNN model M_{Mask} to extract silhouette images from captured images. The other are two CNN models M_{STC} and M_A to estimate the distance between the fingertips. M_{STC} represents a CNN model which is used in Silhouette method, Texture method, and Clipping method. M_A represents a CNN model which is used in Aggregation method.

4.5.1   Structure of CNN Model to Extract the Silhouette Image

M_{Mask} is a model that recognizes a hand area from a given input image and generates a binary image filled with white in the hand area and black in other areas. M_{Mask} has seven layers: four convolution layers, two pooling layers, and one deconvolution layer. Using shorthand notation, the structure of M_{Mask} is $C(64, 5, 2) - P(2, 2) - C(128, 5, 2) - P(2, 2) - C(128, 3, 1) - C(128, 3, 1) - DC(1, 32, 16)$ where $C(d, f, s)$, $P(k, s)$ and $DC(d, f, s)$ represent respectively a convolutional layer with d filters of kernel size $f \times f$ applied to the input with stride s, a pooling layer with kernel size $k \times k$, applied to the input with stride s, and a deconvolutional layer with d filters of kernel size $f \times f$ applied to the input with stride s.

4.5.2   Structure of CNN Model for Three Methods

M_{STC} has seven layers: two convolution layers, two pooling layers, and three fully-connected layers. Using shorthand notation, the structure of M_{STC} is $C(64, 5, 3) - P(2, 2) - C(128, 5, 3) - P(2, 2) - FC(300) - FC(30) - FC(1)$ where $FC(n)$ is a fully-connected layer with n nodes. Figure 6 shows a flow of the distance estimation between the fingertips using Model M_{STC}. The dashed frame in Fig. 6 indicates M_{STC}. Figure 7 shows an internal structure of $Conv \& Pool$ where (d, f, s), (k, s) represent respectively a convolutional layer with d filters of kernel size $f \times f$ applied to the input with stride s and a pooling layer with kernel size $k \times k$, applied to the input with stride s. Figure 8 shows an internal structure of FC where (n) indicates a fully-connected layer with n nodes.

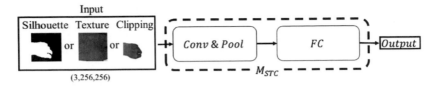

Fig. 6. Flow of the distance estimation between the fingertips using Model M_{STC}

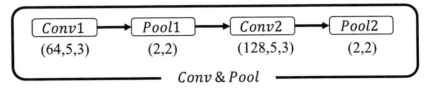

Fig. 7. *Conv* & *Pool*

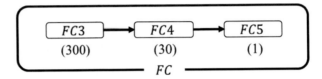

Fig. 8. *FC*: fully-connected layer

4.5.3   Structure of CNN Model for Aggregation Method

Figure 9 shows a flow of the distance estimation between the fingertips using Model M_A. M_A requires two image inputs: a silhouette image and a texture image. Firstly, each input is fed into the same structure including the same convolution layer and pooling layer (*Conv* & *Pool*) as M_{STC}, and its feature maps are outputted. Next, the two outputted feature maps are concatenated by column-wise (*Concat*). Finally, the combined feature maps are fed into the same fully-connected layers (*FC*) as M_{STC}.

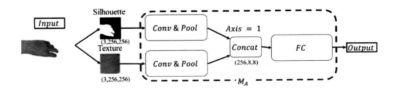

Fig. 9. Flow of the distance estimation between the fingertips using Model M_A

4.6   Experimental Condition

Silhouette method extracts silhouette images using Model M_{Mask}. Texture method extracts texture images by cropping a part of the hand which is a 256×256 pixel area around an MP joint of the forefinger. MP joint is a joint at the base of the hand and the skin texture around the MP joint changes slightly as the forefinger moves. The cropping range needs to include the MP joint, and is not fixed. Clipping method composes a clipping image using an input image and a mask image which is the same as the silhouette image. Also, silhouette, and clipping images are resized to 256×256 pixels for inputs of regressor models.

In the training phase of CNN, the batch size of the input is 100, and the learning rate is 0.1. We used Adam to optimize the learning parameters. The trained model is saved as an estimation model after 200 epochs.

5 Result

RMSE (Root Mean Squared Error) is used as a quantitative measure of estimation errors. RMSE of estimation distance is defined by Eq. (1) where the i-th ground truth and estimated distance are respectively d_i and $\hat{d}_i$, and the number of data is n.

$$RMSE = \sqrt{\frac{\sum_{i=1}^{n}\left(d_i - \hat{d}_i\right)^2}{n}} \tag{1}$$

The unit of distance is in millimeters in this paper. Assume that the model M is trained with training data T, and estimation is performed by applying test data V to the model, and RMSE of the estimation is calculated. This is expressed by $RMSE(M[T], V)$. Figure 10 shows RMSE results for combinations of image processing functions and datasets. In the figure, $RMSE(M_F[F(X_t)], F(X_v))$ is denoted as $M_F(X)$ for simplicity where F is an image processing function, and X is a data set.

$M_C(A)$ for Clipping method was 1.16 mm, which was the smallest. $M_A(A)$ for Aggregation method was 1.64 mm. These showed that Clipping method could estimate with an error smaller than Aggregation method in Dataset A. Meanwhile, $M_C(B)$ and $M_A(B)$ were 3.40 mm and 1.98 mm respectively. This showed that Aggregation method could estimate with the smaller error than Clipping method in Dataset B. Also, the result showed that Clipping and Aggregation methods could estimate with smaller errors than Silhouette and Texture methods.

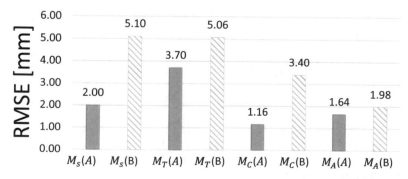

Fig. 10. RMSE for combinations of image processing functions and datasets

6 Discussion

In the proposed methods, the distance between the fingertips of the thumb and the forefinger was estimated with a small error. However, the results of experiments show that it is difficult to estimate the fingertip distance sufficiently by using the Texture method compared with other methods. In this experiment, the area around the MP joint of the forefinger was trimmed to 256 × 256 pixel. The image size could be insufficient to estimate finger distance accurately. This is because, during the pinching movement, wrinkles around MP joints of other fingers are also slightly changed. We need to evaluate how the size of a texture image influences estimation errors in the Texture method.

7 Conclusion

This paper proposed and evaluated the new methods for estimation of the distance between a thumb and a forefinger when the palm of one's hand or fingers is invisible. The experimental results show that the distance between the fingertips of the thumb and the forefinger could be estimated using only the information on the back of the hand, and suggest the proposed method can be utilized in applications. The results also suggest that both the silhouette and the texture of a hand contribute to enhancing the accuracy of estimation. We will investigate a method that is robust for change with time and individual differences.

References

1. Rohrbach, M., Amin, S., Andriluka, M., Schiele, B.: A database for fine grained activity detection of cooking activities. In: IEEE Conference on Computer Vision and Pattern Recognition (CVPR), pp. 1194–1201 (2012)
2. Zhao, W., Zhang, J., Min, J., Chai, J.: Robust realtime physics-based motion control for human grasping. ACM Trans. Graph. (TOG) 32(6), 207 (2013)
3. Sinha, A., Choi, C., Ramani, K.: DeepHand: robust hand pose estimation by completing a matrix imputed with deep features. In: IEEE Conference on Computer Vision and Pattern Recognition (CVPR), pp. 4150–4158 (2016)
4. Kawashima, K.: Vision-based data glove considering the hiding of the thumb by hand-drawn image. Nagoya Institute of Technology Graduation thesis (2014)
5. Katou, H., Mark, B., Asano, K., Tachibana, K.: Augmented reality system and its calibration based on marker tracking. Trans. Virtual Reality Soc. Jpn. 4(4), 607–616 (1999)
6. Kamakura, N.: Hand Shape and Hand Movement. Medical and Tooth Drug Publishing Co., Ltd. (1989)
7. Ichikawa, R.: Motion modeling of finger joints during grasping and manipulation of objects. Wakayama University Bachelor thesis (2002)
8. Yamamoto, S., Funahashi, K., Iwahori, Y.: Study for vision based data glove considering hidden fingertip with self-occlusion. In: Proceedings of SNPD 2012, pp. 315–320 (2012)
9. Mueller, F., Mehta, D., Sotnychenko, O., Sridhar, S., Casas, D., Theobalt, C.: Real-time hand tracking under occlusion from an egocentric RGB-D sensor. In: ICCV (2017)

10. Jang, Y., Noh, S.-T., Chang, H.J., Kim, T.K., Woo, W.: 3D finger CAPE: clicking action and position estimation under self-occlusions in egocentric viewpoint. IEEE Trans. Vis. Comput. Graph. (TVCG) **21**(4), 501–510 (2015)
11. Rogez, G., Supancic, J.S., Ramanan, D.: First-person pose recognition using egocentric workspaces. In: CVPR (2015)
12. Farrell, R., Oza, O., Zhang, N., Morariu, V., Darrell, T., Davis, L.: Birdlets: subordinate categorization using volumetric primitives and pose-normalized appearance. In: ICCV (2011)
13. Branson, S., et al.: Visual recognition with humans in the loop. In: Daniilidis, K., Maragos, P., Paragios, N. (eds.) ECCV 2010. LNCS, vol. 6314, pp. 438–451. Springer, Heidelberg (2010). https://doi.org/10.1007/978-3-642-15561-1_32
14. Yang, S., Bo, L., Wang, J., Shapiro, L.G.: Unsupervised template learning for fine-grained object recognition. In: Pereira, F., Burges, C.J.C., Bottou, L., Weinberger, K.Q. (eds.) Advances in Neural Information Processing Systems 25, pp. 3122–3130. Curran Associates Inc., Red Hook (2012)
15. Yao, B., Khosla, A., Fei-Fei, L.: Combining randomization and discrimination for fine-grained image categorization. In: IEEE Conference on Computer Vision and Pattern Recognition (CVPR), pp. 1577–1584. IEEE (2011)
16. Shimizume, T., Noritaka, O., Umezawa, T.: Contact estimation between thumb and forefinger from hand dorsal image using deep learning. Chiba University Graduation thesis (2018)
17. Schröder, M., Waltemate, T., Maycock, J., Röhlig, T., Ritter, H., Botsch, M.: Design and evaluation of reduced marker layouts for hand motion capture. Comput. Animat. Virtual Worlds **29**(6), e1751 (2017)

Measuring Reflectance of Anisotropic Materials Using Two Handheld Cameras

Zar Zar Tun[1(✉)], Seiji Tsunezaki[1], Takashi Komuro[1], Shoji Yamamoto[2],
and Norimichi Tsumura[3]

[1] Graduate School of Science and Engineering, Saitama University,
255 Shimo-okubo, Sakura-ku, Saitama 338-8570, Japan
`zarzar@is.ics.saitama-u.ac.jp`
[2] Tokyo Metropolitan College of Industrial Technology,
8-17-1 Minami-senju, Arakawa-ku, Tokyo 116-8523, Japan
[3] Graduate School of Science and Engineering, Chiba University,
1-33 Yayoi-cho, Inage-ku, Chiba 263-8522, Japan

Abstract. In this paper, we propose a method for measuring the
reflectance of anisotropic materials using a simple apparatus consisting
of two handheld cameras, a small LED light source, a turning table and
a chessboard with markers. The system is configured to obtain the different incoming and outgoing light directions, and the brightness of pixels
on the surface of the material. The anisotropic Ward BRDF (Bidirectional Reflectance Distribution Function) model is used to approximate
the reflectance, and the model parameters are estimated from the incoming and outgoing angles and the brightness of pixels by using a non-linear
optimization method. The initial values of the anisotropic direction are
given based on the peak specular lobe on the surface, and the best-fitted
one is chosen for the anisotropic direction. The optimized parameters
show the well-fitted results between the observed brightness and the
BRDF model for each RGB channel. It was confirmed that our system
was able to measure the reflectance of different isotropic and anisotropic
materials.

Keywords: Anisotropic materials · Reflectance measurement · Ward
BRDF model

1 Introduction

3D animation is becoming popular and the artists want the CG models to
look more realistic. To fulfill this requirement, it is important to measure the
reflectance of real materials. In particular, the reflectance of anisotropic materials is difficult to measure since the texture on the material surface is rough,
and it has various waving patterns. Some of the incident light on the surface
reflects in different directions. Furthermore, anisotropic reflectance is direction-
ally dependent, and the highlights appear on the surface in different size and

© Springer Nature Switzerland AG 2019
G. Bebis et al. (Eds.): ISVC 2019, LNCS 11844, pp. 482–493, 2019.
https://doi.org/10.1007/978-3-030-33720-9_37

shape such as hair and satin fabric. Measuring reflectance of anisotropic materials is a challenging task due to the complex surface geometry and the variations of reflectance on the surface of the materials. Examples of some anisotropic materials are shown in Fig. 1.

The BRDF (Bidirectional Reflectance Distribution Function) defines how light is reflected at an opaque surface. It is a four dimensional reflectance function of the incoming direction (θ_i, ϕ_i) and the outgoing direction (θ_o, ϕ_o), where θ and ϕ are the elevation and azimuthal angles, respectively.

Dense anisotropic materials are measured using combinations of high-speed cameras and light sources handled by multiple motors [5,8]. Some systems set up automatically integrated acquisition method using a hemispherical gantry, which was equipped with a large number of cameras and light sources [13,17]. They used only a small camera motor and a turntable to avoid using multiple controllers, but their apparatus is expensive and easy to break since it has mechanical part. Anisotropic materials can also be measured using a gonioreflectometer which consists of a camera, lens, light sources, mirrors and a controller [4,11,14,16]. Dana et al. [2] configured a robotic manipulator in which a camera is positioned in seven different intervals. In their setups, a material is oriented by a robot arm to obtain various view and light directions. The detailed reflectance can be measured using such an apparatus, however, the apparatus cost is still high, and the processing time is long due to mechanical controllers. Some systems are customized by combining different cameras, light sources and motors [3,6,10,12,15]. They can reduce the required apparatus than those using a gonioreflectometer and a hemispherical gantry; however, it is still complex in design, and takes time for acquisition. A marker is additionally used in their customized setup [1]. The marker is used for the first frame, and video frame alignment is performed to know the camera pose during image capturing. They can reduce the required apparatus, but their system is limited to align repetitive textures to obtain the correct camera pose.

We propose a measurement method that does not require any large apparatus and control systems. Our system is focused on a simple setup to measure the reflectance of anisotropic materials. In our method, there are two handheld cameras that are used as a light camera for obtaining the light positions and a view camera for capturing the color frames, respectively. A small LED light is attached to the light camera, which is set on a place to light the object. The view camera is moved by hand, facing the target material. A material sample is placed on the chessboard that is mounted on the turning table, and the chessboard is viewed by the two cameras simultaneously. With this configuration, the incoming and outgoing light directions, camera pose and color brightness on the surface of the material can be acquired. The anisotropic Ward model is used to approximate the reflectance. The model parameters are estimated by using a non-linear optimization method. Our system can be used to measure the reflectance of both isotropic and anisotropic materials.

Fig. 1. Examples of some anisotropic materials

2   Related Work

Measuring the reflectance of real materials is a challenging task and many systems have been researched in this fields. Existing methods are categorized into three groups:

Measurement Using a Gonioreflectometer. Some systems measure dense anisotropic reflectance using a gonioreflectometer. Murray-Coleman et al. [11] set up the gonioreflectometer by using a charge-couple device (CCD) camera and a half-silvered plastic hemisphere as the key optical elements that are positioned with a stepping motor. The hemisphere was used to catch the lights reflected from a rotating sample lighted by a fixed fiber optic light, and the movement of the material and light are controlled by a single photometer. Their apparatus is complex and take long time to measure a single surface. Ward [16] updated the setup by changing the very bright light source with a white light lamp and a parabolic reflector that is moved by a controller. They can reduce the rotation time since the material sample is moved by hand.

Filip et al. [4] used an industrial full-frame camera and an array of eleven LEDs, which are separately controlled by different arms depending on the rotating range of the material sample. In this setup, the movements of arms are controlled by a controller which takes lengthy processing time. Rump et al. [14] set up a gonioreflectometer by using a computer-controlled bent rail system, which controls the positions of a high-resolution digital camera. A tunable spectral filter is put behind the lens. The light source is fixed at a place and a material sample is mounted on the robot arm that is placed in the center of the semicircle. The robot arm tilts and turns the sample to synchronize with the moving camera. These setups can obtain different angular directions, but the movements of arms need to synchronize the camera, light and material sample to obtain accurate measurements. Furthermore, these systems used a huge number of combinations of incoming and outgoing angles to obtain the anisotropic reflectance.

Measurement Using Multiple Cameras and Light Sources. Some systems measure dense anisotropic reflectance using multiple cameras and light sources. Hawkins et al. [8] used a semicircular arm with twenty-seven xenon strobe lights, which was rotated around the object and controlled by a computer. Two high-speed video cameras were used, whose frame rates were 110 fps and 60 fps, respectively. Furukawa et al. [5] used two large concentric circles, which were used to equip multiple CCD cameras and multiple halogen lamps. An object was placed at the center of the circle and was rotated by a stepping motor. Another stepping motor was used to control the arm with multiple halogen lamps. These two motors were individually controlled by a PC. Those systems used multiple cameras and light sources, and their movements were handled by multiple controllers.

Rump et al. [13] used a hemispherical gantry where a total of 151 digital cameras were equipped, and built-in flashlights were utilized. A material sample was placed under the gantry in a fixed position. A small electric motor was used to move the lens in cameras during operations. In their apparatus, the number of moving parts can be reduced, and the measurement time is decreased. However, the repeated use of motor can degrade the calibration quality. Weinmann et al. [17] also used a hemispherical gantry in which four projectors and eleven cameras were attached on a vertical arc, and 198 LED lights were distributed over the device. They used a turntable instead of using motors. These systems can capture an image under different lighting conditions at once. However, the apparatus are expensive, and require a wide space to set up.

Measurement Using the Customized Setup. Some systems measure sparse anisotropic reflectance by using their customized setup. Gardner et al. [6] set up their customized apparatus by using a fixed camera, and a translation gantry which was mainly used to control a white neon linear light tube, and that was moved over the material at a fixed distance. Their system allows only printed materials and fabrics to measure the reflectance. Wang et al. [15] updated the system [6] by replacing an array of 40 LEDs, and a color checker pattern for camera calibration in their setup. A stepping motor was used to control a light array, which was used for illuminating the surface from different directions. In this way, they can measure various materials in details.

Ngan et al. [12] used their own apparatus, which consists of a fixed camera and a planer material wrapped on a cylindrical target shape and that was mounted on a precision motor. A light source was also controlled by another precision motor. However, there is a problem that it is difficult to attach the material sample to the cylinder. Fichet et al. [3] set up their own acquisition apparatus in which a light array was rotated around the static material and camera, and the light arm was controlled by a computer. All these systems can reduce the required apparatus cost than using a gonioreflectometer, but they used the light array for which the controller is expensive and the acquisition time is long.

3   Measurement Apparatus

We propose a simple apparatus to measure the reflectance of a target material as shown in Fig. 2. It can obtain the incoming and outgoing light directions, and the brightness of pixels on the surface of the material, which are used to estimate the reflectance parameters.

In this configuration, two handheld cameras, a small LED light, a turning table and a ChArUco board are used. A ChArUco board is a planar chessboard with ArUco markers [7] placed inside the white squares of the chessboard. It provides both the ArUco markers versatility and chessboard corner precision and enables accurate camera pose estimation. A material sample is placed on the center of the chessboard, which is rotated on the turning table. When the images of the material are captured, we set the room dark except that the object was lighted by the LED light to protect entering light from other sources.

The LED light is attached to one camera that is set on a stand, and it is used to light the target object. Another camera is moved by hand from 0 to 90° of outgoing light angles, facing the material. The two cameras capture RGB frames at the rate of 15 frames per seconds, and they are about 0.5 m away from the object. The resolution of colored frames was 1920×1024 pixels. The specifications of the PC were Intel Core i7-7700 CPU, 16 GB memory and NVIDIA GeForce GT×1070 6 GB for GPU. The OpenCV library was used for system implementation, and the Unity game engine was used to visualize the experimental results.

At a surface point on the material, the incoming light directions are changing gradually as the fixed light is pointing to the target material on the turning table. The outgoing light directions are changed as the camera is moved by hand in different directions. By using this configuration, the incoming and outgoing light directions and the brightness of pixels, which are dynamically changing are obtained.

4   Reflectance Estimation

In our method, the anisotropic Ward model [16] is used to estimate the reflectance on the surface of real materials. It is the combination of diffuse and specular reflectance, and it determines how much the light is reflected from the incoming direction i to the outgoing direction o at a surface point as follows:

$$\left(\theta_i, \phi_i, \theta_o, \phi_o\right) = \frac{\rho_d}{\pi} + \frac{\rho_s}{4\pi\alpha_x\alpha_y\sqrt{\cos\theta_i\cos\theta_o}}e^{-\tan^2\theta_h\left(\frac{\cos^2\phi_h}{\alpha_x^2} + \frac{\sin^2\phi_h}{\alpha_y^2}\right)} \tag{1}$$

where

θ and ϕ are the elevation and azimuthal angles,
ρ_d and ρ_s are the diffuse and specular reflection albedos,
α_x and α_y are the surface roughness in X and Y directions,
θ_h and ϕ_h are the elevation and azimuthal angles of the halfway vector, respectively.
$\alpha_x = \alpha_y$ in the case of isotropic materials.

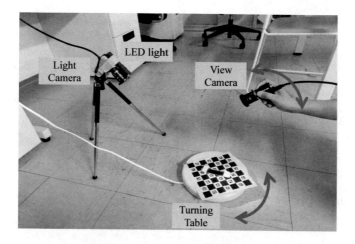

Fig. 2. Our measurement apparatus

4.1 Acquisition of the Camera Pose

In this system, the calibration parameters for the two cameras are acquired simultaneously based on the ChArUco marker [7]. While the images are captured, some of the markers can be missed since the view camera was moved along with the hand. Therefore, more than four markers that can be detected in each frame are used to interpolate the marker corners, otherwise the frames that do not have enough number of markers are skipped.

The camera pose is acquired to know the positions and orientations of the cameras related to the material sample. It is calculated by the coordinate transformation from the world coordinate system based on the marker to the camera coordinate system. The positions of each camera x_c relative to the object are:

$$x_c = -R^{-1}t \tag{2}$$

where R is the rotation matrix and t is the translation vector defined in the world coordinate system based on the marker.

The incoming and outgoing light angles are calculated from the camera positions by taking the inner product. By using the camera pose, the mapping relation between the 3D world coordinates (X, Y, Z) and the 2D image coordinates (x, y) can be obtained by perspective projection.

4.2 Estimation of the BRDF Parameters

The variables used in the anisotropic Ward BRDF model is shown in Fig. 3. We assume that there is a unit normal vector $N\ (0, 0, 1)$, which is the Z coordinate in the world coordinate system based on the marker. θ_i is the angle between the incoming light direction and the normal vector, θ_o is the angle between the normal vector and the outgoing view direction, θ_h is the angle between the normal vector and the halfway vector, ϕ_h is the azimuthal angle of the halfway vector from the X-axis, a is the anisotropic direction, and φ_a is the angle between the anisotropic direction and the halfway vector projected onto the tangent plane. The reflectance parameters are optimized by using the Levenberg-Marquardt method which is the non-linear optimization method.

θ_i and θ_o are calculated according to each camera position x_c projected to the normal vector N as follows:

$$\cos\theta = \frac{x_c \cdot N}{\|x_c\|\|N\|} \tag{3}$$

where θ represents θ_i or θ_o. θ_h is calculated according to the halfway vector H projected to the normal vector as follows:

$$\cos\theta_h = \frac{H \cdot N}{\|H\|\|N\|} \tag{4}$$

ϕ_h is the angle between the positive X-axis and a vector at which the halfway vector H projected onto the tangent plane as follows:

$$\phi_h = \mathrm{atan2}(H_z, H_x) \tag{5}$$

where H_z and H_x are the x and z coordinates of H.

The correspondence between a point on the material and the color pixel is calculated by projecting the point onto the image plane. As the object is rotating and the view camera is moving, the intensity on the vertex is changing from frame to frame. The average of the color and brightness values at the reprojected points over all frames are used to initialize the diffuse and specular albedos.

The roughness values can express the size and shape of the specular highlights on the surface. The initial roughness values for X and Y directions are set to 0.5 and 1.0, respectively.

Estimation of the Anisotropic Direction. The initial values of the anisotropic direction are given based on the azimuthal angle of halfway vector. Some BRDF models including the Ward model are based on the halfway vector, and provide visually plausible reflectance results than those based on the incident light vector. These models show the peak specular lobe around the halfway vector. Another reason is that in a microfacet-based BRDF model, the halfway vector is equal to the normal vector of microfacets. In Ward [16], a vector that can form the azimuthal angle of the halfway vector is used as the anisotropic direction of a brushed material. Kaplanyan et al. [9] assumed that a specular light path is a series of halfway vectors and generates the light transport path by using small perturbations to the halfway vectors for glossy materials.

In our method, the initial values for the angle φ_a are given by adding small perturbations to the azimuthal angle of the halfway vector as follows:

$$\varphi_a \approx \phi_h + \phi_p, \qquad \phi_p = 0, \pm r_i, \pm 2r_i, \pm 3r_i \tag{6}$$

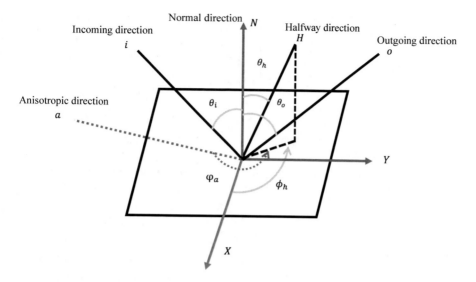

Fig. 3. Variables used in the anisotropic Ward BRDF model: i and o are the incoming and outgoing light directions, N is the unit normal vector, H is the halfway vector, θ_i is the angle between the incoming light direction and the normal vector, θ_o is the angle between the normal vector and the outgoing view direction, θ_h is the angle between the normal vector and the halfway vector, ϕ_h is the azimuthal angle of the halfway vector, a is the anisotropic direction, and φ_a is the angle between the anisotropic direction and the halfway vector projected onto the tangent plane.

where ϕ_h is the azimuthal angle of the halfway vector and $r_i = 5°$. Firstly, the azimuthal angle ϕ_h is given as an initial value for the anisotropic direction. If that angle is not well fitted after non-linear optimization, the initial values are given by increasing or decreasing the azimuthal angle by 5, 10 and 15°. In this way, the best-fitted one is chosen for the anisotropic direction.

5   Experimental Result

In our experiment, real materials were used to measure both the isotropic and anisotropic reflectance. To carry out the experiment for isotropic materials, colored paper, wrapping paper, and a metallic material were used, and for anisotropic materials, fabric, plastic cables, and hair were used. The number of frames used in our experiment were from 50 to 70 frames for each material. The fitting results and the rendering results for these materials are shown.

Fitting Result. The fitting results between the observed brightness of each RGB component and the estimated reflectance with regard to frame numbers are shown in Fig. 4. The fitting results show that the estimated reflectance was well-fitted with the observed brightness for each color channel.

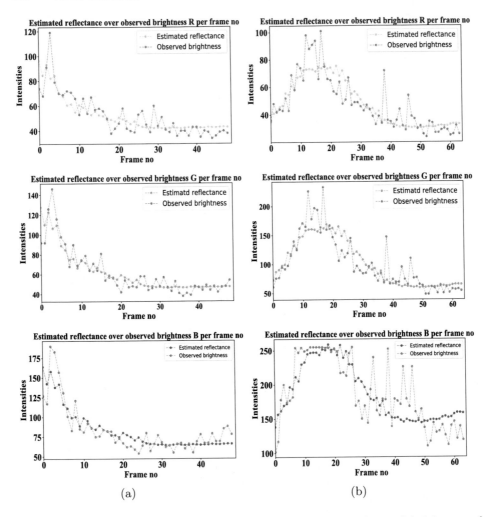

Fig. 4. The fitting results for the estimated reflectance and observed brightness of RGB components with regard to the frame numbers: (a) Fitting result for an isotropic material (b) Fitting result for an anisotropic material.

Rendering Result. The rendering results for the isotropic materials are shown in Fig. 5. The materials were isotropic, but the estimation was performed using the anisotropic Ward model. The rendered materials had uniform specular highlights, and the surface was totally smooth. We can see that the color of the original objects and the rendered materials were matched.

The rendering results for the anisotropic materials are shown in Fig. 6. The estimation of anisotropic materials was performed also using the anisotropic Ward model. We can see different directions of reflectance, and correct colors on the rendered materials.

Wrapping paper   Colored paper   Metallic

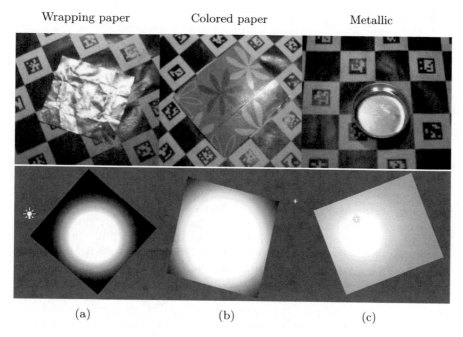

(a)   (b)   (c)

Fig. 5. The original objects and the rendering results of different isotropic materials. upper row: original objects, lower row: rendering results (a) wrapping paper, (b) colored paper, and (c) metallic.

Fabric   Plastic cable1   Plastic cable2   Hair

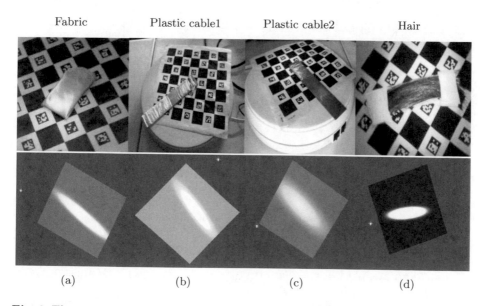

(a)   (b)   (c)   (d)

Fig. 6. The original objects and the rendering results of different anisotropic materials. upper row: original objects, lower row: rendering results (a) fabric, (b) plastic cable 1, (c) plastic cable 2, and (d) hair.

6   Conclusion and Future Work

In our system, a simple setup was used to measure the reflectance of anisotropic materials with lower cost and shorter acquisition time. There are some limitations in our systems that only planer materials are allowed, and the Fresnel term is not considered. In the future, we will extend our method to support spatially-varying reflectance, and estimation of the normal map is needed to support non-planer materials.

References

1. Albert, R.A., Chan, D.Y., Goldman, D.B., O'Brien, J.F.: Approximate svBRDF estimation from mobile phone video. In: Proceedings of the Eurographics Symposium on Rendering: Experimental Ideas & Implementations, SR 2018, pp. 11–22. Eurographics Association, Goslar (2018). https://doi.org/10.2312/sre.20181168
2. Dana, K.J., van Ginneken, B., Nayar, S.K., Koenderink, J.J.: Reflectance and texture of real-world surfaces. ACM Trans. Graph. **18**(1), 1–34 (1999)
3. Fichet, A., Sato, I., Holzschuch, N.: Capturing spatially varying anisotropic reflectance parameters using Fourier analysis. In: Proceedings of the 42nd Graphics Interface Conference, GI 2016, Canadian Human-Computer Communications Society, School of Computer Science, University of Waterloo, Waterloo, Ontario, Canada, pp. 65–73 (2016). https://doi.org/10.20380/GI2016.09
4. Filip, J., Vávra, R., Haindl, M., Zid, P., Krupicka, M., Havran, V.: BRDF slices: accurate adaptive anisotropic appearance acquisition. In: Proceedings of the IEEE Computer Society Conference on Computer Vision and Pattern Recognition, June 2013
5. Furukawa, R., Kawasaki, H., Ikeuchi, K., Sakauchi, M.: Appearance based object modeling using texture database: acquisition, compression and rendering. In: Proceedings of the 13th Eurographics Workshop on Rendering, EGRW 2002, Aire-la-Ville, Switzerland, Switzerland, pp. 257–266. Eurographics Association (2002). http://dl.acm.org/citation.cfm?id=581896.581929
6. Gardner, A., Tchou, C., Hawkins, T., Debevec, P.: Linear light source reflectometry. ACM Trans. Graph. **22**(3), 749–758 (2003). https://doi.org/10.1145/882262.882342. http://doi.acm.org/10.1145/882262.882342
7. Garrido-Jurado, S., Muñoz Salinas, R., Madrid-Cuevas, F., Marín-Jiménez, M.: Automatic generation and detection of highly reliable fiducial markers under occlusion. Pattern Recogn. **47**(6), 2280–2292 (2014). https://doi.org/10.1016/j.patcog.2014.01.005
8. Hawkins, T., Cohen, J., Debevec, P.: A photometric approach to digitizing cultural artifacts. In: Proceedings of the 2001 Conference on Virtual Reality, Archeology, and Cultural Heritage, pp. 333–342. ACM (2001)
9. Kaplanyan, A.S., Hanika, J., Dachsbacher, C.: The natural-constraint representation of the path space for efficient light transport simulation. ACM Trans. Graph. **33**(4), 102:1–102:13 (2014). https://doi.org/10.1145/2601097.2601108. http://doi.acm.org/10.1145/2601097.2601108
10. Luongo, A., et al.: Modeling the anisotropic reflectance of a surface with microstructure engineered to obtain visible contrast after rotation. In: 2017 IEEE International Conference on Computer Vision Workshops (ICCVW), pp. 159–165, October 2017. https://doi.org/10.1109/ICCVW.2017.27

11. Murray-Coleman, J., Smith, A.: The automated measurement of BRDFs and their application to luminaire modeling. J. Illum. Eng. Soc. **19**(1), 87–99 (1990). https://doi.org/10.1080/00994480.1990.10747944
12. Ngan, A., Durand, F., Matusik, W.: Experimental analysis of BRDF models. In: Proceedings of the Eurographics Symposium on Rendering, pp. 117–226. Eurographics Association (2005)
13. Rump, M., Müller, G., Sarlette, R., Koch, D., Klein, R.: Photo-realistic rendering of metallic car paint from image-based measurements. Comput. Graph. Forum **27**(2), 527–536 (2008)
14. Rump, M., Sarlette, R., Klein, R.: Groundtruth data for multispectral bidirectional texture functions. In: Proceedings of the CGIV/MCS 2010, pp. 326–330. Society for Imaging Science and Technology, June 2010
15. Wang, J., Zhao, S., Tong, X., Snyder, J., Guo, B.: Modeling anisotropic surface reflectance with example-based microfacet synthesis. In: ACM SIGGRAPH 2008 Papers, SIGGRAPH 2008, pp. 41:1–41:9. ACM, New York (2008). https://doi.org/10.1145/1399504.1360640. http://doi.acm.org/10.1145/1399504.1360640
16. Ward, G.J.: Measuring and modeling anisotropic reflection. SIGGRAPH Comput. Graph. **26**(2), 265–272 (1992)
17. Weinmann, M., Ruiters, R., Osep, A., Schwartz, C., Klein, R.: Fusing structured light consistency and Helmholtz normals for 3D reconstruction. In: BMVC (2012)

FunPlogs – A Serious Puzzle Mini-game for Learning Fundamental Programming Principles Using Visual Scripting

Robin Horst[✉], Ramtin Naraghi-Taghi-Off, Savina Diez, Tobias Uhmann,
Arne Müller, and Ralf Dörner

RheinMain University of Applied Sciences, Wiesbaden, Germany
{robin.horst,ramtin.naraghi-taghi-off,savina.diez,
tobias.uhmann,arne.muller,ralf.dorner}@hs-rm.de
http://www.hs-rm.de

Abstract. Learning to program can be a tedious task for students. The intrinsic motivation towards games can help to facilitate the first steps in such learning tasks. In this paper we introduce FunPlogs – a serious puzzle mini-game for learning fundamental programming principles. We use visual scripting aspects within this game. These must be used by the students to solve spatial puzzle-like tasks. Within this game we integrate a user-driven content creation approach for the game, so that students can cooperatively create new levels. We show the feasibility of the game concept in a prototype implementation and indicate a high joy of use during a user study.

Keywords: Computer games · Content creation · Computer science education · Visual scripting language · Virtual reality

1 Introduction

Getting students interested in nature sciences is a challenge that also applies for the sub-field of computer science. Motivating to learn programming-principles can be a tough challenge, as well, since students often have intrinsic motivation towards games but tend to have a lack of interests in learning activities [20]. However, existing research has shown that games can also be used as a beneficial medium for computer science education [5,11,17,24] and especially programming education [1,16]. Such games that have a primary focus other than entertainment are called serious games. Approaches in the educational domain do vary depending on aspects like the target audience, spatial setting, learning type, utilization time, game genre and many more. One field of application of short mini games is microlearning [7,8], where learning content may only endure few minutes and should be used as independent self-contained learning sessions.

Another challenge in this domain is creating content (e.g. different levels) for such serious games [12]. Providing predefined levels created by game designers

© Springer Nature Switzerland AG 2019
G. Bebis et al. (Eds.): ISVC 2019, LNCS 11844, pp. 494–504, 2019.
https://doi.org/10.1007/978-3-030-33720-9_38

increases development effort and results in a finite set of learning content. Integrating user-generated content for serious learning games can help to decrease such development effort and increase the reusability of the software [15]. Specifically letting users create content within the game itself is mentioned to be promising and engaging, for example letting users create their own story [22].

In this paper we introduce FunPlogs – a serious puzzle mini-game for learning fundamental programming principles using visual programming. With this work we make the following contribution:

1. We propose a serious game concept to give students an understanding of basic principles of modern procedural programming, like loops and if-then-else decisions. The core of the game for the students is to solve puzzle tasks. They have to use visual scripting to express spatial moving tasks.
2. A user-driven level creation method is provided within this game concept. Content is created collaboratively and asymmetrically by the students themselves. The creation process involves virtual reality (VR) methodology.
3. With a prototype and a user study we show the feasibility of the concepts and indicate that students have fun by using our learning application.

2   Related Work

We relate our work to existing work on computer science education games and user-driven content creation.

Pioneering and famous work by Resnick et al. [21] introduce the visual programming language Scratch. It indicates the success of visual approaches in programming education. It is not directly a learning game, but enables laymen to program and create their own games by providing fundamental programming aspects as visual components that can be connected. Predecessors of Scratch and further pioneering work, such as Squeak [3,10], Etoys[1] and Alice [6,18] provide further insights in the matter of visual programming, VR and learning purposes. These works provide a basis for several follow-up projects (e.g. [12,19]).

Mildner et al. [15] propose a system for the creation of custom-made serious games with user-generated learning content. They enable teacher to create mini games for their students. Web-based authoring is used to create content for their Knowledge Defence game, which lies in the genre of tower defence.

QuizPACK [4], by Brusilovsky and Sosnosovsky uses quizzes to communicate knowledge about programming and follows a similar idea as Mildner et al. Both use a dedicated authoring application and a separate game client application similar as described in the paper on Word Domination [14]. Word Domination draws from first person shooters and quiz elements concerning its game genre.

Work by Johnson and Valente [9] and by Mehm et al. [13] specifically addresses collaborative authoring paradigms for serious games. They propose such concepts for different application areas, which are games for language and culture and health respectively. Johnson and Valente differentiate between two

---

[1] www.squeakland.org (Accessed 22.08.2019).

types of author groups which are domain experts and game experts, such as artists, designers and programmers. The relation between these groups is that the game experts provide authoring tools for the domain experts in consultation with them. Mehm et al., however, propose a similar relation, but subdivides the game experts group into the specific roles in a game creation cycle, which are game designers, game programmers, authoring tool programmers and expert authoring tool users. They describe a fixed process in which these groups work together to create serious games for the field of health education. Masuch and Rueger [12] investigate further challenges in collaborative game design and developing learning environments for creating games. Based on their experience with Squeak [3,10] they perform an analysis of game design processes with OpenCroquet [23] as a platform for collaborative design for online games.

Torrente et al. [26] and Yessad et al. [27] propose instructor-oriented authoring tools for educational video games. They do not draw conclusions on collaborative aspects, but propose systems that help domain experts author entire games in visual editors. Barron-Estrada et al. [2] build on similar concepts as Torrente et al. and Yessad et al. and propose "CodeTraining", an authoring tool for creating content for a gamified programming environment. They enable authors to define specific programming exercises for students. Students can earn points and rise in a leader board visible by other students.

All games and authoring procedures mentioned above provide a static game scenario and genre and let expert-users create content for this scenario, whereas Pex4Fun [25] serves several genres in the form of mini games. One is a puzzle game that takes parameters and return values and let users choose appropriate arguments. The authors of Pex4Fun, however, do not provide direct authoring possibilities, but provide suggestions on how to integrate the puzzles and other mini games in classes. No work was found where learners create their own content for the field of computer science education within the actual game, or in a gamified process – mostly dedicated authoring tools are provided to facilitate the game and content creation.

3 FunPlogs Game Concept

FunPlogs is a serious puzzle and building mini game that makes use of user-created levels to learn fundamentals of programming, as concepts of while-loops and if-then-else decisions. The game concept of FunPlogs is divided into two playable scenes: (1) One for creating playable content together with other students – the *building scene*. And (2) one for actually playing the learning game – the *scripting scene*.

The game flow is build up by iteratively switching between the building scene and the scripting scene. However, the building scene and the scripting scene can be use several times, so that a reflexive and symmetric game flow graph results (Fig. 1). Both scenes are described in detail in the following sections.

Fig. 1. Game flow of FunPlogs. Building new levels and playing the learning game is illustrated as an iterative process. Built level can also be saved for later usage, so that playing or building can also be repeated.

3.1 Scripting Scene

The scripting scene is the core of the learning application. It represents a casual puzzler mini game. Users must guide the player character from an initial starting point to a specific goal position. For this the character must find a way on which he does only use predefined blocks for his path. He must not drop down from the blocks to the bottom of the play area. An example level can be seen in Fig. 2.

Users can direct the virtual character along the path by executing an instruction (Fig. 2 instruction panel) that is made up from several scripting commands (Fig. 2 scripting command menu). The commands in the instruction panel are processed sequential.

A level for FunPlogs is formed by building blocks of different colors. The colors have no impact on the game logic, but contribute to the aesthetic of the game and establish clues for users to orient. The blocks are aligned on a grid, and they can only be stacked upwards or placed on the ground-plane as the lowest level of the grid.

We provide basic movement tasks for solving the spatial task of navigating the character on these blocks: (1) Move forward, (2) move upward, (3) move downward, (4) turn right and (5) turn left. All levels that are designed with the building blocks and the constraints mentioned above can be solved with these basic commands.

Both complex and easy levels can be solved with just using a longer sequence of the basic commands. But users can also use if-/while-statements to see how the instructions can be simplified and how the command count can be reduced. This illustrates to them the use and benefits of if-/while-statements. Whether levels are rather complex or easy is decided by the actual users that create the levels themselves within the building scene.

3.2 Building Scene

The building scene is a sandbox mode of the play area from the scripting scene. The basic principle for creating levels for FunPlogs contrary to the scripting scene involves two players – a *desktop-player* and a *VR-player*. The desktop-player interacts with the system similar as in the scripting scene through a desktop-PC. Players can throw building blocks onto the ground-plane within his top-down view (Fig. 3) and sees the point of view (POV) of the VR-player on his interface in the top left corner.

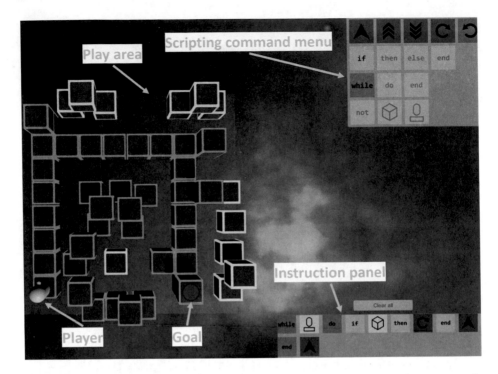

Fig. 2. The top-down point of view of the desktop player during the scripting mode. The interface contains the play area, the scripting command menu and the instruction panel. We furthermore show the virtual player as the starting point and the goal of the puzzle.

The VR-player is located on the initially empty ground-plane. These players see the play area from a first person point of view (Fig. 4). They place the dropped down building blocks on the grid to form the foundation for a walkable path for the virtual character. The VR-player furthermore chooses a starting point for the virtual character and the goal.

Both player-types can suggest certain positions for a drop down or block placement by positioning a marker cube (Fig. 4 purple cube top left) which then hovers over a specific rectangle of the grid. By collaborating and interacting with each other the level is finished. This collaboration within the virtual environment is of asymmetric nature, since one player uses immersive VR technology and the desktop player uses abstracted desktop interactions.

3.3   Prototype Implementation

For our prototype implementation we used the Unity3D game engine as a foundation. The graphical user interface, like the instruction panel of the scripting command menu (Fig. 2, was realized using basic Unity UI-elements. Remaining

Fig. 3. The view of the desktop-player during building mode.

game objects like the ground-plane, the blocks and the player character were made from Unity primitive objects and textures.

The integration of the asymmetric aspect of the virtual environment was more challenging. We explored two possibilities for implementing the multi-player building scene that uses both VR and desktop hardware and interactions. (1) The game can have been developed as a common distributed multi-player game. Two distinct applications are being synchronized, each handling one player class and controlling one specific set of hardware. (2) We decided to implement both classes in one game application that runs the whole game logic and controls the VR and the desktop part. This eliminates the need of a synchronization and facilitates implementations of asymmetric interaction features, like providing the first person view of the VR-player to the desktop-player (Fig. 3 top left). To implement these and all other VR-relating features we used the Virtual Reality Toolkit (VRTK)[2]. We used an HTC Vive VR setup.

4   Evaluation

We conducted an initial user study for evaluating the game concept and draw conclusions about the proposed learning effect of the visual scripting aspects and the user-driven content creation method. This study involved 8 participants (5 male; from 15 to 53 years with Ø 29,6 years). Half of them stated to have little prior experience in programming.

The study started with a user test. Two users tested simultaneously. The test scenario is illustrated in Fig. 5. Participants first tested an example level in the scripting mode to make familiar with the game. After some minutes of free

---
[2] https://vrtoolkit.readme.io/ (Accessed 03.04.2019).

Fig. 4. The view on a FunPlogs level through the eyes of the virtual reality player within the building scene of the game.

testing, the two participants joined in a game. They were asked to build a level in the building scene together. The participants were asked to switch the player roles (VR/desktop) during this step and then could use their own levels within the scripting scene.

After further testing, the participants were asked to fill out an anonymized questionnaire. This questionnaire consisted of demographic questions, followed by 4 questions on the perceived joy of use, the comprehensibility and the scripting tasks. These questions were translated into German as the participants were native Germans: (Q1) How much fun did you have during the creation of the game scenes at the desktop PC? (2) How much fun did you have during the creation of the game scenes using the VR? (3) Do you feel confident that you have understood how an "if"-clause works? (4) Do you feel confident that you have understood how an "while"-loop works? A 5-point likert-scale was used to capture the data. There was also space for free text comments. The answers are illustrated in Fig. 6.

4.1 Analysis of the User Study Results

With an average of Ø 5.0 points and a SD of 0.0 participants stated to have fun in both roles during the collaborative and asymmetric creation of the Fun-Plogs levels. With Ø 4.85 and SD 0.34 they stated to have understood how if-clauses and with Ø 4.83 and SD 0.37 how while-loops do work. Only considering

Fig. 5. The valuation took place in a loose but controlled laboratory environment. Left: VR-player. Right: Desktop-player

participants who explicitly had no programming experience, the values were Ø 4.66 and SD 0.57 for both questions.

In observations during the tests and in free text comments participants stated that they specifically found the collaborative building scene very playful. They furthermore expressed they like the very simple principle of the visual scripting game. Participants also stated that the collaboration during the content-authoring did "randomize" the design of the levels. One participant explicitly mentioned a lack of the VR-player during the actual scripting mode.

4.2   Discussion of the Results

The study generally indicates that participants perceived a high joy of use while playing FunPlogs. Furthermore, it is indicated that despite the simple game concept, complex matters as the while-loop or an if-clause could be transported to programming laymen. Participants needed only few minutes to complete a level of FunPlogs so that an application in the educational field of microlearning could be beneficial for learners.

It can be seen as an advantage that participants found that the collaborative user-driven content creation did veil the level design. The levels therefore were not too clear or predictable during the scripting mode even though they were self-created minutes before the actual usage.

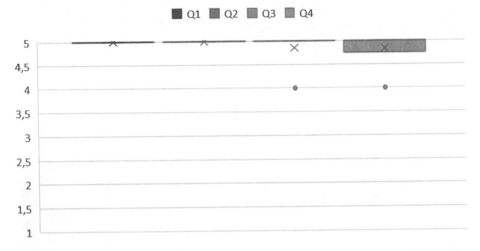

Fig. 6. Box-plot diagrams that illustrate the outcome of the 4 questions. High values represent a positive connotation.

5   Conclusions and Future Work

In this paper we have proposed FunPlogs – a serious puzzle mini-game for learning fundamental programming principles using visual scripting. We have described the concept of the learning game and proposed a collaborative and asymmetric way of user-driven level creation for the game. We could indicate a high joy of use during the usage of FunPlogs on the one hand and exemplary creating a basic understanding of while-loops and if-clauses on the other hand.

In future work, we will investigate in two major aspects. (1) We will maintain more programming aspects in the scripting mode, so that future implementations can transport more knowledge to students. (2) The collaborative VR-aspect of the game will be increased since participants mentioned a high level of joy during collaborating in the building scene. Integrating a VR-player within the actual scripting scene could therefore be beneficial to communicate knowledge within the serious learning game.

Acknowledgements. The work is supported by the Federal Ministry of Education and Research of Germany in the project Innovative Hochschule (funding number: 03IHS071).

References

1. Adams, J.C., Webster, A.R.: What do students learn about programming from game, music video, and storytelling projects? In: Proceedings of the 43rd ACM Technical Symposium on Computer Science Education, pp. 643–648. ACM (2012)

2. Barrón-Estrada, M.L., Zatarain-Cabada, R., Lindor-Valdez, M.: CodeTraining: an authoring tool for a gamified programming learning environment. In: Pichardo-Lagunas, O., Miranda-Jiménez, S. (eds.) MICAI 2016. LNCS (LNAI), vol. 10062, pp. 501–512. Springer, Cham (2017). https://doi.org/10.1007/978-3-319-62428-0_41

3. Bouras, C.J., Poulopoulos, V., Tsogkas, V.: Squeak Etoys: interactive and collaborative learning environments. In: Handbook of Research on Social Interaction Technologies and Collaboration Software: Concepts and Trends, pp. 417–427. IGI Global (2010)

4. Brusilovsky, P., Sosnovsky, S.: Individualized exercises for self-assessment of programming knowledge: an evaluation of quizpack. J. Educ. Resour. Comput. (JERIC) 5(3), 6 (2005)

5. Chandel, P., Dutta, D., Tekta, P., Dutta, K., Gupta, V.: Digital game based learning in computer science education. CPUH Res. J. 1(2), 33–37 (2015)

6. Cooper, S., Dann, W., Pausch, R.: Alice: a 3-D tool for introductory programming concepts. J. Comput. Sci. Coll. 15(5), 107–116 (2000)

7. Hug, T.: Micro learning and narration: exploring possibilities of utilization of narrations and storytelling for the design of "micro units" and didactical micro-learning arrangements. In: Proceedings of Media in Transition (2005)

8. Hug, T.: Microlearning: a new pedagogical challenge (introductory note) (2005)

9. Johnson, W.L., Valente, A.: Collaborative authoring of serious games for language and culture. In: Proceedings of SimTecT, vol. 2008 (2008)

10. Kay, A.C.: Computers, networks and education. Sci. Am. 265(3), 138–149 (1991)

11. Liu, E.Z.F., Chen, P.K.: The effect of game-based learning on students' learning performance in science learning-a case of "conveyance go". Procedia-Soc. Behav. Sci. 103, 1044–1051 (2013)

12. Masuch, M., Rueger, M.: Challenges in collaborative game design developing learning environments for creating games. In: Third International Conference on Creating, Connecting and Collaborating Through Computing (C5 2005), pp. 67–74. IEEE (2005)

13. Mehm, F., Hardy, S., Göbel, S., Steinmetz, R.: Collaborative authoring of serious games for health. In: Proceedings of the 19th ACM International Conference on Multimedia, pp. 807–808. ACM (2011)

14. Mildner, P., Campbell, C., Effelsberg, W.: Word domination. In: Göbel, S., Wiemeyer, J. (eds.) GameDays 2014. LNCS, vol. 8395, pp. 59–70. Springer, Cham (2014). https://doi.org/10.1007/978-3-319-05972-3_7

15. Mildner, P., John, B., Moch, A., Effelsberg, W.: Creation of custom-made serious games with user-generated learning content. In: Proceedings of the 13th Annual Workshop on Network and Systems Support for Games, p. 17. IEEE Press (2014)

16. Moreno, J.: Digital competition game to improve programming skills. J. Educ. Technol. Soc. 15(3), 288–297 (2012)

17. Papastergiou, M.: Digital game-based learning in high school computer science education: impact on educational effectiveness and student motivation. Comput. Educ. 52(1), 1–12 (2009)

18. Pausch, R., et al.: Alice: rapid prototyping system for virtual reality. IEEE Comput. Graphics Appl. 15(3), 8–11 (1995)

19. Pinna, S., Mauri, S., Lorrai, P., Marchesi, M., Serra, N.: XPSwiki: an agile tool supporting the planning game. In: Marchesi, M., Succi, G. (eds.) XP 2003. LNCS, vol. 2675, pp. 104–113. Springer, Heidelberg (2003). https://doi.org/10.1007/3-540-44870-5_14

20. Prensky, M.: Digital game-based learning. Comput. Entertain. (CIE) **1**(1), 21 (2003)
21. Resnick, M., et al.: Scratch: programming for all. Commun. ACM **52**(11), 60–67 (2009)
22. Robertson, J., Good, J.: Story creation in virtual game worlds. Commun. ACM **48**(1), 61–65 (2005)
23. Smith, D.A., Kay, A., Raab, A., Reed, D.P.: Croquet-a collaboration system architecture. In: Proceedings of the First Conference on Creating, Connecting and Collaborating Through Computing, C5 2003, pp. 2–9. IEEE (2003)
24. Steiner, B., Kaplan, N., Moulthrop, S.: When play works: turning game-playing into learning. In: Proceedings of the 2006 Conference on Interaction Design and Children, pp. 137–140. ACM (2006)
25. Tillmann, N., De Halleux, J., Xie, T., Bishop, J.: Pex4Fun: teaching and learning computer science via social gaming. In: 2012 IEEE 25th Conference on Software Engineering Education and Training, pp. 90–91. IEEE (2012)
26. Torrente, J., Moreno-Ger, P., Fernández-Manjón, B., Sierra, J.L.: Instructor-oriented authoring tools for educational videogames. In: 2008 Eighth IEEE International Conference on Advanced Learning Technologies, pp. 516–518. IEEE (2008)
27. Yessad, A., Labat, J.M., Kermorvant, F.: SeGAE: a serious game authoring environment. In: 2010 10th IEEE International Conference on Advanced Learning Technologies, pp. 538–540. IEEE (2010)

Automatic Camera Path Generation from 360° Video

Hannes Fassold$^{(\boxtimes)}$

DIGITAL - Institute for Information and Communication Technologies,
JOANNEUM RESEARCH, Graz, Austria
hannes.fassold@joanneum.at

Abstract. Omnidirectional (360°) video is a novel media format, rapidly becoming adopted in media production and consumption as part of today's ongoing virtual reality revolution. The goal of automatic camera path generation is to calculate automatically a visually interesting camera path from a 360° video in order to provide a traditional, TV-like consumption experience. In this work, we describe our algorithm for automatic camera path generation, based on extraction of the information of the scene objects with deep learning based methods.

Keywords: 360° video · Object detection · Tracking · VR · Storytelling

1 Introduction

Omnidirectional (360°) video content recently got very popular in the media industry, because it allows the viewer to experience the content in an immersive and interactive way. Omnidirectional consumer video cameras like the Samsung Gear 360 or the Ricoh Theta V have multiple lenses and capture images which cover the whole viewing sphere, typically in 4K or UltraHD resolution. The whole viewing sphere is encoded in one 2D image for each timepoint, usually in equirectangular projection [5] (see Fig. 1 for the relation between the viewing sphere and the 2D image). Omnidirectional videos are typically consumed with a head-mounted display (HMD), so that the user is free to choose the area (viewport) within the sphere he is currently interested in. However, not all devices support this kind of navigation possibility. E.g., older TV sets (prior to Smart TVs) don't provide any kind of interactive players for 360° video. Furthermore, even on devices capable of consuming 360° videos interactively, an user might prefer a *lean-back* mode, without the need to navigate around actively in order to explore the content. The goal of *automatic camera path generation* is therefore to calculate automatically a visually interesting camera path from a 360° video, in order to provide a traditional, TV-like consumption experience. The goal is to generate a conventional 2D video from the 360° video automatically, by determining a smooth camera path which captures the salient (most interesting)

© Springer Nature Switzerland AG 2019
G. Bebis et al. (Eds.): ISVC 2019, LNCS 11844, pp. 505–514, 2019.
https://doi.org/10.1007/978-3-030-33720-9_39

regions of the viewing sphere. These regions often correspond to persons performing specific actions, e.g. for a concert scene the salient regions will correspond to
the members of the music band performing the act. In order to generate automatically a pleasing and visually interesting camara path, a high-level semantic
spatio-temporal description of the video is desired. The semantic information is
typically calculated by fusing information gathered from low-level base detectors.
These base detectors operate mostly in the visual domain and employ computer
vision approaches in order to do extract information from the scene. With the
advent of deep learning-based algorithms and GPUs, the performance and speed
of all this classical computer vision tasks has increased dramatically, making the
usage of these algorithms practical.

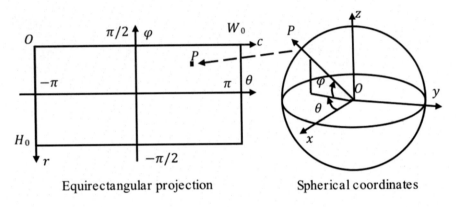

Equirectangular projection   Spherical coordinates

Fig. 1. Coordinate systems employed for an omnidirectional image. Image courtesy
of [9].

For the automatic camera path algorithm, we will mainly rely on the detection and tracking of all objects (persons, animals etc.) which occur in the scene.
The knowledge about the scene objects allows us to calculate saliency (i.e. "inter-
estingness") scores for all scene objects, from which then the camera path is calculated for a certain shot, by tracking the most salient scene object. The paper
is organized as follows. Section 2 gives information about related work in the
literature. In Sect. 3, the *Yoco* algorithm for multi-object detection and tracking
will be described. In Sect. 4, the current algorithm prototype for automatic camera path generation will be described, which relies heavily on the information
provided by the Yoco algorithm. Finally, Sect. 5 provides an outlook of potential
directions to investigate in the future.

2   Related Work

There are a few works for automatic camera path generation from a 360° video.
The approach proposed in [8] first learns a discriminative model from conventional 2D videos collected from the web. It then uses this model to identify

candidate viewpoints and events of interest to capture in the 360° video and determines an optimal camera trajectory using dynamic programming. A disadvantage of this approach is that the learned model is specific to a certain category of 360° video (e.g. soccer videos or hiking videos), as the conventional 2D videos have been collected on the web via domain-specific query keywords. The work [7] extends the algorithm proposed in [8] so that zoom shots (with a small field of view) and wide-angle shots are also supported. Furthermore, the runtime of the algorithm is reduced via a coarse-to-fine strategy for camera trajectory search. In [3], a method is presented for piloting through 360° sports videos. Their method learns an online policy to focus on foreground objects (like a skateboarder) and simultaneously minimizes both view angle loss from human annotated ground truth and smoothness loss between consecutive frames. A deep learning based object detector (Faster R-CNN) is employed for generating candidate hypotheses for objects of interest. In [10], design guidelines for extracting conventional 2D video shots from a 360° video are given (e.g. subject should be centered, people should not be cropped), derived from user studies. Based on these guidelines, a method is presented for extracting a conventional 2D video shot, relying on face and pose detection.

3   Yoco Algorithm

The robust detection and tracking of all objects occurring in the scene is very important for the automatic camera path algorithm in order to calculate a pleasing camera path. Therefore, we researched and developed the novel *Yoco* algorithm for this task (**Yo** for YoloV3 object detector, and **co** for combined with optical flow). The Yoco algorithm is inspired by recent real-time capable online multi-object tracking algorithms like [1], which employs a combination of a deep learning based object detector (Faster Region CNN), Kalman filters for prediction and simple association techniques. The Yoco algorithm employs more powerful components instead, namely the recently introduced YoloV3 object detector [6] and a dense optical flow algorithm for prediction of the object movement. In the following, the respective components will be described, as well as the Yoco algorithm itself.

3.1   YoloV3 Object Detector

The YoloV3 object detector [6] is a state of the art deep learning based algorithm, which provides a very good compromise between detection capability and runtime. It processes the input image in a single phase, in contrast to other popular approaches like Faster-RCNN, which work in two phases (generation of region proposals, classification of regions). The algorithm divides the image into a fixed $n \times n$ grid. For each cell of the grid, it predicts a fixed number of bounding boxes together with their confidence scores and class IDs. A 53-layer network called Darknet-53 is proposed by the author as backbone of the YoloV3 object detector.

Since the original implementation employs only a fixed-size receptive field of quadratic size, an important algorithmic extension has been added in order to support adaptive receptive fields. The idea is that the receptive field size is adapted dynamically, so that it has the same aspect ratio as the input image. This makes sure that the receptive field of the neural network is exploited in an optimal way. For typical 360° video in equirectangular projection, this means that the aspect ratio of the receptive field is 2 : 1 (we set it to 896×448 pixel). We did several experiments with diverse content from 360° video in equirectangular projection, which indicates that the detector is quite robust to the distortions in the image due to the projection. One example output of the detector for an image from a 360° video can be seen in Fig. 2.

Fig. 2. Example output of the YoloV3 object detector.

3.2 Optical Flow Engine

The optical flow problem deals with the calculation of a dense pixel-wise motion-field between two images and has many important applications, as in our case the prediction of the object position in the next frame (tracking). We employ a GPU implementation of the TV-L1 algorithm [11], a classical variational algorithm. It formulates the problem in a disparity preserving, spatially continuous way with a L1 norm data term and anisotropic TV regularization, employing the Huber Norm [2] and solving it numerically with a projected gradient descent scheme. The GPU optical flow implementation is programmed in CUDA and runs in realtime for Full HD resolution on a decent GPU (like a Geforce GTX 1070). The input images for the optical flow algorithm are preprocessed via a structure-texture decomposition in order to be more robust against brightness variation (e.g. due to flicker) in the video.

3.3   Overall Algorithm

In the following, the overall workflow of the Yoco algorithm for multi-object detection and tracking is described briefly. Let I_{t-1} and I_t be two consecutive frames for timepoints $t-1$ and t, and S_{t-1} be the list of already existing scene objects which have been tracked so far until timepoint $t-1$. The workflow for each frame can be roughly divided into four phases:

- In the *preprocessing* phase, the optical flow between the frames I_{t-1} and I_t is calculated, which gives a dense motion field M_{t-1}. Additionally, the YoloV3 object detector is invoked for I_t, yielding a list of detected objects D_t.
- In the *prediction* phase, for all scene objects S_{t-1} their motion is predicted in order to calculate their predicted position S_t for timepoint t. The prediction for each object is calculated as the average of the motion vectors in M_{t-1} for the object bounding box.
- In the *matching* phase, a matching is done of the predicted scene objects S_t against the detected objects D_t. The matching is done in a globally optimal way with the Hungarian algorithm [4], and the *IOU* (intersection-over-union) metric is employed as the matching score.
- In the *update* phase, all scene objects in S_t which could not be matched are considered as lost and a flag is set to exclude them from further processing. In contrast, all detected objects in D_t which could not be matched are considered as newly appearing and therefore added to the scene objects list S_t.

The overall algorithm has been tested on several challenging videos and shows a good performance on them despite its relatively straightforward design. This can be likely attributed due the high quality of the underlying components like the state of the art object detector. The average runtime of the Yoco algorithm is roughly 110 ms for one frame in Full HD resolution on a system with a Geforce GTX 1070 GPU.

4   Automatic Camera Path Algorithm

The automatic camera path generator algorithm works in an iterative fashion, shot by shot. Firstly, a shot length is determined for the next shot. The shot length is fluctuating randomly around a base value, which has to be set by a user and is typically in the range of two to twelve seconds[1]. After setting the shot length, the Yoco multi-object detector and tracker (see Sect. 3) is invoked in order to detect all scene objects and track them through the shot. All scene objects which could not be tracked throughout the whole shot are discarded, as we need the whole trajectory path of each object for calculating its saliency score. In the next step, a global visited map is calculated, which will serve as a tool in order to steer the camera path for the current shot towards areas of the 360° video which have not been viewed in the previous shots. The visited map for a shot is calculated by iterating over the previously visited viewports in the last few shots,

---

[1]   https://stephenfollows.com/many-shots-average-movie/.

projecting them into the image (in equirectangular projection) and accumulating all projected viewports. Each viewport is damped down multiplicatively with a factor, which depends on the timepoint of the viewport (viewports with an earlier timepoint are damped down more) and a user-defined constant which can be interpreted as a *forget factor*. In Fig. 3, the visited maps for three consecutive shots are visualized. Black areas are regions which have not been explored yet in recent history, and white areas denote regions which have been viewed recently.

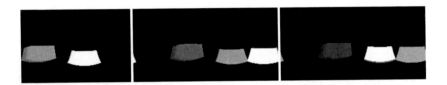

Fig. 3. Visualisation of the visited map for three consecutive shots.

For each scene object, now a set of measures is calculated, from which the saliency score for the object will be calculated. For each object, we calculate the average rectangle location (x, y) and dimension $(width, height)$ of the object. The average is taken over all frames of the current shot. We calculate the average motion magnitude of the object within the current shot in the same way. Additionally, a novel *neighbourhood score* is calculated, which gives a rough indication of how isolated the object is, with respect to other objects in the same frame (of the same object class). It is computed by counting for each frame the number of objects of the same class which are within a distance smaller than a user-defined constant D, and averaging the values over all frames of the shot. As last measure, a visited score is calculated for the object from the overlapping area of the average rectangle of the object and the visited map. A visualisation of the calculated measures for each object can be seen in Fig. 4.

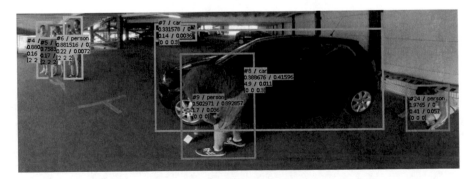

Fig. 4. Visualisation of the calculated measures for each scene object.

After having calculated for each object the set of measure, a saliency score is calculated for each object. The score gives an estimation of how "interesting" the specific object is for a human viewer. E.g., persons in a scene are usually more interesting than e.g. animals or cars. Furthermore, persons which are moving around (e.g., because they are performing a specific action) are usually more interesting than persons which are static (e.g., persons sitting in the audience). The saliency score for an object is calculated from several cues:

- *Object class*: Naturally, persons are more interesting (usually) than other object classes like animals or cars. Therefore, the saliency score for objects of type "person" is increased.
- *Object size*: The saliency score for the object is modulated via the objects average bounding box size so that larger objects (which are supposedly more important) have a higher score. This principle is also known as the *Hitchcock rule* [2].
- *Object motion*: Moving objects are more interesting, as they might perform some actions, compared to static objects (like the audience watching a music concert). Therefore, the saliency score is modulated by the average motion magnitude.
- *Neighbourhood*: We make the assumption that isolated objects (like the musicians in a music event) are more important than objects of the same class which are coalescing together (like the audience). Therefore, the saliency score for objects with less neighbours is increased.
- *Visited score*: We employ the visited score to decrease the saliency score of objects which have been already viewed in recent history.

For each of these cues, we calculate a respective *modulation factor* by which the saliency score gets multiplied. For calculating the modulation factor, we employ linear functions (with clamping) mapping a source interval to a target interval. E.g. for the average bounding box size (measured in percent of the whole image size), we map the interval $[0.2, 1.0]$ to the interval $[1.0, 2.0]$. The interval borders have been determined heuristically for a specific content type (in our case, stage performances like music concerts or shows) and might have to be adapted slightly for another type of content.

After having calculating the saliency score for each object, we determine the *focus object* as the object with the highest saliency score. This is the object we will track in the generated automatic camera path for this shot. Prior to calculating the viewport information for each timepoint, we smooth the object path (the object's bounding box positions) temporally, in order to generate a smooth camera path. For blurring the object path, we employ a box filter with kernel size 5 separately on the x and y coordinate.

For each timepoint, we calculate now a viewport where the viewport center is the center of the object's bounding box. For persons which are quite near to the camera, we steer the viewport center to the upper half of the bounding box in order to avoid cropping the person's head. The viewport has a fixed horizontal field-of-view of 75°, and a 4 : 3 aspect ratio.

Fig. 5. Visualisation of the result of the automatic camera path for a music video (first row). Each row shows two frames from the generated shot (four consecutive shots in total)

The result of the automatic camera path algorithm for a 360° video showing a live music concert is shown in Fig. 5. The base shot length has been chosen as three seconds, in order to account for the dynamic in the content and generate a fast-paced video.

5 Conclusion and Outlook

Although the current prototype of the automatic camera path algorithm works well, there is definitely room for improvements in several directions. Firstly, more semantic information should be extracted from the scene with deep learning methods, in order to understand the video better – which in turn should allow the algorithm to generate a more interesting camera path. Especially the information from face (and face orientation) detection, person action recognition and from semantic segmentation (detect ground/sky/...) could be very valuable. More cinematographic techniques and visual grammar rules for editing/framing should be added, in order to make the generated video more diverse from an artistic point and consequently more interesting to watch. In the current prototype, the field-of-view (FOV) is fixed at 75°, and no zoom, pan or close-up shots are generated, only tracking shots. These constraints should be relaxed, in order to e.g. be able to generate a close-up shot of the face of a person. Furthermore, the current prototype of the algorithm relies heavily on the presence of salient objects (especially persons) in the 360° video. If no such objects exist in the video (e.g. for a 360° video showing a nature scene like an empty beach), an alternative mode should be developed which relies on complementary information.

Acknowledgment. This work has received funding from the European Union's Horizon 2020 research and innovation programme, grant n° 761934, Hyper360 ("Enriching 360 media with 3D storytelling and personalisation elements"). Thanks to Rundfunk Berlin-Brandenburg (RBB) for providing the 360° video content.

References

1. Bewley, A., Ge, Z., Ott, L., Ramos, F., Upcroft, B.: Simple online and realtime tracking. In: 2016 IEEE International Conference on Image Processing (ICIP), pp. 3464–3468 September 2016. https://doi.org/10.1109/ICIP.2016.7533003
2. Galvane, Q., Ronfard, R.: Implementing hitchcock - the role of focalization and viewpoint. In: Bares, W., Gandhi, V., Galvane, Q., Ronfard, R. (eds.) Eurographics Workshop on Intelligent Cinematography and Editing. The Eurographics Association (2017). https://doi.org/10.2312/wiced.20171065
3. Hu, H.N., Lin, Y.C., Liu, M.Y., Cheng, H.T., Chang, Y.J., Sun, M.: Deep 360 pilot: learning a deep agent for piloting through 360° sports videos. In: 2017 IEEE Conference on Computer Vision and Pattern Recognition (CVPR), pp. 1396–1405, July 2017. https://doi.org/10.1109/CVPR.2017.153
4. Kuhn, H.W., Yaw, B.: The hungarian method for the assignment problem. Naval Res. Logist. Q. **2**(1–2), 83–97 (1955)

5. Lee, H., Tateyama, Y., Ogi, T.: Realistic visual environment for immersive projection display system. In: 2010 16th International Conference on Virtual Systems and Multimedia, pp. 128–132, October 2010. https://doi.org/10.1109/VSMM.2010.5665954

6. Redmon, J., Farhadi, A.: Yolov3: an incremental improvement. CoRR abs/1804.02767 (2018). http://arxiv.org/abs/1804.02767

7. Su, Y.C., Grauman, K.: Making 360° video watchable in 2d: Learning videography for click free viewing. In: 2017 IEEE Conference on Computer Vision and Pattern Recognition (CVPR), pp. 1368–1376, July 2017. https://doi.org/10.1109/CVPR.2017.150

8. Su, Y.C., Jayaraman, D., Grauman, K.: Pano2Vid: automatic Cinematography for Watching 360° Videos. In: Bares, W., Gandhi, V., Galvane, Q., Ronfard, R. (eds.) Eurographics Workshop on Intelligent Cinematography and Editing. The Eurographics Association (2017). https://doi.org/10.2312/wiced.20171071

9. Suzuki, T., Yamanaka, T.: Saliency map estimation for omni-directional image considering prior distributions. In: IEEE International Conference on Systems, Man, and Cybernetics, SMC 2018, Miyazaki, Japan, 7–10 October 2018, pp. 2079–2084 (2018). https://doi.org/10.1109/SMC.2018.00358

10. Truong, A., Chen, S., Yumer, E., Li, W., Salesin, D.: Extracting regular FOV shots from 360 event footage. In: Human-Computer Interaction (CHI 2018), Montreal, April 2018

11. Werlberger, M., Trobin, W., Pock, T., Wedel, A., Cremers, D., Bischof, H.: Anisotropic huber-l1 optical flow. In: Proceedings of the British Machine Vision Conference (BMVC), London, UK, September 2009

Highlighting Techniques for 360° Video Virtual Reality and Their Immersive Authoring

Robin Horst[✉], Savina Diez, and Ralf Dörner

RheinMain University of Applied Sciences, Wiesbaden, Germany
{robin.horst,savina.diez,ralf.dorner}@hs-rm.de
http://www.hs-rm.de

Abstract. Highlighting important elements is a fundamental task to guide the user's attention in Virtual Reality (VR) applications. Besides the authoring process of a VR application, the creation of these cues for highlighting in 360° video VR already is a non-trivial task itself. It is even more challenging for laymen in the field of VR.

This paper has three main contributions: (1) We investigate existing highlighting methods for VR scenes setting that are based on 3D models and explore on their suitability for a 360° video VR setting. We involve six highlighting methods. (2) We propose immersive authoring methods suitable for laymen to create these highlights within a 360° video VR application. (3) In a knowledge communication use-case that demonstrates a virtual laboratory, we evaluate the highlighting techniques and their authoring methods. In the user study we indicate that the "outlining" method is highly suitable for a 360° setting and that the according immersive authoring method we propose is appropriate for laymen authoring.

Keywords: Virtual reality · Highlighting techniques · Content creation · Immersive authoring · Laymen authoring

1 Introduction

Current Virtual Reality (VR) technology, such as 360° video cameras, can easily be utilized to capture illustrations of real environments, such as rooms, touristic sites or museums, besides other locations. These 360° videos then can be used to create virtual environments. Users of these virtual environments are able to perceive these locations. But as users wear an HMD, they cannot easily be guided through such locations by co-located persons, so that highlighting distinct objects becomes and important task in such settings. In common VR settings these objects are mostly 3D models, but in video-based VR, these objects lie on the video so that common highlighting techniques for VR may not be suitable or perceived differently by users.

© Springer Nature Switzerland AG 2019
G. Bebis et al. (Eds.): ISVC 2019, LNCS 11844, pp. 515–526, 2019.
https://doi.org/10.1007/978-3-030-33720-9_40

In this paper, we make the following contributions:

1. We propose a set of different established highlighting techniques for common VR settings that are suitable for 360° video VR.
2. For each of these suitable techniques, we introduce an immersive authoring method to be performed by people novel to VR.
3. In a specific use-case, we show the feasibility of our proposed approaches. We evaluate the proposed set of highlighting and immersive authoring methods. We indicate that the demo was well-accepted by the participants. We point out the highlighting method "outline" to be most appropriate for our use-case and indicate that the relating immersive authoring method was rated best within our study by the laymen, as well.

This paper is organized as follows: After this introductory section we present related approaches regarding highlighting in VR, authoring of VR systems and presenting a real-world room within a virtual demo. Section 3 describes the main concepts of (1) different suitable highlighting methods for a 360° video VR setting and (2) immersive authoring interactions to create them within the virtual environment. In Sect. 4, we describe a prototype implementation and show the feasibility of the proposed techniques. In Sect. 5, we present a user study that evaluates the highlighting on the one hand and the authoring techniques on the other hand. A conclusion and future work section completes this paper.

2   Related Work

In this section, we relate our work to state of the art in the fields of highlighting in VR and authoring of VR. We focus on work in a specific sub-setting of VR, which is 360° video VR and authoring concepts that involve immersive authoring interactions.

2.1   Highlighting in Virtual Reality

Trapp et al. [20] present a visualization framework that unifies various highlighting techniques suitable for different types of 3D environments. The authors classify existing highlighting methods into either *style-variance techniques*, *outlining techniques*, and *glyph-based techniques*. Style-variance refers to methods that alter the objects' appearance directly, such as changing the color of their texture. Outlining techniques add an outline or silhouette effect to the object to highlight it. Glyph-based techniques use icons or glyphs and attach them to an object to draw the user's attention to it. All highlights are created by VR-experts themselves. They relate to a VR setting that is based on 3D models. These techniques might not be transferable to 360° video VR, as the highlighted objects are not represented as 3D models, but are displayed on a video texture.

Peter et al. [18] refer to existing highlighting techniques and investigate their integration within an asymmetric VR setting. In this setting, objects can be highlighted by a second user of the system that uses a laptop screen. The user can make use of the highlighting techniques while the first user experiences the virtual environment to guide the user through it. The authors focus on an implementation of light-beam technique to steer the attention of users.

There also exists work about highlighting in the related field of AR which explores opportunities to highlight regions of interest on videos or images of real-world surroundings. Fuchs et al. [12] present techniques for highlighting real entities in augmented reality and point out 9 novel approaches. They rely on the use of particle systems, distortion and contouring. These approaches are based on real-time computer vision methods to find specific objects and then highlight them. Further work in the field of AR proposes to use saliency modulation for guiding the users view based on their spatial attention [21]. Using visual saliency is based on changing the border color of an object – either an object of the virtual environment or an additional object added to the VR scene for this purpose (e.g. a wire-frame cube to highlight a volume). This method also uses real-time computer vision methods to find out about the attention of the users.

We did not find recent work that explores existing or novel highlighting techniques that relate specifically to a 360° video VR setting, where highlighted objects are displayed on a video texture together with several background objects.

2.2 Authoring for Virtual Reality Systems

From early work in the field of VR until today, content creation for VR systems still involves many challenges [7,13,14,16,19,22]. These challenges often depend on the area of application of the VR system, as for example archeology [2], history museums [23], assembly and maintenance prototyping [6] or prototyping for telecommunication products [15]. Besides the application domain, the requirements for a VR authoring system furthermore change according to its targeted end users.

Pioneering work in the field of authoring 3D systems for novices by Conway et al. [4] describes the implementation of Alice, a 3D programming environment targeting novice undergraduates. They describe lessons learned based on this implementation. These lessons learned indicate that users preferred abstractions of the authoring interactions, so that programming related functionality was hidden in favor of more natural metaphors. Defining the position of objects for example was preferred by using forward-left-up metaphors over changing XYZ-coordinates and commands were animated by default. Generally a 2D UI was proposed in this work.

3D UI can furthermore help to facilitate authoring of 3D virtual environments. Work by Dunk et al. [9,10] introduces the gMenu which is a UI that reflects common desktop metaphors (e.g. a virtual keyboard and a virtual screen) in a 3D virtual environment. They point out a set of immersive authoring interaction methods (specifically selection methods) developed for the CAVE [5]. Dunk et al. indicate [8] that laymen in the field of VR can benefit from these immersive interactions during the authoring process of a VR.

The pARnorama system [1] makes use of an interactive 360° video VR to prototype augmented reality (AR) interfaces and applications. Berning et al.

provide here a 2D authoring environment that creates these VR applications for smartphones. They provide interactions for recording the 360° panorama video and editing the video, for example cutting or trimming. A viewer application is used to actually play the video VR prototype. Similarly, recent work by Nguyen et al. [17] (Vremiere) provides user interactions for editing 360° videos. However, they use immersive interactions so that authors have to wear HMDs during the process. Additionally, visual markers can be placed to augment the video scene with virtual content. These markers are used in the editing process to highlight specific regions in the video. These markers are also visualized on a timeline so that users can jump to these markers while watching the video. They furthermore propose to set these pin-like markers on the video texture by pointing and clicking on the video in real time.

These studies indicate a great potential for using immersive authoring inter-actions within laymen-based authoring procedures in 3D model-based VR. Immersive authoring therefore might also offer potential for authoring highlight-ing techniques within 360° video VR.

3   Highlighting Techniques and Immersive Authoring

In this section we describe potential highlighting techniques for a 360° video VR setting and their immersive authoring methods.

3.1   Highlighting Techniques for 360° Video VR

As we rely on 360° video VR, not every established highlighting method can be used similar to a VR that consists of 3D models. Objects are only visible on the surface of an inverted sphere where the video is projected on. Techniques that rely on the 3D geometry of objects might not be suitable for our specific case. In contrast to highlighting in AR applications, we cannot use any sensory data, such as from a depth sensor, but only have the visual data from the video material.

In our work we consider the following six techniques for the 360° setup. Figure 1 shows the techniques from a conceptual view.

1. Label – A panel with name and button in front of the object. The label rectangle is always oriented towards the user's view. This method could be used if the objects are difficult to recognize anyway and the user should see the name at a glance.
2. Boxes – Simple colored, semi-transparent shapes on the objects. In contrast to the label method, the boxes are three dimensional.
3. Scaffold meshes – Instead of the filled boxes, here only cuboid contours are on the objects. These contours are displayed as scaffold meshes. Unlike the boxes, they leave the view of the object almost completely unobstructed.
4. Frame – A frame placed as close as possible to the object in the video leaves the view of the object in question unobstructed. The frame is an outlined rectangle that is, in contrast to the label, adjusted in the orientation. The exact contours of the object play a subordinate role.

5. Halo – A glowing halo effect is spread over the object from the center of it.
6. Outline – An exact contour drawn around the object in the video clearly highlights its components and shape.

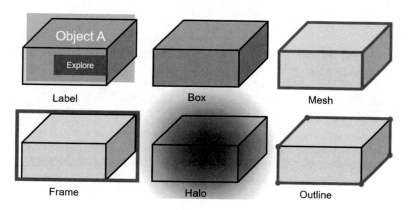

Fig. 1. Highlighting techniques considered for 360° video VR. (Color figure online)

3.2 Immersive Authoring Methods

We provide authoring concepts that are performed directly in the immersive environment, i.e. when the author wears a VR HMD. For authoring the mentioned highlighting methods, we divide necessary interactions into four separate categories. Different subsets of these interactions allow users to create all the highlighting methods in VR:

1. Adding a label – The author can insert individual labels for the objects. Here a virtual keyboard can be useful or also the possible selection from a predefined list of phrases.
2. Positioning a highlight – The author can freely translate, scale and rotate a highlight within the virtual room. A suitable control panel is used to allow the author to transform the object in all possible directions at the push of a button.
3. Creating scene connections – The author can link scenes together so that clicking on a button in one scene takes the user to the next. The accessible scenes must have been stored beforehand.
4. Outlining an object – The author can freely create hulls around objects.

The following procedures for authoring, respectively highlighting selected objects in a 360° virtual space, consist of combinations and variations of the discussed authoring methods.

Label Authoring. For the label highlight, the authoring methods "adding a title" and "creating scene connections" are integrated. First the authors mark a direction, respectively they aim with a controller at the object of interest. Then a new label appears at the selected position. The label is oriented towards the authors. Authors then are asked to enter a title for the label. Then they select an object point to which this highlight should transition to.

Box, Mesh and Frame Authoring. With these three methods a 3D model superimposes the object of interest in such a way that the impression is created that it completely encloses the object. The highlighting object can be a box that superimposes the object, a mesh that encloses the object in a kind of grid, or a simple rectangular frame.

The box, the mesh and the frame methods are similar to each other in terms of authoring. They all rely on interactions to resize, reposition and rotate them. These interactions are used by the authors until the shape of the highlight fits their expectations. Then scene connections are set.

Outline Authoring. The interactions "creating scene connections" and "outlining an object" are used here. With the help of a discrete interaction with the controller (e.g. trigger or button) the users can create vertices in the virtual space that lie on the inverted sphere on which the video is projected on. When they indicate to be finished with an object, lines between these points are generated automatically. A convex hull algorithm is used to calculate the form from the points, since the order of creation of the points should not matter. A naive line-algorithm otherwise would connect the points in the order they were set. Refining the outline therefore would be complicated.

Halo Authoring. A halo is defined by a single point on the inside of the sphere. The halo can be scaled uniformly until it covers the extent of the object.

4   Prototype Implementation

The following highlighting methods were implemented and could be authored. Figures 2 and 3 show examples of the different authoring methods in the virtual environment. We used Unity3D as basis of the prototype.

For the label technique, Unity UI was used. A canvas with a single button was sufficient to represent labels. To author this label we implemented a point and click interaction which instantiated the canvas with a button. The method is illustrated in Fig. 2(left). The label faces the direction towards the author.

The box, mesh and frame authoring methods on the other hand needed a more complex set of interactions. It includes creating a new highlighting object, moving and rotating the object to a position that best fits the current object, scaling the object in different dimensions and selecting a scene to enter when the user clicks on the highlighting object. Figure 2(right) shows the implemented

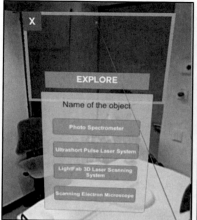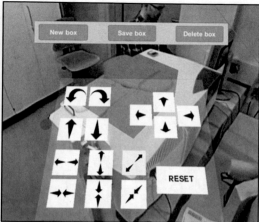

Fig. 2. Left: Label method. The author has just created a new label using the touch-pad and now chooses the scene connection. Right: Box/Mesh/Frame method. The author moves the box using the arrow keys. The red dot on the right illustrates the cursor/pointer of the user. (Color figure online)

interface. A 2D menu was attached to the view of the author and point-and-click gestures were used to activate the buttons. This menu can be used for all three methods in the same way. The box, mesh and frame differ only in their selected Unity prefab. The interaction with these prefabs stays the same. Here the authoring methods "positioning a highlight" and "creating scene connections" are used. In the example of the box, the users first instantiate a box at a position in front of the author within the virtual environment. This box is moved to the correct position using a positioning panel (Fig. 2 middle). This panel also provides possibilities to scale, rotate and translate the box. If the box is at the position of the object of interest, it can be saved on clicking the "Save"-button. Thereafter, the corresponding scene must be selected which should be accessed when the user clicks on the box. The user then has the option to create additional boxes to cover the object more precisely or to realign an already created box again.

The outline method is based on Unity's LineRenderer. This component of a Unity GameObject renders lines between predefined points in 3D space in a predefined order. During authoring the users can use the touch-pad to point on positions on the inverted sphere to define these points. These lie on an invisible sphere that is minimally smaller than the video spheres. For visual support, the points are marked with small sphere-objects (Fig. 3 left). When the author clicks on the UI button "Draw outline", the lines between the corner points are generated and the markers disappear. Instead of just adding the chosen points to a list and pass this list to the LineRenderer, a convex hull algorithm sorts the points so that the points then are connected in a counterclockwise or clockwise order. Otherwise, the lines of the LineRederer would create a hairball that does not outline but cross the object of interest.

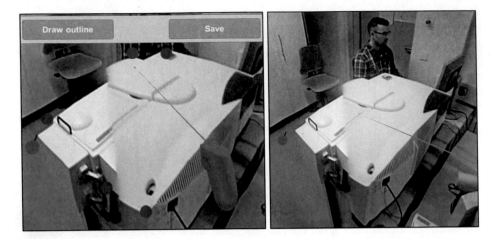

Fig. 3. Left: Outline method. The author sets the corner points for the outline. Right: The author has just created the halo. The red dot depicts the cursor/pointer of the user (Color figure online).

The halo technique was implemented using Unity's visual effect reference "Halo", which creates a halo at the position of a specific Unity GameObject. This GameObject is placed similar to a single point of the outline method, just that the empty GameObject contains a halo component. This halo component creates a 3D halo effect. For our setting, 2D implementations of a halo would have been sufficient, as well. A 2D halo texture for example could have been projected onto the 360° video texture. We decided to use the 3D implementation to address the three dimensional visual perception of users. The 3D effect creates a continuously increasing nebulous fall off towards the user (Fig. 3 right).

5   Evaluation

Besides implementing a prototype of the concepts we conducted a user study for evaluating the highlighting techniques in a 360° video VR setting and their immersive authoring methods we proposed. We used the described implementations within a knowledge communication scene: A professor wants to introduce the laser laboratory of the local university in VR and therefore captured 360° videos.

The study involved 11 unpaid, voluntary participants (5 female, aged between 22 and 55 with Ø 28.54 and SD 8.84 years) and focused on evaluating the highlighting and authoring concepts. Participants were asked to indicate their level of experience with VR hardware from 0 (no experience) to 3 (high experience). These indications ranged from 0 to 3 with Ø 0.63 and SD 0.88, so that the majority of the participants had none or little experience.

We evaluated six different highlighting methods and four immersive authoring methods for them. After an introduction into the VR hardware and the laser laboratory setting, the first part of the study focused on the highlighting methods. In a randomized order, the experimenters gave the participants a VR scene where a single object of interest was highlighted with a distinct highlighting method. Participants were asked to identify the object and communicate when they found it. After each method, they filled out a brief questionnaire with five questions, which were translated into German as their native language: (HQ1) How well or how quickly could you identify the highlighted object? (HQ2) How strongly did you feel disturbed in the virtual world by the highlighting? (HQ3) How much did you feel disturbed because parts of the background and nearby objects were covered by the highlighting? (HQ4) How great were the difficulties in perceiving the highlighted object itself? (HQ5) How well could you perceive the contour of the object?

The immersive authoring methods were evaluated in the second part. In a randomized order, the experimenters gave the participants a VR scene where one of the authoring methods could be carried out for a distinct object. After each method, they filled out a brief questionnaire with four questions: (AQ1) How satisfied are you with the highlight you created? (AQ2) How well or how quickly were you able to highlight the object? (AQ3) How precise could you highlight the object? (AQ4) How much fun did you have creating the highlight? The duration of each authoring method were recorded.

Analysis of the Results. The overall ratings of the participants for each highlighting method for and each question HQ1–HQ5 were tested on significant differences. We conducted the non-parametric and dependent Friedman test [11] for each question. Under a significance level of $p \leq 0.05$, the test showed significant differences for HQ1, HQ3, HQ4 and HQ5, with $p = 0.00016$, $p \leq 0.00001$, $p \leq 0.00001$ and $p \leq 0.00001$ respectively. We conducted further post-hoc tests (after Conover [3]) to identify between which highlighting methods the differences were significant. The resulting ranks of the tests are illustrated in Fig. 4. High values indicate a positive perception concerning HQ1 and HQ5 and low values for HQ3 and HQ4.

We conducted the same tests on significance for the four questions concerning the authoring concerning each method. The Friedman test showed significant differences for all four questions AQ1, AQ2, AQ3 and AQ4 with $p = 0.00085$, $p \leq 0.00001$, $p = 0.00472$ and $p = 0.00002$ respectively. The post-hoc test was used as before. Mean ranks are illustrated in Fig. 4. High values indicate a positive perception concerning all four questions.

Discussion of the Results. Figure 4 illustrates that the outline highlighting method holds the highest absolute rank-values for HQ1 and HQ5 and the lowest for HQ3 and HQ4 and therefore was rated by the participants the most positive. The post-hoc tests revealed that it differs significantly in HQ1 from box and label, in HQ3 from all except frame, in HQ4 from all except mesh and in HQ5 from all methods. The mesh method was rated second-best after Fig. 4. It does

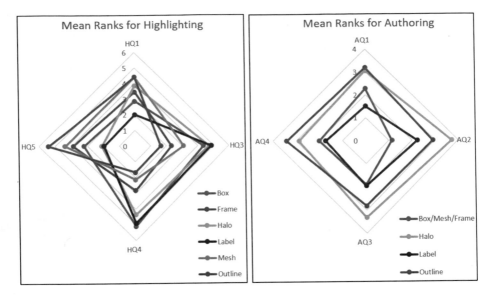

Fig. 4. Illustration of the mean ranks resulting from the Friedman tests for the highlighting techniques (left) and the authoring methods (right) concerning the distinct questions of the questionnaire. (Color figure online)

only differ significantly from the outline method in HQ3 and was rated significantly worse than outline, so that it is indicated that the outline method is the most suitable in our use-case.

Figure 4 furthermore illustrates that the halo and the outline authoring methods were rated the two best methods within the set we consider. For AQ1, halo differs significantly from label, and outline differs significantly from outline and the box/mesh/frame (bmf) method. Both differ significantly from each other method concerning AQ2, whereby halo also was ranked significantly higher than outline. In AQ3 both the halo and the authoring method differ significantly from label and bmf. The same applies for AQ4. Since there was only one significant difference between the best-rated methods, the halo highlighting is indicated to hold the most suitable authoring method for the participants within our study.

The halo highlighting method was rated considerably low compared to the outline highlighting. For being the best-rated highlighting method and holding the second best authoring method, it is therefore strongly indicated that the outline highlighting method is the most suitable method to use for our 360° VR use-case, also concerning immersive laymen authoring.

6   Conclusion and Future Work

In this work we investigated in suitable highlighting techniques for a 360° video VR setting that differs from common VR that uses 3D models. We proposed immersive authoring methods for each of the highlighting techniques that are usable for laymen. We explored how laymen perceive implementations of the techniques, and we pointed out in a user study that the outlining method was rated suitable for both highlighting objects and authoring it.

Potential future work is located in investigating comprehensive immersive authoring environments for 360° VR applications, so that laymen would be able to create these applications entirely. Therefore, future work must provide experts with a toolkit that enables them to (1) actually shoot the required videos themselves and (2) integrate them in a VR environment, together with additional text. We furthermore focused on highlighting static objects in these videos. Moving objects should be regarded in future work so that more complex interactions, such as animating highlights, gain important. Investigating combinations of the proposed highlighting techniques could be of interest for the community, as well.

Acknowledgements. The work is supported by the Federal Ministry of Education and Research of Germany in the project Innovative Hochschule (funding number: 03IHS071).

References

1. Berning, M., Yonezawa, T., Riedel, T., Nakazawa, J., Beigl, M., Tokuda, H.: Parnorama: 360 degree interactive video for augmented reality prototyping. In: Proceedings of the 2013 ACM conference on Pervasive and ubiquitous computing adjunct publication, pp. 1471–1474. ACM (2013)
2. Bruno, F., Bruno, S., De Sensi, G., Luchi, M.L., Mancuso, S., Muzzupappa, M.: From 3D reconstruction to virtual reality: a complete methodology for digital archaeological exhibition. J. Cult. Heritage **11**(1), 42–49 (2010)
3. Conover, W.: Practical Nonparametric Statistics. Wiley, New York (1999)
4. Conway, M., Audia, S., Burnette, T., Cosgrove, D., Christiansen, K.: Alice: lessons learned from building a 3D system for novices. In: Proceedings of the SIGCHI Conference on Human Factors in Computing Systems, pp. 486–493. ACM (2000)
5. Cruz-Neira, C., Sandin, D.J., DeFanti, T.A., Kenyon, R.V., Hart, J.C.: The cave: audio visual experience automatic virtual environment. Commun. ACM **35**(6), 64–73 (1992)
6. De Sa, A.G., Zachmann, G.: Virtual reality as a tool for verification of assembly and maintenance processes. Comput. Graph. **23**(3), 389–403 (1999)
7. Dörner, R., Kallmann, M., Huang, Y.: Content creation and authoring challenges for virtual environments: from user interfaces to autonomous virtual characters. In: Brunnett, G., Coquillart, S., van Liere, R., Welch, G., Váša, L. (eds.) Virtual Realities. LNCS, vol. 8844, pp. 187–212. Springer, Cham (2015). https://doi.org/10.1007/978-3-319-17043-5_11
8. Dunk, A.: Immersive authoring for virtual reality. Ph.D. thesis, University of Reading (2013)
9. Dunk, A., Haffegee, A.: The gMenu user interface for virtual reality systems and environments. In: Allen, G., Nabrzyski, J., Seidel, E., van Albada, G.D., Dongarra, J., Sloot, P.M.A. (eds.) ICCS 2009. LNCS, vol. 5545, pp. 746–753. Springer, Heidelberg (2009). https://doi.org/10.1007/978-3-642-01973-9_83
10. Dunk, A., Haffegee, A., Alexandrov, V.: Selection methods for interactive creation and management of objects in 3D immersive environments. Procedia Comput. Sci. **1**(1), 2609–2617 (2010)

11. Friedman, M.: The use of ranks to avoid the assumption of normality implicit in the analysis of variance. J. Am. Stat. Assoc. **32**(200), 675–701 (1937)

12. Fuchs, S., Sigel, M., Dörner, R.: Highlighting techniques for real entities in augmented reality. In: Proceedings of the 11th Joint Conference on Computer Vision, Imaging and Computer Graphics Theory and Applications - Vol. 1, GRAPP, (VISIGRAPP 2016), pp. 259–270. INSTICC, SciTePress (2016). https://doi.org/10.5220/0005674002570268

13. Gerken, K., Frechenhäuser, S., Dörner, R., Luderschmidt, J.: Authoring support for post-WIMP applications. In: Kotzé, P., Marsden, G., Lindgaard, G., Wesson, J., Winckler, M. (eds.) INTERACT 2013. LNCS, vol. 8119, pp. 744–761. Springer, Heidelberg (2013). https://doi.org/10.1007/978-3-642-40477-1_51

14. Green, M., Jacob, R.: Siggraph'90 workshop report: software architectures and metaphors for non-wimp user interfaces. ACM SIGGRAPH Comput. Graph. **25**(3), 229–235 (1991)

15. Kerttula, M., Salmela, M., Heikkinen, M.: Virtual reality prototyping-a framework for the development of electronics and telecommunication products. In: RSP, p. 2. IEEE (1997)

16. Nebeling, M., Speicher, M.: The trouble with augmented reality/virtual reality authoring tools. In: 2018 IEEE International Symposium on Mixed and Augmented Reality Adjunct (ISMAR-Adjunct), pp. 333–337. IEEE (2018)

17. Nguyen, C., DiVerdi, S., Hertzmann, A., Liu, F.: Vremiere: in-headset virtual reality video editing. In: Proceedings of the 2017 CHI Conference on Human Factors in Computing Systems, pp. 5428–5438. ACM (2017)

18. Peter, M., Horst, R., Dörner, R.: Vr-guide: a specific user role for asymmetric virtual reality setups in distributed virtual reality applications. In: Proceedings of the 15th Workshop Virtual and Augmented Reality of the GI Group VR/AR. Gesellschaft für Informatik (2018)

19. Steed, A.: Some useful abstractions for re-usable virtual environment platforms. In: Software Engineering and Architectures for Realtime Interactive Systems-SEARIS (2008)

20. Trapp, M., Beesk, C., Pasewaldt, S., Dollner, J.: Interactive rendering techniques for highlighting in 3D geovirtual environments. In: Kolbe, T., König, G., Nagel, C., et al. (eds.) Advances in 3D Geo-information Sciences. LNGC, pp. 197–210. Springer, Heidelberg (2010). https://doi.org/10.1007/978-3-642-12670-3_12

21. Veas, E.E., Mendez, E., Feiner, S.K., Schmalstieg, D.: Directing attention and influencing memory with visual saliency modulation. In: Proceedings of the SIGCHI Conference on Human Factors in Computing Systems, CHI 2011, pp. 1471–1480. ACM, New York (2011). https://doi.org/10.1145/1978942.1979158. http://doi.acm.org/10.1145/1978942.1979158

22. Wingrave, C.A., LaViola, J.J.: Reflecting on the design and implementation issues of virtual environments. Presence **19**(2), 179–195 (2010)

23. Wojciechowski, R., Walczak, K., White, M., Cellary, W.: Building virtual and augmented reality museum exhibitions. In: Proceedings of the 9th International Conference on 3D Web Technology, pp. 135–144. ACM (2004)

Applications I

Jitter-Free Registration for Unmanned Aerial Vehicle Videos

Pierre Lemaire[1]([⊠]), Carlos Fernando Crispim-Junior[1], Lionel Robinault[2],
and Laure Tougne[1]

[1] Université Lyon 2, LIRIS, UMR5205, 69676 Bron Cedex, France
{pierre.lemaire,carlos.crispim-junior,laure.tougne}@liris.cnrs.fr
[2] Foxstream, 69120 Vaulx-en-Velin, France
l.robinault@foxstream.fr

Abstract. Unmanned Aerial Vehicles (UAVs), such as tethered drones, become increasingly popular for video acquisition, within video surveillance or remote, scientific measurement contexts. However, UAV recordings often present an unstable, variable viewpoint that is detrimental to the automatic exploitation of their content. This is often countered by one amongst two strategies, video registration and video stabilization, which are usually affected by distinct issues, namely jitter and drifting. This paper proposes a hybrid solution between both techniques that produces a jitter-free registration. A lightweight implementation enables real time, automatic generation of videos with a constant viewpoint from unstable video sequences acquired with stationary UAVs. Performance evaluation is carried out using video recordings from traffic surveillance scenes up to 15 min long, including multiple mobile objects.

Keywords: Motion estimation · Video registration · Video stabilization · Unmanned Aerial Vehicles

1 Introduction

Unmanned Aerial Vehicles (UAVs), are becoming increasingly popular for tasks such as video surveillance or remote data acquisition [15]. Tethered drones [10] can now fly during several hours up to 50 m above ground in stationary flight. Their video flux looks a lot like that of a classic surveillance camera. However, their lack of stability makes tasks such as background subtraction or objects tracking more complex than with a fixed viewpoint (Fig. 1a and b). This paper proposes a real-time, online method to convert videos acquired from a stationary drone into jitter-free, single viewpoint videos as much as possible.

Real-world applications for stationary UAVs such as traffic monitoring or crowd surveillance often present a high density of mobile objects, which may provoke drifting and jitter issues over time. Yet, prior works on UAVs image stabilization techniques have been studied on datasets that include very few mobile objects and rather short sequences [2,13].

© Springer Nature Switzerland AG 2019
G. Bebis et al. (Eds.): ISVC 2019, LNCS 11844, pp. 529–539, 2019.
https://doi.org/10.1007/978-3-030-33720-9_41

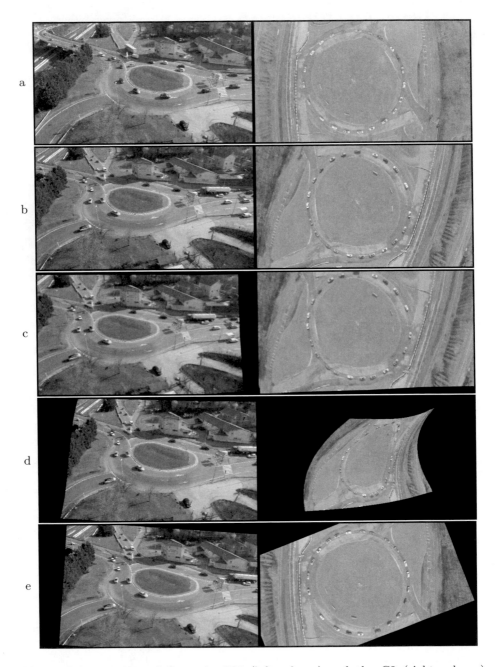

Fig. 1. Images extracted from the M4 (left column) and the C2 (right column) sequences in our database. a: first frame, used as a reference image. b: current frame, after approx. 15 s (resp. 45 s) on left M4 (resp. C2), which we want to register to the first frame of the sequence. c: the output of StabNet [16]. d: the output of CNN-Registration [18]. e: the output of the proposed method.

We propose to tackle the problem of lengthy sequences with multiple mobile objects. In order to leave room for further analysis processes, our solution needs to be online and computationally low-cost. For this purpose, we propose a generic model which can be applied to 2D rigid motion estimation methods. We show how to combine stabilization and registration techniques, and we apply this method to a lightweight 2D-rigid transformation registration algorithm.

2 Prior Work

Producing a constant viewpoint video from a mobile camera is quite equivalent to determining the camera orientation. Determining the extrinsic parameters of a monocular camera within a 3D environment is a problem typically studied by Structure from Motion (SfM) [12] or Simultaneous Localization and Mapping (SLAM) approaches, some of which can operate in real time [11]. However, the latter are mostly designed to work on static environments and rely on parallax, *ie.* when there is enough camera movements to infer the 3D structure of the scene.

Video registration and video stabilization tackle this problem by searching for an image transformation that optimally compensates for camera motion. In the first case, this transformation is estimated between the current frame and a reference image. In the stabilization case, we calculate a trajectory, defined as a combination of consecutive inter-frame motion estimations. This trajectory is then filtered and the image is reprojected so to follow the desired, smooth trajectory.

In the UAV context, authors have stated that the direct application of a registration method to a reference frame leads to unsatisfying, jittery results [1,2,13]. Jitter is often linked to an unstable image source (handheld camera, mechanical high frequency noise, *etc.*). However, it can also correspond to a high-frequency noise caused by the image motion compensation itself. To our understanding, this happens because most registration methods are based on a sparse feature points matching solution, generally accompanied by a selection of inliers and outliers technique such as RANSAC. The intermittent presence of points caused by thresholds in the matching or the inliers selection processes may cause such high-frequency noise.

Classic video stabilization methods such as [8] and [6] have been adapted to the UAV context, sometimes associated with video stitching [7]. The motion estimation is often performed with a very popular approach known as Kanade Lukas Tracker (KLT) [14] but other techniques have been proposed, such as a specific optical flow model which enforces spatial coherence [9]. Most methods are able to handle mobile camera, and thus do not assume the existence of a constant background, which however applies in our context. They eliminate jitter very well, but they tend to imply drifting, which is the tendency to slowly change viewpoint over time.

More recently, convolutional neural networks have been applied to both registration [18] and stabilization [16] domains. Both methods have proposed to use a rich warping model based on Thin Plate Splines (TPS). While such approaches look promising, their direct application on our data proved problematic. We may observe on Figs. 1c (both columns) and d (right column) that 3 out of 4 frames are misaligned relatively to the reference image (Fig. 1a). Authors of StabNet [16] based their approach on a siamese convolutional network that was trained thanks to a stabilization database. This database was acquired with the help of a single handling device to which 2 different cameras were attached, only one of which was physically stabilized with a gimbal. Such ground-truth is not available in our settings. Moreover, this method still does not assume the presence of a constant background to which it should register. CNN-Registration [18] is able to handle large appearance changes and seems suitable to handle long-term registration with important lighting variations and the presence of multiple mobile objects. However, our experiments have shown that this approach is not invariant to rotation (e.g., it is not able to handle a video rotated to some extent, Fig. 1d) or to very large displacement. In our context, applying it would thus require some prior alignment step, which confirms the need for a simple and robust registration method that takes temporal data into account.

3   Modelling the Problem

The idea behind a video stabilization or registration algorithm is to compensate for undesired camera motion, while preserving the image content variability over time. At first, we need to define the degrees of freedom of our problem.

In first approximation, the effects of camera movements can be modeled and compensated through 2D-rigid warping transforms. On stationary drones, the camera is mostly affected by undesired, relatively low magnitude Yaw, Pitch and Roll motion (following the Tait Bryan chained rotations convention). Since the drone is never perfectly stationary, additional undesired 3D translational motion of the camera in space as well as the 3D geometry of the scene add up to the complexity of our problem.

Eventually, we estimate the camera motion between two images Im_i and Im_j through a 2D linear transformation matrix $\tilde{\mathcal{M}}(i,j)$. It is defined by an unique quartet of parameters (t_x, t_y, α, s) (resp. translation along the horizontal and vertical axis, rotation of angle α, and a positive scale in the 2D plane) which are used to approximate the effects on the image of a physical 3D motion performed by the drone (resp. Yaw, Pitch, Roll and translation along the optical axis). Warping Im_i according to the transformation matrix $\tilde{\mathcal{M}}(i,j)$ aims at setting it in the closest possible viewpoint to Im_j. Conversely, warping Im_j according to $\tilde{\mathcal{M}}(j,i) = \tilde{\mathcal{M}}(i,j)^{-1}$ sets it to the closest possible viewpoint to Im_i.

In any case, we rely on the estimation of the motion between two images Im_i and Im_j, for which we propose the following decomposition:

$$\tilde{\mathcal{M}}(i,j) = \mathcal{E}_{\tilde{\mathcal{M}}}(i,j) \times \mathcal{M}_{cam}(i,j) \tag{1}$$

where:

– $\tilde{\mathcal{M}}(i,j)$ is the estimated camera motion between Im_i and Im_j

– $\mathcal{M}_{cam}(i,j)$ corresponds to the motion associated to the actual, physical camera movement, measured as background motion between Im_i and Im_j
– $\mathcal{E}_{\tilde{\mathcal{M}}}(i,j)$ corresponds to a motion estimation error.

$\mathcal{E}_{\tilde{\mathcal{M}}}(i,j)$, $\tilde{\mathcal{M}}(i,j)$ and $\mathcal{M}_{cam}(i,j)$ are all expressed as linear transformation matrices.

A lot of motion estimation or registration methods are available in the literature, ranging from holistic [5] to sparse [14], with various properties and advantages. Equation (1) can be used to characterize any movement estimation algorithm that outputs a 2D linear transform.

Registering a video is the problem of canceling the term $\mathcal{M}_{cam}$ over the course of a video. With a reference frame denoted as 0, the applied warping can be expressed as

$$W(i) = \tilde{\mathcal{M}}(0,i)^{-1} = \mathcal{M}_{cam}(0,i)^{-1} \times \mathcal{E}_{\tilde{\mathcal{M}}}(0,i)^{-1} \tag{2}$$

Stabilizing a video is the problem of smoothing $\mathcal{M}_{cam}$ over the course of a video. This is performed by constructing a trajectory, which is defined as

$$\begin{cases} \mathcal{T}_{\tilde{\mathcal{M}}}(0) = \mathcal{I} \\ \mathcal{T}_{\tilde{\mathcal{M}}}(i) = \tilde{\mathcal{M}}(i-1,i) \times \mathcal{T}_{\tilde{\mathcal{M}}}(i-1) \text{ with } i > 0 \end{cases} \tag{3}$$

which we denote as:

$$\mathcal{T}_{\tilde{\mathcal{M}}}(i) = \overset{\frown}{\prod_{k=1}^{i}} \tilde{\mathcal{M}}(k-1,k) \tag{4}$$

The left arrow sign ($\frown$) means that we perform a left-hand product.

Then, we filter $\mathcal{T}_{\tilde{\mathcal{M}}}$ over time: the warping applied to the original images can be seen as the difference between the filtered trajectory and the original trajectory.

$$W(i) = \mathcal{F}(\mathcal{T}_{\tilde{\mathcal{M}}})(i) \times \mathcal{T}_{\tilde{\mathcal{M}}}(i)^{-1} \tag{5}$$

where $\mathcal{F}(\mathcal{T}_{\tilde{\mathcal{M}}})(i)$ is the output at frame i of a smoothing filter applied on the set of trajectories $\mathcal{T}_{\tilde{\mathcal{M}}}$. It is also expressed as a 2D linear transform matrix. Any output of $\mathcal{F}$ should be a plausible approximation given the physical constraints of the problem. In practice, one can filter independently t_x, t_y, α and s. For real-time, online application, a Kalman Filter [17] can be used.

Given Eq. (1), we can reformulate Eq. (3) as follows:

$$\mathcal{T}_{\tilde{\mathcal{M}}}(i) = \overset{\frown}{\prod_{k=1}^{i}} \left(\mathcal{E}_{\tilde{\mathcal{M}}}(k-1,k) \times \mathcal{M}_{cam}(k-1,k) \right) \tag{6}$$

By definition,

$$\mathcal{M}_{cam}(0, i) = \prod_{k=1}^{\overset{\frown}{i}} \mathcal{M}_{cam}(k - 1, k) \tag{7}$$

In the general case, we cannot develop any further Eq. (6). However, we can introduce an equivalent error term such as Eq. (3) becomes:

$$\mathcal{T}_{\tilde{\mathcal{M}}}(i) = \mathcal{E}_{\tilde{\mathcal{M}}}^{equiv}(0, i) \times \mathcal{M}_{cam}(0, i) \tag{8}$$

The more dissimilar Im_i and Im_j, the more significant $\mathcal{E}_{\tilde{\mathcal{M}}}(i, j)$ is likely to be. Consecutive images being rather similar, they usually yield a $\mathcal{E}_{\tilde{\mathcal{M}}}$ term of low magnitude. However, in such cases, foreground objects often perform little movement from Im_i to Im_j. When i and j are close in time, a part of the term $\mathcal{E}_{\tilde{\mathcal{M}}}(i, j)$ may correspond to light foreground motion that was wrongly considered as background motion by the motion estimator. Such error accumulates into Eq. (6) to form a drifting trajectory (Eq. (8)). This drifting error term explains why it is not recommended to simply use $\mathcal{T}_{\tilde{\mathcal{M}}}^{-1}$ as a registration solution.

Most of the literature in stabilization and registration topics is focused on minimizing the term $\mathcal{E}_{\tilde{\mathcal{M}}}$ within the motion estimation step. This minimization is essential towards achieving good performance, but the existence of such error is unavoidable. However, its nature tends to vary from jitter in a registration case to drifting in a stabilization case. We show how to take advantage of both jittery and drifting behaviors to propose an efficient and low-cost solution towards jitter-free constant viewpoint generation.

4   Proposed Method

In this section, we show how to efficiently combine registration and stabilization approaches into a single hybrid method (Fig. 2). From now on, we will denote by $\tilde{\mathcal{M}}^s$ (resp. $\tilde{\mathcal{M}}^r$ the specific motion estimator for the stabilization (resp. registration) part of the proposed method.

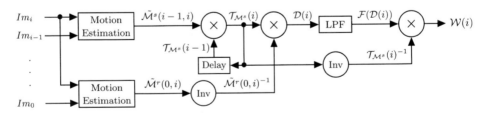

Fig. 2. Overview of the proposed method. Inv corresponds to a matrix inversion; LPF stands for Low-Pass Filter.

The idea is to calculate the product between the trajectory $\mathcal{T}_{\tilde{\mathcal{M}}^s}$ of a stabilization method, and the correction $\tilde{\mathcal{M}}^r(0, i)^{-1}$ applied in a registration method.

$$\mathcal{D}(i) = \mathcal{T}_{\tilde{\mathcal{M}}^s}(i) \times \tilde{\mathcal{M}}^r(0, i)^{-1} \tag{9}$$

Following the model proposed in Eq. (1), as reported in Eqs. (2) and (8), we can reformulate Eq. (9) as:

$$\mathcal{D}(i) = \mathcal{E}_{\tilde{\mathcal{M}}^s}^{equiv}(0, i) \times \left(\mathcal{E}_{\tilde{\mathcal{M}}^r}(0, i)\right)^{-1} \tag{10}$$

As suggested previously, this matrix is essentially a product of a smooth, low frequency drifting error $(\mathcal{E}_{\tilde{\mathcal{M}}^s}^{equiv}(0, i))$ and a jittery, high frequency error $(\mathcal{E}_{\tilde{\mathcal{M}}^r}(0, i))$. Filtering $\mathcal{D}$ allows us to isolate the drifting component.

$$\mathcal{F}\left(\mathcal{D}(i)\right) \approx \mathcal{E}_{\tilde{\mathcal{M}}^s}^{equiv}(0, i) \tag{11}$$

Combining the output of this filter to $\mathcal{T}_{\tilde{\mathcal{M}}^s}^{-1}$ finally allows us to obtain a jitter-free video registration on long sequences, without the need for particularly elaborate motion estimation techniques. Finally, the applied correction is the following:

$$\mathcal{W}(i) = \mathcal{F}\left(\mathcal{D}(i)\right) \times \mathcal{T}_{\tilde{\mathcal{M}}^s}(i)^{-1} \tag{12}$$

5   Evaluation

5.1   Dataset

Our evaluation dataset consists in 8 Full HD, 30 fps RGB video sequences, acquired outdoor at daylight, which include multiple mobile vehicles except 'C0'. 'C0', 'C1' 'C2' and 'C4' were acquired with a light drone on overhead viewpoint, equipped with a GoPro camera. The 4 min long sequence 'C1' and 'C4' feature few vehicles and only light motion in overhead configuration; 'C0' is a 15 s long subset of 'C1' where all objects are static. To challenge the robustness of our approach, the dataset includes the 4 min long sequence 'C2', where the human operator performs two fast clockwise 180° rotation around the vertical axis. 'M1', 'M2', 'M3' and 'M4' are successive 15 min long videos which were acquired with a tethered drone equipped with a CMOS camera, at approximately 50 m above ground in stationary flight. The sequence 'M4' is subject to heavy motion, probably caused by windy conditions. None of those videos displayed significant rolling shutter issues. Figures 1a and b provide examples from sequences 'M4' and 'C2'.

5.2   Implementation

This approach was implemented using computationally lightweight algorithms provided by the OpenCV library [4] and C++ language. Both $\tilde{\mathcal{M}}^s$ and $\tilde{\mathcal{M}}^r$ were estimated on a sparse image representation basis using the KLT approach. The image is first resized to 576×324 (30% of a 1080p resolution) and set to one-channel grayscale. The first frame was adopted as the reference frame for the tested videos. $\tilde{\mathcal{M}}^r(0, i)$ (resp. $\tilde{\mathcal{M}}^s(i - 1, i)$) was estimated by extracting 200 Shi-Tomasi corners [14] on Im_0 (resp. Im_{i-1}), further tracked on Im_i using the Lukas and Kanade Pyramidal Optical Flow (LKPOF) algorithm [3]. A Least

Square Regression (LSR) was used for the motion estimation matrix solving. We used a Kalman Filter [17] on the four motion estimation parameters (t_x, t_y, α, s) independently for the implementation of $\mathcal{F}$ in Eq. (12). The LKPOF algorithm being sensitive to its initialization, we used the KF prediction as the initialization for all of the tracked points locations on the registration part.

The experimentation was carried out on a 2.5 GHZ Intel Core i7 MacBook Pro with 16 Go DDR3 of memory under High Sierra OS. Under these settings, each frame is processed in less than 16 ms using CPU operation only, enabling real time applications and leaving space for further processing analysis.

5.3   Evaluation Protocol

To show the benefits of the proposed combination, we have compared it with different combinations of its elementary components. The following settings were tested:

- Raw: the original, unprocessed video.
- StabilizationKalman: the video stabilized by the algorithm described on Eq. (5), using the same computation of $\mathcal{M}^s$ and filter as described in Sect. 5.2.
- RegistrationLastPos: the video registered by the algorithm described as $\mathcal{M}^r$ in Sect. 5.2, with the registration proposed at frame $i - 1$ as an initialization for the registration of frame i.
- RegistrationKalman: the video registered by the algorithm described as $\tilde{\mathcal{M}}^r$ in Sect. 5.2, with a KF set as described in Sect. 5.2 for both the initialization and the filtering.
- Ours: the proposed method.

Evaluating a stabilization and registration algorithm in our context is a delicate task, since we do not benefit from ground-truth data about the actual camera movements or the image content on our dataset.

To quantify the registration performances of our approach, we propose to track a set of feature points from the reference frame to the current frame, using the same tracker setting as in Sect. 5.2 for $\mathcal{M}^r(0, i)$. The median displacement of all tracked reference points was used as a measure of registration quality. This measure, denoted as frame displacement (fd), was computed on each frame independently.

To quantify the stabilization performances of our approach, we propose to calculate the mean absolute difference of pixel grayscale values between two consecutive frames, over the length of a video sequence. To avoid parts of the image where we had no data, this measurement was performed on the overlapping regions between both consecutive images ($mpvd$).

5.4   Results

The first property that we wanted to quantify is whether our solution is capable of keeping registered to a constant viewpoint. We computed the proposed mean *fd* over the whole course of tested sequences (Table 1). Results empha-size the idea that a stabilization technique, such as StabilizationKalman, is not designed to guarantee a constant viewpoint over the course of a video. On videos 'C0', 'C1' and 'M2', which are subject to little camera motion, all tested regis-tration methods (RegistrationLastPos, RegistrationKalman) and the proposed method perform very similarly. RegistrationKalman suffers from inertia, which degrades its performance, eventually leading to being badly registered during several hundreds of frames on 'C2'. On all tested videos, the difference between the proposed method and the better evaluated registration method is well within subpixel range. This suggests that the proposed algorithm effectively preserves the registration performances of its base component.

Table 1. Mean frame displacement (*fd*) on our test sequences (pixels). In bold: the best performance; underlined: the second best performance.

Settings	M1	M2	M3	M4	C0	C1	C2	C4
Raw	17.43	17.91	14.81	27.1	11.19	11.79	20.04	9.15
StabilizationKalman	18.83	18.11	15.18	25.96	13.78	13.40	20.28	10.46
RegistrationLastPos	**4.85**	_3.84_	**6.51**	**11.85**	**0.74**	**1.29**	**4.70**	**1.09**
RegistrationKalman	6.21	**3.83**	7.33	12.49	0.96	1.40	14.07	1.19
Ours	_4.86_	3.85	_6.55_	_11.87_	_0.75_	_1.30_	**4.70**	_1.12_

The second evaluation focused on assessing the stability properties of the dif-ferent methods based on the *mpvd* values (Table 2). The assumption here is that on stable sequences, only mobile objects should cause pixel values to change sig-nificantly from one frame to the next one. On the other hand, jitter would cause pixel values to change suddenly over significant parts of the image, including the background. Stability here is assessed by the lowest possible *mpvd* value. This is verified in our experiment. In general, the poorest performance is visible on the original image, which is unstable. RegistrationLastPos, where jitter occurs despite the image being overall well registered, displays important values. Filter-ing the output of the registration (RegistrationKalman) significantly improves the results, which shows that this solution was able to tackle most of the jitter issues. On all of the sequences, the better performances are observed with Stabi-lizationKalman, and the proposed combination. The proposed method displays the highest performances because of its ability to keep consistently registered to the same viewpoint.

This quantitative outcome confirms the robustness of the proposed method and the qualitative impression given by visual inspection of the videos[1]. Our proposed approach can be effectively labeled as a jitter-free registration method.

---

[1] http://liris.univ-lyon2.fr/~pi/stationair/.

Table 2. Mean pixel value difference (*mpvd*) between consecutive frames (grayscale value). In bold: the best performance; underlined: the second best performance.

Settings	M1	M2	M3	M4	C0	C1	C2	C4
Raw	6.80	7.20	7.15	7.25	2.02	2.20	2.71	2.26
StabilizationKalman	**3.24**	<u>3.32</u>	**3.38**	**3.30**	<u>1.49</u>	**1.60**	<u>2.09</u>	<u>1.65</u>
RegistrationLastPos	6.46	4.96	6.54	7.88	2.22	2.39	3.92	2.11
RegistrationKalman	5.37	5.60	5.61	5.80	1.50	1.65	2.21	1.67
Ours	**3.24**	**3.25**	**3.38**	<u>3.41</u>	**1.43**	**1.60**	**1.59**	**1.62**

6 Conclusion and Perspectives

In this paper, we have addressed the problem of generating a constant viewpoint from videos acquired by stationary UAVs. The camera being subjected to small movements, the view is unstable and poses a problem for applying automatic processing techniques, or long term analysis such as trajectory registration. In this context, we have proposed a generic model to describe the inherent error of motion estimation algorithms. We have used it as the foundation on how to combine registration and stabilization techniques into one single hybrid method. The method is real time and online. It prevents both jittery and drifting behavior, even in the presence of multiple mobile objects. Results show that it retains the better properties out of the tested stabilization and registration techniques.

Further work will focus on two main aspects. One of them is to investigate how to handle situations where linear 2D-rigid warping is inappropriate, for instance when significant parallax is observed. The second aspect is how to update the reference image during the course of a day. This should enable us to better cope with appearance changes on the background, such as lighting conditions, which is a common problem during video surveillance applications.

Acknowledgements. This work was funded by AURA region (Pack Ambition Recherche 2017). Station'air project, number 1701104601-40893.

References

1. Abdelli, A.: Recursive motion smoothing for online video stabilization in wide-area surveillance. In: 2016 International Conference on Big Data and Smart Computing (BigComp), pp. 40–45. IEEE (2016)
2. Aguilar, W.G., Angulo, C.: Real-time model-based video stabilization for microaerial vehicles. Neural Process. Lett. **43**(2), 459–477 (2016)
3. Bouguet, J.Y.: Pyramidal implementation of the affine Lucas Kanade feature tracker description of the algorithm. Intel Corporation **5**(1–10), 4 (2001)
4. Bradski, G., Kaehler, A.: Opencv. Dr. Dobb's J. Soft. Tools **3** (2000)
5. Evangelidis, G.D., Psarakis, E.Z.: Parametric image alignment using enhanced correlation coefficient maximization. IEEE Trans. Pattern Anal. Mach. Intell. **30**(10), 1858–1865 (2008)

6. Grundmann, M., Kwatra, V., Essa, I.: Auto-directed video stabilization with robust l1 optimal camera paths. In: 2011 IEEE Conference on Computer Vision and Pattern Recognition (CVPR), pp. 225–232. IEEE (2011)
7. Guo, H., Liu, S., He, T., Zhu, S., Zeng, B., Gabbouj, M.: Joint video stitching and stabilization from moving cameras. IEEE Trans. Image Process. **25**(11), 5491–5503 (2016)
8. Liu, F., Gleicher, M., Wang, J., Jin, H., Agarwala, A.: Subspace video stabilization. ACM Trans. Graph. (TOG) **30**(1), 4 (2011)
9. Liu, S., Yuan, L., Tan, P., Sun, J.: Steadyflow: spatially smooth optical flow for video stabilization. In: 2014 IEEE Conference on Computer Vision and Pattern Recognition (CVPR), pp. 4209–4216. IEEE (2014)
10. Lupashin, S., D'Andrea, R.: Stabilization of a flying vehicle on a taut tether using inertial sensing. In: 2013 IEEE/RSJ International Conference on Intelligent Robots and Systems, pp. 2432–2438 (2013). https://doi.org/10.1109/IROS.2013.6696698
11. Mur-Artal, R., Tardós, J.D.: ORB-SLAM2: an open-source slam system for monocular, stereo, and RGB-D cameras. IEEE Trans. Rob. **33**(5), 1255–1262 (2017)
12. Schonberger, J.L., Frahm, J.M.: Structure-from-motion revisited. In: Proceedings of the IEEE Conference on Computer Vision and Pattern Recognition, pp. 4104–4113 (2016)
13. Shen, H., Pan, Q., Cheng, Y., Yu, Y.: Fast video stabilization algorithm for UAV. In: 2009 IEEE International Conference on Intelligent Computing and Intelligent Systems, ICIS 2009, vol. 4, pp. 542–546. IEEE (2009)
14. Shi, J., et al.: Good features to track. In: 1994 IEEE Computer Society Conference on Computer Vision and Pattern Recognition, Proceedings CVPR 1994, pp. 593–600. IEEE (1994)
15. Tauro, F., Porfiri, M., Grimaldi, S.: Surface flow measurements from drones. J. Hydrol. **540**, 240–245 (2016)
16. Wang, M., Yang, G.Y., Lin, J.K., Zhang, S.H., Shamir, A., Lu, S.P., Hu, S.M.: Deep online video stabilization with multi-grid warping transformation learning. IEEE Trans. Image Process. **28**(5), 2283–2292 (2019)
17. Welch, G., Bishop, G.: An introduction to the Kalman filter. Technical report, Chapel Hill, NC, USA (1995)
18. Yang, Z., Dan, T., Yang, Y.: Multi-temporal remote sensing image registration using deep convolutional features. IEEE Access **6**, 38544–38555 (2018)

Heart Rate Based Face Synthesis
for Pulse Estimation

Umur Aybars Ciftci$^{(\boxtimes)}$ and Lijun Yin

State University of New York at Binghamton, Binghamton NY, USA
{uciftci,lyin}@binghamton.edu

Abstract. With the technological advancements in non-invasive heart rate (HR) detection, it becomes more feasible to estimate heart rate using commodity digital cameras. However, achieving high accuracy in HR estimation still remains a challenge. One of the bottlenecks is the lack of sufficient facial videos annotated with corresponding HR signals. In order to prevent this bottleneck, we propose to create videos enriched with different HR values from existing data sets with an attempt to increase the data size in a controllable manner. This paper presents a new method to generate facial videos with various heart rate values through a video synthesis procedure. Our method involves the synthesis of heart beat effects from skin colors of a face. New face video is generated with various heart rate values while taking identity information into account. The quality of the synthetic videos is evaluated by comparing to the original ground truth videos at the pixel level as well as by computing their differentiability across the synthetic face videos. Furthermore, the usability of the new data is assessed through the application of HR estimation from remote video approaches.

Keywords: Heart rate synthesis · Remote heart rate estimation · Face synthesis and analysis

1 Introduction

The recently increasing availability of affordable sensor technologies has been facilitating measuring the heart rate using non-contact portable devices. This caused a proliferation of interest in self-care and self-monitoring. As one of the important vital signs, heart rate estimation is essential for determining the physiological and pathological state of an individual and thus has been gaining increased attention by the research community over the past years.

In clinical settings, heart rate can be monitored either through an electro-cardiogram (ECG) [36] or a pulse oximetry sensor [2]. Heart rate monitoring through ECG requires electrodes to be placed on an individual's skin around the chest area. Depending on the type of ECG data collected, there could be between 3 to 12 electrodes in place. Moreover, data collection requires cables or chest straps to be connected to electrodes for signal acquisition. Even though

© Springer Nature Switzerland AG 2019
G. Bebis et al. (Eds.): ISVC 2019, LNCS 11844, pp. 540–551, 2019.
https://doi.org/10.1007/978-3-030-33720-9_42

ECG gives the most accurate result [27] in terms of heart rate monitoring, its feasibility in daily environment is hindered by the non-trivial set up and the discomfort associated with the use of electrodes. Calculating heart rate through pulse oximetry is another non-invasive method that utilizes a light sensor placed on a finger. The light sensor determines the change in the absorbency of light, which is directly correlated with the change in arterial blood volume. Although pulse oximetry sensors are more convenient to use compared to ECG monitors, they still suffer from limited lifetime due to deterioration and the discomfort associated with the pressure on the finger caused by the sensor.

The heart rate of an individual can also be measured without any physical contact. Existing methods include microwave distance measurement [19], ultrasound [22], thermal imaging [7] and RGB imaging [13,32]. They eliminate the discomfort associated with the electrode placement in ECG monitoring and the pressure on the finger in pulse oximetry monitoring. Among the non-contact heart rate measurement methods, RGB imaging is the most widely used due to the ubiquity of digital cameras [32].

Heart rate measurement through RGB imaging using cameras is based on the concepts of photoplethysmography (PPG) [39] and ballistocardiography(BCG) [12]. Both of these methods require RGB input from an individual's face. The discovery of these two methods opened up new ways of heart rate monitoring in health care [18], telemedicine, rehabilitation, sports, ergonomics [20], living-skin tissue detection [6,41,43] and security [4,11,23].

In each cardiac cycle, the heart pumps blood to the rest of the body. The sudden increase of blood volume in the veins creates a mechanical motion. This motion makes the head move subtly and repetitively in each cardiac cycle, which can be detected using BCG [16]. The increased blood volume during cardiac cycle also results in an increase in hemoglobin in veins. The changes in hemoglobin volume affects the degree of which facial skin reflects and absorbs light, which in turn is reflected as subtle changes in skin color. These changes can be detected using PPG [39] techniques.

The accuracy of results obtained using BCG are sensitive to the motion of the head. Thus, PPG techniques are preferred in real world settings where the noise introduced by the head motion is unavoidable.

There are also challenges associated with the application of PPG to RGB imaging in heart rate estimation. Most of these challenges arise from the noise introduced by the environment such as sub-optimal illumination conditions, occlusions, etc. Various methods have been proposed in the literature to address some of these challenges. [30] propose the rPPG (raw PPG) extraction method that uses blind source separation. The authors use a simple web camera to extract PPG signals from the face of the subject. Raw PPG_R, PPG_G, PPG_B signals of the face region are calculated using the partial mean of the pixel values of each frame over a time period. Those traces are later normalized and decomposed into independent source signals using independent component analysis (ICA) [24]. The ICA signal resembling the PPG signal the most is chosen as the source for heart rate estimation. Authors later extend their work in [31], where they refine the RGB signal used for the ICA by applying de-trending and smoothing. They further refine the selected ICA signal by applying a band pass filter. Finally, the heart rate is extracted using the power spectrum density of the selected signal. Recent work on noise reduction has been reported. For example, Li et al. [26] has done noise reduction by illumination rectification and handled the non-rigid movements. Yan et al. [44] used weighted average of raw traces of the RGB spectrum by maximizing PPG signals and minimizing noises with wavelet transform. Tulyakov et al. [38] segmented the face into multiple patches and used a matrix completion approach to reduce temporal signal noises.

In addition to the heuristic approaches proposed by the researchers, recently supervised remote heart rate recognition approaches have emerged, for example, by using a support vector regression model [15], generated time-frequency maps [14], and a HR regression model and spatio-temporal maps [29].

Currently, very few publicly available data sets are available for the heart rate estimation task. MAHNOB-HCI [37] dataset, is a multi-modal data set for emotion recognition and implicit tagging, enriched with heart rate annotations. However the data set is still limited in terms of spontaneity of their subject responses. In addition, it only contains 27 participants with 34 video sequences for each participant. MMSE-HR [38] data set is a subset of the MMSE database [46], targeting to challenge heart rate estimation algorithms. MMSE-HR data set includes 102 RGB video sequences from 40 participants with diverse ethnic and racial backgrounds. The data set contains RGB videos in addition to physiological signals including heart rate. The blood pressure data was collected using Biopac MP150 data acquisition system [5] at the sample rate of 1kHZ, and the heart rate is derived from the raw blood pressure signal. Details regarding the data collection process in addition to the other collected physiological signals can be found in [46].

The above two datasets are lacking a good coverage for all possible heart rate scenarios. First, they do not have enough data to be used in training and testing a subject independent supervised model. When tried to train one, most of the data is used during the training process and the test does not show real accuracy which makes the comparison to the heuristic approaches unfair as the number of comparison samples and cases are not equal. These datasets do not contain enough extreme case samples (e.g., HR over 90 [17]). Lastly, heart rate values in publicly available datasets are uneven due to heart rate distribution, thus affecting trained parameters in supervised approaches.

Traditionally, the existing work has addresses the heart rate estimation problem under controlled laboratory environments, however, it is demanded to extend the work for real-world and real-time applications. We observed that, the demand on publicly available data sets and the cost of data collection can both be resolved by generative approaches. A possible remedy is to augment the data set from existing data through a synthesis procedure with controlled parameters, which enables the investigation for heart rate estimation methods using diverse synthesized heart rate data with various health conditions, providing control over all training and test videos. Note that there are existing methods for ECG signal synthesis [34], however to our knowledge, there is no existing work done on heart rate synthesis through the modification of heart rate values of given individuals' face videos. In this paper, we propose a new method for heart rate synthesis from a video sequence. As a result, a set of realistic face videos are generated with different heart rate values while taking identity information into account.

The rest of the paper is organized as follows: In Sect. 2 we describe our method for heart rate synthesis, in Sect. 3 we evaluate the performance of our method using the state of the art heart rate estimation approaches, and lastly in Sect. 4 we conclude with a discussion on the limitations of our work and give rise to a future research direction.

2   Heart Rate Synthesis for Facial Video Generation

In this section, we describe our facial heart rate change synthesis method for portrait videos. For each set of frames contained within a single heart beat, our method performs the following three steps: First, it derives the change in the RGB color from the change due to consequence of beating of the heart in the facial skin color. Then, it calculates the new RGB color signal of the desired heart rate value for the synthetic frames based on identity information. Lastly, it replaces the original RGB color change signal of the original heart rate with the synthesized RGB color change signal for the new heart rate value. These three steps can be expressed by the following equation, which is computed for each pixel on the face:

$$C_{Syn}(t) = C_{Org}(t) - S_{Org}(t) + S_{Syn}(t) \tag{1}$$

where t represents the frame and $C_{Syn}(t)$ represents the RGB values for the synthesized pixel, $C_{Org}(t)$ represents the original color of the same pixel, $S_{Org}(t)$ is the color change on the face as a result of the cardiac cycle, and $S_{Syn}(t)$ is the desired change in facial color.

Our method assumes that each captured pixel in human face gathers its color from three different sources [40]. These sources and their relation to each pixel in human face can be expressed as follows:

$$C(t) = I(t) \circ (F_{skin} + F_{BVP}(t)) \tag{2}$$

where $C(t)$ represents RGB channels of the facial pixels at frame t, $I(t)$ represents the luminance level of the frame t, F_{skin} represents the skin reflection, $F_{BVP}(t)$ represents the change in skin reflection due to the fluctuations in blood volume at frame t. This suggests that there is a direct correlation between the change in facial skin color and the skin reflection when there is no change in luminance ($I(t) = 0$).

Measuring the changes in facial skin color is complicated due to the fact that human face contains various veins of different sizes, whose distance to human skin and thus the degree to which they interact with light, is non-uniform [32]. Existing solutions that address this issue focus on prioritizing different regions of interest (ROI) in their calculations. To increase the PPG signal quality, different regions are selected by existing works, for example, Poh et al. [31] used 60% width of the full face and full height; Lewandowska et al. [25] and Scalise et al. [35] used the forehead region only; Aarts et al. [1] used the cheek region, while Yu et al. [45] focused on the area below the eye line as the region of interest. Additionally, patch based methods [20] or methods using facial landmarks [21,28] were also exploited. The variety in facial regions of attention poses a challenge to the facial video synthesis because the synthetic data must be generated correctly for all the regions covering the entire face, consistently in time. In order to overcome this challenge, we create our own facial region patches based on the density of the veins in the human face. The image of these patches is illustrated in Fig. 1. These patches are derived from the landmarks which are defined in OpenFace [3].

After each patch is calculated and extracted, we calculate the raw remote imaging photoplethysmography ($RIPPG_R$) signal [10]. $RIPPG_R$ of each region is calculated as follows:

$$RIPPG_R(t) = \frac{\sum_{P_i \in R} C_i(t)}{|R|} \tag{3}$$

where P_i stands for a pixel within the region, C_i represents the RGB channels of the pixel P_i, and $|R|$ is the number of pixels within the region.

$RIPPG_R$ signal consists of $S_{Org}(t)$ and $I(t)$ signals combined. In order to the $RIPPG_R$ signal into $S_{Org}(t)$ we need to remove the pixel color changes due to illumination. In MMSRHR dataset that we have used, lighting is a linear and the background is stable. So we have utilized these two properties and use the background to calculate the $I(t)$ signal which we subtract from $RIPPG_R$ to get the $S_{Org}(t)$ signal.

To preserve the identity information of a subject and to account for different skin colors, we calculate a set of identity signals, including three possibilities for skin color and two possibilities for the gender of each individual. Thus the synthesized identity signals of an individual are derived from the following equations:

$$S_G(HR) = \alpha S_{Male}(HR) + \beta S_{Female}(HR) \tag{4}$$

where $\alpha + \beta = 1$ and $S_{Male}(HR)$, $S_{Female}(HR)$ are the signals for the Male and Female identity classes for the given heart rate value, and

$$S_P(HR) = \alpha S_{DS}(HR) + \beta S_{LS}(HR) + \gamma S_{WS}(HR) \tag{5}$$

where $\alpha + \beta + \gamma = 1$ and $S_{DS}(HR)$, $S_{LS}(HR)$, $S_{WS}(HR)$ are the signals of skin color (e.g., identity classes of Dark Skin, Light (Pale) Skin, White Skin) for the given heart rate value.

The RGB pixel color change for each identity class is detected from the MMSE-HR [46] data set. By utilizing the diversity in racial and gender identities within the MMSE-HR, we have manually labeled each subject belonging to one skin color(SC) and one gender class. The range of the available heart rate values with in the MMSE-HR data set for each class is shown in Table 1. Once the labeling process is done, the heart beat sequence of each subject of MMSE-HR

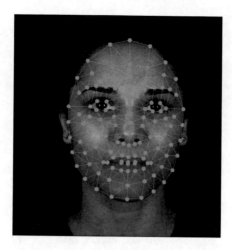

Fig. 1. Triangle Patch Regions

is categorized based on the HR-Gender-SC combination. We then extract the $RIPPG_R$ signals of each patch region from those categories. According to those changes, the estimated signal difference of each patch region is calculated using the following formula:

$$S_{Syn}(HR) = \frac{S_G(HR) + S_P(HR)}{2} \tag{6}$$

where $S_G(HR)$ and $S_P(HR)$ are the identity signals for the given patch region based on the gender and skin color values. For each heart rate value, $S_{Syn}(HR)$ gives different signal size because the duration of each heart beat for individual heart rate is different.

Table 1. Heart rate differences to the each identity class

Identity class	Min heart rate	Max heart rate
Male	50	142
Female	48	139
Dark skin	60	142
Light skin	50	125
White skin	48	133

After obtaining $S_{Syn}(HR)$, we calculate $S_{Org}(HR)$ for each patch region of the face in order to get rid of the RGB color changes introduced by cardiac-cycle of the heat beat in the original video. This formulation requires the heart rate, for which we have used the ground truth data that is already present in the

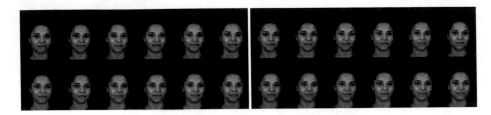

Fig. 2. Visual Comparison Between Synthesized and Original frame sequence for 6 frames. Upper Left: Original frames with heart rate value of 78. Upper Right: Synthesized frames with the same heart rate as the original as 78. Lower Left: Synthesized frames with heart rate value of 60. Lower Right: Synthesized frames with heart rate value of 90

MMSE-HR data set. Using the original heart rate, we calculate $S_{Org}(HR)$ for each patch region following the same procedure to calculate $S_{Syn}(HR)$.

By subtracting the $S_{Org}(HR)$ value of each patch region from the corresponding original patch region, we calculate the skin color. This process only synthesizes the skin color for one heart beat duration. Therefore, the same process of calculating the heart rate, extracting signal, and performing subtraction must be done for each heart beat for the duration of the intended synthesized video. Since the duration of a cardiac cycle is determined by the heart beat rate, the duration of the synthesized video may differ from the original one depending on the intended heart rate values. If the total duration of intended heart rate value sequence to be synthesized is longer than the duration of the original video, the extra section of the intended heart rate value sequence will be removed. Otherwise the last heart beat value will be added to the intended heart rate sequence until the same duration with the original video is reached for protecting the integrity of the video.

3   Evaluation

To validate the usability and the quality of our synthesized videos, three experiments are carried out. First, we use the heart rate values in a source video as the input to our synthesis tool in an attempt to create a replica and assess the authenticity of the synthesized video by comparing it to the source at the pixel level from frame to frame. Second, we show that the heart rate values extracted from synthetic videos by current remote PPG systems match the intended heart rate values used for synthesis. Lastly, we have trained a supervised model using solely synthesized videos for heart rate estimation task.

In our experiments, we employed data from the MMSE-HR data set [38,46]. MMSE-HR data set calculates the heart rate through the raw blood pressure signal from a finger pressure sensor. Involuntary hand or finger movements by subjects during experiments introduce noise to blood pressure data, which reflects as sudden, drastic increase or decreases in the calculated heart rate. Thus, we preprocess the data by identifying these segments of anomalous heart rate values and replacing them with synthetic values that are calculated using the duration of the segment and neighboring heart rate values.

MMSR-HR data set contains 108,117 frames from 102 video sequences of 40 subjects. For all the sequences combined, there are 5,725 heart beats. For each heart beat, we synthesized the same heart beat value for the RGB pixel color comparison. After we synthesized the 5,725 heart beats with their original heart rate values and compared the pixel color difference between synthesized pixels and the original pixels, 88.8% of the synthesized facial pixels share the same RGB values with their original counterparts. Percentages for the same RGB color information for each identity class can be seen in the Table 2. For illustration, Fig. 2 shows a synthesized frame and the original frame next to each other.

Table 2. Synthesized pixel difference between original facial pixel values and synthesized ones

Identity class	Heart beat count	Same RGB color percentage
Male	2124	89.2%
Female	3601	88.6%
Dark skin	910	84.3%
Light skin	1740	88.3%
White skin	3075	90.4%
All	5725	88.8%

In the second experiment, we have tested our synthesis method using different remote PPG methods. We have used approaches specified in [9, 26, 33, 42]. Using the MMSE-HR set we created a subset of video sequences by selecting one video sequence from each subject. Our resulting subset contained 40 video sequences and 1,660 heart beats. In our experiment we applied different methods through our subset three times and obtained the root mean square error (RMSE) rates for the estimated heart rate values. First, those methods are tested on the original data set in order to obtain the error rates for the ground truth. We then synthesize the same heart rate for the entire data set and apply those methods through the synthesized video data. Finally, we synthesize the entire data set with a single heart rate value of 78, which is a common heart rate value among all subjects, and apply the methods on the synthesized videos. The error rates between the synthetic videos and the ground truth data are presented in Table 3. The second column contains results for the subset of MMSE-HR, third column contains results for the synthesized subset with the same heart rate, and the last column is synthesized with the fixed 78 heart rate value.

As documented in Table 3, the accuracy of existing approaches is not drastically affected by using our synthesized videos. This result, in addition to the comparison experiment, has demonstrated that synthesized heart rate video sequences are sufficiently representative to provide realistic appearances in heart rate data augmentation as well as for algorithm training and testing.

In our last experiment we have designed a supervised testing approach in order to test the usability of the synthesized heart rate videos. To do so, we have selected 6 subjects, one for each identity class combination, as a base for heart rate synthesis. Using those 6 subjects we synthesized 6818 different portrait videos with various hear rate values that are equally distributed. Then extracted a ROI with the face witch then deformed into a rectangular shape. This rectangular ROI image is further segmented into 32 equally sized non-colluded squares. Lastly, we calculate the average RGB colors for each of these squares. These calculations give us average RGB colors for 32 aligned squares across the video. In our training data we encode the color changes in these aligned squares of 32 frames into the training images which is used for training the Xception [8] model from scratch. We have tested the trained model using the remaining 34 subjects in the MMSE-HR dataset for the HR estimation and achieved comparable results to the methods which utilized the real videos. Table 3 shows our accuracy in heart rate estimation.

Table 3. Comparison of RMSE rates for the remote PPG methods.

Approaches	RMSE original	RMSE synth	RMSE fixed
Li et al. [26]	18.45	19.23	19.48
De Haan et al. [9]	12.72	14.60	15.22
Wang et al. [42]	11.80	13.95	14.47
Rouast et al. [33]	22.56	24.62	25.97
XceptionNet [8] trained on synthetic data	10.91	N/A	N/A

4   Conclusions and Future Work

In this paper we presented a new method to synthesize realistic facial heart rate videos. The key of the method is to detect the changes that are caused by sudden increase of the blood volume in the facial veins due to the heart beat, and replace those facial pixel changes with synthesized heart rate's changes. Our method is then compared with the ground truth data and evaluated using the state of art approaches on the MMSE-HR data set as a benchmark. The experimental evaluation has demonstrated the utility and feasibility of the synthesized videos for heart rate data augmentation, potentially leading to improvements in algorithm development with more diversified training and test data.

Our future work will further improve our algorithm in order to generate more realistic facial videos with including a variety of heart beat factors. Currently, the skin color changes occurring only on the face region are addressed. Since blood circulates throughout human body, similar skin color changes in the remaining parts of the body are expected. We will investigate heart rate video generation by multi-region skin color detection and fusion in order to further increase the realism of synthetic heart rate videos.

Acknowledgement. The material is based upon the work supported in part by the National Science Foundation under grants CNS-1629898 and CNS-1205664.

References

1. Aarts, L.A., Jeanne, V., Cleary, J.P., Lieber, C., Nelson, J.S., Oetomo, S.B., Verkruysse, W.: Non-contact heart rate monitoring utilizing camera photoplethysmography in the neonatal intensive care unit-a pilot study. Early Human Dev. **89**(12), 943–948 (2013)
2. Al-Ali, A., Diab, M.K., Coverston, R., Maurer, G., Schmidt, J., Schulz, C.: Pulse oximetry sensor, 9 October 2007, patent 7,280,858
3. Baltrusaitis, T., Robinson, P., Morency, L.P.: Openface: an open source facial behavior analysis toolkit. In: WACV, pp. 1–10. IEEE Computer Society (2016)
4. Bao, S.D., Zhang, Y.T., Shen, L.F.: Physiological signal based entity authentication for body area sensor networks and mobile healthcare systems. In: IEEE Engineering in Medicine and Biology (2006)
5. Biopack. https://www.biopac.com
6. Bobbia, S., Benezeth, Y., Dubois, J.: Remote photoplethysmography based on implicit living skin tissue segmentation. In: IEEE ICPR, pp. 361–365 (2016)
7. Chekmenev, S.Y., Rara, H., Farag, A.A.: Non-contact, wavelet-based measurement of vital signs using thermal imaging. In: The 1st International Conference on Graphics, Vision, and Image Processing (GVIP), pp. 107–112 (2005)
8. Chollet, F.: Xception: deep learning with depthwise separable convolutions. In: IEEE CVPR (2017)
9. De Haan, G., Jeanne, V.: Robust pulse rate from chrominance-based rPPG. IEEE Trans. Biomed. Eng. **60**(10), 2878–2886 (2013)
10. Feng, L., Po, L., Xu, X., Li, Y., Ma, R.: Motion-resistant remote imaging photoplethysmography based on the optical properties of skin. IEEE Trans. Circuits Syst. Video Technol. **25**(5), 879–891 (2015)
11. Gibert, G., D'Alessandro, D., Lance, F.: Face detection method based on photoplethysmography. In: IEEE International Conference on Advanced Video and Signal Based Surveillance (AVSS) (2013)
12. Gordon, J.W.: Certain molar movements of the human body produced by the circulation of the blood. J. Anat. Physiol. **11**(Pt 3), 533–536 (1877)
13. Hassan, M., et al.: Heart rate estimation using facial video: a review. Biomed. Signal Process. Control **38**, 346–360 (2017)
14. Hsu, G., Ambikapathi, A., Chen, M.: Deep learning with time-frequency representation for pulse estimation from facial videos. In: 2017 IEEE International Joint Conference on Biometrics (IJCB), pp. 383–389, October 2017
15. Hsu, Y., Lin, Y., Hsu, W.: Learning-based heart rate detection from remote photoplethysmography features. In: 2014 IEEE International Conference on Acoustics, Speech and Signal Processing (ICASSP), pp. 4433–4437 (2014)
16. Inan, O.T., et al.: Ballistocardiography and seismocardiography: a review of recent advances. IEEE J. Biomed. Health Inf. **19**(4), 1414–1427 (2015)
17. Jose, A.D., Collison, D.: The normal range and determinants of the intrinsic heart rate in man. Cardiovasc. Res. **4**(2), 160–167 (1970)
18. Kakria, P., Tripathi, N.K., Kitipawang, P.: A real-time health monitoring system for remote cardiac patients using smartphone and wearable sensors. Int. J. Telemed. Appl. **2015**, 373474 (2015)

19. Kranjec, J., Beguš, S., Geršak, G., Drnovšek, J.: Non-contact heart rate and heart rate variability measurements: a review. Biomed. Sig. Process. Control **13**, 102–112 (2014)
20. Kumar, M., Veeraraghavan, A., Sabharwal, A.: DistancePPG: robust non-contact vital signs monitoring using a camera. Biomed. Optics Express. **6**(5), 1565–1588 (2015)
21. Lam, A., Kuno, Y.: Robust heart rate measurement from video using select random patches. In: Proceedings of the IEEE International Conference on Computer Vision, pp. 3640–3648 (2015)
22. Lawson, G., Belcher, R., Dawes, G., Redman, C.: A comparison of ultrasound (with autocorrelation) and direct electrocardiogram fetal heart rate detector systems. Am. J. Obstet. Gynecol. **147**(6), 721–722 (1983)
23. Lee, A., Kim, Y.: Photoplethysmography as a form of biometric authentication. In: IEEE SENSORS, pp. 1–2 (2015)
24. Lee, T.W.: Independent component analysis. In: Lee, T.W. (ed.) Independent Component Analysis, pp. 27–66. Springer, Boston (1998). https://doi.org/10.1007/978-1-4757-2851-4_2
25. Lewandowska, M., Rumiński, J., Kocejko, T., Nowak, J.: Measuring pulse rate with a webcam a non-contact method for evaluating cardiac activity. In: IEEE Federated Conference on Computer Science and Information Systems (FedCSIS) (2011)
26. Li, X., Chen, J., Zhao, G., Pietikäinen, M.: Remote heart rate measurement from face videos under realistic situations. In: 2014 IEEE Conference on Computer Vision and Pattern Recognition, pp. 4264–4271, June 2014
27. Lu, G., Yang, F., Taylor, J.A., Stein, J.F.: A comparison of photoplethysmography and ECG recording to analyse heart rate variability in healthy subjects. J. Med. Eng. Technol. **33**(8), 634–641 (2009)
28. Mestha, L.K., Kyal, S., Xu, B., Lewis, L.E., Kumar, V.: Towards continuous monitoring of pulse rate in neonatal intensive care unit with a webcam. In: IEEE Engineering in Medicine and Biology Society (EMBC) (2014)
29. Niu, X., Han, H., Shan, S., Chen, X.: SynRhythm: learning a deep heart rate estimator from general to specific. In: 2018 24th International Conference on Pattern Recognition (ICPR), pp. 3580–3585 (2018)
30. Poh, M.Z., McDuff, D.J., Picard, R.W.: Non-contact, automated cardiac pulse measurements using video imaging and blind source separation. Opt. Express **18**(10), 10762–10774 (2010)
31. Poh, M.Z., McDuff, D.J., Picard, R.W.: Advancements in noncontact, multiparameter physiological measurements using a webcam. IEEE Trans. Biomed. Eng. **58**(1), 7–11 (2011)
32. Rouast, P.V., Adam, M.T., Chiong, R., Cornforth, D., Lux, E.: Remote heart rate measurement using low-cost RGB face video: a technical literature review. Front. Comput. Sci. **12**(5), 858–872 (2018)
33. Rouast, P.V., Adam, M.T.P., Cornforth, D.J., Lux, E., Weinhardt, C.: Using contactless heart rate measurements for real-time assessment of affective states. In: Davis, F.D., Riedl, R., vom Brocke, J., Léger, P.-M., Randolph, A.B. (eds.) Information Systems and Neuroscience. LNISO, vol. 16, pp. 157–163. Springer, Cham (2017). https://doi.org/10.1007/978-3-319-41402-7_20
34. Sameni, R., Clifford, G.D.: A review of fetal ECG signal processing; issues and promising directions. Open Pacing Electrophysiol. Ther. J. **3**, 4 (2010)

35. Scalise, L., Bernacchia, N., Ercoli, I., Marchionni, P.: Heart rate measurement in neonatal patients using a webcamera. In: IEEE International Symposium on Medical Measurements and Applications (MeMeA) (2012)

36. Sodi-Pallares, D.: Electrophysiology of the heart. Am. J. Cardiol. (1961)

37. Soleymani, M., Lichtenauer, J., Pun, T., Pantic, M.: A multimodal database for affect recognition and implicit tagging. IEEE Trans. Affect. Comput. **3**(1), 42–55 (2012)

38. Tulyakov, S., Alameda-Pineda, X., Ricci, E., Yin, L., Cohn, J.F., Sebe, N.: Self-adaptive matrix completion for heart rate estimation from face videos under realistic conditions. In: The IEEE Conference on Computer Vision and Pattern Recognition (CVPR) (2016)

39. Verkruysse, W., Svaasand, L.O., Nelson, J.S.: Remote plethysmographic imaging using ambient light. Opt. Express **16**(26), 21434–21445 (2008)

40. Wang, W., den Brinker, A.C., Stuijk, S., de Haan, G.: Algorithmic principles of remote PPG. IEEE Trans. Biomed. Eng. **64**(7), 1479–1491 (2017)

41. Wang, W., Stuijk, S., De Haan, G.: Unsupervised subject detection via remote PPG. IEEE Trans. Biomed. Eng. **62**(11), 2629–2637 (2015)

42. Wang, W., Stuijk, S., De Haan, G.: A novel algorithm for remote photoplethysmography: spatial subspace rotation. IEEE Trans. Biomed. Eng. **63**(9), 1974–1984 (2016)

43. Wang, W., Stuijk, S., de Haan, G.: Living-skin classification via remote-PPG. IEEE Trans. Biomed. Eng. **64**(12), 2781–2792 (2017)

44. Yan, Y., Ma, X., Yao, L., Ouyang, J.: Noncontact measurement of heart rate using facial video illuminated under natural light and signal weighted analysis. Biomed. Mater. Eng. **26**(s1), S903–S909 (2015)

45. Yu, Y.P., Kwan, B.H., Lim, C.L., Wong, S.L., Raveendran, P.: Video-based heart rate measurement using short-time Fourier transform. In: Intelligent Signal Processing and Communications Systems (ISPACS), pp. 704–707. IEEE (2013)

46. Zhang, Z., et al.: Multimodal spontaneous emotion corpus for human behavior analysis. In: Proceedings of the IEEE Conference on Computer Vision and Pattern Recognition, pp. 3438–3446 (2016)

Light-Weight Novel View Synthesis
for Casual Multiview Photography

Inchang Choi, Yeong Beum Lee, Dae R. Jeong, Insik Shin, and Min H. Kim[✉]

KAIST School of Computing, Daejeon, South Korea
minhkim@kaist.ac.kr

Abstract. Traditional view synthesis for image-based rendering requires various processes: camera synchronization with professional equipment, geometric calibration, multiview stereo, and surface reconstruction, resulting in heavy computation, in addition to manual user interactions throughout these processes. Therefore, view synthesis has been available exclusively for professional users. In this paper, we address these expensive costs to enable view synthesis for casual users even with mobile-phone cameras. We assume that casual users take multiple photographs using their phone-cameras, which are used for view synthesis. First, without relying on any expensive synchronization hardware, our method can capture synchronous multiview photographs by utilizing a wireless network protocol. Second, our method provides light-weight image-based rendering on the mobile phone, where heavy computational processes, such as estimating geometry proxies, alpha mattes, and inpainted textures, are processed by a server to be shared in an interactable time. Finally, it allows us to render novel view synthesis along a virtual camera path on the mobile devices, enabling bullet-time photography from casual multiview captures.

Keywords: View synthesis · Computational photography · Multiview

1 Introduction

Novel view synthesis from multiview photographs is an image-based rendering method and requires various computational processes to synthesize new viewpoints from captured photographs. Starting from camera synchronization with a professional camera synchronization hardware, heavy computational processes need to be conducted, such as camera tracking for unstructured cameras, geometric calibrations of camera properties, multiview stereo matching for dense point clouds, surface reconstruction, inverse rendering, and so on. Also, these computational processes require user interaction for synchronization, segmentation, inpainting, geometric reconstruction, etc. Therefore, novel view synthesis has

Electronic supplementary material The online version of this chapter (https://doi.org/10.1007/978-3-030-33720-9_43) contains supplementary material, which is available to authorized users.

© Springer Nature Switzerland AG 2019
G. Bebis et al. (Eds.): ISVC 2019, LNCS 11844, pp. 552–564, 2019.
https://doi.org/10.1007/978-3-030-33720-9_43

been limited to professional setups, not available on casual computing devices, such as mobile phones.

In this work, by addressing these cost challenges of expensive hardware, heavy computations, and manual user interaction, our practical solution enables a casual, automated view synthesis for general users. We developed an efficient automated image-based rendering method on a casual setup that consists of multiple mobile devices connected to a server with a wireless network. Once multiple mobile cameras capture a scene, our method creates bullet-time photography automatically played on the mobile devices, where it freezes time to navigate the scene from novel viewpoints.

Overview. Figure 1 provides overview of our *automated* process of casual view synthesis for mobile multiview photography. Since multiple cameras need to capture a scene simultaneously, we first develop a synchronization method for mobile camera devices using a network time protocol (Sect. 3.1). We then transfer synchronous photographs to a server that computes geometry and texture elements. In the geometry processing step, we estimate the camera parameters of the unstructured (hand-held) mobile devices and the point clouds, which forms the geometry proxy of the scene (Sect. 3.2). Concurrently, we convert multiview photographs to texture elements for rendering. In this step, we separate the foreground and background objects in input images. We also inpaint occlusions in background images rapidly (Sect. 3.3). Once conversion processes are finished, graphics components are transferred to mobile devices through a wireless network, yielding real-time rendering of a virtual scene along the virtual camera path that shows bullet-time photography (Sect. 3.4).

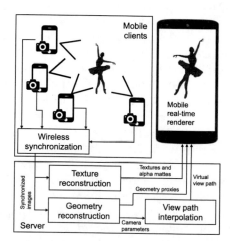

Fig. 1. Overview of our view synthesis.

2   Related Work

Prior works in image-based rendering synthesize novel views from a set of images. They can be classified into three categories according to what geometry information is required [7]. First, a light field can represent light transport of a scene, which can be interpolated to render a novel view from a captured light field. Instead of requiring the geometry information of a scene, light-field rendering exploits a large number of image data. These images are sampled from a dense and uniform camera grid, to approximate the plenoptic function of the scene. To avoid uniform grid sampling, Buehler et al. [1,13,14] proposed unstructured lumigraph rendering, but it requires a rough geometry proxy of an object. Second, view-dependent texture mapping (VDTM) can render a novel view by utilizing the geometry model of a scene as an input [17]. Debevec et al. [5] proposed a VDTM method, where images are projected on to a given input geometry model and a new view is rendered with those projected textures. However, the geometry models used in VDTM need to be either modeled manually or scanned by a 3D scanner. Sinha et al. [16] proposed a view synthesis that uses a geometry model produced by approximating planes on the scene, but the approximation is valid only for planar objects such as buildings. Lastly, depth image-based rendering (DIRB) utilizes a camera projection mechanism and textured depth layers [4]. Instead of taking a geometry model as an input, it estimates the depth information from the corresponding feature points between stereo images, but this approach restricts a novel viewpoint to be close to the real viewpoints. A few studies have performed view synthesis using depth maps [11] or layered depth images [3,15]. Unlike these prior works, we generate geometry proxies from the point cloud of the scene using a multiview stereo approach [18], instead of using any scanned geometry or depth maps. This work enables an automated, efficient image-based rendering with plausible view synthesis. The geometry proxies in our method are subject to a two-pass rendering process like the textured depth layers in DIRB. Refer to Sect. 3.2 for more details.

Recently, Wang et al. [21] introduced a novel view synthesis method, targeting a mobile platform. The study explores potentials of mobile application preliminarily; however, it does not focus on both automation and efficiency of view synthesis, taking *more than an hour* to process with the help of manual input for each stage. To address the impracticability of the prior work, we focus on both *automation and efficiency* for casual view synthesis, enabling us to produce plausible results for about a minute on a mobile platform even without requiring manual interactions.

3   Casual View Synthesis

3.1   Mobile Camera Synchronization

For practical synchronization for the casual setup, we adopt the network time protocol (NTP) [12] to synchronize the clock of every mobile device. In our setup, one of the mobile devices acts as a sync host device that triggers shooting, and the others work as clients (Fig. 2). To synchronize the clocks of devices, all the client devices send the host device an NTP request packet that records a timestamp t_0 of the time when the packet is sent. When the host device receives the packet, it records a timestamp t_1 on the packet and then returns it to the client with a new timestamp t_2 when it departs. The client then records a timestamp t_3 when it receives the packet.

Finally, the time difference t_d between devices is calculated as $\{(t_1 - t_0) + (t_2 - t_3)\}/2$ to adjust the clock on each client device. Each device's clock is then updated by adding t_d on its clock from the time of receiving the return packet. When the host mobile device triggers the synchronous shooting command to make

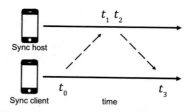

Fig. 2. Packet-based synchronization.

each client device capture a scene simultaneously, we allow a short delay of the one-way trip time of the packet t_r as $\{(t_3 - t_0) - (t_2 - t_1)\}/2$ with an additional allowance of approximately $\sim$100 ms to account for the fluctuation of the wireless network speed in our experiments. Note that since the accuracy of NTP is highly affected by the network environments, all mobile devices are connected via WiFi Direct [2] to minimize any potential error caused by the network environments.

3.2   Automated Estimation of Geometry Proxies

Since the server receives multiple synchronous photographs, it performs the bundle adjustment [20] to obtain point cloud representations of the scene with camera parameters and then approximates geometry proxies of surfaces from clouds for rendering. Through this process, we obtain the point clouds of the foreground and background objects and camera parameters. From the estimated point clouds, we generate geometry proxies for rendering.

Multiview Stereo. We follow the standard multiview stereo method, so-called structure-from-motion, to obtain point clouds and camera parameters. Given a set of synchronized multiview images $\mathbf{I} = \{I_1, I_2, \ldots, I_n\}$, we estimate a set of point clouds $\mathbf{P} = \{P_1, P_2, \ldots, P_m\}$ of the scene and a set of camera parameters $\mathbf{C} = \{C_1, C_2, \ldots, C_n\}$. The bundle adjustment process begins by performing feature matching between input images [20], where SIFT feature points [9] are paired and filtered through RANSAC [6]. We use a set of n camera devices to yield a set of m point clouds, where q_{ij} is the *observed* projection of feature points of the j-th point cloud in the i-th camera. Then the objective function for obtaining both $\mathbf{P}$ and $\mathbf{C}$ can be defined using a pinhole-projection function Φ that projects point P_j to image I_i of camera C_i as $\min_{\mathbf{C},\mathbf{P}} \sum_{i=1}^{n} \sum_{j=1}^{m} w_{ij} \|q_{ij} - \Phi(C_i, P_j)\|^2$, where the weight term w_{ij} is set to 1 when P_j is visible from C_i so that P_j exists in image I_i. Otherwise, it is set to 0. The objective function is solved through a state-of-the-art parallel optimization method [22]. Figure 3(a) shows an example of a point cloud of a scene and the camera frustums estimated by the bundle adjustment. Figure 3(b) shows the estimated geometric proxies for the foreground and background objects.

Geometry Proxy. We next separate the point cloud $\mathbf{P}$ into two sets using the k-means clustering algorithm [10]. The k-means clustering algorithm with $k = 2$ quantizes the input point cloud $\mathbf{P}$ to the point cloud for an object in the foreground $\mathbf{F}$ and the point cloud of the background $\mathbf{B}$. The clustering process is performed by optimizing the cost function: $\min_{F,B} \sum_{P \in F} \|P - \mu_F\|^2 + \sum_{P \in B} \|P - \mu_B\|^2$, where μ_F and μ_B indicate the center of the foreground and the background cluster, respectively. Given the separated point clouds, we generate geometry proxies for them. For the foreground point cloud $\mathbf{F}$, we build a cylinder of radius r, of which the center is μ_F. The background point cloud $\mathbf{B}$ is approximated by a plane containing the center point μ_B with the normal vector of $(0, 0, 1)$. We denote the foreground cylindrical proxy and the background planar as $\mathbf{G}^{\mathcal{F}}$ and $\mathbf{G}^{\mathcal{B}}$, respectively.

3.3   Efficient Production of Textures

We found that the prior work [21] is based on a piece-wise planar stereo approach [16], which is significantly expensive and less compatible with ordinary scenes to determine depth. We therefore introduce a novel rendering workflow that combines learning-based segmentations of synchronized photographs with an efficient rendering approach based on geometry proxies to achieve both efficiency and plausibility. To this end, we convert multiview photographs to textures of the foreground and the background for layered geometric structures.

Foreground Segmentation. Since we produce two separate geometry proxies of the foreground and the background, we segment the input images into two sets of textures, respectively. To exclude any necessity of extra user inputs, we adopt a state-of-the-art semantic image segmentation method based on a convolutional neural network (CNN) [23]. This semantic segmentation method enables us to generate the foreground masks $\mathbf{M}^{\mathcal{F}} = \{M_1^{\mathcal{F}}, M_2^{\mathcal{F}}, \ldots, M_n^{\mathcal{F}}\}$ and the background masks $\mathbf{M}^{\mathcal{B}} = \{M_1^{\mathcal{B}}, M_2^{\mathcal{B}}, \ldots, M_n^{\mathcal{B}}\}$ for the input images $\mathbf{I} = \{I_1, I_2, \ldots, I_n\}$ without any user input. Masks $M_i^{\mathcal{F}}$ and $M_i^{\mathcal{B}}$ for image I_i are binary-valued arrays, where i represents that the pixel is classified as the corresponding label. Note that we assume that the main subject for multiview photography is one or more people for simplicity. The masks are then used for alpha-blending when rendering view synthesis.

Background Inpainting. Using the foreground and background masks, we obtain two sets of textures $\mathbf{T}^{\mathcal{F}} = \{T_i^{\mathcal{F}} | T_i^{\mathcal{F}} \triangleq I_i \circ M_i^{\mathcal{F}}\}$ and $\mathbf{T}^{\mathcal{B}} = \{T_i^{\mathcal{B}} | T_i^{\mathcal{B}} \triangleq I_i \circ M_i^{\mathcal{B}}\}$, where $\circ$ is the Hadamard product operator. There exist empty regions in each background texture in $\mathbf{T}^{\mathcal{B}}$ caused by the background mask. The missing regions particularly in the background occur by the occlusion of the foreground object. It causes inevitable artifacts when a virtual camera V_k renders a novel, synthetic view. To alleviate this occlusion problem, we fill the empty regions by applying an inpainting algorithm. Targeting the interactable performance of our method, we employ a fast-marching inpainting algorithm [19] that approximates unknown pixel values with the weighted sum of pixel known neighboring pixels. After holes are inpainted in the background textures $\mathbf{T}^{\mathcal{B}}$, they are passed to the rendering pipeline on a mobile device, together with the foreground texture $\mathbf{T}^{\mathcal{F}}$, to synthesize novel frames. Figure 3 (c) and (d) compare background textures by different inpainting methods.

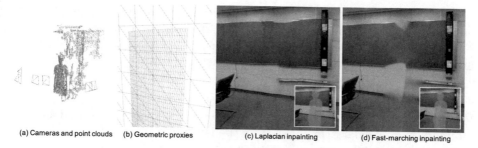

(a) Cameras and point clouds   (b) Geometric proxies   (c) Laplacian inpainting   (d) Fast-marching inpainting

Fig. 3. An example of estimated point clouds (a) and proxy geometry (b) of a scene. (c) is inpainted by a Laplacian-based method [8] in 362 s. (d) is completed by a fast-marching method [19] that we chose in 1.07 s. Insets show inpainted regions.

3.4   Automated Image-Based Rendering

For synthetic view rendering, we aim to automatically create novel view synthesis for bullet-time photography to yield a frozen-time animation. We therefore generate a trajectory array of virtual cameras at novel viewpoints from the array of the real cameras.

Virtual Camera Orientations. We sort the set of camera parameters $\mathbf{C} = \{C_1, C_2, \ldots, C_n\}$ by the x coordinates of the cameras, and we assume that C_1 indicates the leftmost located camera and C_n refers to the rightmost located camera. From the i-th camera parameters C_i, we then extract orientation parameters for rotation R_{C_i} and position parameters for translation T_{C_i}, respectively. The intrinsic parameters of the virtual cameras are set to those of the real cameras. See Fig. 4 for our view path generation.

Suppose we want to build a set of l novel virtual camera parameters $\mathbf{V} = \{V_1, V_2, \ldots, V_l\}$. The orientation parameters R_{V_k} of the k-th virtual camera V_k are estimated by accounting for neighboring cameras' orientations $R_{\mathbf{C}}$ with spatially-varying weights so that the virtual cameras look at a similar position in the scene. We found that this makes users feel comfortable while watching view synthesis. The weight is defined by the distance between the virtual camera V_k and the i-th real camera C_i in the camera set $\mathbf{C}$. The rotation parameter R_{V_k} is calculated as follows:

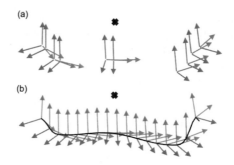

Fig. 4. (a) an object at the cross position is captured by ten cameras. (b) presents the interpolated virtual camera frames.

$$R_{V_k} = \frac{\sum_{i=1}^{n} w_{ik} R_{C_i}}{\sum_{i=1}^{n} w_{ik}}, \qquad w_{ik} = \frac{1}{\sqrt{2\pi\sigma^2}} e^{-\frac{\|T_{V_k} - T_{C_i}\|^2}{2\sigma^2}}$$

where the weight w_{ik} is set to have a Gaussian distribution of the distance between the virtual camera position T_{V_k} and the i-th real camera position T_{C_i}. Therefore, the interpolated orientation of the virtual camera is more influenced by that of closer real cameras than those of distant real cameras. The parameter σ controls how fast the weight decreases as the distance between two camera positions increases.

Virtual Camera Positions. We first create a set of k virtual cameras that are uniformly distributed along the x-axis from the leftmost located camera $T_{C_1}^x$ to the rightmost camera $T_{C_n}^x$. For both y and z positions, we interpolate intermediate values using a cubic spline function $\Psi(x)$ for given x coordinates. For instance, we determine y coordinates using $y = \Psi_y(x)$ in the x-y plane using the set of original camera points $\{(T_{C_i}^x, T_{C_i}^y)|C_i \in \mathbf{C}\}$, where the spline function $\Psi_y(x)$ is in the form of the third-order polynomials. The corresponding z-coordinates of the virtual cameras are computed by the same procedure, estimating a cubic spline $\Psi_z(x)$ spanning the x-z plane.

Two-Pass Rendering. We have prepared all the graphics components including the foreground/background geometries $\mathbf{G}^{\mathcal{F}}$ and $\mathbf{G}^{\mathcal{B}}$, the virtual viewpoints $\mathbf{V}$, and the foreground and background textures $\mathbf{T}^{\mathcal{F}}$ and $\mathbf{T}^{\mathcal{B}}$ in addition to the alpha masks $\mathbf{M}^{\mathcal{F}}$ for the foreground object. For a target virtual viewpoint V_k, we first retrieve the real camera C_m having the minimum distance to V_k. We adopt a two-pass rendering approach that draws the background object and the foreground object separately and blends the two images by a generated alpha matte. The procedure of rendering the background starts from unprojecting texture T on geometry g from the perspective of the real camera C. The scene from the target viewpoint V_k is then rendered. Rendering the foreground object is performed similarly, but it further outputs an alpha matte of the foreground object by warping the binary mask M from the view of C to V_k. Since we use a geometry proxy $\mathbf{G}^{\mathcal{F}}$, which is the very rough approximation for the real geometry of the object, the alpha matte is necessary to refine the rough rendering, not in the model space but the image space. As mentioned earlier, the final output frame is produced via alpha blending of two intermediate images. We iterate the rendering procedure for all virtual cameras in $\mathbf{V}$.

4   Results

We conducted experiments on our view synthesis workflow using eight Google Nexus 5X mobile phones. Our server is equipped with Intel Core i7-3770 CPU with 32 GB memory and NVIDIA GeForce GTX 970 GPU. We took images of a scene in 1440×1080 resolution, but they were scaled to 800×600 when transmitting to the server for both computational and communicational efficiency.

Novel View Synthesis. Given the accurately synchronized mobile devices, we generated synthetic views using our view synthesis method. In Fig. 5, we present interpolated novel views (b) between two real camera views, shown in Images (a) and (c). These novel views in Column (b) were created to enable the bullet-time effect along the virtual camera path automatically. Image (d) presents a point cloud with real camera frustums. The two rightmost camera frustums correspond to two real views shown in (a) and (c), respectively. Images (e) and (f) reveal intermediate geometry proxies for projective camera mapping and an alpha map for foreground segmentation yielding the foreground image (g), which is rendered on top of the inpainted background (h). Six cameras were used to capture this scene.

Figure 6 compares our view synthesis of bullet-time photography to a state-of-the-art method [21]. Wang et al. [21] adopt a piecewise planar stereo method [16] to estimate depth information of the scene for depth image-based rendering. While the planar stereo method is devised initially to estimate the depth of an urban scene that comprises many planar objects such as walls, houses, buildings, etc., we found that it often fails for natural outdoor scenes and human subjects, as shown in Fig. 6(a). Therefore, Wang et al. present frequent DIBR artifacts over rendering results due to erroneous depth estimation. In contrast, our method outperforms the state-of-the-art method regarding DIBR rendering artifacts.

Figure 7 shows additional results, where input real views, point clouds, alpha mattes, and synthesized novel views are presented in each column. Columns (d) and (e) compare the impact of our background inpainting. The inpainting process of the background helps the novel views appear more natural and plausible without requiring severe computational costs. Refer to the supplemental material for more video results.

Performance Analysis. Although our view synthesis is rendered on a mobile device in an interactable time, we have to employ a server to perform heavy computational pre-processing such as texture segmentation, bundle adjustment for geometry, and view path generation to achieve interactive performance. We evaluate a performance analysis on our system by measuring the running time for each process to process a scene. Figure 8 compares the computational costs of our method with Wang et al. [21]. The total running time for our method was 78.79 s (1 min 18 s). In contrast, the state-of-the-art method of Wang et al. took 4506.13 s (1 h 15 mins) for handling the same scene. Note that our method is near the interactive time, which is about 57 times faster than the other method. The most time-consuming step in our method is the semantic segmentation part, which took 57.92 s; i.e., it accounts for about 74 % of the total processing time. We believe that the bottleneck of the segmentation step can be alleviated by substituting the current segmentation method with a more efficient state-of-the-art method in the future.

Camera Synchronization. To assess the accuracy of our synchronization, we experimented with taking synchronized images of a running stopwatch. The stopwatch is capable of displaying time in milliseconds. Using eight mobile devices, we performed ten trials to capture the synchronized images of the time on the stopwatch. We demonstrate the results of the experiment in Fig. 9. As a criterion for the precision, we used the standard deviation of the sample times captured in the synchronized images. Smaller standard deviation indicates less error for synchronization. The average standard deviation for ten trials was only

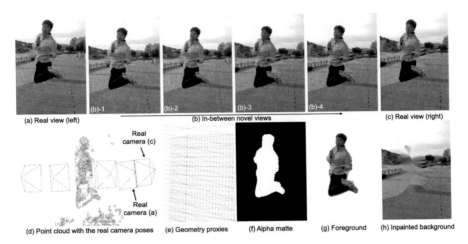

Fig. 5. Automated view interpolation for bullet-time photography along with a synthetic view path. Between two real views (a) and (c), we created intermediate views (b)s synthetically. Image (d) shows a point cloud with the real camera frustums, where the two rightmost frustums show real views (a) and (c) in the upper row, respectively. Images (e)–(h) present graphics components for the image-based rendering of a synthetic view: geometric proxies, an alpha mask, a segmented foreground image, and an inpainted background image.

Fig. 6. Images (a) and (b) compare view interpolations of our method with Wang et al.

(a) Real view   (b) Point cloud   (c) Alpha matte   (d) Novel view w/o inpainting   (e) Novel view w/ inpainting

Fig. 7. Column (a) shows an input image. Columns (b) and (c) demonstrate intermediate point clouds and corresponding alpha mattes. Columns (d) and (e) compare novel view images with/without background inpainting. Column (e) presents a synthetic novel view.

						[Unit: second]
	Wang et al.			Ours		
Geometry processor	Bundle Adjustment (BA)	11.00	Geometry processor	Bundle Adjustment (BA)	11.00	
	3D Line Reconstruction (LR)	1.13		Proxy Generation (PG)	0.0020	
	Plane Detection (PD)	13.00	Texture processor	Segmentation	57.92	
				Background Inpainting (BI)	9.54	
	Depth-map Generation (DG)	4481.00	View path generator	Point and Pose Estimation (PPE)	0.33	
Total		1hour 15mins. (=4506.13secs)	Total		1min. 18secs. (=78.79 secs)	

(a)
- BA 0.24%
- LR 0.03%
- PD 0.29%
- DG 99.44%

Total: 1hour 15mins. (=4506.13 secs)

(b)
- PPE 0%
- BI 12%
- BA 14%
- PG 0%
- Segmentation 74%

Total: 1min. 18secs. (=78.79 secs)

Fig. 8. Performance analysis for computing a bullet-time video. The table on the top compares the time performance in seconds for each step of Wang et al. [21] and our method. The pie charts (a) and (b) compare the proportion of computational times spent for each step of both methods, respectively.

15.77 ms. For the fourth and sixth trials, the standard deviations were virtually zero, meaning no errors.

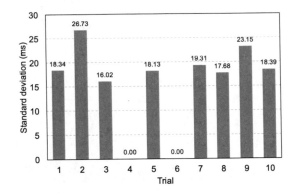

Fig. 9. Synchronization results of ten trials using eight mobile devices. The vertical axis shows the standard deviation of the captured time differences in milliseconds. The horizontal axis represents the trial number. We had the perfect synchronization of eight devices for the 4th and 6th trials. The average standard deviation was only 15.77 ms.

5   Discussion and Conclusion

In summary, we have presented an automated casual view synthesis method that bridges the gap between pervasive mobile computing and multiview photography. Our method enables bullet-time photography of frozen-time animation on wirelessly connected mobile devices in an interactable time. The current method is implemented for still shots. The synthetic video navigation will be our future work. The performance of our synthetic view rendering could be affected by the accuracy of the CNN-based semantic segmentation algorithm [23] that we used. An advanced segmentation method could improve results.

Acknowledgements. Min H. Kim acknowledges Korea NRF grants (2019R1A2C-3007229, 2013M3A6A-6073718) and additional support by Cross-Ministry Giga KOREA Project (GK17-P0200), Samsung Electronics (SRFC-IT1402-02), ETRI(19ZR1400), and an ICT R&D program of MSIT/IITP of Korea (2016-0-00018).

References

1. Buehler, C., Bosse, M., McMillan, L., Gortler, S., Cohen, M.: Unstructured lumigraph rendering. In: Proceedings of the 28th Annual Conference on Computer Graphics and Interactive Techniques, SIGGRAPH 2001. ACM (2001)
2. Camps-Mur, D., Garcia-Saavedra, A., Serrano, P.: Device-to-device communications with wi-fi direct: overview and experimentation. IEEE Wirel. Commun. **20**(3), 96–104 (2013)

3. Chang, C.F., Bishop, G., Lastra, A.: Ldi tree: a hierarchical representation for image-based rendering. In: Proceedings of the 26th Annual Conference on Computer Graphics and Interactive Techniques, SIGGRAPH 1999. ACM Press/Addison-Wesley Publishing Co. (1999)
4. Chen, S.E., Williams, L.: View interpolation for image synthesis. In: Proceedings of the 20th Annual Conference on Computer Graphics and Interactive Techniques, SIGGRAPH 1993 (1993)
5. Debevec, P., Yu, Y., Borshukov, G.: Efficient view-dependent image-based rendering with projective texture-mapping. In: Drettakis, G., Max, N. (eds.) Rendering Techniques '98. Eurographics, pp. 105–116. Springer, Vienna (1998)
6. Fischler, M.A., Bolles, R.C.: Random sample consensus: a paradigm for model fitting with applications to image analysis and automated cartography. Commun. ACM **24**(6), 381–395 (1981)
7. Kang, S.B., Shum, H.Y.: A review of image-based rendering techniques. Institute of Electrical and Electronics Engineers, Inc., June 2000
8. Lee, J.H., Choi, I., Kim, M.H.: Laplacian patch-based image synthesis. In: Proceedings of IEEE Computer Vision and Pattern Recognition (CVPR 2016), pp. 2727–2735. IEEE, Las Vegas (2016)
9. Lowe, D.G.: Distinctive image features from scale-invariant keypoints. Int. J. Comput. Vision **60**(2), 91–110 (2004)
10. Macqueen, J.: Some methods for classification and analysis of multivariate observations. In: In 5-th Berkeley Symposium on Mathematical Statistics and Probability, pp. 281–297 (1967)
11. McMillan, Jr., L.: An image-based approach to three-dimensional computer graphics. Ph.D. thesis, Chapel Hill, NC, USA (1997). uMI Order No. GAX97-30561
12. Mills, D.L.: Internet time synchronization: the network time protocol. IEEE Trans. Commun. **39**(10), 1482–1493 (1991)
13. Scharstein, D.: Stereo vision for view synthesis. In: Proceedings CVPR IEEE Computer Society Conference on Computer Vision and Pattern Recognition, pp. 852–858, June 1996
14. Seitz, S.M., Dyer, C.R.: View morphing. In: Proceedings of the 23rd Annual Conference on Computer Graphics and Interactive Techniques, SIGGRAPH 1996, pp. 21–30. ACM, New York (1996)
15. Shade, J., Gortler, S., He, L.W., Szeliski, R.: Layered depth images. In: Proceedings of the 25th Annual Conference on Computer Graphics and Interactive Techniques, SIGGRAPH 1998, pp. 231–242. ACM, New York (1998)
16. Sinha, S., Steedly, D., Szeliski, R.: Piecewise planar stereo for image-based rendering. In: Twelfth IEEE International Conference on Computer Vision (ICCV 2009). IEEE, Kyoto, September 2009
17. Siu, A.M.K., Lau, R.W.H.: Image-based modeling and rendering with geometric proxy. In: Proceedings of the 12th ACM International Conference on Multimedia, New York, NY, USA, 10–16 October 2004, pp. 468–471 (2004)
18. Snavely, N., Seitz, S.M., Szeliski, R.: Photo tourism: exploring photo collections in 3D. In: SIGGRAPH Conference Proceedings, pp. 835–846. ACM Press, New York (2006)
19. Telea, A.: An image inpainting technique based on the fast marching method. J. Graph. GPU Game Tools **9**(1), 23–34 (2004)
20. Triggs, B., McLauchlan, P.F., Hartley, R.I., Fitzgibbon, A.W.: Bundle adjustment — a modern synthesis. In: Triggs, B., Zisserman, A., Szeliski, R. (eds.) IWVA 1999. LNCS, vol. 1883, pp. 298–372. Springer, Heidelberg (2000). https://doi.org/10.1007/3-540-44480-7_21

21. Wang, Y., Wang, J., Chang, S.: Camswarm: instantaneous smartphone camera arrays for collaborative photography. CoRR abs/1507.01148 (2015)
22. Wu, C., Agarwal, S., Curless, B., Seitz, S.M.: Multicore bundle adjustment. In: Proceedings of the 2011 IEEE Conference on Computer Vision and Pattern Recognition. IEEE Computer Society (2011)
23. Zheng, S., et al: Conditional random fields as recurrent neural networks. CoRR (2015)

DeepPrivacy: A Generative Adversarial Network for Face Anonymization

Håkon Hukkelås[✉] ⓘ, Rudolf Mester ⓘ, and Frank Lindseth ⓘ

Department of Computer Science, Norwegian University of Science and Technology,
Trondheim, Norway
{hakon.hukkelas,rudolf.mester,frankl}@ntnu.no

Abstract. We propose a novel architecture which is able to automatically anonymize faces in images while retaining the original data distribution. We ensure total anonymization of all faces in an image by generating images exclusively on privacy-safe information. Our model is based on a conditional generative adversarial network, generating images considering the original pose and image background. The conditional information enables us to generate highly realistic faces with a seamless transition between the generated face and the existing background. Furthermore, we introduce a diverse dataset of human faces, including unconventional poses, occluded faces, and a vast variability in backgrounds. Finally, we present experimental results reflecting the capability of our model to anonymize images while preserving the data distribution, making the data suitable for further training of deep learning models. As far as we know, no other solution has been proposed that guarantees the anonymization of faces while generating realistic images.

Keywords: Image anonymization · Face de-identification · Generative adversarial networks

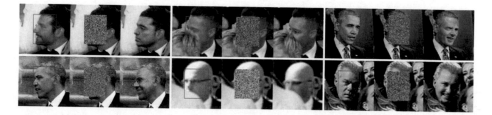

Fig. 1. DeepPrivacy Results on a diverse set of images. The left image is the original image annotated with bounding box and keypoints, the middle image is the input image to our GAN, and the right image is the generated image. Note that our generator never sees any privacy-sensitive information.

G. Bebis et al. (Eds.): ISVC 2019, LNCS 11844, pp. 565–578, 2019.
https://doi.org/10.1007/978-3-030-33720-9_44

1   Introduction

Privacy-preserving data-processing is becoming more critical every year; however, no suitable solution has been found to anonymize images without degrading the image quality. The General Data Protection Regulation (GDPR) came to effect as of 25th of May, 2018, affecting all processing of personal data across Europe. GDPR requires regular consent from the individual for any use of their personal data. However, if the data does not allow to identify an individual, companies are free to use the data without consent. To effectively anonymize images, we require a robust model to replace the original face, without destroying the existing data distribution; that is: the output should be a realistic face fitting the given situation.

Anonymizing images, while retaining the original distribution, is a challenging task. The model is required to remove all privacy-sensitive information, generate a highly realistic face, and the transition between original and anonymized parts has to be seamless. This requires a model that can perform complex semantic reasoning to generate a new anonymized face. For practical use, we desire the model to be able to manage a broad diversity of images, poses, backgrounds, and different persons. Our proposed solution can successfully anonymize images in a large variety of cases, and create realistic faces to the given conditional information.

Our proposed model, called *DeepPrivacy*, is a conditional generative adversarial network [3,18]. Our generator considers the existing background and a sparse pose annotation to generate realistic anonymized faces. The generator has a U-net architecture [23] that generates images with a resolution of 128×128. The model is trained with a progressive growing training technique [12] from a starting resolution of 8×8 to 128×128, which substantially improves the final image quality and overall training time. By design, our generator never observes the original face, ensuring removal of any privacy-sensitive information.

For practical use, we assume no demanding requirements for the object and keypoint detection methods. Our model requires two simple annotations of the face: (1) a bounding box annotation to identify the privacy-sensitive area, and (2) a sparse pose estimation of the face, containing keypoints for the ears, eyes, nose, and shoulders; in total seven keypoints. This keypoint annotation is identical to what Mask R-CNN [6] provides.

We provide a new dataset of human faces, *Flickr Diverse Faces* (FDF), which consists of 1.47M faces with a bounding box and keypoint annotation for each face. This dataset covers a considerably large diversity of facial poses, partial occlusions, complex backgrounds, and different persons. We will make this dataset publicly available along with our source code and pre-trained networks[1,2].

We evaluate our model by performing an extensive qualitative and quantitative study of the model's ability to retain the original data distribution. We

---

[1] Code: www.github.com/hukkelas/DeepPrivacy.

[2] FDF Dataset: www.github.com/hukkelas/FDF.

anonymize the validation set of the WIDER-Face dataset [27], then run face detection on the anonymized images to measure the impact of anonymization on Average Precision (AP). DSFD [14] achieves 99.3% (95.9% out of 96.6% AP), 99.3% (95.0%/95.7%), and 99.3% (89.8%/90.4%) of the original AP on the easy, medium, and hard difficulty, respectively. On average, it achieves 99.3% of the original AP. In contrast, traditional anonymization techniques, such as 8×8 pixelation achieves 96.7%, heavy blur 90.5%, and black-out 41.4% of the original performance. Additionally, we present several ablation experiments that reflect the importance of a large model size and conditional pose information to generate high-quality faces.

In summary, we make the following contributions:

- We propose a novel generator architecture to anonymize faces, which ensures 100% removal of privacy-sensitive information in the original face. The generator can generate realistic looking faces that have a seamless transition to the existing background for various sets of poses and contexts.
- We provide the FDF dataset, including 1.47M faces with a tight bounding box and keypoint annotation for each face. The dataset covers a considerably larger diversity of faces compared to previous datasets.

2   Related Work

De-identifying Faces: Currently, there exists a limited number of research studies on the task of removing privacy-sensitive information from an image including a face. Typically, the approach chosen is to alter the original image such that we remove all the privacy-sensitive information. These methods can be applied to all images; however, there is no assurance that these methods remove all privacy-sensitive information. Naive methods that apply simple image distortion have been discussed numerous times in literature [1,4,5,19,20], such as pixelation and blurring; but, they are inadequate for removing the privacy-sensitive information [4,19,20], and they alter the data distribution substantially.

K-same family of algorithms [4,11,20] implements the k-anonymity algorithm [25] for face images. Newton *et al.* prove that the k-same algorithm can remove all privacy-sensitive information; but, the resulting images often contain "ghosting" artifacts due to small alignment errors [4].

Jourabloo *et al.* [11] look at the task of de-identification grayscale images while preserving a large set of facial attributes. This is different from our work, as we do not directly train our generative model to generate faces with similar attributes to the original image. In contrast, our model is able to perform complex semantic reasoning to generate a face that is coherent with the overall context information given to the network, yielding a highly realistic face.

Generative Adversarial Networks (GANs) [3] is a highly successful training architecture to model a natural image distribution. GANs enables us to generate new images, often indistinguishable from the real data distribution. It has a broad diversity of application areas, from general image generation [2,12,13,30], text-to-photo generation [31], style transfer [8,24] and much more. With the numerous contributions since its conception, it has gone from a beautiful theoretical idea to a tool we can apply for practical use cases. In our work, we show that GANs are an efficient tool to remove privacy-sensitive information without destroying the original image quality.

Ren *et al.* [22] look at the task of anonymizing video data by using GANs. They perform anonymization by altering each pixel in the original image to hide the identity of the individuals. In contrast to their method, we can ensure the removal of all privacy-sensitive information, as our generative model never observes the original face.

Progressive Growing of GANs [12] propose a novel training technique to generate faces progressively, starting from a resolution of 4 × 4 and step-wise increasing it to 1024 × 1024. This training technique improves the final image quality and overall training time. Our proposed model uses the same training technique; however, we perform several alterations to their original model to convert it to a conditional GAN. With these alterations, we can include conditional information about the context and pose of the face. Our final generator architecture is similar to the one proposed by Isola *et al.* [9], but we introduce conditional information in several stages.

Image Inpainting is a closely related task to what we are trying to solve, and it is a widely researched area for generative models [10,15,17,29]. Several research studies have looked at the task of face completion with a generative adversarial network [15,29]. They mask a specific part of the face and try to complete this part with the conditional information given. From our knowledge, and the qualitative experiments they present in their papers, they are not able to mask a large enough section to remove all privacy-sensitive information. As the masked region grows, it requires a more advanced generative model that understands complex semantic reasoning, making the task considerably harder. Also, their experiments are based on the Celeb-A dataset [17], primarily consisting of celebrities with low diversity in facial pose, making models trained on this dataset unsuitable for real-world applications.

3   The Flickr Diverse Faces Dataset

FDF (Flickr Diverse Faces) is a new dataset of human faces, crawled from the YFCC-100M dataset [26]. It consists of 1.47M human faces with a minimum resolution of 128 × 128, containing facial keypoints and a bounding box annotation for each face. The dataset has a vast diversity in terms of age, ethnicity, facial pose, image background, and face occlusion. Randomly picked examples from the dataset can be seen in Fig. 2. The dataset is extracted from scenes related to traffic, sports events, and outside activities. In comparison to the FFHQ [13] and Celeb-A [17] datasets, our dataset is more diverse in facial poses and it contains significantly more faces; however, the FFHQ dataset has a higher resolution.

The FDF dataset is a high-quality dataset with few annotation errors. The faces are automatically labeled with state-of-the-art keypoint and bounding box

Fig. 2. The FDF dataset. Each image has a sparse keypoint annotation (7 keypoints) of the face and a tight bounding box annotation. We recommend the reader to zoom in.

models, and we use a high confidence threshold for both the keypoint and bounding box predictions. The faces are extracted from $1.08M$ images in the YFCC100-M dataset. For keypoint estimation, we use Mask R-CNN [6], with a ResNet-50 FPN backbone [16]. For bounding box annotation, we use the Single Shot Scale-invariant Face Detector [32]. To combine the predictions, we match a keypoint with a face bounding box if the eye and nose annotation are within the bounding box. Each bounding box and keypoint has a single match, and we match them with a greedy approach based on descending prediction confidence.

4 Model

Our proposed model is a conditional GAN, generating images based on the surrounding of the face and sparse pose information. Figure 1 shows the conditional information given to our network, and Appendix A has a detailed description of the pre-processing steps. We base our model on the one proposed by Karras *et al.* [12]. Their model is a non-conditional GAN, and we perform several alterations to include conditional information.

We use seven keypoints to describe the pose of the face: left/right eye, left/right ear, left/right shoulder, and nose. To reduce the number of parameters in the network, we pre-process the pose information into a one-hot encoded image of size $K \times M \times M$, where K is the number of keypoints and M is the target resolution.

Progressive growing training technique is crucial for our model's success. We apply progressive growing to both the generator and discriminator to grow the networks from a starting resolution of 8. We double the resolution each time we expand our network until we reach the final resolution of 128×128. The pose information is included for each resolution in the generator and discriminator, making the pose information finer for each increase in resolution.

4.1 Generator Architecture

Figure 3 shows our proposed generator architecture for 128×128 resolution. Our generator has a U-net [23] architecture to include background information. The encoder and decoder have the same number of filters in each convolution, but the decoder has an additional 1×1 bottleneck convolution after each skip

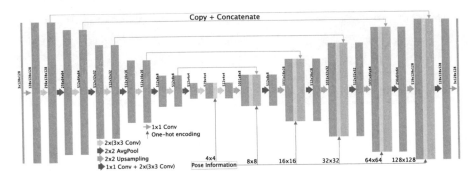

Fig. 3. Generator Architecture for 128×128 resolution. Each convolutional layer is followed by pixel normalization [12] and LeakyReLU ($\alpha = 0.2$). After each upsampling layer, we concatenate the upsampled output with pose information and the corresponding skip connection.

connection. This bottleneck design reduces the number of parameters in the decoder significantly. To include the pose information for each resolution, we concatenate the output after each upsampling layer with pose information and the corresponding skip connection. The general layer structure is identical to Karras *et al.* [12], where we use pixel replication for upsampling, pixel normalization and LeakyReLU after each convolution, and equalized learning rate instead of careful weight initialization.

Progressive Growing: Each time we increase the resolution of the generator, we add two 3×3 convolutions to the start of the encoder and the end of the decoder. We use a transition phase identical to Karras *et al.* [12] for both of these new blocks, making the network stable throughout training. We note that the network is still unstable during the transition phase, but it is significantly better compared to training without progressive growing.

4.2   Discriminator Architecture

Our proposed discriminator architecture is identical to the one proposed by Karras *et al.* [12], with a few exceptions. First, we include the background information as conditional input to the start of the discriminator, making the input image have six channels instead of three. Secondly, we include pose information at each resolution of the discriminator. The pose information is concatenated with the output of each downsampling layer, similar to the decoder in the generator. Finally, we remove the mini-batch standard deviation layer presented by Karras *et al.* [12], as we find the diversity of our generated faces satisfactory.

The adjustments made to the generator doubles the number of total parameters in the network. To follow the design lines of Karras *et al.* [12], we desire that the complexity in terms of the number of parameters to be similar for the discriminator and generator. We evaluate two different discriminator models, which we will name the *deep discriminator* and the *wide discriminator*. The deep discriminator doubles the number of convolutional layers for each resolution. To mimic the skip-connections in the generator, we wrap the convolutions for each resolution in residual blocks. The wider discriminator keeps the same architecture; however, we increase the number of filters in each convolutional layer by a factor of $\sqrt{2}$.

5 Experiments

Fig. 4. Anonymized Images from DeepPrivacy. Every single face in the images has been generated. We recommend the reader to zoom in.

DeepPrivacy can robustly generate anonymized faces for a vast diversity of poses, backgrounds, and different persons. From qualitative evaluations of our generated results on the WIDER-Face dataset [27], we find our proposed solution to be robust to a broad diversity of images. Figure 4 shows several results of our proposed solution on the WIDER-Face dataset. Note that the network is trained on the FDF dataset; we do not train on any images in the WIDER-Face dataset.

We evaluate the impact of anonymization on the WIDER-Face [27] dataset. We measure the AP of a face detection model on the anonymized dataset and compare this to the original dataset. We report the standard metrics for the different difficulties for WIDER-Face. Additionally, we perform several ablation experiments on our proposed FDF dataset.

Our final model is trained for 17 days, 40M images, until we observe no qualitative differences between consecutive training iterations. It converges to a Frèchect Inception Distance (FID) [7] of 1.53. Specific training details and input pre-processing are given in Appendix A.

5.1 Effect of Anonymization for Face Detection

Table 1 shows the AP of different anonymization techniques on the WIDER-Face validation set. In comparison to the original dataset, DeepPrivacy only degrades the AP by 0.7%, 0.7%, and 0.6% on the easy, medium, and hard difficulties, respectively.

Table 1. Face Detection AP on the WIDER Face [27] validation dataset. The face detection method used is DSFD [14], the current state-of-the-art on WIDER-Face.

Anonymization method	Easy	Medium	Hard
No anonymization [14]	96.6%	95.7%	90.4%
Blacked out	24.9%	36.3%	54.8%
Pixelation (16 × 16)	95.3%	94.9%	**90.2%**
Pixelation (8 × 8)	91.4%	92.3%	88.9%
9 × 9 Gaussian blur ($\sigma = 3$)	95.3%	92.8%	84.7%
Heavy blur (filter size = 30% face width)	83.4%	86.3%	86.1%
DeepPrivacy (ours)	**95.9%**	**95.0%**	89.8%

Fig. 5. Different Anonymization Methods on a face in the WIDER Face validation set.

We compare DeepPrivacy anonymization to simpler anonymization methods; black-out, pixelation, and blurring. Figure 5 illustrates the different anonymization methods. DeepPrivacy generally achieves a higher AP compared to all other methods, with the exception of 16 × 16 pixelation.

Note that 16 × 16 pixelation does not affect a majority of the faces in the dataset. For the "hard" challenge, 0% of the faces has a resolution larger than 16 × 16. For the easy and medium challenge, 43% and 29.9% has a resolution larger than 16 × 16. The observant reader might notice that for the "hard" challenge, 16 × 16 pixelation should have no effect; however, the AP is degraded in comparison to the original dataset (see Table 1). We believe that the AP on the "hard" challenge is degraded due to anonymizing faces in easy/medium challenge can affect the model in cases where faces from "hard" and easy/medium are present in the same image.

Experiment Details: For the face detector we use the current state-of-the-art, Dual Shot Face Detector (DSFD) [14]. The WIDER-Face dataset has no facial keypoint annotations; therefore, we automatically detect keypoints for each face with the same method as used for the FDF dataset. To match keypoints with a bounding box, we use the same greedy approach as earlier. Mask R-CNN [6] is not able to detect keypoints for all faces, especially in cases with high occlusion, low resolution, or faces turned away from the camera. Thus, we are only able to anonymize 43% of the faces in the validation set. Of the faces that are not anonymized, 22% are partially occluded, and 30% are heavily occluded. For the remaining non-anonymized faces, 70% has a resolution smaller than 14×14. Note that for each experiment in Table 1, we anonymize the same bounding boxes.

5.2 Ablation Experiments

We perform several ablation experiments to evaluate the model architecture choices. We report the Fréchet Inception Distance [7] between the original images and the anonymized images for each experiment. We calculate FID from a validation set of 50,000 faces from the FDF dataset. The results are shown in Table 2 and discussed in detail next.

Table 2. Ablation Experiments with our model. We report the Fréchet Inception Distance (FID) on the FDF validation dataset, after showing the discriminator $30.0M$ images (lower is better). For results in Table 2a and b, we use a model size of $12M$ parameters for both the generator and discriminator. *Reported after $20.0M$ images, as the deep discriminator diverged after this.

(a) Result of using conditional pose.

Model	FID
With Pose	**2.71**
Without Pose	3.36

(b) Result of the deep and wide discriminator.

Discriminator	FID
Deep Discriminator*	9.327
Wide Discriminator*	**3.86**

(c) Result of different model sizes.

#parameters	FID
12M	2.71
46M	**1.84**

Effect of Pose Information: Pose of the face provided as conditional information improves our model significantly, as seen in Table 2a. The FDF dataset has a large variance of faces in different poses, and we find it necessary to include sparse pose information to generate realistic faces. In contrast, when trained on the Celeb-A dataset, our model completely ignores the given pose information.

Discriminator Architecture: Table 2b compares the quality of images for a deep and wide discriminator. With a deeper network, the discriminator struggles to converge, leading to poor results. We use no normalization layers in the discriminator, causing deeper networks to suffer from exploding forward passes and vanishing gradients. Even though, Brock *et al.* [2] also observe similar results; a deeper network architecture degrades the overall image quality. Note that we also experimented with a discriminator with no modifications to number of parameters, but this was not able to generate realistic faces.

Model Size: We empirically observe that increasing the number of filters in each convolution improves image quality drastically. As seen in Table 2c, we train two models with $12M$ and $46M$ parameters. Unquestionably, increasing the number of parameters generally improves the image quality. For both experiments, we use the same hyperparameters; the only thing changed is the number of filters in each convolution.

6   Limitations

Fig. 6. Failure Cases of DeepPrivacy. Our proposed solution can generate unrealistic images in cases of high occlusion, difficult background information, and irregular poses.

Our method proves its ability to generate objectively good images for a diversity of backgrounds and poses. However, it still struggles in several challenging scenarios. Figure 6 illustrates some of these. These issues can impact the generated image quality, but, by design, our model ensures the removal of all privacy-sensitive information from the face.

Faces occluded with high fidelity objects are extremely challenging when generating a realistic face. For example, in Fig. 6, several images have persons covering their faces with hands. To generate a face in this scenario requires complex semantic reasoning, which is still a difficult challenge for GANs.

Handling non-traditional poses can cause our model to generate corrupted faces. We use a sparse pose estimation to describe the face pose, but there is no limitation in our architecture to include a dense pose estimation. A denser pose estimation would, most likely, improve the performance of our model in cases of irregular poses. However, this would set restrictions on the pose estimator and restrict the practical use case of our method.

7   Conclusion

We propose a conditional generative adversarial network, *DeepPrivacy*, to anonymize faces in images without destroying the original data distribution. The presented results on the WIDER-Face dataset reflects our model's capability to generate high-quality images. Also, the diversity of images in the WIDER-Face dataset shows the practical applicability of our model. The current state-of-the-art face detection method can achieve 99.3% of the original average precision on the anonymized WIDER-Face validation set. In comparison to previous solutions, this is a significant improvement to both the generated image quality and the certainty of anonymization. Furthermore, the presented ablation experiments on the FDF dataset suggests that a larger model size and inclusion of sparse pose information is necessary to generate high-quality images.

DeepPrivacy is a conceptually simple generative adversarial network, easily extendable for further improvements. Handling irregular poses, difficult occlusions, complex backgrounds, and temporal consistency in videos is still a subject for further work. We believe our contribution will be an inspiration for further work into ensuring privacy in visual data.

Appendix A - Training Details

We use the same hyperparameters as Karras *et al.* [12], except the following: We use a batch size of 256, 256, 128, 72 and 48 for resolution 8, 16, 32, 64, and 128. We use a learning rate of 0.00175 with the Adam optimizer. For each expansion of the network, we have a transition and stabilization phase of 1.2M images each. We use an exponential running average for the weights of the generator as this improves overall image quality [28]. For the running average, we use a decay β given by:

$$\beta = 0.5^{\frac{B}{10^4}}, \tag{1}$$

where B is the batch size. Our final model was trained for 17 days on two NVIDIA V100-32 GB GPUs.

Image Pre-processing

Figure 7 shows the input pre-processing pipeline. For each detected face with a bounding box and keypoint detection, we find the smallest possible square bounding box which surrounds the face bounding box. Then, we resize the expanded bounding box to the target size (128×128). We replace the pixels within the face bounding box with a constant pixel value of 128. Finally, we shift the pixel values to the range $[-1, 1]$.

Tensor Core Modifications

To utilize tensor cores in NVIDIA's new Volta architecture, we do several modifications to our network, following the requirements of tensor cores. First, we ensure that each convolutional block use number of filters that are divisible by 8. Secondly, we make certain that the batch size for each GPU is divisible by 8. Further, we use automatic mixed precision for pytorch [21] to significantly improve our training time. We see an improvement of 220% in terms of training speed with mixed precision training.

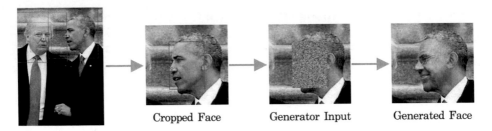

Cropped Face   Generator Input   Generated Face

Fig. 7. Input Pipeline: Each detected face is cropped to a quadratic image, then we replace the privacy-sensitive information with a constant value, and feed it to the generator. The keypoints are represented as a one-hot encoded image.

References

1. Boyle, M., Edwards, C., Greenberg, S.: The effects of filtered video on awareness and privacy. In: Proceedings of the 2000 ACM Conference on Computer Supported Cooperative Work, pp. 1–10. ACM (2000). https://doi.org/10.1145/358916.358935
2. Brock, A., Donahue, J., Simonyan, K.: Large scale GAN training for high fidelity natural image synthesis. In: International Conference on Learning Representations (2019). https://openreview.net/forum?id=B1xsqj09Fm
3. Goodfellow, I., et al.: Generative adversarial nets. In: Ghahramani, Z., Welling, M., Cortes, C., Lawrence, N.D., Weinberger, K.Q. (eds.) Advances in Neural Information Processing Systems 27, pp. 2672–2680. Curran Associates, Inc. (2014). http://papers.nips.cc/paper/5423-generative-adversarial-nets.pdf
4. Gross, R., Sweeney, L., de la Torre, F., Baker, S.: Model-based face de-identification. In: 2006 Conference on Computer Vision and Pattern Recognition Workshop, CVPRW 2006. IEEE (2006). https://doi.org/10.1109/cvprw.2006.125
5. Gross, R., Sweeney, L., Cohn, J., de la Torre, F., Baker, S.: Face de-identification. In: Senior, A. (ed.) Protecting Privacy in Video Surveillance, pp. 129–146. Springer, London (2009). https://doi.org/10.1007/978-1-84882-301-3_8
6. He, K., Gkioxari, G., Dollar, P., Girshick, R.: Mask r-CNN. In: 2017 IEEE International Conference on Computer Vision (ICCV). IEEE, October 2017. https://doi.org/10.1109/iccv.2017.322
7. Heusel, M., Ramsauer, H., Unterthiner, T., Nessler, B., Hochreiter, S.: GANs trained by a two time-scale update rule converge to a local Nash equilibrium. In: Guyon, I., et al. (eds.) Advances in Neural Information Processing Systems 30, pp. 6626–6637. Curran Associates, Inc. (2017)
8. Huang, X., Belongie, S.: Arbitrary style transfer in real-time with adaptive instance normalization. In: 2017 IEEE International Conference on Computer Vision (ICCV), pp. 1501–1510. IEEE, October 2017. https://doi.org/10.1109/iccv.2017.167
9. Isola, P., Zhu, J.Y., Zhou, T., Efros, A.A.: Image-to-image translation with conditional adversarial networks. In: 2017 IEEE Conference on Computer Vision and Pattern Recognition (CVPR). IEEE, July 2017. https://doi.org/10.1109/cvpr.2017.632
10. Jo, Y., Park, J.: SC-FEGAN: face editing generative adversarial network with user's sketch and color. arXiv preprint arXiv:1902.06838 (2019)

11. Jourabloo, A., Yin, X., Liu, X.: Attribute preserved face de-identification. In: Proceedings of 2015 International Conference on Biometrics, ICB 2015, pp. 278–285 (2015). https://doi.org/10.1109/ICB.2015.7139096

12. Karras, T., Aila, T., Laine, S., Lehtinen, J.: Progressive growing of gans for improved quality, stability, and variation. In: International Conference on Learning Representations (2018). https://openreview.net/forum?id=Hk99zCeAb

13. Karras, T., Laine, S., Aila, T.: A style-based generator architecture for generative adversarial networks. In: 2019 IEEE Conference on Computer Vision and Pattern Recognition (CVPR), pp. 4401–4410 (2019)

14. Li, J., et al.: DSFD: dual shot face detector. In: 2019 IEEE Conference on Computer Vision and Pattern Recognition (CVPR) (2019)

15. Li, Y., Liu, S., Yang, J., Yang, M.H.: Generative face completion. In: 2017 IEEE Conference on Computer Vision and Pattern Recognition (CVPR), pp. 5892–5900. IEEE, July 2017. https://doi.org/10.1109/cvpr.2017.624

16. Lin, T.Y., Dollár, P., Girshick, R., He, K., Hariharan, B., Belongie, S.: Feature pyramid networks for object detection. In: 2017 IEEE Conference on Computer Vision and Pattern Recognition (CVPR), pp. 2117–2125. IEEE, July 2017. https://doi.org/10.1109/cvpr.2017.106

17. Liu, G., Reda, F.A., Shih, K.J., Wang, T.-C., Tao, A., Catanzaro, B.: Image inpainting for irregular holes using partial convolutions. In: Ferrari, V., Hebert, M., Sminchisescu, C., Weiss, Y. (eds.) ECCV 2018. LNCS, vol. 11215, pp. 89–105. Springer, Cham (2018). https://doi.org/10.1007/978-3-030-01252-6_6

18. Mirza, M., Osindero, S.: Conditional generative adversarial nets. arXiv preprint arXiv:1411.1784 (2014)

19. Neustaedter, C., Greenberg, S., Boyle, M.: Blur filtration fails to preserve privacy for home-based video conferencing. ACM Trans. Comput. Hum. Interact. 13(1), 1–36 (2006). https://doi.org/10.1145/1143518.1143519

20. Newton, E.M., Sweeney, L., Malin, B.: Preserving privacy by de-identifying face images. IEEE Trans. Knowl. Data Eng. 17(2), 232–243 (2005). https://doi.org/10.1109/tkde.2005.32

21. NVIDIA: A pyTorch extension: tools for easy mixed precision and distributed training in PyTorch (2019). https://github.com/NVIDIA/apex

22. Ren, Z., Lee, Y.J., Ryoo, M.S.: Learning to anonymize faces for privacy preserving action detection. In: Ferrari, V., Hebert, M., Sminchisescu, C., Weiss, Y. (eds.) ECCV 2018. LNCS, vol. 11205, pp. 639–655. Springer, Cham (2018). https://doi.org/10.1007/978-3-030-01246-5_38

23. Ronneberger, O., Fischer, P., Brox, T.: U-Net: convolutional networks for biomedical image segmentation. In: Navab, N., Hornegger, J., Wells, W.M., Frangi, A.F. (eds.) MICCAI 2015. LNCS, vol. 9351, pp. 234–241. Springer, Cham (2015). https://doi.org/10.1007/978-3-319-24574-4_28

24. Ruder, M., Dosovitskiy, A., Brox, T.: Artistic style transfer for videos. In: Rosenhahn, B., Andres, B. (eds.) GCPR 2016. LNCS, vol. 9796, pp. 26–36. Springer, Cham (2016). https://doi.org/10.1007/978-3-319-45886-1_3

25. Sweeney, L.: K-anonymity: a model for protecting privacy. Int. J. Uncertainty Fuzziness Knowl. Based Syst. 10(05), 557–570 (2002)

26. Thomee, B., et al.: YFCC100M: the new data in multimedia research. arXiv preprint arXiv:1503.01817 (2015). http://arxiv.org/abs/1503.01817

27. Yang, S., Luo, P., Loy, C.C., Tang, X.: WIDER FACE: a face detection benchmark. In: 2016 IEEE Conference on Computer Vision and Pattern Recognition (CVPR). IEEE, June 2016. https://doi.org/10.1109/cvpr.2016.596

28. Yazıcı, Y., Foo, C.S., Winkler, S., Yap, K.H., Piliouras, G., Chandrasekhar, V.: The unusual effectiveness of averaging in GAN training. In: International Conference on Learning Representations (2019). https://openreview.net/forum?id=SJgw_sRqFQ

29. Yeh, R.A., Chen, C., Lim, T.Y., Schwing, A.G., Hasegawa-Johnson, M., Do, M.N.: Semantic image inpainting with deep generative models. In: 2017 IEEE Conference on Computer Vision and Pattern Recognition (CVPR), pp. 6882–6890. IEEE, July 2017. https://doi.org/10.1109/cvpr.2017.728

30. Zhang, H., Goodfellow, I., Metaxas, D., Odena, A.: Self-attention generative adversarial networks. In: Proceedings of the 36th International Conference on Machine Learning, vol. 97, pp. 7354–7563. PMLR (2019). http://proceedings.mlr.press/v97/zhang19d.html

31. Zhang, H., et al.: StackGAN: text to photo-realistic image synthesis with stacked generative adversarial networks. In: Proceedings of the IEEE International Conference on Computer Vision, pp. 5908–5916 (2017). https://doi.org/10.1109/ICCV.2017.629

32. Zhang, S., Zhu, X., Lei, Z., Shi, H., Wang, X., Li, S.Z.: S^3FD: single shot scale-invariant face detector. In: 2017 IEEE International Conference on Computer Vision (ICCV), pp. 192–201. IEEE, October 2017. https://doi.org/10.1109/iccv.2017.30

Swarm Optimization Algorithm for Road Bypass Extrapolation

Michael A. Rowland[✉], Glenn M. Suir, Michael L. Mayo, and Austin Davis

U.S. Army Engineer Research and Development Center, Vicksburg, MS, USA
Michael.A.Rowland@usace.army.mil

Abstract. Ant Colony Optimization (ACO) algorithms work by leveraging a population of agents that communicate through interaction with deposited "pheromone," and have been applied in various configurations to the long-standing problem of identifying trafficable terrain from aerial imagery. While these approaches have proven successful in highlighting paved roads in urban, highly-developed sites, they tend to fail in peri-urban and rural locations due to the lower frequency of unnatural features. In this work, we describe a workflow that uses site-specific, near-infrared and first-return LIDAR data to predict the "accessible space" of an image–i.e., the more open regions with shallow elevation gradient that may be readily traversible by both mounted (e.g., all-terrain vehicles) and dismounted forces. Collectively, these regions are supplied as input to an ACO algorithm, modified so that the agents perform a random walk weighted by local elevation change, which allows for a more comprehensive exploration of increasingly featureless imaged terrain. Performance of this workflow is evaluated using two study sites in the continental United States: the Muscatatuck Urban Training Center in rural Indiana, and Camp Shelby in Mississippi. Comparison of results with ground-truth datasets show a high degree of success in predicting areas trafficable by a wide variety of mobile units.

Keywords: Image analysis · Swarm optimization · Trafficability

1 Introduction

The identification of trafficable regions in geospatial information is an important task that directly informs mobility decisions when prior in-situ knowledge of the terrain is lacking. Unfortunately, features of the environment can change rapidly requiring regular updates to the set of geospatial information used to make immediate mobility decisions. For example, the presence or absence of dense foliage, paralyzing mud, or flooding in an ephemeral stream are all dynamic conditions that effect mobility. As vehicles become more autonomous, the underlying datasets used to guide mobility-related decisions will become increasingly scrutinized for their potential to limit property damage and bodily harm.

G. Bebis et al. (Eds.): ISVC 2019, LNCS 11844, pp. 579–590, 2019.
https://doi.org/10.1007/978-3-030-33720-9_45

Existing course forecasting methods rely on models that abstract the complexity of a roadway system into a more organized network of passable segments [1–6]. Such a networked representation is suitable for fast route generation, but becomes extremely limited when off-road mobility is desired. Additionally, data describing conditions of the off-road surfaces and obstacles are often inappropriately assigned the hazards associated with well-developed roadways. To address these concerns, we adapt an Ant Colony Optimization (ACO) algorithm to identify trafficable areas subject to geospatial information datasets that are readily available for many locations around the world. The ACO algorithm is a stochastic swarm intelligence method in which a swarm of agents (or "ants") explore paths charted over desired terrain, such that the mobility decisions of each ant is informed by the extent of "pheromone" deposited by its predecessors [7]. ACO has been used successfully in the past to identify features within images with high confidence. For example, ACO methods have been applied to structured urban environments for road network extraction tasks using aerial imagery at input [8,9]. This method excels in heavily developed cities that exhibit a high degree of contrast between the aligned edges of an inner-city roadway, because pheromone is deposited more densely near street-like features.

Dense urban environments inevitably give way to peri-urban and rural settings as one moves farther away from the city center, where the need to address mobility related questions is arguably more pressing, given the greater variety of movement decisions available there. Because less urbanized sites exhibit fewer developed features, such as the straight edges and sharp contrasts of highly urbanized locales, additional input data are required to extract data features that inform mobility decisions. To this end, we report how ACO workflows can be readily modified to annotate accessible areas beyond paved roads by supplementing aerial imagery with elevation and LIDAR data in peri-urban and rural regions. We demonstrate the improved workflow on two locations: Muscatatuck Urban Training Center in Indiana, and Camp Shelby in Mississippi, each of which contain detail for both urban and rural elements (Fig. 1).

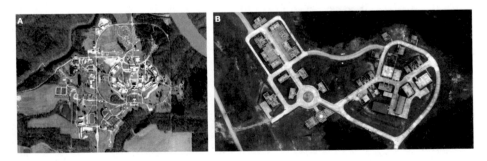

Fig. 1. Imagery of study sites. (*A*) WorldView-2 imagery of the Muscatatuck Urban Training Center. (*B*) Unmanned Aircraft System (UAS) imagery of the Camp Shelby study site.

2 Methods

2.1 Imagery Acquisition and Pre-processing

Muscatatuck Urban Training Center - Satellite. There are a plethora of commercial high-resolution satellite imaging platforms that are commonly available for data acquisition. Several high-resolution satellite image sources are available for acquisition at no cost to the US Army Corps of Engineers through the National Geospatial-Intelligence Agency EnhancedView contract. All acquisitions (archived and new data collections) are coordinated through the Army Geospatial Center Army Imagery Office [10]. WorldView sensors (WorldView-2 and WorldView-3) are among the most spectrally diverse commercial satellites available to date. The WorldView-2 (WV-2) sensor (47 cm panchromatic and 185 cm multispectral, launched 2009) collects eight multispectral bands (coastal, yellow, blue, green, red, red edge, near-infrared (NIR) 1 and NIR 2). The WV-2 sensor was tasked to collect multispectral imagery of the Muscatatuck project area. The multispectral data were collect on 6 November 2016, and acquired using the DigitalGlobe Enhanced Viewer Web Hosting Service. We used the Environment for Visualizing Images (ENVI) version 5.5 (ITT Visual Information Solutions, Inc. 2018) to perform radiometric, atmospheric, and geometric corrections on the WV2 imagery [11].

Camp Shelby - Unmanned Aircraft System (UAS). On 1 June 2017, we used a SkyCrane G4 UAS to collect over 2800 aerial images in one flight over the Camp Shelby study site. The payload included the Micasense RedEdge-M sensor with five narrow spectral bands: blue (475 nm center, 20 nm bandwidth), green (560 nm center, 20 nm bandwidth), red (668 nm center, 10 nm bandwidth), red-edge (717 nm center, 10 nm bandwidth), NIR (840 nm center, 40 nm bandwidth), and a ground sample distance of 8 cm per pixel (per band) at 120 m (~400 ft) above ground level from the launch location [12]. We evenly placed three ground control point (GCP) photo targets throughout the project area. The targets were wooden panels (121×121 cm) with an iron cross pattern. We surveyed the center point and four corners using high accuracy GPS equipment (horizontal accuracy = 1 cm, vertical accuracy = 2 cm).

We used the Pix4 photogrammetric software to process the UAS imagery and generate orthomosaic and Digital Surface Model raster data sets. The software used initial approximations of the sensor's orientation (i.e., approximate latitude, longitude, altitude, roll, pitch, and yaw) to extract tie point locations (i.e., those locations that could be identified in multiple photos). We used the precise location of the GCPs identified within each available image to refine the initial orientation. We added an additional sixteen manual tie points, and four check points, corresponding to keypoints in the images, to improve and assess the reconstructive accuracy and to tightly georeference the orthomosaics to the World Geodetic System 1984 datum. The root mean square error of the final orthomosaics were 0.378 cm and 0.262 cm for the horizontal and vertical control. The ground sample distance was as low as 4.41 cm for the orthomosaic.

Table 1. Trafficability rating by feature class and mode of transportation.

Class	Soldier	ATV	Light truck	Heavy truck
Agriculture	7	8	3	1
Bare ground	9	9	7	3
Barrier	1	0	0	0
Deep water	0	0	0	0
Gravel	8	8	7	5
Pavement	9	9	9	9
Shallow water	4	3	2	2
Slope (25–35%)	5	3	1	0
Slope (<35%)	0	0	0	0
Structure	5	1	0	0
Trees	6	5	1	0
Turf	9	9	8	3

2.2   Imagery Post-processing

Image Classification. The purpose of this study is to classify, based on landscape trafficability, moderate and high spatial resolution imagery to inform and assist in the development of a direction-guided ACO method. The initial trafficability classification serves as a baseline which the ACO method will attempt to emulate. Table 1 provides a list of feature classes (i.e., agriculture, pavement, structure, water, etc.), mode of transportation (i.e., soldier, all-terrain vehicle, light truck, heavy truck), and the trafficability score (TS) for each combination. The TS consists of a range of values (from 0 to 9) where zero (0) represents a feature that is not traversable and nine (9) represents a feature with high trafficability. For example, the agriculture feature class could reasonably be assigned a relatively high trafficability by a soldier on foot (TS = 7), but relatively low trafficability by a heavy truck (TS = 1).

Feature Classification. Recent studies have used object-based image analysis classification methods to analyze air- and space-borne imagery [13]. For the Muscatatuck and Camp Shelby sites, we used the ENVI Feature Extraction module [14] to delineate the imagery into objects based on similar spectral values, texture, and size, including the context of other neighboring objects. We developed a rule set based on the characteristics of objects that shared a common target classification to methodically classify objects into one of twelve possible target classes (Table 1). We then used the ENVI Edit Classification tool [15] to assess and correct the accuracies of the initial classifications [16]. Figure 2 displays the final feature classifications for the Muscutatuck and Camp Shelby sites. We used confusion matrices to measure the accuracies of the WV-2- and UAS-derived classification data; the classified data were highly accurate with Cohen's κ values of 0.94 and 0.97 for the Muscutatuck and Camp Shelby Sites.

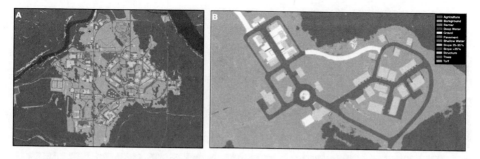

Fig. 2. Feature classification for (*A*) the Muscatatuck Urban Training Center and (*B*) Camp Shelby

2.3 Modified ACO Workflow

Identifying Edge Features and the 'Accessible Space'. The first step in our workflow is to analyze the imagery for sudden shifts in elevation that would be indicative of an artificial structure, trees, or sharp precipices, as well as identifying significant bodies of water. Image analysis was performed using the scikit-image library in Python [17]. We input the aligned first-return LIDAR data and the NIR images (Fig. 3). We then performed a logarithmic correction on the LIDAR imagery with a gain of 2 to increase the contrast. This was followed by edge detection in the corrected LIDAR image using the Canny edge detector ($\sigma = 1.375$). Simultaneously, we obtained the magnitude and orientation of image gradients with the Sobel filter, keeping only the magnitudes and orientations of gradients located on edges identified by the Canny detector. The remaining magnitudes were set to 0, and their associated orientations were saved for use in our modified ACO algorithm.

The array of edge-associated gradient magnitudes were then blurred with a Gaussian filter ($\sigma = 0.089$) to produce an 'influence map' of LIDAR edges on their immediate surroundings; a position surrounded by steep elevation shifts will have a larger influence value than a position in the middle of a featureless plain (Fig. 4). We then built a discrete cumulative distribution function from the values of each pixel in the influence map. A cumulative probability distribution can be constructed from these values, and we define the set of pixels associated with the bottom 90% of this distribution as "accessible space." Accessible space can therefore be interpreted as those regions of the image free of sudden elevation shifts, which would generally hinder mobility through the region.

Accessible space was further refined using NIR imagery to identify bodies of water in the study sites. This was achieved using pixel grayscale values (i.e., RGB color values, (c, c, c), with $c \in [0, 1]$) of $c < 0.15$ to indicate water. The intersection between the accessible space and water was removed from the accessible space identified from the influence map. Finally, we then found all accessible space connected components (regions in which any 2 labeled pixels are connected by a continuous chain of similarly labeled pixels) and removed those that were either very small (<400 pixels for the study site imagery) or did not reach

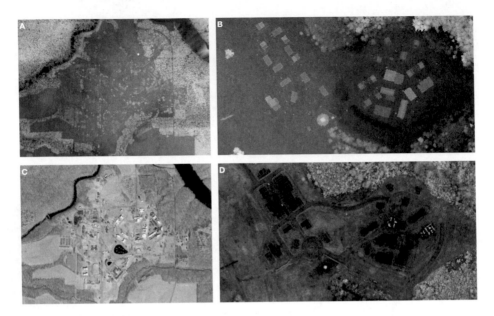

Fig. 3. First return LIDAR (*A&B*) and near-infrared imagery (*C&D*) for the Muscu-tatuck (*A&C*) and Camp Shelby (*B&D*) sites.

the image's border; for example, accessible space associated with building roofs. The remaining identified regions were saved to be used as input to our ACO algorithm.

Modified ACO Algorithm. Our modified ACO algorithm takes in data files containing the gradient orientations and magnitudes of the edges from the first-return LIDAR imagery, the accessible spaces, and bodies of water identified as described above. The edge gradient orientations are rounded to the nearest $\pi/4$ radians, so that they point toward one of the 8 immediate neighboring pixels.

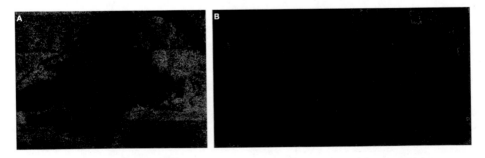

Fig. 4. Influence map of LIDAR edges on their immediate surroundings for Mus-catatuck (*A*) and Camp Shelby (*B*).

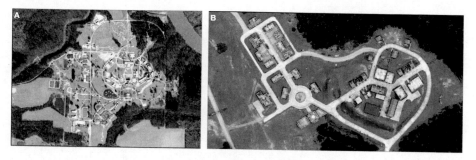

Fig. 5. Accessible spaces (red) identified for the Muscatatuck (A) and Camp Shelby (B) study sites. (Color figure online)

The pheromone map is initialized with a bias towards accessible space (initial pheromone = 10 units) over the rest of the terrain (initial pheromone = 1 unit).

We refer to an "ant" as an agent which navigates the image, but is also capable of modifying the pheromone state of any pixel it encounters. Ants are individually simulated, changing the pheromone state along its path to instruct future ants. Each ant is initially placed at a random location outside of the accessible space with uniform probability. Simulation time, $t_n = \sum_i^n \Delta t$, is the sum of all n previous time steps; at $t_0 = 0$, each of the 8 potential movement directions available to each ant (every $\pi/4$ from $[-\pi, \pi)$) is equally likely, with the exception of those that would transport the ant over water or beyond the image border. For each timestep $t_n > 0$, each ant observes all edges and their magnitudes (resultant from the Canny edge detection & Sobol filter method described above) within a vision box, centered on itself, with side-length of 4 pixels. The magnitude of each edge within this vision box, the sum of these magnitudes, and the two possible directions in which an edge may be pointing (the gradient's orientation $\pm\pi/2$) are recorded to memory. Each ant then adds the ratio of the magnitude of each edge to the sum of all edge magnitudes within its vision box to the weightings for each of the directions in which the edge is pointing. Finally, the ratio of the pheromone in the neighboring position for each direction to the sum of all pheromone in the 8 neighboring positions is also added to the weights of the respective directions. The weights are then normalized and used to determine the movement decision of the ant using a random number generator (See Fig. 6 for an example of the decision process).

The decision-making and movement process is repeated for the ant until it reaches the edge of the image. Once it reaches the edge, it revisits each location along its path and lays down 1 unit of pheromone for each unique position (a position visited multiple times receives the same amount of pheromone as a position visited once). The half of the pheromone above the initial amounts for each location is then removed, allowing paths least followed to dissipate. The algorithm then initializes a new ant and begins the exploration again until it reaches a preset number of ants (1000 ants in this work). The final pheromone map is output for the algorithm.

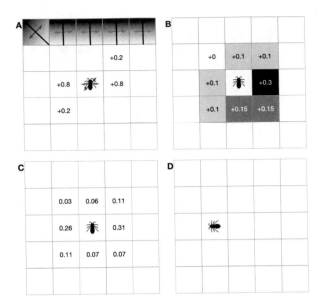

Fig. 6. An example of an ant judging its immediate environment and making a choice in movement. (*A*) The ant is able to see an edge ahead. The 5 segments of the edge have equal gradient magnitudes. The furthest left, however, is turned diagonally relative to the others (black arrows represent the orientation of the edge gradient). The influence of each edge segment on the ant's decision is marked for each destination. (*B*) The ant detects stronger pheromones to its right and behind it (darker gray representing stronger pheromones). The influence of the pheromones on the ant's decision is marked for each destination. (*C*) The probability of moving to any of the 8 potential neighboring positions, based on an even initial distribution of weight, modified by detected edges and pheromones. (*D*) The ant decides to move left based on a random number generator. The decision process repeats itself until the ant reaches the edge of the imaged area. (Color figure online)

Pheromone Smoothing and Comparison to Ground Truth. After the modified ACO is finished, we perform two more steps to the pheromone map to smooth the final output. First, we remove pheromones in the lower 12.5 percentile, ignoring paths laid by later ants that were not well traveled by others. Then we performed a median blur, where each pixel's pheromones is set to the median of the pheromones within a 5 × 5 pixel box centered on that pixel. At this point, any position with non-zero pheromone is counted as trafficable terrain (Fig. 7).

We contrasted the workflow's predicted trafficable terrain against the ground truth presented in Fig. 2. For each mode of transportation, we count terrain with a trafficability rating of 7 or greater as trafficable. We then do an element-wise contrast of the ground truth trafficable terrain to the trafficable terrain predicted by our modified ACO workflow.

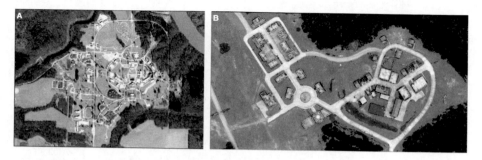

Fig. 7. Final results from the modified ACO workflow for Muscatatuck (*A*) and Camp Shelby (*B*). (Color figure online)

Table 2. Comparison of predicted trafficable terrain against ground truth

Study site	Metric	Soldier	ATV	Light truck	Heavy truck
Muscatatuck	Completeness	89.9%	89.9%	49.1%	84.2%
	Correctness	79.7%	79.7%	97.4%	13.5%
	F$_1$-score	84.5%	84.5%	65.3%	23.2%
Camp Shelby	Completeness	88.2%	88.2%	88.2%	94.3%
	Correctness	94.6%	94.6%	94.6%	16.9%
	F$_1$-score	91.3%	91.3%	91.3%	28.7%

We focused on three metrics to assess the quality of the results with regard to the ground truth for each mode of transportation: (1) the completeness, the fraction of trafficable segments correctly identified by the workflow, (2) the correctness, the fraction of predicted trafficable segments that are truly trafficable, and (3) the F$_1$-score, which integrates both completeness and correctness into a single measurement [8,9]. These measurements are defined mathematically:

$$\text{Completeness } (\%) \equiv 100 \times \frac{|TP|}{|TP| + |FN|},$$

$$\text{Correctness } (\%) \equiv 100 \times \frac{|TP|}{|TP| + |FP|}, \text{ and}$$

$$\text{F}_1\text{-score } (\%) \equiv 100 \times \frac{2 \cdot \text{Completeness} \cdot \text{Correctness}}{\text{Completeness} + \text{Correctness}},$$

where $|TP|$ is the number of true positive segments, $|FN|$ is the number of false negative segments, and $|FP|$ is the number of false positive segments.

3 Results

The stepwise results of the workflow on the Muscatatuck and Camp Shelby study sites are presented throughout the Methods section, ultimately returning the terrain highlighted in Fig. 7. The workflow's predictions cover a sizable portion of the terrain identified as trafficable for Soldiers and ATVs, and Heavy Trucks, while only predicting half of the potential terrain for Light Trucks in Muscatatuck (Table 2). This is likely due to false negatives in unpaved, open terrain, such as bare ground, gravel, or turf, over which Light Trucks can traverse whereas Heavy Trucks are limited to pavement.

The workflow's predictions in Muscatatuck demonstrate a high level of correctness for Soldiers, ATVs, and Light Trucks, indicating that the algorithm generally captures and identifies the trafficable terrain with a low number of false positives. The correctness is actually higher for Light Trucks than Soldiers and ATVs; with agriculture being the main difference in trafficability between these modes of transportation, this indicates a direction for future work towards improving predictions in farmland. The correctness of the predictions for Heavy Trucks are comparatively low. This, however, could easily be explained by the high number of false positives due to the nature of the algorithm to favor open, unpaved terrain.

The assessments of the algorithm's predictions present a similar results for the Camp Shelby study site. The predicted trafficable terrain generally includes a significant fraction of the observed trafficable terrain for all modes of transportation. The workflow, however, demonstrates a low level of correctness for the heavy truck. This is, once again, explainable by the algorithm's affinity for open, unpaved terrain.

4   Discussion and Conclusions

Existing methods fail to traverse open fields due to their reliance on visible edges and segments with obvious directionality, both of which are generally lacking in wide open spaces. The goal of this work was to expand upon previous approaches to applying the ACO algorithm to road identification from aerial imagery [8,9] to identify potentially trafficable terrain in peri-urban and rural locations. To this end, we present a workflow that first identifies the accessible space in a site based on near-infrared and first-return LIDAR data. The accessible space is used as an input to our modified ACO, in which an ant's movement resembles random diffusion in some aspects, allowing the ants to explore feature-less terrain. Our workflow performs well for Soldiers and ATVs, with F_1-scores of 94.5% and 91.3% for the Muscatatuck Urban Training Center and Camp Shelby study sites.

While the algorithm works well for Soldiers and ATVs, comparisons against terrains identified as potentially trafficable for Light and Heavy Trucks indicate areas in which there is room for improvement. The increase in the correctness of the predictions for Light Trucks in Muscatatuck indicate a higher number of false positives associated with agricultural land. On the flip-side, the differences in the completeness of the results suggest that the algorithm's exploration of bare ground, gravel, and turf could be improved further.

Ultimately, we describe here a workflow to use near-infrared and first-return LIDAR data to predict trafficable terrain in peri-urban and rural spaces. In its current form, the algorithm works relatively well for the study sites used. In the future, application of this workflow to other sites could provide crucial insights into improving and optimizing the algorithm for multiple modes of transportation.

Acknowledgments. Opinions, interpretations, conclusions, and recommendations are those of the author(s) and are not necessarily endorsed by the U.S. Army.

References

1. Dijkstra, E.W.: A note on two problems in connexion with graphs. Numerishe Math. **1**(1), 269–271 (1959). https://doi.org/10.1007/BF01386390
2. Danzig, G.B.: Linear Programming and Extensions. Princeton University Press, Princeton (1962)
3. Hart, P.E., Nilsson, N.J., Raphael, B.: A formal basis for the heuristic determination of minimum cost paths. IEEE Trans. Syst. Sci. Cybern. **4**(2), 100–107 (1968). https://doi.org/10.1109/TSSC.1968.300136
4. Meyer, U.: Single-source shortest-paths on arbitrary directed graphs in linear average-case time. In: 12th Symposium on Discrete Algorithms, pp. 797–806 (2001). https://doi.org/10.1145/365411.365784
5. Thorup, M.: Integer Priority queues with decrease key in constant time and the single soruce shortest paths problem. In: 35th ACM Symposium on Theory of Computing, pp. 149–158 (2003). https://doi.org/10.1016/j.jcss.2004.04.003
6. Goldbeter, A.V., Harrelson, C.: Computing the shortest path: A* meets graph theory. In: 16th ACM-SIAM Symposium on Discrete Algorithms, pp. 156–165. ACM Press, New York (2005)
7. Dorigo, M., Brattari, M.: Ant Colony Optimization. MIT Press, Cambridge (2004)
8. Yin, D., Du, S., Wang, S., Guo, Z.: A direction-guided ant colony optimization method for extraction of urban road information from very-high-resolution images. IEEE J. Sel. Top. Appl. Earth Obs. Remote Sen. **8**(10), 4785–4794 (2015). https://doi.org/10.1109/JSTARS.2015.2477097
9. Maboudi, M., Amini, J., Hahn, M., Saati, M.: Object-based road extraction from satellite images using ant colony optimization. Int. J. Remote Sens. **38**(1), 179–198 (2017). https://doi.org/10.1080/01431161.2016.1264026
10. Suir, G.M., Reif, M., Hammond, S., Jackson, S., Brodie, K.: Unmanned Aircraft Systems to Support Environmental Applications within USACE Civil Works. No. ERDC SR-18-3, U.S. Engineer Research and Development Center, Vicksburg, MS (2018)
11. Suir, G.M., Sasser, C.E.: Redistribution and impacts of nearshore berm sediments on the Chandeleur barrier islands, Louisiana. Ocean Coast. Manag. **168**, 103–115 (2018)
12. RedEdge by MicaSense. http://www.micasense.com/rededge/. Accessed 16 Apr 2019
13. Broussard III, W., Suir, G.M., Visser, J.M.: Unmanned Aircraft Systems (UAS) and Satellite Imagery Collections in a Coastal Intermediate Marsh to Determine the Land-Water Interface, Vegetation Types, and Normalized Difference Vegetation Index (NDVI) Values. No. ERDC/TN WRAP-18-1, U.S. Engineer Research and Development Center, Vicksburg, MS (2018)
14. ENVI: ENVI Field Guide - ENVI Feature Extraction Module User's Guide. ITT Visual Information Solutions, Boulder, CO (2008)

15. ENVI: ENVI Classification Tools. ITT Visual Information Solutions, Boulder, CO (2019) https://www.harrisgeospatial/docs/editclassificationimages.html
16. Suir, G.M., Jones, W.R., Garber, A.L., Gailani, J.Z: Landscape Evolution of the Oil Spill Mitigation Sand Bern in the Chandeleur Islands, Louisiana. No. ERDC-TR-16-15, US Army Engineer Research and Development Center, Vicksburg, MS (2016)
17. van der Walt, S., et al.: Scikit-image: image processing in Python. PeerJ **2**, e453 (2014). https://doi.org/10.7717/peerj.453

ST: Vision for Remote Sensing and Infrastructure Inspection

Concrete Crack Pixel Classification Using an Encoder Decoder Based Deep Learning Architecture

Umme Hafsa Billah, Alireza Tavakkoli[ID], and Hung Manh La[(✉)][ID]

University of Nevada, Reno, NV 89557, USA
hla@unr.edu
https://ara.cse.unr.edu

Abstract. Civil infrastructure inspection in hazardous areas such as underwater beams, bridge decks, etc., is a perilous task. In addition, other factors like labor intensity, time, etc. influence the inspection of infrastructures. Recent studies [11] represent that, an autonomous inspection of civil infrastructure can eradicate most of the problems stemming from manual inspection. In this paper, we address the problem of detecting cracks in the concrete surface. Most of the recent crack detection techniques use deep architecture. However, finding the exact location of crack efficiently has been a difficult problem recently. Therefore, a deep architecture is proposed in this paper, to identify the exact location of cracks. Our architecture labels each pixel as crack or non-crack, which eliminates the need for using any existing post-processing techniques in the current literature [5,11]. Moreover, acquiring enough data for learning is another challenge in concrete defect detection. According to previous studies, only 10% of an image contains edge pixels (in our case defected areas) [31]. We proposed a robust data augmentation technique to alleviate the need for collecting more crack image samples. The experimental results show that, with our method, significant accuracy can be obtained with very less sample of data. Our proposed method also outperforms the existing methods of concrete crack classification.

Keywords: Crack detection · Pixel labeling · Deep learning architecture · Data augmentation

1 Introduction

Modern transportation system consists of a variety of civil infrastructures such as roads, bridge decks, highways, etc. Potential defects or deterioration in these structures can lead to unwanted situation e.g., road accidents. Civil infrastructure inspection is an essential for ensuring a well performing transportation system. The main element of these structures, is concrete. Concrete is composed of an aggregate mixture of various type of rocks, limestone, clay, and water. This liquid paste is altogether known as cement. The cement hardens over time as

© Springer Nature Switzerland AG 2019
G. Bebis et al. (Eds.): ISVC 2019, LNCS 11844, pp. 593–604, 2019.
https://doi.org/10.1007/978-3-030-33720-9_46

water evaporates from the mixture. This leads to various type of deterioration such as cracking, spalling, abrasion, etc. Cracking in concrete occurs more frequently than any other defects. The cement of concrete suffers from cracking mostly in comparison to other defects. Shrinkage in concrete elements, expansion, overloading, heaving, chemical exposure, corrosion with metals infused in concretes, improper drying, etc is some of the most common reasons for concrete cracking.

The longevity and performance of civil infrastructure are immensely affected by the defects of the concrete. Moreover, rebuilding infrastructure is time-consuming, uneconomic as well as time-consuming. Thus, continuous inspection of concrete health is necessary for maintaining a fully functional transportation system.

Earlier civil infrastructure inspection was performed manually by experts. However, the time consuming and labor-intensive manner of such method necessitated autonomous inspection. Autonomous inspection robotic systems [11,16,20] integrated with various sensors e.g., non-destructive evaluation (NDE) sensors [13] and camera can access infrastructure location to collect NDE data and sample images, which are further processed for defect identification. Autonomous inspection systems can reach dangerous areas where it is unsafe for humans to reach. The less error-prone nature of the autonomous systems also made them a convenient technique to adopt for maintenance [10,14,15].

One of the main challenges in identifying concrete defect autonomously is to provide the machine with enough knowledge of unhealthy concrete. Therefore, the need for an extensive amount of concrete samples is undeniable. In addition, an efficient architecture that can extract distinguishing features of concrete defect is also necessary. Recently many studies have proposed many architectures or methods for extracting such features. In the remainder of this section we have elaborated about the recent works of concrete crack inspection, the challenges associated and our contribution to the research problem.

1.1 Literature Review

Concrete defect classification and localization have enticed the attention of the research community very recently. The state of the art image processing techniques e.g., thresholding [19,24,29], morphological operations [2,7,17,22,28,30] and edge detection algorithms [21,25,32], have been proven efficient for defect localization [5]. The most significant advantage of these approaches is the extraction of both local and global feature of crack location with less computational complexity. However, the extensive amount of noise (crack like areas) present in real-world images induces extraction of unnecessary feature points. 'These unnecessary feature points increase the number of falsely identified crack pixels. Moreover, perfect parameter selection is also a conundrum for these type of methods.

Since the machine learning architectures are adaptive to real-world situations, it is intuitive to use them for defect classification and localization. In this paper, we categorize the machine learning architectures into two divisions such as (a) shallow architectures and (b) deep architectures. Some of the shallow machine learning architectures in the literature, for defect classification are Support Vector Machines (SVM) [8,25,28], Adaboost [25], Multi-Layer Perceptron (MLP) [4]. The conundrum of selecting perfect parameter set is solved by these architectures. An accurate classification using these architectures, require a balanced data-set having uniform instances of both healthy and defected areas of concrete. However, recent studies show that defected pixels occur only 10% of the time in an image [31]. Thus, the scarcity of well-balanced instances of both classes significantly drops accuracy. On the other hand, the recent advent of deep architectures [18] in solving classification problem,

Since the deep architectures [18] achieved significant performance gain in image classification, some studies [3,5,6,11,12,27] used them for crack image classification. These approaches apply image processing techniques on the extracted crack blocks, to localize the cracks. However, the rate of false classification and parameter selection of image processing techniques affects the performance of crack localization. Moreover, the computational complexity, as well as the number of parameters of deep architectures increases as the network, goes deeper. The growing number of parameters degrades with a deeper layer which, drops the performance of the network. In addition, the deep architectures require an extensive amount of data to train the networks on. Collection and processing of such data-set are time-consuming and memory intensive.

1.2 Contributions

From the above discussion we postulate that the main challenges in concrete defects detection in previous studies are :

1. Generating distinguishing feature maps for crack and non-crack pixels with a deep architecture.
2. A deep architecture that is less affected by parameter degradation problem of deep architecture.
3. Generation of a balanced data-set with enough instances of both crack and non-crack pixels.

In this paper, we proposed a robust deep network architecture alleviating the effect of parameter degradation. Our architectures use a series of encoder and decoder to generate distinguishing feature descriptor for crack and non-crack class. Lastly, our data augmentation technique enables to generate a substantial amount of instances for training. The rest of the paper is organized as follows: Sect. 2 elaborately explains our Proposed architecture. In Sect. 3, we discuss our training process, data augmentation and results. Lastly, we conclude in Sect. 4.

2 Methodology

The deep network architectures eliminated the need for feature extraction using traditional image processing techniques. In this paper, we introduce an encoder-decoder based deep network architecture to extract definitive features of crack and non-crack pixels. There exists, a number of different encoder-decoder based deep convolutional network architectures in literature, such as, UNet [26], SegNet [1], DeconvNet [23], FCN [12] etc. These networks are designed for semantic segmentation of generic object classes in natural images, and therefore, are not quite suitable for crack detection. To address the generic nature of these networks, we have designed the Proposed network architecture inspired by the architecture of SegNet [1]. In this section, we briefly reviewed the architecture of SegNet and then discussed our proposed network architecture.

2.1 SegNet

The SegNet architecture is composed of five encoders and five decoders. The encoders consist of a series of convolution layers, followed by ReLu, Batch Normalization, and max-pooling layer. The first two encoders have three consecutive convolution layers with 64 and 128 filters of size 3×3 respectively. The remaining encoders are composed of two convolution layers with 256, 512 and 512 filters of size 3×3 respectively. The convolution operations are performed with 3×3 filters. Each max-pooling layer uses a 2×2 window with stride 2 to obtain translation in-variance as mentioned in [1]. The max pooled indices are stored in memory to use in their respective decoder. Each decoder consists of a bilinear upsampling layer, followed by the convolution, ReLu, Batch Normalization layers using the same convention as their corresponding encoder layers. The upsampling operations are performed using memorized pool indices from the max-pooling layers. The SegNet architecture does not add a fully connected layer at the end of the network. Alternatively, it maps the output of the decoder layer to the softmax layer and assigns a label to each pixel.

2.2 Proposed Architecture

SegNet architecture uses a 3×3 window for the convolution operations in the encoder layers. Performing convolution operation with smaller windows causes significant boundary information loss. Since the pixels in a crack location are connected, such information loss has an enormous effect on classification. For example, if a $256 \times 256 \times 3$ (196,608 pixels)image is convolved with eight filters of size 3×3, a feature map of size $128 \times 128 \times 8$ (131,072 pixels)is generated. The reduced feature map on this particular operation loses the information of 65,536 pixels. The deeper the network goes, the more pixel information is lost. Our proposed network architecture accumulates for this lost pixel values in SegNet.

Since significant feature information is lost during the convolution process of each encoder, we have added a side output function [31] to each encoder. The side output function accommodates for the feature loss in each encoding operation. The side output function takes the output feature map of its corresponding encoder layer and up-samples it to original size. To up-sample the feature maps to its original size, we use a transposed convolution operation, followed by sigmoid activation. Since the transposed convolution includes learn-able parameters, it feeds the network with more information about the feature space. Our Proposed

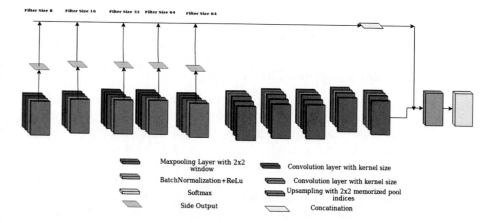

Fig. 1. Proposed architecture for detecting pixels

network architecture is shown in Fig. 1. The side outputs from each encoder layer are concatenated together in the final layer. The output of the merged layer is passed to a convolution layer with filter size 1. The number of filters in the final convolution layer is the number of desired classes. A softmax layer is added at the end of the convolution layers.

2.3 Data Augmentation

The deep network architectures require a balanced data-set with enough instances of each class. In this section, we discuss our data augmentation technique which alleviates the need to collect the huge number of data instances.

The deep network architecture proposed in this paper labels each pixel as crack or non-crack. Thus, a pixel map of each training sample from the original data set is generated manually. We define a pixel map as a binary image of the same size as the training sample images. Each pixel in the pixel map is assigned a value. The crack pixels in the original image are assigned the value 1 in the pixel map. The non-crack pixels are assigned the value 0.

Our data augmentation method generates thousands of sub-sample from a single image sample and its pixel map. We take each image randomly from our data set. At first, A random center position (x, y) is generated for that image. Then we sub-sample an image and its corresponding pixel map of height h and width w from the large image. After that, it is randomly decided if the image and its pixel map should be flipped (horizontally or vertically). Lastly, we perform gamma correction on the image randomly.

3 Experiment Results

We performed multiple experiments to train and evaluate our method. We compared our method with recent crack detection architectures in literature. In this section, we elaborately discussed our experimental setup, comparison with different methods and result interpretation.

3.1 Experimental Setup and Parameters

We optimized our proposed network architecture with Adam optimizer with a constant learning rate of 0.001. Since we have only two classes, a binary cross-entropy loss was used. It was trained for 100 episodes on a 1080Tx GPU.

We collected our data using an autonomous robotic system with NDE sensor fusion method [11] from various roads and bridges. These images contain many noises such as oil spilling, paint, stones, strips from tire screeching and many more. To generate the pixel map of each image we used Gimp software. To train our method we have generated pixel maps 33 large resolution images of $2304 \times 3456 \times 3$ (height $\times$ width $\times$ channel).

Using our data augmentation technique we have generated 5000 sub-sampled images of size 512×512 (height $\times$ width) for training and 1000 images of size 512×512 (height $\times$ width) for validation from the large resolution images of the database. In each episode of training, a different set of 6000 images (training + validation) is generated. We evaluated the performance of our network with recent deep architectures for crack classification. At first, we compared our results with the image block classification method [9,11] to demonstrate the nature of the segmentation problem affecting crack detection. Since the proposed network architecture labels pixel and uses an encoder-decoder architecture, we have also compared our results with recent encoder-decoder architecture for pixel-level labeling such as Unet [26], SegNet [1].

3.2 Comparative Analysis

For evaluation, we generated 200 images of size $1024 \times 1024 \times 3$ (height $\times$ width $\times$ channel) from our validation data set using our data augmentation technique. In this section, we elaborately explained the quantitative and qualitative results on different architectures based on our data-set.

Quantitative Comparisons. For evaluating our Proposed network architecture, we have taken into account different state-of-the-art statistical measurements such as true positive, false positive, true negative, false negative, accuracy, error rate, specificity, precision, recall, and F-1 score. We defined the crack pixels as the positive class and non-crack pixels as the negative class.

Thus, true positive (TP) is defined as the number of correctly detected crack pixels. True negative (TN) is defined as the number of pixels detected as non-crack that are labeled non-crack pixels in the ground truth. False-positive (FP) is the number of pixels that are erroneously detected as crack pixels. Finally, False negative (FN) is the number of crack pixels detected as non-crack pixels. A summary of the evaluation results performed on different methods are shown in Table 1.

Table 1. Quantitative Comparisons of the Proposed Network Architecture with Existing Crack Detection Methods.

Method	TP%	FP%	TN%	FN%	Acc.$^\diamond$	E.R.*	Spc.§	Prec.†	Rec.‡	F-1*
Gibbs [11]	25.2	23.0	77.0	25.2	76.9	23.1	77.0	0.004	0.25	0.007
Unet [26]	53.5	1.3	98.7	46.5	98.6	1.4	98.7	12.9	53.5	20.8
SegNet^1 [1]	55.4	1.3	98.7	44.6	98.5	1.5	98.7	13.2	55.4	21.3
SegNet^2 [1]	55.1	1.3	98.7	44.9	98.6	1.4	98.7	13.5	55.1	21.7
Proposed^1	56.1	**1.1**	**98.9**	43.9	**98.7**	**1.3**	**98.9**	**15.3**	56.1	**24.1**
Proposed^2	**57.2**	1.3	98.7	**42.8**	98.5	1.5	98.7	13.1	**57.2**	21.4

1: Conv-Layer Sizes (8-16-32-64-64)

2: Conv-Layer Sizes (16-32-64-128-128)

TP: True Positive, FP: False Positive, TN: True Negative, FN: False Negative

$\diamond$: Accuracy=$\frac{TP+TN}{TP+FP+TN+FN}$ $*$: Error Rate=$\frac{FP+FN}{TP+FP+TN+FN}$

$\S$: Specificity=$\frac{TN}{TN+FP}$ $\dagger$: Precision=$\frac{TP}{TP+FP}$

$\ddagger$: Recall=$\frac{TP}{TP+FN}$ $\star$: F-1 Measure=$2 \times \frac{Pre.\times Rec.}{Pre.+Rec.}$

In Table 1 we compared our results with both block-wise crack detection and pixel-wise crack detection techniques from the recent literature. The block detection method [11] under-performs than all the other existing pixel labeling method. The false-positive rate of this method is much higher than the other methods. Moreover, each detected crack block is a mixture of crack and non-crack pixels. This makes the block detection method to suffer from unacceptably high false positive, false negative and error rates compared to pixel labeling methods. It is evident from these measures, that a model with such a high error rate is not feasible for any classification.

We also compared our method with recent pixel classification methods from the literature, such as SegNet [1] and UNet [26]. For uniform comparison, we have employed two filter banks of size (8-16-32-64-64) and (16-32-64-128-128) for SegNet and our Proposed Architecture. The Unet architecture is designed with a regular number of filter banks of VGG-16, which is (64-128-256-512-512).

The SegNet^1 architecture uses a fewer number of filters compared to Unet, which reduces the number of learning parameters. The SegNet^1 architecture achieves more true positive rate, precision, recall and F1 score in comparison to Unet [26]. The false-positive rate, true negative rate, specificity measures are similar in both SegNet^1 and UNet. It under-performs than Unet in case of false-negative rate and error rate. Therefore, we can deduce that the SegNet^1 architecture acceptable in terms of less computational complexity and slightly better result than Unet.

The SegNet^2 model uses filter bank of size (16-32-64-128-128), which is larger than SegNet^1 but smaller than Unet. SegNet^2 achieves higher true positive rate, precision and F1 score than both Unet and SegNet^1. It has a similar false-positive rate, true negative rate, specificity measures with both SegNet^1 and

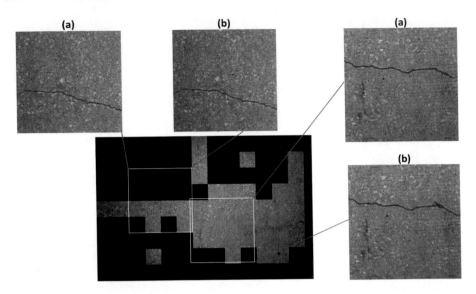

Fig. 2. Qualitative comparison of the proposed method with Gibbs [11] block detection architecture. The result shown in the middle is the crack detection using the Gibbs method, while (a) shows the pixels-wise crack detection results of the Proposed[1] architecture, and (b) shows the results of the Proposed[2] architecture on two random 1024×1024 sub-regions of the original image.

Unet. It reduces the error rate of SegNet[1], which is higher than Unet. In addition, it improves the accuracy in comparison to SegNet[1]. However, the higher false-negative rate and lower recall rate in comparison to SegNet[1] represent the effect of gradient degradation. Though the overall method shows higher F1 score than the previous methods, this method is not suitable for crack classification considering the degradation of gradient problem.

The Proposed[1] architecture shows significant performance gain in all of the statistical measure. It achieves more true positive rate, false-positive rate, true negative rate, accuracy, specificity, precision, F-1 score and less error rate, the false-negative rate in comparison to SegNet[1], SegNet[2] and Unet.

To reveal the effect of parameter degradation in our architecture we have experimented our architecture by increasing the filter bank to (16-32-64-128-128). The Proposed[2] architectures achieve more true positive rate, recall rate and less false-negative rate than all the previous methods in Table 1. However, because of parameter degradation the error rate increases as well as the accuracy drops. Therefore, we can deduce that the Proposed[1] architecture is more suitable for crack pixel classification in comparison to other recent methods. Moreover, the Proposed[2] architecture is less affected by the gradient degradation problem in comparison to SegNet[2].

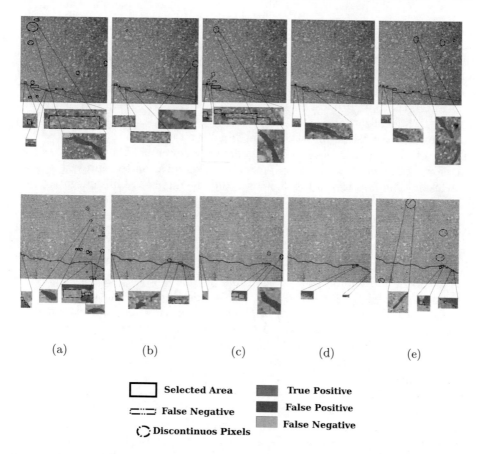

(a)   (b)   (c)   (d)   (e)

☐ Selected Area	■ True Positive
⊏╌╌⊐ False Negative	■ False Positive
◯ Discontinuos Pixels	■ False Negative

Fig. 3. Qualitative comparison of the proposed method with the state-of-the-art: (a) Unet [26]. (b) Segnet[1]. (c) Segnet[2]. (d) Proposed[1] Architecture. (e) Proposed[2] Architecture

It is worth noting that crack pixels exist in such small numbers, considering the vast majority of pixels in an image being normal. This makes the evaluation result biased toward the effective detection of non-crack pixels. To accommodate for this bias, we do not solely, rely on true positive rates. Instead, better measures of the unbiased performance of the crack detection methods are the accuracy, and the Error Rate, shown in Table 1. As observed from the table, both of the proposed methods outperform the existing techniques from the literature, while the Proposed[1] shows the highest Accuracy and lowest Error Rate.

Qualitative Comparisons. In this section, we have discussed the comparative results on sample images from our validation data set. We have shown comparative results from both block detection methods and pixel classification methods.

In Fig. 2 the comparative result of block detection method and our proposed method is shown. The Gibbs [11] architecture, divides an image into smaller sub-blocks of size 256×256. Each block is identified as crack and non-crack. The non-crack blocks are labeled as black in the image. Moreover, we have shown some results from the Proposed architecture on the same block. It is evident from Fig. 3, that our Proposed[1] architecture outperforms Gibbs [11] method in case of crack localization.

Figure 3 shows the result of different pixel-level classification methods. The number of crack pixels occurs are significantly lower than non-crack pixels. Therefore, we zoomed out some of our crack pixel location to represent a more clear result. The first row in Fig. 3, shows that the number of false-negative pixels in the same area is higher in Unet. It is reduced in both SegNet[1] and SegNet[2] architecture. However, in the same area, our Proposed[1] architecture significantly reduces the number of false-negative pixels in comparison to SegNet[1], SegNet[2] and Unet. The Proposed[2] have more false-negative pixels than Proposed[1] but it has less false negative pixels than the other previous architectures.

One of the most important observations in this study is, the pixel labeling method is affected by pixel discontinuity. We define pixel discontinuity is the detection of the anomalous length of pixels (not continuous pixels as crack) as cracks. These discontinuous pixels are the effect of gradient degradation. The discontinuous pixels are shown by the circled area in Fig. 3.

Our results show that the Proposed[1] architecture removes most of these discontinuous pixels significantly. From Figure 3, we can see that the Unet architecture have many discontinuous pixels. SegNet[1] and SegNet[2] reduces the length and number of these pixels. On the other hand, the discontinuous pixels affect the Proposed[1] architecture very little. Moreover, the Proposed[2] architecture have some discontinuous pixels (last image of row 2). However, the length of the discontinuous pixels is reduced in comparison to Unet. In addition, it has more true-positive pixels in comparison to Unet and SegNet architecture.

4   Conclusions and Future Work

We presented in this paper, a deep convolutional network architecture while accommodating for the feature loss. Our architecture shows that with a limited number of filters we can alleviate the feature loss. The main motivation of this work is to design an efficient crack detection system for civil infrastructure inspection. Our method also shows significant improvement over existing methods. Moreover, we presented data augmentation techniques, which can significantly improve the performance of any architecture. On the contrary, our architecture consumes more memory because of its large number of parameters. In the future, we would optimize the memory structure as well as achieve better performance.

References

1. Badrinarayanan, V., Handa, A., Cipolla, R.: Segnet: A deep convolutional encoder-decoder architecture for robust semantic pixel-wise labelling. arXiv preprint arXiv:1505.07293 (2015)
2. Bai, X., Zhou, F., Xue, B.: Multiple linear feature detection based on multiple-structuring-element center-surround top-hat transform. Appl. Opt. **51**(21), 5201–5211 (2012)
3. Billah, U.H., La, H.M., Tavakkoli, A., Gucunski, N.: Classification of concrete crack using deep residual network. In: 9th International Conference on Structural Health Monitoring of Intelligent Infrastructure (SHMII-9), pp. 1–6, August 2019
4. Bray, J., Verma, B., Li, X., He, W.: A neural network based technique for automatic classification of road cracks. In: 2006 International Joint Conference on Neural Networks, IJCNN 2006, pp. 907–912. IEEE (2006)
5. Cha, Y.J., Choi, W., Büyüköztürk, O.: Deep learning-based crack damage detection using convolutional neural networks. Comput. Aided Civil Infrastruct. Eng. **32**(5), 361–378 (2017)
6. Dinh, T.H., Ha, Q., La, H.M.: Computer vision-based method for concrete crack detection. In: 2016 14th International Conference on Control, Automation, Robotics and Vision (ICARCV), pp. 1–6. IEEE (2016)
7. Elbehiery, H., Hefnawy, A., Elewa, M.: Surface defects detection for ceramic tiles using image processing and morphological techniques (2005)
8. Gavilán, M., et al.: Adaptive road crack detection system by pavement classification. Sensors **11**(10), 9628–9657 (2011)
9. Gibb, S., La, H.M., Louis, S.: A genetic algorithm for convolutional network structure optimization for concrete crack detection. In: 2018 IEEE Congress on Evolutionary Computation (CEC), pp. 1–8, July 2018
10. Gibb, S., Le, T., La, H.M., Schmid, R., Berendsen, T.: A multi-functional inspection robot for civil infrastructure evaluation and maintenance. In: 2017 IEEE/RSJ International Conference on Intelligent Robots and Systems (IROS), pp. 2672–2677, September 2017
11. Gibb, S., La, H.M., Le, T., Nguyen, L., Schmid, R., Pham, H.: Nondestructive evaluation sensor fusion with autonomous robotic system for civil infrastructure inspection. J. Field Rob. **35**(6), 988–1004 (2018)
12. Krizhevsky, A., Sutskever, I., Hinton, G.E.: ImageNet classification with deep convolutional neural networks. In: Advances in neural information processing systems, pp. 1097–1105 (2012)
13. La, H.M., Gucunski, N., Kee, S.H., Nguyen, L.: Data analysis and visualization for the bridge deck inspection and evaluation robotic system. Vis. Eng. **3**(1), 1–16 (2015)
14. La, H.M., Gucunski, N., Kee, S.-H., Yi, J., Senlet, T., Nguyen, L.: Autonomous robotic system for bridge deck data collection and analysis. In: 2014 IEEE/RSJ International Conference on Intelligent Robots and Systems, pp. 1950–1955, September 2014
15. La, H.M.: Mechatronic systems design for an autonomous robotic system for high-efficiency bridge deck inspection and evaluation. IEEE/ASME Trans. Mechatron. **18**(6), 1655–1664 (2013)
16. La, H.M., Gucunski, N., Dana, K., Kee, S.H.: Development of an autonomous bridge deck inspection robotic system. J. Field Rob. **34**(8), 1489–1504 (2017)

17. Landstrom, A., Thurley, M.J.: Morphology-based crack detection for steel slabs. IEEE J. Sel. Top. Signal process. **6**(7), 866–875 (2012)

18. LeCun, Y., Bengio, Y., Hinton, G.: Deep learning. Nature **521**(7553), 436 (2015)

19. Li, Q., Liu, X.: Novel approach to pavement image segmentation based on neighboring difference histogram method. In: 2008 Congress on Image and Signal Processing, CISP 2008, vol. 2, pp. 792–796. IEEE (2008)

20. Lim, R.S., La, H.M., Shan, Z., Sheng, W.: Developing a crack inspection robot for bridge maintenance. In: 2011 IEEE International Conference on Robotics and Automation, pp. 6288–6293, May 2011

21. Lim, R.S., La, H.M., Sheng, W.: A robotic crack inspection and mapping system for bridge deck maintenance. IEEE Trans. Autom. Sci. Eng. **11**(2), 367–378 (2014)

22. Maode, Y., Shaobo, B., Kun, X., Yuyao, H.: Pavement crack detection and analysis for high-grade highway. In: 2007 8th International Conference on Electronic Measurement and Instruments, ICEMI 2007, pp. 4–548. IEEE (2007)

23. Noh, H., Hong, S., Han, B.: Learning deconvolution network for semantic segmentation. In: Proceedings of the IEEE International Conference on Computer Vision, pp. 1520–1528 (2015)

24. Oliveira, H., Correia, P.L.: Automatic road crack segmentation using entropy and image dynamic thresholding. In: 2009 17th European Conference on Signal Processing, pp. 622–626. IEEE (2009)

25. Prasanna, P., Dana, K., Gucunski, N., Basily, B.: Computer-vision based crack detection and analysis. In: Sensors and Smart Structures Technologies for Civil, Mechanical, and Aerospace Systems 2012, vol. 8345, p. 834542. International Society for Optics and Photonics (2012)

26. Ronneberger, O., Fischer, P., Brox, T.: U-Net: convolutional networks for biomedical image segmentation. In: Navab, N., Hornegger, J., Wells, W.M., Frangi, A.F. (eds.) MICCAI 2015. LNCS, vol. 9351, pp. 234–241. Springer, Cham (2015). https://doi.org/10.1007/978-3-319-24574-4_28

27. Simonyan, K., Zisserman, A.: Very deep convolutional networks for large-scale image recognition. arXiv preprint arXiv:1409.1556 (2014)

28. Sun, Y., Salari, E., Chou, E.: Automated pavement distress detection using advanced image processing techniques. In: 2009 IEEE International Conference on Electro/Information Technology, EIT 2009, pp. 373–377. IEEE (2009)

29. Sy, N., Avila, M., Begot, S., Bardet, J.C.: Detection of defects in road surface by a vision system. In: 2008 14th IEEE Mediterranean Electrotechnical Conference, MELECON 2008, pp. 847–851. IEEE (2008)

30. Tanaka, N., Uematsu, K.: A crack detection method in road surface images using morphology. MVA **98**, 17–19 (1998)

31. Xie, S., Tu, Z.: Holistically-nested edge detection. In: Proceedings of the IEEE International Conference on Computer Vision, pp. 1395–1403 (2015)

32. Zhao, H., Qin, G., Wang, X.: Improvement of canny algorithm based on pavement edge detection. In: 2010 3rd International Congress on Image and Signal Processing. vol. 2, pp. 964–967. IEEE (2010)

A Geometry-Based Method
for the Spatio-Temporal Detection
of Cracks in 4D-Reconstructions

Carl Matthes[(✉)], Adrian Kreskowski, and Bernd Froehlich

Virtual Reality and Visualization Research Group,
Bauhaus-Universität Weimar, Weimar, Germany
`carl-feofan.matthes@uni-weimar.de`

Abstract. We present a novel geometry-based approach for the detection of small-scale cracks in a temporal series of 3D-reconstructions of concrete objects such as pillars and beams of bridges and other infrastructure. The detection algorithm relies on a geometry-derived coloration of the 3D surfaces for computing the optical flow between time steps. Our filtering technique identifies cracks based on motion discontinuities in the local crack neighborhood. This approach avoids using the material color which is likely to change over time due to weathering and other environmental influences. In addition, we detect and exclude regions with significant local changes in geometry over time e.g. due to vegetation. We verified our method with reconstructions of a horizontal concrete beam under increasing vertical load at the center. For this case, where the main crack direction is known and a precise registration of the beam geometries over time exists, this approach produces accurate crack detection regardless of substantial color variations and is also able to mask out regions with simulated growth of vegetation over time.

1 Introduction

A timely, accurate and reliable detection of damages of built infrastructure is essential to prevent potential failure and increased costs for maintenance and repair. While monitoring of buildings, bridges and other infrastructure objects by various acquisition and 3D reconstruction technologies is slowly becoming feasible (e.g. [1,2]), the algorithmic detection of damages such as small-scale cracks is difficult due to changes of the radiometric properties of surfaces under varying lighting conditions, weathering and other environmental influences.

In this work, we developed a crack detection pipeline that relies on at least two 3D-reconstructions of a real-world object from two different points in time. In a first step, we replace the radiometric information of the surfaces by a

Electronic supplementary material The online version of this chapter (https://doi.org/10.1007/978-3-030-33720-9_47) contains supplementary material, which is available to authorized users.

G. Bebis et al. (Eds.): ISVC 2019, LNCS 11844, pp. 605–618, 2019.
https://doi.org/10.1007/978-3-030-33720-9_47

geometry-derived color, which is based on a local geometric feature invariant under transformations as well as large-scale non-rigid deformations. We establish correspondences between the two time steps through means of optical flow [3] and search for motion discontinuities which may correspond to cracks. We also developed a novel geometric descriptor which helps to identify incorrect correspondences between time steps and allows us to exclude regions that are subject to geometric occlusions e.g. by vegetation. In our current implementation, a precise registration of the geometry over time is required and the main crack direction has to be known or manually found.

Our work is inspired by Chaudhury et al. [4] who suggested to find cracks by exploiting local discontinuities in 2D optical flow along the crack line. Their approach relies on a sequence of images that are acquired under constant lighting conditions and, in their use case, in rapid succession. It is our goal to develop an approach for outdoor environments where radiometric variations of the material due to weathering and lighting conditions as well as occlusions caused by the growth of vegetation are common side effects of longer time spans between acquisitions. In related work, the often image-based crack detection approaches commonly attempt to reduce the amount of false positive matches arising from these real-world influences by a posteriori filtering or connected component analysis. However, substantial detection disturbances cannot easily be removed in postprocessing and impose obstacles on the applicability of image-based methods. Therefore, we argue that in many cases the color of the material is not ideally suited for detecting small-scale cracks.

Our geometry-based crack detection approach is centered around the following contributions:

- the development of a local geometric feature to be used in optical flow computations that performs similarly well as the surface color of 3D objects made from concrete if no radiometric changes are present but remains to enable the robust detection of correspondences with radiometric variations when color-based optical flow estimations fail
- an efficient verification of uncertain correspondences in 3D optical flow caused by occlusions using a novel SSIM-based geometric descriptor for point clouds
- a sparse voxel octree-based filtering approach for the detection of small-scale cracks which operates on material displacement, rather than the color offset of the cracks themselves

We integrated all proposed techniques into a framework for the spatio-temporal detection of cracks in a temporal series of large point clouds and demonstrated their effectiveness with 3D-reconstructions of a horizontal concrete beam under increasing vertical load at the center.

2   Related Work

With few exceptions, the detection of cracks has been driven by image-based methods in the past. Combinations of percolation [5,6], genetic programming [7] and, more recently, machine learning [8,9] have been applied successfully to detect and measure minuscule-scale cracks in single images. Advances have been made to produce crack detection from image sequences. Benning et al. [10] first proposed to compute deformation of material under stress using photogrammetry. Since then, a number of researchers employed digital image correlation (DIC) to detect micro-scale cracks in 2D displacement fields [11–14].

More recently, Chaudhury et al. [4] suggested the detection of early stage cracks in image sequences by filtering for discontinuities in optical flow. Similar to DIC-based methods, their approach relies on the surface color of concrete material and is not ideally suited for outdoor environments, when radiometric variations over time other than those along cracks are significant. In addition, potential occlusions over time in photo sequences can lead to an unreliable image-based detection of cracks and were left unattended in previous work.

Detection disturbances caused by uneven illumination and shadows in images have been addressed in previous work. Qu et al. [15] eliminate detection noise through percolation processing of images while Li et al. [16] improve detection performance by predicting per-pixel crack probabilities through convolutional neural networks. We propose a distinct and novel approach to perform the crack detection, which is particularly robust against variations of material color, shadows and illumination.

We establish correspondences between two point clouds through means of optical flow. Optical flow estimation is a technique for computing relative motion in image sequences. Especially global methods [3] are useful for the dense and accurate determination of non-rigid displacements. We utilize a GPU-accelerated implementation of a coarse-to-fine variational optical flow algorithm [17] and store the resulting motion information in an auxiliary data structure based on sparse voxel octrees (SVO) [18].

3   Detection of Small-Scale Cracks

For the autonomous localization of structural risks on a regular basis, we analyze geometric deformations over time to inform crack detection. Regular 3D acquisition and reconstruction of built infrastructure enables the detection and observation of geometric deformations and changes of the surface since references from the past are available.

In this work, a 3D-reconstruction at a point in time t is represented by a point cloud C_t which is constituted by points residing on surfaces of the reconstructed object. Each point is associated with a color and a normal vector. We detect the formation of small-scale cracks over time by filtering for discontinuities in geometric deformations between C_t and a second point cloud $C_{t+\delta}$, which was acquired at a later point in time.

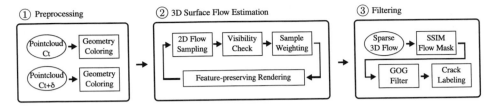

Fig. 1. Overview of our proposed crack detection pipeline.

Figure 1 depicts an overview of our proposed crack detection pipeline. In a preprocessing step, we derive geometric features from both point clouds to establish a basis for optical flow estimation between our data sets. Next, we compute 2D optical flow [17] for a set of viewing points onto the point clouds and combine coinciding samples through a weighted blending based on surface normals and viewing directions to obtain a 3D surface flow field. The 3D surface flow field describes the displacement between surface points in C_t to corresponding positions in $C_{t+\delta}$. Finally, we filter the 3D surface flow to detect motion discontinuities, which correspond to cracks residing on the surface. The detected cracks are already registered into the coordinate system of the two input point clouds for subsequent analysis.

Initially, we replace per-point radiometric information with a geometry-based coloring, which is introduced in Sect. 4. For the 3D surface flow estimation, we synthesize renderings of both point clouds from predefined viewing points generated from the camera extrinsics used for the structure-from-motion-based 3D reconstruction of both point clouds. At each viewing point, we compute 2D optical flow between the two data sets and combine coinciding optical flow samples from all viewing points to estimate an accurate 3D surface flow. The estimation of 3D surface flow is presented in Sect. 5. In a postprocessing step, we verify the established correspondences by considering the geometric similarity in both point clouds using a novel SSIM-based descriptor. To produce our crack labeling, we determine a suitable filter orientation locally and convolve the 3D surface flow using a Gradient of Gaussian kernel. Section 6 describes our postprocessing and filtering in detail. The detection accuracy of the proposed pipeline is evaluated in Sect. 7.

4 Geometry-Based Coloring

The material color is often not ideal for detecting small-scale cracks, as radiometric variations due to weather and lighting conditions, graffiti or markings are frequent side effects of longer periods between acquisitions and can cause detection problems. In addition, vegetation growing in the vicinity of concrete surfaces introduces geometric occlusions which may inhibit detection even in areas where cracks remain visible otherwise.

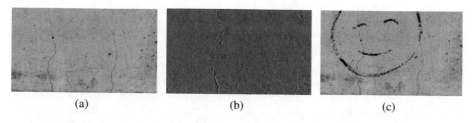

Fig. 2. In previous work, the detection of cracks is based purely on the color of the material (a). We propose to replace the original material colors by a geometry-based artificial coloring (b), which allows us to perform crack detection even in the presence of severe radiometric disturbances (c) that would otherwise introduce a considerable amount of false positive matches and therefore result in unreliable crack detection.

To mitigate these limitations, we replace per-point RGB information with a local geometric recoloring which is not influenced by uneven illumination, shadows or dirt and therefore well-suited to inform the detection of cracks. The geometry-based coloring should be invariant under transformations as well as large-scale non-rigid deformations of our data sets over time. Per-point surface normals provide a suitable starting point for our feature. We compute a best-fitting plane through a sufficiently large neighborhood $p_i \in C_t$, $|x - p_i| < \varepsilon$ of any point x and replace the color associated with point x by a gray-scale value based on $n_x^T n_{plane}$, where n_x and n_{plane} are the normals of point x and the plane respectively. Contrast stretching improves the saliency of the feature and leads to a better utilization of the available color range.

Figure 2 depicts our recoloring of a point cloud alongside the original material color for comparison. This pseudo-coloring is exclusively based on a local deviation from planarity of surface normals and enables the estimation of accurate 3D surface flow which is not disturbed by radiometric variations between the point clouds over time.

5   3D Surface Flow Estimation

In our approach, the 3D surface flow serves two purposes. Firstly, it allows us to infer correspondences of points on object surfaces in the presence of non-rigid displacements between our data sets. Secondly, we exploit motion discontinuities alongside crack boundaries to inform our crack detection. Thus, our detection is not based on the color offset of the cracks themselves as in most previous work, but on the displacements of the surrounding material. This is advantageous, because crack detection based on color offset can lead to false positives in outdoor areas, e.g. discoloration due to rust may be classified as a crack.

Since our data sets consist of points residing on object surfaces, we require 3D flow information only for those regions which contain surfaces. Therefore, we do not apply a global variational optical flow algorithm in three dimensions directly. Instead, we estimate the optical flow in 2D, and project the flow vectors back onto the 3D surfaces. The resulting representation can then be filtered in three dimensions to obtain crack labels in the coordinate system of the two input point clouds. We use an auxiliary sparse voxel octree (SVO) [18] to store and validate the computed 3D surface flow in a discretized space. The SVOs spatial resolution is based on the local point density such that it is high close to surfaces and low in empty regions. This representation also allows for adaptive precision when filtering for discontinuities.

To compute a 3D surface flow between two point clouds, we sample both data sets from the set of viewing points used for 3D-reconstruction, which guarantees that all surfaces are covered. First, we render both data sets in two separate passes and use a GPU-accelerated optical flow implementation to determine the 2D flow between our point clouds as seen by a virtual camera positioned and oriented according to a specific extrinsic at a time. The synthesized images used for the estimation of optical flow are based on the artificial recoloring presented in Sect. 4. Then, we project each leaf-level voxel corresponding to point cloud C_t onto the image plane of the current view and interpolate the optical flow at this position. Next, we add the estimated motion vector and unproject the resulting position using the depth buffer corresponding to $C_{t+\delta}$. Thus, we obtain two world positions residing on the surface of the two data sets and the vector connecting them contributes to the per-voxel 3D surface flow. The flow contributions of flow samples from all viewing points are weighted into the adaptive SVO data structure based on the cosine similarity between the current viewing direction and the surface normal at the voxel under consideration, which has the effect of weighting samples taken from viewing directions orthogonal to the local surface higher than oblique ones. For each viewing point, we prevent the sampling of flow for voxels which are occluded by other parts of the data set by intersecting a ray connecting the voxel center and the viewing point with the SVO data-structure.

In our system, the 3D points are rendered as oriented, circular surfels [19] to approximate a closed surface. We achieve a high feature preservation by blending overlapping surfels smoothly using a 2-pass surface splatting approach [20]. For this purpose, we estimate the radii of all surfels such that a visually watertight surface is constructed.

Our data sets consist of hundreds of millions of colored points and their memory footprint can exceed the gigabyte-range. To scale our pipeline to very large, highly-detailed 3D data sets, we suggest a level-of-detail (LOD) approach similar to Goswami et al. [21], designed to effectively reduce the amount of data persistent in memory while optimizing the resolution of the data set for each viewing point. Alternatively, it is possible to split large point clouds into several overlapping sub point clouds before processing.

6   Post-processing and Filtering

Optical flow is prone to artifacts arising from geometric occlusions in particular and therefore, geometric changes in close proximity of the concrete surface (e.g. growth of vegetation) cause unreliable optical flow estimations. To reliably prevent false positive matches caused by erroneous correspondences, we propose to mask out regions where correspondences are uncertain by exploiting geometric information available in our point cloud reconstructions.

6.1   Masking of Uncertain Correspondences

For any 3D surface flow sample s, we compare the geometric and radiometric similarities of two regions $C_t(x)$ and $C_{t+\delta}(x')$ in our point clouds, where $x' = x + s$. We consider the regions similar if $C_{t+\delta}(x') \approx C_t(x)$ according to a suitable similarity measure.

Previous work has invented a number of geometric descriptors for the comparison of point clouds [22–25]. Commonly, these descriptors consider the local neighborhood of a query point through binning approaches [26] and score the similarity of two queries. Alexandre [26] concludes that descriptors for point clouds should incorporate radiometric information to improve their performance. Palma et al. [25] propose a multi-scale shape descriptor based on a moving least square spherical fit through a local patch of the point cloud. They report strong change segmentation results, however, similar to most point cloud descriptors, their method does not account for radiometric information associated with points.

We introduce a customized descriptor based on our geometry-derived coloring to verify correspondences in our pipeline. First, we employ a unique, unambiguous local reference frame established in [27] to orient our descriptors relative to the underlying local surface. This greatly improves the potential similarity of the descriptors even if the orientation of the surface under consideration changed. Next, we divide the neighborhood $p_i \in C_t, |x-p_i| < \varepsilon$ and $p_j \in C_{t+\delta}, |x'-p_j| < \varepsilon$ of the query points x and x' into spherical bins. We found a multiple of the voxel edge length to be a suitable choice for ε. In our weighting scheme, we first assign a unit-length central axis n_b to each bin b. The contribution of points to each bin b is inverse-distance weighted by $acos(n_b^T(\frac{p_i-x}{\|p_i-x\|}))$ or $acos(n_b^T(\frac{p_j-x'}{\|p_j-x'\|}))$, which are the angular deviations between the bin axes n_b and the normalized vectors connecting the query points x and x' with the points p_i and p_j, respectively (Fig. 3a). Finally, we perform a weighted averaging of our geometry-derived coloring for each bin.

For our choice of a suitable similarity measure, we use the structural similarity index (SSIM) [28] and we require the number of bins in both descriptors under comparison to be equal. For the comparison of two descriptors, we follow Wang et al. [28]:

$$SSIM(x,y) = \frac{(2\mu_{b_x}\mu_{b_y} + C_1)(2\sigma_{b_x b_y} + C_2)}{(\mu_{b_x}^2\mu_{b_y}^2 + C_1)(\sigma_{b_x}\sigma_{b_y} + C_2)} \tag{1}$$

In our case b_x and b_y denote the set of bins of two descriptors, μ denotes the average and σ the variance of the per-bin values, and $\sigma_{b_x b_y}$ corresponds to the covariance of b_x and b_y. If the structural similarity of two SSIM-descriptors is too low to support a correspondence, we remove the associated flow information and mask the region for the remainder of our pipeline. We only mask leaf-level voxels of the SVO directly, and propagate masking information to the inner voxels of the hierarchy. If any child voxel is masked, we also mask its parent, but we stop propagating masking information at a voxel edge length of 2 cm. This provides for cleaner, more reliable albeit more coarse masks.

Our masking of voxels prevents false positive matches in regions of the data sets where considerable geometric changes between acquisitions would otherwise introduce erroneous optical flow correspondences. The resulting masks are used to prohibit crack detection during filtering and crack labeling.

6.2   Filtering and Crack Labeling

To derive a crack labeling from our 3D surface flow, we use the adaptive representation of the sparse voxel octree. Initially, only a subset of leaf-voxels contain flow information. To propagate flow information to all voxels, including the interior ones, we apply a push-and-pull algorithm on the SVO. Starting from the leaf level voxels, we average existing flow information in a bottom-up process to the inner voxels of the hierarchy. When we reach the root-voxel, we start a top-down propagation of flow information from parent voxels to any children which do not contain flow yet. During this process, we avoid the traversal of any masked voxels and their descendants. After this process, all non-masked voxels of the SVO contain flow information.

We use a Gradient of Gaussian filter to detect discontinuities in our surface flow and obtain a per-voxel crack response. To perform filtering on our sparse voxel octree, we choose the size of the filter based on the edge length of the voxel at the center of the filter and use efficient point insertions to look-up values of adjacent voxels.

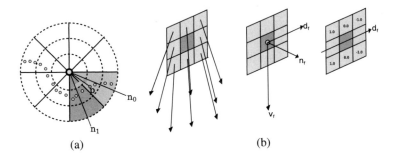

(a)   (b)

Fig. 3. (a) Illustration of our SSIM-based geometric descriptor for point clouds. For simplicity, it is shown in two dimensions but the principle extends in a straightforward manner to three dimensions. We divide the space around the query point in radial bins. The contribution of a point p to any bin is computed through inverse distance weighting of the angular deviations (depicted in yellow) to the nearest central bin axes n_0 and n_1. (b) Illustration of the tangential reference frame used in our filtering approach. For each filtering step, we average per-voxel flow directions in the neighborhood (left) to produce v_f. Our filtering direction d_f is orthogonal to the surface normal n_f and v_f (middle). We filter for discontinuities in flow directions along d_f (right) using a Gradient of Gaussian kernel. (Color figure online)

Our data sets are registered into a joint coordinate system and we focus on the detection of cracks in a concrete beam which is put under increasing vertical load at its center. Thus, the local crack directions roughly agree with the direction of non-rigid displacement of the concrete material. In this case, the most decisive spatial axis d_f to detect cracks lies tangential to the local surface patch and orthogonal to the direction of the crack. The filter response is highest along this axis when cracks are present. Therefore, we construct a local reference frame to orient our filter tangential to the local surface patch for any filtering step (Fig. 3b).

7 Results and Discussion

We conducted an evaluation of our spatio-temporal crack-detection method by example of a 240 cm long concrete beam which was put under increasing load at its center and captured for 3D-reconstruction using 327 images. We tested our implementation with three point cloud series (Fig. 4), each of which consists of two time steps; one without stress and one with high vertical load that shows a moderate amount of vertical cracks. To simulate the application of graffiti and growth of vegetation between acquisitions, we added radiometric and geometric variations to the second time steps of our data sets. Each point cloud consists of 579 million points and amounts to approx. 9 GB.

Commonly, ground-truth comparisons are burdened by the difference in width of strokes made during manual annotation and the detected crack labels. This difference is a decisive factor as it can cause considerable disagreement during cell-by-cell comparisons. To alleviate this quality factor, we propose a hierarchical comparison.

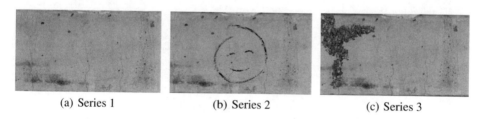

(a) Series 1   (b) Series 2   (c) Series 3

Fig. 4. This figure shows the second time step of three point cloud series used in our evaluation. Each series consists of two time steps, the first of which remains unchanged for all three data sets. *Series 1* features no substantial variations of color or geometry over time. We added color variations to the surface of *Series 2* in the second time step to simulate application of graffiti over time and to evaluate our approach when facing significant radiometric variations over time. In addition, we used an ivy generator to simulate the growth of vegetation over time in the second point cloud of *Series 3*. (Color figure online)

We consider precision and recall with respect to the granularity of our comparisons. First, we label all leaf-level voxels in our SVO data structure that contain cracks according to our detection. Next, we propagate labels to the interior voxels of the hierarchy until the root node is reached. This representation of hierarchical labels allows us to perform a ground-truth comparison at different resolutions corresponding to a spectrum of detection accuracy at different scales. Finally, we created a manually annotated ground-truth SVO for comparisons which contains hierarchical labels created in a similar manner.

Figure 5 presents precision and recall scores when comparing our detection to manually annotated ground-truth cracks. We perform the comparison at 8 depths of our SVO data structures corresponding to specific voxel edge lengths in millimeters. Our results show, that we achieve a precision greater than 0.8 for accuracy in the millimeter range. At the sub-millimeter scale, a number of false positive matches decreases the precision. The propagation of crack labels to interior nodes of the SVO allows for coarser comparisons which improve the precision score. Above a voxel edge length of 2 mm, our high recall scores indicate that cracks were completely detected. False negative matches caused by disagreements in stroke widths start to appear below 2 mm and cause recall scores to drop.

Our approach avoids the use of original material color for crack detection and is therefore particularly robust against radiometric variations in 3D-reconstructions (*Series 2*). A complete detection of cracks in *Series 3*, which features considerable geometric occlusions in the second point cloud, is impossible and the corresponding recall score is upper-bounded by 0.85 in our case. However, the consistent precision scores show that the pipeline is able to mitigate false positive matches commonly arising from severe geometric changes between acquisitions.

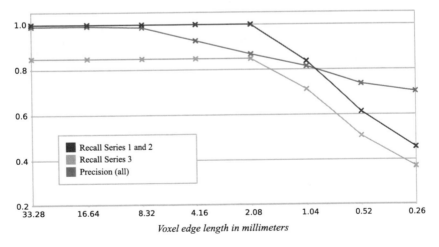

Fig. 5. The plots show precision and recall scores of detected cracks in comparison with a ground-truth annotation. We perform a hierarchical comparison and the voxel edge length corresponds to the depth of our SVOs chosen for comparison. (Color figure online)

We implemented the approach described in [4] which operates on a series of photographs in order to derive crack detection from discontinuities in optical flow. To allow for hierarchical comparisons with their work, we used two photographs of our concrete beam with their pipeline and propagated hierarchical crack labels in a quad-tree approach. Table 1 presents a comparison of f1-scores with respect to cell edge lengths chosen for comparison. The comparison suggests that all approaches perform well for *Series 1*, where no significant color variations or geometric occlusions between time steps exist. The lower f1-score of our method at very high detection accuracy can be attributed to the granularity of the 3D-reconstructions used for evaluation.

When tested with *Series 2* and *Series 3*, the image-based method proposed in [4] yields recall and precision scores between 0.02 and 0.2. These very low scores are caused by false positives due to considerable changes in color and geometry of these data sets over time. In comparison, our results show that the use of 3D point clouds and the inherent geometric information can alleviate false positive matches caused by radiometric variations of the original material color as well as occlusions in overgrown regions.

Before correspondence estimation, we replace material colors by a geometry-based coloring as described in Sect. 4. The similarity between 3D surface flow estimated using this recoloring and 3D surface flow created using the original material color is very high (PSNR = 56.01, SSIM = 0.9978). This confirms that the flow estimation based on our artificial recoloring results in a very similar 3D surface flow as the original color. In practice, the f1-scores based on flow obtained from the original material color, and flow estimated with our geometry-based coloring differ marginally.

Without taking the 3D-reconstruction into account, our pipeline takes approx. 1 h and 41 min to process two time steps of our concrete beam data set (Fig. 6).

Table 1. Comparison of f1-scores for *Series 1* with respect to cell edge lengths. All f1-scores decrease at higher comparison accuracy because the ground-truth annotation stroke width does not agree perfectly with the detection, causing lower recall values. Our f1-scores are computed by comparing crack labels at specific depths of a ground-truth SVO with detected crack labels at the corresponding depths. F1-scores for [4] are obtained by analogously comparing 2D-layers of a ground-truth image pyramid of crack labels with a second image pyramid derived from the detected crack labels.

Accuracy	Color-based	Geometry-based	[4]
8.333 mm	0.995	0.995	0.987
4.166 mm	0.963	0.963	0.941
2.083 mm	0.932	0.929	0.865
1.042 mm	0.841	0.821	0.791
0.521 mm	0.687	0.669	0.732
0.260 mm	0.572	0.554	0.695

In this work, we primarily focused on the detection of cracks caused by vertical bending stress and we assumed crack directions to agree with the surrounding directions of displacement. The supplementary video shows a GPU-accelerated SVO-filtering to produce crack labels on the fly based on an interactively chosen filtering direction in the local surface plane. In our case, filtering directions orthogonal to the direction of the crack in the surface plane produce stronger crack detection results.

Illumination conditions and shadows may occasionally limit the reconstruction quality of surfaces in practice and we do not expect 3D-reconstructions to be available for an entire building or bridge everywhere in the wild. It would be sufficient to produce 3D-reconstructions in critical regions where cracks are most likely to occur. The accuracy of our method strongly depends on the significance of small-scale discontinuities with respect to the surrounding motion and therefore, a precise registration is required. Further improvements will be necessary to use our method with series of point clouds that are unregistered or deformed substantially between acquisitions.

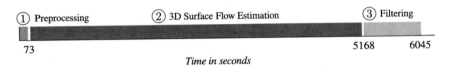

Fig. 6. This figure illustrates the overall time in seconds taken to process each of our point cloud series shown in Fig. 4.

8   Conclusion

We presented an algorithm for the detection of small-scale cracks in outdoor environments based on motion discontinuities in 3D surface flow. Optical flow estimation based on our local geometric feature produces correct correspondence information even in the presence of significant color variations, provided that 3D-reconstructions from two different points in time are available. As a result, our sparse voxel octree-based 3D filtering technique identifies cracks by exploiting local material displacement information, rather than the color offset of the cracks themselves. Our pipeline also incorporates a novel SSIM-based descriptor for point clouds to mask out poor correspondence estimations that may originate from geometric occlusions over time. We have shown that our filter identifies overgrown regions which allows us to limit the detection to those areas where cracks are visible.

In the future, we plan to generalize our method to enable the detection of all types of cracks in concrete and other materials, including cases where crack directions are not known in advance. Currently, we estimate motion from synthesized image pairs corresponding to a set of view points. An improved pipeline should estimate 3D surface flow directly and geometrically from the point cloud representations.

Acknowledgments. This work was supported by the German Federal Ministry of Education and Research (BMBF) under the project number 13N14657 (Project AIS-TEC). The concrete beam data set used in this work is courtesy of Bauhaus-Universität Weimar.

References

1. Agnisarman, S., Lopes, S., Madathil, K.C., Piratla, K., Gramopadhye, A.: A survey of automation-enabled human-in-the-loop systems for infrastructure visual inspection. Autom. Constr. **97**, 52–76 (2019)
2. Morgenthal, G., Hallermann, N., Kersten, J., Taraben, J., Debus, P., Helmrich, M., Rodehorst, V.: Framework for automated UAS-based structural condition assessment of bridges. Autom. Constr. **97**, 77–95 (2019)
3. Horn, B., Schunck, B.: Determining optical flow. Artif. Intell. **17**, 185–203 (1981)
4. Chaudhury, S., Nakano, G., Takada, J., Iketani, A.: Spatial-temporal motion field analysis for pixelwise crack detection on concrete surfaces. In: 2017 IEEE Winter Conference on Applications of Computer Vision (WACV), pp. 336–344. IEEE (2017)
5. Yamaguchi, T., Nakamura, S., Saegusa, R., Hashimoto, S.: Image-based crack detection for real concrete surfaces. IEEJ Trans. Elect. Electron. Eng. **3**, 128–135 (2008)
6. Yamaguchi, T., Hashimoto, S.: Fast crack detection method for large-size concrete surface images using percolation-based image processing. Mach. Vis. Appl. **21**, 797–809 (2010)
7. Nishikawa, T., Yoshida, J., Sugiyama, T., Fujino, Y.: Concrete crack detection by multiple sequential image filtering. Comput. Aided Civil Infrastruct. Eng. **27**, 29–47 (2012)
8. Cha, Y.J., Choi, W., Büyüköztürk, O.: Deep learning-based crack damage detection using convolutional neural networks. Comput. Aided Civil Infrastruct. Eng. **32**, 361–378 (2017)
9. Chen, F.C., Jahanshahi, M.R.: NB-CNN: deep learning-based crack detection using convolutional neural network and Naive Bayes data fusion. IEEE Trans. Ind. Electron. **65**, 4392–4400 (2018)
10. Benning, W., Lange, J., Schwermann, R., Effkemann, C., Görtz, S.: Monitoring crack origin and evolution at concrete elements using photogrammetry. In: ISPRS Congress Istanbul Commission, vol. 2004. (2004)
11. Bruck, H., McNeill, S., Sutton, M.A., Peters, W.: Digital image correlation using newton-raphson method of partial differential correction. Exp. Mech. **29**, 261–267 (1989)
12. Hutt, T., Cawley, P.: Feasibility of digital image correlation for detection of cracks at fastener holes. NDT & E Int. **42**, 141–149 (2009)
13. Poissant, J., Barthelat, F.: A novel "subset splitting" procedure for digital image correlation on discontinuous displacement fields. Exp. Mech. **50**, 353–364 (2010)
14. Rupil, J., Roux, S., Hild, F., Vincent, L.: Fatigue microcrack detection with digital image correlation. J. Strain Anal. Eng. Des. **46**, 492–509 (2011)
15. Qu, Z., Lin, L.D., Guo, Y., Wang, N.: An improved algorithm for image crack detection based on percolation model. IEEJ Trans. Electr. Electron. Eng. **10**, 214–221 (2015)
16. Li, Y., Li, H., Wang, H.: Pixel-wise crack detection using deep local pattern predictor for robot application. Sensors **18**, 3042 (2018)

17. Brox, T., Bruhn, A., Papenberg, N., Weickert, J.: High accuracy optical flow estimation based on a theory for warping. In: Pajdla, T., Matas, J. (eds.) ECCV 2004. LNCS, vol. 3024, pp. 25–36. Springer, Heidelberg (2004). https://doi.org/10.1007/978-3-540-24673-2_3

18. Laine, S., Karras, T.: Efficient sparse voxel octrees. IEEE Trans. Vis. Comput. Graph. **17**, 1048–1059 (2011)

19. Pfister, H., Zwicker, M., Van Baar, J., Gross, M.: Surfels: surface elements as rendering primitives. In: Proceedings of the 27th Annual Conference on Computer Graphics and Interactive Techniques, pp. 335–342. ACM Press/Addison-Wesley Publishing Co. (2000)

20. Botsch, M., Hornung, A., Zwicker, M., Kobbelt, L.: High-quality surface splatting on today's GPUs. In: 2005 Eurographics/IEEE VGTC Symposium Proceedings on Point-Based Graphics, pp. 17–141. IEEE (2005)

21. Goswami, P., Erol, F., Mukhi, R., Pajarola, R., Gobbetti, E.: An efficient multiresolution framework for high quality interactive rendering of massive point clouds using multi-way kd-trees. Vis. Comput. **29**, 69–83 (2013)

22. Frome, A., Huber, D., Kolluri, R., Bülow, T., Malik, J.: Recognizing objects in range data using regional point descriptors. In: Pajdla, T., Matas, J. (eds.) ECCV 2004. LNCS, vol. 3023, pp. 224–237. Springer, Heidelberg (2004). https://doi.org/10.1007/978-3-540-24672-5_18

23. Tombari, F., Salti, S., Di Stefano, L.: Unique signatures of histograms for local surface description. In: Daniilidis, K., Maragos, P., Paragios, N. (eds.) ECCV 2010. LNCS, vol. 6313, pp. 356–369. Springer, Heidelberg (2010). https://doi.org/10.1007/978-3-642-15558-1_26

24. Thanou, D., Chou, P.A., Frossard, P.: Graph-based compression of dynamic 3D point cloud sequences. IEEE Trans. Image Process. **25**, 1765–1778 (2016)

25. Palma, G., Cignoni, P., Boubekeur, T., Scopigno, R.: Detection of geometric temporal changes in point clouds. In: Computer Graphics Forum, vol. 35, pp. 33–45. Wiley Online Library (2016)

26. Alexandre, L.A.: 3D descriptors for object and category recognition: a comparative evaluation. In: Workshop on Color-Depth Camera Fusion in Robotics at the IEEE/RSJ International Conference on Intelligent Robots and Systems (IROS), Vilamoura, Portugal, vol. 1 (2012)

27. Tombari, F., Salti, S., Di Stefano, L.: Unique shape context for 3D data description. In: Proceedings of the ACM Workshop on 3D Object Retrieval, pp. 57–62. ACM (2010)

28. Wang, Z., Bovik, A.C., Sheikh, H.R., Simoncelli, E.P.: Image quality assessment: from error visibility to structural similarity. IEEE Trans. Image Process. **13**, 600–612 (2004)

An Automatic Digital Terrain Generation Technique for Terrestrial Sensing and Virtual Reality Applications

Lee Easson, Alireza Tavakkoli[✉], and Jonathan Greenberg

University of Nevada, Reno, NV 89557, USA
leasson@nevada.unr.edu, {tavakkol,jgreenberg}@unr.edu

Abstract. The identification and modeling of the terrain from point cloud data is an important component of Terrestrial Remote Sensing (TRS) applications. The main focus in terrain modeling is capturing details of complex geological features of landforms. Traditional terrain modeling approaches rely on the user to exert control over terrain features. However, relying on the user input to manually develop the digital terrain becomes intractable when considering the amount of data generated by new remote sensing systems capable of producing massive aerial and ground-based point clouds from scanned environments. This article provides a novel terrain modeling technique capable of automatically generating accurate and physically realistic Digital Terrain Models (DTM) from a variety of point cloud data. The proposed method runs efficiently on large-scale point cloud data with real-time performance over large segments of terrestrial landforms. Moreover, generated digital models are designed to effectively render within a Virtual Reality (VR) environment in real time. The paper concludes with an in–depth discussion of possible research directions and outstanding technical and scientific challenges to improve the proposed approach.

Keywords: Digital Terrain Model · Terrestrial Remote Sensing · Geological Landmass Modeling

1 Introduction

Terrains are among the most fundamental features in any virtual application simulating a landmass, ranging from computer games to geological simulations. For example, in an open-world massively multiplayer online role playing game, large-scale natural environments maybe designed for players to explore, where a vast terrain is usually the first part of the authoring pipeline to be subsequently augmented with props that represent rocks, trees, plants and buildings. On the other hand, real-world terrain are usually more complex and varied and may include plains, mountain ranges, and eroded valleys in a single environment. Terrain formation is a combination of long-term and complex geological events with complicated physical and geological interactions amongst different

© Springer Nature Switzerland AG 2019
G. Bebis et al. (Eds.): ISVC 2019, LNCS 11844, pp. 619–630, 2019.
https://doi.org/10.1007/978-3-030-33720-9_48

components comprising the landmass. In addition, different geological features are dominant at difference range scales. These complexities contribute to many unsolved challenges in terrain modeling.

One definition of Digital Terrain Models (DTM), [3], relates to geometrical aspects of the 3D environment acquired from Laser scanning and is a continuous function mapping a 2D position (x, y) to the terrain elevation $z = f(x, y)$. In this definition, the terrain is defined as the boundary between the ground and the air. Yet, there are certain geographical feature, such as overhangs [12], ground vegetation [10], and large man-made structures, that may render the assumptions required for this definition inaccurate [14].

The aforementioned DTM will require utilizing a large amount of data collected by aerial or ground-based Laser scanning technology. This data is generally combined to produce a collection of points referred to as Point Clouds (PC). In essence, each point in a point cloud represented a location in the world from which the light emitted from the scanner is reflected back. The massive amount of data within even a small scanned region makes it necessary to represent the DTM using a more efficient structure.

Several data structures are utilized in the literature that represent DTMs with varied levels of performance [14]. These structures range from pixel-level representation of the elevation data by quantizing the 2D planimetric locations of the point clouds to a hybrid approach by interpolating points on the surface of a grid-mesh structure [1]. To improve the quality of the structure of the DTM, and with the popularity of triangulation techniques in computer graphics, several Triangulated Irregular Networks (TINs) are proposed with the goal of improving storage efficiency of the point cloud representation of the DTM [2], with recent attempts to improve the performance of the triangulation approaches [8,9,11,19]. Most of these methods assume that the terrain is smooth and continuous with a large height difference between neighbouring points on ground and non-ground objects. Therefore, the performance of these methods often decreases through wrongly filtering hilly regions and large buildings.

Because of the simplicity and ease of implementation, morphology-based methods [5–7,13] are mostly used in ground filtering. However, finding the correct structuring element size is a problem in these methods. While a small structuring element is needed for filtering points on vegetation, tree, and cars, a large structuring element should be used for filtering points on buildings.

In this paper we propose an fast ground filtering approach with an efficient DTM representation capable of preserving detailed geological features and applicable to both urban and non-urban landmasses. Unlike most other methods that try to extract ground points via many iterations for DTM generation, the proposed technique extracts all ground points via a series of atomic operations geared towards preserving geological features and eliminating non-ground points. The main hypothesis in the proposed method is that non-ground objects produce sharp variations in elevation within a spacial neighborhood. Hence, we propose using region growing for segmenting non-ground objects. The method is tested on a number of point cloud data sets obtained the United States Geological Survey. The proposed method is also compared with the existing methods.

2   The Proposed Approach

Figure 1 shows an overview of the proposed Point Cloud Filtering and DTM generation pipeline. The proposed architecture is comprised of three components, i.e., preprocessing stage, map generation module, and terrain generation module, shown as the vertical tracks. These components in turn process three different data structures in the form of Point Clouds, Heightmaps, and Landscape mesh.

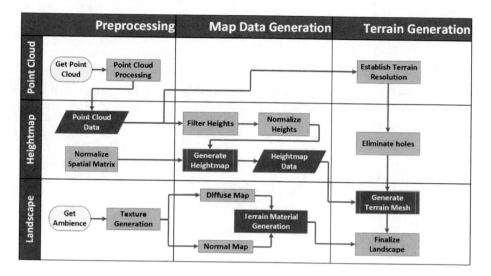

Fig. 1. The proposed processing pipeline.

The first stage of the proposed pipeline is the preprocessing step. In this stage the Lidar point cloud data is processed to represent a gridded topological form. To accomplish this task, we perform the nearest neighbor interpolation in conjunction with a kernel-based statistical outlier removal to generate the raster grid from the Lidar point cloud. In this step, the three data structures representing the point cloud data, the spatial matrix of the map data, and the landscape texture and material data will be established and ready for processing. The texture data is extracted from the point clouds photometric information, if this information is available. The photometric information will be used to produce a diffuse map as well as a normal map for the terrain materials.

The second stage in the pipeline is responsible for generating the heightmap data representing a topological formation of the terrain as well as shader models for rendering a physically realistic view of the material applied on the surface of the terrain. In this stage, the topological spatial matrix is processed in order to accomplish two tasks. First, the overall topological and geological statistics of the terrain is learned by employing Singular Value Decomposition (SVD). Second, the learned statistics of the overall terrain topology is combined with the first and second order statistics of the point cloud data to eliminate the non-terrain objects while preserving details of the geological features of the terrain.

The last step in the pipeline is the terrain generation stage. In this stage, the resolution of the final landscape is calculated from the overall point cloud data. This information is then used to fill the holes introduced in the topological heightmap as a result of non-terrain object segmentation. Once the overall heightmap of the terrain is established, the terrain mesh generation process will generate an efficient digital mesh model for the terrain represented at various Level of Detail (LoD) information. At this stage the shader models for the terrain materials are also computed and applied to render the terrain.

2.1   The Preprocessing Step

The preprocessing stage of the proposed pipeline, shown in Algorithm 1, is responsible for initializing the gridded and rasterized data structures for the Terrain heightmaps, texture maps, and shader materials.

Algorithm 1: Preprocessing Stage of the DTM Generation Pipeline.

Data: P : Input-Point Cloud. // point $P_i = (x_i, y_i, z_i, r_i, g_i, b_i)$
Result:
L : Landscape Point Cloud Data File.
T : Landscape Texture.
M : Landscape Layered Material.
begin
 $L(x, y) \leftarrow$ Stat_Outlier(P, th) // Eq. (1)
 for *all* P_i **do**
  Find $L_l(x, y, z)$ lowest and $L_h(x, y, z)$ highest Lidar Returns Eq. (2)
 Set texture Coordinates: **begin**
  $T(u, v) = new\_Texture(u, v)$ // coordinate map from Eq. (3)
 Set Shader Material: **begin**
  $M \leftarrow new\_Material(Diff(u, v), Norm(u, v))$

Statistical Outlier Removal: The first step in cleaning out the input Lidar point-cloud data is to eliminate outliers. Outliers include points introduced to the point cloud due to noise or small moving objects, such as airplanes, located at drastically different heights than the terrain, need to be eliminated. In order to perform this task, we first build a non-parametric density estimation of the point cloud in a local spatial neighborhood [17].

Assuming an outlier threshold of th, we eliminate points from the point cloud data whose probability of belonging to the known distribution from which the

Lidar data is generated falls below th. This probability is calculated using the non-parametric kernel density estimation, below:

$$P(z_i|inlier) = \frac{1}{|N_k(z_i)|} \sum_{z_j \in N_k(z_i)} \frac{1}{\sigma\sqrt{(2\pi)}} exp\left(-\frac{\sigma(p_j, p_i)}{2h^2}\right) \tag{1}$$

where z_i is the height value of the ith point p_i in the point cloud data p_j at a spatial neighborhood location of $N_k \in \mathbb{R}^2$.

Top and Bottom Returns: Once the statistical outliers are eliminated, we will need to determine the most likely ground points. In order to accomplish this task, we will set two rasterized data structures for the lowest return and the highest return points at a location (x, y) denoted as $L_l(x, y, z)$ and $L_h(x, y, z)$:

$$\forall P_i \quad \begin{bmatrix} L_l(x,y,z) \\ L_h(x,y,z) \end{bmatrix} = \begin{bmatrix} \min\limits_{z_i}(P_i : x = x_i \& y = y_i) \\ \max\limits_{z_i}(P_i : x = x_i \& y = y_i) \end{bmatrix} \tag{2}$$

where $x \in [min(x_i), max(x_i)]$ and $y \in [min(y_i), max(y_i)]$.

Shader and Texture Initialization: In order to render physically realistic materials on the surface of the final DTM, we will establish the data structures $T(u, v)$ and M as the texture map and the landscape material, respectively. First, a mapping between the spatial domain of the point cloud $(x, y) \in \mathbb{R}^2$ and the texture-coordinates (u, v) is determined:

$$(u, v)^T = \begin{bmatrix} \Phi_u : (x_{min}, x_{max}) \to (0, 1) \\ \Phi_v : (y_{min}, y_{max}) \to (0, 1) \end{bmatrix} \tag{3}$$

Next, the shader material for the landscape is initialized based on the photogrametric information, if this information is included in the Lidar point cloud data. Suppose for each point P_i in the point cloud data, the photogrametric information is given in the form of $C_i = (r_i, g_i, b_i)$ color components. The details about the computation of the diffuse and normal channels of the landscape material are discussed later in the paper in Sect. 2.3.

2.2   The Heightmap Generation Step

Once the point cloud data is refined during the pre-processing step, it is passed through the heightmap generation stage of the algorithm to produce a two-dimensional structure maintaining the overall height associated with the terrain surface. This heightmap object is then utilized to generate a three-dimensional model of the terrain surface as a 3D mesh object. This section discusses the process of generating the terrain heightmap by removing non-terrain objects while preserving significant geological features.

Algorithm 2 shows the overall pipeline of generating the terrain surface heightmap. The process starts by taking the top and bottom point cloud data

---

Algorithm 2: Heightmap Generation Stage of the DTM Pipeline.

Data:
L_l, L_h : Landscape Top and Bottom Point Cloud Data.
P : Point Cloud Data.
Result:
H : Landscape Heightmap Data File.
begin
    for *all P_i* **do**
        $\hat{L} = L_l \cap L_h$ // Non-ground overhangs
        $L = (L_l \cup L_h) - \hat{L}$ // Potential ground points
        $\hat{H} \leftarrow L.Heights$ // Eq. (4)
        Find $\hat{g} \leftarrow$ S.V.D. $(\hat{H})$ // Eq. (7)
        $g \leftarrow$ **inPaint**$(\hat{g})$ // Fill holes

---

structures generated from the pre-processing phase to determine the potential ground points and eliminate the over-hangs. Then a polynomial function with sufficient local variance and smooth global consistency is fit onto the data to estimate the overall structure of the terrain ground. This is utilized to computer the ground heightmap values for each point in the landmass.

Terrain Height Estimation. With the Lowest L_l and the highest L_h LiDar returns from the point cloud data, we start modeling the heightmap of the terrain. Each point (x, y, z) in a point cloud belongs to one of two classes, i.e., the ground or the non-ground objects. Both L_l and L_h are quantized in such a way as to represent 2D grids ranging from (x_{min}, y_{min}) to (x_{max}, y_{max}).

It is trivial to eliminate overhangs (or points covering the ground area) if both the ground position and the overhang points are visible within the point cloud data. Points within a spatial location $\mathcal{R}(x, y)$ are considered to belong to the non-ground object covering the surface of the ground if they exist in both L_l and L_h structures. Therefore, the first iteration of the heightmap is generate by interpolating the height values of all points in L_l that do not belong to L_h as:

$$\hat{H} = h(x, y) = \frac{1}{Size(\mathcal{R})} \sum_{(x,y,z) \in \mathcal{R}} \{z | (x, y, z) \in L\} \tag{4}$$

The height of the ground in a landmass may be considered as a low-degree polynomial with the non-ground objects, e.g. shrubbery, biomass, and man-made structures, disrupting the natural curvature and geological features of the terrain. Therefore, we postulate that the heightmap of the terrain is a combination of a ground function $g(x, y)$ and an anomalous function $\mathcal{N}(x, y)$:

$$h(x, y) = g(x, y) + \mathcal{N}(x, y) \tag{5}$$

where h is a heightmap calculated from raw point cloud data (Fig. 2(a)), g is a low-order polynomial function with high degrees of smoothness over a large

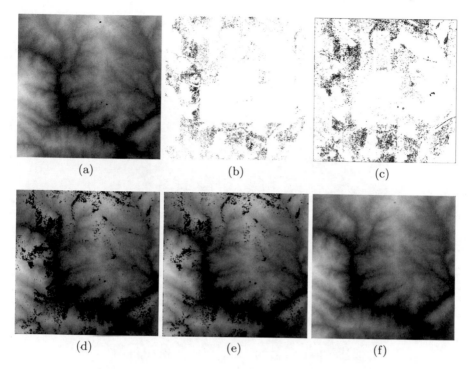

Fig. 2. Terrain modeling heightmap generation step performed on Idaho dataset. (a) Original data with no-terrain elements. (b) Dark areas are non-terrain LiDar returns. (c) Dark areas are non-terrain geological features. (d) Non-terrain geological features are removed. (e) Non-terrain areas are removed. (f) Final terrain heightmap.

spatial area representing the ground heightmap (Fig. 2(f)), and $\mathcal{N}$ represents the non-ground geological and man-made features shown in Fig. 2(b) and (c).

This formulation represents the terrain heightmap modeling as a novelty detection question [15]. Therefore, we represent the ground region of the terrain heightmap data g as a polynomial with degree N of the following form:

$$g(x,y) = \sum_{i,j=0}^{N} a_i b_j (x^i \cdot y^j) \tag{6}$$

Using the above formulation, and given the heightmap from Eq. (4), we need to solve the linear system of equations resulting from all (x, y) values of $\hat{H}$ as follows:

$$[h(x_1,y_1)\cdots h(x_N,y_N)]^T = \begin{bmatrix} a_0 b_0 & a_1 b_0 & \cdots & a_N b_N \\ \vdots & \vdots & \ddots & \vdots \\ a_0 b_0 & a_1 b_0 & \cdots & a_N b_N \end{bmatrix} \begin{bmatrix} 1 & x & y & \cdots & x^N y^N \end{bmatrix} \tag{7}$$

This terrain function may be visualized as the combination of Fig. 2(d) and (e), in which the darker areas represent non-ground objects encoded as $\mathcal{N}$. These dark areas produce holes in the ground heightmap and are filled using an automatic inpainting algorithm similar to [18]. The final terrain heightmap is shown in Fig. 2(f).

(a)

(b)

Fig. 3. Terrain meshes: (a) Terrain mesh from the original point cloud. (b) Terrain mesh with the proposed heightmap generation technique.

2.3   The Terrain Modeling Step

Digital Terrain Models are employed in a number of applications ranging from geographical analysis, biomass and environmental studies, etc. In order for a DTM to be useful for its intended application, it must be generated in such an efficient manner as to allow for realistic rendering, interactivity, and efficient manipulation. To this end, we propose the use of the Unreal Engine 4's Landscapes [16]. Algorithm 3 provides an overview of this stage of the pipeline responsible for generating the 3D mesh of the terrains as well as shader materials employed for physically realistically rendering of the terrain (Fig. 3).

Terrain Mesh Modeling: The 3D mesh representing the ground surface is generated by applying a polygonal mesh based on the heightmap generated from the previous step. In this stage of the algorithm, a 2D grid is generated for each pair of (x, y) coordinates associated with pixels in the heightmap.

Terrain Texture Modeling: With the mapping between the heightmap data and the point cloud data established, an interpolation technique is used to sample

---

Algorithm 3: Mesh Generation and Shader Programming of the DTM Pipeline.

Data:
P : Point Cloud Data
H : Heightmap
Result:
M : Terrain Mesh. H : Terrain Heightmap. T : Terrain Texture. Mat : Shader Material.
begin

    Mesh.Vert: M.(vertex.x,vertex.y)$\xleftarrow{\Phi}$ ($H.x, H.y$)
    $M \leftarrow$ Interpolate[$h(\text{Grid}(x, y))$]
    for *all P_i* **do**
        $T \leftarrow$PC2Texture(P, H) // Generate Texture from Point Cloud
    Calculate Terrain Extent
    $(U, V) \leftarrow$ Texture Coordinate Mapping
    $Mat \leftarrow (Diffuse_{uv}, Normal_{uv})$ // Shader Program

---

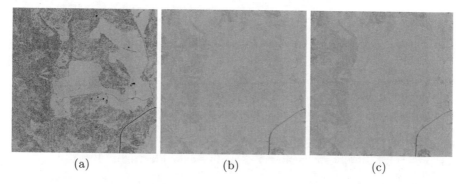

(a)   (b)   (c)

Fig. 4. Terrain texture: (a) Original sparse texture. (b) Dense texture. (c) Modified dense texture.

the color (or intensity) values from point clouds in a neighborhood that map onto the terrain mesh object. Figure 4 shows the results of the interpolation steps taken to generate a photorealistic texture for the terrain from the Point Cloud data.

Terrain Material Modeling: The material applied to the surface of the terrain mesh is comprised of two main channels, a diffuse channel and a normal channel. The diffuse channel of the material utilizes the texture coordinates to map the color (or intensity) values of the terrain texture on the surface of the 3D terrain mesh. The normal channel is computing using a normal map generation technique [4].

Figure 5 shows the final rendering of the Digital Terrain Model with the material applied. As it can be seen, the quality of the rendering is quite realistic. Note the various geological features preserved, while the man-made structures or

Fig. 5. Final terrain model with shader parameters applied.

non-ground objects are effectively removed from the terrain model. The texture applied on the surface of the terrain in the form of a physically-based material drastically enhances the visualization of the DTM.

3   Experimental Results

This section presents the results of the proposed DTM technique performed on a variety of point cloud data from the USGS datasets. The first set of results (Fig. 6) demonstrates that quality of the modeled DTM compared to the rendering of the point cloud data. The point cloud data rendered in the Cloud Compare software is shown in Fig. 6(a). The main issue is the lack of discrimination between points belonging to the ground surface and other structural elements. The proposed technique has the ability to eliminate the non-terrain elements while preserving significant geological features as evident from Fig. 6(b).

(a)   (b)

Fig. 6. The results of the proposed framework. (a) The original point cloud data rendered in Cloud Compare software. (b) The 3D landscape DTM generated by the proposed framework and rendered in Unreal Engine 4.

Figure 7 shows the generated heightmaps (Fig. 7(a)) and the 3D landscape mesh associated with each heightmap (Fig. 7(b)). As seen from the figures, the proposed DTM mesh objects represent the geological features quite accurately.

(a)   (b)

Fig. 7. Heightmaps (a) and their associated terrains (b) generated by the proposed framework. From top: California Calaveras-Tuolumne (CA), Washington County (FL), and Oahu (HI), respectively.

4   Conclusions and Future Work

In this paper we proposed a pipeline for generating Digital Terrain Models (DTM) from a variety of Lidar-based point cloud datasets. The proposed pipeline automatically generates heightmaps by eliminating non-ground points from the point cloud and interpolating the surface height values from the remaining points. The texture and materials are also created to provide photorealistic rendering of the terrain 3D mesh. There are a number of future directions to this work. Performing semantic segmentation on the 3D point cloud data may add higher level information to the data useful for effective generation of heightmaps.

References

1. Ackermann, F.E., Kraus, K.: Grid based digital terrain models. na (2004)
2. Axelsson, P.: Dem generation from laser scanner data using adaptive tin models. Int. Arch. Photogrammetry Remote Sens. **33**(4), 110–117 (2000)
3. El-Sheimy, N., Valeo, C., Habib, A.: Digital Terrain Modeling: Acquisition, Manipulation and Applications (Artech House Remote Sensing Library). Artech House, Norwood (2005)
4. Gimp: Normal map plugin (2019). https://code.google.com/archive/p/gimp-normalmap/
5. Kobler, A., Pfeifer, N., Ogrinc, P., Todorovski, L., Oštir, K., Džeroski, S.: Repetitive interpolation: a robust algorithm for DTM generation from aerial laser scanner data in forested terrain. Remote Sens. Environ. **108**(1), 9–23 (2007)
6. Li, Y., Yong, B., Wu, H., An, R., Xu, H.: An improved top-hat filter with sloped brim for extracting ground points from airborne lidar point clouds. Remote Sens. **6**(12), 12885–12908 (2014)
7. Mongus, D., Lukač, N., Žalik, B.: Ground and building extraction from lidar data based on differential morphological profiles and locally fitted surfaces. ISPRS J. Photogrammetry Remote Sens. **93**, 145–156 (2014)
8. Mongus, D., Žalik, B.: Parameter-free ground filtering of lidar data forautomatic DTM generation. ISPRS J. Photogrammetry Remote Sens. **67**, 1–12 (2012)
9. Mongus, D., Žalik, B.: Computationally efficient method for the generation of a digital terrain model from airborne lidar data using connected operators. IEEE J. Sel. Top. Appl. Earth Observations Remote Sens. **7**(1), 340–351 (2013)
10. Næsset, E.: Vertical height errors in digital terrain models derived from airborne laser scanner data in a boreal-alpine ecotone in Norway. Remote Sens. **7**(4), 4702–4725 (2015)
11. Özcan, A.H., Ünsalan, C.: Lidar data filtering and dtm generation using empirical mode decomposition. IEEE J. Sel. Top. Appl. Earth Observations Remote Sens. **10**(1), 360–371 (2016)
12. Pfeifer, N.: A subdivision algorithm for smooth 3D terrain models. ISPRS J. Photogrammetry Remote Sens. **59**(3), 115–127 (2005)
13. Pingel, T.J., Clarke, K.C., McBride, W.A.: An improved simple morphological filter for the terrain classification of airborne lidar data. ISPRS J. Photogrammetry Remote Sens. **77**, 21–30 (2013)
14. Shan, J., Toth, C.K.: Topographic Laser Ranging and Scanning: Principles and Processing. CRC Press, Boca Raton (2018)
15. Tavakkoli, A.: Novelty detection: an approach to foreground detection in videos. In: Pattern Recognition. IntechOpen (2009)
16. Tavakkoli, A.: Game Development and Simulation with Unreal Technology, 2nd edn. AK Peters/CRC Press, Boca Raton (2018)
17. Tavakkoli, A., Nicolescu, M., Bebis, G.: Automatic robust background modeling using multivariate non-parametric Kernel density estimation for visual surveillance. In: Bebis, G., Boyle, R., Koracin, D., Parvin, B. (eds.) ISVC 2005. LNCS, vol. 3804, pp. 363–370. Springer, Heidelberg (2005). https://doi.org/10.1007/11595755_44
18. Van Sinh, N., Ha, T.M., Thanh, N.T.: Filling holes on the surface of 3D point clouds based on tangent plane of hole boundary points. In: Proceedings of the 7th Symposium on Information and Communication Technology, pp. 331–338 (2016)
19. Zhang, J., Lin, X.: Filtering airborne lidar data by embedding smoothness-constrained segmentation in progressive tin densification. ISPRS J. Photogrammetry Remote Sens. **81**, 44–59 (2013)

Rebar Detection and Localization for Non-destructive Infrastructure Evaluation of Bridges Using Deep Residual Networks

Habib Ahmed[1], Hung Manh La[1(✉)], and Gokhan Pekcan[2]

[1] Advanced Robotics and Automation Lab, Department of Computer Science and Engineering, University of Nevada, Reno, NV 89557, USA
hahmed@nevada.unr.edu, hla@unr.edu
[2] Department of Civil and Environmental Engineering, University of Nevada, Reno, NV 89557, USA

Abstract. Nondestructive Evaluation (NDE) of civil infrastructure has been an active area of research for the past few decades. Traditional inspection of civil infrastructure, mostly relying on visual inspection is time-consuming, labor-intensive and often provides subjective and erroneous results. To facilitate this process, different sensors for data collection and techniques for data analyses have been used to effectively carry out this task in an automated manner. The purpose of this research is to provide a novel Deep Learning-based method for detection of steel rebars in reinforced concrete bridge elements using data from Ground Penetrating Radar (GPR). At the same time, a novel technique is proposed for the localization of rebar in B-scan images. In order to examine the performance of the rebar detection and localization system, results are outlined to demonstrate the feasibility of the proposed system within relevant practical applications.

Keywords: Structural Health Monitoring (SHM) · Non-Destructive Evaluation (NDE) · Ground Penetrating Radar (GPR) sensor · Convolutional Neural Networks (CNNs) · Deep Residual Networks (ResNets)

1 Introduction

The monitoring, maintenance and rehabilitation of critical civil infrastructure during their life-cycle is of paramount importance. Of the different components of civil infrastructure, the need for periodic assessment, evaluation and maintenance of highway bridges has been emphasized by studies in the recent past [1–4]. According to the National Bridge Inventory (NBI), there are more than 600,000 bridges in the United States [5]. Although, the number of marginally or seriously damaged bridges has been declining over the past few decades, the recent statistics provided by the US Department of Transportation have classified around 67,000 bridges as structurally deficient and 85,000 as functionally obsolete [5]. For many decades, health and status assessment of these structures have been performed primarily through visual inspection using human inspectors. While this approach remains essential for system health assessment, it presents significant limitations that hinder the detection of various defect types and

© Springer Nature Switzerland AG 2019
G. Bebis et al. (Eds.): ISVC 2019, LNCS 11844, pp. 631–643, 2019.
https://doi.org/10.1007/978-3-030-33720-9_49

Fig. 1. State-of-the-art robotic platforms employing a wide-range of sensors for infrastructural monitoring, such as: (a) 7 channel impact-echo apparatus [15], (b) RABIT platform [12] (c) Seekur Jr. robotic platform [9], and (d) Roadmap system [10]

extent of damage that may lead to undesired consequences. In addition to other types of structural health monitoring (SHM) methods, non-destructive evaluation (NDE) techniques have the potential to streamline various forms of periodic inspections and to minimize the direct and indirect costs associated with failure of aging bridges. Therefore, the timely evaluation, monitoring and rehabilitation of bridges can reduce the overall direct as well as indirect costs and prevent loss of lives due to a possible structural failure and collapse.

This paper is presented in five sections. First, the motivation towards furthering the existing state-of-the-art for bridge deck evaluation and maintenance is discussed. Section 2 is dedicated to the discussion related to existing research conducted in the field of civil infrastructure assessment and evaluation. Section 3 presents the development of the proposed Deep Learning-based methodology for rebar detection and localization. Section 4 demonstrates the performance of the proposed approach. Finally, the overall conclusions are drawn and recommendations for future research has been provided in Sect. 5.

2   Related Works

Structural health monitoring (SHM) of civil infrastructure by means of NDE techniques has been a growing research area of interest in the recent past. Some of the major emerging themes in recent studies can be classified into research related to technological platforms, sensors and instrumentation modules for data collection, and algorithms for data analyses. Traditionally, tasks related to NDE have been performed visually by trained personnel [6]. However, in recent years, robotic platforms are being leveraged for infrastructure evaluation to enhance the overall efficiency and reduce the time-consumption and error in data collection. The usage of bridge-climbing robot for monitoring the condition of steel bridges was also proposed in a previous research [7]. An underwater robotic platform has been developed to monitor the condition of bridge piers [8]. Similarly, for the case of bridge evaluation, Gibb et al. [9] discussed the feasibility of a multi-functional, multi-sensor-based mobile platform containing GPR, electrical resistivity (ER) probe, and vision sensors. Figure 1(c) highlights the proposed robotic platform taking samples from an underground garage. Diamanti and Redman [10] used data from GPR sensors to examine surface and subsurface layer cracks using a ground-coupled Roadmap system, which has been outlined in Fig. 1(d). However, the

Roadmap platform cannot be considered as a truly robotic platform, as it requires manual assistance in terms of towing and driving with the help of a human driver.

Another novel robotic platform, namely the Robotics Assisted Bridge Inspection Tool (RABIT) has been designed for efficient automated evaluation of bridge decks [11–14]. This particular robotic platform has been equipped with different sensor technologies (e.g. impact echo, ultrasonic surface waves, electrical resistivity and GPR), which enable the classification of some of the most common defects in bridge decks, such as concrete degradation, delamination and rebar corrosion [11, 12]. Figure 1(b) shows the *RABIT* platform during the actual inspection and evaluation of a bridge deck. Its application and functionality have been further developed by La et al. [6] towards the automated monitoring of civil infrastructure using on-surface crack detection and bridge evaluation. In another recent research, a novel re-configurable platform spanning a maximum length of 12-ft was deployed that used seven channel impact-echo apparatus for infrastructure evaluation [15]. Figure 1(a) outlines the utilization of the re-configurable multi-channel impact-echo-based infrastructure evaluation platform towed at the back of human-operated vehicle.

The usage of GPR data for infrastructure evaluation has been in practice for as far back as the 1970s with applications that include void space detection, depth of concrete cover on bridges, locating metallic objects in concrete spaces, and general inspection and maintenance of reinforced concrete structures [16]. Some of the earlier studies have used GPR data for underground pipe detection [17], detection of underground objects, e.g. landmines and pipes [8], and examining defects in tunnels [18]. It is only recently that the shift has focused towards using GPR for bridge evaluation with particular emphasis on rebar detection and localization [12, 16, 19–23]. In the following discussion, the emphasis will be towards discussing the salient features of the proposed rebar detection and localization system. The rationale for using Deep Residual Networks for rebar detection will also be provided in view of the state-of-the-art in relevant research area.

3 System Methodology

In this section, a comprehensive evaluation of the different elements within the proposed method for rebar detection and localization will be highlighted. Earlier studies focusing on rebar detection and classification have used a number of different methods, ranging from Support Vector Machines [12] and Naïve Bayesian classifier [19] to the use of primitive Neural networks in some of the early studies using GPR for non-destructive infrastructure evaluation [8, 17]. One of the recent studies by Dinh et al. [24] has utilized a convolutional neural network for rebar detection. From a machine learning perspective, the detection and recognition of rebar from other non-rebar anomalies and artifacts detected in B-scans can be considered as a two-class classification problem. Earlier studies employing Residual Networks and their variants have attested to their superior performance towards tackling a vast range of research problems [25–27]. To the knowledge of the authors, there is no published work, which provides evaluation of Deep Residual Networks (ResNet-50) towards rebar detection and localization. It is for this reason that the present study employs one of the variants of the Deep Residual Networks (i.e. ResNet-50) [28] as a critical sub-component of the overall system for rebar detection and localization. A preliminary analysis has been discussed in one of the recent works by the authors [20]. The present study is essentially a continuation and in-depth evaluation of the performance of Deep Residual Networks, along with its various pros and cons for the application towards NDE of bridges. Figure 2 depicts some of the salient features of the proposed system for rebar detection and localization.

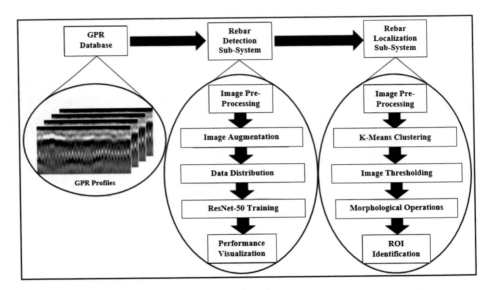

Fig. 2. Proposed system for rebar detection and localization

3.1   Proposed Model for Rebar Detection and Localization

Figure 2 outlines some of the basic building blocks for the rebar detection and rebar localization sub-systems. The first block of the proposed model is the GPR database, which leverages B-Scan data from different bridges to separate data for the two classes (i.e. rebar and non-rebar classes). The statistical information regarding the data and its distribution for testing and validation will be highlighted in the proceeding sections. Figure 3 provides details regarding the basic building block for ResNet-50. For system training using Deep Residual Network architecture (i.e. ResNet-50), a number of different operations have been performed, which include *image pre-processing* (different image operations are performed to reduce image noise and de-blurring), *image augmentation* (different transformation functions are applied to each image, which increases the dataset size and system performance), *data distribution* (random distribution of data into training and validation sets), ResNet-50 *model training* (use of data set for model training and validation to assess the performance of the rebar classification system) and *performance evaluation and visualization* (different performance measures are used to evaluate and visualize the system performance). Table 1 can be used to examine the different layers of the underlying network architecture for ResNet-50 used in this study.

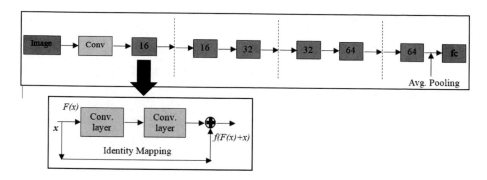

Fig. 3. Basic building block used for the development of Deep Residual Networks [28].

Table 1. Different properties of the Residual Network (ResNet-50) architecture [28]

Layer name	Input blocks	Output size
Conv1	7 × 7, 64, stride 2	112 × 112
Conv2	3 × 3 max pool, stride 2 [1 × 1, 64 3 × 3, 128 1 × 1, 512]	56 × 56
Conv3	[1 × 1, 128 3 × 3, 128 1 × 1, 512]	28 × 28
Conv4	[1 × 1, 256 3 × 3, 256 1 × 1, 1024]	14 × 14
Conv5	[1 × 1, 512 3 × 3, 512 1 × 1, 2048]	7 × 7
	Average pool, 1000-d fc Softmax	1 × 1

With regard to the overall system for rebar detection and localization, it is important to understand that there is a sequential order between the consecutive blocks. This means that before the data is available to the different processes in the rebar localization sub-system, the data undergoes processing through the different functions outlined in rebar detection sub-system, which are given in Fig. 2. Once the rebar detection sub-system is able to differentiate between the rebar and non-rebar images, the images belonging to the former category are acquired by rebar localization sub-system to establish the physical presence of rebar artefact within the available data. Similar to the rebar detection sub-system, image pre-processing functions are used in the rebar localization sub-system to sharpen the intricate details and enhance the overall boundary between the background and parabolic artefact outlining the presence of underground steel rebars. K-means clustering algorithm [29] is used to segment the *background* (image pixels that do not contain rebar artefact information) and *foreground* (pixels that contain information related to rebar artefacts) information. In order to extract relevant information, the Image Thresholding technique has been used, which leads to the binarization of the original RGB image, along with some non-rebar artefacts [30]. In order to separate noise from rebar artefacts, a number of different morphological operations are utilized, namely morphological opening and closing operations [30]. Finally, the Region-of-Interest (ROI) is highlighted using the bounding box approach. The proceeding section will discuss some of the important findings in relation to the performance of the overall rebar detection and localization system.

4   Results and Discussion

4.1   Dataset

For the development of the proposed system for rebar detection and localization, GPR data has been acquired from a number of different sources. The dataset 1 has been acquired from a bridge located in Warren County, NJ, which was included as part of the data in one of the earlier studies [15]. Table 2 summarizes the dataset sizes for the different dataset used and their distribution between the training and validation phases for the two classes. To the knowledge of the authors, this dataset is the only publicly-available data of bridge inspection using GPR sensors. Dataset 2 is one segment of the overall GPR data collected from the inspection and evaluation performed on 40 different bridges in the United States between the time period of 2013 and 2014 [6, 11]. A portion of the available GPR data has also been used in a previous study [6, 18]. Since, dataset 2 contains GPR data from five different bridges, the overall number of images is considerably higher in comparison to dataset 1. Furthermore, the two datasets used in this study allow demonstration of the effect of data sizes on the system training as discussed in subsequent sections.

Table 2. Data set sizes used for training and validation

Name	Class rebar		Class no rebar		Total
	Training	Validation	Training	Validation	
Dataset 1	1,200	300	2,400	600	4,500
Dataset 2	1,043	228	7,027	2,040	10,338
Total	2,243	528	9,427	2,640	14,838

4.2   Rebar Detection Sub-system

In this section, the results obtained during the training and validation of the proposed system are presented. One of the most important system characteristics is the trained system accuracy, which is shown in Figs. 4 and 6 for dataset 1 and 2 respectively. In these figures, it can be seen that for the case of systems trained for different batch sizes, the overall system accuracy converges when the system is trained for 20 epochs, which means that training beyond this point does not result is significant gains in system performance. When examining Figs. 4 and 6 collectively it is important to realize that the y-axis scales vary for both these figures. In general, systems trained for higher epochs have higher accuracy than system trained for lower epochs. Figures 5 and 7 demonstrate the overall trend between number of epoch and time (in seconds) for the different values specified for batch size during training of the proposed system using dataset 1 and 2 respectively. From Fig. 5, it can be seen that when comparing the time taken for successful training of systems with different batch sizes, the batch size with the highest overall training time is 4. This shows that in order to optimize the training of the proposed system, a high level of batch size should be preferred. In order to fully appreciate the scale of improvement in computational performance of the proposed system, Fig. 3 shows that the time necessary for training with batch size of 32 and 16 epochs is comparable to the training time for batch size of 4 and 8 epochs.

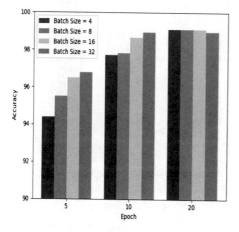

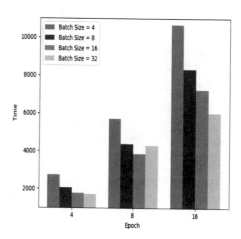

Fig. 4. Relationship between number of epochs and system accuracy for dataset 1.

Fig. 5. Relationship between number of epochs and training time for dataset 1.

In this regard, Fig. 6 presents the results of system training for dataset 2 in terms of accuracy with increase in batch size and epochs for a specific range of values chosen for different system parameters. In contrast to the results obtained for dataset 1, it can be seen that the overall improvement in accuracy with increase in number of epochs is not pronounced for dataset 2. Similarly, it can be seen in Fig. 6, that increase in batch size does not necessarily result in considerably higher performance, specifically for the case of dataset 2. At the same time, there is very small variation in accuracy for the systems trained with different batch sizes. Furthermore, the results obtained for the case of batch size of 32 do not correspond to the highest performance. Due to the increased size of dataset 2, the training time is much higher in comparison to dataset 1, as highlighted in Fig. 5, which shows that system trained with smaller batch sizes undergo higher increase in training time. In general, for the training of the rebar detection subsystem, the inverse relationship between batch size and training time is evident, i.e. increase in batch size reduces the overall time taken for system training. In order to fully benefit from the magnitude of available GPR data, both dataset 1 and 2 had been concatenated. It has been examined in the relevant studies that the performance of Deep Learning-based algorithms is highly dependent on the scale of dataset being used for the system training [28].

Table 3 outlines the overall performance of the system trained using data from different dataset. It can be seen that the system trained after concatenation of the dataset 1 and 2 lead to the highest accuracy and lowest system loss metrics. However, in contrast to the training of dataset 1 and 2 separately, which were trained for 20 epochs each, the system utilizing both dataset 1 and 2 had to be trained for 100 epochs. It can be seen in Table 3 that the training time for system trained on the total data has the

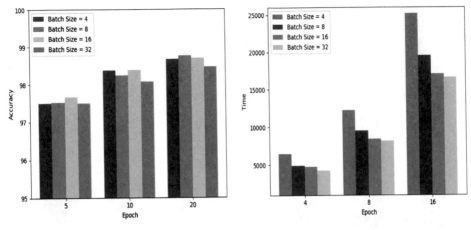

Fig. 6. Relationship between number of epochs and system accuracy for dataset 2.

Fig. 7. Relationship between number of epochs and training time for dataset 2.

highest training time. The learning rate for all of the instances of system training was 0.005, which allowed for steady convergence with reduced probability of overfitting. The size of images in the dataset 1 and 2 had been fixed to 81 × 81 pixels. The system used for performing the different computations had the following specifications: *Intel*® i5 processor with 2.3 GHz clock speed, 4 GB RAM, and 500 GB hard disk. In comparison with relevant studies [12, 19, 23, 24], the results highlighted in this research provide the highest system-level performance for rebar detection system. In the following sub-section, some of the relevant results and associated discussion regarding rebar localization sub-system will be provided.

Table 3. Summary of results for the Rebar Detection System trained using different dataset

Dataset	System performance		
	Accuracy	System loss	Training time
Dataset 1	99.11%	2.91%	7,229 s
Dataset 2	98.75%	3.73%	17,067 s
Total	99.42%	1.88%	21,687 s

4.3   Rebar Localization Sub-system

In this subsection, some of the important details regarding rebar localization sub-system will be outlined. The rebar localization sub-system is the final component of the overall system proposed for rebar detection and localization in this research. Figure 8 presents the step-by-step transition and transformation of the input image from the output of the rebar detection sub-system, which is further processed in order to outline the specific region in which the rebar is present. The main goal within this sub-system is to ensure that the regions in the GPR B-scan images containing the rebar profiles can be effectively highlighted, which can allow for the assessment of different rebar within the bridges. The automation of the rebar localization process can allow the bridge inspection personnel to examine the structural health of individual rebars within bridges.

It can be seen that image segmentation is performed with the help of K-mean clustering algorithm, which allows the segmentation of the different regions based on the varying color intensities. K-means clustering is an unsupervised learning-based algorithm, which separates image regions based on the level of color variations into different clusters [30]. As, it can be seen in Fig. 8, there are considerable variations between the foreground and background regions in rebar images. This particular aspect is leveraged to separate out the different image regions using the Image Thresholding technique, which transforms the image from RGB channels with varying color intensities to a single-channel-based binary image. In this manner, the essential foreground regions are highlighted in images, along with noise and high-intensity regions from the background regions. In order to ensure the ROI only contain regions with rebar profile hyperbolic signatures, the different morphological operations (e.g. opening, closing) are used to separate the foreground regions from the noise artefacts and background regions.

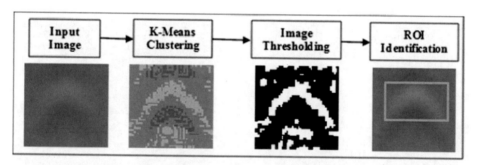

Fig. 8. Results for the different processes in the rebar localization sub-system

Table 4 outlines the overall performance of rebar localization sub-system in terms of accuracy and precision. The performance of the proposed rebar localization sub-system was evaluated on images with single and multiple rebar signatures. It can be seen from Table 4 that the overall accuracy for single rebar images is higher than for B-scan images containing multiple rebar signatures. For images with multiple rebar profiles, the sliding window-based approach was used to highlight different rebars within B-scan images. The overall accuracy of the rebar localization sub-system is at par with the different rebar localization systems developed in the previous studies [12, 19, 24]. A number of factors can affect the overall accuracy of localization of rebars in the B-scan images, such as high-level of noise artefacts in images, presence of multiple wave reflections, overlapping rebar signatures in B-scan images for multiple rebars, use of construction materials with varying properties (e.g. density, permittivity) and presence of non-rebar underground objects (e.g. pipes, utility lines, void spaces and underground metal objects) that exhibit similar hyperbolic signatures.

Table 4. Summary of results for Rebar Localization on dataset 1 and 2

Dataset	Single rebar localization		Multiple rebar localization	
	Accurate localization	Inaccurate localization	Accurate localization	Inaccurate localization
Dataset 1	1,426	73	854	64
Dataset 2	1,299	45	869	76
Total (%)	2,725 (95.85%)	118 (4.15%)	1,723 (92.49%)	140 (7.51%)
Total accuracy		94.52%	Total precision	95.18%

Figures 9 and 10 outline the results of rebar localization sub-system on a segment of B-Scan image obtained from dataset 1 and 2 respectively. It can be seen in Fig. 10 that the proposed system for rebar localization should be able to differentiate between actual rebar profiles and shadow effects, which can be seen in the lower portion of Fig. 10. It can also be observed that these shadow effects are much less pronounced in Fig. 9. Some of the examples of positive and negative results for rebar localization have been provided in Fig. 11.

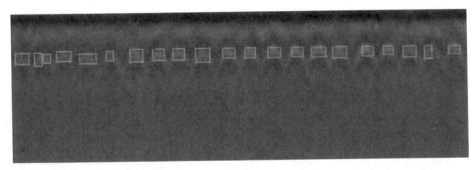

Fig. 9. Results for the rebar localization on a segment of B-Scan image from dataset 1

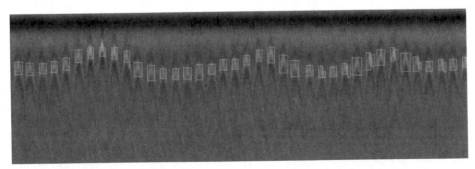

Fig. 10. Results for the rebar localization on a segment of B-Scan image from dataset 2

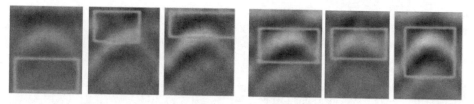

Fig. 11. Examples of negative (first three samples) and positive results for rebar localization

5 Conclusion

In this paper, a novel method for rebar detection has been developed, which utilizes the Deep Learning-based ResNet-50 architecture to train the system to differentiate between rebar and non-rebar images. At the same time, a novel method for rebar localization has also been presented, which uses image processing functions and bounding-box-based approach to outline the location of rebar within the B-scan images. The performance of the rebar detection and rebar localization sub-systems is comparable to some of the relevant state-of-the-art systems developed in the recent past [9, 12, 20, 24]. It can be concluded that this study has revealed compelling results, which warrant further investigation towards the usage of Deep Learning-based architectures to address the research problems related to NDE in general as well as rebar detection and localization in particular. Future comparative studies may provide insight into performance of different Deep Learning-based frameworks for the purpose of system development for rebar detection and localization. At the same time, additional data from different bridges can facilitate the assessment of the overall system performance and robustness due to varying *internal properties* (e.g. length and width of bridges, construction materials used, depth of rebar, total number of rebar used) and *external conditions* (e.g. levels of concrete delamination, rebar corrosion, weather conditions).

Acknowledgment. Financial support for this INSPIRE UTC project is provided by the U.S. Department of Transportation, Office of the Assistant Secretary for Research and Technology (USDOT/OST-R) under Grant No. 69A3551747126 through INSPIRE University Transportation Center (http://inspire-utc.mst.edu) at Missouri University of Science and Technology. The views, opinions, findings and conclusions reflected in this publication are solely those of the authors and do not represent the official policy or position of the USDOT/OST-R, or any State or other entity.

References

1. Penn, A.: The deadliest bridge collapses in the US in the last 50 years. CNN, 15 March 2018
2. Kirk, R.S., Mallett, W.J.: Highway Bridge Conditions: Issues for Congress. US Congressional Research Service, Washington, D.C. (2013)
3. Wright, L., Chinowsky, P., Strzepek, K., et al.: Estimated effect of climate change on flood vulnerability of US bridges. Mitig. Adapt. Strat. Glob. Change **17**(8), 939–955 (2012)

4. Briaud, J.-L., Brandimarte, L., Wang, J., D'Odorico, P.: Probability of scour depth exceedance owing to hydrologic uncertainty. Georisk 1(2), 77–88 (2014)
5. US Department of Transportation Report: 2015 Status of the Nation's Highways, Bridges, and Transit: Conditions and Performance, Pub. No: FHWA-PL-17-001. US Department of Transportation, Washington, DC (2015)
6. La, H.M., Gucunski, N., Dana, K.J., Kee, S.-H.: Development of an autonomous bridge deck inspection robotic system. J. Field Robot. 34, 1489–1504 (2017)
7. DeVault, J.E.: Robotic system for underwater inspection of bridge piers. IEEE Instrum. Meas. Mag. 3(3), 32–37 (2000)
8. Al-Nuaimy, W., Huang, Y., et al.: Automatic detection of buried utilities and solid objects with GPR using neural networks and pattern recognition. J. Appl. Geophys. 43(2), 157–165 (2000)
9. Gibb, S., La, H.M., Le, T., Nguyen, L., Schmid, R., Pham, H.: Nondestructive evaluation sensor fusion with autonomous robotic system for civil infrastructure inspection. J. Field Robot. 35, 988–1004 (2018)
10. Diamanti, N., Redman, N.: Field observations and numerical models of GPR response from vertical pavement cracks. J. Appl. Geophys. 81, 106–116 (2012)
11. Gucunski, N., Kee, S.-H., La, H.M., Basily, B., Maher, A.: Delamination and concrete quality assessment of concrete bridge decks using a fully autonomous RABIT platform. Struct. Monit. Maintenance 2(1), 19–34 (2015)
12. Kaur, P., Dana, K.J., Romero, F.A., Gucunski, N.: Automated GPR rebar analysis for robotic bridge deck evaluation. IEEE Trans. Cybern. 46(10), 2265–2276 (2016)
13. La, H.M., Lim, R.S., Du, J., Zhang, S., Yan, G., Sheng, W.: Development of a small-scale research platform for intelligent transportation systems. IEEE Trans. Intell. Transp. Syst. 13(4), 1753–1762 (2012)
14. La, H.M., Gucunski, N., Kee, S.-H., Nguyen, L.V.: Data analysis and visualization for the bridge deck inspection and evaluation robotic system. J. Visual. Eng. 3(6), 1–16 (2015)
15. Mazzeo, B.A., Larsen, J., McElderry, J., Guthrie, W.S.: Rapid multichannel impact-echo scanning of concrete bridge decks from a continuously moving platform. In: Proceedings of 43rd Annual Review of Progress in Quantitative Nondestructive Evaluation, vol. 1806, pp. 1–6 (2017)
16. Wang, Z.W., Zhou, M., Slabaugh, G.G., Zhai, J., Fang, T.: Automatic detection of bridge deck condition from ground penetrating radar images. IEEE TASE 8(3), 633–640 (2011)
17. Gamba, P., Lossani, S.: Neural detection of pipe signatures in ground penetrating radar images. IEEE Trans. Geosci. Remote Sens. 38(2), 790–797 (2000)
18. Protopapadakis, E., Doulamis, N.: Image based approaches for tunnels' defects recognition via robotic inspectors. In: Bebis, George, et al. (eds.) ISVC 2015. LNCS, vol. 9474, pp. 706–716. Springer, Cham (2015). https://doi.org/10.1007/978-3-319-27857-5_63
19. Gibb, S., La, H.M.: Automated rebar detection for ground-penetrating radar. In: Bebis, George, et al. (eds.) ISVC 2016. LNCS, vol. 10072, pp. 815–824. Springer, Cham (2016). https://doi.org/10.1007/978-3-319-50835-1_73
20. Ahmed, H., La, H.M., Gucunski, N.: Rebar detection using Ground Penetrating Radar with state-of-the-art Convolutional Neural Networks. In: Proceedings of 9th SHMII, St. Louis, Missouri, 4–7 August 2019
21. La, H.M., Gucunski, N., Kee, S.H., Yi, J., Senlet, T., Nguyen, L.: Autonomous robotic system for bridge deck data collection and analysis. In: Proceedings of IEEE/RSJ International Conference on Intelligent Robots and Systems (IROS), Chicago, IL, USA, 14–18 September 2014
22. Lim, R.S., La, H.M., Sheng, W.: A robotic crack inspection and mapping system for bridge deck maintenance. IEEE Trans. Autom. Sci. Eng. 11(2), 367–378 (2014)

23. La, H.M., Lim, R.S., Basily, B., Gucunski, N., Yi, J., Maher, A., Romero, F.A., Parvardeh, H.: Mechatronic and control systems design for an autonomous robotic system for high-efficiency bridge deck inspection and evaluation. IEEE Trans. Mechatron. **18**(6), 1655–1664 (2013)
24. Dinh, K., Gucunski, N., Duong, T.H.: An algorithm for automatic localization and detection of rebars from GPR data of concrete bridge decks. Autom. Constr. **89**, 292–298 (2018)
25. Yu, L., Chen, H., Dou, Q., Qin, J., Heng, P.-H.: Automated melanoma recognition in dermoscopy images via very deep residual networks. IEEE Trans. Med. Imaging **36**(4), 994–1015 (2017)
26. Zhang, K., Sun, M., Han, T.X., Yuan, X., Guo, L., Liu, T.: Residual networks of residual networks: multilevel residual networks. IEEE TCSVT **28**(6), 1303–1314 (2018)
27. Kim, J.-H., Lee, J.-S.: Deep residual network with enhanced upscaling module for super-resolution. In: IEEE CVPR, pp. 913–922 (2018)
28. He, K., Zhang, X., Ren, S., Sun, J.: Deep Residual learning for image recognition. In: Proceedings of ICCV, pp. 770–778 (2016)
29. Chen, C.W., Luo, J., Parker, K.J.: Image segmentation via adaptive K-mean clustering and knowledge-based morphological operations with biomedical applications. ITIP **7**(12), 1673–1683 (1998)
30. Gonzales, R.C., Woods, R.E.: Digital Image Processing, 4th edn. Pearson, New York (2017)

Computer Graphics II

Intrinsic Decomposition by Learning from Varying Lighting Conditions

Gregoire Nieto[1], Mohammad Rouhani[2]($\boxtimes$) (iD), and Philippe Robert[2]

[1] Technicolor R&I, Rennes, France
[2] InterDigital R&D, 975 Avenue des Champs Blancs, 35576 Cesson-Sevigne, France
{mohammad.rouhani,philippe.robert}@interdigital.com

Abstract. Intrinsic image decomposition describes an image based on its reflectance and shading components. In this paper we tackle the problem of estimating the diffuse reflectance from a sequence of images captured from a fixed viewpoint under various illuminations. To this end we propose a deep learning approach to avoid heuristics and strong assumptions on the reflectance prior. We compare two network architectures: one classic 'U' shaped Convolutional Neural Network (CNN) and a Recurrent Neural Network (RNN) composed of Convolutional Gated Recurrent Units (CGRU). We train our networks on a new dataset specifically designed for the task of intrinsic decomposition from sequences. We test our networks on MIT and BigTime datasets and outperform state-of-the-art algorithms both qualitatively and quantitatively.

1 Introduction

Intrinsic image decomposition describes an image based on its reflectance and shading components with many applications ranging from stabilization, re-colorization, relighting to texture and virtual object insertion, to mention a few. Given an image I, this problem aims at disentangling the *shading component* S from the *diffuse reflectance* R: $I = S.R$, where the earlier depends on the shape and lighting conditions while the latter reflects the intrinsic surface color. The problem of Single Image Intrinsic Decomposition (SIID) is an ill-posed problem as we have an infinite number of potential solutions for a single image. To reduce the ambiguity of the decomposition, the given image can be accompanied by a sequence of images captured under different lighting conditions. This prevents common failure cases of single image methods such as difficulties to handle hard cast shadows and bright specularities. We refer to it as Multiple Image Intrinsic Decomposition (MIID).

Traditional approaches, regardless of using a single input image or a sequence of images, estimate the reflectance through direct optimization. The quality of the result highly depends on heuristics modeling and hand-crafted priors on shading and reflectance. Classical optimization-based methods like [13] disentangle reflectance and shading by formulating strong assumptions on reflectance that are derived from prior knowledge. For instance, in [13], it is assumed that pixels with similar normalized intensity profiles over time are likely to have the same shading. The result shown in Fig. 2(a) clearly depicts seams between clusters of pixels that are supposed to share the

© Springer Nature Switzerland AG 2019
G. Bebis et al. (Eds.): ISVC 2019, LNCS 11844, pp. 647–660, 2019.
https://doi.org/10.1007/978-3-030-33720-9_50

Fig. 1. Our neural network processes a sequence of images $(I)_t$ captured under various (uncorrelated) illuminations, and produces the time-invariant reflectance image R.

(a)   (b)   (c)   (d)

Fig. 2. Reflectance by [13]: (a) with c = 20 pixel clusters and $\alpha = 100$. (b) c = 60, $\alpha = 100$. (c) c = 20, $\alpha = 50.0$. (d) using a different set of shaded images, parameters of (a).

same shading over time. Increasing the number of clusters (Fig. 2(b)) does not improve the result, which implies that these methods strongly depend on the *assumption* over the reflectance priors. One of the main advantages of using deep learning over classic approaches is to get rid of explicit priors, and rather, to learn them implicitly.

Another flaw of prior-based approaches lies in *how* these priors are tuned. Figure 2(a, c) display results with different settings for α coefficient that modulates the regularization term. This term forces the solution to be close to the mean chromaticity image. Since the heuristics used to disambiguate the intrinsic decomposition are not directly derived from a mathematical formulation of the problem, but rather from prior knowledge of how we expect the reflectance to be, finding the right coefficient to balance the cost function ends up to unhandy parameter tuning.

Moreover, intrinsic image decomposition should be consistent over a sequence of frames with varying illumination, i.e. diffuse reflectance should be invariant to illumination changes. This is the objective that [17] aims at, by training on sequences of various illuminations and forcing the predicted reflectance to be similar over a sequence. However, there is no guaranty that the network can learn this property at the inference time.

In this paper we propose a new intrinsic image decomposition method that estimates the diffuse reflectance from a sequence of images captured from a viewpoint under various illuminations (Fig. 1). To this end we propose a deep learning approach to avoid heuristics and strong assumptions on reflectance priors. We compare two network architectures: one classic 'U' shaped Convolutional Neural Network (CNN) and a Recurrent Neural Network (RNN) composed of Convolutional Gated Recurrent Units (CGRU). We train our network on a new dataset specifically designed for the task of intrinsic decomposition from sequences. We test our network on MIT [8] and Big-Time [17] datasets and outperform state-of-the-art algorithms both qualitatively and quantitatively.

2   Related Work

Intrinsic Image Decomposition from a Single Image. The intrinsic image decomposition domain is mainly represented by methods that estimate the reflectance by using priors-based optimization, from a single image and without any additional data. For a long time they were largely dominated by the Color Retinex algorithm [8]. It decomposes the image by assuming that a change in color is due to a change in shading when the chromaticity remains constant, and due to a change in reflectance otherwise. This idea derives from the prior knowledge that the reflectance is somehow closely related to the chromaticity. In [28], a non-local reflectance constraint is included to the Retinex formalism, by enforcing reflectance similarity between pixels that share similar chromaticities. Non-local reflectance priors were adopted by subsequent works [11,15,19,20,27], as well as non local shading priors [11,15] by adding valuable improvement to widely used local reflectance and shading priors. Given the ill-posed nature of the intrinsic decomposition problem, formulating novel hand-crafted priors has been a crucial issue. Deep learning is proposed as an alternative to bypass this approach by learning implicit priors *from the data itself.*

Intrinsic Image Decomposition with Deep Learning. Machine learning has been proposed as a solution to the problem in the seminal work on relative reflectance judgments [22], trained on human judgment dataset [2]. Likewise in [29], it is proposed to learn relative reflectance judgments, but as a first step before recovering dense reflectance map like in [2]. Indeed, machine learning is used as a way to estimate priors, not to estimate the final reflectance itself. Direct reflectance estimation by a CNN was an original idea by [21], improved by [24] that introduces the use of a U-net [23] for intrinsic decomposition. There has been many variations of these approaches [1,6,10,16] but to our knowledge, only [17] suggests the use of sequences of illumination-varying images to train a neural network. However, it is still a one-to-one process at inference time, thus well-adapted to classic CNN encoder-decoder architecture. On the other hand, our method is a many-to-one process at training time *and* inference time.

Intrinsic Decomposition from Image Sequences. Methods that benefit from temporal constraints by processing videos are numerous [11,15,19,20,27]. On the contrary, our approach does not require any temporal consistency between views in our sequences. Our problem formulation was initially addressed by [25]. They produce reasonable results by taking advantage of prior knowledge on natural images. However, in [18] it is shown that such results may severely be altered by a biased illumination. More recent solutions were provided to the multi-view problem [5,14]. In [14], the inferred 3D geometry imposes shading constraints for intrinsic decomposition. In [13], a state-of-the-art solution is proposed to solve the initial fixed viewpoint problem [18,25]; they alleviate the lack of geometry by cleverly clustering pixels that share the same radiance profile over time. But like previous optimization-based work, their decomposition algorithm strongly depends on reflectance heuristics, hand-made priors and coefficient tuning. In the present work, we have adopted neural network to solve this problem.

Recurrent Neural Network (RNN). RNNs are networks that loop over themselves, so the output is passed as an input at the next iteration. They are ideal to process sequences of correlated data, such as words in a sentence of frames in a video. The number of times the network loops over itself is not part of its architecture, which makes it flexible to any sequence length; this is analogous to how convolution is flexible for the spatial size of inputs. However, during the training, the back-propagated loss gradient tends to vanish at every iteration: an issue known as *vanishing gradients* [9]. To overcome this problem, Long Short-Term Memory (LSTM) units have been proposed. They are composed of a memory cell that *remembers* information of previous sequences. The information flow over sequences is regulated by three *gates* inside the cell. Applied to images, convolutional LSTMs [26] replace the traditional dense matrix to vector operations by convolutions. In Gated Recurrent Units [4], the memory cell is also used as hidden layer, requiring fewer parameters while performing similarly.

3   Model

In this section we describe two architectures that we compare in Sect. 5: a fully convolutional U-net and convolutional GRU, referred to as CGRU. To describe precisely the architectures, we refer to T as the number of frames in a sequence, C the number of input image channels, F the number of output features (or output channels) and (H, W) the spatial dimensions of input/output images. We feed the network with tensors of shape $T \times C \times H \times W$, and obtain a prediction tensor of size $F \times H \times W$. In practice we want to obtain RGB reflectance images, so $F = C = 3$. Images are resized so that their spatial dimensions are either 256×384, 384×256 or 256×256 depending on their original ratio.

3.1   U-Net

We implemented a 'U' shaped architecture, that has already shown some potential in SIID [1,10,17,24]. The original architecture used for medical segmentation [23], is composed of an encoder and a mirrored decoder. This classic U-net architecture has been modified for adapting with our application. Like [17] it takes a sequence of images but stacks them along the channel dimension, so that the shape of the input tensor is $T.C \times H \times W$. It is composed of 6 convolutional layers for the encoder, 6 for the decoder and one central. Our U-net is lighter than [17]: each convolutional module consists of a single 2D convolution (with a stride of 2 for the encoder), a batch normalization and a *RELU*. Indeed, due to the limited amount of data (every sequence is one single training example), we need to decrease the number of parameters to a reasonable level to avoid overfitting. In addition, each convolutional layer of the decoder possesses a bilinear interpolation (that doubles the spatial dimension) and a concatenation of the input signal of corresponding spatial dimensions (skip-connection).

Since input images are stacked together in the channel dimension, the length of a sequence has to be fixed, otherwise the architecture changes (the number of convolutions of the first encoding layer). The flexible nature of RNNs makes them better-suited than CNNs to process sequences of images.

3.2 Convolutional Gated Recurrent Unit (CGRU)

Our second architecture is a Recurrent Neural Network. Using such RNNs has several advantages over CNNs:

- it needs fewer parameters (thousands instead of millions) because every image in the sequence is processed by units that share the same weights;
- since it loops over the sequence, it can process any number of frames;
- it requires less GPU memory because the recurrent loop can be run sequentially.

Following the idea that our model should have as few parameters as possible so it generalizes to any kind of scene, we opt for Gated Recurrent Unit (GRU). Like [26] with LSTMs, we implemented a convolutional version of the GRU (CGRU), that replaces matrix-vector operations by convolutions, so that it processes information both *temporally* and *spatially*. Let I_t be the current input frame and h_t the hidden layer (or output) at time t, the next hidden layer h_{t+1} or output of the unit is computed as follows:

$$z_t = \sigma(W_{zi} * I_t + W_{zh} * h_t + b_z). \tag{1}$$

$$r_t = \sigma(W_{ri} * I_t + W_{rh} * h_t + b_r). \tag{2}$$

$$\tilde{h}_t = \tanh(W_{hi} * I_t + W_{hh} * (r_t \circ h_t) + b_h). \tag{3}$$

$$h_{t+1} = (1 - z_t) \circ h_t + z_t \circ \tilde{h}_t. \tag{4}$$

with $*$ denoting the convolution operation, W and b the weights and biases of the convolutions, $\circ$ the element-wise product, σ the sigmoid function and $\tanh$ the hyperbolic tangent. Hidden layers h_t are tensors of shape $F \times H \times W$ and input frames I_t are tensors of shape $C \times H \times W$.

The hidden layer h behaves like the memory cell of a LSTM unit, forgetting and learning information from the successive frames that are fed to the unit. Intuitively we can think of it as containing all the illumination-invariant information of the sequence, which is expected to be the reflectance. At each iteration, a new input frame passes through the gates that select the information h, forget with the reset gate image r_t, and update h with the update gate image z_t. Initially the hidden layer is set to 0, which means we have no prior memory. Eventually when we have iterated over the whole sequence, the prediction R is the final hidden layer h_T.

It is also possible to *stack* several layers of CGRUs. In Fig. 3 we represent two layers 0 and 1. Each recurrent unit output h_t^l is not only passed *horizontally* to the next iteration to be jointly processed with I_{t+1} by the same unit, but also *vertically* to another unit as a new input. Units from other layers do not share the same weights. Stacked layers can be seen as if the sequence was processed by successive convolutional layers, which enables deeper feature processing and structure extraction. The final prediction R is the output h_T^L of the last layer L (h_T^1 in Fig. 3).

3.3 Achromatic Illumination Assumption

The assumption of the achromatic illumination is common in the SIID literature [2, 6, 29]. However, it is not clear whether it improves or deteriorates the prediction. It

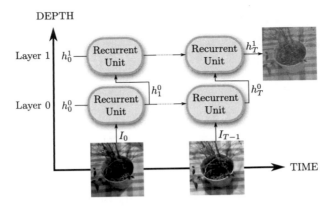

Fig. 3. CGRUs can be stacked vertically to enable deep feature processing. The output sequence of each layer is passed to the next one till reaching the final prediction R.

assumes that the lighting intensity is constant over the sequence, which is the case in most scenes but not always (multiple light sources, colored illumination, dimming light). As a consequence, the shading is greyscale; we can predict a greyscale reflectance r and recover the tricolor reflectance R with the median chromaticity of the sequence:

$$R = 3 . r . \text{median}_t \left(\frac{I_t^c}{\sum_c I_t^c} \right) \text{ with } I_t^c \text{ the } c^{th} \text{ channel of } I_t. \tag{5}$$

The relevance of using such assumption is discussed in Sect. 5, where both models (achromatic that predicts r with $F = 1$ and chromatic that predicts R with $F = 3$) are confronted.

3.4   Loss

Our model fitting is supervised by comparing the prediction R and the ground truth reflectance R^* in the loss function. We force the prediction to be close to the ground truth not only in terms of color, but also in terms of gradient [21]. In [21] however, a L2-norm is used; we use instead an L1, known to be more robust to outliers. We do not apply the loss to the shading because our model implies that it is directly derived from the input sequence and the predicted reflectance. We tried to add the same shading smoothness constraint as in [13], but we obtained worse results.

In addition, we apply a total variation [7] on the predicted reflectance. It comes from the observation that natural images are generally piecewise smooth. In Sect. 5 we study the influence of the total variation term on the quality of the images. The final loss function is

$$\mathcal{L}(R, R^*) = \|R^* - R\|_1 + \|\nabla R^* - \nabla R\|_1 + \|\nabla R\|_1. \tag{6}$$

4   Dataset

Traditionally, SIID methods train their models and evaluate their results on 4 datasets: MIT [8], MPI Sintel [3], IIW [2] and SAW [12]. Nevertheless, only MIT is suited to the task of MIID, since the rest only contain single image examples. Recently a new dataset called BigTime [17] was introduced, with images sequences but no ground truth.

Because the MIT dataset alone is not sufficient neither for training or for evaluation, we crafted our own dataset, called Washington, composed of real and synthetic images. Our dataset combines the better of two worlds: sequences of real images with changing illumination and an image used as reflectance ground truth. Washington is made of indoor scenes of various objects on a table. Indoor scenes are chosen over outdoor, so we are able to capture a large diversity of illuminations in a controlled environment, which makes it possible to estimate a pseudo-reflectance for supervised training. Indeed, to obtain an acceptable ground truth and reference image, we capture an image under pseudo-ambient lighting, which makes the shading almost constant everywhere. Such image, called *pseudo-reflectance*, is not the proper reflectance since it still contains ambient occlusion (inter-shadowing of concave surfaces), but it suits many AR applications such as texturing and relighting.

We create our real dataset (see the first two rows in Fig. 4) by capturing sequences of frames from a fixed viewpoint, and changing the illumination. We used 10 sets of objects; for each set we create ten various scenes, changing the position of the objects and the camera viewpoint, which makes a total of 100 scenes. From every of these 100 captured videos, we randomly extract 10 sequences of 30 frames (with no continuous variation of shading over time). The complete dataset of 1000 sequences of real images is split into a training set, a validation set and a test set with a respective proportion of (80%/10%/10%). We make sure that the splits do not share any scenes or objects.

To cope with our issue of not having a ground truth reflectance (in particular for evaluation since a pseudo-reflectance image suits well to MIID supervision) we enhance our Washington dataset with 780 supplementary sequences of synthetic views (see the last two rows in Fig. 4). The synthetic scenes were created and rendered using Unity; they simulate a plane carrying various 3D objects from the daily life. Up to 3 point light sources of different intensities lit the scenes. In addition, we use a large collection of textures and materials to render specularities. The dataset is split into a training set (700 sequences) and a test set (80 sequences).

5   Experiments

We perform several experiments to validate the performance of our models. First, we study the relevance of the achromatic illumination assumption. Second, we observe the influence of the number of input views on the predicted reflectance, and validate the recurrent model (CGRU) by decomposing the result frame by frame. Then we compare our models to state-of-the-art methods, in term of numerical, visual and runtime performance. Last but not least, we address some limits of our models.

Training. Our models (U-net and CGRU) are trained on our Washington training set (real images), unless otherwise stated. The 800 training sequences contain 15 images

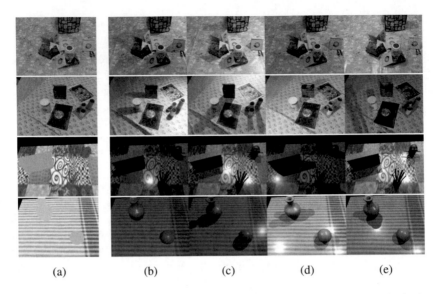

(a)   (b)   (c)   (d)   (e)

Fig. 4. A sample of our training set. First two rows: real data. Last two rows: synthetic data. (a) Pseudo-reflectance (reference). (b–e) Some images from sample sequences.

that are resized to 384×256. At each iteration, network is fed a single sequence, which means the batch size is one (huge due to memory requirement). We perform 40 epochs and the training lasts approximately 10 h on an NVidia GTX 1080. We save the model for which the validation loss (computed on the real Washington validation set) is minimum. We use Adam optimizer with a learning rate of 0.0005.

Evaluation Metrics. Like previous experiments in the literature [17,21,24], we use the metrics MSE, LMSE and DSSIM to evaluate our results. MSE is a scale-invariant version of the Mean Square Error introduced by [8] to account for relative reflectance. LMSE is the Local Mean Square Error [8], which is the MSE computed on 16×16 overlapping patches (the size matters little according to the authors). DSSIM is the structural dissimilarity index. Predicted reflectance images are compared to reference image. In the case of real Washington dataset, for which we have no proper ground truth, we compare the prediction to the pseudo-reflectance.

5.1 Chromatic Versus Achromatic Illumination Assumption

In this experiment we validate the use of the achromatic assumption that models the shading as being greyscale. Therefore, as detailed in Sect. 3, instead of predicting tri-color reflectance we predict a greyscale reflectance and recover the color thanks to the median chromaticity of the sequence (Eq. 5). This assumption is validated on the Washington real test set and on the MIT dataset. The model used for this experiment is CGRU with a depth (number of layers L) of 1. Although there is no significant numerical difference between the chromatic and the achromatic model on Washington dataset, we notice a strong difference on MIT dataset in favor of the achromatic model

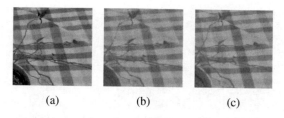

(a)   (b)   (c)

Fig. 5. Qualitative validation of the achromatic illumination assumption of a sample of the Washington set. (a) Reference. (b) Chromatic model. (c) Achromatic model.

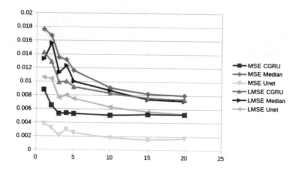

Fig. 6. Performance of U-net and CGRU on Washington real test set with an increasing number of input frames. The median image of the sequence is used as baseline.

(LMSE = 0.0581 against 0.0866). The superiority of the achromatic model is qualitatively validated on Washington, as highlighted in Fig. 5. The achromatic model tends to produce images with colors that are more faithful to the original. In addition, we observe that the obtained tricolor reflectance from the chromatic model becomes more and more greyish as we increase the depth of the recurrent network ($L > 1$). For all these reasons we performed the next experiments with the use of the achromatic model.

5.2   The Influence of the Number of Images in a Sequence

We analyze the influence of the number of images on the predicted reflectance by testing the U-net and CGRU ($L = 1$) models on our Washington real test set. The Fig. 6 illustrates the results obtained with a number of input images T that varies between 1 and 20. The figure clearly shows the superiority of U-net against CGRU on this test set. As expected, increasing the number of input frames increases the performance. However, CGRU behaves differently: it quickly converges towards its maximum performance after a few frames, contrarily to U-net whose performance with respect to the number of input frames appears more linear.

We show the non-linear behavior of the CGRU in Fig. 7, that displays two sequences of the validation set and the predicted output over time (b–i). Notice that the shadow formed by the flower pot on the top sequence quickly disappears from the prediction. Although the convergence is fast, the output is not disturbed by new challenging

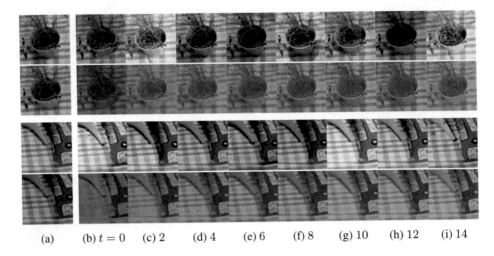

| (a) | (b) $t = 0$ | (c) 2 | (d) 4 | (e) 6 | (f) 8 | (g) 10 | (h) 12 | (i) 14 |

Fig. 7. Validating for 2 sequences. (a) Top: median image. Bottom: pseudo-reflectance. (b–i) Input images I_t (top) and output images h_t (bottom) for iterations $t = 0 \ldots 14$.

input frames that contain hard cast shadows (Fig. 7(f)) nor over/under-exposed frames (Fig. 7(h–i)). The bottom sequence is another example of a robust prediction: when the light direction abruptly changes from Fig. 7(h–i), no shadow is added at the right of the green hose, but the left shadow of the hose and the coffin are largely attenuated. This is a case where the prediction overperforms the reference. It means that the recurrent model, by its simplicity, easily generalizes to produce reflectance images that are even better than the pseudo-reflectance images.

A clear disadvantage of U-net is that it needs to be re-trained each time we change the number of input frames, because of its rigid architecture. On the contrary the prediction of CGRU ($L = 1$) is improved only by feeding it another image, because it processes the input images sequentially. The length of the sequence processed by CGRU ($L = 1$) is virtually infinite. Note that it is the case for most optimization-based methods like [13,18,25]. We also tested [13] with different numbers of input images and it is always outperformed by our models (Fig. 6) ([13]: LMSE = 0.0198 for $T = 5$ or LMSE = 0.017 for $T = 20$). In the next subsection we will see further comparisons with state-of-the-art methods.

5.3   Comparison with State-of-the-Art Methods

We compare our models to state-of-the-art methods [13,17,18,25]. The first three ones are tested via sequences of 15 images with static viewpoint. For [13], the α parameter value that produces best results in our dataset is 100; we set the number of clusters to 20. We choose to compare to [25], an early method that competes with [13]. For [18], we keep the same parameters as in the original paper. We also compare our models to the recent single image method [17]: we obtain the results by computing the temporal median of the predicted reflectance over the sequence. Note that we use the temporal median of the input raw sequence as baseline.

Table 1. Numerical results on our test dataset. The lower the better (in bold). VAR is $10^5 \times$ the measured variance value. The first five rows show the state of the art.

Metric	Washington virtual dataset			Washington real dataset				MIT dataset		
	MSE	LMSE	DSSIM	VAR	MSE	LMSE	DSSIM	MSE	LMSE	DSSIM
Median	0.1498	0.0586	0.3613	125	0.0082	0.0074	0.2139	0.0573	0.1511	0.1400
[25]	0.1334	0.0689	0.3556	111	0.0087	0.0105	0.3039	0.0497	0.1364	0.1470
[18]	0.1378	0.0748	0.3433	103	0.0077	0.0076	0.2001	0.0448	0.1089	0.1289
[17] (median)	0.0770	0.1062	0.3138	**2**	0.0095	0.0303	0.2363	0.0292	0.0892	0.1498
[13]	0.0718	0.0885	0.3002	79	0.0107	0.0173	0.2541	0.0381	0.0920	0.1426
Our methods:										
CGRU-2-TV	**0.0661**	0.0598	0.3179	15	0.0049	0.0097	0.2206	0.0377	0.0770	0.1462
CGRU-2-L1*	0.0718	0.0596	0.2914	27	0.0046	0.0093	0.2394	0.0266	0.0662	0.1335
CGRU-2-L1	0.1017	0.0611	0.3701	46	0.0037	0.0066	0.2060	0.0365	0.0698	0.1374
CGRU-1-TV	0.0820	0.0506	0.3149	69	0.0061	0.0067	0.2198	0.0264	0.0592	0.1354
CGRU-1-L1*	0.0712	0.0596	**0.2780**	40	0.0064	0.0096	0.2365	0.0263	0.0632	0.1315
CGRU-1-L1	0.0715	0.0533	0.3216	58	0.0052	0.0076	0.2192	0.0246	0.0581	0.1342
U-net-TV	0.0836	**0.0439**	0.3222	35	0.0023	0.0057	0.2071	0.0283	0.0755	0.1418
U-net-L1*	0.0824	0.0536	0.3305	32	0.0019	0.0058	0.2046	0.0407	0.0862	**0.1271**
U-net-L1	0.0847	0.0509	0.3233	23	**0.0015**	**0.0056**	**0.1993**	**0.0236**	**0.0578**	0.1309

Numerical Results: Numerical results are presented in Table 1. It is shown that our models largely outperform all other methods. U-net performs the best, followed by CGRU with a single depth layer (CGRU-1). Surprisingly deep recurrent networks ($L > 1$) do not outperform the single layer one; networks with 3 and 4 layers are not shown because they produce worse results, only CGRU-2 is showed. Visually we observe that the deeper the CGRU, the blurrier the predictions tend to be. Training on the virtual train set in addition to the real train set (models marked with a * in Table 1) only improves results on the virtual test set. However, the performance of deep CGRU $L > 1$ are improved when additional synthetic data is used, from which we can infer that their mediocre performance compared to simpler models is due to overfitting.

Illumination Invariance Criterion: In addition to the presented metrics, we add an illumination invariance criterion. It is the variance of the reflectances from several *sequences* of images of the same scene captured under different illuminations. Since in our Washington dataset we have 10 different sequences of illuminations per scene, we compute the variance over the 10 predicted reflectances; the lower variance the better. The SIID method [17] outperforms the others by far. We believe the way the model was trained enforced the illumination invariance of their output (a key contribution of their work). Nevertheless, the quality of the predicted reflectance is inferior to ours.

Loss Function: We compare the performance of our models trained with either the L1 norm only (written "L1" on Table 1), or with the additional total variation term (written "TV"). We observe that the TV term penalizes the network in general. However, its resulting prediction is visually interesting. In Fig. 8 we can state that the TV network

Reference Median   [25]   [18]   [17]   [13]   CGRU-L1 U-net-TV U-net-L1

Fig. 8. Comparison with state-of-the-art method on real Washington (first two rows) and MIT (last two rows) datasets. The median image is used as baseline for comparison. The three last columns illustrate our methods: "TV" means that the total variation was used in the loss; we write "L1" otherwise.

performs better in the case of a simple uniform reflectance (for the paper on the third row). In contrast it performs poorly in the presence of highly detailed images such as the turtle (last row), smoothing out the details on the shell. The reason why it generally underperforms the simple yet generic L1 loss, is probably because it oversimplifies the predicted reflectance, making it piece-wise constant where texture should be left untouched. Nevertheless, even trained with the TV loss, the U-net model still outperforms state-of-the-art approaches.

Runtime Performance: Like in [19] (where they use a geometric proxy and user scribbles), our implementation is real-time. In contrast, [27] processes a single frame in a minute, and [11] in ten minutes. The faster network is U-net (3 ms to process 15 frames of size 384×256), then CGRU-1 (7 ms) and finally CGRU-2 (17 ms). [17] is also quite fast even when applied to the whole sequence (4 ms). Other methods [13, 18, 25] are iterative and take approximately 30 s. Note that we could obtain the reflectance with [25] faster if we computed the pseudo-inverse directly instead of solving the problem iteratively as we did.

5.4 Limitations

Our model is not exempt of limits, especially when it comes to decompose images that have a complex shading, such as the panther in the MIT dataset. Although cast shadows are removed or at least well attenuated, shading in the form of ambient occlusion is still visible. It is clearly due to the fact that most of the pseudo-reflectance images display ambient occlusion and other weak lighting effects. However, this is not a problem for most of AR applications (e.g. relighting), as such image remains closer to true reflectance than chromaticity-like images often displayed by other methods.

6 Conclusion

We have presented an end-to-end method to estimate the reflectance from a sequence of images that are captured from the same view under various illuminations. Contrary to state-of-the-art approaches, we do not rely on any prior knowledge on reflectance, nor hand-crafted priors, but rather learn from the data itself. As a consequence, no parameter tuning is needed at inference time. Two different models are proposed to solve this problem, based on U-net and recurrent network (CGRU), while the earlier has the advantage of being fast and provides better results, the latter is more flexible and requires less memory storage as it processes any number of views sequentially. Both networks process sequences in real-time and outperform state-of-the-art methods. Moreover, a new dataset has been provided, including sequences of images and their ground truth reflectances. We hope this will encourage people to train and evaluate their networks for the tasks of single and multiple image intrinsic decomposition.

References

1. Baslamisli, A.S., Le, H.-A., Gevers, T.: CNN based learning using reflection and retinex models for intrinsic image decomposition. In: The IEEE Conference on Computer Vision and Pattern Recognition (CVPR), June 2018
2. Bell, S., Bala, K., Snavely, N.: Intrinsic images in the wild. ACM Trans. Graph. (SIGGRAPH) **33**(4), 159 (2014)
3. Butler, D., Wulff, J., Stanley, G., Black, M.: MPI-Sintel optical flow benchmark: supplemental material. Technical report, MPI-IS-TR-006, MPI for Intelligent Systems (2012)
4. Cho, K., et al.: Learning phrase representations using RNN encoder-decoder for statistical machine translation. arXiv preprint arXiv:1406.1078 (2014)
5. Duchêne, S., et al.: Multi-view intrinsic images of outdoors scenes with an application to relighting. ACM Trans. Graph. **34**(5) (2015)
6. Fan, Q., Yang, J., Hua, G., Chen, B., Wipf, D.: Revisiting deep intrinsic image decompositions. In: The IEEE Conference on Computer Vision and Pattern Recognition (CVPR), June 2018
7. Goldluecke, B., Cremers, D.: An approach to vectorial total variation based on geometric measure theory. In: 2010 IEEE Conference on Computer Vision and Pattern Recognition (CVPR), pp. 327–333, June 2010
8. Grosse, R., Johnson, M.K., Adelson, E.H., Freeman, W.T.: Ground truth dataset and baseline evaluations for intrinsic image algorithms. In: 2009 IEEE 12th International Conference on Computer Vision, pp. 2335–2342, September 2009
9. Hochreiter, S., Bengio, Y., Frasconi, P.: Gradient flow in recurrent nets: the difficulty of learning long-term dependencies. In: Kolen, J., Kremer, S. (eds.) Field Guide to Dynamical Recurrent Networks. IEEE Press, Piscataway (2001)
10. Janner, M., Wu, J., Kulkarni, T.D., Yildirim, I., Tenenbaum, J.: Self-supervised intrinsic image decomposition. In: Advances in Neural Information Processing Systems, pp. 5938–5948 (2017)
11. Kong, N., Gehler, P.V., Black, M.J.: Intrinsic video. In: Fleet, D., Pajdla, T., Schiele, B., Tuytelaars, T. (eds.) ECCV 2014. LNCS, vol. 8690, pp. 360–375. Springer, Cham (2014). https://doi.org/10.1007/978-3-319-10605-2_24
12. Kovacs, B., Bell, S., Snavely, N., Bala, K.: Shading annotations in the wild. In: Computer Vision and Pattern Recognition (CVPR) (2017)
13. Laffont, P., Bazin, J.: Intrinsic decomposition of image sequences from local temporal variations. In: 2015 IEEE International Conference on Computer Vision (ICCV), pp. 433–441, December 2015
14. Laffont, P.-Y.: Intrinsic image decomposition from multiple photographs. Ph.D. thesis, Inria/University of Nice Sophia-Antipolis, October 2012

15. Lee, K.J., et al.: Estimation of intrinsic image sequences from image+depth video. In: Fitzgibbon, A., Lazebnik, S., Perona, P., Sato, Y., Schmid, C. (eds.) ECCV 2012. LNCS, vol. 7577, pp. 327–340. Springer, Heidelberg (2012). https://doi.org/10.1007/978-3-642-33783-3_24

16. Lettry, L., Vanhoey, K., Gool, L.V.: DARN: a deep adversarial residual network for intrinsic image decomposition. In: 2018 IEEE Winter Conference on Applications of Computer Vision (WACV), pp. 1359–1367 (2018)

17. Li, Z., Snavely, N.: Learning intrinsic image decomposition from watching the world. In: The IEEE Conference on Computer Vision and Pattern Recognition (CVPR), June 2018

18. Matsushita, Y., Lin, S., Kang, S.B., Shum, H.-Y.: Estimating intrinsic images from image sequences with biased illumination. In: Pajdla, T., Matas, J. (eds.) ECCV 2004. LNCS, vol. 3022, pp. 274–286. Springer, Heidelberg (2004). https://doi.org/10.1007/978-3-540-24671-8_22

19. Meka, A., Fox, G., Zollhöfer, M., Richardt, C., Theobalt, C.: Live user-guided intrinsic video for static scenes. IEEE Trans. Vis. Comput. Graph. 23(11), 2447–2454 (2017)

20. Meka, A., Zollhöfer, M., Richardt, C., Theobalt, C.: Live intrinsic video. ACM Trans. Graph. 35(4), 109:1–109:14 (2016)

21. Narihira, T., Maire, M., Yu, S.X.: Direct intrinsics: learning albedo-shading decomposition by convolutional regression. In: Proceedings of the 2015 IEEE International Conference on Computer Vision (ICCV), ICCV 2015, pp. 2992–2992. IEEE Computer Society, Washington, DC (2015)

22. Narihira, T., Maire, M., Yu, S.X.: Learning lightness from human judgement on relative reflectance. In: Proceedings of the IEEE Conference on Computer Vision and Pattern Recognition, pp. 2965–2973 (2015)

23. Ronneberger, O., Fischer, P., Brox, T.: U-net: convolutional networks for biomedical image segmentation. In: Navab, N., Hornegger, J., Wells, W.M., Frangi, A.F. (eds.) MICCAI 2015. LNCS, vol. 9351, pp. 234–241. Springer, Cham (2015). https://doi.org/10.1007/978-3-319-24574-4_28

24. Shi, J., Dong, Y., Su, H., Stella, X.Y.: Learning non-lambertian object intrinsics across shapenet categories. In: 2017 IEEE Conference on Computer Vision and Pattern Recognition (CVPR), pp. 5844–5853. IEEE (2017)

25. Weiss, Y.: Deriving intrinsic images from image sequences. In: Eighth IEEE International Conference on Computer Vision, ICCV 2001, Proceedings, vol. 2, pp. 68–75. IEEE (2001)

26. Xingjian, S., Chen, Z., Wang, H., Yeung, D.-Y., Wong, W.-K., Woo, W.-C.: Convolutional LSTM network: a machine learning approach for precipitation nowcasting. In: Advances in Neural Information Processing Systems, pp. 802–810 (2015)

27. Ye, G., Garces, E., Liu, Y., Dai, Q., Gutierrez, D.: Intrinsic video and applications. ACM Trans. Graph. 33(4), 80:1–80:11 (2014)

28. Zhao, Q., Tan, P., Dai, Q., Shen, L., Wu, E., Lin, S.: A closed-form solution to retinex with nonlocal texture constraints. IEEE Trans. Pattern Anal. Mach. Intell. 34(7), 1437–1444 (2012)

29. Zhou, T., Krähenbühl, P., Efros, A.A.: Learning data-driven reflectance priors for intrinsic image decomposition. In: 2015 IEEE International Conference on Computer Vision (ICCV), pp. 3469–3477, December 2015

Pixel2Field: Single Image Transformation to Physical Field of Sports Videos

Liang Peng(⊠)

Verizon Media, Sunnyvale, CA 94089, USA
plg519@gmail.com

Abstract. Locating players on a 2D field plane for sports match is the first step towards developing many types of sports analytics applications. Most existing mechanisms of locating players require them to wear sensors during sports play. Sports games can be easily recorded by cameras with low cost. Current human detection and tracking techniques can be used to locate players in the video, which is typically distorted for panorama view. We propose an end-to-end system named Pixel2Field, which can transform every pixel location into their scaled 2d field image. This is done by first undistorting the image by estimating the distortion coefficients, followed by a homography recovery. Experiments using detected soccer players from a distorted video show the proposed transformation method works well. To the best of knowledge, this is the first end-to-end system that can transform frame pixel location to field location without any human intervention. This unlock a lot of opportunities for developing sports analytics applications.

Keywords: Image distortion · Homograph transformation · Camera calibration · Sports analytic

1 Introduction

Obtaining players' locations serves the basis for sports analytics. For different sports, once the players' locations are known, variety of analytics can be done such as speed estimation, distance estimation, tactics analysis and highlights summarization. Currently, letting players wear sensors [1, 3] during match play is the most common way to obtain their positions. However, this way has obvious drawbacks. First, letting players wear sensors has obstacle due to its tedious process before the game. Second, wearing sensors bring uncomfortable feel to the players during the game play. Third, sensors come with a certain cost. On the other hand, video capturing devices become more commonly used today for both professional players and ammeter players. Large number of sports games are recorded every day. Currently, sports videos are mainly used for viewers to watch either live or re-play version of the game. Using videos for sports analytics have many advantages since it does not require players to wear anything and also has low cost compared with the sensors.

© Springer Nature Switzerland AG 2019
G. Bebis et al. (Eds.): ISVC 2019, LNCS 11844, pp. 661–669, 2019.
https://doi.org/10.1007/978-3-030-33720-9_51

There are mainly two types of techniques needed for conducting video-based sporting analytics. The first type is object and human detection. For object detection, a lot of research has been done. Feature-engineering-based approaches include using color [12], intrinsic structure [10], and materials [20] to develop features for object detection in images. Feature-learning-based methods [9,13,18] mainly reply on deep neural networks do detect objects. Video contains temporal info. as additional property than images, so some video-based object detection techniques [7,11] were developed using temporal info. or key frames [14,15,22] from videos to detect objects. Face-detection-based methods [16] [21] have been used detect humans, but sports videos typically contains humans that are small on the filed which was captured from camera far away. Face-detection-based methods can not be directly employed. Some motion-based method [2] has been developed to track sports players in moving scene. The second type is transformation from video to physical field, some exiting work have studied the transformation techniques about distortion and homograph, but it requires human intervention for calibration. To the best of our knowledge, there is no system existing that can do the fully automatic transformation in an end-to-end fashion.

There are some existing challenges when using videos for locating players and conducting analytics. First, most cameras can only cover partial field when requiring to be placed relative close to the field to record clear videos for the types of sports with large field (e.g. soccer, football), due to their covering angles. Second, even though panorama video can be obtained by wide-angle video camera or stitching several partial videos recorded by an array of cameras, distortion is inevitable for the recorded videos. From distorted videos, players' pixel location from frames could be obtained by using computer vision techniques (e.g. human detection, tracking, object detection). However, sports analytics require players physical 2d location on the field. Therefore, there is a gap of transforming the pixel location of players to their physical location on a 2d plane (i.e. scaled play-field from bird-view).

Two main challenges exist in transforming distort frame to 2d field map. The first one is to undistort the image by calibration. This typically requires the distortion coefficients from the camera which was used to record the video. If we only have access to the video without the camera parameters info., calibration cannot be done. Some latest work [5] proposed the approach of calibration using only a single image. However, even after the calibration, the undistorted frame is still a homography transformation of the scaled rectangle field. Recover of the scaled rectangle field remains challenges. Some existing methods [6,19] require human to pick up the matching points between the homography image and original image to estimate the transformation parameters, but it is hard to scale due to the human intervention.

In this paper, we propose a fully automatic end-to-end system that can transform each frame in sports video to a 2d field map without any camera info. There are three major contributions of our work: First, we formulate an objective function and provide the solution for estimating the radial distortion coefficients leveraging hough transformation from a single image. Second, we propose a fully automatic homography recovery method utilizing key-points detection. Last but not least, we integrate these modules to an end-to-end system which is capable of transforming pixel location to field location. To the best of our knowledge, it is the first system that can transform pixel location from distorted sports video to a 2d field map without any human intervention. Experiments using a professional soccer game recording show our proposed system achieve good transformation results.

The rest of the paper is organized as follows: Sect. 2 introduces our proposed system starting from overview followed by detailed explanation of each module; Sect. 3 presents the experiment and results. Last, we conclude the work with future directions in Sect. 4.

2 Transformation from Frame Pixel to 2D Field

2.1 System Overview

Figure 2 shows the architecture of the proposed system. The input is a frame of recorded video from sports game. The output we want to get is a scaled 2d map which directly corresponds to the physical field from which the video was recorded (Fig. 1).

Looking backward from the output (i.e.: 2d field image) to the input (recorded video frame), two types of transformation occurred during the video recording. First, due to the perspective view of the camera, homography transformation occurred from 2d field. This means that the actual rectangle physical field is mapped to a trapezoid. Second, the video frame is a distortion of the trapezoid. Therefore, the proposed system aims to reverse this process by first undistorting the input frame followed by homography restoring to obtain the scaled 2d field image. For easier discussion, let's divide the whole flow into two phases: undistortion and homography recovery. In undistortion phase, for the input frame, we want to find out a mapping function to transform each position of input frame to an undistorted image. According to Brown's distortion model [4], two key distortion coefficients need to be estimated to decide the mapping. They are called radial distortion coefficients. Typically, the camera have the values of these parameters. However, as mentioned in Sect. 1, camera-related parameters are not always available and we want to develop an approach to estimate the distortion coefficients solely based on the image itself. This typically requires some manual work of labeling some matching points between the distorted image and the undistorted one. Unlike general video scenes, we have some prior knowledge in sports video scenes. For example, the borderlines and reference lines from playground suppose to be straight. These prior knowledge can be leveraged to formulate an optimization problem to solve for distortion coefficients. For each input frame, we apply hough transformation to automatically detect the border lines of the play-field. Then sample points can be taken from these lines. Once the sample points are obtained, we can use them to solve the optimization problem to find the distortion coefficients. Finally, we apply brown's distortion model to transform the video frame into the undistorted image. In phase 2, since the undistorted frame is a homography transformation of the scaled 2d field map, Hessian matrix need to be estimated to decide the transformation function. Just like in undistortion, this typically require the manual labeling on some matching

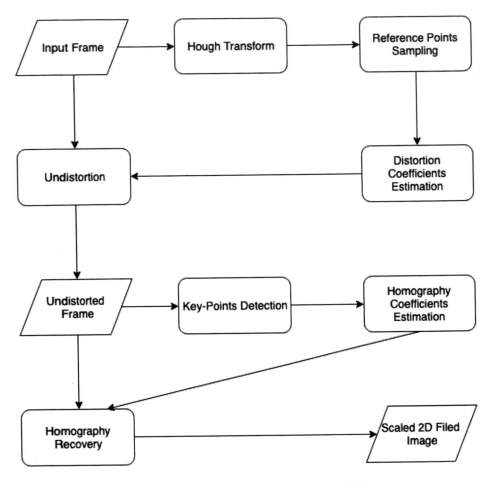

Fig. 1. Architecture overview of the Proposed System

points between the original image and homography transformation of the image. Thanks to the special property of sports video scene, key points based on the reference lines and border lines can be leveraged to find these points. Therefore, for the undistorted frame, we first employ the key-points detection module to find some key points on the play-field. Then we estimate the homography coefficients (i.e.: hessian matrix) by these key points and the standard physical map of the sports play-field. Finally, we use these coefficients to apply the homography recovery function to obtain the scaled 2d field map. Sections 2.2 and 2.3 will explain how each phase works in detail.

2.2   Image Undistortion

In this module, we want to obtain the undistorted image from the distorted video frame. According to Brown's model, letting x_d, y_d represent the horizontal and vertical coordinates of a point on distorted image, respectively, and c_x, c_y represent the center coordinates of the distorted image. The corresponding horizontal coordinate x_i, and vertical coordinate y_i, of the undistorted image can be expressed as:

$$x_i = x_d + (x_d - c_x)(k_1 r^2 + k_2 r^4) \tag{1}$$

$$y_i = y_d + (y_d - c_y)(k_1 r^2 + k_2 r^4) \tag{2}$$

where r is the distance of the point (x_d, y_d) to the center (c_x, c_y), and k_1, k_2 are the radial distortion coefficients.

It can be seen from above that the undistortion mapping function can be fixed once radial distortion coefficients k1 and k2 are estimated.

Without the camera parameters, we propose an approach to estimate these parameters leveraging sports' scenes special properties. In any sports game with the borderlines being straight (e.g.: soccer, football), some of these borderlines can be distorted to curves. If we can obtain some sample points on these lines from distorted image, we know each group of points on the same line with possible curve shape should be from a straight line in undistorted image. Therefore, first, we apply color-based segmentation and hough transformation to automatically detect the m borderlines of the field. Second, we random some sample points each of these borderlines. Finally, the corresponding points on the undistorted image should have the shortest total distance between each point and fitted straight border lines. Therefore, radial distortion coefficients k1 and k2 can be estimated by solving the minimization problem.

$$argmin \sum_{j=1}^{m} \sum_{p_j^i} min||P_j^i - R_j|| \tag{3}$$

where P_j^i is ith point from jth borderline, and R_j is the fitted straightline using the points from jth borderline using least square for regression.

We use a pre-grid-search and fine-tune algorithm to find k1 and k2.

2.3   Homography Recovery

Once the undistorted image is obtained, which is a homography transformation of the scaled 2d field image. We can apply the following mapping function for homography transformation:

$$s_i[x_i', yi', 1]^T = H[x_i, y_i, 1]^T \tag{4}$$

where left-side represents the source points on 2d coordinates and right-side represent the mapped homography coordinates.

To estimate the hessian matrix H, some matching points between the original image and the homograph transformed image need to be provided. Instead of manual labeling, we take advantage of the prior knowledge for sports playground. Since most sports games have a standard sizes or range of sizes for the whole field and each sub-region. On the undistorted frame, we first apply color-based image segmentation and hough transformation to detect the borderline and reference lines for the play-field. Then we form a set of key-points by the union set of sampled points on reference lines and the intersection between borderlines and reference lines. On the standard field map, we know the coordinates of the points corresponding key-points based on the sports filed specification. We can scale the physical field to a small image by a fixed scale ratio and obtain these scaled key points. Now the detected key-points on the undistorted image and the scaled key-points on the scaled 2d map form the matching points to estimate the hessian matrix. Once the hessian matrix is obtained, we can apply the homography transformation to map every point from undistorted image to a scaled 2d field map.

3   Experimental Results

To evaluate the proposed approach, we use a dataset of video recording of a professional soccer game [17]. The video was recorded using a five 2k-cameras array fixed at 3 positions (one in the middle, one on each side) of audience field for the match between Tromsø IL and Tottenham. The game was held at Alfheim Stadium in Norway. A panorama video was generated to cover the whole play-field by stitching videos from five cameras. The stitched panorama video has obvious distortion.

If the proposed system of transforming frame pixel to scaled 2d field perform well, it will serve as a foundation to develop many sports analytics applications. For instance, not only the frame of play-field can be mapped to 2d, but also every single pixel on the frame could be transformed to their corresponding location on 2d field. That means, if the pixel positions of the players from the video frame can be detected using some players detection and tracking algorithms, then we can map all players' locations to a bird-view 2d field map. This unlocks the door of developing different types of analytics about the sports video and players, such as generating players' statistics of running speed, distance, and heat map. Tactics analyzer and recommendation system for coaching are some other examples.

The dataset comes with 241 video clips from the game, with each clip lasts approximately 3 seconds. Since all the video clips are from one video recording with static camera and the proposed transformation applies to each frame, the mapping function are the same across frames from the video. However, since we also want to test the performance of transformation for players and players keep moving through the video sequence, we select multiple frames to evaluate the proposed transformation system. First, we randomly selected 5 video clips, followed by randomly selecting one frame from each video clip. Then these 5 frames are used as input to test the proposed method. For each frame, we employ a players detection algorithm to detect the players' locations. Then, we apply color-based segmentation and hough transformation to detect the four borderlines of the play-field. Based on the 4 detected borderlines, we sample total of 34 points

(8 points for each goal line, 9 points for each side line). These 34 points are used to estimate distortion coefficients by minimizing the cost function (3). The estimated values of k1 and k2 are 4.608e-7 and -1.024e-15, respectively. These two values are plugged back into formula (1) and (2) to obtain the undistortion function. We then do frame distortion by transforming the position of each pixel to its new position on undistorted frame.

After obtaining the undistorted frame, we apply key-points detection algorithm to detect the pixel positions of 26 key-points based on the intersection of all borderlines and reference lines. On the other hand, we find an image (width: 1920, height: 1080) of a standard soccer field as a scaled soccer field. The locations of these corresponding key-points on this image are estimated by standard soccer field specifications. Using the detected 26 key-points from video frame and the corresponding 26 key-points from scaled 2d soccer field, we estimate the values of homography coefficients (i.e. hessian matrix).

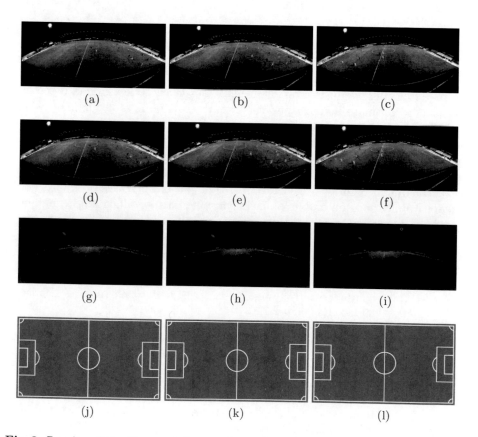

Fig. 2. Results of the Proposed System from Three Frames (each sampled from one video clip): each column is a frame; row 1: original fame; row 2: frame with classified players, row 3: undistorted frame, row 4: transformed 2d scaled field with classified players

Then we use the obtained hessian matrix to do homography recovery by transforming the position of every point on the distorted frame to the scaled 2d map.

Figure 2 shows the qualitative results of our proposed system. Five rows corresponding to five sampled frames. On each column, the four image from top to bottom are: original video frame, original video frame with detected players, undistorted frame, and scaled 2d field image with detected players' positions. Since the dataset do not have the players' physical locations, we don't have the ground-truth to quantitatively measure the transformation performance. However, we can observe two things from the qualitative results: First, the four borderlines on the undistorted frame are close to straight lines compared with the original video frame with the obvious distortion. Second, the mapped players' position are pretty accurate using their positions from the original video frame as reference.

4   Summary

In this paper we proposed an end-to-end system of transforming distorted frame into 2d field of sports videos. In the system, we formulate an optimization problem for estimating the distortion coefficients and leverage key-points detection to automatic estimate homography coefficients. To the best of our knowledge, this is the first fully-automatic system that can transform distorted video frames into scaled 2d field map. Detected players show the transformation achieve good performance. The proposed system can be used to unlock the opportunities for developing many sports-analytics applications, since all sports video recorded by static camera can by used to generate real-time player activities on a bird-view 2d map. Applications on mobile phone with some battery offloading techniques [8] could be developed to do real-time sports analytics using the proposed system.

References

1. Alonso, R.A.: Sports telemetry system for collecting performance metrics and data, US Patent 8,289,185, 16 October 2012
2. Baysal, S., Duygulu, P.: Sentioscope: a soccer player tracking system using model field particles. IEEE Trans. Circuits Syst. for Video Technol. **26**(7), 1350–1362 (2015)
3. Carlock, C.R.: Apparatus for locating and positioning a football on a football playing field, US Patent 3,985,356, 12 October 1976
4. Fryer, J.G., Brown, D.C.: Lens distortion for close-range photogrammetry. Photogram. Eng. Remote Sens. **52**(1), 51–58 (1986)
5. Lopez, M., Mari, R., Gargallo, P., Kuang, Y., Gonzalez-Jimenez, J., Haro, G.: Deep single image camera calibration with radial distortion. In: Proceedings of the IEEE Conference on Computer Vision and Pattern Recognition, pp. 11817–11825 (2019)
6. Pavić, D., Schönefeld, V., Kobbelt, L.: Interactive image completion with perspective correction. Vis. Comput. **22**(9–11), 671–681 (2006)

7. Peng, L.: Enhanced camera capturing using object-detection-based autofocus on smartphones. In: 2016 4th Intl Conf on Applied Computing and Information Technology/3rd Intl Conf on Computational Science/Intelligence and Applied Informatics/1st Intl Conf on Big Data, Cloud Computing, Data Science & Engineering (ACIT-CSII-BCD), pp. 208–212. IEEE (2016)

8. Peng, L.: Gscheduler: Reducing mobile device energy consumption. In: 2016 4th Intl Conf on Applied Computing and Information Technology/3rd Intl Conf on Computational Science/Intelligence and Applied Informatics/1st Intl Conf on Big Data, Cloud Computing, Data Science & Engineering (ACIT-CSII-BCD), pp. 1–6. IEEE (2016)

9. Peng, L.: Object Recognition in Videos Utilizing Hierarchical and Temporal Objectness with Deep Neural Networks. Ph.D. dissertation, Utah State University (2017)

10. Peng, L., Qi, X.: A hierarchical model to learn object proposals and its applications. J. Intell. Fuzzy Syst. **31**(5), 2543–2551 (2016)

11. Peng, L., Qi, X.: Temporal objectness: model-free learning of object proposals in video. In: 2016 IEEE International Conference on Image Processing (ICIP), pp. 3663–3667. IEEE (2016)

12. Peng, L., Qian, H.: Automatic red-eye detection in consumer photographs. In: International Conference on Computer Applications in Industry and Engineering (2018)

13. Peng, L., Qian, H.: A three-stage object detection framework using compact features and deep CNN. In: International Conference on Computer Applications in Industry and Engineering (2018)

14. Peng, L., Wang, H.: Object identification system and method, US Patent 9,122,931, 1 September 2015

15. Peng, L., Yang, Y., Qi, X., Wang, H.: Highly accurate video object identification utilizing hint information. In: 2014 International Conference on Computing, Networking and Communications (ICNC), pp. 317–321. IEEE (2014)

16. Peng, L., Yang, Y., Wang, H.: Automatic face annotation method and system, US Patent 9,176,987, 3 November 2015

17. Pettersen, S.A., et al.: Soccer video and player position dataset. In: Proceedings of the 5th ACM Multimedia Systems Conference, pp. 18–23. ACM (2014)

18. Redmon, J., Divvala, S., Girshick, R., Farhadi, A.: You only look once: Unified, real-time object detection. In: Proceedings of the IEEE conference on computer vision and pattern recognition, pp. 779–788 (2016)

19. Wang, Q., Zhang, Y.: High speed stereoscopic shadowgraph imaging and its digital 3D reconstruction. Meas. Sci. Technol. **22**(6), 065302 (2011)

20. Yu, J., Skaff, S., Peng, L., Imai, F.: Leveraging knowledge-based inference for material classification. In: Proceedings of the 23rd ACM International Conference on Multimedia, pp. 1243–1246. ACM (2015)

21. 彭亮，杨益敏，汪灏泓: 面部自动标注方法及系统, cN Patent CN105100894A, 25 November 2015

22. 彭亮，汪灏泓: 一种物体图像识别方法及其系统, cN Patent CN104573706A, 29 April 2015

UnrealGT: Using Unreal Engine to Generate Ground Truth Datasets

Thomas Pollok[1]([✉]), Lorenz Junglas[1], Boitumelo Ruf[1,2], and Arne Schumann[1]

[1] Fraunhofer IOSB, Video Exploitation Systems, Karlsruhe, Germany
{thomas.pollok,lorenz.junglas,boitumelo.ruf,
arne.schumann}@iosb.fraunhofer.de
[2] Institute of Photogrammetry and Remote Sensing,
Karlsruhe Institute of Technology, Karlsruhe, Germany
boitumelo.ruf@kit.edu

Abstract. Large amounts of data have become an essential requirement in the development of modern computer vision algorithms, e.g.
the training of neural networks. Due to data protection laws, overflight
permissions for UAVs or expensive equipment, data collection is often a
costly and time-consuming task. Especially, if the ground truth is generated by manually annotating the collected data. By means of synthetic
data generation, large amounts of image- and metadata can be extracted
directly from a virtual scene, which in turn can be customized to meet
the specific needs of the algorithm or the use-case. Furthermore, the use
of virtual objects avoids problems that might arise due to data protection issues and does not require the use of expensive sensors. In this
work we propose a framework for synthetic test data generation utilizing
the Unreal Engine. The Unreal Engine provides a simulation environment that allows one to simulate complex situations in a virtual world,
such as data acquisition with UAVs or autonomous diving. However, our
process is agnostic to the computer vision task for which the data is
generated and, thus, can be used to create generic datasets. We evaluate
our framework by generating synthetic test data, with which a CNN for
object detection as well as a V-SLAM algorithm are trained and evaluated. The evaluation shows that our generated synthetic data can be
used as an alternative to real data.

Keywords: Simulation · Unreal Engine · Ground truth · Annotated
data · Object detection · SLAM

1 Introduction

The recent advancements in the field of deep learning have significantly improved
results for a number of computer vision tasks, e.g. object detection, semantic
segmentation, person re-identification and pose estimation [2,7,10,17]. However,
such data-driven approaches require a large amount of training data, which is
typically cost intensive and time consuming to acquire, assess and annotate.
The annotation of the acquired data and generation of ground truth by drawing

© Springer Nature Switzerland AG 2019
G. Bebis et al. (Eds.): ISVC 2019, LNCS 11844, pp. 670–682, 2019.
https://doi.org/10.1007/978-3-030-33720-9_52

bounding box or segmenting the image is a especially time consuming and critical process, as erroneous data can have a great impact on the convergence of the training and the resulting accuracy that is achieved by the model. Furthermore, not only do data-driven approaches benefit from large and versatile datasets, but the classical computer vision algorithms are also improved, if they can be evaluated and tested on large amounts of data. Apart from the time needed to generate suitable ground truth, a number of other aspects need to be considered when acquiring image data. First and foremost are measures to protect the privacy of individuals, such as blurring faces or car license plates that appear in the data. Other aspects involve guidelines and approvals by public authorities, especially when acquiring data using unmanned aerial vehicles (UAVs) or other special equipment, e.g. lasers.

In recent years, more and more work has focused on using synthetic data for training and evaluating computer vision algorithms, in order to avoid the challenges mentioned above. Such data can be generated by using modern video games [14] or 3D game engines [3,12,15,16]. This allows to extract a large number of accurate ground truth data, such as bounding boxes, segmentation maps, depth maps or camera poses, as this information is already available in the virtual world from which the data is rendered. In particular the Unreal Engine (UE)[1] is utilized by a number of frameworks for the generation of synthetic datasets, i.e. [3,12,15,16]. While the UE was originally designed for the development of video games, it has evolved into a modern 3D rendering engine [5], which is used in numerous areas of application such as computer vision, architecture or the automotive industry. The UE allows to perform real-time renderings of a virtual environment at frame rates of over 60 Hz. With the use of modern rendering techniques, such as Physical Based Rendering (PBR) and Ray tracing, photorealistic datasets can be synthesized. Through its extensive application programming interface (API), the UE enables the user to dynamically modify the virtual environment and extract the desired metadata during the runtime of the simulation. At the same time, the integrated development environment (IDE), in combination with the UE Marketplace, enables the user to easily design and create a custom environment, specific for his or her needs.

Our main contribution is a plugin for the Unreal Engine that is available to the community under an open source license. The plugin allows computer vision researchers to export ground truth datasets from 3D scenes that are created using the Unreal Editor. Our approach allows for exporting a large set of typically used image and metadata that is useful for deep learning, 3D reconstruction and other tasks. In contrast to the popular approach UnrealCV, we can also automatically enrich existing scenes with arbitrary objects while being able to specify allowed placement regions, e.g. ensuring that vehicles are places only on streets. Furthermore, our approach is highly configurable through the Unreal Editor interface and easy to extend. We think that the benefits of this plugin will grow in the future as the Unreal Engine is very popular and keeps improving, e.g. through ray tracing for more realistic lighting and reflections.

---

[1] www.unrealengine.com.

The remainder of this paper is structured as follows. First, an overview about related work is presented, followed by the description of our approach. Afterwards, experiments with a neural network for object detection and a popular visual SLAM algorithm are presented.

2   Related Work

In the computer vision community there exists a number of frameworks that rely on the Unreal Engine to generate synthetic datasets. Among these are Microsoft AirSim [15], CAR Learning to Act (CARLA) [3], UnrealCV [12] and the NVIDIA Deep learning Dataset Synthesizer (NDDS) [16]. Since the algorithms, which are evaluated in the scope of this work address different computer vision tasks, namely, object detection and Visual Simultaneous Localization and Mapping (V-SLAM), we will focus our discussion on how effectively the data required for these tasks can be generated, using existing frameworks. While deep learning based detection approaches are typically trained upon RGB images together with ground truth annotations represented as 2D bounding boxes, the evaluation of V-SLAM algorithms requires RGB-D data together with camera poses.

AirSim and CARLA are open-source simulation environments that allow to simulate the data acquisition using UAVs or cars. They provide a number of sensors, which are typically attached to the vehicles and can be used to extract various types of information from the virtual scene. This includes semantic segmentation, depth maps and surface orientations encoded in normal maps. While AirSim only allows one to attach sensors to airborne or terrestrial vehicles, and only supports one client at a time, CARLA also supports the possibility to attach the desired sensors to objects other than vehicles and the use of multiple, independent clients at the same time within the scene. However, since the primary focus of both frameworks is the use of UAVs or cars, the virtual environments are typically comprised of outdoor scenes and the movement of the sensors is restricted to the degrees of freedom (DoF) inherent to the type of client to which the sensors are attached. This does not always allow to move the camera freely or simulate appropriate scenes, making the use of AirSim and CARLA impractical for the task of creating generic synthetic datasets intended for a wide range of computer vision tasks. Furthermore, both frameworks thus far do not allow one to automatically extract bounding boxes around objects of interest or extract the camera poses, which in turn are required for training and evaluating algorithms used for object detection and V-SLAM.

UnrealCV, in contrast, is a framework that does not focus on a specific use-case but rather allows one to generically extract image data together with the corresponding metadata from a virtual scene within the UE. In addition to the data, which can be extracted by AirSim and CARLA, i.e. images, segmentation maps, depth maps and normal maps, the UnrealCV framework also allows one to extract information about scene objects, such as their position. Since UnrealCV focuses on a more general use-case for synthetic data generation, the user is not restricted to attach the sensors to a specific scene object. However, the API only provides a limited interface, hiding many functionalities from the user, e.g. annotation objects of interest with 2D bounding boxes.

The focus of the NVIDIA Deep learning Dataset Synthesizer lies more on generating large synthetic datasets used for the task of object detection and object pose estimation. As the name implies, the main focus of NDDS is on methods in the field of deep learning and the framework thus especially provides functionality to improve the training of deep neural networks. NDDS, for example, provides a plugin that implements Domain Randomization [16], allowing to randomly scatter objects within the scene. Unlike the previously mentioned frameworks, NDDS allows one to extract 2D and 3D bounding boxes around scene objects. However, the NDDS only provides a plugin for the UE and directly saves the generated data into files stored on the system. The AirSim, CARLA and UnrealCV frameworks, on the otherhand, utilize the plug-in mechanism of the Unreal Engine API in combination with a client-server architecture to generate and pass on the image and metadata to a program running independently of the UE.

In principle, all mentioned frameworks can create similar data. The main differences lie in the usability and extensibility. Our architecture allows implementing an arbitrary type of data and can be exported as text, images or binary data. Our approach only consists of a single plugin for the Unreal Engine that has direct access to all data from the Unreal Engine, and it does not require a separate client. Furthermore, our approach does not require programming knowledge, as the interaction with the Unreal Engine is based on a graphical user interface.

3   Approach

The goal of this work is to provide a toolkit that allows creating synthetic datasets from virtual scenes together with a large variety of different meta data (i.e. ground truth) to support a wide range of computer vision tasks. Our approach is based on the Unreal Engine v4.22. An important advantage of using the Unreal Engine is that it has a flexible architecture, which can be extended with custom functionality through plugins. Our toolkit is realized as such an UE plugin and therefor has full access to the UE via the Unreal API, which allows for interaction with the virtual scene and all its objects and metadata.

An overview of our approach is shown in Fig. 1. We use a modular architecture, which can be extended by new functionality as needed. The basis of the plugin are data generators, which can generate image data and metadata. We provide image data generators for RGB images, depth maps, semantic segmentations, instance segmentations and normal maps (see Fig. 2). Further data generators can be implemented and added conveniently. Besides image data, the plugin also provides metadata. This includes camera parameters, camera position and orientation, fine object bounding boxes and information about the object classes. Figure 3 shows two available bounding box modes that handle object visibility differently. The first creates large boxes that does not handle regions with partially occluded regions due to semi-transparent objects like fences and

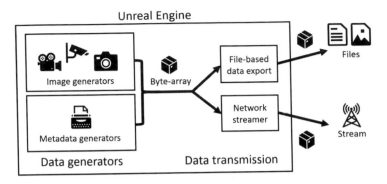

Fig. 1. Overview of the Unreal Engine Plugin for data extraction.

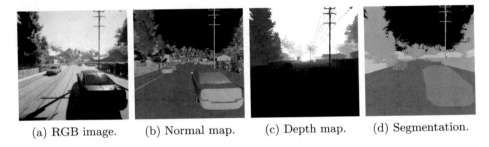

  (a) RGB image.   (b) Normal map.   (c) Depth map.   (d) Segmentation.

Fig. 2. Example images from different image generators.

vegetation while the second allows for very fine bounding boxes using a morphological closing operator. Many camera parameters like exposure, aperture, focal length, field of view, color correction, resolution and even the option for a random resolution per image are configurable in the user interface. All data is stored in the form of byte-arrays to be able to handle the data in an easy and uniform way. For data export we provide a file-based approach for offline processing as well as a stream-based approach for live processing of the data. Offline data is typically used for performance and accuracy benchmark datasets or training datasets. The stream based output can be used to connect the Unreal scene to live processing, like a real-time object detector, while freely navigating in the scene. Out of the box the plugin supports live data transfer via HTTP and a simple TCP protocol, which allows one to easily receive the live stream data in a variety of programming languages. For controlling the virtual camera, two different modes are supported. In the first mode, the active viewer in the scene is followed, thus allowing direct control of the resulting output data during simulation. In the second mode, a virtual path is followed that can be manually specified beforehand as a spline through the scene. This allows to simulate, for example, a virtual car ride or a drone flight. Furthermore, our toolkit supports multiple cameras and thus allows for the creation of, for example, stereo or trifocal camera setups. All image and meta data are obtained synchronously with a specifiable framerate for all cameras.

The toolkit can be configured in detail through several UI elements, which are displayed directly in the Unreal Editor. The editor also allows objects and actors to be placed in the virtual world. Editing using the UI is intuitive and requires very little technical knowledge of the engine.

(a) More accurate bounding box with additional segmentation with only the visible regions of an object.

(b) A closing morphological operator is used to get an even more accurate bounding box of objects behind semitransparent objects, such as the fence on the left.

Fig. 3. Different bounding box modes.

3.1 Scene Generator

To generate data, the plugin requires a 3D scene. The user can either use an existing scene or create their own using the Unreal Editor. Generating data usually requires at least a modification of the scene, for example, by placing additional objects. Since creating or extending a scene can be very time consuming, generators are often used to facilitate the process. In this work, a hybrid approach is implemented. A landscape (the floor of the scene), optionally with already placed objects, such as plants or houses, is assumed.

The landscape can be automatically filled with objects that are randomly selected from a list. Objects can be placed only in a specific area, which is configurable. It is also possible to randomize several scene parts with different objects.

The random distribution of the objects takes place with a modified version of the Poisson Disk Sampling algorithm [1]. Poisson Disk Sampling generates a list of random points with a fixed minimum distance to each other. The point distribution of the sampling algorithm has been changed so that a different minimum distance can be set for each point. This minimum distance depends on the size of the object, which is placed later on this point by the actor. This ensures that objects do not physically overlap.

In addition, it is possible to use object filters to specify objects on which no objects are placed. The distribution can thus be configured such that vehicles are placed only on roads, for example. Whether or not objects may overlap with existing objects in the scene is also configurable. This prevents the placement of a vehicle into a house or tree that is already part of the scene. Also random rotations and random materials of the objects can be enabled. Furthermore, it is possible to manually add specific objects.

 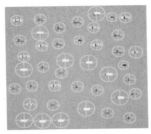 

(a) A selection of vehicles that are placed in the scene.

(b) Vehicles are randomly placed on a flat plane.

(c) Vehicles are placed on the road in an existing scene.

Fig. 4. Example object placements. The points that were created by Poisson Disk Sampling algorithm are depicted as circles. A green circle indicates that a point is valid, a red circle indicates that a point is blocked. (Color figure online)

4   Experiments

To show the utility and quality of the data generated using UnrealGT, two typical but very different computer vision tasks are evaluated. First, we assess the training of a well known CNN object detection framework for the task of vehicle detection in the generated data. 2D object bounding boxes are required for this task. Second, we apply a Visual SLAM approach that is used in robotics for robot path reconstruction and scene mapping. This task requires depth information and camera pose data for application and evaluation.

4.1   Object Detection with CNNs

For this experiment we train a popular real-time object detection framework, YOLOv3 [13], for the task of vehicle detection on data generated using UnrealGT. Our goal is not to achieve state of the art vehicle recognition accuracy, but rather to demonstrate that the data created using UnrealGT is suitable for CNNs to learn meaningful concepts and aid in object detection.

Data Generation. For creation of suitable training data, we rely on a popular Unreal demo scene from the Modular Neighborhood Pack (see Fig. 5a) available in the Unreal Marketplace. The scene depicts a suburban neighborhood and contains several vehicles. However, the overall number and visual variety of the available vehicles is very limited. The existing vehicles further have a very low level of detail. We thus remove the existing vehicles and employ the scene generator of UnrealGT to randomly place new vehicles. Vehicle models from the CARLA project [3] are used for placement. These vehicle models include different types of cars from different manufacturers, Coupés, sedans, SUVs and vans (see Fig. 4a). The models correspond to real vehicles and are modeled with a sufficiently high level of detail. Each placed vehicle receives a randomly chosen material with different surface properties and colors. The resulting visual variety and random placement of the vehicles aids the network in learning a representation that can generalize to the test set.

An image generator and metadata generator are configured in UnrealGT to extract camera images and vehicle bounding boxes. The image generator is configured for images between 512×512 and 1920×1280 pixels resolution to achieve different scales and aspect ratios. Both generators are synchronized and configured to generate 12 images per second while the actor to which both generators are attached moves along a predefined camera path. Two paths are configured to cover the entire scene, one for training and one for testing (see Fig. 5b). Between train and test data generation, new vehicles are randomly placed to avoid overlap between the two sets. The final dataset contains 1438 training images and 440 test images.

(a) Demo scene of the used Modular Neighbourhood Pack. The scene contains a suburb with different houses, trees and plants.

(b) Manually chosen camera paths for training (magenta) and testing (blue).

Fig. 5. Aspects of the data creation process for object detection.

Training. The YOLOv3 detector is configured for a uniform input resolution of 416×416 pixels. All generated images are scaled to this input size. Standard parameters of the YOLOv3-416 model are applied for training. The only modification is a limitation to a single vehicle class. The model is trained for 4000 iterations at a batch size of 64.

Results. We evaluate the quality of the resulting model by relying on the established metric of mean average precision (mAP). Therefore, we consider a detection as correct, if the intersection-over-union with a groundtruth box is larger than 0.5.

Table 1. Evaluation results for different testsets.

Testset	mAP
UnrealGT	75.3%
Stanford Cars	79.9%
KITTI	32.7%

The results of our evaluation are given in Table 1. When evaluated on the generated UnrealGT test set, the trained model achieves a mAP of 75.3%. Compared to other datasets, such as COCO [9] and PascalVOC [6], where similar models achieve about 55% mAP, this is a comparatively high value. A main reason for this is the still somewhat limited visual variety within the UnrealGT dataset. For example, lighting conditions are similar and nearly ideal across the entire dataset. This makes the detection task easier than on diverse real world datasets. Several detection results on the UnrealGT test set are depicted in Fig. 6. The main source of errors are missing detections for distant or strongly occluded vehicles.

(a) Both vehicles are detected.

(b) Vehicles at different scales successfully detected.

(c) Storm drain wrongly detected as vehicle.

Fig. 6. Example detections from the UnrealGT test set.

We further evaluate the application of our UnrealGT trained model to real world data. When evaluated on the Stanford Cars test dataset [8], the model achieves a similar accuracy of 79.9% mAP. The Stanford Cars dataset contains 8041 images of nearly format filling vehicles. Image quality and object size are thus well suited for detection tasks and similar in appearance to the vehicles in UnrealGT, which are located closely to the camera. More exotic vehicle types, which are not included in the UnrealGT training data are detected without issue, indicating that the model has learned a generalizing representation of vehicles. This smaller domain gap between simulated and real-world data is thus successfully bridged by the model.

Lastly, the model is evaluated on the KITTI dataset, which contains street scenes recorded from the perspective of a driving vehicle. The resulting mAP is much lower at 32.7%. Qualitative results on KITTI are displayed in Fig. 7. Vehicles at close range and under good lighting conditions, similar to UnrealGT, are detected well. The main issue impacting the mAP arises with more distant vehicles and more complex and different lighting conditions than in UnrealGT. This larger domain gap thus requires additional addressing and a direct transfer of models is only of limited value. A promising avenue to reduce this gap is to increase the visual variety in the simulated training data. This could be done by relying on additional features and functionalities available in the Unreal Engine or via the Unreal Marketplace, such as methods to vary lighting conditions while creating the training data.

(a) Close range vehicles are often found cor- (b) No vehicles recognized due to lighting.
recly.

Fig. 7. Results on the KITTI dataset. Complex lighting conditions can lead to completely missed detections across the image.

(a) Birds view.   (b) Example camera view.

Fig. 8. Virtual camera path for synthetic data and ground truth generation.

4.2   Visual SLAM

Visual SLAM is a typical robotics and computer vision task that describes the problem of simultaneously localizing a sensor and mapping the environment [4] from visual sensors. ORB-SLAM2 is a popular real-time approach that uses ORB image features for tracking and mapping. It supports the use of either a monocular, stereo or RGBD camera [11].

ORB-SLAM2 is just one of a variety of approaches, but the goal is to show a proof of concept that different sensors can be evaluated using synthetic data. For evaluation we use the Standard Neighbourhood Scene in which a virtual camera path was defined to sample images (see Fig. 8a). Images were rendered with a resolution of 752 × 480 pixels at 10 fps. However, to avoid aliasing effects, the image was rendered in 1504 × 960 and then downsampled to 752 × 480 pixels. Intrinsic camera parameters are automatically provided by the UnrealGT and can be directly extracted.

For evaluation we compared the computed trajectory with the ground truth trajectory for which we used the RMSE metric, the absolute positioning error (APE) in meter, which was also used by the authors of ORB-SLAM2. The achieved APEs (see Fig. 9), are comparable with the APEs, that ORB-SLAM2 achieved on KITTI, where it achieved on different sub-datasets an error between 6 and 50 m for monocular sensors and 0.5 to 10 m for stereo sensors. Compared to that ORB-SLAM2 achieves comparable or even better results on the created synthetic datasets. The reason here is that the sensors are perfectly calibrated and the RGBD sensor gives ground truth depth values. To further evaluate ORB-SLAM2 researchers can easily generate more challenging datasets with less translation and stronger rotation or add noise to the sensor data.

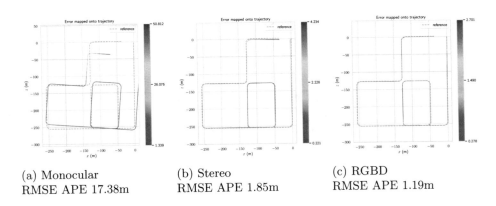

(a) Monocular
RMSE APE 17.38m

(b) Stereo
RMSE APE 1.85m

(c) RGBD
RMSE APE 1.19m

Fig. 9. ORB-SLAM2 evaluation results on different using synthetic sensors data. Monocular SLAM suffers from scale drift, stereo SLAM recovers absolute scale properly, RGBD SLAM shows most accurate results.

5   Conclusion

This paper presented UnrealGT, a plugin for the Unreal Engine, that allows for exporting ground truth datasets from 3D scenes created using the Unreal Editor. The most typical image and metadata types like RGB images, depth maps, semantic segmentations, normal maps, camera poses, intrinsic camera parameters, object bounding boxes, and more, are supported out of the box. The plugin architecture is designed for easy extension in the future. As shown in our experiments, the data is useful for training neural networks like object detectors or for the evaluation of 3D reconstruction approaches like V-SLAM where accurate ground truth is often difficult to acquire but crucial for evaluation. The plugin contains a vast amount of configuration options and is also able to randomly enrich an existing scene with new objects whose placement can be limited to semantically relevant areas. Our plugin[2] is available under the MIT license on Github. We think that the community will benefit from our contribution, particularly considering the ever improving capabilities of the Unreal Engine and the vast amount of scenes, assets and plugin extensions, e.g. simulating day and night time or seasons, that can be downloaded directly from the Unreal Engine marketplace.

Acknowledgment. This work has received funding from the European Union's Horizon 2020 research and innovation program in the context of the VICTORIA project under grant agreement No. 740754.

References

1. Bridson, R.: Fast Poisson disk sampling in arbitrary dimensions. In: Proceedings of ACM SIGGRAPH Sketches (2007)
2. Dang, Q., Yin, J., Wang, B., Zheng, W.: Deep learning based 2D human pose estimation: a survey. Tsinghua Sci. Technol. **24**(6), 663–676 (2019)
3. Dosovitskiy, A., Ros, G., Codevilla, F., Lopez, A., Koltun, V.: CARLA: an open urban driving simulator. In: Proceedings of Annual Conference on Robot Learning, pp. 1–16 (2017)
4. Durrant-Whyte, H., Bailey, T.: Simultaneous localization and mapping: part I. IEEE Robot. Autom. Mag. **13**(2), 99–110 (2006)
5. Eberly, D.: 3D Game Engine Design: A Practical Approach to Real-Time Computer Graphics. CRC Press, Boca Raton (2006)
6. Everingham, M., Van Gool, L., Williams, C.K.I., Winn, J., Zisserman, A.: The PASCAL Visual Object Classes (VOC) challenge. Int. J. Comput. Vis. **88**(2), 303–338 (2010)
7. Guo, Y., Liu, Y., Georgiou, T., Lew, M.S.: A review of semantic segmentation using deep neural networks. Int. J. Multimedia Inf. Retrieval **7**(2), 87–93 (2018)
8. Krause, J., Stark, M., Deng, J., Fei-Fei, L.: 3D object representations for fine-grained categorization. In: Proceedings of IEEE International Conference on Computer Vision Workshops, pp. 554–561 (2013)
9. Lin, T.Y., et al.: Microsoft COCO: common objects in context. In: Proceedings of European Conference on Computer Vision, pp. 740–755 (2014)
10. Liu, L., et al.: Deep learning for generic object detection: a survey. arXiv preprint arXiv:1809.02165 (2018)
11. Mur-Artal, R., Tardós, J.D.: ORB-SLAM2: an open-source SLAM system for monocular, stereo, and RGB-D cameras. IEEE Trans. Robot. **33**(5), 1255–1262 (2017)
12. Qiu, W., Yuille, A.: UnrealCV: connecting computer vision to unreal engine. In: Proceedings of European Conference on Computer Vision, pp. 909–916 (2016)

---

[2] http://unrealgt.github.io.

13. Redmon, J., Farhadi, A.: YOLOv3: an incremental improvement. arXiv preprint arXiv:1804.02767 (2018)
14. Richter, S.R., Vineet, V., Roth, S., Koltun, V.: Playing for data: ground truth from computer games. In: Leibe, B., Matas, J., Sebe, N., Welling, M. (eds.) ECCV 2016. LNCS, vol. 9906, pp. 102–118. Springer, Cham (2016). https://doi.org/10. 1007/978-3-319-46475-6_7
15. Shah, S., Dey, D., Lovett, C., Kapoor, A.: AirSim: high-fidelity visual and physical simulation for autonomous vehicles. In: Proceedings of Field and Service Robotics, pp. 621–635 (2018)
16. Tremblay, J., et al.: Training deep networks with synthetic data: bridging the reality gap by domain randomization. In: Proceedings of IEEE Conference on Computer Vision and Pattern Recognition Workshops, pp. 1082–10828 (2018)
17. Zheng, L., Yang, Y., Hauptmann, A.G.: Person re-identification: past, present and future. arXiv preprint arXiv:1610.02984 (2016)

Fast Omnidirectional Depth Densification

Hyeonjoong Jang, Daniel S. Jeon, Hyunho Ha, and Min H. Kim[✉]

KAIST School of Computing, Daejeon, Korea
minhkim@kaist.ac.kr

Abstract. Omnidirectional cameras are commonly equipped with fish-eye lenses to capture 360-degree visual information, and severe spherical projective distortion occurs when a 360-degree image is stored as a two-dimensional image array. As a consequence, traditional depth estimation methods are not directly applicable to omnidirectional cameras. Dense depth estimation for omnidirectional imaging has been achieved by applying several offline processes, such as patch-matching, optical flow, and convolutional propagation filtering, resulting in additional heavy computation. No dense depth estimation for real-time applications is available yet. In response, we propose an efficient depth densification method designed for omnidirectional imaging to achieve 360-degree dense depth video with an omnidirectional camera. First, we compute the sparse depth estimates using a conventional simultaneous localization and mapping (SLAM) method, and then use these estimates as input to a depth densification method. We propose a novel densification method using the spherical pull-push method by devising a joint spherical pyramid for color and depth, based on multi-level icosahedron subdivision surfaces. This allows us to propagate the sparse depth continuously over 360-degree angles efficiently in an edge-aware manner. The results demonstrate that our real-time densification method is comparable to state-of-the-art offline methods in terms of per-pixel depth accuracy. Combining our depth densification with a conventional SLAM allows us to capture real-time 360-degree RGB-D video with a single omnidirectional camera.

Keywords: Omnidirectional stereo · 3D imaging · Depth densification

1 Introduction

Omnidirectional cameras have been popularly used for capturing 360-degree images and are essential for virtual reality (VR)/augmented reality (AR) applications to mix rendered virtual objects in real scenes. Omnidirectional cameras are equipped with fisheye-lenses to capture a very wide field of view (FOV)

Electronic supplementary material The online version of this chapter (https://doi.org/10.1007/978-3-030-33720-9_53) contains supplementary material, which is available to authorized users.

© Springer Nature Switzerland AG 2019
G. Bebis et al. (Eds.): ISVC 2019, LNCS 11844, pp. 683–694, 2019.
https://doi.org/10.1007/978-3-030-33720-9_53

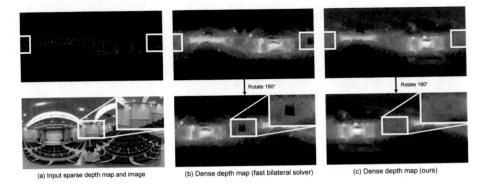

(a) Input sparse depth map and image   (b) Dense depth map (fast bilateral solver)   (c) Dense depth map (ours)

Fig. 1. (a) shows an example of a sparse depth map as input obtained from a visual SLAM method [5] and an equirectangular color image captured by an omnidirectional camera. (b) presents a densification result in two different orientations using the fast bilateral solver [1] on the equirectangular depth map. When the 360-degree image is rotated, the simple densification on the equirectangular image suffers from the seam artifacts. (c) shows our densification result. Our densification does not suffer from seam artifacts when the depth map is rotated in a different orientation. The closeup of the white/beige-colored wall compares the artifacts for the two methods.

with even more than 180° for each lens, yielding 360-degree images with a single camera. Different from ordinary 2D images, 360-degree images have special properties that give rise to new **challenges** in terms of image processing. First, in order to store 360-degree image data in the conventional 2D image array, a geographic projection mapping between spherical and image coordinates is required additionally: e.g., equirectangular projection, latitude-longitude projection, cube-map projection, concentric projection, etc. [22]. However, when 360-degree image data are geographically projected and stored as a 2D image array, severe geometrical *warp* inevitably occurs in the stored 360-degree image; for example, a straight line of the object may appear warped like an arc in the equirectangular image (see the white arc in the middle in Fig. 1 as an example), where certain parts are distorted, enlarged, or shrunk unevenly and nonlinearly depending on their geometric positions. In particular, spherical distortion in geographic projection mapping is a severe problem when applying existing image processing operators for 360-degree images as they have been developed for ordinary 2D images. These challenges have been resolved by additionally applying several offline processes, such as patch-matching, optical flow, and convolutional propagation filtering, resulting in additional heavy computation. To the best of our knowledge, no fast depth densification method for 360-degree images is available yet.

Second, the ordinary 2D image data have four boundaries: the leftmost, rightmost, topmost, and bottommost ends of the image. In contrast, the 360-degree image data have *no ends*; i.e., parts of the image are *circularly connected without ends*. For example, when a patch-wise operator is applied for depth densification on an unfolded 360-degree image (such as an equirectangular image, shown in Fig. 1), the leftmost and rightmost parts are different after applying the densification operator. The difference becomes clear when the processed depth map is wrapped in the 360-degree image data. The traditional algorithms are not free from the inconsistency artifacts because they cannot satisfy the circular constraints when the results are wrapped in 360-degree images.

Figure 1 compares depth densification results from the sparse depth input (a) using a state-of-the-art method, the fast bilateral solver [1] (b) and ours (c). The top rows of (b) and (c) show densification results by two different methods, and the bottom rows below present 180-degree rotated images of the same scene. The top depth map in (b) is densified from the left sparse, an equirectangular depth map by the densification method, and the map below in (b) shows the 180-degree rotation of the same propagated depth map. Note that the leftmost and rightmost regions indicate the same area, the white/beige-colored wall, in (b) and (c). When the resulting 360-degree images are rotated, the naïve densification method presents seam artifacts on the stitched area due to inconsistent computation over edges.

In this work, we propose an efficient dense densification method specially designed for omnidirectional imaging such that it allows the 360-degree dense depth video to be captured with a single omnidirectional camera. First, we obtain sparse depth estimates per each subframe from the input 360-degree video using a real-time simultaneous localization and mapping (SLAM) method [5] as input for our densification method. As our key contribution, we introduce a novel spherical pull-push method by means of a *joint spherical pyramid* for color and depth information, based on multi-level icosahedron subdivision surfaces. Our method accounts for not only the aforementioned characteristics of 360-degree images (i.e., distortion and circularity), but also is computationally efficient. It takes just an additional 15 ms for propagating the sparse depth estimates to every pixel with awareness of edge structures using a conventional GPU. Combining our depth densification with the conventional SLAM allows us to capture 360-degree dense depth video in real-time with a single omnidirectional camera.

2   Related Work

Multi-camera Methods. In order to cover the entire field of view in 360-degree angles, several multi-camera omnidirectional methods have been proposed. They are equipped with an array of multiple cameras with ordinary lenses on a circle structure [2,24]. They then apply the traditional stereo matching algorithm, assuming a cylindrical projection model with an ordinary field of view. They can search stereo correspondence based on epipolar geometry through rectification. However, these methods can capture depth along the azimuthal angles only. Their results cannot obtain complete 360-degree depth information, due to the lack of cameras and image formation at the top and bottom directions.

The form factor of multi-camera systems is significantly increased by having many cameras and consequently they are not portable. With efforts focused on reducing the form factor, multiple fisheye lenses have been installed in omnidirectional camera systems [16–18]. The FOV of fisheye lenses is significantly larger at about 180°–190° than those of ordinary lenses. Thus the pinhole-based perspective projection model is invalid with fisheye lenses. They, therefore, employ the spherical rectification method, which is devised on the inverse-equirectangular projection model, a.k.a. the latitude-longitude (LL) projection model. On the rectified images in the spherical domain, they use the conventional stereo algorithm, scanning stereo correspondence along the horizontal line on a pair of LL projection images. They produce a complete 360-degree depth map, but the computation is time consuming. For instance, Lin et al. [18] took about 12 min for rectification and depth estimation for processing one 360-degree image.

Single-Camera Methods. Recently, extensive efforts have been made to enable *monoscopic* 360-degree depth imaging. Caruso et al. [3] introduced a visual SLAM method for a hemispherical fisheye-lens camera that covers 185° angles. They estimate sparse depth points and propagate them partially while tracking the camera motion. Their method is devised for navigation using a fisheye-lens camera and therefore they only provide partially depth information, which is not applicable for 360-degree image-based rendering. Im et al. [12] and Huang et al. [11] make use of a single 360-degree RGB camera (equipped with two front/back fisheye lenses). They both take video frames as input and apply the structure-from-motion algorithm to estimate the camera pose parameters. Im et al. densify the sparse depth using the sphere-sweeping method based on the stereo algorithm. Huang et al. propagate the sparse depth using Delaunay Triangulation-based densification [21]. However, similar to the previous spherical stereo methods, these monoscopic methods also require more than 10 min to densify the sparse depth for one omnidirectional depth map. The proposed method is 40,000 times faster than the state-of-the-art methods of omnidirectional depth densification, reducing the computational time from 10 min to 15 ms.

Depth Densification for Traditional 2D Images. Depth densification is a long-lasting problem and has been researched for many years in computer vision. For brevity, we simplify the overview of depth densification methods for traditional 2D images. Sparse depth information as points or edges has been propagated to every pixel in a dense depth map using the colorization solver [15], the guided image filter [9], or the fast bilateral solver [1]. Different from the simple interpolation of sparse point, the main objective of these methods is to densify the sparse information while preserving sharp edges of objects in the scene. Densification is time consuming in nature [8,15]. To address the speed, a fast bilateral solver [1] and a fast depth densification [10] were also proposed for traditional 2D images, in addition to an optimization approach [8] and neural network-based inference [4,13,19]. However, all these methods are suitable for traditional 2D images, and are not directly applicable for the projected views of 360-degree image data, resulting in inconsistency artifacts (as shown in Fig. 1). In contrast, we propose a novel depth densification method using a joint spherical pyramid on a multiscale architecture with icosahedron subdivision, which satisfies the characteristics of 360-degree images.

3   Omnidirectional Depth Densification

3.1   360-degree Sparse Depth Estimation

We capture 360-degree video using a conventional omnidirectional camera and then obtain sparse depth information and extrinsic camera parameters for each frame using a visual SLAM method [5]. We use the sparse depth information of the 360-degree depth map as input for our densification method.

360-degree to 2D Images. The visual SLAM method that we used is a fast open source method, but is designed for traditional 2D images [5], rather than 360-degree images. The camera stores the input video in the equirectangular format. When the SLAM method runs on the original format of 360-degree video, the number of detected features decreases significantly due to geographic distortion by spherical projection. To address this challenge, we project the input 360-degree video frames to the cube-map representation model, as shown in Fig. 2. We first divide each input 360-degree image into six-face images that look outward in six orthogonal directions to each other in the spherical domain.

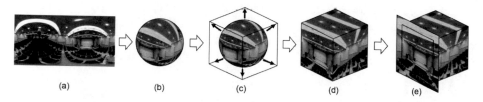

Fig. 2. (a) An equirectangular image that represents a 360-degree image. (b) A sphere mapping of the equirectangular image. (c) Projection from the sphere to a cube. (d) A cube map of the 360-degree image. (e) The extension of each face with FOV margins for robust depth estimation near borders.

Depth Estimation. It is worth noting that when we subdivided and projected to six faces (shown in (d)) and ran the SLAM method for six cameras toward each face, we found that SLAM features cannot be captured well near square boarders of each face. We extended the camera FOV from 90° to 102° for each face direction. Once we could obtain features well within the square face, we cut out the extra margins when they were combined every detected feature to a 360-degree depth map via the spherical representation. However, since we estimate sparse depth on each face separately, the depth scales from each face camera may be different from each other. Thus we normalize depth values in each face camera using the magnitude of the six estimated camera translation vectors and depth values overlapped in the extra margins. This allows us to capture sparse features well with the omnidirectional camera input and traditional 2D SLAM method. This preprocess can be substituted with any available 360-degree SLAM method [3].

3.2   Omnidirectional Depth Densification

Now we describe a fast depth densification method that densifies the sparse depth to obtain a complete 360-degree depth map using our spherical pull-push algorithm.

Joint Spherical Pyramid. Since we estimate the sparse depth for the six faces in the cube map, we then project them to the unit sphere domain, as shown in the top-left sphere in Fig. 3(a). The spherical image pyramid was initially proposed to achieve scale-invariance for effectively detecting visual features in omnidirectional SLAM methods [7,23]. In contrast, we devise a novel spherical architecture for fast depth densification. We propose a *joint spherical pyramid* that includes multiscale color and depth information in the spherical domain by subdividing icosahedron in multiple resolutions, where each level of pyramid corresponds to each level of subdivision.

Figure 3(a) shows an example of our joint spherical pyramid. For example, level 0 represents a 20-face icosahedron and level 1 represents an 80-face structure[1]. The number of triangles increases by four times when the level increases; i.e., four triangles in level $n+1$ corresponds to one triangle in level n (see Fig. 3b). Suppose we subdivide the 20-face icosahedron up to the 8th level. The number of polygons increases to $20 \times 4^8 = 1,310,720$ faces, the number of which is similar to the number of pixels in a cube map with 6 faces of each face resolution of 480×480 (1,382,400 pixels in total). We set the finest level of subdivision to level 8 for our experiment.

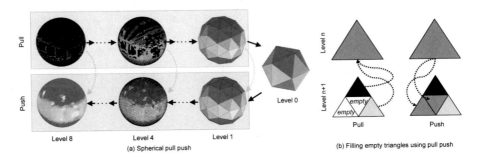

Fig. 3. (a) Spherical pull-push algorithm using multiple subdivision levels of icosahedron. (b) Four triangles in the current level corresponds to one triangle in the upper level. We compute the mean of existing values in the pull phase, and fill empty triangles with the mean value in the push phase.

---

[1] Note that contrary to the labeling convention of the image pyramid, we label each level from the coarse to fine level in ascending order, following the subdivision labeling convention.

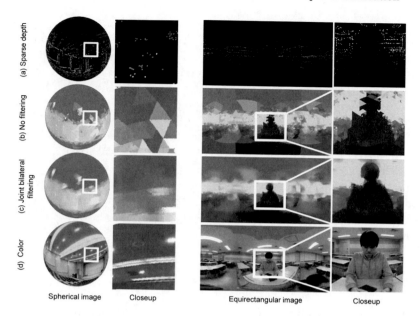

Fig. 4. (a) shows the sparse depth input. (b) presents the initial depth map filled by the pull-push process. (c) In the push phase, we refine the initial depth map using the joint bilateral filter at each level to remove triangle artifacts, starting from level 5 to 8. It refines and preserves edges in the final depth map. (d) shows the guide color images used for filtering.

Lookup Tables. Our method allows for precomputing the geographic relationship between pixels and polygons of the spherical pyramid. We make use of two precomputed lookup tables: (a) each pixel in the cube map to each polygon in each level of the spherical pyramid, and (b) nearest neighbors for each polygon at each level. Unlike in 2D images, we need to define the neighbor set N with nearest neighbors as we use the spherical structure with triangle polygons. Since we know every 3D position of triangles on the unit sphere, we can find neighbors by calculating the Euclidean distance. The number of polygons is very large in our case. Thus, we precompute the neighbors using an approximating nearest neighbor algorithm [20] and save them as a lookup table for each level in advance.

Spherical Densification. Our densification procedure consists of two main parts: First, we fill empty depth pixels coarsely using the pull-push algorithm [6] in our joint spherical pyramid. Second, we refine the coarsely filled depth values to have fine edge details with joint bilateral filtering [14] at each fine level of the spherical pyramid.

Our pull-push algorithm has two phases, the pull phase and the push phase. In the pull phase, we compute the average of existing depth values for every four triangles at the level $n+1$ and assign the average to the polygon at the level n. See Fig. 3(b). In case none of the four triangles at the level $n+1$ have depth values, we treat the triangle as empty at the n-level. We found that setting level 0 with the 20-face icosahedron can fill every polygon at the end of the pull phase with natural scenes. In the push phase, we fill every empty triangle in the $n+1$ level with the average depth values of the coarse triangles in the n level. Note that we do not change existing values of the triangle in the push phase. This allows us to fill empty regions while preserving low-frequency edge structures.

Edge-Aware Filtering. In order to preserve high-frequency details, we refine depth values with joint bilateral filtering [14] on the spherical space at each level before pushing the current depth values to the next finer level. For each triangle p and its neighbor triangle q in the neighbor field N, the refined depth $\tilde{D}_p$ is calculated by the Gaussian weighted sum of neighbor depths D_q. We employ two different weights: spatial distance in the spherical space and the color difference as follows:

$$\tilde{D}_p = \frac{1}{W_p} \sum_{q \in N} \exp \left(-\frac{\|X_p - X_q\|_2^2}{2\sigma_s} - \frac{\|C_p - C_q\|_2^2}{2\sigma_c} \right), \tag{1}$$

where X_p and C_p are a 3D coordinate vector and an RGB color vector of triangle p, respectively. In addition, σ_s and σ_c are the parameters for spatial distance and color difference, respectively, and W_p is the normalization constant, the sum of the products of the Gaussian weights. We found that filtering the coarse depth information at level 0 to 4 does not provide positive effects because each triangle covers an excessively large area. Thus, we apply the filter from level 5 to level 8 (finest) only. Lastly, we reproject the dense depth values in the cube map into the final output format, the equirectangular image. In addition, we apply the temporal median filter among three neighboring frames (previous/current/next) to reduce noise in the densified depth video. See Fig. 4 for an example.

4   Results

We tested our algorithm with 360-degree videos (1920×960 pixels) captured by a Ricoh Theta camera. Our algorithm is implemented using C++ with CUDA. We used a machine with an Intel i7-6700 4.00 GHz processor with 32 GB RAM and NVIDIA GeForce GTX 1080 Ti. We configured a total of eight levels of subdivisions of an icosahedron to compose the joint spherical pyramid. In the push phase, the joint bilateral filter is applied from level 5 to level 8 only. The color weight parameter σ_c is set to 4.02 and the spatial parameter σ_s is set to 40.2. N is set to 500 to ensure the filter preserves edges effectively. Our algorithm takes less than 15 ms with our CUDA implementation to densify a sparse depth map obtained from the visual SLAM method [5].

For a quantitative evaluation of our algorithm, we rendered two virtual scenes and captured the ground-truth (GT) depth in the equirectangular image format. We also obtained sparse depth maps from the virtual scenes as input for densification algorithms. We compared the accuracy of our method compared

(15 ms per frame on GPU) with other densification methods: fast bilateral solver (0.49 s per frame on CPU) [1], colorization solver (96.83 s per frame on CPU) [15], and guided image filter (0.36 s per frame on CPU) [9]. We used the authors' original publicly available implementations, which are written in Python. Therefore, performance is not directly comparable. As shown in Table 1, our method provides accurate dense depth maps compared to other methods. We measured the mean squared error (MSE) values for each result with GT. The colorization solver and ours show the highest accuracy among four methods. However, as shown in Fig. 5, the colorization solver presents severe color dependency when densifying depth and also cannot preserve high-frequency details in dense depth maps, compared to our method.

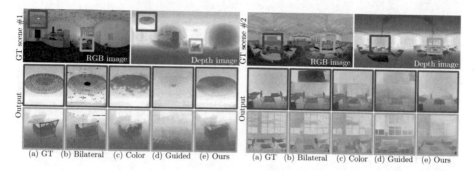

Fig. 5. Closeup results compared to the ground-truth image. (a) Ground-truth depth image. (b) Fast bilateral solver. (c) Colorization solver. (d) Guided image filter. (e) Ours.

Table 1. The MSE errors between each result (Fig. 5) and the ground-truth depth map with the four different methods. The colorization solver and our method provide the highest accuracy. However, the colorization solver cannot preserve edge structures well, while our method preserves high-frequency edge structures clearly with overall high accuracy.

Method	Fast bilateral solver	Colorization solver	Guided image filter	Ours
GT scene #1	0.5758	0.0448	0.2040	0.0336
GT scene #2	0.3764	0.0518	0.2463	0.1659

Figure 6 presents dense depth map results from real monoscopic, omnidirectional camera input. Our method outperforms other densification methods in two aspects: First, as shown in the first row of closeups, our method can propagate sparse depth more independently of color properties than the compared methods. Second, as shown in the second row of results, our method is free from the seam artifacts at the stitched border of the 360-degree image. This is because our method takes the spherical characteristics into account. Note that the flickering artifacts in videos are originated from the inaccurate depth estimates of the used SLAM method [5].

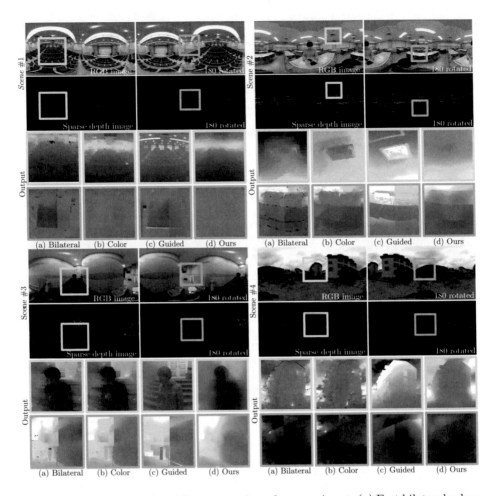

Fig. 6. Comparison results with monoscopic real camera input. (a) Fast bilateral solver. (b) Colorization solver. (c) Guided image filter. (d) Ours.

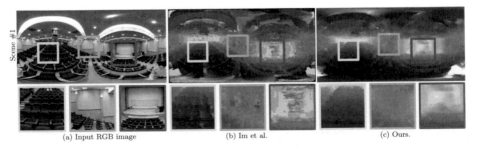

Fig. 7. Comparison with other monocular, omnidirectional dense depth imaging. (a) Input image. (b) Im et al. [12]. (c) Ours.

Finally, we compared our results with the monocular, omnidirectional dense depth imaging method proposed by Im et al. [12]. Our method is based on the SLAM input and allows for dynamic motion, yielding real-time dense depth output. However, 30 frames with *small* motion are required to estimate one depth frame. Therefore, their method is not applicable to large motion. Moreover, their computation is time consuming. It took 5 min per frame, thus not allowing for real-time applications. Figure 7 qualitatively compares dense depth maps captured by two methods.

5   Conclusion

We have presented a novel depth densification algorithm using a joint spherical pyramid that considers color and depth simultaneously. The joint spherical pyramid is made of a total of eight levels of subdivision of a 20-face icosahedron. Our algorithm consists of two phases; in the pull phase, we average up the sparse depth values and store them in the spherical pyramid from the fine to the coarse level. In the push phase, we filled empty polygons from the averaged depth values of the upper level of the pyramid. In order to preserve high-frequency details, we filter each level with the joint bilateral filter with the input color image. Our method accounts for the characteristics of the 360-degree images and as such it shows no seam effects of propagation. Moreover, our method is computationally efficient, taking less than 15 ms, because it is parallelizable and implemented with CUDA and make use of precomputed lookup tables. It is adoptable for other real-time VR/AR applications that require dense depth maps for handling occlusion in rendering.

Acknowledgements. Min H. Kim acknowledges Korea NRF grants (2019R1A2C-3007229, 2013M3A6A-6073718) and additional support by Cross-Ministry Giga KOREA Project (GK17-P0200), Samsung Electronics (SRFC-IT1402-02), ETRI (19ZR1400), and an ICT R&D program of MSIT/IITP of Korea (2016-0-00018).

References

1. Barron, J.T., Poole, B.: The fast bilateral solver. In: Leibe, B., Matas, J., Sebe, N., Welling, M. (eds.) ECCV 2016. LNCS, vol. 9907, pp. 617–632. Springer, Cham (2016). https://doi.org/10.1007/978-3-319-46487-9_38
2. Bunschoten, R., Krose, B.: Robust scene reconstruction from an omnidirectional vision system. IEEE Trans. Robot. Autom. **19**(2), 351–357 (2003)
3. Caruso, D., Engel, J., Cremers, D.: Large-scale direct slam for omnidirectional cameras. In: 2015 IEEE/RSJ International Conference on Intelligent Robots and Systems (IROS), pp. 141–148. IEEE (2015)
4. Chen, Z., Badrinarayanan, V., Drozdov, G., Rabinovich, A.: Estimating depth from RGB and sparse sensing. In: Proceedings of the European Conference on Computer Vision (ECCV), pp. 167–182 (2018)
5. Engel, J., Koltun, V., Cremers, D.: Direct sparse odometry. IEEE Trans. Pattern Anal. Mach. Intell. **40**(3), 611–625 (2018)

6. Gortler, S.J., Grzeszczuk, R., Szeliski, R., Cohen, M.F.: The lumigraph. Siggraph **96**, 43–54 (1996)
7. Guan, H., Smith, W.A.: Brisks: binary features for spherical images on a geodesic grid. In: Proceedings of the IEEE Conference on Computer Vision and Pattern Recognition, pp. 4516–4524 (2017)
8. Hawe, S., Kleinsteuber, M., Diepold, K.: Dense disparity maps from sparse disparity measurements. In: 2011 International Conference on Computer Vision, pp. 2126–2133. IEEE (2011)
9. He, K., Sun, J., Tang, X.: Guided image filtering. IEEE Trans. Pattern Anal. Mach. Intell. **35**(6), 1397–1409 (2013)
10. Holynski, A., Kopf, J.: Fast depth densification for occlusion-aware augmented reality. In: SIGGRAPH Asia 2018 Technical Papers, p. 194. ACM (2018)
11. Huang, J., Chen, Z., Ceylan, D., Jin, H.: 6-DOF VR videos with a single 360-camera. In: 2017 IEEE Virtual Reality (VR), pp. 37–44. IEEE (2017)
12. Im, S., Ha, H., Rameau, F., Jeon, H.-G., Choe, G., Kweon, I.S.: All-around depth from small motion with a spherical panoramic camera. In: Leibe, B., Matas, J., Sebe, N., Welling, M. (eds.) ECCV 2016. LNCS, vol. 9907, pp. 156–172. Springer, Cham (2016). https://doi.org/10.1007/978-3-319-46487-9_10
13. Jaritz, M., De Charette, R., Wirbel, E., Perrotton, X., Nashashibi, F.: Sparse and dense data with CNNs: depth completion and semantic segmentation. In: 2018 International Conference on 3D Vision (3DV), pp. 52–60. IEEE (2018)
14. Kopf, J., Cohen, M.F., Lischinski, D., Uyttendaele, M.: Joint bilateral upsampling. In: ACM Transactions on Graphics (ToG), vol. 26, p. 96. ACM (2007)
15. Levin, A., Lischinski, D., Weiss, Y.: Colorization using optimization. In: ACM Transactions on Graphics (ToG), vol. 23, pp. 689–694. ACM (2004)
16. Li, S.: Binocular spherical stereo. IEEE Trans. Intell. Transp. Syst. **9**(4), 589–600 (2008)
17. Li, S., Fukumori, K.: Spherical stereo for the construction of immersive VR environment. In: IEEE Proceedings, VR 2005, Virtual Reality, pp. 217–222. IEEE (2005)
18. Lin, H.S., Chang, C.C., Chang, H.Y., Chuang, Y.Y., Lin, T.L., Ouhyoung, M.: A low-cost portable polycamera for stereoscopic 360° imaging. IEEE Trans. Circ. Syst. Video Technol. **29**(4), 915–929 (2018)
19. Mal, F., Karaman, S.: Sparse-to-dense: depth prediction from sparse depth samples and a single image. In: 2018 IEEE International Conference on Robotics and Automation (ICRA), pp. 1–8. IEEE (2018)
20. Muja, M., Lowe, D.G.: Scalable nearest neighbor algorithms for high dimensional data. IEEE Trans. Pattern Anal. Mach. Intell. **36**(11), 2227–2240 (2014)
21. Shen, S.: Accurate multiple view 3D reconstruction using patch-based stereo for large-scale scenes. IEEE Trans. Image Process. **22**(5), 1901–1914 (2013)
22. Shirley, P., Chiu, K.: A low distortion map between disk and square. J. Graph. Tools **2**(3), 45–52 (1997)
23. Zhao, Q., Feng, W., Wan, L., Zhang, J.: SPHORB: a fast and robust binary feature on the sphere. Int. J. Comput. Vision **113**(2), 143–159 (2015)
24. Zhu, Z.: Omnidirectional stereo vision. In: Proceedings of the Workshop on Omnidirectional Vision, Budapest, Hungary (2001)

Correction to: DeepGRU: Deep Gesture Recognition Utility

Mehran Maghoumi and Joseph J. LaViola Jr.

Correction to:
Chapter "DeepGRU: Deep Gesture Recognition Utility" in:
G. Bebis et al. (Eds.): *Advances in Visual Computing*,
LNCS 11844, https://doi.org/10.1007/978-3-030-33720-9_2

The given name and family name of an author were not tagged correctly in the originally published article. The author's given name is "Joseph J." and his family name is "LaViola." This was corrected.

The updated version of this chapter can be found at
https://doi.org/10.1007/978-3-030-33720-9_2

© Springer Nature Switzerland AG 2020
G. Bebis et al. (Eds.): ISVC 2019, LNCS 11844, p. C1, 2020.
https://doi.org/10.1007/978-3-030-33720-9_54

Author Index

Printed in the United States
By Bookmasters